Student Engagement in Higher Education

In the updated edition of this important volume, the editors and chapter contributors explore how diverse populations of students experience college differently and encounter group-specific barriers to success. Informed by relevant theories, each chapter focuses on engaging a different student population, including low-income students, Students of Color, international students, students with disabilities, religious minority students, student-athletes, part-time students, adult learners, military-connected students, graduate students, and others. New in this third edition is the inclusion of chapters on Indigenous students, student activists, transracial Asian American adoptee students, justice-involved students, student-parents, first-generation students, and undocumented students.

The forward-thinking, practical, anti-deficit-oriented strategies offered throughout the book are based on research and the collected professional wisdom of experienced educators and scholars at a range of postsecondary institutions. Current and future faculty members, higher education administrators, and student affairs educators will undoubtedly find this book complete with fresh ideas to reverse troubling engagement trends among various college student populations.

Stephen John Quaye is Past President of ACPA: College Student Educators International, and Associate Professor of Higher Education and Student Affairs at The Ohio State University, USA.

Shaun R. Harper is President-Elect of the American Educational Research Association, Executive Director of the USC Race and Equity Center, and a Provost Professor in the Rossier School of Education and Marshall School of Business at University of Southern California, USA.

Sumun L. Pendakur is the Chief Learning Officer and Director of the USC Equity Institutes at the USC Race and Equity Center at University of Southern California, USA.

Student Engagement in Higher Education

Theoretical Perspectives and
Practical Approaches for Diverse Populations

Third Edition

EDITED BY
STEPHEN JOHN QUAYE, SHAUN R. HARPER,
AND SUMUN L. PENDAKUR

Routledge
Taylor & Francis Group

NEW YORK AND LONDON

Third edition published 2020
First published in paperback 2020

First published 2020
by Routledge
52 Vanderbilt Avenue, New York, NY 10017

and by Routledge
2 Park Square, Milton Park, Abingdon, Oxon OX14 4RN

Routledge is an imprint of the Taylor & Francis Group, an informa business

© 2020 Taylor & Francis

The right of Stephen John Quaye, Shaun R. Harper, and Sumun L. Pendakur to be identified as the authors of the editorial material, and of the authors for their individual chapters, has been asserted in accordance with sections 77 and 78 of the Copyright, Designs and Patents Act 1988.

All rights reserved. No part of this book may be reprinted or reproduced or utilised in any form or by any electronic, mechanical, or other means, now known or hereafter invented, including photocopying and recording, or in any information storage or retrieval system, without permission in writing from the publishers.

Trademark notice: Product or corporate names may be trademarks or registered trademarks, and are used only for identification and explanation without intent to infringe.

First edition published by Routledge 2009
Second edition published by Taylor & Francis 2015

Library of Congress Cataloging-in-Publication Data
Names: Quaye, Stephen John, 1980– editor. | Harper, Shaun R., 1975– editor. |
   Pendakur, Sumun L., editor.
Title: Student Engagement in Higher Education : Theoretical Perspectives and
   Practical Approaches for Diverse Populations / Edited by Stephen John Quaye,
   Shaun R. Harper, Sumun L. Pendakur.
Identifiers: LCCN 2019046445 (print) | LCCN 2019046446 (ebook) |
   ISBN 9780367002220 (hardback) | ISBN 9780367002244 (paperback) |
   ISBN 9780429400698 (ebook)
Subjects: LCSH: Student affairs services—United States. | Student activities—
   United States. | College students—Services for—United States. | Muticultural
   education—United States.
Classification: LCC LB2342.92 .S78 2020 (print) | LCC LB2342.92 (ebook) |
   DDC 378.1/97—dc23
LC record available at https://lccn.loc.gov/2019046445
LC ebook record available at https://lccn.loc.gov/2019046446

ISBN: 978-0-367-00222-0 (hbk)
ISBN: 978-0-367-00224-4 (pbk)
ISBN: 978-0-429-40069-8 (ebk)

Typeset in Times
by Apex CoVantage, LLC

We dedicate the third edition of this book to postsecondary educators who take seriously the responsibility of equitably engaging every student at their institutions.

Contents

Acknowledgements

We salute the thoughtful educators and administrators who will use this book to guide bold, imaginative institutional efforts to engage student populations across all axes of identity—those who will do the authentic work of aligning espoused values concerning equity, diversity, inclusivity, and justice with the deliberate actions necessary to actualize those ideals.

A book of this magnitude does not come to fruition without the support of family, friends, and mentors. First, we owe an enormous amount of gratitude to Sebastian James Quaye (Stephen's son), Shawn K. Hill (Shaun's husband), and Sunil Malhotra, Shashi Veer, and Shama Shakti (Sumun's partner and children) for their unwavering encouragement and love throughout the completion of this book. We also thank Rebecca Collazo and Heather Jarrow at Routledge for their support. We also appreciate Cynthea Jackson's assistance.

We also extend gratitude to the 45 authors in this book for their wisdom, clarity, and insight on how to authentically engage students while strategically shaping the institutional conditions to do so with excellence. Finally, we acknowledge all the mentors and supporters who have shaped and transformed our perspectives about engagement over the decades.

Stephen John Quaye
The Ohio State University

Shaun R. Harper
University of Southern California

Sumun L. Pendakur
University of Southern California
July 2019

Foreword

The concept of student engagement has traveled across the landscape of higher education and student affairs literature for the last several decades. Researchers, institutional leaders, and policymakers have constructed student engagement as a central characteristic of success in college. The idea of student engagement focuses on the role of postsecondary institutions in providing students with multiple opportunities for experiences to which they might not otherwise be exposed without pursuing a college degree. More importantly, student engagement encourages institutional leaders to implement strategies that ensure students experience a learning environment that promotes their psychological, social, emotional, and physical well-being. Despite the positive and idealistic assumptions undergirding student engagement, the concept is situated in a much more problematic reality framed by four looming questions: 1) Who are the students? 2) In what are they engaging? 3) Where is the engagement occurring? and 4) With whom are they engaging? A review of the robust student engagement literature would suggest that the students are White; they are engaging in opportunities afforded primarily to White, affluent students; their engagement is occurring on predominantly White campuses, in predominantly white spaces with other White people.

In a chapter I co-authored with Shaun R. Harper (one of the co-editors for this book) and Jessica Harris in 2015, we stated,

> The most cited student engagement pioneers are all white; they decided which experiences and activities add value to a student's college experience. They are unlikely familiar with particular activities and practices in which minoritized students are engaged that bolster their sense of belonging and keep them engaged and retained.
>
> (p. 210)

Our assertion remains relevant. Student engagement as a concept is largely misunderstood by institutional leaders, resulting in their inadequate measurement and observation of engagement on their campuses. Scholars rarely examine this important aspect of student development through a critical lens (Patton, Renn, Guido, & Quaye, 2016), leaving educators ill-equipped to rethink, critique, and disrupt hegemonic notions of who engaged students are and the opportunities they are afforded.

Student Engagement in Higher Education has and continues to be a major catalyst for shifting the dominant narrative associated with student engagement. This edited volume is undeniably the most important contribution to moving the student engagement literature to a critical space that broadens how readers think about the four aforementioned questions. Readers will notice several critical themes that not only reflect earlier editions, but also reveal the direction in which the study of student engagement is and should be going. First, contributors rearticulate student engagement by identifying structural deficits embedded within the operation of postsecondary institutions, rather than problematizing students. This approach allows space for readers to consider student engagement through an equity-oriented lens. As a result, opportunities for engagement, particularly for marginalized groups, can focus on remedying oppressive systems and structures instead of fixing students.

Another broad theme that resonates throughout this book is that everyone can and should have a vested interest in student engagement, regardless of their institutional affiliation or status. Although institutional leaders, student affairs administrators, and faculty are specifically positioned to equitably promote and implement student engagement, a more communal approach is possible by involving staff, students and their families, and members of the surrounding community. A communal approach holds promise for centering minoritized students whose voices, cultures, and experiences are typically absent from engagement opportunities. This theme is particularly significant, given the contentious political and social climate in the United States, the continued presence of oppressive immigration laws, the surge in White supremacy, and the increasingly blurred lines between higher education and society.

A third noticeable theme is the importance of critically understanding the dynamic nature of students' experiences. Student engagement can never be effective through a one-size-fits-all approach. Instead, institutional leaders, student affairs educators, and faculty should have a heightened awareness of both external and internal forces that shape students' experiences and affect their levels of engagement. This book encourages readers to move beyond examining student characteristics in a simplistic way, toward viewing these characteristics within the larger sociopolitical context. Educators must consider the depths and diversity of students' identities, the strengths they bring to campus, and the innovative ways that student engagement can be leveraged to promote their success.

Overall, the third edition of *Student Engagement in Higher Education* continues to push the envelope of its predecessors by presenting the complexities and experiences of students whose lives are rarely the center of attention in the larger body of work on student engagement, such as students who are incarcerated/formerly incarcerated, student activists, parenting students, and undocumented students. Contrary to dominant beliefs regarding student engagement, there are highly diverse student populations who engage in diverse campus environments, such as community colleges and historically Black colleges and universities. More importantly, we need critical frameworks in order to understand the depth and breadth of possibilities for understanding student engagement beyond its current limitations. If educators espouse a commitment to student engagement, then their knowledge of the concept must be broadened and challenged. *Student Engagement in Higher Education* is precisely the resource that researchers, institutional leaders, and policymakers need in order to truly meet the needs of all students who aspire to attain a college degree.

Lori D. Patton

The Ohio State University

May 16, 2019

References

Patton, L. D., Harper, S. R., & Harris, J. C. (2015). Using critical race theory to (re)interpret widely-studied topics in US higher education. In A. M. Martinez-Aleman, E. M. Bensimon, & B. Pusser (Eds.), *Critical approaches to the study of higher education* (pp. 193–219). Baltimore, MD: The Johns Hopkins University Press.

Patton, L. D., Renn, K., Guido, F. M., & Quaye, S. J. (2016). *Student development in college: Theory, research, and practice* (3rd ed.). San Francisco, CA: Jossey Bass.

Preface

This third edition of *Student Engagement in Higher Education: Theoretical Perspectives and Practical Approaches for Diverse Populations* brings together 45 authors to devote focused attention to populations that continue to remain underserved on college and university campuses. Since the publication of the first edition in 2009, two key features of the book have made it especially appealing for classroom adoption. First, readers have appreciated the expansive coverage of diverse populations—from international students to student veterans to students from low-income backgrounds and so on. A chapter is devoted entirely to each population. Second, the structural similarity of chapters makes it especially readable—each begins with a creative introduction and synthesis of literature concerning population-specific needs and issues, followed by a theoretical framework that attempts to help readers make sense of challenges and realities faced by that population, and ends with a set of sensible and innovative strategies for student engagement. In light of the praise received for these aspects of the book, we maintained the same structure for the third edition.

The intended audience for this book is anyone who wishes to better engage students on college and university campuses. Most notably, faculty in graduate-preparation programs in student affairs and higher education can use this book to help students understand the challenges, needs, and assets of specific populations; students might also feel seen in reading the stories and experiences of people who identify similarly to them. In addition, student affairs educators working in various functional areas can utilize this book in their programming and efforts to retain and engage students in their learning, using anti-deficit lenses.

Since publication of the last edition, the social landscape of higher education has changed, given the political climate following the 2016 election of Donald J. Trump to the White House. Although oppression, stratification, and violence are not new in the United States, with Trump's election, hate crimes and bias incidents have increased on campuses, making the climate for minoritized students extremely more challenging to navigate (Balsamo, 2018). As higher education continues to evolve, so, too, must educators' practices and inclusion of populations previously not centered. As such, this third edition offers attention to seven populations unaddressed in previous volumes: justice-involved students, first-generation students, transracial Asian American adoptee students, student activists, undocumented students, Indigenous students, and parenting students. These new chapters respond to feedback from readers and offer educators a stronger understanding of how to adapt their practices to better meet these students' needs. This volume also works to help readers think beyond traditional four-year institutions, as well as use intersectional frameworks to guide their practice.

Although the book is organized in a specific format, each chapter can stand on its own. Those using the book in courses might devote the beginning part of the semester or quarter to understanding the needs, challenges, and assets of the populations covered before moving to thinking through creative strategies for better engaging students toward the latter part of the semester or quarter. Instructors can also invite students to use their own experiences to develop strategies not offered in this book, as well as to investigate populations outside the scope of this book. Instructors can also leverage theories from different paradigms to help students understand how addressing students' needs is different based on the theories one employs in their work.

Finally, while this book is comprehensive, it is far from exhaustive. We cannot adequately cover all populations in one volume, so we encourage readers to suggest new populations and to use their own knowledge in applying this work to their own contexts. Engaging in dialogues with colleagues about the unique challenges of one's campus can enable readers to see what gaps remain and what supplemental information is needed to best engage students in proactive, equity-minded ways.

Reference

Balsamo, M. (2018, November 13). FBI Report shows 17 percent spike in hate crimes in 2017. *AP News*. Retrieved from https://www.apnews.com/e5e7bb22f8474408becd2fcdc67f284e

Chapter 1
The Heart of Our Work

Equitable Engagement for Students in US Higher Education

Sumun L. Pendakur, Stephen John Quaye, and Shaun R. Harper

In the fraught summer of 2019, we brought this third edition to life under difficult circumstances—rising inequality, emboldened White supremacy, a climate crisis, and so much more, all under the ominous eye of an oppressive political administration. These circumstances, however, provide a clarion call for all in staff, faculty, and administrator roles in higher education to do better by students, particularly those who experience the range of exclusion and harm embedded in their collegiate environments. This is the practitioner's locus of control, the sphere of influence, and practitioners must act. Colleges and universities are diversifying at the fastest rate in history, reflective of broader demographic changes. The student activism that emerged in 2015 around identity and campus sexual violence is a powerful reminder that students still face oppression on their campuses and beyond. In addition, the student protests were powerful reminders that the original demands of the 1970 Black Action Movement at the University of Michigan are, as yet, largely unmet. And yet, many campuses operate via traditional forms of student engagement, with narrow visions of the dynamic and intersectional needs, assets, and opportunities presented by today's and tomorrow's students. None of these statements is intended to induce hopelessness. On the contrary, our writing here speaks to an opportunity: a chance to learn more, transform one's knowledge and skills, equitably alter institutions of higher education from the inside out, and meaningfully impact the experiences and futures of all the students educators serve.

We posit that developing a nuanced, specific understanding of community-based needs and assets is essential for the 21st-century student affairs educator or faculty member. Simply having broad-stroke knowledge about minoritized communities is not enough. Specificity is essential for faculty and student affairs educators' ability to be strategic and intentional about fostering conditions that compel students to make the most of college, both inside and outside the classroom. In their 1991 book, *Involving*

Colleges: Successful Approaches to Fostering Student Learning and Development Outside the Classroom, Kuh and colleagues concluded:

> *Involving Colleges* are committed to pluralism in all its forms, and they support the establishment and coexistence of subcommunities that permit students to identify with and receive support from people like themselves, so they can feel comfortable in becoming involved in the larger campus community.
>
> (p. 369)

This declaration and subsequent related perspectives guided the conceptualization and writing of the first and second editions of this book. Although we differentiate involvement from engagement later in this chapter, transforming today's campuses into *Involving Colleges* for all students is very much the vision with which this work was undertaken. This third edition draws from that wellspring and also broadens the boundaries of student engagement considerations through an intersectional and anti-deficit lens. Intersectional, in that each author in this edition has attempted to articulate the social, economic, and political ways in which identity-based systems of oppression connect, overlap, and influence each other (Crenshaw, 1989). Anti-deficit, in that while the authors present the very real and complex challenges populations of students face, this does not mean they are operating from deficits. The question the authors answer is "Where are the challenges placed?" In this book, authors ask readers to take an equity-minded approach to systems, institutional mechanisms, and educator gaps in knowledge as the problem, not the students (Bensimon, 2007). By looking at the problem systemically, educators can better engage and honor students because they are addressing the root of the problem, not the symptoms.

In this third edition, we amplify the specific challenges faced by diverse populations on college campuses and offer guidance for accepting institutional responsibility for the engagement of students. We trust that readers will be moved to respond with deliberation through conversations, collaborative planning, programs, services, curricular enhancements, and assessment. A cursory scan of the table of contents will confirm that this book is not exclusively about "minority students." Rather, authors focus on a range of populations for whom the published research confirms that engagement, sense of belonging and affirmation, and connectivity to the college experience are in various ways problematic. Emphasis is also placed on enhancing outcomes and development among different populations. New for this volume is the inclusion of chapters on student activists, formerly incarcerated/justice-involved students, parenting students, undocumented students, first-generation college students, transracial Asian American adoptees, and Native and Indigenous students.

The practical implications presented at the end of each chapter are in response to issues noted in the literature, informed by relevant theories, and based on the collective professional wisdom of those who have written. The authors bring to this book decades of full-time work experience in various capacities (faculty, student affairs educators, academic affairs administrators) at a wide range of two-year and four-year institutions of higher education. Indeed, they are experts in the field who have taken an intricate look at the various populations represented in this book and have devoted a large part of their careers to understanding the needs of these students. Notwithstanding, we neither claim to furnish all the answers nor contend that this book contains prescriptive solutions for all engagement problems facing every student population. Instead, experienced educators and scholars have collaborated to produce a resource for the field of higher education and the student affairs profession that will hopefully ignite dialogue, agency, and strategic thinking and action on behalf of undergraduates who should be at the heart of the work.

The remainder of this chapter sets the stage for the population-specific chapters that follow. We begin by making clear what we mean by "student engagement" and synthesizing what decades of empirical research contend about the associated gains, educational benefits, and outcomes. Next, we discuss the importance of shifting the onus for engagement from students to educators and administrators, as we advocate strategy, intentionality, and reflective action. We then justify the role of theory in this book and in engagement practice. The chapter concludes with an urgent note for campuses to better align espoused values of equity and inclusion with concrete institutional actions.

Understanding the Landscape and Significance of Engagement

Student engagement is simply characterized as participation in educationally effective practices, both inside and outside the classroom, which leads to a range of measurable outcomes. We borrow this operational definition from Kuh, Kinzie, Buckley, Bridges, and Hayek (2007), who also note:

> Student engagement represents two critical features. The first is the amount of time and effort students put into their studies and other educationally purposeful activities. . . . The second component of student engagement is how the institution deploys its resources and organizes the curriculum, other learning opportunities, and support services to induce students to participate in activities that lead to the experiences and desired outcomes such as persistence, satisfaction, learning, and graduation.
>
> (p. 44)

We are persuaded by a large volume of empirical evidence that confirms strategizing ways to increase the engagement of various student populations, especially those for whom engagement is known to be problematic, is a worthwhile endeavor. However, the gains and outcomes are too robust to leave to chance, and social justice will not ensue if some students come to enjoy the beneficial byproducts of engagement, but others do not.

Engagement and Student Outcomes

"The impact of college is largely determined by individual effort and involvement in the academic, interpersonal, and extracurricular offerings on a campus" (Pascarella & Terenzini, 2005, p. 602). However, as the authors of this book elucidate in myriad ways, countless cultural and contextual obstacles exist on the path of students being able to fully engage with all the campus offerings. That disparity is especially sharp, given that researchers have found that educationally purposeful engagement leads to the production of gains, benefits, and outcomes in numerous domains. These include: cognitive and intellectual skill development (Anaya, 1996; Baxter Magolda, 1992); college adjustment (Cabrera, Nora, Terenzini, Pascarella, & Hagedorn, 1999; Kuh, Palmer, & Kish, 2003); moral and ethical development (Evans, 1987; Rest, 1993); practical competence and skills transferability (Kuh, 1993, 1995); the accrual of social capital (Harper, 2008); and psychosocial development, productive racial and gender identity formation, and positive images of self (Patton, Renn, Guido, & Quaye, 2016; Harper & Quaye, 2007; Okello, 2018; Torres, Howard-Hamilton, & Cooper, 2003). In addition, Tross, Harper, Osher, and Kneidinger (2000) found that students who devote more time to academic preparation activities outside of class earn higher grade-point averages. While all these benefits are important, the nexus between engagement and persistence has garnered the most attention.

Engagement and Persistence

As noted in the first edition of this book (and elsewhere), differences in first- to second-year persistence, as well as in four-year and six-year graduation rates, continually disadvantage many Students of Color, undergraduate men, lower-income students, first-generation college-goers, undergraduates who commute to their campuses, and a handful of other student populations. While the reasons for student persistence through degree attainment are multifaceted and not easily attributed to a narrow set of explanatory factors (Braxton, Hirschy, & McClendon, 2004), we know one point for certain: Those who are actively engaged in educationally purposeful activities, both inside and outside the classroom, are more likely to persist through graduation. This assertion has been empirically proven and consistently documented by numerous higher education researchers (e.g., Astin, 1975, 1993; Bean, 1990, 2005; Berger & Milem, 1999; Braxton, Milem, & Sullivan, 2000; Bridges, Cambridge, Kuh, & Leegwater, 2005; Milem & Berger, 1997; Pascarella & Terenzini, 2005; Peltier, Laden, & Matranga, 1999; Stage & Hossler, 2000; Tinto, 1993, 2000, 2005). Museus (2014) expands on this body of research by describing the *site* of student engagement through the Culturally Engaging Campus Environments Model, which focuses on cultural relevance and cultural responsiveness.

Tinto, the most frequently cited scholar on college student retention, contends that engagement (or "academic and social integration," as he called it) is positively related to persistence. In fact, his research shows that engagement is the single most significant predictor of persistence (Tinto, 2000). He notes that many students discontinue their undergraduate education because they feel disconnected from peers, professors, and administrators at the institution. "Leavers of this type express a sense of not having made any significant contacts or not feeling membership in the institution" (Tinto, 2000, p. 7). In his 1993 book, *Leaving College: The Causes and Cures of Student Attrition*, Tinto argues that high levels of integration into academic and social communities on campus lead to higher levels of institutional commitment, which in turn compel a student to persist (Tinto, 1993).

Similarly, Bean (1990, 2005) proposes that students leave when they are marginally committed to their institutions. Institutional commitment is strengthened when undergraduates are actively engaged in educationally purposeful endeavors that connect them to the campus and in which they feel some sense of enduring obligation and responsibility (Bean, 2005; Swail, Redd, & Perna, 2003; Tinto, 1993). Those who hold leadership positions in student organizations, for example, assume responsibilities in their groups and know that others depend on them for service, guidance, and follow-through on important initiatives. Thus, they feel committed to their respective organizations and the institution at large and are less likely than students who are not engaged to leave. The same could be applied to a student who feels like an important contributor to learning and discussions in their classes. While the relationships between engagement, student outcomes, and retention are powerful, it is important to acknowledge the conditions under which these are likely to occur.

Distinguishing Educationally Purposeful Engagement

Over 30 years ago, Astin defined student involvement as "the amount of physical and psychological energy that the student devotes to the academic experience" (1984, p. 297). Astin's conceptualization of involvement refers to behaviors and what students actually do, instead of what they think, how they feel, and the meanings they make of their experiences. His theory of student involvement is principally concerned with how college students spend their time and how various institutional actors, processes, and opportunities facilitate development. "The extent to which students can achieve particular developmental goals is a direct function of the time and effort they devote to activities designed to produce these gains" (p. 301). This theory is among the most frequently cited in the higher education literature.

While conceptually similar, there is a key qualitative difference between involvement and engagement: it is entirely possible to be involved in something without being engaged. For example, a student who is present and on time for every weekly meeting of an organization but sits passively in the back of the room, never offers an opinion or volunteers for committees, interacts infrequently with the group's advisor or fellow members outside weekly meetings, and would not dare consider running for an office could still legitimately claim that she is involved in the group. However, few would argue this student is actively engaged, as outcomes accrual is likely to be limited. The same could be said for the student who is involved in a study group for his psychology class but contributes little and asks few questions when the group meets for study sessions. Action, purpose, and cross-institutional collaboration are requisites for engagement and deep learning (Kinzie & Kuh, 2004; Kuh, Kinzie, Schuh, Whitt, & Associates, 2005; Kuh et al., 2007).

The National Survey of Student Engagement (NSSE), an instrument through which data have now been collected from approximately four million undergraduates at more than 1,500 different four-year colleges and universities since 2000, is constructed around ten engagement indicators and a set of high-impact educational practices:

Academic Challenge—Including Higher-Order Learning, Reflective and Integrative Learning, Quantitative Reasoning, and Learning Strategies.

Learning with Peers—Including Collaborative Learning and Discussions with Diverse Others.

Experiences with Faculty—Including Student-Faculty Interaction and Effective Teaching Practices.

Campus Environment—Including Quality of Interactions and Supportive Environment.

High-Impact Practices—Special undergraduate opportunities such as Service Learning, Study Abroad, Research with Faculty, and Internships that have substantial positive effects on student learning and retention.

Student engagement in the activities associated with each NSSE indicator is considered educationally purposeful, as it leads to deep levels of learning and the production of enduring and measurable gains and outcomes (Kuh et al., 2005). This focus on student learning and outcomes creates another distinction between involvement and engagement. We offer one additional defining characteristic: the dual responsibility for engagement. As Tanaka (2002) writes, the major works by scholars on engagement and persistence all have in common "(1) an interest in measuring the impact of student participation in the institution and (2) a tendency not to examine the underlying cultures of that institution (often Western European, straight, upper middle class, and male)" (p. 264). Patton, Harper, and Harris (2015) expand this critique by noting that the most-cited scholars of student engagement are "unlikely familiar with particular activities and practices in which minoritized students are engaged that bolster their sense of belonging and keep them (and their same-race peers) engaged and retained" (p. 208). Therefore, while we see the critical need for the full engagement of all students, particularly those who experience minoritization, the extant literature often employs frameworks that place the majority of the burden for involvement and engagement on students, without regard for the historical ways in which engagement has been structured to be more readily available for some, but not all.

In the next section, we argue that students should not be chiefly responsible for engaging themselves, but that faculty and student affairs educators must foster the conditions that enable diverse populations of students to be engaged, persist, and thrive.

On Whose Shoulders? Shifting the Onus of Engagement

Put simply, institutional leaders ought not to expect students to engage themselves. Kuh (2001) suggests student engagement is a measure of institutional quality. That is, the more engaged its students are in educationally purposeful activities, the better the institution. Similarly, Pascarella (2001) maintains, "An excellent undergraduate education is most likely to occur at those colleges and universities that maximize good practices and enhance students' academic and social engagement" (p. 22). Given this, we deem it essential for faculty and student affairs educators to view engaging diverse populations as "everyone's responsibility," including their own. Student affairs educators and faculty must alter the structure of the institution (e.g., their department, program) to best meet the dynamic needs of today's students, rather than continuing to operate from deficit-minded frameworks. Additionally, engagement does not occur in a vacuum. The "what" and "how" of students' experiences are dramatically shaped by multiple factors, some of which are outside the institutions—market forces, the sociopolitical landscape, key legislation, the defunding of higher education by the state, and history. Without a strong historical and political lens, it is easy for educators to lose sight of how their campuses have evolved and, yet, continue to fail students. Presidents, deans, and other senior administrators must also hold themselves and everyone else on campus accountable for ensuring institutional quality in this regard. A clear signal of institutional deficiency is when there are few ramifications for those who either blatantly refuse or unintentionally neglect to enact the practices known to produce rich outcomes for students.

From Negligence to Intentionality

Quaye and Harper (2007) describe the ways in which faculty neglect to incorporate culturally-relevant perspectives into their class discussions and assigned materials. The onus is often placed on students with minoritized identities to find readings that appeal to their unique backgrounds and to bring up topics related to their sociocultural identities in class discussions. There is little accountability for ensuring that professors are thoughtful and strategic about creating classroom experiences that enable students to learn about differences. Interactions with peers across differences inside and outside of class have been positively linked to benefits and outcomes in the following domains: self-concept (intellectual and social), cultural awareness and appreciation, racial understanding, leadership, engagement in citizenship activities, satisfaction with college, high post-baccalaureate degree aspirations, and readiness for participation in a diverse workforce (Antonio et al., 2004; Chang, Astin, & Kim, 2004; Chang, Denson, Sáenz, & Misa, 2006; Gurin, Dey, Hurtado, & Gurin, 2002; Harper & Antonio, 2008; Hu & Kuh, 2003; Pascarella, Edison, Nora, Hagedorn, & Terenzini, 1996; Villalpando, 2002). "Knowing that students and society could ultimately benefit from new approaches to cross-cultural learning, but failing to take the necessary steps to intentionally create enabling conditions [inside and] outside the classroom is downright irresponsible" (Harper & Antonio, 2008, p. 12).

The negligence described here is partially explained by the "magical thinking" philosophy that often undergirds practices of student engagement:

The [magical thinking] rationale provides no guidance for campuses on assembling the appropriate means to create environments conducive to realization of the benefits of diversity or on employing the methods necessary to

facilitate the educational process to achieve those benefits. Under this rationale, the benefits will accrue as if by magic.

(Chang, Chang, & Ledesma, 2005, pp. 10–11)

Negligence is synonymous with magical thinking; simply providing services for students is not sufficient to enrich their educational experiences. Rather, we defend a position of intentionality where faculty and student affairs educators are conscious of every
action they undertake and are able to consider the long-range implications of decisions.

Across the collegiate landscape, relations across various forms of difference are often
inequitable and serve to reinscribe forms of hierarchy. Minoritized students often report
there is infrequent interaction between them and their peers in dominant groups, and
that there is a lack of attention paid to improving the climate (Ancis, Sedlacek, & Mohr,
2000; Cabrera et al., 1999; Garvey, Sanders, & Flint, 2017; Harper & Hurtado, 2007;
Hurtado, 1992; Rockenbach, Mayhew, & Bowman, 2015; Wells & Horn, 2015). When
campus climates are hostile and antagonistic toward certain students, disengagement,
dropping out, and maladjustment are likely unintended, yet nearly inevitable, outcomes.

As Chang et al. (2005) and Harper and Antonio (2008) note, an erroneous assumption is
often made that students will naturally learn about their peers simply by coming into contact with those who share different views, experiences, and identities. For example, simply
increasing the numbers of queer and trans students on campus will not automatically create more opportunities for cisgender heterosexual students to interact with them. Rather,
as authors of chapters throughout this book maintain, educators must facilitate structured
opportunities for these dialogues to transpire. Meaningful strategies are necessary that enable
institutions to realize the benefits of engaging the full swath of college-goers today. These
solutions must be grounded in students' actual experiences, reflective of their unique backgrounds and interests, and designed with both broad and specific implications in mind.

The insights presented in this book are consistent with Strange and Banning's (2001)
design vision for postsecondary institutions. They call for campuses that are "intentionally designed to offer opportunities, incentives, and reinforcements for growth and
development" (p. 201). Such a philosophy of engagement responds to the multifaceted and complex needs of campus populations today. When an institution provides
reinforcements for students, it means educators have envisioned and enacted the types
of learning opportunities that will contribute to student development and engagement.
This, of course, requires knowing who students are and understanding their prior knowledge and experiences, the types of educational contexts from which they have come, and
what they view as necessary for enabling engagement (Harper, 2007, 2011). Devoting
attention to those students who are not as engaged in educationally purposeful activities
is an important way to be deliberate in one's practices.

Understanding Before Acting

Creating optimal learning environments in which all students feel connected is difficult, but nonetheless important. Educators must have the requisite skills and expertise to analyze the campus environment and determine where gaps in engagement and

achievement exist. More importantly, they must resist the urge to act without consider-ing the effects of potential solutions and instead, spend time understanding the obstacles facing students who are not as engaged. Otherwise, creating programs, mentoring, or teaching without a knowledgeable, strategic, and equitable approach to engagement only serve to reify the dominant norms of the institution (which reflect the centrality of White, cisgender male, middle-class norms) (Pendakur, 2016).

Faculty who are interested in providing avenues for Students of Color to be engaged in predominantly White classroom contexts might decide to incorporate readings that reflect the scholarly contributions of Writers of Color. On the surface, this practice seems logical and consistent with research that demonstrates the influence of culturally-relevant literature on student learning (Ladson-Billings, 1995). However, what this pro-fessor might fail to consider is the reactions of White students to these readings. How might the faculty member deal with White students who believe the course is primarily focused on Students of Color and accuse the instructor of attempting to indoctrinate them with a politically liberal agenda? After thinking about this practice, the faculty member might still decide to proceed in the same manner, but the outcomes will be dif-ferent since they have considered not only the needs of Students of Color, but also the reactions of and growth opportunities for White students in the course.

Repeatedly emphasized throughout this book is the importance of listening to stu-dents in order to understand how to enhance their educational experiences. Since September 11, 2001, and again under the Trump administration, we have seen the docu-mented rise in hate crimes and everyday forms of hostility and violence toward Muslim and Arab students. Seeking to improve engagement among these students, institutional leaders might plan campus-wide programs that include cross-cultural dialogues, Arab and Muslim speakers, and panels comprised of religious minority students sharing their experiences on campus. As educators strive to determine why these hateful behaviors persist, they may gradually learn that religious minority students are not only experienc-ing prejudice and oppression from their peers, but also in their courses from professors. The decision to incorporate a wide array of programs aimed at students is often missing in trainings for faculty and student affairs educators on teaching about difference in all its forms. In the current example, if educators failed to ask Arab and Muslim students about their needs and developed interventions to improve their experiences based on assumptions about the issues students face, such efforts would be void of a complex understanding of the challenges confronting these students and would likely be, at best, marginally effective. As alluded to earlier, situating student engagement at the conflu-ence of history, institutional practices, practitioner efforts, and sociopolitical pressures is highly necessary; otherwise, student affairs educators run the risk of problematizing the population, rather than the structures and systems that surround them.

This example demonstrates the importance of analyzing problematic trends and outcomes from students' vantage points. One of the most effective ways to improve student engagement is to invite those who are the least engaged to share their knowl-edge and experiences (Harper, 2007, 2011). As the authors of *Learning Reconsidered* recommend: "All institutions should establish routine ways to hear students' voices, consult with them, explore their opinions, and document the nature and quality of their experience as learners" (ACPA & NASPA, 2004, p. 33). When educators speak with students from diverse backgrounds, they will begin to see patterns in their stories emerge and gain a more nuanced understanding of their needs. In addition, educators can observe the particularities in students' experiences and begin to develop customized services to improve student outcomes.

Barriers to achievement and engagement can result from making decisions without qualitative input from students (Harper, 2007, 2011). Strange and Banning (2001) discuss how a renovation project of a campus building should include insights from multiple people (including students) prior to the construction. Allowing future users of the facilities to comment on its accessibility and openness to multiple groups enables students to feel included in the decision-making process. This sense of ownership can facilitate engagement for various campus members. Some chapters in this book explore the impact of space and campus design on student engagement. For instance, providing opportunities for students with disabilities and Students of Color to share their opinions about the physical design of a building as well as select potential artwork for the walls, confirms that educators are taking their needs into consideration prior to proceeding. This practice will facilitate the construction of buildings that align with students' needs and interests, thereby leading to a campus environment that is emblematic of the varied experiences, backgrounds, and perspectives of students.

In an era in which student engagement is receiving increasing attention, providing undergraduates with numerous, sustained opportunities to actively participate in determining the appropriate methods for enriching their academic and social experiences in higher education cannot be overstated. Several scholars (e.g., Baxter Magolda & King, 2004; Harper, 2007, 2011; Harper & Antonio, 2008; Kuh et al., 2005, 2007; Strange & Banning, 2001) propose educational practices that are student-centered, well-planned, researched, and guided by student input and assessment data. As Freire (1970) notes, acting without reflecting on why people are oppressed can lead to further oppression. He advises that educators utilize praxis—combining reflection with action. Throughout the book, authors write in this manner and advocate inviting students into dialogues about improving their engagement.

Theory, Practice, Praxis

One of the primary premises of *Student Engagement in Higher Education* is that educators make informed decisions when they utilize relevant theories to guide practice. As such, theories related to identity development, racial/ethnic awareness, stereotypes, deconstructing Whiteness, and others are tied to the needs of the populations considered in each chapter that follows. "Theory is a framework through which interpretations and understandings are constructed. Theory is used to describe human behavior, to explain, to predict, and to generate new knowledge, [practices], and research" (McEwen, 2003,

p. 166). In this book, authors use theories to frame the issues students face and to inform the strategies they propose. In essence, there is interplay between theory and practice, as theory is used to recommend tentative solutions to educational disparities, keeping in mind that those approaches should be continually assessed and revised given the learners and institutional context. Similarly, alternative theories are available as one evaluates the effectiveness of interventions intended to improve engagement. Reason and Kimball (2012) cite Schön (1987) in order to amplify this approach by offering a powerful theory to practice framework that embeds institutional context and feedback loops such that the educator is deeply situated in the knowledge of the field and is able to apply theory effectively in practice, through reflective learning in action. Authors in this edition of *Student Engagement in Higher Education* also utilize a variety of critical theoretical frameworks and lenses to make their cases: theories of indigeneity, critical race theory, critical Whiteness studies, queer theory, feminist theory, and more. As indicated by Abes, Jones, and Stewart (2019), the educator's ability to fluidly navigate and integrate the praxis emerging from both the "canon" of student development theory, as well as critical, cutting-edge frameworks is paramount to today's equity-minded student affairs educator.

The use of theoretical frameworks in each chapter is consistent with current student affairs expectations. Moreover, as detailed in ACPA's Strategic Imperative for Racial Justice and Decolonization (Quaye, Aho, Beard Jacob, Domingue, Guido, Lange, Squire, & Stewart, 2019), educators must openly name the myriad ways racism, White supremacy, and colonization, continue to manifest in the theories that guide their practice to the structures of their institutions. The Strategic Imperative pushes educators to employ liberatory practices that yield outcomes related to critical consciousness, radical democracy, and humanization (Aho & Quaye, 2018). It also emphasizes the importance of educators working to heal from their own trauma so that they can best support students in doing the same.

For decades, there has existed a superficial separation between faculty and student affairs educators, as the former were thought to be responsible for students' classroom learning, while the latter group focused on students' involvement in co-curricular activities (ACPA, 1994). Even though student affairs educators have sought to challenge and transform this demarcation between students' academic and personal selves, there still continues to be an expectation that professors focus on theory and research, while student affairs educators devote their time to practice (ACPA & NASPA, 2004; Harper & Antonio, 2008). Authors in *Student Engagement in Higher Education* reject this false dichotomy and show how educators in both areas are responsible for facilitating a holistic learning environment. The authors model this by using, for example, psychological, environmental, and student development theories to guide the interventions proposed at the end of each chapter. They share concrete strategies for how faculty and student affairs educators can build on each other's expertise to improve the educational experiences of students.

We recognize that educators are often busy and must react quickly to crises that occur on campus. Decisions can still be made promptly and effectively if one keeps current with theory and reflectively strives to understand the changing needs and demographics of today's college students. Linking theory with practice is not simple; it requires a willingness to rethink one's assumptions about classroom and out-of-class learning and embrace a holistic approach to education that places students' needs at the forefront. One of the central aims of the book is to offer a wealth of examples where theoretical insights converge with practical solutions.

Purposeful Engagement: Cultivating an Environment of Thriving

Diversity, multiculturalism, pluralism, equity and equality, inclusiveness, and social justice are among the many buzzwords used to espouse supposed institutional values. Colleges and universities use these terms liberally in mission statements, on websites, and in recruitment materials. Consequently, various groups of students show up expecting to see evidence of what they have been sold. The most obvious contradiction to these espoused values is the carelessness with which engagement is treated. Students of Color and White student participants in Harper and Hurtado's (2007) study expressed extreme disappointment with the institutional rhetoric concerning diversity and inclusiveness. The misalignment of espoused and enacted institutional values must be addressed if students across various groups are to equitably accrue the full range of benefits associated with educationally purposeful engagement—there must be a greater demonstration of institutional seriousness.

"At-risk students" is perhaps one of the most unfair terms used in American education, in P–12 and higher education alike. This suggests that some students are in jeopardy of not succeeding. Our view is that students are *placed* at risk for dropping out of college when educators are negligent in customizing engagement efforts that connect them to the campus. While some may enter with characteristics and backgrounds that suggest they need customized services and resources, we maintain that student affairs educators and faculty should be proactive in assessing those needs and creating the environmental conditions that would enable all students to thrive (Love, 2019). They are placed at risk when engagement is treated the same and population-specific efforts are not enacted. Concerning the engagement of diverse populations of college students, our position is very much consistent with the title of Manning, Kinzie, and Schuh's (2006) book, *One Size Does Not Fit All*. In the chapters that follow, authors advocate moving beyond sameness to customize educational practices and maximize meaningful, intentional engagement and outcomes for all.

Finally, while the goal may seem lofty, learning to transform institutions and engagement practices through theoretically-grounded, praxis-oriented, equity-minded lenses is a skill that all educators can develop, no matter where they sit in their colleges and universities. When the larger landscape seems hopeless at times, this point should serve as a motivator for all: that the capacity to be agents for justice-centered engagement, the heart of our work, lies within us all.

References

Abes, E. S., Jones, S. R., & Stewart, D-L. (2019). *Rethinking college student development theory using critical frameworks.* Sterling, VA: Stylus.

Aho, R., & Quaye, S. J. (2018). Applied critical leadership: Centering racial justice and decolonization in professional associations. *The Journal of Critical Scholarship on Higher Education and Student Affairs, 3*(3), 8–19.

American College Personnel Association. (1994). *The student learning imperative: Implications for student affairs.* Washington, DC: Author.

American College Personnel Association & National Association of Student Personnel Administrators. (2004). *Learning reconsidered: A campus-wide focus on the student experience.* Washington, DC: Authors.

Anaya, G. (1996). College experiences and student learning: The influence of active learning, college environments, and cocurricular activities. *Journal of College Student Development, 37*(6), 611–622.

Ancis, J., Sedlacek, W., & Mohr, J. (2000). Student perceptions of campus cultural climate by race. *Journal of Counseling and Development, 78*(2), 180–185.

Antonio, A. L., Chang, M. J., Hakuta, K., Kenny, D. A., Levin, S., & Milem, J. F. (2004). Effects of racial diversity on complex thinking in college students. *Psychological Science, 15*(8), 507–510.

Astin, A. W. (1975). *Preventing students from dropping out.* San Francisco, CA: Jossey-Bass.

Astin, A. W. (1984). Student involvement: A developmental theory for higher education. *Journal of College Student Personnel, 25*(2), 297–308.

Astin, A. W. (1993). *What matters in college? Four critical years revisited.* San Francisco, CA: Jossey-Bass.

Baxter Magolda, M. B. (1992). Cocurricular influences on college students' intellectual development. *Journal of College Student Development, 33*, 203–213.

Baxter Magolda, M. B., & King, P. M. (Eds.). (2004). *Learning partnerships: Theory and models of practice to educate for self-authorship.* Sterling, VA: Stylus.

Bean, J. P. (1990). Why students leave: Insights from research. In D. Hossler & J. P. Bean (Eds.), *The strategic management of college enrollments* (pp. 147–169). San Francisco, CA: Jossey-Bass.

Bean, J. P. (2005). Nine themes of college student retention. In A. Seidman (Ed.), *College student retention: Formula for student success* (pp. 215–244). Washington, DC: ACE and Praeger.

Bensimon, E. M. (2007). The underestimated significance of practitioner knowledge in the scholarship of student success. *The Review of Higher Education, 30*(4), 441–469.

Berger, J. B., & Milem, J. F. (1999). The role of student involvement and perceptions of integration in a causal model of student persistence. *Research in Higher Education, 40*(6), 641–664.

Braxton, J. M., Hirschy, A. S., & McClendon, S. A. (2004). *Understanding and reducing college student departure. ASHE-ERIC Higher Education Report* (Vol. 30, No. 3). San Francisco, CA: Jossey-Bass.

Braxton, J. M., Milem, J. F., & Sullivan, A. S. (2000). The influence of active learning on the college departure process: Toward a revision of Tinto's theory. *The Journal of Higher Education, 71*(5), 569–590.

Bridges, B. K., Cambridge, B., Kuh, G. D., & Leegwater, L. H. (2005). Student engagement at minority-serving institutions: Emerging lessons from the BEAMS project. *New Directions for Institutional Research, 125*, 25–43.

Cabrera, A. F., Nora, A., Terenzini, P. T., Pascarella, E. T., & Hagedorn, L. S. (1999). Campus racial climate and the adjustment of students to college: A comparison between White students and African American students. *Journal of Higher Education, 70*(2), 134–202.

Chang, M. J., Astin, A. W., & Kim, D. (2004). Cross-racial interaction among undergraduates: Some consequences, causes, and patterns. *Research in Higher Education, 45*(5), 529–553.

Chang, M. J., Chang, J. C., & Ledesma, M. C. (2005). Beyond magical thinking: Doing the real work of diversifying our institutions. *About Campus, 10*(2), 9–16.

Chang, M. J., Denson, N., Sáenz, V., & Misa, K. (2006). The educational benefits of sustaining cross-racial interaction among undergraduates. *Journal of Higher Education, 77*, 430–455.

Crenshaw, K. (1989). Demarginalizing the intersection of race and sex: A black feminist critique of antidiscrimination doctrine, feminist theory and antiracist politics. *University of Chicago Legal Forum,* 139–167.

Evans, N. J. (1987). A framework for assisting student affairs staff in fostering moral development. *Journal of Counseling and Development, 66*, 191–193.

Freire, P. (1970). *Pedagogy of the oppressed*. New York, NY: The Continuum International Publishing Group.

Garvey, J. C., Sanders, L. A., & Flint, M. A. (2017). Generational perceptions of campus climate among LGBTQ undergraduates. *Journal of College Student Development, 58*(6), 795–817.

Gurin, P., Dey, E. L., Hurtado, S., & Gurin, G. (2002). Diversity and higher education: Theory and impact on educational outcomes. *Harvard Educational Review, 72*, 330–366.

Harper, S. R. (2007). Using qualitative methods to assess student trajectories and college impact. In S. R. Harper & S. D. Museus (Eds.), *Using qualitative methods in institutional assessment*. New Directions for Institutional Research (No. 136, pp. 55–68). San Francisco, CA: Jossey-Bass.

Harper, S. R. (2008). Realizing the intended outcomes of *Brown*: High-achieving African American male undergraduates and social capital. *American Behavioral Scientist, 51*(7), 1–24.

Harper, S. R. (2011). Strategy and intentionality in practice. In J. H. Schuh, S. R. Jones, & S. R. Harper (Eds.), *Student services: A handbook for the profession* (5th ed., pp. 287–302). San Francisco, CA: Jossey-Bass.

Harper, S. R., & Antonio, A. L. (2008). Not by accident: Intentionality in diversity, learning, and engagement. In S. R. Harper (Ed.), *Creating inclusive campus environments for cross-cultural learning and student engagement* (pp. 1–18). Washington, DC: NASPA.

Harper, S. R., & Hurtado, S. (2007). Nine themes in campus racial climates and implications for institutional transformation. In S. R. Harper, & L. D. Patton (Eds.), *Responding to the realities of race on campus* (New directions for student services, No. 120) (pp. 7–24). San Francisco, CA: Jossey-Bass.

Harper, S. R., & Quaye, S. J. (2007). Student organizations as venues for Black identity expression and development among African American male student leaders. *Journal of College Student Development, 48*(2), 133–159.

Hu, S., & Kuh, G. D. (2003). Diversity experiences and college student learning and development. *Journal of College Student Development, 44*(3), 320–334.

Hurtado, S. (1992). The campus racial climate: Contexts for conflict. *Journal of Higher Education, 63*(5), 539–569.

Kinzie, J., & Kuh, G. D. (2004). Going deep: Learning from campuses that share responsibility for student success. *About Campus, 9*(5), 2–8.

Kuh, G. D. (1993). In their own words: What students learn outside the classroom. *American Educational Research Journal, 30*(2), 277–304.

Kuh, G. D. (1995). The other curriculum: Out-of-class experiences associated with student learning and personal development. *Journal of Higher Education, 66*(2), 123–155.

Kuh, G. D. (2001). Assessing what really matters to student learning: Inside the National Survey of Student Engagement. *Change, 33*(3), 10–17.

Kuh, G. D., Kinzie, J., Buckley, J. A., Bridges, B. K., & Hayek, J. C. (2007). *Piecing together the student success puzzle: Research, propositions, and recommendations*. ASHE Higher Education Report (Vol. 32, No. 5). San Francisco, CA: Jossey-Bass.

Kuh, G. D., Kinzie, J., Schuh, J. H., Whitt, E. J., & Associates (2005). *Student success in college: Creating conditions that matter*. San Francisco, CA: Jossey-Bass.

Kuh, G. D., Palmer, M, & Kish, K. (2003). The value of educationally purposeful out-of-class experiences. In T. L. Skipper, & R. Argo (Eds.), *Involvement in campus activities and the retention of first-year college students*. The First-Year Experience Monograph Series (No. 36, pp. 19–34). Columbia, SC: University of South Carolina, National Resource Center for the First-Year Experience and Students in Transition.

Ladson-Billings, G. (1995). Toward a theory of culturally relevant pedagogy. *American Educational Research Journal, 32*(3), 465–491.

Love, B. L. (2019). *We want to do more than survive: Abolitionist teaching and the pursuit of educational freedom*. Boston, MA: Beacon Press.

Manning, K., Kinzie, J., & Schuh, J. H. (2006). *One size does not fit all: Traditional and innovative models of student affairs practice*. New York, NY: Routledge.

McEwen, M. K. (2003). The nature and uses of theory. In S. R. Komives, & D. B. Woodard (Eds.), *Student services: A handbook for the profession* (4th ed., pp. 147–163). San Francisco, CA: Jossey-Bass.

Milem, J. F., & Berger, J. B. (1997). A modified model of college student persistence: Exploring the relationship between Astin's Theory of Involvement and Tinto's Theory of Student Departure. *Journal of College Student Development, 38*(4), 387–400.

Museus, S. D. (2014). The culturally engaging campus environments (CECE) model: A new theory of college success among racially diverse student populations. In M. B. Paulsen (Ed.), *Higher education: A handbook of theory and research* (pp. 189–227). New York, NY: Springer.

Okello, W. K. (2018). From self-authorship to self-definition: Remapping theoretical assumptions through Black feminism. *Journal of College Student Development, 59*(5), 528–544.

Pascarella, E. T. (2001). Identifying excellence in undergraduate education: Are we even close? *Change, 33*(3), 19–23.

Pascarella, E. T., Edison, M., Nora, A., Hagedorn, L. S., & Terenzini, P. T. (1996). Influence of students' openness to diversity and challenge in the first year of college. *Journal of Higher Education, 67*, 174–195.

Pascarella, E. T., & Terenzini, P. T. (2005). *How college affects students, Volume 2: A third decade of research*. San Francisco, CA: Jossey-Bass.

Patton, L. D., Harper, S. R., & Harris, J. (2015). Using critical race theory to (re)interpret widely-studied topics related to students in US higher education. In A. M. Martínez Alemán, E. M. Bensimon, & B. Pusser (Eds.), *Critical approaches to the study of higher education* (pp. 193–219). Baltimore: Johns Hopkins University Press.

Patton, L. D., Renn, K. A., Guido, F. M., & Quaye, S. J. (2016). *Student development in college: Theory, research, and practice* (3rd ed.). San Francisco, CA: Jossey-Bass.

Pendakur, S. L. (2016). Empowerment agents: Developing staff and faculty to support students at the margins. In V. Pendakur (Ed.), *Closing the opportunity gap: Identity-conscious strategies for retention and student success*. Sterling, VA: Stylus Publishing.

Peltier, G. L., Laden, R., & Matranga, M. (1999). Student persistence in college: A review of research. *Journal of College Student Retention, 1*(4), 357–375.

Quaye, S. J., Aho, R. E., Beard Jacob, M., Domingue, A. D., Guido, F. M., Lange, A. C., Squire, D., & Stewart, D-L. (2019). *A bold vision forward: A framework for the strategic imperative for racial justice and decolonization*. Washington, DC: ACPA.

Quaye, S. J., & Harper, S. R. (2007). Faculty accountability for culturally-inclusive pedagogy and curricula. *Liberal Education, 93*(3), 32–39.

Reason, R. D. and Kimball, E. W. (2012). A new theory-to-practice model for student affairs: Integrating scholarship, context, and reflection. *Education Publications, 21*.

Rest, J. R. (1993). Research on moral judgment in college students. In A. Garrod (Ed.), *Approaches to moral development* (pp. 201–213). New York, NY: Teachers College Press.

Rockenbach, A. N., Mayhew, M. J., & Bowman, N. A. (2015). Perceptions of the campus climate for nonreligious students. *Journal of College Student Development, 56*, 181–186.

Schön, D. A. (1987). *Educating the reflective practitioner: Toward a new design for teaching and learning in the professions*. San Francisco, CA: Jossey-Bass.

Stage, F. K., & Hossler, D. (2000). Where is the student? Linking student behaviors, college choice, and college persistence. In J. M. Braxton (Ed.), *Reworking the student departure puzzle* (pp. 170–195). Nashville, TN: Vanderbilt University Press.

Strange, C. C., & Banning, J. H. (2001). *Educating by design: Creating campus learning environments that work*. San Francisco, CA: Jossey-Bass.

Swail, W. S., Redd, K. E., & Perna, L. W. (2003). *Retaining minority students in higher education: A framework for success*. ASHE-ERIC Higher Education Report (Vol. 30, No. 2). San Francisco, CA: Jossey-Bass.

Tanaka, G. K. (2002). Higher education's self-reflexive turn: Toward an intercultural theory of student development. *Journal of Higher Education, 73*(2), 263–296.

Tinto, V. (1993). *Leaving college: Rethinking the causes and cures of student attrition* (2nd ed.). Chicago, IL: University of Chicago Press.

Tinto, V. (2000). Taking retention seriously: Rethinking the first year of college. *NACADA Journal, 19*(2), 5–10.

Tinto, V. (2005). Moving from theory to action. In A. Seidman (Ed.), *College student retention: Formula for student success* (pp. 371–333). Washington, DC: American Council on Education and Praeger.

Torres, V., Howard-Hamilton, M. F., & Cooper, D. L. (2003). *Identity development of diverse populations: Implications for teaching and administration in higher education. ASHE-ERIC Higher Education Report* (Vol. 29, No. 6). San Francisco, CA: Jossey-Bass.

Tross, S. A., Harper, J. P., Osher, L. W., & Kneidinger, L. M. (2000). Not just the usual cast of characteristics: Using personality to predict college performance and retention. *Journal of College Student Development, 41*(3), 325–336.

Villalpando, O. (2002). The impact of diversity and multiculturalism on all students: Findings from a national study. *NASPA Journal, 40*, 124–144.

Wells, A. V., & Horn, C. (2015). The Asian American College experience at a diverse Institution: Campus climate as a predictor of sense of belonging. *Journal of Student Affairs Research and Practice, 52*(2), 149–163.

Chapter 2
Engaging Students of Color

Samuel D. Museus, Kimberly A. Griffin,
and Stephen John Quaye

Despite the investment of significant resources and energy in increasing student engagement opportunities throughout the US higher education system in recent decades, substantial racial disparities in the quality of college student outcomes persist. National data repeatedly highlight that Students of Color—including Black, Latinx, Native American, and Pacific Islander populations—exhibit significantly lower rates of attainment than their majority counterparts (Espinosa, Turk, Taylor, & Chessman, 2019; NCES, 2019). Although Asian Americans have high rates of attainment in the aggregate, some ethnic groups within this racial category exhibit the lowest attainment rates of all racial and ethnic groups within the US (Museus, 2014a).

One factor that arguably reinforces the aforementioned inequities is the way efforts to increase student engagement and success are approached. Specifically, engagement opportunities—similar to other structures on college campuses—do not serve all racial groups equally well. Existing evidence indicates that Students of Color face disparities in access to some engagement opportunities (Brownell & Swaner, 2009; Kuh, Cruce, Shoup, Kinzie, & Gonyea, 2008; Kuh, 2008; Seifert, Gillig, Hanson, Pascarella, & Blaich, 2014). In addition, while there is evidence that engagement can lead to positive outcomes for Students of Color (e.g., Espinosa, 2011; Jones, Barlow, & Villarejo, 2010), evidence that the engagement opportunities *equalize* the quality of college experiences and outcomes is limited at best. These realities warrant a revisiting of the concept of student engagement and consideration of how it can be redefined and reframed in ways that are more equitable.

Scholars have noted that student engagement discourse is often framed in a one-size-fits-all way (Museus, 2014b; Museus, Chang, & Zilvinskis, in press). Such discourse perpetuates assumptions that if an institution offers ample engagement opportunities, such as first-year seminars and learning communities, then all students will have equal ability to thrive on their campuses. This deracialized and acultural way of thinking about engagement ignores the vast body of knowledge that is generated from Communities of Color and highlights the salient role of social and cultural context, as well as students' social identities, in shaping their experience within higher education (Museus, Ledesma, & Parker, 2015). This chapter is based on our well-founded belief that in order to create engagement opportunities that serve students in equitable ways, knowledge from Communities of Color must be considered and incorporated into the design and delivery of engagement programs and practices.

In the following section, we present important context for our discussion about engagement, highlighting some key concepts that center environment and identity in the discussion about engagement. Next, we discuss the ways in which college educators might reenvision and redesign engagement opportunities to be more racially equitable. In the final section, we offer a set of recommendations for policy and practice, which serves as a starting point for educators wanting to adopt a serious commitment to serving Students of Color equitably.

Critical Concepts

Two concepts provide a useful backdrop for the current discussion: campus racial climate and campus racial culture. In discussing these two concepts, we also highlight potential barriers to engagement that exist for Students of Color by not utilizing these frameworks. Campus climate is an inherently ambiguous concept. Bauer (1998) defined *campus climate* as "the current perceptions, attitudes, and expectations that define the institution and its members" (p. 2). By this definition, climate is a relatively tacit and flexible aspect of the campus environment. The malleable nature of campus climates makes them an easy target for institutional efforts to change environments to get immediate results and improve the experiences of Students of Color. The drawback of this malleability, however, is that the impact of institutional efforts to improve campus climates can also quickly change or diminish. Thus, efforts to improve campus environments for historically oppressed groups via climate initiatives can sometimes be immediate and short-lived and may only influence the experiences of a small proportion of students on college campuses on which they are implemented. Thus, it is important for educators focusing on changing their institutional climates to consider both comprehensive and long-term transformation approaches.

In contrast to campus climate, the concept of *campus culture* refers to what Kuh and Whitt (1988) called the following:

> Deeply-embedded, persistent patterns of norms, values, practices, beliefs, and assumptions that shape the behavior of individuals and groups in a college or university and provide a frame of reference within which to interpret the meaning of events and actions on and off the campus.
>
> (pp. 12–13)

Campus culture, therefore, refers to the very fabric that permeates all aspects of university life and that shapes and defines the behavior and experiences of people within that organization. In the remainder of this section, we discuss the concepts of *campus racial climate and campus racial culture*. In doing so, we underscore how race permeates and shapes these two aspects of the environment on college and university campuses.

Campus Racial Climate

Initially proposed by Hurtado, Milem, Clayton-Pedersen, and Allen (1999), the campus racial climate framework can provide important insights, informing our understanding of the multidimensional nature of climate and how it can influence interest in engagement among Students of Color. The campus racial climate is defined as the current attitudes, perceptions, and expectations within an institutional community about issues of race, ethnicity, and diversity (Hurtado et al., 1999). More hostile campus racial climates can negatively influence the interactions of Students of Color with other members of the campus community, both in and outside the classroom, by diminishing the quality, frequency, and potential of positive outcomes of their interactions on campus. This, in turn, can inhibit students' patterns of engagement, which ultimately has poor implications for student growth, development, and retention (Cabrera, Nora, Terenzini, Pascarella, & Hagedorn, 1999; Hurtado, 1992).

Based on the framework, an institution's campus racial climate is created by internal and external forces, which together shape the climate at each individual campus. The acknowledgement of external forces, namely government policies and the sociohistorical contexts of the region, state, or United States, draws attention to how broad societal trends and public policies can influence campus racial climates. For example, legislation and court decisions eliminating affirmative action do not only exist outside institutions. Rather, they influence campus policies, practices, and attitudes about race and diversity, which may help institutions increase the number of Students of Color on campuses and the safe spaces that those students construct for themselves but may also make these students feel less welcome in various campus spaces and less interested in participating in various activities in and outside the classroom.

According to the framework, climate is shaped by five internal dimensions: (1) an institution's history and legacy of inclusion or exclusion, (2) compositional diversity, (3) psychological climate, (4) behavioral climate, and (5) organizational/structural diversity (Milem, Chang, & Antonio, 2005). These dimensions are interconnected; however, each dimension of the framework can be specifically targeted to facilitate institutional transformation. First, an institution's historical legacy of inclusion or exclusion can continue to shape current racial dynamics on college and university campuses (Hurtado et al., 1999). For example, many institutions have a history of perpetuating hostile environments for Students of Color. Without addressing or acknowledging this history, Students of Color may feel their campuses are still hostile, unwelcoming places that only enrolled them because of forced desegregation policies.

Compositional diversity is frequently described as the first step that must be taken in developing an environment that fosters positive cross-racial interactions and refers to the actual representation of People of Color on campus (Hurtado et al., 1999;

Milem et al., 2005). This dimension involves any efforts to increase the physical presence of students, staff, and faculty from underrepresented groups. Despite its importance, the singular act of increasing the number of People of Color on campuses will not necessarily create more positive campus racial climates (Cabrera et al., 1999; Chang, 2002; Hurtado et al., 1999; Milem et al., 2005). Rather, the psychological and behavioral dimensions of those racial climates must be addressed. The psychological dimension includes "individuals' views of group relations, institutional responses to diversity, perceptions of discrimination or racial conflict, and attitudes held towards others from different racial/ethnic backgrounds" (Hurtado et al., 1999, p. 25). The behavioral dimension, or quality of interactions and relationships between people from diverse backgrounds, reminds readers that they must attend to the nature of interactions between different groups on campus to promote a more hospitable environment. The psychological and behavioral dimensions of racial climates can be perceived as working in tandem, particularly in relation to fostering the engagement of Students of Color. Negative perceptions of racial climates can make students more reluctant to engage with those from different backgrounds than their own. Similarly, a lack of interactions across difference can lead to negative perceptions of the racial climate and level of inclusion for People of Color on campus.

Finally, Milem et al. (2005) added organizational/structural diversity to the original Hurtado et al. (1999) campus racial climate framework. This dimension highlights the important roles that established institutional processes, curricular requirements, and campus decision-making processes play in shaping racial climates. For example, curricular requirements that emphasize Eurocentric principles and disregard work from Scholars of Color can shape students' interest and engagement in the classroom; similarly, policies that give student organizations funding and space based on their length of time at their institutions can privilege predominantly White student groups based on the historical demography of their campuses.

Campus Racial Culture

While many of the scholars who study institutional culture discuss it as a deracialized phenomenon (e.g., Kuh, Kinzie, Schuh, Whitt, & Associates, 2005; Whitt, 1993, 1996), several scholars have highlighted the fact that race shapes the cultures of postsecondary institutions and the experiences of Students of Color within these cultures (Guiffrida, 2006; Guiffrida, Kiyama, Waterman, & Museus, 2012; Jayakumar, 2012; Jayakumar & Museus, 2012; Kuh & Love, 2000; Museus, 2007, 2008a, 2008c, 2011a, 2011b; Museus & Harris, 2010; Museus & Liverman, 2011; Museus & Quaye, 2009; Museus, Ravello, & Vega, 2012; Quaye & Chang, 2012; Rendón, Jalomo, & Nora, 2000). Building on the work of these scholars, Museus et al. (2012) defined the *campus racial culture* as:

> Collective patterns of tacit values, beliefs, assumptions, and norms that evolve from an institution's history and are manifest in its mission, traditions, language, interactions, artifacts, physical structures, and other symbols,

which differentially shape the experiences of various racial and ethnic groups and can function to oppress racial minority populations within a particular institution.

(p. 32)

The concept of the campus racial culture is based on the notion that most, if not all, predominantly White institutions are founded on deeply embedded Eurocentric values, beliefs, and assumptions that shape the norms and behaviors of faculty, staff, and students on college campuses (Jayakumar & Museus, 2012; Museus et al., 2012). Moreover, the campus racial culture suggests that Eurocentric cultural values, assumptions, and norms that permeate postsecondary institutions can shape the experiences of Undergraduates of Color in powerful ways. To offer an example of how campus racial cultures can significantly affect the experiences of Students of Color, we highlight the difference between individualistic and collectivist cultural orientations. Because college Students of Color are more likely to come from cultures with collectivist orientations, institutions and programs that perpetuate individualistic and competitive values and assumptions might create conditions in which Students of Color have difficulty engaging, have low levels of satisfaction, and are less likely to succeed (Guiffrida, 2006; Guiffrida et al., 2012). In contrast, institutions and programs that emphasize fostering community and family in academic environments and collaborative learning activities that reflect the values, assumptions, and norms of the racial communities of Students of Color can increase these students' abilities to connect with the cultures of the campus and their likelihood of success (Fullilove & Treisman, 1990; Guiffrida, 2006; Guiffrida et al., 2012).

There are three other concepts that help better understand the nature of the campus racial culture and how it shapes the experiences of undergraduates of color: cultural (in) congruence, cultural dissonance, and cultural integration (Kuh & Love, 2000; Museus, 2008a, Museus & Quaye, 2009). *Cultural incongruence* refers to the distance between the cultures of students' campuses and the cultures of their home communities (Kuh & Love, 2000; Museus & Quaye, 2009); *cultural dissonance* denotes the tension that students experience as a result of the distance between these campus and home cultures (Museus, 2008a), and excessive cultural dissonance can result in culture shock, or a condition in which students leave cultures with familiar cultural signs and symbols and consequently experience feelings of anxiety, frustration, and helplessness (Oberg, 1960). Scholars have suggested that when Students of Color encounter Eurocentric cultures on their college campuses that are incongruent with those from their home communities, they are likely to feel increased cultural dissonance, which is inversely related to engagement and success (Museus & Quaye, 2009). Thus, postsecondary educators can increase engagement and success among Students of Color by decreasing the amount of cultural dissonance these students feel as they navigate predominantly White institutions.

One way educators can diminish the cultural dissonance that Students of Color experience as they transition to and navigate their institutions is by utilizing the concept of cultural integration. While the term *integration* has been used for decades to describe students' assimilation into the academic and social subsystems on campus (Tinto, 1987,

1993), the concepts of academic and social integration have been critiqued for being culturally biased and placing an unfair expectation on Students of Color to assimilate to the dominant cultures of predominantly White institutions (Attinasi, 1989; Tierney, 1999). To reclaim the term *integration* and reframe it in a culturally responsive light, higher education researchers have introduced the concept of *cultural integration* to refer to the incorporation of academic and social elements, as well as students' cultural backgrounds and identities, into educational spaces, programs, practices, events, and activities (Museus, 2011b; Museus et al., 2012). They suggest that educators can integrate these academic, social, and cultural elements to bridge the various spheres of students' lives and lead to the creation of stronger connections between Students of Color and their respective campuses. Empirical evidence indicates that cultural integration can positively influence the engagement and success of Students of Color because it facilitates students' connections to the academic and social subsystems of campus, while simultaneously strengthening ties to their cultural backgrounds (Museus et al., 2012).

The term *cultural integration* is based on the underlying assumption that educators can, and sometimes do, bridge academic and co-curricular divides, as well as the notion that such bridging can have positive effects on engagement and success among Students of Color. Nevertheless, we recognize that many researchers and college educators distinguish between the academic (i.e., classroom) and social (i.e., out-of-class) experiences of students in higher education. Thus, in the last section, we discuss strategies for fostering engagement among Students of Color in these two domains. We acknowledge, however, that many of our recommendations encompass both aspects of campus life.

Creating Equitable Environments and Engagement Opportunities

More recently, scholars have generated models that more effectively reflect the lives and realities of students from diverse backgrounds. For example, Museus (2014a) utilized over 20 years of scholarship on the conditions that affect success among diverse college students to propose a model that describes the types of environments that allow these populations to thrive in college. The CECE model provides a framework to understand equitable environments that might maximize engagement and success among diverse populations but can also be used to think about how engagement opportunities can be constructed in equitable ways. It outlines nine indicators that characterize environments in which diverse populations can thrive. The first five indicators focus on *cultural relevance* or the ways in which institutional environments are relevant to the cultural backgrounds and communities of diverse populations:

1. *Cultural Familiarity:* Campus spaces for undergraduates to connect with faculty, staff, and peers who share or understand their cultural backgrounds, identities, and experiences.
2. *Culturally Relevant Knowledge:* The extent to which students have opportunities to learn about their own cultural communities via culturally relevant curricular and co-curricular opportunities.

3. *Cultural Community Service:* Opportunities for students to give back to and positively transform their cultural communities.
4. *Meaningful Cross-Cultural Engagement:* Opportunities to engage in positive and purposeful interactions with peers from different cultural backgrounds.
5. *Cultural Validation:* Educators validating students' background, identities, and experiences.

The remaining four indicators focus on *cultural responsiveness* or the ways in which campus environments respond to the norms and needs of diverse students:

1. *Collectivist Cultural Orientations:* The ways in which campus cultures and educators focus on shared, rather than only individual, success.
2. *Humanized Educational Environments:* Availability of opportunities for students to develop meaningful relationships with faculty and staff members who care about and are committed to their success.
3. *Proactive Philosophies:* Educators who use proactive philosophies go above and beyond to actively reach out, encourage, and sometimes pressure students to take advantage of available information, opportunities, and support.
4. *Holistic Support:* College students' access to at least one educator who students are confident will provide them with the support and information they need or connect them with someone who can provide adequate support.

A significant and growing body of evidence suggests that these types of environments are associated with students' positive connections to their campuses, engagement, and eventual outcomes. While not intended to be exhaustive, we provide an overview of themes in this research, which highlights how the following factors facilitate engagement and eventual success among Students of Color in college: (1) culturally relevant (co-)curricula, (2) culturally familiar campus organizations, (3) opportunities to give back to cultural communities, and (4) safe and validating spaces.

Culturally Relevant (Co-)Curricula

Researchers show how curricula that reflect and engage the cultural backgrounds of Students of Color positively influence their engagement and success (e.g., Kiang, 2002, 2009; Museus, Lam, Huang, Kem, & Tan, 2012; Museus, Mueller, & Aquino, 2013). For example, ethnic studies programs can offer curricula that reflect the cultural communities and identities of Students of Color, thereby permitting those students to identify with the course content while simultaneously building community with faculty and peers of similar racial, ethnic, and cultural backgrounds (Kiang, 2002, 2009; Museus, Lam et al., 2012).

Culturally Familiar Campus Organizations

In response to the challenges many Students of Color face as they seek opportunities to engage in activities outside the classroom, many may seek and participate in culturally-based living options, groups, and organizations to establish a connection to the campus community (Bourke, 2010; Guiffrida, 2003; Museus, 2008c; Patton, 2006). Over the past decade, researchers have called attention to the critical role that culturally-based co-curricular activities and spaces play in the engagement patterns and outcomes of Students of Color at predominantly White institutions. Although these organizations are sometimes regarded as evidence of "balkanization" or "self-segregation" on many college campuses, Hurtado and colleagues (1999) suggest culturally based groups serve as valuable support mechanisms, social outlets for the students, and facilitators of further involvement in campus activities.

Opportunities to Give Back to Cultural Communities

As mentioned, many Students of Color report that mainstream campus organizations and activities seldom reflect their cultural identities or interests (Davis, 1991; Person & Christensen, 1996; Rooney, 1985). This is problematic because there is some evidence indicating that Students of Color are more likely to become engaged when they can access opportunities to connect with their cultural heritages (Comp, 2008; Guiffrida, 2003; Harper & Quaye, 2007; Museus, 2008b; Museus et al., 2012; Rubin, 2004). For example, researchers have written about how Students of Color engage in study abroad for the purposes of heritage seeking, in order to acquire knowledge related to their community and family histories and cultures (Comp, 2008; Rubin, 2004). Additionally, scholars have written about students who engage in various campus activities so that they can connect with people who have similar cultural backgrounds and give back to their cultural communities (Guiffrida, 2003; Harper & Quaye, 2007; Museus, 2008b).

Safe and Validating Campus Spaces

Subcultures and spaces that reflect the cultural backgrounds of students can function as "safe spaces," instrumental in reducing feelings of isolation, marginality, and alienation among Communities of Color (Guiffrida, 2003; Kiang, 2002, 2009; Murguia, Padilla, & Pavel, 1991; Museus, 2008b, 2011a; Museus, Lam et al., 2012; Patton, 2006; Solórzano, Allen, & Carroll, 2002; Wang, Sedlacek, & Westbrook, 1992). Work by Person and Christensen (1996), Guiffrida (2003), and Museus (2008c) suggests students experience a sense of mattering and validation in ethnic student organizations, providing a space where students are accepted rather than isolated or alienated. Similarly, Patton (2006) describes the importance of Black cultural centers, noting that, in addition to providing students a place where they can relax, these centers enable students to feel a sense of belonging and family that they were lacking within the larger institution.

Further, cultural organizations and multicultural spaces provide opportunities for students to connect with others they perceive to be "like them," sharing similar backgrounds, experiences, and interests. Museus's (2008c) analysis of interviews conducted with Black and Asian American students suggests they perceive ethnic student organizations as an important means to meet and connect with students who share their cultural background, having similar upbringings and struggles navigating their predominantly

White institution. Through this sense of shared experience and identity, cultural organizations appear to provide avenues for comfort, support, and opportunities to connect with peers in an authentic way (Guiffrida, 2003; McClure, 2006; Museus, 2008c). Cultural organizations also provide students with a sense of cultural connection, allowing them to share in and express their identities through their participation. Participants in Harper and Quaye's (2007) study of Black male leaders noted that they chose to engage in cultural organizations based on their desire to give back to their communities and support other Black students. Similarly, Inkelas (2004) and Museus (2008c) found that students developed a stronger sense of racial and ethnic identity through their participation in ethnic organizations.

Student Engagement Strategies

A multipronged method is necessary to engage Students of Color in predominantly White campus and classroom environments. We encourage departments and units across campus to leverage their unique strengths to develop programs and strategies that meet the needs and concerns of the students they serve. In this section, we outline several approaches that can be utilized independently; however, at the same time, we urge student affairs professionals, faculty, and institutional leaders to resist the tendency to work in isolated silos and collaborate as they develop interventions.

Examine Institutional and Programmatic Missions

Mission statements are intended to guide organizational priorities and actions and are a critical aspect of the cultures that exist within institutions and within specific academic programs. While many missions state that increasing diversity or supporting a diverse student body is valued and a priority, too often these values fall short of being fully enacted. Despite their inclusion in mission statements, some may argue that supporting and engaging campus diversity is too difficult and conflict with other important institutional goals, such as maintaining selectivity and prestige, celebrating tradition, and affirming free speech. However, we remind readers that these values and priorities can certainly coexist, and institutional leaders must periodically and critically examine whether and how practices, pedagogy, and policies align with mission statements and affirm a meaningful commitment to Students of Color. Further, faculty and academic administrators should engage in periodic reflection on the missions of their programs in order to better understand whether their campuses and programs reflect the needs of Students of Color.

Conduct Climate Assessments and Cultural Audits

Assessment plays a central role in promoting the engagement of Students of Color, and it is important for institutions to conduct regular campus racial climate assessments. Such assessments are integral to ensuring that campus administrators, faculty, and staff understand how students are experiencing campus racial climates, how various groups experience these climates in disparate ways, and how they can improve these climates for Students of Color. While institutional leaders are increasingly hiring external consultants to conduct these assessments, student affairs assessment offices can and should play a critical role in climate assessment work. Student affairs assessment offices can focus institutional attention on how climate manifests outside the classroom in co-curricular spaces, interpreting and collecting new data that can inform the development of strategies to enhance climate in residence halls, student organizations, and shared social spaces.

In addition, institutions must attend to how culture, or the complex web of values, beliefs, assumptions, norms, and behaviors (Jayakumar & Museus, 2012; Kuh & Whitt, 1988; Museus, 2007), drives students' experiences and opportunities to engage on campus. In fact, some aspects of campus cultures (e.g., cultural assumptions) are so deeply embedded in the organizational fabric of institutions and taken for granted by their members that people within these campuses never reflect on and do not completely understand these cultural elements or their impact. For example, assumptions about who is smart and college-ready, what rigor and merit look like, and what is "normal" in a campus community can drive the daily behavior of faculty and staff on college campuses, often negatively affecting the experiences and outcomes of Students of Color (Jayakumar & Museus, 2012). Thus, it is imperative that institutional leaders engage in cultural audits that can uncover these aspects of culture and unpack how they impact Students of Color (Museus, 2007; Whitt, 1993). Additionally, given that campus cultures often appear as "normal" and can be invisible to those who feel a sense of community membership, it is important for institutions to involve external assessment specialists who can "make the familiar strange" and prompt institutional members to engage in a critical analysis of their taken-for-granted assumptions (Museus, 2007; Whitt, 1993).

As campuses assess their environments, it is critical to incorporate and respect the voices of Students of Color. Students are in the best positions to evaluate whether their social and educational needs are being met, and providing students with opportunities to be heard by those who have the power to make changes can lead to more intentional and successful support strategies. There are multiple ways to ensure that students' voices and perspectives are amplified. First, data collected during climate assessments and cultural audits must be carefully disaggregated so the voices of the smallest populations on campus do not get lost. Further, care must be taken to examine trends at the intersections of students' identities, examining within-group differences based on, for example, gender identity, sexual orientation, ability, and religion. Also, student advisory committees can be composed to provide feedback to academic and institutional leaders about deficiencies in academic content and department offerings, cultural awareness of faculty and staff members, and potential ways to engage them and their peers in leadership opportunities. An advisory committee can be particularly helpful in shifting the climate and culture of an academic department by recommending revisions to syllabi and suggesting readings reflective of students' cultural groups that faculty can incorporate into their courses. Sharing these insights with academic deans and department chairs who can filter information to faculty can ultimately improve the climate and culture for Students of Color, creating a more positive environment for engagement.

Foster Peer Networks

Peer support is critical to fostering the engagement of Students of Color. Engagement opportunities that foster a connection to peers and a sense of community can promote belonging and, ultimately, student persistence (Harris & Wood, 2013; Strayhorn, 2012). Providing activities and spaces in which Students of Color can connect with other students who share their identities enables them to reenergize in the company of others who share similar experiences. Therefore, educators should provide opportunities for Students of Color to formulate networks with other Peers of Color.

Strategies to foster students' connections to peers can vary greatly, and we encourage institutions to think creatively about how to create space and opportunities for connection. For instance, periodic forums comprising Students of Color provide a space for students to develop and sustain relationships with their peers across multiple majors and disciplines. These forums provide opportunities for students to candidly discuss climate-related challenges and their experiences at predominantly White institutions. Further, these forums can enable students to build friendships through their positive experiences and share strategies for navigating academic and social spaces. Creating opportunities for more senior students to academically and socially support new students through peer mentoring relationships can also be a successful strategy. Several institutions have established programs in which third- and fourth-year students serve as peer mentors for incoming students and provide them with the social networks necessary to succeed during their collegiate tenures.

Academic programs can also be leveraged to foster peer networks. Institutions can utilize summer bridge programs, which can enable Students of Color to develop peer networks and engage in classroom settings prior to the start of the academic year. Students in these programs gather support and confidence from peers involved at the institution, while also gaining knowledge and skills that will prepare them for their upcoming academic experience. Summer bridge programs enable students to navigate the campus environment in the company of peers who are also striving to do the same. Ethnic studies departments and programs can also be important resources in helping students connect with peers who share their identities and supporting Communities of Color. Cross-disciplinary courses, panels, and symposia that center on identity and race can draw Students of Color together, facilitating their connections with each other as they engage in academic content that connects with their experiences as People of Color.

Support Culturally-Focused Organizations and Spaces

Culturally-focused campus spaces and organizations, such as culture centers and ethnic student organizations, are critical to the engagement of Students of Color. Many scholars documenting the challenging campus climates in which Students of Color live and learn note the importance of counter-spaces that Students of Color create, spaces in which they create their own supportive campus climates, receive validation and encouragement, and openly challenge stereotypes and microaggressions (e.g., Harper & Hurtado, 2007; Nuñez, 2011; Solórzano, Ceja, & Yosso, 2000). In addition to serving as a source of support within a larger environment that is sometimes unwelcoming, these organizations provide opportunities for students to interact and build connections with peers who share their backgrounds and interests (Griffin & McIntosh, 2015; Guiffrida, 2003; Museus, 2008c, 2011b; Museus et al., 2012). They may also offer Students of Color much-needed opportunities to develop important professional skills and competencies as they take on leadership roles within these groups and serve as an entryway to more broad engagement with faculty and other members of the campus community (Guiffrida, 2003; Harper & Quaye, 2007; Patton, Bridges, & Flowers, 2011).

In addition to serving as "safe spaces" of support and solace, cultural centers and organizations can be "brave spaces" from which Students of Color engage in acts of protest and resistance. Campus activism is also an important form of campus engagement, creating opportunities for students to engage across and appreciate differences and develop their voices and perspectives as they work towards social and institutional change (Linder, Quaye, Lange, Roberts, Lacy, & Okello, 2019). Cultural centers and organizations often offer students opportunities to learn more about social issues, build critical mass, and gain access to resources that can promote their engagement in social action. While activism can often make senior leaders uncomfortable by making incidents of individual and structural racism more visible and forcing transformational change, it is important to listen to and support student activism and the organizations that foster engagement in social action.

It is important to note that calls for the elimination of cultural centers and organizations in order to create more opportunities for engagement across difference and fewer options for self-segregation do not acknowledge the important positive role that these organizations play in the lives of Students of Color. In fact, given the positive outcomes stemming from student participation and leadership in culturally-based organizations, institutions must begin or continue to support their goals and efforts. As noted by Patton (2006), cultural centers are often underdeveloped spaces located far from the center of campus activity. Similarly, student organizations focused on addressing the needs of Students of Color may be allocated fewer resources, be marginalized, or face more stringent disciplinary sanctions than predominantly White organizations (Bourke, 2010). Investing financial resources in culturally-based organizations, providing cultural centers with adequate space and staffing, and providing student groups with guidance and mentorship can promote the efficacy of these entities as they aim to engage and support students.

In addition to providing spaces and organizations that affirm students' racial and ethnic identities, institutional leaders and student affairs professionals must be mindful of how they recognize and support the multiple identities that students embrace and embody. Intersectional theory and current research suggest that there is a unique benefit to students connecting with peers in organizations that recognize their racial identity along with their ethnicity, sexual identity, religious identity, and ability (e.g., Griffin &

McIntosh, 2015; Stewart, 2008). Developing and supporting efforts that recognize students' integrated identities can enable students who feel overlooked or marginalized when their identities are only supported or recognized in isolation to find these spaces particularly important.

Provide Professional Development for Student Leaders

To engage Students of Color in a wider range of campus activities and encourage students to more often engage with those from different racial and ethnic backgrounds, we urge institutional leaders to develop trainings and workshops that arm student leaders with tools to promote intercultural interactions across their organizations. Although students might believe they have the skills to engage across racial differences, many are raised in homogeneous neighborhoods and attend segregated schools (Saenz, 2010). Their confidence may exceed their cross-cultural experience and abilities, and students receive little guidance or support in their efforts to engage across differences when they enter diverse campus environments. Thus, despite students' potential interest in and understanding of the importance of the learning that can take place when they interact with someone from a different racial background, they may not engage because of uncertainty, discomfort, or fear and the lack of preparation to deal with these negative emotions (Fisher & Hartmann, 1995; Harper & Hurtado, 2007). This may be a particularly salient concern for White students, considering that they tend to engage across differences outside the classroom at rates lower than Students of Color before and during college (Fisher & Hartmann, 1995; Gurin, Dey, Hurtado, & Gurin, 2002; Hurtado, Griffin, Arellano, & Cuellar, 2008; Saenz, 2010).

A series of workshops for student leaders from diverse backgrounds may help students develop the skills and competencies to engage in difficult conversations and learn with and from peers from different racial and ethnic backgrounds. The workshops would help student leaders develop strategies that would promote inclusion and racial interactions across their organizations. For example, campus administrators and student affairs professionals can help students think about how to coordinate programs and activities that provide students with opportunities to engage in difficult dialogues and assess whether or not they have created a comfortable environment within the group for students from diverse racial and ethnic backgrounds. Furthermore, holding these training sessions creates opportunities for student leaders to engage with each other, building their individual efficacy, which is necessary to effectively participate in cross-racial interaction and form a foundation for future collaborations and partnerships between student groups and organizations.

Offer and Incentivize Faculty Training and Development

Many faculty were not socialized to utilize culturally-broad literature during their graduate tenures, and many still teach in culturally-exclusive ways. When Students of Color are exposed to mainly White, Eurocentric perspectives, they come to believe the contributions of their cultural groups are trivial or nonexistent. Furthermore, when

Undergraduates of Color peruse the syllabi on the first day of class, they immediately receive a subtle message concerning the importance (or lack thereof) of their racial or ethnic communities.

Faculty and student affairs educators should utilize a diverse array of academic content to demonstrate the contributions of People of Color in various disciplines. First, faculty who wish to engage Students of Color must intentionally incorporate readings that pertain to the experiences of these undergraduates and their respective communities. This practice recognizes that students are more likely to be engaged when culturally diverse perspectives are integrated into curricula. Further, faculty must consider how they can integrate principles associated with difficult dialogues (Placier, Kroner, Burgoyne, & Worthington, 2012), facilitating opportunities to have meaningful dialogues across difference. At the same time, faculty should not expect or rely on Students of Color to discuss their experiences or insights in order to educate White students when the topic of race surfaces in classroom discourse. Instead, inviting White students to discuss their racial and ethnic backgrounds and identities can lessen the pressure placed on Students of Color to speak as experts on race and ethnicity. Workshops on White privilege should also be conducted so that White students have opportunities to reflect on and ask questions about their Whiteness and how they benefit from systemic privilege and racial oppression. Additionally, educators should not assume that Students of Color speak using a racial or ethnic lens at all times. They should also recognize that all racial and ethnic groups have multiple, intersecting identities (e.g., socioeconomic, gender, sexual orientation), which influence their experiences with and perspectives on race and ethnicity.

College educators should support training and development to help faculty integrate these principles in their classrooms. This professional development will include readings, writing reflections, and sharing of culturally-relevant learning material and pedagogies, which can become incorporated into faculty courses. In-services or faculty conferences provide forums for modeling to occur through sharing culturally-inclusive approaches and syllabi from faculty who utilize varied methods of teaching Students of Color. Faculty who are knowledgeable about inclusive classroom settings can be asked to observe, evaluate, and give feedback to professors who are working toward changing their teaching practices.

While this work is valuable and can lead to better outcomes for all students, institutions rarely recognize or reward activities that focus on teaching and learning or developing more inclusive curricula. Thus, institutions should recognize the time and effort that this work requires and provide meaningful incentives and rewards for faculty members who develop and implement culturally-relevant teaching methods. Upper-level administrators should provide incentives and rewards to those who continuously embrace diverse curricular and learning practices and are recognized by students as providing inclusive and culturally-relevant learning environments. By giving recognition to faculty who connect with students, positive norms are established at the faculty level that students matter. Other faculty will be more willing to change and incorporate alternative learning approaches into their classroom settings in order to improve their performance and receive recognition. These rewards can and should vary based on what is valuable in each institutional context, but could include supplemental funding, institution-wide recognition, and consideration in the tenure and promotion processes.

Conclusion

College Students of Color often encounter campus classrooms and environments that are not attuned to their needs. In this chapter, we highlighted several challenges that face Undergraduates of Color as they navigate curricular and co-curricular campus environments. We offered campus racial climates and campus racial cultures as theoretical lenses that can be used to explore how to best engage Students of Color in college. Students of Color are not a monolithic group, and as our recommendations illuminate, better engaging these students warrants strategies that are attuned to their backgrounds and needs in both classroom and out-of-class experiences. When used thoughtfully, these strategies respond to the increasing rates of enrollment of Students of Color within higher education by placing their racial and ethnic identities and cultures at the forefront of the learning process.

References

Attinasi, L. C. Jr. (1989). Getting in: Mexican Americans' perceptions of university attendance and the implications for freshman year persistence. *The Journal of Higher Education, 60*(3), 247–277.

Bauer, K. W. (1998). Editor's notes. In K. W. Bauer (Ed.), *New directions for institutional research* (No. 98, pp. 1–5). San Francisco, CA: Jossey-Bass.

Bourke, B. (2010). Experiences of Black students in multiple cultural spaces at a predominantly White institution. *Journal of Diversity in Higher Education, 3*(2), 126–135.

Brownell, J. E., & Swaner, L. E. (2009). High-impact practices: Applying learning outcomes literature to the development of successful campus programs. *Peer Review, 11*(2), 26–30.

Cabrera, A. F., Nora, A., Terenzini, P. T., Pascarella, E., & Hagedorn, L. S. (1999). Campus racial climate and the adjustment of students: A comparison between White students and African-American students. *The Journal of Higher Education, 70*(2), 134–160.

Chang, M. J. (2002). Preservation or transformation: Where's the real educational discourse on diversity. *The Review of Higher Education, 25*(2), 125–140.

Comp, D. (2008). US heritage-seeking students discover minority communities in Western Europe. *Journal of Studies in International Education, 12*(1), 29–37.

Davis, R. (1991). Social support networks and undergraduate student academic-success-related outcomes: A comparison of Black students on Black and White campuses. In W. R. Allen, E. G. Epps, & N. Z. Haniff (Eds.), *College in Black and White: African American students in predominantly White and in Historically Black Public Universities* (pp. 143–158). Albany, NY: SUNY Press.

Espinosa, L. L. (2011). Pipelines and pathways: Women of color in undergraduate stem majors and the college experiences that contribute to persistence. *Harvard Educational Review, 81*(2), 209–241.

Espinosa, L. L., Turk, J. M., Taylor, M., & Chessman, H. M. (2019). *Race and ethnicity in higher education: A status report.* Washington, DC: American Council on Education.

Fisher, B. J., & Hartmann, D. J. (1995). The impact of race on the social experiences of college students at a predominantly White university. *Journal of Black Studies, 26*(2), 117–133.

Fullilove, R. E., & Treisman, E. M. (1990). Mathematics achievement among African American undergraduates at the University of California, Berkeley: An evaluation of the mathematics workshop program. *Journal of Negro Education, 59*(3), 463–478.

Griffin, K. A., & McIntosh, K. L. (2015). Finding a fit: Understanding Black immigrant students' engagement in campus activities. *Journal of College Student Development, 56*(3), 243–260.

Guiffrida, D. A. (2003). African American student organizations as agents of social integration. *Journal of College Student Development, 44*(3), 304–319.

Guiffrida, D. A. (2006). Toward a cultural advancement of Tinto's theory. *The Review of Higher Education, 29*(4), 451–472.

Guiffrida, D. A., Kiyama, J. M., Waterman, S., & Museus, S. D. (2012). Moving from individual to collective cultures to serve students of color. In S. D. Museus & U. M. Jayakumar (Eds.), *Creating campus cultures: Fostering success among racially diverse student populations* (pp. 68–87). New York, NY: Routledge.

Gurin, P., Dey, E., Hurtado, S., & Gurin, G. (2002). Diversity and higher education: Theory and impact on educational outcomes. *Harvard Educational Review, 72*(3), 330–366.

Harper, S. R., & Hurtado, S. (2007). Nine themes in campus racial climates. In S. R. Harper & L. D. Patton (Eds.), *Responding to the realities of race on campus* (New directions for student services, pp. 7–24). San Francisco, CA: Jossey-Bass.

Harper, S. R., & Quaye, S. J. (2007). Student organizations as venues for Black identity expression and development among African American male student leaders. *Journal of College Student Development, 48*(2), 127–144.

Harris III, F., & Wood, J. L. (2013). Student success for men of color in community colleges: A review of published literature and research, 1998–2012. *Journal of Diversity in Higher Education, 6*(3), 174–185.

Hurtado, S. (1992). The campus racial climate: Contexts of conflict. *The Journal of Higher Education, 63*(5), 539–569.

Hurtado, S., Griffin, K. A., Arellano, L., & Cuellar, M. (2008). Assessing the value of climate assessments: Progress and future directions. *Journal of Diversity in Higher Education, 1*(4), 204–221.

Hurtado, S., Milem, J., Clayton-Pedersen, A., & Allen, W. (1999). *Enacting diverse learning environments: Improving the climate for racial/ethnic diversity in higher education. ASHE-ERIC Higher Education Report, 26*(8). Washington, DC: The George Washington University, Graduate School of Education and Human Development.

Inkelas, K. K. (2004). Does participation in ethnic cocurricular activities facilitate a sense of ethnic awareness and understanding? A study of Asian Pacific American undergraduates. *Journal of College Student Development, 45*(3), 285–302.

Jayakumar, U. M. (2012). Social praxis in shaping supportive cultures and traditionally White institutions. In S. D. Museus & U. M. Jayakumar (Eds.), *Creating campus cultures: Fostering success among racially diverse student populations* (pp. 130–149). New York, NY: Routledge.

Jayakumar, U. M., & Museus, S. D. (2012). Mapping the intersection of campus cultures and equitable outcomes among racially diverse student populations. In S. D. Museus & U. M. Jayakumar (Eds.), *Creating campus cultures: Fostering success among racially diverse student populations* (pp. 1–27). New York, NY: Routledge.

Jones, M. T., Barlow, A. E., & Villarejo, M. (2010). Importance of undergraduate research for minority persistence and achievement in biology. *The Journal of Higher Education, 81*(1), 82–115.

Kiang, P. N. (2002). Stories and structures of persistence: Ethnographic learning through research and practice in Asian American Studies. In Y. Zou & H. T. Trueba (Eds.), *Advances in ethnographic research: From our theoretical and methodological roots to post-modern critical ethnography* (pp. 223–255). Lanham, MD: Rowman & Littlefield.

Kiang, P. N. (2009). A thematic analysis of persistence and long-term educational engagement with Southeast Asian American college students. In L. Zhan (Ed.), *Asian American voices: Engaging, empowering, enabling* (pp. 21–58). New York, NY: NLN Press.

Kuh, G. D. (2008). *High impact educational practices: What they are, who has access to them, and why they matter*. Washington, DC: Association of American Colleges and Universities.

Kuh, G. D., Cruce, T. M., Shoup, R., Kinzie, J., & Gonyea, R. M. (2008). Unmasking the effects of student engagement on first-year college grades and persistence. *The Journal of Higher Education, 79*(5), 540–563.

Kuh, G. D., Kinzie, J., Schuh, J. H., Whitt, E. J., & Associates (2005). *Student success in college: Creating conditions that matter*. San Francisco, CA: Jossey-Bass.

Kuh, G. D., & Love, P. G. (2000). A cultural perspective on student departure. In J. M. Braxton (Ed.), *Reworking the student departure puzzle* (pp. 196–212). Nashville, TN: Vanderbilt University Press.

Kuh, G. D., & Whitt, E. J. (1988). The invisible tapestry: Culture in American colleges and universities: *ASHE-ERIC Higher Education Report, 17*(1). Washington, DC: Association for the Study of Higher Education.

Linder, C., Quaye, S. J., Lange, A. C., Roberts, R. E., Lacy, M. C., & Okello, W. K. (2019). "A student should have the privilege of just being a student": Student activism as labor. *The Review of Higher Education, 42*, 37–62.

McClure, S. M. (2006). Voluntary association membership: Black Greek men on a predominantly White campus. *The Journal of Higher Education, 77*(6), 1036–1057.

Milem, J., Chang, M. J., & Antonio, A. L. (2005). *Making diversity work on campus: A research-based perspective*. Washington, DC: Association of American Colleges and Universities.

Murguia, E., Padilla, R. V., & Pavel, M. (1991). Ethnicity and the concept of social integration in Tinto's model of institutional departure. *Journal of College Student Development, 32*(5), 433–439.

Museus, S. D. (2007). Using qualitative methods to assess diverse campus cultures. In S. R. Harper & S. D. Museus (Eds.), *Using qualitative methods in institutional assessment: New Directions for Institutional Research* (No. 136, pp. 29–40). San Francisco, CA: Jossey-Bass.

Museus, S. D. (2008a). Focusing on institutional fabric: Using campus culture assessments to enhance cross-cultural engagement. In S. R. Harper (Ed.), *Creating inclusive environments for cross-cultural learning and engagement in higher education* (pp. 205–234). Washington, DC: National Association of Student Personnel Administrators.

Museus, S. D. (2008b). The model minority and inferior minority myths: Stereotypes and their implications for student learning. *About Campus, 13*(3), 2–8.

Museus, S. D. (2008c). The role of ethnic student organizations in fostering African American and Asian American students' cultural adjustment and membership at predominantly White institutions. *Journal of College Student Development, 49*(6), 568–586.

Museus, S. D. (2011a). Generating Ethnic Minority Success (GEMS): A collective-cross case analysis of high-performing colleges. *Journal of Diversity in Higher Education, 4*(3), 147–162.

Museus, S. D. (2011b). Using cultural perspectives to understand the role of ethnic student organizations in Black students' progress to the end of the pipeline. In D. E. Evensen & C. D. Pratt (Eds.), *The end of the pipeline: A journey of recognition for African Americans entering the legal profession* (pp. 162–172). Durham, NC: Carolina Academic Press.

Museus, S. D. (2014a). *Asian American students in higher education*. New York, NY: Routledge.

Museus, S. D. (2014b). The culturally engaging campus environments (CECE) model: A new theory of success among racially diverse college student populations. In *Higher education: Handbook of theory and research* (pp. 189–227). New York, NY: Springer.

Museus, S. D., Chang, T., & Zilvinskis. (in press). Merging cultural diversity and academic quality to (re)envision 21st century college campuses: The promise and power of culturally relevant high-impact practices in promoting racial equity in higher education. In C. B. Newman, C. S. Platt, A. A. Hilton, & B. Hinnant-Crawford (Eds.), *Multicultural education in the 21st century: Innovative research and practices*. Charlotte, NC: Information Age Publishing.

Museus, S. D., & Harris, F. (2010). The elements of institutional culture and minority college student success. In T. E. Dancy II (Ed.), *Managing diversity: (Re)visioning equity on college campuses* (pp. 25–44). New York, NY: Peter Lang.

Museus, S. D., Lam, S., Huang, C., Kem, P., & Tan, K. (2012). Cultural integration in campus subcultures: Where the cultural, academic, and social spheres of college life collide. In S. D. Museus & U. M. Jayakumar (Eds.), *Creating campus cultures: Fostering success among racially diverse student populations* (pp. 106–129). New York, NY: Routledge.

Museus, S. D., Ledesma, M. C., & Parker, T. L. (2015). *Racism and racial equity in higher education*. San Francisco, CA: Jossey-Bass.

Museus, S. D., & Liverman, D. (2011). Analyzing high-performing institutions: Implications for studying minority students in STEM. In S. R. Harper, C. Newman, & S. Gary (Eds.), *Students of color in STEM: Engineering a new research agenda: New directions for institutional research* (No. 148, pp. 17–27). San Francisco, CA: Jossey-Bass.

Museus, S. D., Mueller, M. K., & Aquino, K. (2013). Engaging Asian American and Pacific Islander culture and identity in graduate education. In S. D. Museus, D. C. Maramba, & R. T. Teranishi (Eds.), *The misrepresented minority: New insights on Asian Americans and Pacific Islanders, and the implications for higher education* (pp. 106–123). Sterling, VA: Stylus.

Museus, S. D., & Quaye, S. J. (2009). Toward an intercultural perspective of racial and ethnic minority college student persistence. *The Review of Higher Education, 33*(1), 67–94.

Museus, S. D., Ravello, J. N., & Vega, B. E. (2012). The campus racial culture: A critical race counterstory. In S. D. Museus& U. M. Jayakumar (Eds.), *Creating campus cultures: Fostering success among racially diverse student populations* (pp. 28–45). New York, NY: Routledge.

National Center for Education Statistics [NCES]. (2019). *Status and trends in the education of racial and ethnic groups*. Washington, DC: Author.

Nuñez, A. M. (2011). Counterspaces and connections in college transitions: First-generation Latino students' perspectives on Chicano studies. *Journal of College Student Development, 52*(6), 639–655.

Oberg, K. (1960). Culture shock: Adjustment to new cultural environments. *Practical Anthropology, 7*, 177–182.

Patton, L. D. (2006). The voice of reason: A qualitative examination of Black student perceptions of their Black culture center. *Journal of College Student Development, 47*(6), 628–646.

Patton, L. D., Bridges, B. K., & Flowers, L. A. (2011). The effects of Greek affiliation on African American students' engagement. *College Student Affairs Journal, 29*(2), 113–123.

Person, D. R., & Christensen, M. C. (1996). Understanding Black student culture and Black student retention. *NASPA Journal, 34*, 47–56.

Placier, P., Kroner, C., Burgoyne, S., & Worthington, R. (2012). Developing difficult dialogues: An evaluation of classroom implementation. *The Journal of Faculty Development, 26*(2), 29–36.

Quaye, S. J., & Chang, S. H. (2012). Creating a culture of inclusion in the classroom: From marginality to mattering. In S. D. Museus & U. M. Jayakumar (Eds.), *Creating campus cultures: Fostering success among racially diverse student populations* (pp. 88–105). New York, NY: Routledge.

Rendón, L. I., Jalomo, R. E., & Nora, A. (2000). Theoretical considerations in the study of minority student retention in higher education. In J. Braxton (Ed.), *Reworking the student departure puzzle* (pp. 127–156). Nashville, TN: Vanderbilt University Press.

Rooney, G. D. (1985). Minority students' involvement in minority student organizations: An exploratory study. *Journal of College Student Personnel, 26*(5), 450–456.

Rubin, K. (2004). Going to study. *International Educator, 13*, 26–33.

Saenz, V. B. (2010). Breaking the segregation cycle: Examining students' precollege racial environments and college diversity experiences. *The Review of Higher Education, 34*(1), 1–37.

Seifert, T. A., Gillig, B, Hanson, J. M., Pascarella, E. T., & Blaich, C. F. (2014). The conditional nature of high impact/good practices on student learning outcomes. *The Journal of Higher Education, 85*(4), 531–564.

Solórzano, D. G., Allen, W. R., & Carroll, G. (2002). Keeping race in place: Racial microaggressions and campus racial climate at the University of California Berkeley. *Chicano Latino Law Review, 23*, 15–112.

Solórzano, D. G., Ceja, M., & Yosso, T. (2000). Critical race theory, racial microaggressions, and campus racial climate: The experiences of African American college students. *Journal of Negro Education,* 60–73.

Stewart, D. L. (2008). Being all of me: Black students negotiating multiple identities. *The Journal of Higher Education, 79*(2), 183–207.

Strayhorn, T. L. (2012). *College students' sense of belonging: A key to educational success for all students.* New York, NY: Routledge.

Tierney, W. G. (1999). Models of minority college-going and retention: Cultural integrity versus cultural suicide. *Journal of Negro Education, 68*(1), 80–91.

Tinto, V. (1987). *Leaving college: Rethinking the causes and cures of student attrition*. Chicago, IL: University of Chicago Press.

Tinto, V. (1993). *Leaving college: Rethinking the causes and cures of student attrition* (2nd ed.). Chicago, IL: University of Chicago Press.

Wang, Y., Sedlacek, W. E., & Westbrook, F. D. (1992). Asian Americans and student organizations: Attitudes and participation. *Journal of College Student Development, 33*, 214–221.

Whitt, E. J. (1993). Making the familiar strange. In G. D. Kuh (Ed.), *Cultural perspectives in student affairs work* (pp. 81–94). Lanham, MD: University Press of America and American College Personnel Association.

Whitt, E. J. (1996). Assessing student cultures. In M. L. Upcraft & J. H. Schuh (Eds.), *Assessment in student affairs: A guide for practitioners* (pp. 186–216). San Francisco, CA: Jossey-Bass.

Chapter 3
Engaging Multiracial Students

C. Casey Ozaki, Marc P. Johnston-Guerrero,
and Kristen A. Renn

Leila stood at the top of the stairs that led to the administration building's courtyard. She often passed through the building and courtyard on her way back to her residence hall after class; most students passed through this part of campus sometime during their day. Today, as Leila was watching students walk by, it occurred to her that they all seemed to look alike and that she didn't really look like any of them. This realization was a contrast to what she experienced at the suburban Chicago community college from which she had transferred to Bowden College. In her home community and at Lakeshore Community College, Leila had been surrounded by all kinds of people. Her friends represented a spectrum of races and cultures. When Leila decided to transfer to Bowden College, she knew she was going to a small, predominantly White college and that she would look different from most of the other students, but she was unprepared for how different she would feel. While at Lakeshore, Leila had lived at home, worked in a local rehabilitation residence, and focused on getting good grades to transfer to a bachelor of nursing degree program like the one at Bowden. Her classmates came from a host of backgrounds—people of all genders, recent immigrants, adults returning for career changes—forming a community through their shared commitment to advancing their lives through education. But now that Leila was among a homogeneous group of students—in age, social class backgrounds, and (for the most part) race—she began to realize that college might be about more than good grades and preparation for a career; it was also challenging her to figure out who she was—especially when she didn't necessarily see a space for the person she was envisioning.

During the transfer process, Leila had been reminded of how she didn't quite fit into the racial categories that existed. Leila identified as half Filipino and half White. Some of the many surveys and information-gathering forms she completed when she applied and was admitted allowed her to select more than one racial option, but others forced her to choose one race or give an "other" option. She often felt uneasy, given that her options seemed to be either to deny one of her parent's heritage or to identify herself as an "other"—an alien of sorts.

Living away from home for the first time, Leila missed having friends with whom she could laugh about the idiosyncrasies of having an Asian family or lament over missing home-cooked meals. Unlike Lakeshore, Bowden seemed to have a student group for everything. Leila had visited the Asian Pacific Islander student group on campus, but when multiple students acted surprised that she was Filipino, teasing her about being a "watered-down" Asian, Leila decided not to return. She understood they were just teasing and did not mean to hurt her feelings, but it had made her doubt whether or not she belonged in the group even more. At the same time, people at Bowden talked about race a lot more than they did at Lakeshore—Students of Color were invested in making changes at Bowden. All these experiences prompted Leila to examine her racial and ethnic identity even more and left her wondering if there were any other "mixed" students on campus experiencing the same thing.

Leila loved being at Bowden College, but these experiences left her feeling isolated at times and without peers with whom she could discuss these kinds of issues. The majority students had each other, and the Students of Color who identified as monoracial had their groups, but where were the "mixed" students supposed to go? For that matter, were there any other "mixed" students on campus?

Leila's story is one example of the challenges multiracial students—those with parents from more than one racial or ethnic group—may face when they enter a college environment. One of the developmental undertakings often faced by traditional-aged college students is the task of establishing an identity; race and ethnicity are often particularly relevant to determining an answer to the question "Who am I?" (Chickering & Reisser, 1993). As college students engage in this task, they not only consider their own feelings and thoughts in the process of identity development, but are also influenced by family, friends, peers, social groups, and organizational structure and policies (Patton, Renn, Guido, & Quaye, 2016). When the cultural and structural norms across these influences are focused on the monoracial student experience and identity, multiracial students may struggle to find social and physical places of belonging (Harris, 2017; King, 2011; Renn, 2004).

In this chapter, we begin by describing the issues multiracial students encounter within higher education. We include consideration of the current societal context, campus policies, and campus culture, in addition to interpersonal interactions among students individually and within student organizations. Next, we demonstrate how ecological, critical, and intersectional theoretical approaches frame and enlighten a discussion of multiracial students' needs and challenges. Finally, based on these needs and challenges, we recommend strategies for administrators, staff, and faculty to enhance services to further engage multiracial students in various college campus environments and institutional types.

Prior to the 1990s, there was little attention given to mixed race and multiracial individuals' experiences in general and specifically in higher education (Renn, 2008). As the theoretical literature grew and investigation into the identity development of multiracial people emerged (Renn, 2000, 2004; Root, 1990; Wijeyesinghe, 2001, 2012), recognition of this often invisible population grew. During this time, the US Office of Management and Budget (OMB) issued Statistical Directive 15 (in 1995, with a revised version in 1997). This directive expanded to five racial and two ethnic categories[1] available to individuals when identifying their demographic information to federal agencies and required such agencies to allow individuals to choose more than one racial category, taking effect on the 2000 US Census. This change in US policy allowed Americans for the first time to respond with a fuller range of racial categories with which they might identify. Yet we note that the categories themselves have limitations and may not fully capture one's complex identity, for instance, with Middle Eastern and North African (MENA) groups being categorized as White (Strmic-Pawl, Jackson, & Garner, 2018).

In addition to the events that contributed to an increase in awareness of the multiracial population among the American social consciousness, data from the 2010 US Census indicate that the multiracial population continues to grow. The census (US Census Bureau, 2012) found that 2.9% of the population self-identify as more than one race, demonstrating an increase of 0.5% since the 2000 Census. More recent surveys found even higher percentages. The 2017 American Community Survey 1-Year Estimates (US Census Bureau, n.d.) found 3.3% of Americans claimed two or more racial ancestries. A 2015 Pew Research Center survey of US multiracial individuals found that a potential 6.9% of the population could be considered mixed race depending on how they are counted and what information is used. In common across these surveys, all project the continued growth of the US multiracial population, particularly in comparison to the broader population. The median age of the mixed race individuals is 19, compared to single-race individuals with a median age of 38, and the share of multiracial babies has risen from 1% in 1970 to 10% in 2013 (Pew Research Center, 2015). Multiracial American demographics have grown three times as fast as the whole population and are projected to triple by 2060 (Pew Research Center, 2015).

The concentration of multiracial Americans among youth and younger adults is reflected in the percentage of multiracial students who make up postsecondary enrollment. In 2015, 3.5% of the total enrollment in higher education identified as more than one race. Among four-year institutions, that share is 3.6%, while it is 3.0% in two-year institutions (Snyder, de Brey, & Dillow, 2018). Although multiracial students make up a somewhat smaller percentage of two-year versus four-year college students, there is no research that specifically examines mixed race students at two-year institutions; rather, literature is concentrated at the four-year institutional type.

In addition to the dearth of research on two-year institutions, the experiences of multiracial college students across varied institutional types, such as minority-serving institutions, remains minimal as well, although this is beginning to expand. A recent study by Harris and BrckaLorenz (2017) on the differences in engagement between Black, White, and biracial students at historically Black colleges and universities (HBCUs) and non-HBCUs found that differences in engagement experiences do exist by group and institutional type. For example, in "discussions with diverse others" at HBCUs, biracial students engaged more than Black students, but biracial and Black students engaged in such discussions more than White students at non-HBCUs. Yet, biracial students were less engaged on seven out of eleven engagement measures when compared to their Black peers at non-HBCUs and White peers at HBCUs. Similarly, biracial students at HBCUs and non-HBCUs had poorer quality of interactions with faculty, staff, and students than Black and White students at both institutions. This study indicates that there are differences in biracial students' engagement on campuses and that this may interact with institutional type.

Based on these figures, projections, and findings, an increasing number of college students across the higher education landscape are likely to identify as multiracial in the coming years. How educators fully serve, support, and engage this growing collegiate population continues to be an area of growth and development on campuses.

"Which Box(es) Do I Check?"

As multiracial students anticipate their transition from secondary to higher education, their racial and ethnic identities are often engaged by institutions even before arriving on campus. As 98% of racial data is collected at application (Renn, 2009), the reporting of demographic information is often one of the first interactions with a college that students encounter. Despite federal requirements that institutions must at some point provide students with the opportunity to report race using more than one category (e.g., at application), institutional-level assessments or research questionnaires are often not under the same scrutiny. Thus, although traditional-aged multiracial college students have come of age knowing they should be able to "mark one or more" given the 2000 Census, they may still be faced with feelings of discomfort, resentment, and exclusion at being limited to checking one racial category when identifying themselves even outside of admissions applications (Renn, 2004; Shih & Sanchez, 2005; Townsend, Markus, & Bergseiker, 2009). Contrary to these negative outcomes, being able to have and claim their multiracial identity in private and public (e.g., demographic forms, social media, student organizing) contexts is psychologically beneficial to mixed heritage people (Binning, Unzueta, Huo, & Molina, 2009; Shih & Sanchez, 2005; Townsend et al., 2009). During a developmental period in which students are actively constructing who they want to be, privately and publicly (Chickering & Reisser, 1993), encountering institutional contexts in which those identifications are limited can not only be psychologically distressing, but can also influence the social construction of those identities (Renn & Lunceford, 2004; Townsend et al., 2009).

As the twenty-first century marches on, multiracial identification has become more solidified as a viable racial self-identification through the work of advocacy organizations, inclusion in racial demographic options, and the growth of mixed-race individuals in the population. From this position, Curington (2016) discussed the movement into and influence of the internet and social media as both spaces where media representations of multiraciality have become more mainstream and where these cyber-spaces "constitute(s) an important space for performing and negotiating multiracial identities at the level of everyday interaction" (p. 38). She also critically contextualizes the examination of multiraciality within the historical and societal power structures and among the intersections of social identities.

"What Are You?"

As students enter the college setting, they are not only engaged with developing their identities, but are also challenged to do this while establishing peer groups and friendships and developing a sense of belonging (Chaudhari, 2016; Patton et al., 2016). Navigating the complex physical and social environment of college is challenging for most students, but for multiracial students, there is the additional task of managing and responding to perceptions about their race and ethnicity (Museus, Lambe Sariñana, Yee, & Robinson, 2016; Renn, 2004; Talbot, 2008). Students live and learn in complex ecologies where race is a central organizing concept of student culture and life.

Race and ethnicity are among the characteristics that we in the United States draw upon in an effort to understand and categorize people around us. When multiracial individuals do not fit into the predetermined categories of race and ethnicity into which we are conditioned to organize people, a common question asked is "What are you?" Such a question infers that the person being questioned does not fit or belong within the expected five standard monoracial categories. Johnston-Guerrero and Renn (2016) identified the driving social force behind such questioning as monoracialism, where society prefers individuals with only one race and perpetuates monoracial as "superior to being multiracial [which] is rooted in inaccurate, racist, and pseudo-scientific notions of so-called racial purity" (pp. 139–140). The presumption that a person should look or act in particular ways or have specific cultural knowledge associated with monoracial categories often has the consequence of asking the multiracial person to legitimize their racial and ethnic identity (King, 2008, 2011; Renn, 2004; Talbot, 2008).

Another repercussion of the predominantly monoracial construction of race in the US consciousness is the invisibility of multiraciality. As others have difficulty identifying and placing multiracial students into known categories, assumptions are made about what their race and ethnicity are or should be depending on physical appearance. These assumptions lead to miscategorization and invisibility of multiraciality as a valid racial option and require students to explain, legitimize, and educate about their identities to peers and friends on campus in ways that are not required by students who identify, personally and phenotypically, with the predominant monoracial categories (King, 2008, 2011; Renn, 2004; Talbot, 2008). These interactions are commonly experienced as multiracial microaggressions, or the subtle, everyday, and often unintended behaviors that demean or invalidate multiraciality or contribute to environments that perpetuate monoracial norms (Harris, 2017; Hurtado, Alvarado, & Guillermo-Wann, 2015; Johnston & Nadal, 2010).

Furthermore, the physical appearance of multiracial students may contribute to how others choose to accept or reject them as a part of a monoracial group. A student's skin color, hair color and texture, or eye shape may lead others to make assumptions about the groups to which they belong. Further, for example, a multiracial Black and White student may be "too" dark or light skinned, leading them to feel pressured to identify as Black without identifying other heritage(s) or to be rejected by other Black students (Ozaki & Parson, 2017; Renn, 2004; Rockquemore, 2002; Shang & Gasser, 2016; Talbot, 2008).

The experience of having to negotiate the "in" and "out" groups of racial politics on college campuses proves particularly tricky for multiracial students. While they are attempting to explore and develop their racial and ethnic identities, they are also asked to publicly identify, legitimate, and educate about their racial identities to others, potentially causing additional stress and confusion. Deciding which boxes to check and answering "What are you?" questions draw attention to racial identity in ways that it may not for students from monoracial groups (Kellogg & Liddell, 2012).

Navigating Racially and Ethnically Focused Student Services and Organizations

One arena where the negotiation of race and identity for multiracial students often plays out in the college environment is among race- and ethnicity-based student services and organizations. Race- and ethnicity-based student organizations were originally established to support students of color in meeting others from similar racial and ethnic backgrounds and having a space to identify and share relevant issues (Patton, 2010). These groups also serve to organize and advocate on behalf of students from underrepresented groups (Young & Hannon, 2002). On predominantly monoracial campuses, multiracial students may encounter and engage with their peers, faculty, and staff differently than their monoracial peers, as such exploring and seeking to understanding how institutional type, structural diversity, and campus structures and practices influence multiracial students' overall quality of engagement and experiences is critical to their support (Ford & Malaney, 2012; Harris & BrckaLorenz, 2017).

For the multiracial student looking for a place to meet others, explore issues of identity, and find a sense of belonging within the greater college campus, negotiating participation and belonging among race-based student organizations can be challenging and confusing. Monoracial student organizations can create communities that multiracial students perceive as exclusionary, whether due to the organization's actions or students' perceptions of belonging based on their physical features and cultural/language knowledge (Ford & Malaney, 2012; King, 2011; Literté, 2010; Ozaki & Johnston, 2008; Renn, 2000, 2004).

Literté (2010) found that because monoracial student organizations exist to institutionalize and legitimize the identities of "Black," "Latino/a," and "Asian American," they also implicitly deny the existence and veracity of biracial identity and persons. Hence, many biracial students view ROSS (race-oriented student services) with discomfort because they seemingly inhibit students' ability to develop "true self-consciousness" and secure institutional validation (p. 126). As a result, multiracial student organizations have developed on many campuses (Malaney & Danowski, 2015; Ozaki & Johnston, 2008), but many institutions lack the resources, leadership, or number of multiracial students needed in order to support and sustain such organizations. Therefore, students on campuses without multiracial student organizations are often required to negotiate the ROSS terrain in environments that are often ambivalent at best toward multiraciality.

Theoretical Perspectives

To provide a theoretical background for understanding multiracial students' experiences, success, and impediments to success in college, we describe three theoretical approaches: ecology, critical mixed-race studies, and intersectionality. These theories are the foundation for the engagement strategies we present in the next section.

Campus Ecology

Ecological approaches to student development emerged from multiple areas of study, including human ecology, developmental ecology, and campus ecology (Patton et al., 2016; Renn & Patton Davis, 2017). The underlying premise of this family of theories is that individuals exist in dynamic contexts of mutual influence. A person interacts with his or her environment, and those interactions influence both the person and the environment. Akin to biological conceptions of ecology, an individual's characteristics make them well-suited to some environments; but when there is a mismatch, the person must adapt the environment or adapt to the environment in order to thrive.

In translating the ecological concept to student development, scholars have relied heavily on the work of developmental psychologist Urie Bronfenbrenner (1979, 1993) for his model that integrates personal characteristics with developmental contexts and processes over time (see Patton et al., 2016). Key to this approach is understanding how people invite varied responses from the context and react differently to them according to personal traits; thus, two people from the same background may experience an environment very differently, and two people from very different backgrounds may have similar experiences in the environment.

Kristen Renn (2003, 2004) is a scholar of bi- and multiracial college student identities and experiences. She takes an explicitly ecological perspective, consistent with the work of Maria P. P. Root (1990, 1998, 1999), who was an early integrator of ecological frameworks into studies of bi- and multiracial youth. Based on a multi-campus qualitative study of mixed race students, Renn (2000, 2003, 2004) proposed five patterns of bi- and multiracial identity among college students. The five patterns are:

1. **Monoracial identity**, in which students claim a single, monoracial identity from among their heritage groups.
2. **Multiple monoracial identities**, in which students alternate between/among heritage group identities. Alternation may be over an extended period of time

("Last year I generally hung out with my Asian friends, but this year I'm more with my Latina group") or may be more frequent ("I'll be going to Black Gospel Choir practice tonight after I have dinner with my mostly White housemates in the Vegan Co-op").

3. **Multiracial identity**, in which students claim a biracial, multiracial, mixed-race, or other named identity that represents more than one heritage at the same time. For example, students might call themselves Hapa (Asian and White) or Blaxican (Black and Mexican) or use some other term.

4. **Extraracial identity**, in which students "opt out" of racial categorization or denounce/deconstruct the system of racial classification in the United States. For no student in Renn's study was this the *only* identity, but about one-quarter of participants fit this pattern some of the time.

5. **Situational identity**, in which students shift identity based on circumstances. A highly ecological concept, this pattern is based on how interactions between person and environment shape the individual's racial identity over time and in differing conditions.

In every pattern, Renn (2000, 2003, 2004) located mutual influences between person and environment, the hallmarks of an ecological approach to understanding identity and development. Peers, academic settings, family, faculty, friendship groups, and extracurricular activities were forces acting on and with multiracial students to send messages about racial identities. Key factors included students' appearance, their knowledge of culture (e.g., language, traditions, food, holidays) related to their various heritage groups, and academic exposure to material about their heritage groups and about the concept of race itself. Another factor in students' ability to move among multiracial identity patterns was the campus ethos regarding membership in different student communities. On campuses where they could move easily among social groups (such as a sports team, the choir, and the progressive student activists), students reported more ease in identifying situationally than did their multiracial peers on campuses where the boundaries between student subcultures were less permeable.

It is important to note here that Renn did not propose anything like a stage model of multiracial identity. Indeed, she joined Root in eschewing this approach. Renn offered a model for understanding the processes of and influences on multiracial identity. These areas offer guidance for higher education programs, policies, and practices as we describe at the end of this chapter.

Critical Mixed-Race Studies

An emerging, interdisciplinary field of critical mixed-race studies (CMRS) is furthering the integration of more critical paradigms and epistemologies to multiracial scholarship broadly (e.g., Daniel et al., 2014) and higher education specifically (e.g., Johnston-Guerrero & Chaudhari, 2016; Malaney & Danowski, 2015). Yet, Daniel et al. (2014) remind us that just because past scholarship did not use the term "critical" should not deem it "uncritical" or that it "is now irrelevant and should be relegated to the dustbin"

(p. 7). This call for highlighting historical accuracy aligns with tenets of Critical Race Theory (CRT) that Harris (2016) adapted to develop critical multiracial theory (Multi-Crit), which may more adequately account for and explain multiracial college students' experiences with race and racism. Similar to other offshoots or adaptations of CRT in education to various populations (e.g., LatCrit, TribalCrit), Harris (2016) proposed eight tenets of MultiCrit, with the first four being pulled directly from CRT and the second four added/adjusted to better align with multiraciality. These tenets include: (1) challenge to ahistoricism, (2) interest convergence, (3) power of experiential knowledge, (4) challenge to dominant ideology, (5) monoracial paradigm of race, (6) endemic nature of monoracism and colorism in addition to racism, (7) micro-differential racialization, and (8) intersectionality of multiple racial identities.

Although reviewing each tenet is outside the scope of this chapter, we highlight the monoracial paradigms of race and monoracism here because we argue they are central to enhancing engagement strategies for multiracial students. There is extreme diversity within this group, given the various heritage combinations in addition to different patterns of identification. For instance, what unites a student who has biological parents who are Black and White and who identifies solely as Black with another student whose parents are Mexican and Filipino and who identifies as Mexipino? These students are not united just by being "mixed." What connects these diverse students is that their identities and experiences are influenced by monoracialism, or the preference for a monoracial paradigm of race, and monoracism.

Monoracism is the system of oppression targeting multiracial individuals (Johnston & Nadal, 2010). Also referred to as multiracial oppression, Hamako (2014) succinctly explained that monoracism is "the systemic privileging of things, people and practices that are racialized as 'single-race' and/or 'racially pure' (e.g., 'Monoracial') and the oppression of things, people, and practices that are racialized as being of more than one race (e.g., 'Multiracial,' 'Mixed-Race,' 'Multiethnic,' etc.)" (p. 81). Critical perspectives on multiracial engagement must take monoracism and monoracialism into account, given their pervasiveness within institutions of higher education.

In her examination of multiracial women students' experiences with microaggressions, Harris (2017) argued that institutional monoracism is "the vein that carries and embeds a monoracial-only paradigm of race (the disease) throughout education, a combination that manifests in multiracial microaggressions, a symptom of the disease" (p. 441). Monoracism manifests when multiracial students are not allowed to declare their multiracial heritage on institutional surveys, are forced to question their participation in monoracially designed student events or services (e.g., welcome or graduation ceremonies for monoracial populations), or are not provided with services targeting or inclusive of multiracial students (Harris, 2017; Kellogg & Liddell, 2012).

Intersectionality

In addition to ecological models and critical frameworks, the theory of intersectionality has much to offer the understanding of multiracial students' identities and experiences.

Indeed, intersectionality is a tenet of CRT and MultiCrit (Harris, 2016) yet has been advanced across multiple fields to form its own body of knowledge and warrants specific attention here. Even from a nontheoretical, commonsense interpretation of the concept of intersections, bi- and multiracial students would seem to be included in this idea. They exist, after all, at the biological intersections of heritage groups that for hundreds of years were legally barred from marriage or sexual union in the United States (Pascoe, 2009). But intersectionality as a theoretical perspective takes that commonsense interpretation farther, lending important nuances to understanding multiracial students in higher education.

Intersectionality is a theoretical approach that has gained ground in student development research as a way to understand how race, gender, sexual orientation, social class, and a host of other felt and ascribed identities interact, given their intersecting systems of oppression. After decades of, first, studying all students as though they were the same and, second, breaking down components of identity into separate domains (e.g., race, sexuality, gender, etc.), intersectionality offers a way to put the pieces back together through understanding how the domains are mutually constitutive (Abes & Jones, 2013; Núñez, 2014). Being a gay Black man is different from being a gay White man or a straight Black man because of the intersections of racism and heterosexism/homophobia.

Abes and Jones' (2013) book on multiple dimensions of identity discusses contemporary perspectives on college student identity as the "intersection of context, personal characteristics, and social identities" (p. xxi) and how the nature and structures of power influence identity. Abes and Jones (2013) used this opportunity to reconceptualize their Model of Multiple Dimensions of Identity (MMDI). Foundational to their investigation and treatment of multiple identities is the theory of intersectionality, suggesting that to explore multiple identities is to engage in examination of intersections and borderlands. Wijeyesinghe (2012) uses the MMDI as a primary point for comparison between intersectionality and multiracial identity literature and theories' assumptions and characteristics. She addresses the shared tenets that identity is holistic yet complex whose elements are not dichotomous but influence one another and are influenced by the world. As such, individuals "can simultaneously embody positions of power and marginality by attending to the multiple social positions that each individual inhabits" (Wijeyesinghe, 2012, p. 85) and, given the constant change of the world in which individuals and their identities exist, sense of self and identity are fluid and evolving across context and time. Wijeyesinghe (2012) represents these shared characteristics as core assumptions for the Intersectional Model of Multiracial Identity.

In examination of intersectionality and multiraciality, scholars have identified gender, sexuality, and different racial heritage combinations as intersecting identities. Rockquemore (2002) reported that Black/White biracial women experienced particular gender effects in their experiences; some women found themselves courted by White men because they were seen as "exotic" (but not too threatening), whereas Black men sought them out because they were typically lighter-skinned than monoracially identified Black women on campus. Reactions from Black and White men and from Black women led Rockquemore's participants to have a heightened sense of both racial and gender identities.

Similarly, intersections of multiracial identity and sexual orientation among students have received some attention. King (2011) studied female college students who identified as "multiracial/biracial—bisexual/pansexual" (p. 440). This combination led participants to "try on" different identities (p. 446) and to "negotiate self" understandings (p. 447) while struggling to find a place to fit on campus. Renn (2004) identified intersections of multiracial identity and lesbian/gay/bisexual (LGB) identities among some of her participants, one of whom noted that already knowing that she was biracial helped her understand herself as "outside the box" in terms of sexuality. Different from the students in King's study, this student found that understanding race as socially constructed facilitated her understanding of sexuality as socially constructed.

In considering multiracial students and engagement through an intersectional lens, we urge attention to the ways that college environments sometimes press students to make choices among identities. For example, Ford and Malaney (2012) found that multiracial students at a small liberal arts college found the authenticity of their racial identity challenged in monoracial group settings. King (2011) reported that some participants felt that they had to choose to affiliate with LGB students or with students of color. Museus, Lambe Sariñana, and Ryan (2015) observed that exotification of mixed people might be experienced differently by students of different genders. And though they were writing from the perspectives of faculty members, Jessica Harris (in Harris & Nicolazzo, 2017) pointed to the challenges and opportunities of living in the "borderlands" of intersecting identities in the academy.

Intersectional, critical, and ecological frameworks are compatible and offer unique lenses through which to understand multiracial student identities and experiences. All depend on complex, mutual influences of person and environment and hold racial and other identities as social constructions that may vary within an individual, across contexts, and across the lifespan. They also account for multiple levels of identity-based empowerment and oppression that operate to affect an individual's opportunities in education and elsewhere. For these reasons, we find them to be robust frameworks from which to understand multiracial student identities and experiences.

Student Engagement Strategies

Thus far, we have laid the groundwork for understanding the needs and challenges of multiracial students within higher education and presented theoretical frameworks intended to provide helpful lenses for understanding multiracial students' experiences in relation to their contexts and other identities. With this foundation, we suggest the following approaches and strategies for administrators, faculty, and staff working with these students.

Audit Campus Policies and Procedures

Conduct an audit of campus policies and procedures with an eye toward identifying those that require or imply that individual students, faculty, and staff identify in only one monoracial category. As of 2010, all institutions were required to collect and report data on student race and ethnicity using the same "check all that apply" format used by the US Census and other federal agencies. Many institutions were already ahead of that requirement, but many others waited to change their admissions forms and data systems (see Renn, 2009). Beyond admissions forms—which is where 98% of institutions collect federally required data on student race and ethnicity (Renn, 2009)—a myriad of institutional systems were not required to conform to this standard. Students continue to report instances where they are asked to identify themselves in a single racial category once they arrive on campus. They also report that such inquiries violate their rights to self-identification in more than one category, as multiracial, outside categories, or situationally. These violations lead to a sense of invisibility and not belonging. Conversely, the opportunity to "check all that apply" and to see themselves represented in institutional data provides support.

Recruit, Hire, and Support Multiracial Staff and Faculty and Promote Student Connections

Having multiracial staff and faculty on campus who are available to support and interact with multiracial students is important in order to foster a connection on campus with people with similar experiences. Being able to connect with multiracial students, staff, and faculty is critical for developing a sense of belonging and identity construction (Renn, 2004). Having visible multiracial staff and faculty available to multiracial students may demonstrate the institution's commitment to people "like them." But too often, multiracial faculty and staff may also be faced with questions of being "enough" or feeling forced to identify as monoracial to adhere to the pervasive monoracialism operating on campuses (Harris & Nicolazzo, 2017).

Provide Multiracially Inclusive Diversity Trainings

Work with student affairs educators who conduct workshops and training sessions to help them understand that not all students identify in one racial group. A popular "diversity training" exercise divides students into groups by race (typically, Black, White, Asian, Latino, and Native American). Bi- and multiracial students, if compelled to choose one of these groups, may not feel comfortable or may receive clear verbal and nonverbal feedback from peers that they are not welcome in the group they have chosen. Similarly, talking about student diversity without naming multiraciality excludes this group and continues to keep students invisible in the campus milieu (Johnston-Guerrero & Renn, 2016).

Establish Multiracial Student Organizations

If there is no organization for multiracial students on campus, take steps to create space for such organizations to develop. For example, the Multiracial Beavers group at Oregon State University started as a staff-initiated discussion group for multiracial faculty, staff, and students on campus and has blossomed to include multiracial-focused leadership retreats, weekly "drop-in" meetings, and an oral history project. Outside of the establishment of a student organization, staff and faculty can introduce programming that addresses multiracial student interests. Collaborate with monoracial groups of students of color (e.g., Black Student Union, Asian Pacific Islander Association, La Raza) to sponsor speakers, programs, and events that highlight the contributions of multiracial people. Work with academic departments that are bringing speakers to campus and suggest speakers who are multiracial or focus on multiraciality. Steven Riley created and maintains the resource www.mixedracestudies.org, which can serve as a central place to find such speakers.

Treat Student Organizations Equally

If there is a multiracial student organization on campus, make sure that it is treated similarly to other identity-based student organizations. Whether as "jumping off points" for leadership in other organizations or as "an oasis from the monoracial world" (Renn, 2004), these groups can provide support, social outlets, and educational programs that create a more supportive campus climate for multiracial students (Malaney & Danowski, 2015). Particularly on campuses that have well-established race- and ethnicity-based student organizations, competition for resources can exist when adding a similar organization (Ozaki & Johnston, 2008); therefore, policies that equalize the student organization playing field can help preserve the goals and efforts of such organizations while promoting cooperation.

Foster and Support Strong Student Leadership

For campuses where multiracial student organizations do not currently exist or are new, the process of organizing, gathering, and advocating for multiracial student needs can be a significant task. As described previously in this chapter, accurately identifying multiracial students who do not self-identify but may be interested in starting or participating in a student organization is a challenge given the phenotypic ambiguity that often accompanies multiracial people. Furthermore, at times, information about student organizations and activities that might be of particular interest to students of color is provided to students based on their demographic information collected at application. For institutions that do not provide the option to indicate more than one racial category or do not store data in this format, sharing information about potentially supportive opportunities on campus would be difficult. Therefore, to form formal and informal networks and student organizations, the student, staff, and faculty leadership must be strong and well supported (Ozaki & Johnston, 2008; Wong & Buckner, 2008).

Include Multiracial Issues in the Curriculum

Faculty must take care to include a multiracial perspective in their courses and curriculum. As issues of diversity and equity have established their necessity in general education curricula, information about multiracial issues has yet to be as interwoven. Not only would inclusion in more curricula and courses educate students about multiracial issues, but it would also serve to legitimize multiracial identity while creating a more inclusive environment (Renn, 2003; Williams, Nakashima, Kich, & Daniel, 1996). Furthermore, Renn (2004) found that exposing students to postmodern conceptions of race in the classroom helped provide them with the language and cognitive skill required to understand their experiences. The Critical Mixed Race Studies Association (https://criticalmixedracestudies.com) sponsors a journal and biennial conference with resources useful for integrating multiraciality into curriculum and pedagogy.

Create a Campus Culture of Boundary-Crossing

A campus culture that promotes boundary crossing will inherently acknowledge and legitimize the experiences and identities of multiracial students. Not only will recognizing the cross-racial/ethnic experiences of students promote inclusion of multiracial students in predominantly monoracial environments, but it will also provide greater space for students to explore experiences and meaning across felt and ascribed identities. By encouraging students and groups to interact across different backgrounds and identities, they will not only be exposed to differences but also be exposed to a culture in which differences are valued. One way to stimulate boundary crossing is to encourage student groups and organizations to interact and program together. Furthermore, providing additional resources, such as funding, to programs that promote boundary crossing would likely serve as an incentive. In addition, faculty and student affairs educators can encourage dialogues across monoracial and multiracial groups, in addition to promoting discussions and understanding of intersectionality across all identity-based organizations.

Conclusion

In the vignette at the beginning of this chapter, Leila struggled with many of the needs and issues faced by multiracial students across institutions of higher education. She faced feelings of isolation and invisibility and questions about the legitimacy of her racial identity and belonging. While Leila recognized that the intention of her peers and campus environment was not to make her feel this way, the lack of connection with similar peers and a sense that the campus was not designed to include students who did not fall into a designated monoracial category had the unfortunate consequence of exclusion.

Although Leila is a fictional character, her experience is reminiscent of the needs, issues, and challenges told by multiracial college students anecdotally and through research. Staff, faculty, and administrators can expect multiracial students to come to college in increasing numbers. They must, therefore, critically examine how their institutions are structured and designed. What messages are sent to multiracial college students when they do not have a box to check that reflects their identity or when they see other students on campus who have physical and psychological spaces in which to examine and develop their racial and ethnic identities, but none exists for them? The engagement strategies we propose are designed to help educators responsible for creating campus environments consider how they can be intentionally inclusive of multiracial students at structural, group, and individual levels.

Note

1 Races are Black or African American, American Indian or Alaska Native, Asian, Native Hawaiian or Other Pacific Islander, White; ethnicity is defined as "Hispanic or Latino" or "Not Hispanic or Latino."

References

Abes, E. S., & Jones, S. R. (2013). *Identity development of college students: Advancing frameworks for multiple dimensions of identity*. San Francisco, CA: Jossey-Bass.

Binning, K. R., Unzueta, M. M., Huo, Y. J., & Molina, L. E. (2009). The interpretation of multiracial status and its relation to social engagement and psychological well-being. *Journal of Social Issues, 65*(1), 35–50.

Bronfenbrenner, U. (1979). *The ecology of human development: Experiments by nature and design*. Cambridge, MA: Harvard University Press.

Bronfenbrenner, U. (1993). The ecology of cognitive development: Research models and fugitive findings. In R. H. Wozniak & K. W. Fischer (Eds.), *Development in context: Acting and thinking in specific environments* (pp. 3–44). Hillsdale, NJ: Erlbaum.

Chaudhari, P. (2016). *Understanding mixed race and multiethnic students' sense of belonging in college* (Unpublished dissertation, University of Pittsburgh). Retrieved from http://d-scholarship.pitt.edu/27633

Chickering, A. W., & Reisser, L. (1993). *Education and identity* (2nd ed.). San Francisco, CA: Jossey-Bass.

Curington, C. V. (2016). Rethinking multiracial formation in the United States: Toward an intersectional approach. *Sociology of Race and Ethnicity, 2*(1), 27–41.

Daniel, G. R., Kina, L., Dariotis, W. M., & Fojas, C. (2014). Emerging paradigms in critical mixed race studies. *Journal of Critical Mixed Race Studies, 1*(1), 6–65.

Ford, K. A., & Malaney, V. K. (2012). "I now harbor more pride in my race": The educational benefits of inter-and intraracial dialogues on the experiences of students of color and multiracial students. *Equity & Excellence in Education, 45*(1), 14–35.

Hamako, E. (2014). *Improving antiracist education for multiracial students* (Unpublished doctoral dissertation). University of Massachusetts, Amherst, MA.

Harris, J. C. (2016). Toward a critical multiracial theory in education. *International Journal of Qualitative Studies in Education, 29*(6), 795–813.

Harris, J. C. (2017). Multiracial college students' experiences with multiracial microaggressions. *Race Ethnicity and Education, 20*(4), 429–445.

Harris, J. C., & BrckaLorenz, A. (2017). Black, White, and Biracial students' engagement at differing institutional types. *Journal of College Student Development, 58*(5), 783–789.

Harris, J. C., & Nicolazzo, Z. (2017). Navigating the academic borderlands as multiracial and trans* faculty members. *Critical Studies in Education*, 1–16.

Hurtado, S., Alvarado, A. R., & Guillermo-Wann, C. (2015). Thinking about race: The salience of racial identity at two-and four-year colleges and the climate for diversity. *The Journal of Higher Education, 86*(1), 127–155.

Johnston-Guerrero, M. P., & Chaudhari, P. (2016). "Everyone is just mixed to me": Exploring the role of multiraciality in college students' racial claims. *Equity & Excellence in Education, 49*(3), 254–266.

Johnston, M. P., & Nadal, K. L. (2010). Multiracial microaggressions: Exposing monoracism in everyday life and clinical practice. In D. W. Sue (Ed.), *Microaggressions and marginality: Manifestation, dynamics and impact* (pp. 123–144). New York, NY: Wiley & Sons.

Johnston-Guerrero, M. P., & Renn, K. A. (2016). Multiracial Americans in college. In K. O. Korgen (Ed.), *Race policy and Multiracial Americans* (pp. 139–154). Bristol, UK: Policy Press.

Kellogg, A. H., & Liddell, D. L. (2012). "Not half but double": Exploring critical incidents in the racial identity of multiracial college students. *Journal of College Student Development, 53*(4), 524–541.

King, A. R. (2008). Student perspectives on multiracial identity. In K. A. Renn & P. Shang (Eds.), *Biracial and multiracial college students: Theory, research, and best practices in student affairs* (New directions for student services, pp. 33–42). San Francisco, CA: Jossey-Bass.

King, A. R. (2011). Environmental influences on the development of female college students who identify as multiracial/biracial-bisexual/pansexual. *Journal of College Student Development, 52*(4), 440–455.

Literté, P. E. (2010). Revising race: How biracial students are changing and challenging student services. *Journal of College Student Development, 51*(2), 115–134.

Malaney, V. K., & Danowski, K. (2015). Mixed foundations: Supporting and empowering multiracial student organizations. *Journal Committed to Social Change on Race and Ethnicity, 1*(2), 55–85.

Museus, S. D., Lambe Sariñana, S. A., & Ryan, T. K. (2015). A qualitative examination of multiracial students' coping responses to experiences with prejudice and discrimination in college. *Journal of College Student Development, 56*(4), 331–348.

Museus, S. D., Lambe Sariñana, S. A., Yee, A. L., & Robinson, T. E. (2016). A qualitative analysis of multiracial students' experiences with prejudice and discrimination in college. *Journal of College Student Development, 57*(6), 680–697.

Núñez, A. M. (2014). Employing multilevel intersectionality in educational research: Latino identities, contexts, and college access. *Educational Researcher, 43*(2), 85–92.

Ozaki, C. C., & Johnston, M. P. (2008). The space in between: Issues for multiracial student organizations and advising. In K. A. Renn & P. Shang (Eds.), *Biracial and multiracial college students: Theory, research, and best practices in student affairs* (New directions for student services, pp. 53–62). San Francisco, CA: Jossey-Bass.

Ozaki, C. C., & Parson, L. (2017). Colorism and mixed race college students. C. R. Monroe (Ed.), *Race and colorism in education* (pp. 99–114). New York, NY: Routledge.

Pascoe, P. (2009). *What comes naturally: Miscegenation law and the making of race in America.* New York, NY: Oxford University Press.

Patton, L. D. (Ed.). (2010). *Culture centers in higher education: Perspectives on identity, theory, and practice.* Sterling, VA: Stylus.

Patton, L. D., Renn, K. A., Guido, F., & Quaye, S. J. (2016). *Student development in college: Theory, research, and practice* (2nd ed.). San Francisco, CA: Jossey-Bass.

Pew Research Center (2015). *Multiracial in America: Proud, diverse and growing in numbers.* Washington, DC: Pew Researcher Center.

Renn, K. A. (2000). Patterns of situational identity among biracial and multiracial college students. *The Review of Higher Education, 23*(4), 399–420.

Renn, K. A. (2003). Understanding the identities of mixed race college students through a developmental ecology lens. *Journal of College Student Development, 44*, 383–403.

Renn, K. A. (2004). *Mixed race college students: The ecology of race, identity, and community.* Albany: State University of New York Press.

Renn, K. A. (2008). Research on bi- and multiracial identity development: Overview and synthesis. In K. A. Renn & P. Shang (Eds.), *Biracial and multiracial college students: Theory, research, and best practices in student affairs* (New directions for student services, pp. 13–21). San Francisco, CA: Jossey-Bass.

Renn, K. A. (2009). Education policy, politics, and mixed heritage students in the United States. *Journal of Social Issues, 65*(1), 165–183.

Renn, K. A., & Lunceford, C. J. (2004). Because the numbers matter: Transforming racial and ethnic data in postsecondary education to meet the challenges of a changing nation. *Educational Policy, 18*, 752–783.

Renn, K. A., & Patton Davis, L. (2017). Environments and campus cultures In J. Schuh, S. R. Jones, & V. Torres (Eds.), *Student services: A handbook for the profession* (6th ed.) (pp. 58–72). San Francisco, CA: Jossey-Bass.

Rockquemore, K. A. (2002). Negotiating the color line: The gendered process of racial identity construction among Black/White biracial women. *Gender & Society, 16*(4), 485–503.

Root, M. P. P. (1990). Resolving 'Other' status: Identity development of biracial individuals. *Women and Therapy, 9*(1/2), 185–205.

Root, M. P. P. (1998). Experiences and processes affecting racial identity development: Preliminary results from the Biracial Sibling Project. *Cultural Diversity and Mental Health, 4*(3), 237–247.

Root, M. P. P. (1999). The biracial baby boom: Understanding the ecological constructions of racial identity in the 21st century. In R. H. Sheets & E. R. Hollins (Eds.), *Racial and ethnic identity in school practices: Aspects of human development* (pp. 67–90). Mahwah, NJ: Erlbaum.

Shang, P., & Gasser, H. S. (2016). Mixed race college students and colorism: Considerations for post-secondary institutions. In C. Monroe (Ed.), *Race and colorism in education* (pp. 99–110). New York, NY: Routledge.

Shih, M., & Sanchez, D. T. (2005). Perspectives and research on the positive and negative implications of having multiple racial identities. *Psychological Bulletin, 131*, 569–591.

Snyder, T. D., de Brey, C., & Dillow, S. A. (2018). *Digest of education statistics 2016* (NCES 2017–094). Washington, DC: National Center for Education Statistics.

Strmic-Pawl, H. V., Jackson, B. A., & Garner, S. (2018). Race counts: Racial and ethnic data on the US census and the implications for tracking inequality. *Sociology of Race and Ethnicity, 4*(1), 1–13.

Talbot, D. M. (2008). Exploring the experiences and self-labeling of mixed-race individuals with two minority parents. In K. A. Renn & P. Shang (Eds.), *Biracial and multiracial college students: Theory, research, and best practices in student affairs* (New directions for student services, pp. 23–32). San Francisco, CA: Jossey-Bass.

Townsend, S. S. M., Markus, H. R., & Bergseiker, H. B. (2009). My choice, your categories: The denial of multiracial identities. *Journal of Social Issues, 65*(1), 183–202.

US Census Bureau. (2012). *The two or more races population: 2010* (Brief No. C2010BR-13). Washington, DC: Government Printing Office.

US Census Bureau. (n.d.). *ACS housing and demographic estimates: 2017 American community survey 1-year estimates*. Retrieved from https://factfinder.census.gov/faces/tableservices/jsf/pages/productview.xhtml?pid=ACS_17_1YR_DP05&prodType=table

Wijeyesinghe, C. L. (2001). Racial identity in multiracial people: An alternative paradigm. In C. L. Wijeyesinghe & B. W. Jackson, III (Eds.), *New perspectives on racial identity development: A theoretical and practical anthology* (pp. 129–152). New York, NY: New York University Press.

Wijeyesinghe, C. L. (2012). Racial identity in multiracial people: An alternative paradigm. In C. L. Wijeyesinghe & B. W. Jackson, III (Eds.), *New perspectives on racial identity development: Integrating emerging frameworks* (2nd ed., pp. 129–152). New York, NY: New York University Press.

Williams, T. K., Nakashima, C. L., Kich, G. K., & Daniel, G. R. (1996). Being different together in the university classroom: Multiracial identity as transgressive education. In M. P. P. Root (Ed.), *The multiracial student experience: Racial borders as the new frontier* (pp. 359–379). Thousand Oaks, CA: Sage.

Wong, M. P. A., & Buckner, J. (2008). Multiracial student services come of age: The state of multiracial student services in higher education in the United States. In K. A. Renn & P. Shang (Eds.), *Biracial and multiracial college students: Theory, research, and best practices in student affairs* (New directions for student services, pp. 43–52). San Francisco, CA: Jossey-Bass.

Young, L. W., & Hannon, M. D. (2002, February). The staying power of Black cultural centers. *Black Issues in Higher Education, 18*(26), 104. http://iibp.chadwyck.com/iibp/full_rec?ACTION=byid&ID=00056814

Chapter 4
Engaging Transracial Asian American Adoptees in College

Aeriel A. Ashlee

It's kind of weird for me to say, but I feel like a White person in an Asian body. . . . I just didn't feel Asian, whatever Asian is supposed to feel like. I felt like what people saw on the outside, and what they thought I should act like, didn't match how I felt on the inside.

—Hannah (Ashlee, 2019, p. 125)

Hannah, a senior in college, shared this reflection in a study that explored the racialized experiences of transracial Asian American adoptee collegians (Ashlee, 2019). As Hannah explained, transracial Asian American adoptees—most of whom are Asian Americans adopted into and raised by White families—experience and understand their racial identity in distinctly different ways from their nonadopted Asian American peers. While scholars have long called for the disaggregation of Asian American communities in higher education (Pendakur & Pendakur, 2012), transracial Asian American adoptees have been largely absent from student affairs scholarship (Museus, 2014). This chapter provides an introduction and overview of transracial Asian American adoptees in college, briefly reviews several theories that may help student affairs educators better understand and support this student population, and concludes with recommended strategies for engaging transracial Asian American adoptees in higher education.[1]

Understanding Transracial Asian American Adoptees in College

Transracial Asian American adoptees are a minoritized and underserved student population in part because they are often invisible to their nonadopted peers and college educators (Suda & Hartlep, 2016). Only within the past few years, with the emergence of transracial Asian American adoptee higher education and student affairs scholar-practitioners, has scholarship on this student community become available in the field (Ashlee, 2019; Fry, 2019; Hoffman & Vallejo Peña, 2013; Suda & Hartlep, 2016).

Transracial Asian American adoptees may initially (and phenotypically) present similarly to their nonadopted Asian American counterparts, meaning they may encounter and have to deal with similar anti-Asian racism (Ashlee, 2019; Suda & Hartlep, 2016). However, researchers have also found that transracial Asian American adoptees' adoptee identity and experience facilitates additional, notably different, racialized experiences in college (Ashlee, 2019; Hoffman & Vallejo Peña, 2013; Suda & Hartlep, 2016). The following is a brief overview of some of the unique experiences and needs of transracial Asian American adoptee collegians.

Navigating Racial Liminality

Transracial Asian American adoptees often navigate feeling racially in-between. This feeling is in part because race has been socially constructed through the manufacturing of normative standards for each racial group (Ehlers, 2012). These standards rely upon essentialized depictions of race—which are informed and upheld by monoracism and White supremacy—that often conflate race and culture. For example, while college educators may perceive transracial Asian American adoptees as phenotypically Asian, adoptees may not possess the expected markers of what it means to have or enact an essentialized Asian identity (e.g., having Asian parents, being fluent in an Asian language or familiar with Asian cultural norms). Instead of experiencing race within the rigidity imposed and widely accepted by hegemonic, essentialized definitions, many transracial Asian American adoptees describe experiencing racial liminality. *Liminality* refers to the "state of being betwixt and between social roles and/or identities" (Ibarra & Obodaru, 2016, p. 47). For transracial Asian American adoptees, racial liminality may manifest itself as feeling neither authentically Asian nor fully White, but rather an amorphous mix of racial identities.

Existing beyond essentialized notions of race means that transracial Asian American adoptees may feel an acute disconnect between their ascribed (other-defined) and avowed (self-defined) racial identities. This disconnect can give rise to a differential consciousness, in which transracial Asian American adoptees understand and view race with a unique subjectivity informed by their positionality as outsiders within essentialized renderings of race (Ashlee, 2019; Trenka, Oparah, & Shin, 2006). Depending on the context, transracial Asian American adoptees in college may experience shifting racial salience and sense of belonging. Sometimes, transracial Asian American adoptees may prefer to be in predominantly White spaces because those spaces are most like the environments in which they were raised. Other times, transracial Asian American adoptees may prefer to be in predominantly Asian spaces because they may feel less racially conspicuous. In either case, wherever transracial Asian American adoptees feel a sense of belonging is often informed by whether others acknowledge and include their racial and adoptee identities.

Given the nature of their transracial adoptions and the experience of being raised in and by White adoptive families, transracial Asian American adoptees may feel connected to and simultaneously like caveats from both White and Asian racial groups.

This may appear to college educators as an identity contradiction, as transracial Asian American adoptees may concurrently ache to embody their Asian identity and Whiteness, while also actively rejecting both essentialized racial categories (Ashlee, 2019). This experience of feeling a part of both Asian and White racial groups and also apart from both Asian and White racialized experiences is often intuitive for transracial Asian American adoptees but can be difficult for them to articulate to others, especially as dominant racial discourses privilege monoracial identities (Johnston & Nadal, 2010), thereby obscuring the complexities of navigating racial liminality.

Transracial Asian American adoptees' experience of racial in-betweenness can result in isolation as their nonadopted peers and college educators may perceive their racial liminality as racial confusion. Additionally, transracial Asian American adoptees' racialized experiences may not neatly follow the trajectories of development described by Asian American racial identity theories most regularly referenced in higher education (Alvarez, 2002; Kim, 2001; Kodama, McEwen, Liang, & Lee, 2002). These theories and models foreground ethnic, cultural, and familial factors in racial identity development, which may not resonate with or apply to transracial Asian American adoptees, given their upbringing in predominantly White families and communities (Ashlee, 2019). This does not mean transracial Asian American adoptees are delayed in their racial identity development; rather, it indicates that their racial identity exploration process may not conform to current expectations. Therefore, student affairs educators must think expansively about engaging transracial Asian American adoptee collegians as there is profound potential and insight in the racial liminality embodied by transracial Asian American adoptees. For instance, transracial Asian American adoptees' experience of feeling in-between Asian and White racialized groups calls into question the very racial categories so many colleges and universities adhere to when administering Student of Color support services, which, by their very structure, reinforce limited and limiting essentialized notions of race. As such, an assets-based approach and willingness to explore non-essentialized understandings of race are integral to engaging transracial Asian American adoptees in college; I provide more information about this point in the final section of this chapter related to recommendations for student affairs practice.

Exploring Racial Proximity to Whiteness

As adoptees of color raised in and by White adoptive families, transracial Asian American adoptee collegians grapple with a complex relationship to Whiteness. Often their White adoptive families afford transracial adoptees access to certain privileges (e.g., Anglicized last names, well-resourced neighborhoods, familial networks, social capital, class status). This access to White privilege—or the residual benefits of their adoptive families' White privilege—is contingent on their proximity to their White adoptive families and may not be something of which transracial Asian American adoptees are cognizant. Regardless of their awareness, the conditional nature of transracial Asian American adoptees' access to White privilege often becomes apparent when they go to college as this is regularly the first time peers and educators do not see them primarily as an extension of their White adoptive families, but as People of Color. While some aspects of their conditional access to their adoptive families' White privilege may endure in college, transracial Asian American adoptees must also independently deal with the realities of racism as they are no longer sheltered by their proximity to their White adoptive families.

Although the very nature of transracial adoption gives transracial Asian American adoptee collegians conditional access to White privilege, their transracial adoptions can also facilitate racial isolation and a lack of access to racial mirrors (Hoffman & Vallejo Peña, 2013). This may mean some transracial Asian American adoptees' racial assimilation and tendency toward identifying with their White adoptive families serve as coping strategies for surviving their forced immersion in Whiteness. The strategic and historic triangulation of Asian Americans as a racial wedge between Black and White communities (Kim, 1999) further complicates transracial Asian American adoptees' relationship to Whiteness. This relates to the model minority myth, which is the pervasive positioning of Asian Americans as the ideal or model racialized minority, and which has influenced adoption social workers' tendency to advocate for the placement of Asian children into White adoptive families with greater frequency than other Adoptees of Color (Dorow, 2006). In fact, transracial Asian American adoptees have been referred to as the model, model minority (Park Nelson, 2016), as adoption social workers have depicted them as the most assimilable and culturally compliant transracial adoptee group. Unfortunately, this racial characterization is laden with multiple problematic racist assumptions (e.g., compliance with Whiteness is preferred, Whiteness is the ideal by which all other racial groups are measured and to which they should aspire) and can be internalized by transracial Asian American adoptees in ways that can damage their racial self-confidence (e.g., trying to mimic White standards of beauty, making fun of Asian accents).

For many transracial Asian American adoptees, the desire to develop a sense of belonging in their White adoptive families may contribute to a tendency to aspire to Whiteness. The yearning to fit in with and connect to their White adoptive families can facilitate internalized racism against their own Asianness, which can give rise to a strong disassociation from and prejudice against other Asians and Asian Americans. Chris, a senior transfer student and participant in a study on the racialized experiences of transracial Asian American adoptees in college, shared that when he was younger, he rejected other Asian Americans (Ashlee, 2019). In college, he began to unpack and critically examine his internalized racism. For Chris, his transfer from a community college to a four-year institution propelled him to begin "dismantling and tearing apart a lot of the things that I had done to myself, in terms of my identity . . . self-hatred, internalized racism, and a sense of rejection. . . . I had to work a lot at undoing that" (Ashlee, 2019, p. 70).

Another complex dynamic for transracial Asian American adoptees related to their relationship to Whiteness is the dual minimization of, and lack of preparation for how to cope with, racism. Historically, parents adopting transracially have downplayed—if not entirely rejected—their children's racial differences (Fry, 2019). Often, this means that while some adoptive parents provide opportunities for transracial Asian American adoptees to participate in language camps or to explore their birth/first cultures, most transracial Asian American adoptees are not having conversations with their families about how to deal with race and racism (Ashlee, 2019; Hoffman & Vallejo Peña, 2013). Adoptive families' colorblind mentality may result in White adoptive parents focusing on culture over race (e.g., enrolling adoptees in Korean drumming classes or Chinese cooking lessons instead of addressing systemic racism). While this parenting approach may be grounded in good intentions (aimed at creating a sense of inclusion and cultural celebration for the transracial adoptee, rather than accentuating their racial difference), an unfortunate outcome is that the adoptee is left without adequate preparation for the racist realities they will eventually encounter as People of Color. Additionally, transracial Asian American adoptees may begin to internalize the racial avoidance of their adoptive families to mean that there is something bad or unwanted about their racial identity. In other words, colorblind parenting—regardless of intent—may have the impact of encouraging transracial Asian American adoptees to understand racism through an individualized lens, rather than acknowledging larger systemic realities (e.g., explaining anti-Asian taunts or teasing as the actions of one mean bully instead of naming White supremacy and systemic racism as underlining factors).

Grappling With Racial Authenticity

Separate from, but directly related to, transracial Asian American adoptees' complex relationship to Whiteness is an insecurity about others not perceiving them as Asian enough. This again relates to the idea of racial essentialism and the misperception that there is a finite, immutable set of characteristics that designate a person as racially authentic and, thus, fully belonging to that racial group (Ashlee & Quaye, revise & resubmit). Many transracial Asian American adoptee collegians worry that others (i.e., their non-adopted Asian and Asian American peers, their professors and other college administrators) will regard their upbringing by their White adoptive families as grounds for deeming them racially insufficient. Concerned that their lack of cultural knowledge and limited Asian language proficiency will serve as indicators that they did not have authentic Asian racialized experiences growing up, some transracial Asian American adoptee collegians feel wary of when (or if) they should disclose their adoptee identity to others, for fear that doing so will result in losing racial credibility (Ashlee, 2019).

For many transracial Asian American adoptees, college may be the first time they have access to a critical mass of other Asian Americans, given that many were raised in their adoptive families' predominantly White contexts. While some transracial Asian American adoptees may initially seek out race- and ethnicity-based student organizations and/or Asian American studies courses as a way to explore and cultivate their racial identity, other transracial Asian American adoptee collegians feel ostracized and excluded from these spaces because their Asian racialization differs from the nonadopted dominant narrative (Ashlee, 2019; Hoffman & Vallejo Peña, 2013; Suda & Hartlep, 2016). Thus, it is important for student affairs educators to note that although transracial Asian

American adoptees may seem to belong in and relate to nonadopted Asian American student spaces, many transracial Asian American adoptee collegians may actually avoid these spaces because they fear their peers will deem them racially inauthentic, designating their transracial adoption as grounds for racial fraud.

Given that hegemonic conceptions of race are largely dependent on phenotype, transracial Asian American adoptees must deal with societal interpretations of their racial identity, regardless of whether those perceptions accurately reflect their racial self-concept. This often leads to tension and conflict for transracial Asian American adoptees, as with all Asian Americans, as they are forced to defend themselves and their racialized experiences against anti-Asian racial microaggressions (e.g., others' invasive and persistent questioning, such as "Where are you *really* from?"). For transracial Asian American adoptees, responding to these questions may be additionally complex as they may not have information about their own birth stories or family background. For example, many transracial Asian American adoptees are also transnational adoptees who may know their country of birth but may not know much else about their ancestry; alternatively, they may respond with information about their adoptive family's genealogy or their naturalized citizenship status, which may further confuse or frustrate their questioner. Thus, the very nature of their transracial adoptions makes transracial Asian American adoptees more susceptible to others' racial questioning, which can cause further insecurity about their racial authenticity.

Useful Theories for Engaging Transracial Asian American Adoptees in College

To date, higher education and student affairs scholars have generated two theories specifically about transracial Asian American adoptee collegians. In the first, Hoffman and Vallejo Peña (2013) authored an ethnic identity development model for transracial Korean American adoptees. Their model depicts an identity exploration process involving three elements of personal examination: (1) the salience of and reflection upon one's adoptee identity, (2) activities and experiences that promote ethnic self-identity, and (3) the notion of Whiteness and how being raised by White adoptive families affects adoptees' not feeling Asian enough. According to Hoffman and Vallejo Peña (2013), there are four interrelated themes that interact with how transracial Korean adoptees explore their identity: their environmental context (e.g., predominantly White communities, rural areas); the presence or absence of systems of support (e.g., parents, peers, significant others); missing pieces, such as lack of knowledge of medical history or biological family; and the process of healing (e.g., birth family searching, finding community with other adoptees). Hoffman and Vallejo Peña (2013) contend that Korean adoptees experience identity as fluid and complex. This scholarship can be useful in helping student affairs educators understand the intricate and lifelong process of transracial Asian American adoptees' ethnic identity development.

In 2016, Suda and Hartlep developed a grounded theory model for navigating a transracial adoptee identity in what they describe as "normatively cisracial" (p. 57) college campuses. Suda and Hartlep (2016) extended the gender identity studies term *cisgender* to create *cisracial*, which refers to an alignment between one's perceived race or heritage and that which society projects onto individuals. According to Suda and Hartlep (2016) there are six themes related to the lived experiences of transracial adoptees on college campuses: (1) awareness of adoptee identity, (2) pride in adoptee identity, (3) avoidance of adoptee identity, (4) difficulty for others to understand transracial adoptee identity, (5) "balancing two worlds," and (6) dealing with others' perceptions of transracial adoptees. These experiences are influenced by struggles faced by transracial adoptees on cisracial college campuses (e.g., dealing with racism, adoptee identity not regarded as central to identity, "balancing two worlds" as transracial adoptees, and dealing with others' perceptions of transracial adoptees) and inform ways educators can support the unique needs of transracial adoptee collegians. From these findings, Suda and Hartlep (2016) generated a model of current normative cisracial college campus culture and proposed a reconceptualized model of a transracial college campus. Their theoretical modeling may help student affairs educators identify potential institutional and cultural factors that may impede or conversely facilitate transracial Asian American adoptees' student engagement on college campuses.

In addition to these models, which are descriptive of transracial Asian American adoptees' experiences in college, I want to introduce two additional theories that may be useful for student affairs educators seeking to think expansively and innovatively about how to engage transracial Asian American adoptees in college.

Border Theory

Border Theory foregrounds liminality and a differential consciousness that arises from the ambiguity of (un)belonging and (mis)fitting in historical, social, and spatial contexts (Anzaldúa, 1987). Although Anzaldúa wrote *Borderlands* from her own standpoint as a queer Chicana feminist reflecting on the Mexico/Texas border, the ideological underpinnings of Border Theory have extended to a diverse array of academic fields, including education (Ashlee, 2019; Orozco-Mendoza, 2008). Derived from her own autohistoria *Borderlands/La Frontera: The New Mestiza*, Anzaldúa (1987) contends that those who cannot or do not fit within established binaries of us versus them (e.g., male/female, White/Person of Color, American/foreigner) are deemed deviant. However, rather than solely focusing on the ways in which the border group (i.e., transracial Asian American adoptees) falls short, contests, or complicates the status quo (i.e., monoracial categories), Border Theory urges educators to think expansively and consider the insight and brilliance garnered from a border positionality. According to Border Theory, residing on borders—or existing beyond the rigidity of imposed social categories—gives rise to a nuanced, complex, and valuable perspective. Using a Border Theory lens may enable student affairs educators to regard transracial Asian American adoptees' transgression of monoracial definitions not with a deficit depiction, but as evidence of empowered racial activation that invites more fluid, healing, and liberatory conceptions of race.

Asian Critical Theory

Asian Critical Theory (AsianCrit) is a conceptual lens that applies Critical Race Theory (CRT) to the unique ways in which race and racism shape the everyday lives of Asian Americans (Museus & Iftikar, 2013). It is comprised of seven tenets in total, several of which may be particularly useful for engaging transracial Asian American adoptee collegians. *Asianization* addresses the ways in which members of society lump all Asian Americans in one monolithic group and, through nativistic racism, racializes them as overachieving model minorities and perpetual foreigners (Museus & Iftikar, 2013). This captures the racial conundrum of transracial Asian American adoptees who are simultaneously regarded as the model, model minority (most "ideal" for transracial adoptions) and are also cast as the forever foreigner, forced to perpetually defend themselves, their identities, and their belonging. *Transnational contexts* refers to the relevance of historical and contemporary contexts that extend beyond national borders, such as the ways in which anti–Asian American racism is informed by imperialism, emerging global economies, international war, and transnational migration, all of which are factors influencing transracial Asian American adoption. *Strategic (anti)essentialism* recognizes intra-Asian diversity and the need to disaggregate research on Asian Americans while also acknowledging the political utility of aggregating some scholarship on the community as a whole. This both/and understanding supports the need to acknowledge the unique racialized experiences of transracial Asian American adoptee collegians while also considering their racialized similarities with other Asian American college populations. Finally, *intersectionality* advances the notion that racism is interlocking with all other systems of oppression (e.g., classism, ableism, heterosexism, sexism) to mutually shape the experiences of Asian Americans, which, in the case of transracial Asian American adoption, may play out in who can adopt and who is considered most desirable to adopt. Using an AsianCrit lens may help student affairs educators grasp the multiple factors at play in how transracial Asian American adoptees are racialized and how educators can best engage and support these students on college campuses.

Recommendations for Practice

I now discuss several recommendations for future student affairs practice. These recommendations focus on concrete strategies for student affairs educators to better engage transracial Asian American adoptees in college.

1. **Suspend assumptions and do your own work.** As explained in this chapter, transracial Asian American adoptee collegians often feel that they do not measure up to others' racialized expectations (Ashlee, 2019; Hoffman & Vallejo Peña, 2013; Suda & Hartlep, 2016). In fact, when asked what they most wished college educators knew about their student experience, transracially adopted Asian American collegians replied that they wished educators made fewer assumptions about them and their identities (Ashlee, 2019). Knowing that transracial

Asian American adoptees may (or may not) identify with how student affairs educators perceive them, it is of the utmost importance that educators seeking to engage transracial Asian American adoptees in college suspend their assumptions about this student population and invest in doing their own work to better understand how being transracially adopted impacts these students' collegiate experiences and engagement. One way for educators to learn more about the unique needs of transracial Asian American adoptees and how to best support their student engagement (without projecting this expectation onto transracially adopted Asian American college students to do the educating themselves) is to turn to the field's national conference and professional development network. Within the past few years, research papers and practitioner-based educational sessions on understanding and serving transracial Asian American adoptee collegians have been featured at the ACPA: College Student Educators International annual convention, the NASPA: Student Affairs Administrators in Higher Education annual conference, and the National Conference on Race and Ethnicity in Higher Education annual conference.

2. **Bring an assets-based perspective to transracial Asian American adoptees.** Drawing from Anzaldúa's (1987) Border Theory will enable student affairs educators to bring an assets-based approach to transracial Asian American adoptee collegians. Instead of viewing transracial Asian American adoptees' propensity to identify as racially in-between as evidence of identity confusion or racial incongruence, a Border Theory perspective suggests that there is brilliance in adoptees' racial liminality. Rather than positioning transracial Asian American adoptees as the caveat or exception to hegemonic (i.e., monoracial) models of racial identity development and formation, student affairs educators will be able to more effectively engage transracial Asian American adoptees if they explore the insight and ingenuity that lie within transracial Asian American adoptees' racialized experiences. An important aspect of approaching transracial Asian American adoptees with an assets-based perspective involves refraining from measuring their racial identity development against monoracial renderings of Asian American racial identity. Instead of questioning transracial Asian American adoptees' racial authenticity, given their proximity to Whiteness through their adoptive families, student affairs educators will be more effective in engaging this student population by considering the ways in which their racialized experiences demonstrate racial resiliency and transgressive innovation in light of the oppressive realities of systemic racism.

3. **Introduce adoptee narratives.** Many transracial Asian American adoptees express feeling isolated on their college campuses and in their racialized experiences (Ashlee, 2019; Hoffman & Vallejo Pena, 2013; Suda & Hartlep, 2016). One way to address this isolation and better engage transracial Asian American adoptees in higher education is to feature adoptee narratives in campus programming. Books such as Park Nelson's (2016) *Invisible Asians*, films like

Somewhere Between, and blogs authored by transracial Asian American adoptees, including *Harlow's Monkey* and *Red Thread Broken*, serve as creative platforms for transracial Asian American adoptee identity exploration and articulation. These resources are empowering and affirming for transracial Asian American adoptees. By offering access to these narratives—through featuring an adoptee-related film, a campus keynote, or an Asian Pacific American Heritage Month book club—student affairs educators can will help transracial Asian American adoptees feel less alone in their racialized experience and help them discover language to describe and make sense of transracial Asian American adoptee identity. Additionally, exposure to adoptee narratives will help alleviate tokenizing conditions experienced by transracial Asian American adoptees in college. As student affairs educators are themselves introduced to transracial adoptee narratives, they may be less inclined to exotify the experiences of transracial Asian American adoptee students with whom they work. Similarly, hosting transracial Asian American adoptee speakers and researchers will provide valuable racial mirrors for transracial Asian American adoptee collegians, while simultaneously elevating campus-wide understanding and recognition of the transracial adoptee community, which may help better inform student affairs educators about the unique identity politics and challenges related to transracial adoption.

4. **Encourage explicit inclusion in student organizations.** To help combat the minoritization and underrepresentation of transracial Asian American adoptees in college, student affairs educators might encourage already established student organizations (e.g., the Asian American student union or the multiracial student group on campus) to consider explicitly including transracial Asian American adoptees in their group's mission statement and organization events. The purposeful inclusion of transracial Asian American adoptees in these types of identity-based student organizations may help alleviate some of the insecurities transracial Asian American adoptees have about their sense of belonging in dedicated Asian and Asian American student spaces. Additionally, given that some transracial Asian American adoptee collegians are disinclined to join traditional racial- or ethnic-based student organizations for fear of ostracization or questions about their racial authenticity, student affairs educators should also consider creating transracial adoptee–specific groups based on student interest.

5. **Expand identity-based programming to include experience-based programming.** Another strategy to engage transracial Asian American adoptee collegians is to expand identity-based programming to include not only events and programs for specific racial identity groups (e.g., Asian American college students), but also to explore shared identity experiences (e.g., not feeling racially enough). This programmatic reframe is grounded in a broader philosophical shift from defining the parameters of a community in oppositional contexts (e.g., who is in group and who is out group) to exploring commonalities

and shared aspects of experience as sites for radical interconnectivity (Keating, 2013). Experience-based programming, such as a campus conversation around the topic of racial authenticity, has the potential to create intentional space for transracial Asian American adoptees to reflect on their racialized experiences and facilitate connection with others who may also feel they do not measure up to what it means to be "racially enough." Such programming has the potential to evoke important individual identity exploration, as well as to spur solidarity and empathy building across and between people of different racial categories (Ashlee & Quaye, under review).

6. **Disaggregate Asian American students and revise racial demographic data collection.** Recognizing the importance of a strategic (anti)essentialized understanding of Asian American college students (Museus & Iftikar, 2013), student affairs educators must disaggregate Asian American student communities to accurately understand, and thus be able to address the unique engagement issues for, diverse Asian American subgroups. By taking time to understand intra-Asian diversity, such as the racialized experiences of transracial Asian American adoptees, student affairs educators will be better able to respond to the needs of diverse Asian American students. Related to disaggregating Asian American students is the need for administrators college and university to revise racial demographics data collection strategies. To date, administrators have not collected demographic information about adoptee students. To resolve this oversight, student affairs educators might consider partnering with colleagues in admissions and institutional research offices to reexamine how, when, and which racial demographics information is collected from students. Revisions to demographic data collection may involve providing an open-response field on racial reporting forms rather than asking students to select from a finite list of predesignated racial categories (e.g., allowing a student to write in that they racially identify as a "transracial Asian American adoptee" rather than solely being able to select "Asian/Asian American"). Alternatively, as racial demographics forms have evolved to include the selection of multiple racial categories to better serve bi/multiracial students, "transracial adoptee" might be added as a descriptor from which students can choose (e.g., a respondent could select "Asian/Asian American" and "transracial adoptee"). Additionally, the option to revise or change their reported racial demographic information may enable students to indicate shifts in their racial identity that occur over the course of their collegiate experience (e.g., as they become more involved in ethnic/race-based student groups, take ethnic studies courses, and meet other racially minoritized students on campus, which may introduce new language and inform changes to how students racially identify).

7. **Use social media to facilitate connection and community.** Due in part to the fact that being a transracial adoptee is in many ways an invisible identity unless

purposefully disclosed, transracial Asian American adoptees may experience social isolation, which can further reinforce their sense of otherness and racial marginalization. Therefore, helping transracial Asian American adoptees connect can be necessary to student engagement and encouraging to their racial identity development. Social media can help facilitate these relationships and enable transracial Asian American adoptees to forge networks beyond their individual campuses. These virtual spaces can be useful as transracial Asian American adoptees seek community with people with whom to process racist and anti-adoption microaggressions and understand and validate their racialized experiences. In 2016, a group of transracial adoptee student affairs scholar-practitioners created the Transracial Adoptees in Higher Education Collective, a Facebook group with a mission of creating space for transracial adoptees in higher education to be in community together and share experiences, strategies, and research to support each other and adoptee collegians. While primarily a community of graduate students, student affairs educators, and multidisciplinary adoption scholars who identify as transracial adoptees, some undergraduate students have found the group as well. Members connect across institution type (e.g., community colleges, four-year private, and public institutions) to share reflective content (e.g., blog posts), connect about adoptee activism issues (e.g., intercountry adoptee citizenship rights), and exchange information about transracial adoption resources (e.g., scholarships, conferences, research opportunities). Since its inception, the collective has grown to include more than 130 members from across the country and has led to numerous in-person socials and meet ups. A quick search reveals that there are more than 80 different groups related to transracial adoption on Facebook alone, and many more groups exist for specific racial and ethnic adoptee communities (i.e., Korean adoptees, Chinese adoption).

Conclusion

In this chapter, I reviewed theoretical and empirical literature related to transracial Asian American adoptees in college. I provided an introduction to and overview of this minoritized and underserved student population, as well as reviewed several theoretical frameworks that may help student affairs educators better understand and support this student community. Finally, I offered recommendations for better engaging transracial Asian American adoptees in higher education. College is a catalytic context for student development broadly and may be uniquely so for transracial Asian American adoptees. For many transracial Asian American adoptees, college coincides with a shift from being viewed primarily in relation to their White adoptive families to being viewed primarily as Asian college students, not readily visible as adoptees (Ashlee, 2019). In this regard, college can be a notable and transformative context for transracial Asian American adoptees, especially when student affairs educators are informed about transracial adoptees' unique experiences and prepared to employ targeted student engagement strategies to support their learning and development.

Note

1 The author chose to focus on transracial Asian American adoptees to attend to the unique racialized experiences of this population. While there may be similarities in experiences and engagement strategies across transracial adoptee communities, future research is needed.

References

Alvarez, A. N. (2002). Racial identity and Asian Americans: Supports and challenges. In M. K. McEwen, C. M. Kodama, A. N. Alvarez, S. Lee, & C. T. H. Liang (Eds.), *Working with Asian American college students* (New directions for student services, No. 97) (pp. 33–43). San Francisco, CA: Jossey-Bass.

Anzaldúa, G. (1987). *Borderlands/La Frontera: The new mestiza*. San Francisco, CA: Aunt Lute Book Company.

Ashlee, A. A. (2019). *Neither, nor, both, between: Understanding transracial Asian American adoptees' racialized experiences in college using Border Theory* (Doctoral dissertation). Retrieved from Ohio-LINK. (miami1556291981659086)

Ashlee, A. A., & Quaye, S. J. (revise & resubmit). On being racially enough: A duoethnography across minoritized racial identities. *International Journal of Qualitative Studies in Education*.

Dorow, S. K. (2006*). Transnational adoption: A cultural economy of race, gender, and kinship*. New York, NY: New York University Press.

Ehlers, N. (2012). *Racial imperatives: Discipline, performativity, and struggles against subjection*. Bloomington, IN: Indiana University Press.

Fry, J. J. (2019). Asian American transracial adoptees: Identity development in college. *Journal of Student Affairs, 28*, 61–68.

Hoffman, J., & Vallejo Peña, E. V. (2013). Too Korean to be White and too White to be Korean: Ethnic identity development among transracial Korean American adoptees. *Journal of Student Affairs Research and Practice, 50*(2), 152–170. http://doi.org/10.1515/jsarp- 2013–0012

Ibarra, H., & Obodaru, O. (2016). Betwixt and between identities: Liminal experience in contemporary careers. *Research in Organizational Behavior, 36*, 47–64.

Johnston, M. P., & Nadal, K. L. (2010). Multiracial microaggressions: Exposing monoracism in everyday life and clinical practice. In D. W. Sue (Ed.), *Microaggressions and marginality: Manifestation, dynamics and impact* (pp. 123–144). New York, NY: Wiley & Sons.

Keating, A. (2013). *Transformation now: Toward a post-oppositional politics of change*. Champaign, IL: University of Illinois Press.

Kim, C. J. (1999). The racial triangulation of Asian Americans. *Politics & Society, 27*(1), 105–138.

Kim, C. J. (2001). Asian American identity development theory. In C. L. Wijeyesinghe & B. W. Jackson III (Eds.), *New perspectives on racial identity development: A theoretical and practical anthology* (pp. 67–90). New York, NY: New York University Press.

Kodama, C. M., McEwen, M. K., Liang, C. T. H., & Lee, S. (2002). An Asian American perspective on psychosocial student development theory. In M. K. McEwen, C. M. Kodama, A. N. Alvarez, S. Lee, & C. T. H. Liang (Eds.), *Working with Asian American college students* (New directions for student services, No. 97) (pp. 45–59). San Francisco, CA: Jossey-Bass.

Museus, S. D. (2014). *Asian American students in higher education: Key issues on diverse college students*. New York, NY: Routledge.

Museus, S. D., & Iftikar, J. (2013). *AsianCrit: Toward an Asian critical theory in education*. Paper presented at the 2013 Annual Meeting of the American Educational Research Association, San Francisco, CA.

Orozco-Mendoza, E. F. (2008). *Borderlands theory: Producing border epistemologies with Gloria Anzaldúa* (Master's thesis). Retrieved from Electronic Theses and Dissertations database. (05062008–175949).

Park Nelson, K. P. (2016). *Invisible Asians: Korean American adoptees, Asian American experiences, and racial exceptionalism*. New Brunswick, NJ: Rutgers University Press.

Pendakur, S., & Pendakur, V. (2012). Let's get radical: Being a practitioner-ally for Asian Pacific Islander American college students. In D. Ching & A. Agbayani (Eds.), *Asian American and Pacific Islanders in higher education: Research and perspectives on identity, leadership, and success* (pp. 31–55). Washington, DC: NASPA Student Affairs Professionals in Higher Education.

Suda, D. K., & Hartlep, N. D. (2016). "Balancing two worlds": Supporting transracially adopted Asian/American students on the college campus. *Educational Foundations*, *29*(1–4), 55–72.

Trenka, J. J., Oparah, J. C., and Shin, S. Y. (Eds.). (2006). *Outsiders within: Writing on transracial adoption*. Cambridge, MA: South End Press.

Chapter 5
Engaging Indigenous Students

Erin Kahunawaika'ala Wright and Heather J. Shotton

Our creation stories tell us we have lived on our ancestral lands since time immemorial. Moreover, history tells us we have been part of what we now know as American higher education since its colonial establishment in the 17th century, even in the wake of genocidal campaigns designed to eliminate our physical and cultural presence from these lands (Wolfe, 2006).

Dena'ina scholar Jessica Bissett Perea (2013) opens her piece on Alaska Native presence with this idea of "present absence," which defines the space Indigenous Peoples—who represent a host of distinct peoples and cultures with unique political relationships with the US—have come to occupy in the broader US consciousness. In one way, present absence in higher education speaks to the intentional erasure of Indigenous presence in modern society by US colonialism. Indigenous Peoples are relegated to the past, found only as antiquities in university museums' Native American collection or stored away in carefully labeled boxes in anthropology departments, even though Indigenous students are more than likely enrolled on these same campuses. In another way, present absence "asterisks" (Garland, 2007; Shotton, Lowe, & Waterman, 2013) Indigenous Peoples' stories in higher education due to our small (read "unimportant") population sizes, yet unabashedly appropriates our cultures through college mascots and "Hawaiian luaus," for example. Even in this critically important text guiding our field on engaging minoritized students, Indigenous students have not been included until this third edition. While we are incredibly grateful to the editors for actively addressing this epistemological gap, the benign neglect simply illustrates the point: we are here but rarely considered an integral part of "higher education's story" (Shotton et al., 2013). This is even more troubling when one considers the fact that Indigenous students have been enrolled in this country's colleges and universities for over 350 years (Austin, 2005). These historical and contemporary erasures of our presence emphasize the enduring deleterious impacts of settler colonialism on Indigenous Peoples (Kaomea, 2014). So, given our state of present absence, how do we meaningfully decolonize our student engagement praxis and illuminate the well-traveled, hidden, new, and potential paths supporting Indigenous student engagement?

In this chapter, we have designed an indigenized landscape survey of sorts to build familiarity with the terrain we must first acknowledge and then traverse when considering Indigenous student engagement in higher education. We use "Indigenous Peoples,"[1] "Indigenous," and "Native" interchangeably to refer to the autochthonous peoples of the lands we now know as the United States and its politically affiliated territories. We use "Native American" to denote American Indians and Alaska Natives. You will also notice we identify Indigenous scholars with their Native nation(s) prior to their name or in parentheses after their name as a way to reestablish our presence in the higher education literature. We begin our survey by providing significant contextual information about Indigenous Peoples to establish a particular understanding of this landscape. Theories and concepts key to (re)framing Indigenous students' journeys to and through higher education follows. Moving away from the deficit-oriented perspective that blames Indigenous students for their perceived failures in education, we then offer an analysis of epistemological and structural issues facing Indigenous students as a way to reorient our thinking about higher education's responsibilities to decolonize their epistemologies, methodologies, and methods of engagement with Indigenous students. We end this chapter by identifying multiple paths to nurturing Indigenous student engagement in higher education.

Defining "Indigenous"

Indigenous identity and status in the US are complex and nuanced. In order for higher education professionals, scholars, and policy makers to begin to understand this complexity, it must first be understood that Indigenous people occupy what Lumbee scholar Bryan M. J. Brayboy (2005, 2013) calls a liminal space. That is, our identities are both political and racialized (Brayboy, 2005, 2013). At the root of Indigeneity is the connection to place. Simply stated, the term *indigenous* means "to be of place" (Deloria & Wildcat, 2001, p. 31). For Indigenous Peoples, to be of a particular place denotes a historical, cultural, and spiritual connection. As Indigenous scholars Vine Deloria, Jr. (Lakota) and Daniel Wildcat (Yuchi) (2001) explain, "Indigenous people represent a culture emergent from a place, and they actively draw on the power of that place physically and spiritually" (p. 32). Connection to place for Indigenous People in the US and our status as the original inhabitants of this land are key to understanding our political status. Indigenous peoples inhabited what is now known as the United States long before it was the United States (Salis Reyes, 2014), and prior to colonization, Indigenous people had our own systems of rule and forms of governance.

The sovereign status of Native American tribes is an important distinction when engaging Indigenous students. Today, there are 573 distinct federally recognized tribal nations[2] in the US, all known by various names including tribes, nations, bands, pueblos, communities, and Alaska Native villages (Federal Register, 2018; NCAI, 2016; US Department of Interior, 2018). Native American tribes engage in a government-to-government, or nation-to-nation, relationship with the US federal government. This is based on the recognition of the legal and political relationship between tribes and the US that was established through the process of treaty making (Deloria & Lytle, 1983).

At the heart of tribal sovereignty is the right to self-governance (National Congress of American Indians [NCAI], 2016). As sovereign nations, tribes have their own distinct systems of government that include powers of determining citizenship, establishing civil and criminal laws, taxation, and licensing, as well as the provision and regulation of tribal activities including land management, education, health care, law enforcement, and basic infrastructure (Kalt, 2007; NCAI, 2016). Two key functions of tribal governments as they relate to higher education are that of tribal citizenship and education. As Deloria and Lytle (1983) explain, citizens of tribal nations enjoy the benefit of dual citizenship, where they are both citizens of tribal nations and citizens of the US. This distinction is important when engaging Indigenous students in higher education, and we make this distinction in an attempt to (re)frame the institutional responsibility to Indigenous students.

While Native American tribes and Native Hawaiians have a shared history with settler colonialism, both the history of the occupation of Hawai'i and the relationship between Native Hawaiians and the US is distinct from tribes (Beamer, 2014; Goodyear-Ka'ōpua, Hussey, & Wright, 2014; Salis Reyes & Shotton, 2018). While Native Hawaiians are not "federally recognized" by the US government as a Native nation, they have several federal laws establishing their indigeneity within the context of the US legal system. For example, similar to American Indian reservations, the 1920–1921 Hawaiian Homes Commission Act designated lands in Hawai'i for "native Hawaiians" (individuals able to prove 50% Native blood quantum) to establish homesteads, including agricultural and pastoral lots. Also on the 100th commemoration of the US-aided overthrow of the independent Kingdom of Hawai'i in 1993, President Bill Clinton signed Public Law 103–150, apologizing to Native Hawaiians for the overthrow of their nation and called for a process of reconciliation. Although Native Hawaiians have not been privy to any kind of "reconciliation" with the US thus far, movements for sovereignty and self-determination remain active and strong.

US-occupied territories like American Sāmoa, Puerto Rico, and Guam have their own unique histories and consequent challenges as nations with Indigenous Peoples. The consequences of these histories add to the complexities of what "Indigenous" or "Native" means in the context of American higher education. Wright and Balutski (2013) write,

> The citizens of U.S. colonies [or territories] assume liminal identities, legally and politically [and racially], as "full" citizens of neither the United States nor their island nation. Furthermore, these groups are then identified in the United States as "Native Hawaiian and Other Pacific Islanders," which classifies them racially but erases (or obscures) the legal and political aspects of their identities that impact, for example, issues of access to higher education.
>
> (p. 147)

Like Native Hawaiians, Indigenous Peoples in US colonies literally live in a state of in-betweenness. Needless to say, these complications born of US colonialism and occupation are problematic on multiple levels for Indigenous Peoples.

Theories and Concepts

Settler Colonialism

A succinct understanding of settler colonialism theories is found in Native Hawaiian scholar Noelani Goodyear-Kaʻōpua's book *The Seeds We Planted: Portraits of a Native Hawaiian Charter School*, a portraiture study of a Native Hawaiian culture-based public charter school in Hawaiʻi. Drawing on the analysis of settler colonialism in Hawaiʻi by leading Native Hawaiian political scholar Haunani-Kay Trask, Goodyear-Kaʻōpua (2013) describes settler colonialism in the following way to denote Hawaiʻi as a "settler state":

> As Indigenous studies scholars have established, settler colonialisms seek to rid the land of collective Native presence and permanence in order to make way for and legitimize settler societies. Settler colonialisms are historically rooted, land-centered projects that are never fully complete.
>
> (p. 23)

Goodyear-Kaʻōpua uses the plural "settler colonialisms" to denote the specificity of settler colonialism theories to each place and people. As she illustrates, settler colonialism is a distinctive type of colonialism, which: 1) seeks to permanently replace Indigenous Peoples with invasive settler societies who then assert their "legitimate" juridical, militarized, and cultural dominion over Indigenous lands and resources; and 2) continuously engages in the "logic of elimination" (Wolfe, 2006) over time, using tools of colonialism to maintain the erasure of Indigenous Peoples and, in turn, delegitimize their claims over lands, resources, and peoplehood.

In essence, settler colonialism "destroys to replace" (Wolfe, 2006, p. 388) by asserting that settlers and settler societies, regardless of how one settles, benefits from the displacement and/or containment of Native people, whether it is through genocide, relocation, English-only laws, reservations, boarding schools/educational systems, political status, or assertions of eminent domain. These features of settler colonialism are clearly visible through an analysis of the histories of Native North America and the ongoing displacement of Native peoples as with, for example, the violence against Dakota and Lakota water protectors at Standing Rock by settler state agents (governmental and private) and the "asterisking" of Indigenous students by researchers in the higher education literature. To place a finer point on the settler colonial endgame, Native Hawaiian scholar J. Kēhaulani Kauanui (2016) writes, "the logic of elimination is about the elimination of the native as *native*" (emphasis in original, p. 1).

In 2000, *Amerasia Journal* published an issue guest edited by Candace Fujikane and Jonathan Y. Okamura, two Japanese American scholars from Hawaiʻi, titled, "Whose

Vision? Asian Settler Colonialism in Hawai'i" to examine the ways settler colonialism operates when Indigenous Peoples (Native Hawaiian) are displaced by what Trask calls "settlers of color" (Asian Americans) (Trask, 2000). In their revised edition, retitled *Asian Settler Colonialism: From Local Governance to the Habits of Everyday Life in Hawai'i*, Fujikane (2008) says the Native Hawaiian and non–Native Hawaiian contributors to the book "work collectively to examine Asian settler colonialism as a constellation of colonial ideologies and practices of Asian settlers who currently support the broader structure of the US settler state" as well as "identify their [Asian settlers'] responsibilities to Hawaiians" (p. 6).

Unsurprisingly, Asian settler colonialism has been a controversial framework because it is premised upon the idea that people of color *participate in and benefit from* the displacement of Native people, regardless of their arrival histories and positionalities in the US social hierarchy. Fujikane (2008) addresses the critiques of Asian settler colonialism as "dishonor[ing] the struggles of their [Asian Americans in Hawai'i] grandparents and great-grandparents" (p. 6) by complicating our understandings of "histories of oppression and resistance" (p. 7). That is to say, part of "honoring the struggles of those who came before us" (p. 7) means not only to acknowledge Asian American claims of oppression and resistance to US colonialism, but also to acknowledge the ways in which these "histories of oppression and resistance" contribute to the ongoing dispossession of Native Hawaiians. Consequently, Asian settler colonialism views Asian Americans in Hawai'i as victims, survivors, and agents of the US settler state. For Indigenous Peoples, Fujikane and Okamura make a significant contribution to repositioning our thinking about Indigenous settler/settler of color relationships writ large:

> The status of Asians as settlers, however, is not a question about whether they were the initial colonizers or about their relationship with white settlers. The identification of Asians as settlers focuses on their obligations to the indigenous peoples of Hawai'i and the responsibilities that Asian settlers have in supporting Native peoples in their struggles for self-determination.
>
> (Fujikane, 2008, p. 7)

Through the lens of settler colonialism, Indigenous student engagement must first begin with acknowledging that settler colonialism is an ongoing project that calls for using settler practices to erase/contain Native presence. As Tuck and Ree (2013) remind us, settler colonialism requires that Indigenous peoples be made into ghosts. We must engage in critical self-reflection about the conscious and unconscious ways higher education continues to participate in Native people's erasure and develop decolonial engagement practices that foreground Native movements for cultural/political sovereignty and self-determination.

Nation-Building

A central concept for understanding the role of higher education in the lives of Indigenous students is Native nation-building (Benham & Stein, 2003; Brayboy, 2005; Brayboy et al., 2012; Goodyear-Ka'ōpua, 2013; Brayboy et al., 2014; Minthorn & Shotton,

2018; Shotton, 2018; Waterman, Lowe, & Shotton, 2018). Brayboy et al. (2012) frame Native higher education as an integral part of nation-building, not simply as a means for individual social mobility, but as a means to create "independence of mind" (Indigenous Knowledge Systems section, para 1) while also strengthening the economic, political/legal, and intellectual/cultural facets of Native nationhood. To this end, research shows that Indigenous students view their participation in higher education as an important way to "give back" to their Native communities in particular ways (Brayboy, 2005; Keene, 2018; Salis Reyes, 2018).

Native nation-building extends our thinking beyond conventionally defined student outcomes in higher education around citizenship such as civil and community engagement. For Indigenous students with dual citizenship (i.e., US and American Indian tribal nation or Alaska Native tribe, corporation, or village), those from non-federally recognized Native nations (e.g., Gabrieliño-Tongva Tribe (California)) and those from US-occupied Indigenous nations (e.g., Guam, American Sāmoa, Puerto Rico), Native nation-building attends to "uphold[ing] the values, interests, and cultures of Native communities and nations" and "preserv[ing] community, sovereignty, and cultural traditions" (Champagne, 2003). Reasserting Indigenous presence by perpetuating political/legal as well as cultural sovereignty and self-determination for Native nations and communities is fundamental to the higher education journeys of Indigenous students.

To better understand this orientation, Brayboy et al. (2012) contextualize Native nation-building within the broader discussion of Indigenous knowledge, particularly as it relates to the strong connections Indigenous students have to their Native nations and communities and the lands Indigenous students come from. They write:

> At the heart of Indigenous knowledge systems are notions of community and its concomitant survival; an understanding that lived experience is a very important form of knowledge (and subsequently informs theory); the importance of relationality, respect, and reciprocity; as well as the recognition of the importance of place/space and land. In this paradigm, the survival of Indigenous community is more important than any individual.
>
> (Indigenous Knowledge Systems section, para 2)

Brayboy and Maughan (2009) remind us that Indigenous knowledge is deeply rooted in the relationship between individuals and their communities, that community is "at the core of our existence" (p. 15). Native nation-building is inextricably tied to higher education because of the importance placed on collective well-being. That is to say, the collective is valued over the individual, and success and prestige depend more on the extent to which an individual shares accumulated wealth and contributes to the well-being of the community (Deyhle & Swisher, 1997). This is in sharp contrast to the individualistic and neoliberal forms of achievement that are traditionally prized in higher education, in which individual achievement, status gained through degree attainment, and the promise of securing desirable employment are valued (Shotton, 2018).

Research on Indigenous students confirms that supporting relationally oriented life-ways in higher education praxis positively impacts traditional measures of student success like transfer, persistence, and graduation while also, unsurprisingly, helping Indigenous students maintain/sustain their cultural identities (e.g., HeavyRunner & DeCelles, 2002; Thomas, Kanaʻiaupuni, Frietas, & Balutski, 2012; Minthorn & Shotton, 2018; Waterman et al., 2018). As an example, in her study of Haudenosaunee students, Onondaga scholar Stephanie J. Waterman (2012) finds that, given this community orientation of Native American students, "home-going" is a key strategy in supporting their successful matriculation. This finding contrasts traditional higher education literature which tells us one of the best strategies to retain students is to increase their on-campus engagement (e.g., Astin, 1984; Pascarella & Terenzini, 2005). This is not to say on-campus engagement is not important for Indigenous students—it is vitally important. Rather, our assertion is that both engagement on campus *and* home-going are important for Indigenous student engagement. Furthermore, Chippewa scholar Duane Champagne (2003) writes that creating opportunities for Indigenous students to cultivate relationships with Indigenous communities is essential to preparing them for Native nation-building. Indigenous student engagement through the lens of Native nation-building actively cultivates reciprocal relationships with Indigenous students and their nations and communities and supports students in their goals to "give back."

Tribal Critical Race Theory

A particularly influential framework in understanding the higher education journeys of Indigenous students comes from Brayboy's articulation of Tribal Critical Race Theory (TribalCrit) (2005, 2013). Critical Race Theory (CRT) emerges from the field of critical legal studies as a response to "positivist and legal discourse of civil rights" (Ladson-Billings, 1998, p. 7). CRT is a very useful framework for communities of color because it foregrounds race, racism, intersectionality, and power in its analyses, particularly as it manifests in US legal and institutional structures (like higher education) while simultaneously advocating action-oriented avenues addressing inequality and injustice. For Indigenous Peoples, CRT also methodologically aligns with many of our cultures' preferred means of knowledge transmission and theorizing: that is, through storytelling.

Inspired by his own search to find appropriate theories to fully understand and express Native American experiences with educational institutions (Brayboy, 2005, 2013) and building on the original work of Ladson-Billings and Tate (1995) situating CRT in education, Brayboy (2005) writes,

> TribalCrit emerges from Critical Race Theory (CRT) and is rooted in the multiple, nuanced, and historically—and geographically—located epistemologies and ontologies found in Indigenous communities. Though they differ depending on time, space, place, tribal nation, and individual, there appear to be commonalities in those ontologies and epistemologies. TribalCrit is rooted in these commonalities while simultaneously recognizing the range and variation that exists within and between communities and individuals.
>
> (p. 427)

He then extends CRT's theoretical reach to attend to the "liminal legal/political" and racialized identities of American Indians[3] and their experiences with US colonialism and to move beyond the "black/white binary" of civil rights discourse imbedded in CRT by adding the following nine tenets to Matsuda, Lawrence, Delgado, and Crenshaw's (1993) foundational six:

1. Colonization is endemic to society.
2. US policies toward Indigenous peoples are rooted in imperialism, White supremacy, and a desire for material gain.
3. Indigenous peoples occupy a liminal space that accounts for both the political and racialized natures of our identities.
4. Indigenous peoples have a desire to obtain and forge tribal sovereignty, tribal autonomy, self-determination, and self-identification.
5. The concepts of culture, knowledge, and power take on new meaning when examined through an Indigenous lens.
6. Governmental policies and educational policies toward Indigenous peoples are intimately linked around the problematic goal of assimilation.
7. Tribal philosophies, beliefs, customs, traditions, and visions for the future are central to understanding the lived realities of Indigenous peoples, but they also illustrate the differences and adaptability among individuals and groups.
8. Stories are not separate from theory; they make up theory and are, therefore, real and legitimate sources of data and ways of being.
9. Theory and practice are connected in deep and explicit ways such that scholars must work towards social change.

Like CRT, TribalCrit has galvanized other Indigenous scholars to engage in theory building given the complexities and diversity among Indigenous Peoples and the lack of adequate frameworks to fully understand our experiences with US education. For Native Hawaiians, 'Ōiwi Critical Race Theory (Wright & Balutski, 2013, 2016) and Kanaka Critical Race Theory (Salis Reyes, 2016, 2018) expand upon TribalCrit to theorize Native Hawaiian engagement with higher education as kuleana lāhui (Native nation-building). Pacific Islander Critical Race Theory (PICRiT) (Kukahiko, 2017) also centers the experiences of Pacific Islander student-athletes to reframe the ways we understand their participation (and lack thereof) in higher education beyond their physical labor in collegiate athletics.

While Brayboy fully honors the diversity of Indigenous Peoples in the US and writes against attempts to essentialize our identities and experiences, TribalCrit provides a useful lens to understand the historical, political, and epistemological "commonalities" (p. 427) among Indigenous Peoples, which is helpful to identifying shared spaces to strategize for Indigenous student engagement.

Issues and Challenges of Place

As previously discussed, place cannot be separated from a discussion of Indigenous Peoples. Place is salient for Indigenous students in two specific ways: first, as integral to Indigenous identities and second, as the terra firma on which all institutions of higher education stand. Aleut scholars Eve Tuck and Wayne Yang (2012) explain that Indigenous Peoples have creation stories about "how we/they came to be in a particular place—indeed how we/they came to *be a place* [emphasis in original]. Our/their relationships to land comprise our/their epistemologies, ontologies, and cosmologies" (p. 6). These creation stories are inextricably linked to place, reflecting our ancestral knowledge systems and informing our ways of being in the world, including our spirituality/cultural practices critical to maintaining our Indigenous identities. Further emphasizing the gravity of this relationship, Santa Clara Pueblo science scholar Gregory Cajete (2004) writes,

> Indigenous people are people of place, and the nature of the place is embedded in their language. The physical, cognitive, emotional orientation of a people is a kind of "map" they carry in their heads and transfer from generation to generation. The map is multidimensional and reflects the spiritual as well as the mythic geography of a people.
>
> (p. 46)

Native Hawaiian scholars Lilikalā Kameʻeleihiwa (1992), Kapā Oliveira (2014) and Mehana Vaughan (2018) talk about the Hawaiian word for *place* or *land* (including the sea), *ʻāina*, meaning "that which feeds." Vaughan (2018) says, "The word [*ʻāina*] speaks to a relationship with *ʻāina*, the place that feeds your family, not only physically but spiritually, mentally, and emotionally" (p. 2). This multidimensional map Cajete describes is a crucial guide for Indigenous Peoples as we navigate the world.

Therefore, when Indigenous students attend college away from their Indigenous places, the college-going experience can be a culturally/spiritually and physically jarring one that goes beyond homesickness (HeavyRunner & DeCelles, 2002). Couple this separation with the general invisibility of Indigenous students and the absence of Indigenous knowledge systems, designated campus spaces, and aesthetics in higher education, and the dissonance/disengagement many Indigenous students feel is unsurprising. "Indigenous people are people of place" is a significant aspect culturally (and politically) distinguishing Indigenous students from racially minoritized students and cannot be overstated. Indigenous students draw their identities from their places. So how do we build structures and practices that nurture Indigenous students' relationships with their ancestral places *and* their campus communities?

Place is significant for Indigenous Peoples because it also embodies our collective lived experiences. From the Indian Removal Act of 1830 to the water protectors at Standing Rock and the protectors of the Arctic and Mauna a Wākea, our places also tell our stories about dispossession and survivance.[4] Institutions of higher education are not separate from the lived experiences of Indigenous Peoples as they also embody settler colonial histories of displacement and erasure. In *Ebony and Ivy*, Wilder (2013) demonstrates the critical role American higher education played in upholding the institution of slavery (including the use of enslaved people to build and maintain these campuses) but also in the displacement of Native Americans specifically from their lands. Without Native lands, these institutions would not be among the most prestigious (and wealthiest) in the world.

Native Hawaiian scholar Kaiwipunikauikawēkiu Lipe (2018) advises that stakeholders must acknowledge this history if higher education hopes to fully embrace its liberatory and democratized ideals:

> [I]f we are going to address inequality and inequity in higher education, we have to begin with at least this one truth: Every university in the United States of America and Hawai'i [and other US territories] is situated on Indigenous land (Justice, 2004; Kame'eleihiwa in Lipe, 2012). As such, each of our universities, and each of us who work at those universities, reaps resources from the Indigenous homelands upon which our institutions sit; land that was likely seized from those Indigenous peoples.
>
> (p. 163)

Acknowledging the histories of dispossession (and the historical trauma caused by dispossession (Brave Heart, 2003)) as well as the ongoing benefits derived from dispossession is another critical piece to meaningfully addressing Indigenous student engagement. Wilder's research inspired higher education stakeholders to demand institutions of higher education begin reckoning with their history with slavery—to acknowledge their complicity, make restitution to the descendants of the people enslaved in the building and running of these institutions, and make a commitment toward anti-oppressive higher education praxis. While reconciliation processes are not without their shortcomings, the conversation sets a precedent for Indigenous Peoples to call for reconciliation as well.

Historical Role of Education for Indigenous Peoples

The history of Native peoples and US/colonial education is a complicated one, its impacts still felt today. The most familiar narrative is one of Native erasure. Education was used as a settler colonial tool to, as the oft-quoted founder of the Carlisle Indian School Captain Richard H. Pratt goes, "Kill the Indian in him, and save the man." This history chronicles the forcible removal of Native children from their families and lands, involuntary deculturation, and physical, sexual, and psychological abuse largely in Indian boarding schools and government-run schools (which were also somewhat replicated in Alaska and Hawai'i). It is also a history of resistance to settler colonial attempts to deculturate Indigenous Peoples. In the case of Native Hawaiians, western-style education was viewed as a "modernizing project" preparing Native and non-Native citizens of the independent Kingdom of Hawai'i for its turn toward a global modernity, so by the mid–19th century the Kingdom boasted a well-developed largely Native-led public education system (Goodyear-Ka'ōpua, 2013).

The history of Indigenous peoples and education is also covered by Indigenous scholars (and in partnership with non-Indigenous scholars) (e.g., Benham & Heck, 1998; Lomawaima, 1999; Lomawaima & McCarty, 2006; Reyhner & Eder, 2004). However, it is important to share a baseline understanding of Native experiences with Western education especially since education is often cast as an accessible means for social mobility. Mvskoke/Creek scholar K. Tsianina Lomawaima (1999) identifies four tenets to colonial American Indian education that we would identify as "commonalities" among several Indigenous communities:

(1) That Native Americans were savages and had to be civilized;
(2) That civilization required Christian conversion;
(3) That civilization required subordination of Native communities, frequently achieved through resettlement efforts; and
(4) That Native people had mental, moral, physical, or cultural deficiencies that made certain pedagogical methods necessary for their education. (p. 3)

After decades of unsuccessful warring with Natives (we continued to survive), American colonialists decided "civilizing" the Natives would be the next best option in alignment with the settler colonial logic and agenda. Lomawaima goes on to say, "These [tenets] were not based on natural truths but were culturally constructed and served specific agendas of the colonizing nations . . . Although these ideas have become *naturalized*, or taken for granted over time, they should be questioned and analyzed" (emphasis in original, p. 4). Indigenous scholars have "questioned and analyzed" these historical, taken-for-granted assumptions embedded in American education for years now because education continues to view and treat Native students (and their families and communities) as damaged (Cote-Meek, 2014).

In 2016, Dr. Lomawaima gave an "Equity and Difference" lecture at the University of Washington titled, "More Than Mascots! Less Than Citizens? American Indians Talk: Why Isn't the US Listening?" Her title distills an important lesson for us all: education needs to listen to Indigenous Peoples. More research is always needed, but we believe it is important to point out well-documented, well-traveled Native educational paths already in existence. For example, among the most well-documented paths is culturally responsive schooling (Brayboy & Castagno, 2008; Demmert & Towner, 2003; Kanaʻiaupuni, Ledward & Jensen, 2010). Culturally responsive schooling "transforms deficit-oriented schooling into environments of abundance that utilize ancestral knowledge, culturally relevant pedagogy, Hawaiian ways of being and knowing, and contemporary socio-cultural, socio-political contexts to inspire . . . youth to forge anti-colonial, success-based cultural identities" (Wright, 2018, p. 21). Yet we rarely see these proven paths incorporated into Non-Native Colleges and Universities (NNCUs) (Shotton et al., 2013). From our scholar-practitioner perspectives, countless Native communities have documented these paths in multiple formats such as technical reports, grant awards, program evaluations, and newsletters which are often available online. Furthermore,

Indigenous scholars are working to transform the meaning of "scholarship" by including the research and reflections of Indigenous scholar-practitioners in their publications (e.g., Shotton et al., 2013; Minthorn & Chavez, 2016; Minthorn & Shotton, 2018; and Waterman et al., 2018). It is clear that Indigenous communities, many without sufficient resources, are actively addressing their educational needs and aspirations as acts of sovereignty and self-determination. Learning from Indigenous communities themselves about what works for Indigenous students is vital to overcoming the challenges higher education faces with engaging Indigenous students.

Colonialism and Racism

Anishinaabe scholar Sheila Cote-Meek (2014) reminds us that Indigenous peoples have been "imagined and narrated in a particular way and through a particular lens" (p. 46). That lens has been colonial, and the narration has been one of erasure. As a result, Indigenous students simultaneously encounter issues of colonization and racism. The effects of erasure magnify issues of racism for Indigenous peoples. Because we are not the ones narrating our stories, representation of Indigenous people in the mainstream perpetuates stereotypical ideology that places Indigenous people outside mainstream culture and portrays us as relics of the past (Hill, Kim, & Williams, 2010). Our invisibility allows non-Indigenous people to acquire their understanding of Indigenous People through indirect sources that often perpetuate stereotypes and racist imagery (Castagno, 2005; Fryberg, Markus, Oyserman, & Stone, 2008).

The literature suggests that Indigenous students regularly encounter racism on college campuses (Castagno, 2005; Huffman, 1991; Jackson, Smith, & Hill, 2003; Mihesuah, 2003; Perry, 2002; Shotton, 2017; Tachine, Cabrera, & Yellow Bird, 2017). Indigenous students experience both active and passive racism, marginalization, and generally hostile campus climates, which ultimately results in feelings of isolation (Jackson et al., 2003; Perry, 2002; Tachine et al., 2017). We understand that Indigenous students encounter racism in higher education; it has been well documented. What bears further discussion are the complex intersections of racism and colonialism for Indigenous students and the profoundly different way in which Indigenous people are racialized.

Student Engagement Strategies

Strategies for engaging Indigenous students must be (re)framed and centered in understanding of the nuanced and political identities of Indigenous Peoples. Toward that aim, we offer the following suggestions as paths to nurturing Indigenous student engagement in higher education.

Develop and Maintain Relationships With Indigenous Communities

Develop meaningful and reciprocal relationships with tribal nations and Native Hawaiian communities. Engagement of Indigenous students must begin with a recognition of the role that community plays in the success of Indigenous students. It has been established that a central concept of higher education in the lives of Indigenous students is Native nation-building (Benham & Stein, 2003; Brayboy, 2005; Brayboy et al., 2012; Goodyear-Ka'ōpua, 2013; Brayboy et al., 2014; Minthorn & Shotton, 2018; Shotton, 2018; Waterman et al., 2018). As such, institutions should seek to develop and maintain relationships with tribal nations that honor their status as sovereign nations (Salis Reyes & Shotton, 2018). It is particularly important for public state institutions to engage with tribal nations on a government-to-government basis. Relationships must be reciprocal and continually attended to so that they are maintained in meaningful and respectful ways. Engagement strategies with Indigenous communities might involve the following:

- Engage with Indigenous communities through listening sessions or community dialogues to assess community and student needs.
- Host meetings between institutional leadership (e.g., president, chancellor, provost) and tribal leaders both on campus and in tribal communities to assess tribal and tribal citizen needs.
- Establish memorandums of understanding (MOU) between institutions and tribal nations that address tribal needs and serving Indigenous students.
- Establish administrative offices (e.g., Office of Tribal Liaison or Office of Native Hawaiian Affairs) that work directly with Indigenous communities.

Honor Connections to Place

Connection to place is not only central to Indigenous identity, it is what defines Indigeneity. Indigenous relationships to land shape our epistemological and ontological understanding of who we are. When we discuss land in the context of place, it takes on a much deeper meaning. Engaging Indigenous students must begin with an honoring connection to place and how that relates to the very institutions in which Indigenous students enroll, particularly NNCUs. Indigenous students often have deep ancestral, cultural, spiritual, and historical connections to the lands of the colleges and universities that they attend, especially if they are attending college in their homelands. Institutions must honor those connections.

The first step in honoring place requires institutions of higher education to thoughtfully examine the history of the land, and the Indigenous peoples connected to the land, on which they reside. Furthermore, institutions must interrogate their status as settlers occupying Indigenous land and the multiple ways that institutions benefit from the dispossession of Indigenous land. Every institution in the US occupies Indigenous land, land that was the original homelands of the Indigenous people of this country (Salis Reyes & Shotton, 2018). One step that institutions can take is to develop meaningful land acknowledgement policies and protocols. This requires moving beyond simple land acknowledgement statements that honor Indigenous peoples as the original inhabitants of the land, though this is a good first step. Land acknowledgement policies must be intentional and seek to lay out specific culturally appropriate protocols, critically examine institutional histories, and ultimately have decolonial aims. Most importantly, land acknowledgement policies should be developed with Indigenous communities.

Build Community With Indigenous Students

The value of community is central to understanding Indigenous students. For Indigenous peoples, our understanding of who we are and our place in this world is deeply connected to our relationships with community. As Brayboy et al. (2012) explain, "the knowledge systems, ways of being, and teaching philosophies for many Indigenous peoples are critically focused on community and survival" (p. 16). Engaging Indigenous students then, must honor Indigenous values of the collective and seek to build community with Indigenous students. This requires creating spaces for Indigenous students to gather and be in community with one another, Indigenous faculty and staff, community members, and elders. This may come by way of dedicated Indigenous student centers or creating Indigenous places of learning on campus. These processes should be done in community and in consultation with Indigenous students.

Support and Protect Indigenous Student Cultural Practices

Indigenous students engage in cultural and spiritual practices in various ways. Onondaga scholar Stephanie Waterman (2012) reminds us that participation in ceremonies and maintaining spiritual connections are important for Indigenous student success. This often occurs in the home communities of Indigenous students, but returning home is not always feasible. Institutions should work to ensure that Indigenous students are able to engage in cultural and ceremonial practices when they are on campus. This involves creating protective spaces and policies that allow Indigenous students to freely engage in cultural practices that sustain them. Cultural practices often involve the use of sacred plants, medicines, and tobacco, so institutions should develop and implement policies (e.g., smudging policies or tobacco use policies) that support Indigenous cultural practices on campus (Minthorn, 2014; Salis Reyes & Shotton, 2018; Singson, Tachine, Davidson, & Waterman, 2016). Institutions should also work to connect Indigenous students with local Indigenous communities that may provide resources that help students maintain cultural practices when they are away from home.

Foster Student Connections to Home Communities

It is our assertion that Indigenous student engagement occurs both on campus *and* through the process of home-going. Research consistently supports the importance of family and connections to home on Indigenous student persistence (Guillory, 2009; Guillory & Wolverton, 2008; HeavyRunner & DeCelles, 2002; Lopez, 2018; Makomenaw, 2014; Waterman, 2012). Maintaining connections to home through the process of home-going is a culturally sustaining practice for Indigenous students. Waterman (2012) suggests that "the concept of home needs to be redefined and the language of 'going home' framed positively rather than negatively" (p. 202). Reframing home-going requires institutions of higher education to examine policies and practices that may hinder home-going. Furthermore, policies should aim to honor Indigenous students' connections to home and provide protections for students to return home to participate in cultural ceremonies.

Reframe Concepts of Student Engagement

Finally, institutions and higher education professionals should actively engage in reframing concepts of student engagement. When we consider the political context of Indigenous students' status and the land that US colleges and universities occupy, then it seems appropriate that institutions recognize their status as guests (albeit uninvited guests) on Indigenous lands and engage with Indigenous peoples accordingly. Rather than framing conversations around how students engage with the institution, we should reframe engagement to consider how institutions engage Indigenous students and their communities in culturally appropriate and decolonial ways.

Conclusion

"Ha'ina 'ia mai ana ka puana" is a phrase often found at the end of many Hawaiian lyrical compositions, relaying to the listener the composer's final thoughts. At the end of our journey here, our ha'ina for you, is simple and best expressed by Tuck and Yang (2012): "Decolonization is not a metaphor." Their statement is aspirational as it is instructive for higher education and its stakeholders. Transforming higher education in support of Indigenous students means nothing short of assuming the difficult and discomforting task of deconstructing and dismantling settler colonial structures so familiar to us. As Lipe (2018) says, we cannot address inequality and inequity in higher education without first acknowledging the ways higher education and non-Indigenous Peoples have historically benefitted and continue to benefit from the dispossession of Indigenous Peoples by reproducing colonial structures. Recognition of this truth is a first step.

Borrowing from the immense wisdom of Black lesbian feminist intellectual Audre Lorde (1984), our collective liberation cannot rely on simple acknowledgements of historical trauma or of difference; nor can we rely on the tools of domination to determine our way forward. Rather, she says, "Only within that interdependency of different strengths, acknowledged and equal, can the power to seek new ways of being in the world generate, as well as the courage and sustenance to act where there are no charters" (p. 111). Engaging Indigenous students in higher education thus requires us (individuals and institutions) to also engage *ourselves* in the arduous and continuous work of unlearning and undoing colonialism while simultaneously and interdependently working to envision and actualize liberatory higher education for all.

Notes

1 The United Nations (UN) defines Indigenous Peoples as the "inheritors and practitioners of unique cultures and ways of relating to people and the environment. They have retained social, cultural, economic and political characteristics that are distinct from those of the dominant societies in which they live. Despite their cultural differences, indigenous peoples from around the world share common problems related to the protection of their rights as distinct peoples" (United Nations, 2018).

2 There is a distinction between federally recognized and state recognized tribes. It is important to note that this distinction lies in the relationship of a tribe to the US federal government. State recognized tribes are recognized by their respective state governments but are not officially recognized by the federal government (ANA, 2014). As such, they do not operate on a government-to-government basis with the federal government and are not afforded the benefits and resources available to federally recognized tribes. It is also important to note that there are tribes and other Native peoples in the US and its affiliated territories currently in the process of advocating for federal recognition and other types of political relationships with the US, including independence from the US. We make these distinctions to point out the complex nature and multiple layers of the political status of tribes in the US and not to say federal recognition constitutes Native "legitimacy."

3 Brayboy focuses on the experiences of American Indians in this piece. However, we find significant areas of resonance with the experiences of Indigenous Peoples in his analysis.

4 We intentionally utilize the term "survivance" as reclaimed by Gerald Vizenor (2008) to note the "active sense of presence over absence, deracination, and oblivion" of Indigenous people (p. 1).

References

Administration for Native Americans (ANA). (2014). *American Indians and Alaska natives— What are state recognized tribes?* Retrieved from www.acf.hhs.gov/programs/ana/resource/ american-indians-and-alaska-natives-what-are-state-recognized-tribes

Astin, A. W. (1984). Student involvement: A developmental theory for higher education. *Journal of College Student Personnel, 25*(4), 297–308.

Austin, R. D. (2005). Perspectives of American Indian nation parents and leaders. *New Directions for Student Services, 2005*(109), 41–48.

Beamer, K. (2014). *No Mākou ka mana: Liberating the nation.* Honolulu, HI: Kamehameha Schools Publications.

Benham, M. K. P. & Heck, R. H. (1998). *Culture and educational policy in Hawai'i: The silencing of Native voices.* Mahwah, NJ: Lawrence Erlbaum Associates, Inc.

Benham, M. K. A., & Stein, W. J. (2003). *The renaissance of American Indian higher education: Capturing the dream.* New York, NY: Routledge.

Brave Heart, M. Y. H. (2003). The historical trauma response among natives and its relationship with substance abuse: A Lakota illustration. *Journal of Psychoactive Drugs, 35*(1). Retrieved from https://doi. org/10.1080/02791072.2003.10399988

Brayboy, B. M. J. (2005). Toward a tribal critical race theory in education. *The Urban Review, 37*(5), 425–446.

Brayboy, B. M. J. (2013). Tribal critical race theory: An origin story and future directions. In M. Lynn & A. D. Dixson (Eds.), *Handbook of critical race theory in education* (pp. 108–120). New York, NY: Routledge.

Brayboy, B. M. J., Fann, A. J., Castagno, A. E., & Solyom, J. A. (2012). *Postsecondary education for American Indian and Alaska Natives: Higher education for nation building and self-determination.* ASHE Higher Education Report 37: 5. San Francisco, CA: Jossey-Bass.

Brayboy, B. M. J., & Maughan, E. (2009). Indigenous knowledges and the story of the bean. *Harvard Educational Review, 79*(1), 1–21.

Brayboy, B. M. J., Solyom, J. A., & Castagno, A. E. (2014). Looking into the hearts of Native peoples: Nation building as an institutional orientation for graduate education. *American Journal of Education, 120*(4), 575–596.

Brayboy, B. M. J. and Castagno, A. E. (2008). How might Native science inform "informal science learning"? *Cultural Studies of Science Education, 3*, 731–750.

Cajete, G. (2004). Philosophy of Native science. In A. Waters (Ed.), *American Indian thought* (pp. 45–57). Oxford: Blackwell Publishing.

Castagno, A. E. (2005). Extending the bounds of race and racism: Indigenous women and the persistence of the Black—White paradigm of race. *Urban Review, 37*(3), 447–468.

Cote-Meek, S. (2014). *Colonized classrooms: Racism, trauma and resistance in post-secondary education.* Winnipeg, Manitoba, CA: Fernwood Publishing.

Champagne, D. (December 2003). Education for nation-building. *Cultural Survival Quarterly Magazine.* Retrieved from https://www.culturalsurvival.org/publications/cultural-survival-quarterly/education-nation-building

Deloria Jr., V., & Lytle, C. M. (1983). *American Indians American justice.* Austin, TX: University of Texas Press.

Deloria Jr, V., & Wildcat, D. (2001). *Power and place: Indian education in America.* Golden, CO: Fulcrum Publishing.

Demmert, W. G. & Towner, J. C. (2003). *A review of the research literature on the influences of culturally based education on the academic performance of Native American students.* Portland, OR: Northwest Regional Education Laboratory.

Deyhle, D., & Swisher, K. G. (1997). Research in American Indian and Alaska Native education: From assimilation to self-determination. *Review of Research in Education, 22*(1), 113–194.

Federal Register. (2018). 81 FR 26826. Retrieved from www.federalregister.gov/documents/2018/07/23/2018-15679/indian-entities-recognized-and-eligible-to-receive-services-from-the-united-states-bureau-of-indian

Fryberg, S. A., Markus, H. R., Oyserman, D., & Stone, J. M. (2008). Of warrior chiefs and Indian princesses: The psychological consequences of American Indian mascots. *Basic and Applied Social Psychology, 30*(3), 208–218.

Fujikane, C., & Okamura, J. Y. (2000). Whose vision? Asian settler colonialism in Hawaiʻi, a special issue of *Amerasia Journal, 26*(2).

Fujikane, C., & Okamura, J. Y. (2008). *Asian settler colonialism: From local governance to the habits of everyday life in Hawaiʻi.* Honolulu, HI: University of Hawaii Press.

Garland, J. L. (2007). [Review of the book *Serving Native American students* (New directions for student services)]. *Journal of College Student Development, 48*, 612–614.

Goodyear-Kaʻōpua, N. (2013). *The seeds we planted: Portraits of a Native Hawaiian charter school.* Minneapolis, MN: University of Minnesota Press.

Goodyear-Kaʻōpua, N., Hussey, I., & Wright, E. K. (Eds.). (2014). *A nation rising: Hawaiian movements for life, land, and sovereignty.* Durham, NC: Duke University Press.

Guillory, R. M. (2009). American Indian/Alaska Native college student retention strategies. *Journal of Developmental Education, 33*(2), 12–38.

Guillory, R. M., & Wolverton, M. (2008). It's about family: Native American student persistence in higher education. *The Journal of Higher Education, 79*(1), 58–87.

HeavyRunner, I., & DeCelles, R. (2002). Family education model: Meeting the student retention challenge. *Journal of American Indian Education, 41*(2), 29–37.

Hill, J. S., Kim, S., & Williams, C. (2010). The context of racial microaggressions against Indigenous peoples: Same old racism or something new? In D. W. Sue (Ed.), *Microaggressions and marginality: Manifestation, dynamics, and impact* (pp. 105–122). Hoboken, NJ: Wiley.

Huffman, T. E. (1991). The experiences, perception, and consequences of campus racism among Northern Plains Indians. *Journal of American Indian Education, 30*(2), 25–34.

Jackson, A. P., Smith, S. A., & Hill, C. L. (2003). Academic persistence among Native American college students. *Journal of College Student Development, 44*(4), 548–565.

Justice, D. H. (2004). Seeing (and reading) red: Indian outlaws in the ivory tower. In D. A. Mihesuah & A. C. Wilson (Eds.), *Indigenizing the academy: Transforming scholarship and empowering communities* (pp. 100–123). Lincoln, NE: University of Nebraska Press.

Kalt, J. P. (2007). The role of constitutions in Native nation building: Laying a firm foundation. In M. Jorgensen (Ed.), *Rebuilding Native nations: Strategies for governance and development* (pp. 78–114). Tucson, AZ: University of Arizona Press.

Kameʻeleihiwa, L. K. (1992). *Native lands and foreign desires: Pehea lā e pono ai?* Honolulu, HI: Bishop Museum Press.

Kanaʻiaupuni. S. M., Leward, B., & Jensen, ʻŪ. (September 2010). *Culture-based education and its relationship to student outcomes.* Honolulu, HI: Kamehameha Schools Research & Evaluation Division. Retrieved from http://www.ksbe.edu/_assets/spi/pdfs/CBE_relationship_to_student_outcomes.pdf

Kaomea, J. (2014). Education for elimination in nineteenth-century Hawai'i: Colonialism and the Native Hawaiian Chiefs' Children Boarding School. *History of Education Quarterly*, *52*(2), 123–144.

Kauanui, J. K. (2016). "A structure, not an event": Settler colonialism and enduring indigeneity. *Lateral, 5*(1). http://csalateral.org/issue/5-1/forum-alt-humanities-settler-colonialism-enduring-indigeneity-kauanui/

Keene, A. J. (2018). Tough conversations and "giving back": Native freshmen perspectives on the college application process. In S. J. Waterman, S. C. Lowe, & H. J. Shotton (Eds.), *Beyond access: Indigenizing programs for Native American student success* (pp. 33–45). Sterling, VA: Stylus.

Kukahiko, K. T. (2017). *Pacific Islanders in college football: Getting in, staying in, and moving on* (dissertation). Retrieved from https://escholarship.org/uc/item/35p890gr

Ladson-Billings, G. (1998). Just what is critical race theory and what's it doing in a nice field like education? *International Journal of Qualitative Studies in Education, 11*(1), 7–24.

Ladson-Billings, G., & Tate, W. (1995). Toward a critical race theory of education. *Teachers College Record, 97*, 47–68.

Lipe, K. (2012). Kēia 'Āina: The center of our work. In J. K. K. Osorio (Ed.), *I Ulu i ka 'āina: Land* (pp. 99–109). Honolulu, HI: University of Hawai'i Press.

Lipe, K. (2018). Toward equity and equality: Transforming universities into Indigenous places of learning. In R. S. Minthorn & H. J. Shoton (Eds.), *Reclaiming Indigenous research in higher education* (pp. 162–177). New Brunswick, NJ: Rutgers University Press.

Lomawaima, K. T. (1999). The unnatural history of American Indian education. In K. G. Swisher & J. W. Tippeconnic III (Eds.), *Next steps: Research and practice to advance Indian education* (pp. 1–31). Washington, DC: Office of Educational Research and Improvement.

Lomawaima, K. T. and McCarty, T. L. (2006). *"To remain an Indian": Lessons in democracy from a century of Native American education*. New York, NY: Teachers College Press.

Lopez, J. D. (2018). Factors influencing American Indian and Alaska Native postsecondary persistence: AI/AN millennium falcon persistence model. *Research in Higher Education, 59*(6), 792–811.

Lorde, A. (1984). The master's tools will never dismantle the master's house. In *Sister outsider: Essays and speeches by Audre Lorde* (pp. 110–113). Berkeley, CA: Crossing Press.

Makomenaw, M. (2014). Goals, family, and community: What drives Tribal College transfer student success. *Journal of Student Affairs Research and Practice, 51*(4), 380–391.

Matsuda, M. J., Lawrence, C. R., Delgado, R., and Crenshaw, K. W. (1993). *Words that wound: Critical race theory, assaultive speech, and the First Amendment*. Boulder, CO: Westview Press.

Mihesuah, D. (2003). Introduction: Native student, faculty, and staff experiences in the ivory tower. *American Indian Quarterly, 27*(1–2), 46–49.

Minthorn, R. S. (2014). Accommodating the spiritual and cultural practices of Native American college and university students. *Journal of College and University Student Housing, 41*(1), 154–163.

Minthorn, R. S. and Chavez, A. F. (2016). *Indigenous leadership in higher education*. New York, NY: Routledge.

Minthorn, R. S., & Shotton, H. J. (Eds.). (2018). *Reclaiming Indigenous research in higher education*. New Brunswick, NJ: Rutgers University Press.

National Congress of American Indians (NCAI). (2016). *Tribal nations and the United States: An introduction*. Retrieved from www.ncai.org/about-tribes

Oliveira, K. K. R. N. (2014). *Ancestral places: Understanding Kanaka geographies*. Corvallis, OR: Oregon State University Press.

Pascarella, E. T., & Terenzini, P. T. (2005). *How college affects students: A third decade of research (Vol. 2)*. San Francisco, CA: Jossey-Bass.

Perea, J. (2013). A tribalography of Alaska Native presence in academia. *American Indian Culture and Research Journal, 37*(3), 3–28.

Perry, B. (2002). American Indian victims of campus ethnoviolence. *Journal of American Indian Education, 41*(1), 35–55.

Reyhner, J. and Eder, J. (2004). *American Indian education: A history (1st edition)*. Norman, OK: University of Oklahoma Press.

Salis Reyes, N. A. (2014). The multiplicity and intersectionality of Indigenous identities. In D. Mitchell, Jr. (Ed.), *Intersectionality & higher education: Theory, research, & praxis* (pp. 45–54). New York, NY: Peter Lang.

Salis Reyes, N. A. (2016). *"What am I doing to be a good ancestor?" An indigenized phenomenology of giving back among Native college graduates* (Doctoral dissertation). Retrieved from ProQuest (10127227).

Salis Reyes, N. A. (2018). A space for survivance: Locating Kānaka Maoli through the resonance and dissonance of critical race theory. *Race Ethnicity and Education, 21*(6), 739–756.

Salis Reyes, N. A., & Shotton, H. J. (2018). *Bringing visibility to the needs and interests of Indigenous students in higher education: Implications for research, policy, and practice.* Policy report commissioned by the Association for the Study of Higher Education (ASHE)—National Institute for Transformation and Equity (NITE) Report Series. Las Vegas, NV.

Shotton, H. J. (2017). "I thought you'd call her White Feather": Native women and racial microaggressions in doctoral education. *Journal of American Indian Education, 56*(1), 32–54.

Shotton, H. J. (2018). Reciprocity and nation building in Native women's doctoral education. *American Indian Quarterly, 42*(4), 488–507.

Shotton, H. J., Lowe, S. C., & Waterman, S. J. (Eds.). (2013). *Beyond the asterisk: Understanding Native students in higher education* (pp. 1–24). Sterling, VA: Stylus.

Singson, J. M., Tachine, A. R., Davidson, C. E., & Waterman, S. J. (2016). A second home: Indigenous considerations for campus housing. *Journal of College and University Student Housing, 42*(2), 110–125.

Tachine, A. R., Cabrera, N. L., & Yellow Bird, E. (2017). Home away from home: Native American students' sense of belonging during their first year in college. *The Journal of Higher Education, 88*(5), 785–807.

Thomas, S., Kanaʻiaupuni, S., Freitas, A., & Balutski, B. J. N. (2012). Access and success for students from Indigenous populations: The case of Native Hawaiians and higher education. In J. C. Smart & M. B. Paulsen (Eds.), *Higher education: Handbook of theory and research* (pp. 335–367). New York, NY: Springer Science + Business Media.

Trask, H. (2000). Native social capital: The case of Hawaiian sovereignty and Ka Lahui Hawaii. *Policy Sciences, 33*(3/4), 149–159.

Tuck, E., & Ree, C. (2013). A Glossary of haunting. In S. Holman-Jones, T. Adams & C. Ellis (Eds.), *Handbook of autoethnography* (pp. 639–658). Thousand Oaks, CA: SAGE Publications.

Tuck, E., & Yang, K. W. (2012). Decolonization is not a metaphor. *Decolonization: Indigeneity, Education & Society, 1*(1), 1–40.

United Nations. (2018). *United Nations: Indigenous peoples.* Retrieved from www.un.org/development/desa/indigenouspeoples/about-us.html

US Department of the Interior. (2018). *Frequently asked questions.* Retrieved from www.bia.gov/frequently-asked-questions

Vaughan, M. B. (2018). *Kaiāulu: Gathering tides.* Corvallis, OR: Oregon State University Press.

Vizenor, G. (Ed.). (2008). *Survivance: Narratives of Native presence.* Lincoln, NE: University of Nebraska Press.

Waterman, S. J. (2012). Home-going as a strategy for success among Haudenosaunee college and university students. *Journal of Student Affairs Research and Practice, 49*(2), 193–209.

Waterman, S. J., Lowe, S. C., & Shotton, H. J. (Eds.). (2018). *Beyond access: Indigenizing programs for Native American student success.* Sterling, VA: Stylus.

Wilder, C. S. (2013). *Ebony and ivy: Race. slavery, and the troubled history of America's universities.* New York, NY: Bloomsbury Press.

Wolfe, P. (2006). Settler colonialism and the elimination of the Native. *Journal of Genocide Research, 8*(4), 387–409.

Wright, E. K., & Balutski, B. J. N. (2013). The role of context, critical theory, and counter-narratives in understanding Pacific Islander indigeneity. In *The misrepresented minority: New insights on Asian Americans and Pacific Islanders, and the implications for higher education* (pp. 140–157). Sterling, VA: Stylus.

Wright, E. K., & Balutski, B. J. N. (2016). Ka ʻIkena a ka Hawaiʻi: Toward a Kanaka ʻŌiwi critical race theory. In K. A. R. K. N. Oliveira & E. K. Wright (Eds.), *Kanaka ʻŌiwi methodologies: Moʻolelo and metaphor* (pp. 86–108). Honolulu, HI: University of Hawaiʻi Press.

Wright, E. K. (2018). "It was a process of decolonization and that's about as clear as I can put it": Kuleana-centered higher education and the meanings of Hawaiianness. In R. S. Minthorn & H. J. Shotton (Eds.), *Reclaiming Indigenous research in higher education* (pp. 18–35). New Brunswick, NJ: Rutgers University Press.

Chapter 6
Engaging White Students

Nolan L. Cabrera, Chris Corces-Zimmerman,
and Jamie R. Utt

While this text is entitled *Student Engagement in Higher Education*, we would like to add a modifier for our chapter. Specifically, we are calling for *critical* engagement with White students. We use the term *critical* to indicate that it is work contextualized within contemporary White supremacy and that the work is meant to disrupt and transform this system of oppression (Cabrera, 2019). This is an important distinction when the subject is White students because one of the privileges of Whiteness is not having to constantly consider race (Cabrera, 2017). This also leaves White students in a state of relative racial ignorance (Cabrera & Corces-Zimmerman, 2017), which in turn means they are in a state of *racial arrested development* (Cabrera, Watson, & Franklin, 2016). What does this mean in terms of practice? White students will require a disproportionate amount of attention, energy, and support as they develop their racial selves, and they are frequently the most demanding in terms of the attention they expect (Applebaum, 2010). The more White students demand time, attention, and energy, the less time that the needs of Students of Color can be met. This means there is a balance to engaging White students—understanding their developmental needs while not allowing their needs to dominate classroom (or co-curricular) space (Applebaum, 2010).

As we consider what it means to critically engage White students on college and university campuses, it is important to recognize that this chapter could only exist within the last 25 years. We say this because it is only in the last quarter century that there has been a shift to acknowledging that "student" and "White" are not synonymous. Recent shifts toward treating students in higher education as "customers" who must be pleased make it difficult to more deeply engage White students in interrogating their identities and privileges, but this makes the work all the more important (Cabrera, 2019). Within this context, we offer this chapter to professionals in higher education, challenging them and their White students to move beyond narratives of simple diversity and difference and into critical, intersectional analyses of Whiteness and White identity.

While the majority of the initial research in higher education that focused specifically on Whiteness and White students was largely descriptive and rooted in theories of student identity development (e.g., Helms, 1990), in the past ten years there has been a shift in this work towards a more critical grounding where Whiteness in higher education is critiqued using theories grounded in Critical Whiteness Studies (CWS; Corces-Zimmerman & Cabrera, in press). This is an important development because centrally focusing on White identity development can frequently serve to reinforce White privilege as it overlooks the systemic and institutional ways that Whiteness and White people marginalize and oppress People of Color. Instead, rooting this work in CWS means that we are examining Whiteness at the service of racial equity (Cabrera, 2019). While White students engaging in anti-racist praxis will necessarily develop their racial selves in the process, self-actualization is not the reason to do this work. Racial justice is.

Whiteness, Critical Whiteness Studies, and Intersectionality

Before we can dive too deeply into this type of analysis, some points of definition are necessary. First, there is some colloquial confusion as "Whiteness" is frequently treated as synonymous with "White people." As Leonardo (2009) argued, "'Whiteness' is a racial discourse, whereas the category 'white people' represents a socially constructed identity, usually based on skin color . . . Whiteness is not a culture but a social concept" (pp. 169–170). This concept, which is central to CWS analyses, focuses on a social structure of racial oppression that privileges White-identified people and marginalizes People of Color. While White people necessarily benefit from this system, they are not the same as Whiteness, and this shift in focus from individual White people to Whiteness as an ideology of racial oppression is essential in deflecting individual claims of "But I'm not a racist." As a corollary, wealthy people may benefit from the US economic system, but they are not the same as capitalism (Cabrera, 2019).

Therefore, this chapter is rooted in CWS, which to add more nuance, is frequently confused with Critical Race Theory (CRT). We want to be clear that we are rooting this work in CWS and not CRT because CRT was created to serve as a theorizing space for Scholars of Color to address issues of racial oppression. Part of this also meant validating the cultural knowledge of Communities of Color, which academia continually marginalizes both historically and contemporarily (Delgado & Stefancic, 2001). CWS represents the "other side of this coin," if you will, by critically analyzing Whiteness and racial oppression from the habits and structures of the privileged group.

As this text is frequently used by student affairs professionals, we want to also be clear on a specific term: *intersectionality*. As much of student affairs practice is rooted in identity and identity development, this term is frequently misunderstood to mean the different social identities that people bring with them to college campuses (Harris & Patton, 2018). Instead, we think it is important to return to Crenshaw's (1989) conception of the term as multiple, mutually reinforcing spheres of oppression (e.g., White supremacy and patriarchy) that contextualize and shape the lived experiences of marginalized people.

We then, however, flip this paradigm on its head by examining how these same spheres of oppression inform and shape the lives of people who benefit from these same oppressive social structures. Specific to White male undergraduates, Cabrera (2011) refers to their social identities as *racial hyperprivilege*, or ones where their masculinity in a patriarchal society serves to enhance their White privilege.

Finally, we will use the term *White supremacy*[1] to refer to the system of racial oppression that contextualizes engaging with White students on college campuses and White people more generally. We frequently receive pushback in the form of the question "Don't you think you will alienate some people by using this term?" We instead argue the following. First, the term is accurate (Bonilla-Silva, 2006; Feagin, 2006; Omi & Winant, 2015), and rarely do people question the validity of the term. Rather, they tend to focus on how the term makes "people" feel. This leads to the second issue. The term *people* in these discussions is frequently missing a key adjective: "White." That is, the discomfort experienced hearing the term *White supremacy* is largely located among White people, and we did not write the chapter to cater to *White fragility* (DiAngelo, 2011). This catering to Whiteness and White fragility only serves to reify White supremacy, and we are therefore direct in our terminology usage. As Cabrera (2019) has previously offered, "[P]lease keep in mind that it is far more difficult for People of Color to survive racial oppression than it is for White people to educate themselves on the subject" (p. 8). If White people in general, and White college students in particular, are going to shirk away from racial justice work because of an accurate terminology usage, it is questionable how committed they would actually be. Reason and Evans (2007) argue that pushing students beyond race neutrality to color cognizance is the first step in promoting racial justice ally development; however, it is also where the bulk of time is spent regarding the intersection of White students and race as they tend to be in states of racial arrested development (Cabrera et al., 2016).

White Racial Identity Development and the Campus Environment

As has been previously mentioned, much of the initial work on the intersection of Whiteness and higher education tended to be focused on the processes through which individual White students come to understand and make sense, or fail to make sense, of their White racial identity. Historically, the vast majority of foundational work in higher education and student affairs was essentially research on White students, without any acknowledgement of the racial biases in focus, perspective, or sample population (Cabrera, 2019). This began to change in the 1990s, when the work of Helms (1990) and her White Racial Identity Development Model began to be applied and eventually became foundational in the higher education and student affairs literature. Helms posited that racial identity development for White people occurred in two distinct phases: 1) abandonment of racism and 2) evolution of a non-racist identity, each comprised of three linear substatuses. Within the abandonment of racism phase, Helms identified the statuses of contact, disintegration, and reintegration, followed by the evolution of a nonracist identity through which White students move through the statuses of pseudo-independence, immersion/emersion, and autonomy—the final stage being anti-racist.

Building on Helms's work, Rowe, Bennett, and Atkinson (1994) proposed their White Racial Consciousness Model (WRCM) that they described as focusing on "one's awareness of being White and what that implies in relation to those who do not share White group membership" (pp. 133–134). Where Helms's model was structured through a series of linear stages of development, the WRCM was centered on two types of attitudes that White students may possess in relation to their racial identity: 1) unachieved White racial consciousness and 2) achieved White racial consciousness (Patton, Renn, Guido, & Quaye, 2016). While these two models differ in small ways, they are largely similar in that they focus primarily on the development of White students, they are largely power-neutral in how they are conceptualized, and they fail to address the myriad of oppressive ways in which Whiteness at a systemic level privileges White students and marginalizes Students of Color.

Student development occurs in context, and analyses of the physical environment used to be extremely common (e.g., Banning, 1992, 1993; 1997; Banning & Bartels, 1997; Banning & Kaiser, 1974; Banning & Kuk, 2005; Banning & Luna, 1992). In particular, this vein of scholarship would explore the underlying messages that the campus environments send to different student populations. While this work has waned in recent years, the physical space remains incredibly important in terms of the campus racial climate. Recently, there have been massive controversies about the physical space on college campuses as students (largely Students of Color) have demanded that, for example, statues of the Confederacy's president Jefferson Davis be removed (Cabrera, Franklin, & Watson, 2017). When these statues are removed, there is frequently a predictable backlash, largely by White students and alumni, in part because these actions disrupt the cultural norm of Whiteness on the campus that they took for granted like a fish in water (Cabrera et al., 2016).

It is important to remember that race and space intersect, and at many historically White institutions, White people have cultural ownership of most campus environments (Cabrera et al., 2016; Gusa, 2010; Harper & Hurtado, 2007). This is an important consideration for student affairs practitioners because this also means that these environments cater to White racial comfort (Cabrera et al., 2016; Gusa, 2010). Cabrera et al. (2016) argue that catering to this White racial comfort keeps White students in a state of *racial arrested development*. Cabrera and Corces-Zimmerman (2017) further argue that a great deal of this racial comfort is predicated on structured racial ignorance, which then becomes the basis for anti–Student of Color thoughts and actions on college campuses. The larger point here is that student affairs practitioners sometimes have the ability to manipulate the physical environment to disrupt this White institutional presence (Cabrera et al., 2016; Gusa, 2010). Even when they do not, they still need to be able to take account of it as this will contextualize the development of their White students, or rather, their frequent lack of development of their racial selves (Cabrera et al., 2016). This, in turn, becomes the basis for expressions of anti-racial minority ideology, thought, and action, especially among White male undergraduate students (Cabrera & Corces-Zimmerman, 2017).

While identity development is central to student affairs practice (Patton et al., 2016), identity development in the absence of analyses of power only serves to reinforce White supremacy (Cabrera, 2019). Also, there is an implication that, at the most advanced stages of White racial identity development, White people become fully actualized and "free" of racism (Cabrera, 2012). Instead, Cabrera (2012) argued that "[W]orking through Whiteness is not an end met, but a continual process engaged" (p. 397). Additionally, identity development models that center White student growth also tend to downplay the relationship among White students, Whiteness, White supremacy, and racial oppression. In higher education, however, there have been some recent developments in CWS.

Critical Whiteness Studies and Higher Education Scholarship

Traditionally, the scholarly areas of CWS and higher education have been largely disconnected and divergent fields of study. In higher education, racial analyses tend to be rare (Harper, 2012) as the field tends to focus on the *diversity rationale*—or how diverse learning environments produce increased social and academic development for all students (e.g., Hurtado, Alvarez, Guillermo-Wann, Cuellar, & Arellano, 2012). When scholars in the field do meaningfully engage with issues of race and racism, they tend to be through the lens of CRT and focus primarily on the marginalization of People of Color within institutions of higher education (Harper, 2012). However, if there is a group that is being marginalized, there is another group that is socially privileged: in this case, White people. While CWS-grounded work on higher education is still evolving, to this point there have been some important developments that serve to inform the ways that educators can engage White college students.

Corces-Zimmerman and Cabrera (in press) divide this research into two distinct eras. The first era occurred in the first decade of the 21st century, was centered around student affairs research, and sought to understand how institutions of higher education can support the development of racial justice allies—or White people who leverage their White privilege for racial justice (e.g., Ortiz & Rhoads, 2000; Reason, Millar, & Scales, 2005). This vein of scholarship demonstrated how multicultural course content, structured and sustained cross-racial dialogues, cross-racial friendships, anti-racist White role models, and opportunities for anti-racist action, collectively offer challenges and opportunities for White students to work on their anti-racist selves (Alimo, 2012; Ortiz & Rhoads, 2000; Peet, 2006; Reason et al., 2005; Reason & Evans, 2007; Zuñiga, Nagda, & Sevig, 2002). A great deal of this work was conducted under the larger umbrella of theorizing allyship development and aimed to inform what institutions of higher education in general, and student affairs professionals more specifically, could do to support White students in this development (Broido, 2000; Edwards, 2006; Reason, & Broido, 2005). While scholars in this era made many important empirical and theoretical contributions to the current understanding of Whiteness in higher education, the majority did not tend to orient their scholarship in theories derived from CWS.

In contrast, the second decade of the 2000s has been marked by a direct engagement with the ways in which Whiteness informs higher education policy, practice, and student outcomes (e.g., Ashlee, 2017; Blincoe & Harris, 2009; Cabrera, 2012, 2014a, 2014b, 2014c, 2014d; Cabrera & Corces-Zimmerman, 2017; Cabrera et al., 2017; Cabrera et al., 2016; Case, 2012; Case & Rios, 2017; Doucet, Grayman-Simpson, & Wertheim, 2013; Gusa, 2010; Linder, 2015; Robbins, 2017; Robbins & Jones, 2016; Soble, Spanierman, & Liao, 2011; Stewart & Nicolazzo, in press; Todd, Spanierman, & Poteat, 2011; Yeung, Spanierman, & Landrum-Brown, 2013). These analyses tend to directly critique White supremacy and the role that institutions of higher education play in continuing to support this oppressive system. In addition, much of the scholarship in this period has maintained a strong focus on the ways in which individual White students, faculty, staff, and administrators perpetuate Whiteness through their beliefs and actions. These subsections of CWS work in higher education have explored the intersections of Whiteness and gender (Cabrera, 2014b, 2014c; Linder, 2015; Robbins & Jones, 2016), Whiteness and class (Hamilton, Roksa, & Nielsen, 2018), and the ways in which White individuals perpetrate racially based microaggressions against People of Color through direct interactions (Cabrera & Corces-Zimmerman, 2017), decisions about curriculum (Cabrera, 2019), and even the physical structure of the institution itself (Cabrera et al., 2017). While most scholars and practitioners view this as a positive shift toward a stronger focus on both individual and institutional critiques of Whiteness, some have offered the perspective that this second wave of scholarship has tended to focus so strongly on the role of higher education in maintaining White supremacy that it loses many of the pragmatic, day-to-day implications of the work (Corces-Zimmerman & Cabrera, in press). This is not to say that one area is better or worse than the other, but rather, that each has its relative strengths and limitations.

Implications for Policy and Practice

Having reviewed the evolution and characteristics of the empirical and theoretical work on Whiteness and White students in higher education, a few central implications emerge for student affairs practice for engaging White students regarding issues of race and racism. Before engaging with White students, student affairs professionals must first do their own work to understand how their own views and identity are embedded in and informed by Whiteness and White supremacy (Cabrera, 2019). While this is particularly important for White student affairs educators, the reality is that the ubiquitous and invisible nature of Whiteness and White supremacy allows them to influence people regardless of their racial identity (Cabrera, 2018). Engaging in this personal reflection and pursuit of knowledge involves much more than attending a couple of workshops or reading McIntosh's (1990) "Invisible Knapsack" article. Rather, it necessitates a long-standing commitment to daily explorations of one's complicity in Whiteness (Applebaum, 2010), extensive reading of seminal works on racism and Whiteness (Baldwin, 1963; Du Bois, 1989), and a willingness to accept racism and Whiteness as both systemic and individual ideologies that inform one's perceptions of Students and People of Color, no matter how shameful that may be.

When engaging with White students, student affairs professionals must remember that they are always doing so in spaces that are rooted in Whiteness. This can occur through institutional messages in recruiting materials (Corces-Zimmerman, 2018), institutional diversity statements (Iverson, 2010), allocation of fiscal and human resources, or decisions about curriculum and pedagogy inside and outside the classroom, Whiteness is pervasive in the culture and functioning of institutions of higher education (Gusa, 2010). This means that when White students are challenged to explore their racial identities, Whiteness, and White privilege, they will do so in spaces that are meant for them and likely meant to preserve their safety, reputation, and sense of self (Leonardo & Porter, 2010). As a result, student affairs professionals must consider the many ways in which they must complicate the relationship that White students have to their White-centric campuses in order to create the dissonance and discomfort necessary to challenge Whiteness within White students (Cabrera et al., 2016). A first step is taking account of the university environment before getting to students.

The Social and Policy Campus Environment: Messaging of Whiteness

As previously demonstrated, the college campus serves as a racialized environment (e.g., Banning, 1992, 1997), and the different messages White students receive from this environment will affect how willing or unwilling they are to meaningfully engage around issues of racism. For example, some institutions of higher education require a diversity course, and taking courses like this can support White students working through racial issues (Bowman, 2011). However, not all curricula under the umbrella of "diversity" are equally effective due in large part to the tendency of many diversity classes to treat diversity as a matter of inclusion as opposed to as a problem rooted in past and present-day oppression. As Sleeter (2011) notes, diversity-focused classes rooted in an ethnic studies curriculum tend to be more challenging and high impact when it comes to educating White students about social and racial inequity. Additionally, the method by which diversity curricula are offered is critically important. Simply regurgitating statistics about racial inequality is also inadequate. As Leonardo (2005) argues, "Countering with scientific evidence an ideological mindset that criminalizes people of color becomes an exercise in futility because it does not even touch the crux of the problem, one based upon fear and loathing" (p. 402). Instead, Cabrera (2012; 2019) found in his work with White male undergraduates that diversity curriculum coupled with a *humanizing pedagogy* was centrally important in helping these students develop a sense of connectedness and "linked fate" across racial difference. That is, it was incumbent on the educator to put a human face on the consequences of systemic racism in order to make the issue real in the eyes of White men (Cabrera, 2019). By instilling a sense of personal connection and empathy in these students, educators were able to make the often-invisible lived realities of Whiteness and White privilege more tangible and identifiable. In particular, giving White students a personal stake in efforts to challenge White supremacy appears to take them from a space of lamenting what they are losing and focusing more on how challenging racism ultimately benefits those around them. This shift is comparable to what Edwards (2006) describes as an "ally for self-interest."

The messaging from central administration also plays a role in how White students do or do not engage issues of racism. For example, do institutional leaders only commodify diversity as numbers, or do they actually sanction anti-racism in both discourse and policy? Usually it is the former, but either approach sets the overall tone for the university as to whether or not it supports anti-racism. Does the institution require its chief diversity officer to be responsible for all racial work on campus, or is that equitably distributed to deans and faculty (Milem, Chang, & Antonio, 2005)? Do institutional leaders at public meetings acknowledge that the land upon which their university sits was stolen from Native American peoples? The overall point is that the racial climate of an institution sets the context for whether or not White students are willing to engage race, and student affairs professionals need to be aware of this social environment when doing their work with White students. Moving from institutional policies to interpersonal engagement, one of the most important structured methods of promoting anti-racism among White students is via *sustained*, critical dialogue.

Dialogue Across and Within Difference

On many campuses, the go-to approach to learning about race for White students is intergroup dialogue, and the results of these well-structured, well-executed programs demonstrate that they can help White students gain racial awareness (Zuñiga et al., 2002). The challenge, though, is that these dialogues can also be spaces in which linguistic violence is wrought upon Students of Color by these White students. As noted by Leonardo and Porter (2010), multiracial dialogue might be uncomfortable for Students of Color because "it reaffirms an already hostile and unsafe environment for many Students of Color whose perspectives and experiences are consistently minimized" (p. 140). In particular, Leonardo and Porter (2010) were highly critical of the creation of *safe spaces* in these environments because these tended to mean that they were safe for White student comfort. There is still a great deal of promise within this approach as long as it is implemented with fidelity and well-trained facilitators (Cabrera et al., 2017).

Given this context, it can be important to cultivate carefully designed spaces for White students to explore identity, power, privilege, and oppression in spaces with other White people. As noted by Tatum (1997), "participation in White consciousness-raising groups organized specifically for the purpose of examining one's own racism [is] another way to 'keep moving forward'" (p. 110). The challenge, though, is that there is a long and violent history of White people meeting in White-only spaces to talk about race, so there is a need to construct White caucus spaces for White people to explore topics of race that are simultaneously accountable to People of Color. Accountability can take many forms, and many groups have offered principles of accountability that can help to guide those who wish to start a White caucus space (e.g., Cushing, Cabbil, Greeman, Hitchcock, & Richards, 2010). For example:

- Outreach and dialogue with Leaders of Color on campus prior to forming a White caucus space to determine if they think such a space would be necessary and helpful and ask what boundaries such a group would need to set.
- Establish accountability principles and have an accountability advisory or steering group that consists of a diversity of People of Color from the campus community. Ideally, the labor of the accountability group should be compensated in some way. Having a group opens the possibility for direct observation of a White caucus space, allowing direct feedback about how White caucus spaces can be improved.
- Accountability must be practiced through the context of authentic relationships across difference (Tochluk & Levin, 2010). Asking random People of Color to serve as accountability partners can simply be tokenizing, but when in the context of wider work and relationships together, formal accountability can strengthen relationships and wider commitments to intersectional racial justice work.
- White caucus spaces should balance reflection and action as spaces where White folks meet to discuss their own issues can be helpful but do little to change the material reality of oppression People of Color face on campus. Additionally, social critique without action can lead to counterproductive nihilism (Peet, 2006). Thus, having a component of accountable *action* in community beyond reflective space is important.

Specific to the dialogues themselves, student affairs practitioners need to help White students grapple with these central questions:

- What does it mean to be White? What is White privilege? What are Whiteness and White supremacy?
- How has Whiteness historically and contemporarily oppressed People of Color?
- What responsibility accompanies White privilege? What should White people be doing to combat White supremacy?

These three areas are intended to help White students recognize Whiteness and White privilege within themselves and foster a sense of *racial empathy*[2] regarding the effect racial oppression has on People of Color, while strategizing about actions they can take individually and collectively to combat racism. This is not so much a dialogue space about self-actualization as a way of centering anti-racism. The principles of dialogue cut across social context; however, there are specific considerations for student affairs professionals when engaging White students on campus, and they tend to vary based on how/where students are already engaged.

Engaging Students Through Residence Life and Residential Education

Residence life is incredibly well suited to foster student development (Patton et al., 2016), and therefore, it is an important area to engage White students around topics of Whiteness and White privilege. In fact, there are some who have suggested that this is an important environment to develop and offer living/learning communities dedicated to multiculturalism as a mechanism of White student engagement (Sallee, Logan, Sims, & Harrington, 2009). We modify this slightly and reframe the issue to say that learning/living communities offer a strong opportunity to collectively engage in social justice–oriented anti-racism. That is, a form of multiculturalism that centers difference and tolerance instead of oppression and racism does little to address the issue of Whiteness (Cabrera, 2019). This issue aside, there is an incredible amount of potential in residence life in general, and learning/living communities in particular, to engage issues of racism. Given the ingrained sense of community and shared living experience that are central to the work of residence life professionals, the interactions had with both student staff members and residents of a specific community provide ample opportunity to form the types of relationships and norms necessary for vulnerable conversations about race and Whiteness to occur (Sallee et al., 2009). These can take the form of structured, sustained workshops (Reason, 2014), academic coursework, and co-curricular activities (Barefoot, 2005). Returning to the central theme of this chapter, we highlight that all these efforts need to center critical assessments of power and privilege while offering sustained engagement with White students. As was previously mentioned, utilizing racial caucus or affinity programming in which groups of all-White students come together within a residential setting, or perhaps in student staff training, to discuss their own experiences with Whiteness in a setting that is facilitated by a professional who is well-versed in critical race and Whiteness theories is more likely to push students toward an understanding of the ways in which Whiteness impacts them on both systemic and individual levels. Similarly, repeated programming to explore topics like segregation, criminal justice reform, or access to education can serve as a means to engage White students around larger societal issues that are deeply rooted in Whiteness and White privilege.

Engaging Students in Historically White Greek Life

One of the most challenging spaces to engage White students in critical examinations of Whiteness and their own White identities is also one of the most important spaces to take up that work. White Greek students tend to be some of the most wealth privileged in the country, and the connections built through Greek life can lead to a lifetime of concentrated status and power (Chang, 2014). As Allen (2008) makes clear, we must understand and address White people with wealth as those most able to *act* on Whiteness and racism in ways that hurt People of Color but also poorer Whites. Thus, engaging Greek students in critically understanding Whiteness and how it operates not only to privilege White students on campus but also to harm Students of Color is important not only to avoid overtly racist incidents as have been seen in many Greek organizations in recent years, but also to engage White Greek members in taking up the work of racial justice inside and outside their organizations. As part of this, Greek life professionals must engage historically White Greek organizations in both learning about and wrestling with the overtly racist history of White Greek life, which was created and is maintained as a way to consolidate power among the White elite (Ross, 2016). Further, as noted earlier, sustained education on issues of race, power, and Whiteness is needed to realize change (Cabrera, 2012; Reason, 2014). Greek life professionals and those in deans of students' offices are in a unique position to mandate ongoing education as requisite for membership in historically White Greek organizations. Leveraging mandatory ongoing education from a competent professional with a background in racial justice education and a knowledge of CWS could begin the process of movement toward less racist and more racially aware student engagement in historically White Greek life. Because there is evidence of mixed effects of mandatory "diversity education" in education literature (Kulik & Roberson, 2008), practitioners must move beyond outward-focusing "cultural competency" and strive to empower Greek students to interrogate their own Whiteness through multisession education guided by a well-qualified professional (Tatum, 1997).

Engaging White Students in Leadership Programs

While student leadership programs are fruitful places for engaging White students in considering leadership for social change, too often they are mired in models of leadership that rearticulate Whiteness as normative and neutral. Many of the traditional leadership models (e.g., the Social Change Model) utilized in higher education are rooted in Whiteness, relying overtly or subtly on individualistic notions of leadership and calls for civility, cooperation, and collectivity as desirable traits to which all leaders should aspire (Komives & Wagner, 2016). Even though many of these models do not outwardly express a preference for White ways of leadership, the absence of any direct acknowledgement of or attempt to challenge the historical associations between White behaviors and definitions of leadership also allows for the perpetuation of dominant leadership narratives. For a leadership development program to effectively serve an anti-racist purpose, it would need to challenge White students to examine how their White privilege is connected to their identities as leaders, to actively center examples of leadership styles and histories of People of Color (Boren, 2001; Rhoads, 1998), and to integrate modern perspectives on transformative leadership from activist Scholars of Color (Brown, 2017). This approach recenters the efforts of People of Color in leadership positions, which sends an implicit message about *who* is a leader and *how* leadership is enacted.

Engaging Students Through Conduct Interventions

In 2015, fury erupted from White pundits after Saida Grundy tweeted, "Why is white America so reluctant to identify white college males as a problem population?" (Cabrera, 2019). Grundy (2017) later wrote about how this attack was part of a larger pattern of attacks on Black academics, but amidst the outrage machine working to get Grundy fired, the importance of her question was lost. That is, a disproportionate number of students facing conduct hearings are White and male, and yet institutions are reluctant to make understanding the intersections of Whiteness and patriarchy central to any learning-based sanction. Her statement was factually accurate. That it was controversial says more about the state of race relations than the nature of her words (Cabrera et al., 2017).

Rather than seeing the relationship as simply correlational, student conduct officials must have the courage to consider the relationship among Whiteness, masculinity, and student misbehavior. Acknowledging this reality will open the door to fruitful dialogue and reflection about how Whiteness and patriarchy combine to exacerbate feelings of entitlement and invincibility that are central to the White male college experience (Cabrera, 2019).

Engaging White Students in Racial and Social Justice Spaces

Just because White students are engaged in social justice spaces does not therefore mean they are anti-racist (Cabrera, 2012). A common misunderstanding amongst student affairs professionals is that because of the social values, lived experiences, or activist orientations of White students who participate in racially based centers, LGBTQ groups, or gender-based support communities, these students do not maintain Whiteness and White supremacy in these spaces (Patton, 2011; Renn, 2011). It is true that students in these spaces and from marginalized identities are *more likely* to engage anti-racism (Cabrera, 2012; Cabrera et al., 2017), but it is still possible, and in fact it is likely, that Whiteness and White privilege will be issues they continually grapple with (Cabrera, 2012; Linder, 2015). For example, much scholarship has been written about Whiteness and feminism, specifically the propensity for White women to dominate feminist spaces, both in their leadership and in the actions taken by the group as a whole (Nicolazzo & Harris, 2014). Whether they are the numerical majority or not does not determine the ways in which White students can capitalize on, or in some cases even weaponize, their White privilege to maintain their dominance and security in spaces that are intended to challenge oppression. That said, the presence of conversations and values that advocate for racial and social justice uniquely position student affairs practitioners in these spaces to engage White students in critical reflection on their social power and privilege. In these circumstances it is foundational that practitioners ensure that the responsibility for educating or challenging White students not be placed on Students of Color; this work must be done by White students themselves. Thus, introducing more racially advanced White students to concepts like intersectionality (Crenshaw, 1987), the matrix of domination (Collins, 1993), or the Model of Multiple Dimensions of Identity (Abes, Jones, & McEwen, 2007), are all ways to prompt them to explore how their combination of dominant and marginalized identities are impacted by larger societal and institutional forces. It is critically important in these spaces, especially for White students who have one or more marginalized identities, for them to understand that being oppressed in one way does not negate the ways Whiteness affords them a myriad of privileges in their college experiences and life in general.

Engaging Nontraditional White Students

While the majority of the recommendations provided in the previous sections are not exclusive to what some might call "traditional" college students, we acknowledge that there is a bias in the scholarship that centers the experiences of these students.

Nontraditional students embody a wide range of identities and experiences; among these are older students, part-time students, transfer students, commuter students, student-parents, and veteran students. When working with White students who possess one or more of these nontraditional identities, student affairs educators and practitioners must think intentionally and creatively as to the best ways to engage these students, given their distinct needs and experiences. In describing the work of engaging commuter students, Jacoby (2016) makes the suggestion that educators can tailor existing infrastructures like classes or learning communities to take advantage of the unique perspectives and characteristics that these students bring with them to campus. Wood and Moore (2016) also emphasize that these nontraditional identities be seen as strengths and opportunities to engage students in different and deeper ways. In short, educators must keep in mind that White students are not a monolith in terms of the experiences, needs, and identities that they bring to campus. When acknowledged and incorporated into efforts to engage White students in anti-racist education, these unique identities allow educators to approach the process of challenging Whiteness with novel and innovative practices.

Conclusion

The work of engaging White students in explorations of Whiteness and their White racial identity brings with it a number of challenges and powerful opportunities for development. Given that Whiteness is largely invisible to those who benefit from the system (Cabrera, 2009), broaching these conversations is likely to require intentional acts on behalf of student affairs practitioners. At the same time, when Whiteness is made visible, the beneficiaries tend to either, consciously or otherwise, dodge and dance around issues of race in an example of *White agility* (Cabrera, 2019), or to respond in a manifestation of defensiveness through what many describe as *White fragility* (DiAngelo, 2011). The overall point being that while Whiteness is a source of many of the problems within institutions of higher education (Gusa, 2010), there is more energy invested by both students and administrators in defending Whiteness than in actually engaging and challenging the individual and institutional dynamics that allow it to thrive in institutions of higher education (Cabrera, 2019). While this may paint a seemingly bleak picture of the possibility of engaging White students in critical explorations of Whiteness, we think it is important for student affairs professionals to approach this work with a realistic assessment of the ways in which Whiteness manifests itself in order to best inform their actions and interactions with White students. In acknowledging the normative ways that Whiteness operates in protecting and privileging White students, educators must remember that engaging White students will require that they make otherwise safe and protected spaces into meaningfully uncomfortable ones (Cabrera et al., 2016), creating challenging spaces where White students experience the dissonance necessary to prompt personal growth and development. The absence of this agitation leaves White students in a state of *racial arrested development* via structured racial ignorance (Cabrera et al., 2017), which becomes the basis for anti–Student of Color campus racism (Cabrera & Corces-Zimmerman, 2017).

Notes

1 Describing the historical development and contemporary manifestations of White supremacy are beyond the scope of this chapter. To more thoroughly explore them, we highly recommend readers Bonilla-Silva's (2001) *White Supremacy & Racism in the Post–Civil Rights Era* and his (2006) *Racism without Racists*, Omi and Winant's (2015) *Racial Formation*, Anderson's (2016) *White Rage*, Painter's (2010) *The History of White People*, and Allen's (1997) *The Invention of the White Race*.

2 Please note, we use "empathy" instead of "sympathy" here because the latter implies a sense of pity and social superiority; the former implies a sense of human connectedness. For more on this subject see Cabrera (2019).

References

Abes, E. S., Jones, S. R., & McEwen, M. K. (2007). Reconceptualizing the model of multiple dimensions of identity: The role of meaning-making capacity in the construction of multiple identities. *Journal of College Student Development, 48*(1), 1–22.

Alimo, C. J. (2012). From dialogue to action: The impact of cross-race intergroup dialogue on the development of White college students as racial allies. *Equity & Excellence in Education, 45*(1), 36–59.

Allen, R. L. (2008). What about poor White people? In W. Ayers, T. Quinn, & D. Stovall (Eds.), *The handbook of social justice in education* (pp. 209–230). New York, NY: Routledge.

Allen, T. W. (1997). *The invention of the White race*. Vol. 2: *The origin of oppression in Anglo-America*. New York, NY: Verso.

Anderson, C. (2016). *White rage: The unspoken truth of our racial divide*. Bloomsbury Publishing USA.

Applebaum, B. (2010). *Being White, being good: White complicity, White moral responsibility, and social justice pedagogy*. Lanham, MD: Lexington Books.

Ashlee, K. (2017). Utilizing mindfulness and contemplative practices to promote racial identity development for White College students. *Understanding and Dismantling Privilege, 7*(2), 54–65.

Baldwin, J. (1963). *The fire next time*. New York, NY: Dial.

Banning, J. H. (1992). Visual anthropology: Viewing the campus ecology for messages of sexism. *Campus Ecologist, 11*(1), 1–4.

Banning, J. H. (1993). The pedestrian's visual experience on campus: Informal learning of cultural messages. *Campus Ecologist, 11*(1), 1–4.

Banning, J. H. (1997). Assessing the campus' ethical climate: A multidimensional approach. *New Direction for Student Services, 1997*(77), 95–105.

Banning, J. H., & Bartels, S. (1997). A taxonomy: Campus physical artifacts as communicators of campus multiculturalism. *NASPA Journal, 35*, 29–37.

Banning, J. H., & Kaiser, L. (1974). An ecological perspective and model for campus design. *Personnel and Guidance Journal, 52*, 370–375.

Banning, J. H., & Kuk, L. (2005). Campus ecology and student health. *Spectrum*, 9–15.

Banning, J. H., & Luna, F. (1992). Viewing the campus ecology for messages about Hispanic/Latino culture. *Campus Ecologist, 10*(4), 1–4.

Barefoot, B. O. (2005). Current institutional practice in the first year of college. In M. L. Upcraft, J. N. Gardner, B. O. Barefoot, & Associates (Eds.), *Challenging and supporting the first-year students: A handbook for improving the first year of college* (pp. 47–63). San Francisco, CA: Jossey-Bass.

Blincoe, S., & Harris, M. J. (2009). Prejudice reduction in White students: Comparing three conceptual approaches. *Journal of Diversity in Higher Education, 2*(4), 232–242.

Bonilla-Silva, E. (2001). *White supremacy & racism in the post—civil rights era*. Boulder, CO: Lynne Rienner.

Bonilla-Silva, E. (2006). *Racism without racists: Color-blind racism and the persistence of racial inequality in the United States* (2nd ed.). Lanham, MD: Rowman & Littlefield.

Boren, M. E. (2001). *Student resistance: A history of the unruly subject*. New York, NY: Routledge.

Bowman, N. A. (2011). Promoting participation in a diverse democracy: A meta-analysis of college diversity experiences and civic engagement. *Review of Educational Research, 81*(1), 29–68.

Broido, E. M. (2000). The development of social justice allies during college: A phenomenological investigation. *Journal of College Student Development, 41*(1), 3–18.

Brown, Z. R. (2017, May 10). Problematizing the social change model of leadership. *Thinking Race Blog* [Blog Post]. Retrieved from https://thinkingraceblog.wordpress.com/2017/05/10/problematizing-the-social-change-model-of-leadership-development/

Cabrera, N. L. (2009). *Invisible racism: Male, hegemonic Whiteness in higher education* (Unpublished doctoral dissertation). University of California, Los Angeles.

Cabrera, N. L. (2011). Using a sequential exploratory mixed-method design to examine racial hyper privilege in higher education. In K. A. Griffin and S. D. Museus (Eds.), *Using mixed-methods approaches to study intersectionality in higher education* (pp. 77–91). New Directions for Institutional Research, no. 151. San Francisco, CA: Jossey-Bass.

Cabrera, N. L. (2012). Working through whiteness: White male college students challenging racism. *Review of Higher Education, 35,* 375–401.

Cabrera, N. L. (2014a). Beyond Black and White: How White male college students see their Asian American peers. *Equity & Excellence in Education, 47*(2), 133–151.

Cabrera, N. L. (2014b) But we're not laughing: White male college students' racial joking and what this says about "post-racial" discourse. *Journal of College Student Development, 55*(1), 1–15.

Cabrera, N. L. (2014c). "But I'm oppressed too": White male college students framing racial emotions as facts and recreating racism. *International Journal of Qualitative Studies in Education, 27*(6), 768–784.

Cabrera, N. L. (2014d). Exposing Whiteness in higher education: White male college students minimizing racism, claiming victimization, and recreating White supremacy. *Race, Ethnicity, and Education, 17*(1), 30–55.

Cabrera, N. L. (2018). Where is the racial theory in Critical Race Theory?: A constructive criticism of the Crits. *The Review of Higher Education, 42*(1), 209–233.

Cabrera, N. L. (2019). *White guys on campus: Racism, White immunity, and the myth of 'post-racial' higher education*. New Brunswick, NJ: Rutgers University Press.

Cabrera, N. L., & Corces-Zimmerman, C. (2017). An unexamined life: White male racial ignorance and the agony of education for Students of Color. *Equity & Excellence in Education, 50*(3), 300–315.

Cabrera, N. L., Franklin, J. D., & Watson, J. S. (2017). *Whiteness in higher education: The invisible missing link in diversity and racial analyses*. Association for the Study of Higher Education monograph series. San Francisco, CA: Jossey-Bass.

Cabrera, N. L., Watson, J., & Franklin, J. D. (2016). Racial arrested development: A critical Whiteness analysis of the campus ecology. *Journal of College Student Development, 57*(2), 119–134.

Case, K. A. (2012). Discovering the privilege of whiteness: White women's reflections on anti-racist identity and ally behavior. *Journal of Social Issues, 68*(1), 78–96.

Case, K. A., & Rios, D. (2017). Educational interventions to raise awareness of White privilege. *Journal on Excellence in College Teaching, 28*(1), 137–156.

Chang, C. (2014, August 12). Separate but unequal in college Greek life. *The Century Foundation*. Retrieved from https://tcf.org/content/commentary/separate-but-unequal-in-college-greek-life/?agreed=1

Collins, P. H. (1993). Black feminist thought in the matrix of domination. In *Social Theory: The Multicultural and Classic Readings* (pp. 615–625). San Francisco, CA: Westview.

Corces-Zimmerman, C. (2018). Normalizing whiteness on college campuses: A critical content analysis of college and university viewbooks. *Understanding and Dismantling Privilege, 8*(2), 90–108.

Corces-Zimmerman, C., & Cabrera, N. L. (in press). Whiteness and higher education. In *SAGE encyclopedia of higher education*. Thousand Oaks, CA: SAGE Publications, Inc.

Crenshaw, K. W. (1987). Race, reform, and retrenchment: Transformation and legitimation in antidiscrimination law. *Harvard Law Review, 101,* 1331.

Crenshaw, K. W. (1989). Demarginalizing the intersection of race and sex: A Black feminist critique of antidiscrimination doctrine, feminist theory and antiracist politics. *University of Chicago Legal Forum, 1989*, 139–167.

Cushing, B., Cabbil, L., Greeman, M., Hitchcock, J., & Richards, K. (2010). *Accountability and White anti-racist organizing: Stories from our work*. Roselle, NJ: Crandall, Dostie & Douglass Books.

Delgado, R., & Stefancic, J. (2001). *Critical race theory: An introduction*. New York, NY: New York University Press.

DiAngelo, R. (2011). White fragility. *International Journal of Critical Pedagogy, 3*(3), 54–70.

Doucet, F., Grayman-Simpson, N., & Shapses Wertheim, S. (2013). Steps along the journey: Documenting undergraduate White women's transformative processes in a diversity course. *Journal of Diversity in Higher Education, 6*(4), 276.

Du Bois, W. E. B. (1989). *The souls of black folk*. New York, NY: Penguin Books.

Edwards, K. E. (2006). Aspiring social justice ally identity development: A conceptual model. *NASPA Journal, 43*(4), 39–60.

Feagin, J. R. (2006). *Systemic racism: A theory of oppression*. New York, NY: Routledge.

Grundy, S. (2017). A history of white violence tells us attacks on Black academics are not ending (I know because it happened to me). *Ethnic and Racial Studies, 40*(11), 1864–1871.

Gusa, D. L. (2010). White institutional presence: The impact of Whiteness on campus climate. *Harvard Educational Review, 80*, 464–490.

Hamilton, L., Roksa, J., & Nielsen, K. (2018). Providing a "Leg Up": Parental involvement and opportunity hoarding in college. *Sociology of Education, 91*(2), 111–131.

Harper, S. R. (2012). Race without racism: How higher education researchers minimize racist institutional norms. *Review of Higher Education, 36*(1), 9–29.

Harper, S. R., & Hurtado, S. (2007). Nine themes in campus racial climates and implications for institutional transformation. In S. R. Harper & L. D. Patton (Eds.), *Responding to the realities of race on campus* (New directions for student services, No. 120) (pp. 7–24). San Francisco, CA: Jossey-Bass.

Helms, J. E. (1990). *Black and White identity: Theory, research, and practice*. Westport, CT: Praeger.

Harris, J. C. & Patton, L. D. (2018). Un/doing intersectionality through higher education research. *The Journal of Higher Education, 90*(3), 347–372.

Hurtado, S., Alvarez, C. L., Guillermo-Wann, C., Cuellar, M., & Arellano, L. (2012). A model for diverse learning environments: The scholarship on creating and assessing conditions for student success. In J. C. Smart & M. B. Paulsen (Eds.), *Higher education: Handbook of theory and research* (Vol. 27, pp. 41–122). Dordrecht, The Netherlands: Springer.

Iverson, S. V. (2010). Producing diversity: A policy discourse analysis of diversity action plans. In E. J. Allan, S. V. Iverson, & R. Ropers-Huilman (Eds.), *Reconstructing policy in higher education: Feminist poststructural perspectives* (pp. 193–213). New York, NY: Routledge.

Jacoby, B. (2016). Engaging commuter and part-time students. In S. R. Komives & W. Wagner (Eds.), *Leadership for a better world: Understanding the social change model of leadership development*. Hoboken, NJ: John Wiley & Sons.

Komives, S. R., & Wagner, W. (Eds.). (2016). *Leadership for a better world: Understanding the social change model of leadership development*. Hoboken, NJ: John Wiley & Sons.

Kulik, C., & Roberson, L. (2008). Common goals and golden opportunities: Evaluations of diversity education in academic and organizational settings. *Academy of Management Learning & Education, 7*(3), 309–331.

Leonardo, Z. (2005). Through the multicultural glass: Althusser, ideology and race relations in post-civil rights America. *Policy Futures in Education, 3*, 400–412.

Leonardo, Z. (2009). *Race, whiteness, and education*. New York, NY: Routledge.

Leonardo, Z., & Porter, R. (2010). Pedagogy of fear: Toward a Fanonian theory of "safety" in race dialogue. *Race Ethnicity and Education, 13*(2), 139–157.

Linder, C. (2015). Navigating guilt, shame, and fear of appearing racist: A conceptual model of antiracist White feminist identity development. *Journal of College Student Development, 56*(6), 535–550. Johns Hopkins University Press.

McIntosh, P. (1990). White privilege: Unpacking the invisible knapsack. *Independent School*, Winter, 31–36.

Milem, J. F., Chang, M. J., & Antonio, A. L. (2005). *Making diversity work on campus: A research-based perspective*. Washington, DC: Association of American Colleges and Universities.

Nicolazzo, Z., & Harris, C. (2014). This is what a feminist (space) looks like:(Re) conceptualizing women's centers as feminist spaces in higher education. *About Campus*, *18*(6), 2–9.

Omi, M., & Winant, H. (2015). *Racial formation in the United States* (3rd ed.). New York, NY: Routledge.

Ortiz, A. M., & Rhoads, R. A. (2000). Deconstructing Whiteness as part of a multicultural educational framework: From theory to practice. *Journal of College Student Development*, *41*, 81–93.

Painter, N. I. (2010). *The history of White people*. New York, NY: W. W. Norton & Company.

Patton, L. D. (2011). Promoting critical conversations about identity centers. In P. M. Magolda & M. B. Baxter Magolda (Eds.), *Contested issues in student affairs: Diverse perspectives and respectful dialogue* (pp. 255–260). Sterling, VA: Stylus.

Patton, L. D., Renn, K. A., Guido, F. M., & Quaye, S. J. (2016). *Student development in college: Theory, research, and practice*. San Francisco, CA: Jossey-Bass.

Peet, M. R. (2006). *We make the road by walking it: Critical consciousness, structuration, and social change* (Unpublished doctoral dissertation). University of Michigan, Ann Arbor.

Reason, R. D. (2014). Engaging White students in multicultural campuses. In S. R. Harper & S. J. Quaye (Eds.), *Student engagement in higher education: Theoretical perspectives and practical approaches for diverse populations* (pp. 75–89). New York, NY: Routledge.

Reason, R. D., & Broido, E. M. (2005). Issues and strategies for social justice allies (and the student affairs professionals who hope to encourage them). In R. D. Reason, E. M. Broido, T. L. Davis, & N. J. Evans (Eds.), *Developing social justice allies* (New directions for student services, No. 110) (pp. 81–89). San Francisco, CA: Jossey-Bass.

Reason, R. D., & Evans, N. J. (2007). The complicated realities of Whiteness: From color-blind to racially cognizant. In S. R. Harper & L. D. Patton (Eds.), *Responding to the realities of race on campus* (New directions for student services, No. 120) (pp. 67–75). San Francisco, CA: Jossey-Bass.

Reason, R. D., Millar, E. A. R., & Scales, T. C. (2005). Toward a model of racial justice ally development. *Journal of College Student Development*, *46*(5), 530–546.

Renn, K. A. (2011). Identity centers: An idea whose time has come . . . and gone? In P. M. Magolda & M. B. Baxter Magolda (Eds.), *Contested issues in student affairs: Diverse perspectives and respectful dialogue* (pp. 244–254). Sterling, VA: Stylus.

Rhoads, R. A. (1998). *Freedom's web: Student activism in an age of cultural diversity*. Baltimore, MD: Johns Hopkins University Press.

Robbins, C. (2017). College experiences that generated racial dissonance: Reflections from cisgender White women in graduate preparation programs. *College Student Affairs Journal*, *35*(2), 57–69. Southern Association for College Student Affairs.

Robbins, C. K., & Jones, S. R. (2016). Negotiating racial dissonance: White women's narratives of resistance, engagement, and transformative action. *Journal of College Student Development*, *57*(6), 633–651.

Ross, L. (2016). *Blackballed: The Black and White politics of race on America's campuses*. New York, NY: St. Martin's Press.

Rowe, W., Bennett, S. K., & Atkinson, D. R. (1994). White racial identity models: A critique and alternative proposal. *The Counseling Psychologist*, *22*(1), 129–146.

Sallee, M. W., Logan, M. E., Sims, S., & Harrington, W. P. (2009). Engaging White students on a multicultural campus: Developmental needs and institutional challenges. In S. R. Harper & S. J. Quaye (Eds.), *Student engagement in higher education: Theoretical perspectives and practical approaches for diverse populations* (pp. 199–221). New York, NY: Routledge.

Sleeter, C. E. (2011). *The academic and social value of ethnic studies: A research review*. Washington, DC: National Education Association.

Soble, J. R., Spanierman, L. B., & Liao, H. Y. (2011). Effects of a brief video intervention on White university students' racial attitudes. *Journal of Counseling Psychology*, *58*(1), 151.

Stewart, D-L., & Nicolazzo, Z. (in press). The high impact of [whiteness] on trans* students in postsecondary education. *Equity and excellence in education*.

Tatum, B. D. (1997). *"Why are all the Black kids sitting together in the cafeteria?" And other conversations about race.* New York, NY: Basic Books.

Tochluk, S., & Levin, C. (2010). Powerful partnerships: Transformative alliance building. In B. B. Cushing, L. Cabbil, M. Freeman, J. Hitchcock, & K. Richards (Eds.), *Accountability and White anti-racist organizing: Stories from our work* (pp. 190–219). Roselle, NJ: Crandall, Dostie & Douglass Books.

Todd, N. R., Spanierman, L. B., & Poteat, V. P. (2011). Longitudinal examination of the psychosocial costs of racism to Whites across the college experience. *Journal of Counseling Psychology, 58*(4), 508–521

Wood, J. L., & Moore, C. S. (2016). Engaging community college transfer students. In S. R. Komives & W. Wagner (Eds.), *Leadership for a better world: Understanding the social change model of leadership development.* Hoboken, NJ: John Wiley & Sons.

Yeung, J. G., Spanierman, L. B., & Landrum-Brown, J. (2013). "Being White in a multicultural society": Critical whiteness pedagogy in a dialogue course. *Journal of Diversity in Higher Education, 6*(1), 17.

Zuñiga, X., Nagda, B. A., & Sevig, T. D. (2002). Intergroup dialogues: An educational model for cultivating engagement across difference. *Equity & Excellence in Education, 35*(1), 7–17.

Chapter 7
Engaging International Students

Jenny J. Lee and Santiago Castiello-Gutiérrez

International students constitute a significant and growing student population in many colleges and universities around the world. The OECD (2018) estimates over 4.6 million students were enrolled in institutions outside their country of citizenship in 2017, more than double the number in 2000 (UNESCO, 2018), suggesting that international education will increase in global demand in the years to come. With rising global wealth and improving educational infrastructure and delivery, crossing national borders specifically for higher education purposes is more commonplace than ever before.

Preferred destinations for international study tend to be in North America, Oceania, and Western Europe. The top ten destinations for international students comprise seven countries from the so-called G8 group (only Italy is missing) plus China, Australia, and Spain. Although the countries at the top have shifted a little, the fact is that student mobility is still highly concentrated in just a handful of countries. The top five receivers of international students, the United States, the United Kingdom, China, Australia, and France, constitute almost 60% of all international students combined (Farrugia & Bhandari, 2017; OECD, 2018). The United States continues to be the leading destination for cross-border study, hosting over one million international students (Farrugia & Bhandari, 2017). The top three countries sending students to the US for higher education are China, India, and South Korea, comprising over half (55%) of the total international enrollments (Farrugia & Bhandari, 2017). These three Asian countries similarly account for almost one-third (29%) of all students studying abroad worldwide (UNESCO, 2018). The main driver toward the US in particular has been the prestige associated with studying at a US university, especially given the country's high concentration of the world's most highly ranked universities. (See Academic Ranking of World Universities, compiled by the Shanghai Jiao Tong University (ShanghaiRanking Consultancy, 2018) and Times Higher Education Ranking (THE, 2018).) As such, there has been a relatively steady enrollment rise, with over 85 percent more students than there were a decade earlier (Farrugia & Bhandari, 2017). The absolute number of international students in the US has also grown as a result of changes to immigration processes that now allow students to remain in the country under a student visa even after graduation for an "optional practical training" (OPT) that can go from one to up to three years, depending on the student's academic field.

Benefits of Hosting International Students

To fully appreciate the significance of such concerns and the potential losses at stake, it helps to understand the benefits that overseas students offer to the countries that educate them. Among the most widely cited motivations for attracting international students are their financial contributions. With declining public investments in higher education around the world, international tuition and fees, which are typically much higher than what colleges and universities charge their in-state students, can potentially subsidize university operations. In Australia, for example, international education is the country's third-largest export, with international student fees replacing its public contributions at a growing rate (Australia Department of Education and Training (DET), 2018). Although international students constitute only 5% of all students in the US, their financial contributions are still notable (Farrugia & Bhandari, 2017). In the academic year 2016–2017, these students and their dependents contributed approximately $37 billion to the US economy, with over two thirds coming from sources outside the country, including personal, family, home governments, and sending universities (NAFSA, 2017). The over one million international students in the US also supported or created over 450,000 jobs (NAFSA, 2017).

Many international students, particularly graduate students and postdocs, have become vital to the US in maintaining its competitive edge in areas of science, technology, engineering, and mathematics (STEM) research (Cantwell & Lee, 2010; Haddal, 2008). Data from the National Science Foundation (NSF) Survey of Earned Doctorates indicate that science and engineering doctorates to internationals are increasing and that this population comprises the majority of doctoral degree recipients in the engineering, mathematics, and computer science fields (NSF, 2018). Given domestic skill shortages in the STEM areas, colleges and universities have had to rely increasingly on international students and graduates as researchers to maintain their scientific knowledge production (Cantwell & Lee, 2010). These students work in scientific labs, assist in grant writing, lead major research projects, serve as teaching assistants or instructors, and comprise a significant portion of students and graduates from STEM departments, thereby raising the prestige of many research universities.

Beyond their monetary and scientific contributions, international students provide a wealth of cultural knowledge and diverse perspectives that are vital in preparing future students to compete successfully in the global economy. A narrow US-centric education is no longer sufficient in the current era of globalization. As countries are becoming increasingly interdependent, knowledge about and experiences in diverse cultures, economies, politics, social issues, and languages are being recognized as valuable forms of capital. Moreover, past higher education research has empirically demonstrated the many positive outcomes associated with interacting with diverse international students, such as greater cultural knowledge, cross-cultural communication, self-awareness (Campbell, 2012), reduced stereotypes (Volet & Ang, 2012), and belongingness (Glass & Westmont, 2014). In addition to the learning and associated outcomes that international students offer, they also provide helpful social networks, linking individuals and groups across borders. Given that international students are often among the most privileged citizens in their home countries, they may provide valuable connections to influential individuals and organizations throughout the world. For example, international students have also been found to be vital bridges for faculty and students in cross-border scholarly research, thereby linking institutions globally (Maldonado-Maldonado & Cantwell, 2007).

Challenges for International Students

Although international students offer countless benefits to US colleges and universities, they are vulnerable (Sherry, Thomas, & Chui, 2010) and among the most misunderstood and stereotyped. Many are often mistaken for or categorized with domestic Students of Color despite such major cultural differences. International students' past educational experiences, worldviews, and cultural approaches can be quite different from those of domestic students, even despite sharing the same racial background (Zhou & Cole, 2017). Among the studies that have compared domestic and international students, overall findings concur that international students are likely to experience greater challenges in their adaptation to college than domestic students (Van Horne, Lin, Anson, & Jacobson, 2018; Zhou & Cole, 2017), such as in finding part-time work, fear of failure, workload, and nervousness/tension, to name a few. Although such dissimilarities between international and domestic students are vast and hardly disputed, scant resources targeted to this student population tend to be devoted to a single isolated international affairs office that is somehow responsible for catering to the many complex immigration issues as well as academic and social needs of the often thousands of students from all over the world in a single campus.

Even the category of "international students" implies a homogeneous group that combines together all non-US students. As mentioned by Coate (2009, p. 277), there is a tendency within higher education institutions "to treat them [international students] as economically important but academically deficient." This perception that all international students are the same and that their "defining characteristic" is that they "have more economic than academic capital" (p. 277) dehumanizes the invaluable individual characteristics of each student. Even as a group, the diversity among international students is such that they actually have more differences between them than any commonalities, with the exception of a shared purpose in choosing to study outside their home countries. Their motivations for studying abroad, their past experiences, and their future goals are as varied as the countries from which they originate. Even within a single sending country, there can be many diverse cultural backgrounds.

International students' background factors, such as their primary language, race, or country and region of origin, can greatly shape their experiences and outcomes. Research has shown how international students from non-European countries are less socially engaged with their college than their European peers (Glass, Gómez, & Urzua, 2014). Beyond just socialization, students from different countries and regions also experience different degrees of discrimination, as in the case of African students at US institutions (George Mwangi, Changamire, & Mosselson, 2018). However, despite the broad variety of cultures that international students represent, many of the challenges they face tend to be relatively similar in initially entering any foreign environment with varying degrees of difficulty. Early entry issues regarding mastering the local language, cultural norms, and food tastes, as well as the social "shock" of being away from family and friends back home can be expected, especially for students traveling to countries with very different cultures on opposite ends of the globe. Countless studies have illuminated such anticipated concerns (e.g., Bianchi, 2013; Lee & Rice, 2007; Paton, 2007), and without adequate attention and support, their problems can sometimes manifest to extreme stress and depression (Chavajay & Skowronek, 2008; Constantine, Okazaki, & Utsey, 2004; Yeh & Inose, 2003).

For readers less familiar with the specific challenges of studying in another country, some common issues are reported in the following sections.

English Language and Learning

International students in the US whose first language is not English have the obvious challenge of learning academic content in their non-native language (Cheng & Erben, 2012; Li, Chen, & Duanmu, 2010). Understanding lectures, including professors and teaching assistants speaking too quickly and with unfamiliar jargon, was reported as being especially challenging (Zhang & Mi, 2009). Even proficient English speakers can experience the frustration of not being understood in class due to their pronunciation and accents, while the problems are magnified for those who are less fluent (Park, Klieve, Tsurutani, & Harte, 2017; Sherry et al., 2010). Faculty office hours and even study groups can be quite daunting as simply being able to freely converse and ask questions cannot be taken for granted. Without the ability to confidently question and follow class discussions, silence may be mistaken for disengagement (Reda, 2009). Meanwhile, troubles with being able to freely converse in the host language may not only lead to challenges in daily functions but also result in considerable stress and a negative self-concept (Akanwa, 2015; Andrade, 2006; Byun et al., 2011; Cheng & Erben, 2012; Yeh & Inose, 2003).

Social Isolation

What tends to follow language barriers are social isolation and loneliness, particularly outside the classroom. A study comparing student engagement at US campuses between domestic and international students shows how "international students consistently report lower levels of social satisfaction and feelings of being welcome and respected on campus" (Van Horne et al., 2018, p. 351). Other studies similarly found that when asked to rank their greatest concerns, international students tend to indicate developing social networks as their primary challenge (Chavajay & Skowronek, 2008; Glass, Buus, & Braskamp, 2013; Sawir, Marginson, Deumert, Nyland, & Ramia, 2008), reporting "feelings of loneliness arising in their academic work and institutional relationships" (Sawir et al., 2008, pp. 162–163). Sawir et al. (2008) identified three forms of loneliness: personal, social, and cultural. While personal loneliness (loss of familial contact) and social loneliness (loss of social networks) are commonly understood and anticipated, they also recognized cultural loneliness, based on an absence of their familiar cultural and/or linguistic environment. They further uncovered a strong corresponding relationship between loneliness and problems developing cross-cultural relationships.

Though many students may find social support in international student clubs and organizations (Glass & Gesing, 2018), other universities may not have adequate representation from particular countries, and those students from less-populous nations may feel especially alone. Even among groups where there is a large representation of international students from particular countries, cultural isolation might still exist. Such ethnic balkanization is worrisome as misinformation may be passed around peers and never corrected. Further, they may isolate themselves in self-imposed campus enclaves. Schmitt, Spears, and Branscombe (2003) found that part of the reason that international students gravitate toward each other is a shared identity of rejection. That is, "identification with international students increased in response to perceiving prejudice and suppressed the costs of perceiving oneself as excluded from the host community" (p. 1), and "identification with other international students is not based on similar intragroup traits but is constructed in context based on their common treatment from the majority" (p. 5). Moreover, perceived discrimination was more positively related to identification with other international students than to identification with one's home country. These findings are especially insightful because they challenge the assumption that international students congregate due to any preexisting group identities but rather form alliances based on their shared common challenges. The researchers also found that while perceived discrimination might lead to a decrease in self-esteem, identifying with other international students mediated a positive relationship between perceived discrimination and self-esteem. In other words, a shared international student identity could lead to a healthier and more positive sense of self, helping overcome experiences of mistreatment. Yet, despite tendencies to withdraw into culturally similar or internationally based social networks and their potential benefits, international students nevertheless desire to interact with and befriend local members of the host community (Hotta & Ting-Toomey, 2013).

Positive peer relationships are vital, not only in fostering belonging (Glass & Westmont, 2014), but also in learning (Lee, 2018). Previous research indicated that Asian students from Confucian backgrounds, for example, tend to be more collectivist in their approach to learning, relying more on group interaction in their studies (Wang et al., 2012), and, without adequate social learning environments, they may be especially at academic risk. These findings are most applicable for international students from other collectivist cultures. Peer collaboration may be a preferred style of learning for many international students (Lee, 2018), but forced group work does not automatically lead to an ideal learning environment where everyone benefits (Rose-Redwood & Rose-Redwood, 2018). Without communication and peer group work based on mutual respect and trust, some international students may feel further isolated in a small group setting.

An unwelcoming environment can push students toward further isolation. Research on international students tends to center on university welcomeness and often neglects the larger social environment off campus. The positive relationships that international students can establish should not only be confined to institutional walls. A welcoming environment by the larger community is also crucial in the adaptation process of the students (Gautam, Lowery, Mays, & Durant, 2016; Marangell & Arkoudis, 2018; Marginson et al., 2010; Romerhausen, 2013; Smith & Khawaja, 2011).

Cultural Norms

Understanding the host cultural norms can also be difficult for international students. Ways of interacting with professors, such as how to address them and whether to make eye contact, can be considerably different from what might be expected in the home country. For instance, avoiding eye contact can be perceived as a signal of respect and reverence in one culture but the same gesture might also be perceived as being untrustworthiness in another (Lee & Opio, 2011). Classroom interactions may also widely differ by cultures, especially among countries that uphold greater formality between teachers and students than the United States (Myles & Cheng, 2003). While Asian cultures might frown upon openly questioning authority, criticism and debate tend to be highly valued in the United States. Such forms of learning and interacting may be very unusual, sometimes even culturally unacceptable, and thus challenging for many overseas students. Some students may struggle with internal conflicts about whether to speak out in class and appear disrespectful. Even honoring a professor's allowance of being called by their first name could be a source of tension for some international students. Other academic norms, like avoiding plagiarism, might be unfamiliar to international students whose previous education may have focused on rote memory or failed to socialize students on writing ethics (Adhikari, 2018; Amsberry, 2009; Bethany, 2016). Faculty and student peers might confuse an international student's humility and modesty, two highly valued traits outside the United States, as ignorance and incompetence. Further, cross-cultural miscommunication might also arise, such as different perceptions of gender roles and opposite-sex relationships (Lacina, 2002). Physical touch and socializing with members of a different gender could be interpreted differently based on one's culture. What might be intended harmlessly in one culture could be mistaken as a personal violation in another. The problem with these and other academic norms is that they tend to be addressed as cultural traits, particularly in what has been defined as "big C Culture," meaning the more visible and broad characteristics of one's culture (holidays, food, art, etc.) as opposed to "little c culture," which is more about common but less obvious beliefs, values, accepted styles, etc. (Herron, Cole, Corrie, & Dubreil, 2000).

Despite such potential cultural differences, international students tend to keep their problems to themselves rather than seeking institutional support (Constantine, Anderson, Caldwell, Berkel, & Utsey, 2005; Lee & Rice, 2007). Research on international college students is mostly found within the counselling literature, indicating the psychological "problems" that this student sector tends to face related to their "adjustment." In their examination of Asian students, Heggins and Jackson (2003) suggested that they tend to underutilize counselling and other support services due to cultural norms and stigmas associated with psychological concerns. These students instead seek out existing social networks for support. Similar findings were reported for African students, who indicated they would not seek out support due to unfamiliarity with counselling services and possible distrust (Constantine et al., 2005). Moreover, international students who experience psychological distress may not seek out professional support due to unfamiliarity or fear of being stigmatized. As a result, there may be serious consequences if such problems are left unaddressed, such as depression (Constantine et al., 2004; Rosenthal, Russell, & Thomson, 2008) and lowered career aspirations (Reynolds & Constantine, 2007).

Costs and Visa Procedures

Several studies have also noted the financial burden of studying abroad as a major concern and stressor among overseas students (Glass et al., 2013; Nyland, Forbes-Mewett, & Härtel, 2013). In the Institute of International Education's (IIE) global survey of over 15,000 prospective students, cost was cited as the primary obstacle to studying in the United States; 62% perceived US tuition to be expensive and the primary obstacle to studying in the country (IIE, 2015). Changes in the cost of living, particularly for students from low-income countries, can have a major toll on the mental and physical energy required in seeking supplemental income while being required to maintain their full-time student status. Without readily accessible resources from family in their home countries, these students are often left on their own to cover their basic living and educational necessities. Studying abroad is also dependent on macroeconomic variables like exchange rates (Conlon, Ladher, & Halterbeck, 2017; McKenzie, 2008), leading some students to experience additional financial setbacks with a depreciating home currency while living abroad, resulting in even less monetary support from home. Their financial troubles tend to be considerably greater than those of local students, given that international students have very little to no access to loans and scholarships and must pay out-of-state tuition (Li & Lee, 2018; Su, 2018).

In the same IIE survey, half the respondents indicated that the United States had difficult or complex student visa procedures and the highest requirements of any host destination in the world (IIE, 2015). The US visa procedures are notoriously cumbersome, and delays in processing can create a host of problems in preparing for relocation, ranging from travel arrangements, securing university housing, signing up for classes, and other time-sensitive tasks. Further, the Student Exchange Visitor Information System (SEVIS), a mandatory program that requires all higher education institutions to screen and track international students and scholars, was implemented in 2001. This surveillance program was introduced given that several of those directly involved in the attacks on the World Trade Center on September 11, 2001, arrived in the United States on student visas. Since then, SEVIS has been scrutinized as both costly and inefficient in its intended purpose of identifying potential terrorists (Urias & Yeakey, 2009). Hosting universities have protested that the program is extremely burdensome and that the Department of Homeland Security has provided little training in its implementation (Haddal, 2008). Given the difficulties of obtaining visas as well as problems with national security, some international students have questioned whether studying in the United States is worth facing these bureaucratic challenges (Haddal, 2008).

A common issue related to the burdensome costs of studying in the US as a foreign citizen is how higher education institutions are increasing tuition without offering almost any kind of financial support for internationals (Li & Lee, 2018). A recent study has shown how particularly well-reputed research intense but not top tier institutions have used international student enrolment to compensate for reductions in state appropriations. Bound, Braga, Khanna, and Turner (2016) estimate that for a 10% reduction in public funding, institutions increase their international enrolments by 12% to 17%, depending on the institution type. This phenomenon incentivizes institutions to collect from international students the always-growing full-tuition sticker price. This, combined with the fact that over 80% of international undergraduate students' primary sources of funding are personal and family funds (Farrugia & Bhandari, 2017), less affluent students are especially prone to financial distress (Su, 2018).

Discrimination

There have long been reports of discrimination and hostile acts against international students, in the US and globally. For example, in 2011, nine Chinese students were attacked and robbed in the UK, leading university administrators at Sussex Downs College to educate their four hundred international students on how to protect themselves (BBC, 2011). In their study of African students in the United States, Constantine and her colleagues (2005) identified several acts of mistreatment, including verbal assaults from teaching staff and perceptions of intellectual inferiority and of being uncivilized. Negative stereotypes manifested in social challenges, including finding roommates and developing friendships. Lee and Rice (2007) also identified cases of sexual harassment, verbal assaults, and physical attacks against international students in the United States.

More recently, with the current rise of neo-nationalism and populist sentiments among large proportions of the population at many Western countries (i.e., the United Kingdom, the United States, France, Poland), international students continue to be vulnerable. The hostility toward international students has spiked again in the past two years. In the United States alone, during the 2016 presidential campaigns and after Donald Trump's election, an increase in aggressions and harassment incidents were reported on US campuses (SPLC, 2016). A recent study by Quinton (2018) suggested that Trumpism was associated with negative attitudes among US students against their international peers on campus.

Among the most tragic occurrences was the death of Hussain Saeed Alnahdi, a student from Saudi Arabia, after being brutally assaulted. Other incidents included harassment against students from specific countries like Mexico and some Middle Eastern countries or other groups, regardless of nationality, like Black and Muslim students. Kiecker Royall and Dodson (2017) surveyed over 2,000 students who were at the time considering attending a college in the US; one third expressed a decline in their interest in traveling to the US in light of the current political climate. Over half of them mentioned concerns about their personal safety, 48% were worried about prejudice or discrimination against people from their country, and 45% thought people in the US seem less welcoming to international students.

Such discrimination is not isolated to ethnic majority against ethnic minority groups. The current political climate could foster and target racist and xenophobic perceptions from and across all groups. Ritter (2016) found how some international students learn, for example, negative perceptions of Latinos while in the US. Stereotypes in Asian media about Black and White race relations in the US have resulted in Asian students at US campuses feeling less comfortable interacting with African American students (Smith, Bowman, & Hsu, 2007).

Addressing These Challenges

Despite such accounts, the overriding literature on international students places the burden on international students to adapt, acculturate, and overcome any challenges that are set up by their hosts (Hellstén, 2007; Lee & Rice, 2007). Past dominant theoretical frameworks conceptualized international students towards adaptation (Glass et al., 2014; Ye & Edwards, 2015; Zhou, Jindal-Snape, Topping, & Todman, 2008), adjustment (Lin, Peng, Kim, Kim, & LaRose, 2012; Reynolds & Constantine, 2007; Zhang & Goodson, 2011), acculturation (Gautam et al., 2016; Smith & Khawaja, 2011), and intercultural competence development (Bennett, 2009; Deardorff, 2006), all of which assume international students' incorporation into the host culture's values, beliefs, and behaviors. The fundamental problem with many of such viewpoints is that, while they promote integration, they often place the responsibility to adjust solely on the newcomer, and they also may discount the cultural value that international students offer in bettering the host environment (Lee & Rice, 2007). The acculturation framework, for instance, assumes cultural superiority and devalues what newcomers may offer: that is, that there is a "better way" to be and live, namely from the position of the host society in comparison to the environment of origin. A common strategy in helping international students cope with "culture shock" and then "acculturation" has been "the development of stress-coping strategies and culturally relevant social skills . . . and should result in psychological adjustment and sociocultural adaptation" (Zhou et al., 2008, p. 69).

In her discourse analysis of media regarding international students in Australia, Devos (2003) uncovered ways that these students are perceptually being marginalized as "foreign and 'the other'" (p. 164). They are highly valued for their economic contributions as "fee paying students" (p. 160), but they are also targeted as responsible for lowering academic standards with "corrupt[ion]," "malaise," and metaphors of "disease" and an "epidemic" (p. 162). She elaborated, "International students are simultaneously a source of contempt (for their inadequate English language skills), resentment (that we have to accept them at all) and paradoxically, anxiety ('will they like us?')" (p. 164). Meanwhile, the media constructed local Australian academics as victims of poorly prepared and inferior international students who are overrunning the Australian higher education system (Devos, 2003).

A second major limitation to the existing literature is that most research on international students examined this population as a homogenous group, often in comparison to local students, although some studies have sought to differentiate student experiences by their region or country of origin. Despite the dominance of Asians among international students in the US (Farrugia & Bhandari, 2017), there have been limited attempts to differentiate between them or compare them to students from other regions. Among the few studies, Wilton and Constantine (2003) reported that Latin American international students experienced greater psychological distress than Asian students. Sakurai, Parpala, Pyhältö, and Lindblom-Ylänne (2016) compared the experiences of Asian and European international students and found that the former "exhibited a slightly more surface approach to learning, and were more organised in their studies" than the latter (p. 24). But in another comparison survey of international students from seven regions of the world, Hanassab and Tidwell (2002) found that Africans faced the greatest discriminatory challenges and that Asian students reported the highest psychological distress. The authors also reported minimal difficulties among Canadians and Western Europeans, who reported being more socially involved with US nationals and reported fewer troubles. In a similar vein, African students related "lower self-efficacy, acculturative stress, and depression compared to other international students" (Constantine et al., 2004, p. 237), suggesting that the reasons might have to do with the fact that "African students may face a larger gap between their culture of origin and American culture" (p. 238), and that racism might also be present. Despite a lack of research that systematically differentiates students' experiences by their countries of origin (see IIE, 2015, as an exception), the studies that have included Anglo students have consistently found that these students (i.e., Canadians, Australians, and Western Europeans) studying in the United States and Australia experienced far less social isolation and related challenges than students from Asian and developing countries (IIE, 2015; Lee, 2017; Lee & Opio, 2011; Lee & Rice, 2007).

To address these common shortcomings with literature, we suggest to practitioners and researchers the use of three frameworks: soft power, neo-racism, and academic hospitality. The first one serves as a way of understanding the broader political context for the internationalization of higher education, and student mobility in particular. Based on this framework internationalization is hardly neutral and is built upon histories of power imbalances. Neo-racism involves acknowledging that internationalization could potentially reinforce the cultural stratification and divides between parts of "the North" and "the South" and that discrimination happens throughout campuses—consciously or not—based on the Other's culture and nationality. Lastly, academic hospitality, suggests proactive engagement by creating the conditions on campus to sustain engagement beyond mere tolerance or respect between "locals" and "internationals." The broader goal that we suggest is transforming higher education institutions into "global villages."

Theoretical Perspectives

Soft Power

Given the large number of students who are traveling across borders every year to the top destinations in the Global North, student mobility can be framed as a form of soft power. Soft power refers to persuasion in international relations that involves cultural values to influence agendas over forced coercion (Nye, 2002). Based on this concept, internationalization is hardly neutral and power disparities are evident in international activities. As soft power pertains to higher education, student flows from the Global South to the Global North allow the latter to open communication channels with the former by educating students in Western-based knowledge, theories, and approaches (Lee, 2014). However, soft power can also work in the opposite direction. Recently, the Kingdom of Saudi Arabia threatened to stop funding the more than 8,000 students attending postsecondary institutions in Canada after a diplomatic altercation. Similarly, Turkey's Ministry of Education expressed that they will stop funding graduate scholarships to the US and will send "students to European and Far Eastern universities in line with Turkey's interests" (ICEF, 2018). Overall, soft power provides a more critical lens to examine ways that political relations and agendas shape the various directions of international student flows.

Neo-Racism

Nationalities also matter on arrival. Past studies have demonstrated that many international students experienced innumerable negative encounters with their university hosts, particularly those from non-Western nations. Negative views about the lack of openness to outside cultures held by those in the United States are pervasive. In the IIE survey previously discussed, over 30% of the more than 15,000 respondents indicated disagreement with the statement that the United States welcomes international students (IIE, 2015).

One of the guiding frameworks for this chapter, neo-racism, is based on the premise that international students are being discriminated against, not simply based on the color of their skin, but also based on negative assumptions about their home countries on the basis of culture and national order (Lee & Rice, 2007). The experiences of international students from China, for example, may be exceedingly more difficult than the experiences of US-born Chinese Americans. The concept of neo-racism has its roots in France as immigrants from the Arab regions were being mistreated under the justification of preserving the "French race" (Balibar, 2005, p. 170) and "legitimate policies of exclusion" (Balibar, 2007, p. 81). Balibar (2007) elaborated:

> The new racism is a racism of the era of "decolonization," of the reversal of population movements between the old colonies and the old metropolises, and the division of humanity within a single political space. . . . It is a racism whose dominant theme is not about biological heredity but the insurmountability of cultural differences, a racism which, at first sight, does not postulate the superiority of certain groups or peoples in relation to others but "only" the harmfulness of abolishing frontiers, the incompatibility of life-styles and traditions.
>
> (p. 84)

Balibar (2005) goes on to explain that, even in France, there is no true ethnic basis. He wrote:

> No nation, that is, no national state, has an ethnic basis, which means that nationalism cannot be defined as an ethnocentrism except that precisely in the sense of the product of fictive ethnicity. To reason any other way would be to say that "peoples" do not exist naturally any more than "races" do, either by virtue of their ancestry, a community of culture or pre-existing interests.
>
> (p. 166)

Since then, several studies (i.e., Cantwell & Lee, 2010; Lee, 2017; Lee, Jon, & Byun, 2017; Lee & Opio, 2011; Lee & Rice, 2007) have applied this concept of neo-racism to explain the many documented cases of discrimination against international students. They argued that institutions should consider the value that international students offer to their host institutions but also critically examine ways that faculty, staff, students, and the local community might be in some ways responsible for creating an unwelcome, and sometimes hostile, environment for their international guests. They also found that students from developing and non-Western countries experienced the greatest challenges compared to their international White counterparts. Thus, not all international students face the same difficulties, nor are international students' issues akin to those of Students of Color. For example, research has indicated that Africans encountered prejudicial treatment from African Americans (Constantine et al., 2005; Lee & Opio, 2011). The neo-racism framework suggests universities pay particular attention to the needs of students from non-Western countries as potential targets of xenophobia.

Universities as Global Villages

The emergence of a "new racism" climate on campus requires more than prevention. The obvious first step is to acknowledge that discrimination occurs, but to truly overcome it, university campuses need to become safe spaces that go beyond tolerating diversity and shift towards an embracement of the differences. Bennett (2000) described academic hospitality as "welcoming [O]thers through openness in both sharing and receiving claims to knowledge and insight" (p. 23–24). He highlights the importance of the "sharing" and "receiving" components of the definition by explaining how the former relies on the "recognition that [O]thers' distinctive individualities and overall experience are inherently relevant to their learning" (p. 24) whereas the latter relies on an "awareness that . . . the perspective of the [O]ther could easily supplement . . . correct . . . or even transform one's self-understanding" (p. 24).

Simply being nice is not enough. When international students are dehumanized as either "cash, competition, or charity" (Stein & Andreotti, 2016, p. 226), then genuine engagement becomes difficult to sustain. Academic hospitality requires mutuality (George Mwangi, 2017; Leng, 2016; Leng & Pan, 2013; Marginson, 2007), which is embedded into the three substantive functions of a university: teaching, research, and service (Bennett, 2000). Hospitality in teaching requires faculty throughout campus to develop the intercultural competencies that allows them to "ask the right questions of [O]thers . . . that draw out students so that their own experiences become a valuable and respected resource" (Bennett, 2000, p. 26). Hospitality in research means integrating diverse theories and methods into scholarly inquiry. Finally, hospitality in service is integrating the other two functions and aligning them with a mission toward a greater common good. For international students, being in a "hospitable" environment with the aforementioned characteristics can ease and support their transition into their new educational system (Ploner, 2018). More than that, being part of a global community shifts the more utilitarian approach to student mobility that is characterized by what the students and the institutions can "get" from a "transaction" like studying abroad (Deschamps & Lee, 2015).

Student Engagement Strategies

Higher education institutions play vital roles in fostering global communities by engaging students of all nationalities while promoting the success of all. Engaging international students especially is fundamental to internationalizing universities but also to investing in the futures of higher education institutions. Overseas student experiences can directly impact the flow of future students to the institution as international student choices often are determined by the recommendation of friends, family, and other contacts back home (Lee, 2010; Pimpa, 2003). Faculty, staff, and students are, thus, all responsible for creating a welcoming environment for international guests.

Student engagement approaches must consider international students' unique dispositions and ways that domestic student strategies do not readily apply. All too often, recommendations for supporting the international student population have been as broad based as "choose the right kind of classes," "develop good personal practices," and "study with friends" (Abel, 2002, p. 16). These suggestions ignore the fundamental cultural reasons that might underlie an international student's difficulties in navigating a new environment and the unfamiliar system of obtaining academic and social support. Even the most well-intended suggestions, such as time management advice, may not consider that at least half of all international students are not native English speakers; far more hours are needed to simply comprehend class material. Furthermore, a Western conception and emphasis on time is highly presumed, not taking into account the many different approaches to studying, such as simply until one masters the material, rather than being dictated by the clock.

With the preceding review of the major challenges facing international students in mind, it is important for anyone who interacts with international students to have what we call "international consciousness," entailing global awareness, cultural appreciation, and openness to learning that extends beyond our national borders. Some might find it helpful to place themselves in the position of someone who has not lived in the United States and is traveling here for the first time and perceiving and interacting within the environment with new eyes. Given the wide breadth of cultures and viewpoints that are represented in this population, it is important for faculty, staff, and students to embody an international consciousness. Thus, here are some suggestions in supporting international students.

Forming Connections With International Students

Get to know international students personally. Given the challenges in identifying the specific needs of overseas students from every country or region without overgeneralizing, getting to know these students is a crucial step in best supporting these students. As the literature review demonstrates, negative stereotypes and assumptions about students from "foreign" countries have a dangerous effect on their experiences abroad. The most effective way to dismantle any prejudices would be to get to know international students as individuals with rich cultural backgrounds and new perspectives to offer. Most of these students enter the United States with very few networks, if any, and are prone to social isolation and loneliness. Matching them with domestic student "buddies" and arranging occasional social gatherings are certainly helpful, but they can also appear quite forced and artificial. Less task-oriented attempts, such as kind gestures, a listening ear, and frequent contact, may especially help these students feel welcome and at ease. International student organizations play vital roles in creating a system of social support, but it is also important not to isolate these students to their cultural groups, as they desire to befriend local students as well. Higher education institutions need also to address the development of intercultural competencies among international as well as local students to avoid segregation and future discrimination on their campuses.

Providing Financial Support

While international students are stereotyped as coming from wealthy backgrounds, many international students experience considerable financial stress. Without much access to scholarships or financial aid and with a cap on working on campus part time, many struggle to make ends meet. Particularly older students who might be traveling with dependents also struggle given the work restrictions on students' dependents' visas. Devalued currencies abroad and limited governmental assistance, if any, are additional economic challenges. When part-time job opportunities become available, international students apply but are sometimes turned away, sometimes due to limited English proficiency or prejudice against some foreign accents. With limited opportunities for many students whose language is not English to converse with native English speakers in their home country, their ability to read and write is often much stronger than their oral communication skills. However, international students also tend to be highly motivated and determined as they already made the commitment to learn outside the comforts of their home country. Advocating within the campus on behalf of international students to get part-time jobs could assist in reducing their social isolation and in improving their language proficiency faster. It will also help in reducing financial stress while engaging the student with the university through an increased sense of belonging.

Thinking Practically

For anyone who has traveled abroad, it is easy to consider that even the basic tasks, such as finding and understanding public transportation or opening a bank account, can be taken for granted. When befriending international students, one will soon discover their many practical concerns that are hardly raised by their US counterparts. Chief among them are being met at the airport or arranging transportation from the airport and finding adequate housing. In some cases, students arrive in the United States alone and for the first time, without any knowledge of how to get to the campus or where to live. Due to arduous US visa processes and missing housing registration deadlines, there are some students who live in hotels for the first several weeks of the school term until they find adequate and affordable housing. Helping students with these basic living arrangements can save them considerable stress and anxiety, especially while adjusting to a new country and university for the first time. Further, workshops and/or reading materials on the US culture, particularly on the norms regarding the local area where the university is located, can also be valuable. As there might be negative stereotypes about some students' home countries, they may also have negative stereotypes about the United States or the particular region of the country.

Providing Advocacy

Quite often, attempts to welcome and support international students tend to be limited to their initial orientation to the university. Sometimes the greatest challenges occur after they have settled into their regular schedule and routine. Unexpected maltreatment might occur, whether it is a degrading remark from a professor, sexual harassment from a supervisor, or social isolation from classmates. Though such examples might appear anecdotal and infrequent, previous research has demonstrated that such acts do occur but are often not reported. International students may fear deportation or retribution for causing trouble and may instead suffer silently. Although international affairs offices on campus are the primary source of international student support, they tend to be overburdened with complex immigration procedures, including SEVIS, and a myriad of international student administrative concerns. Other campus offices may be less familiar with the needs and struggles of overseas students. Thus, faculty and students, as well as administrators across the university, should be sensitive to the different circumstances of international students compared to their domestic peers and serve them accordingly. Moreover, creating a welcoming atmosphere is foundational in building trust should problems arise. For instance, the #YouAreWelcomeHere campaign, started by the company StudyGroup and highly promoted by Temple University, now has over 300 higher education institutions from the US promoting the benefits of having a diverse campus community (YouAreWelcomeHere.org, 2016).

Outreach Among Student Affairs Educators

Considerable costs and staffing resources are often used to recruit full-fee-paying students from overseas. But there is far less attention on maintaining their expectations and satisfaction on their arrival. There are countless student support services that international students may not be aware of, particularly because such services may not exist in the universities in their home countries. The student affairs profession is relatively new abroad and may be unfamiliar to those outside the United States. Beyond providing a written directory of support programs, student affairs staff should reach out to international students, educating them on ways they can seek out support and encouraging them to take advantage of what these programs offer and how to participate. Related to this recommendation, student affairs staff should be sensitive to the needs and issues of overseas students and try to avoid a one-size-fits-all program that focuses solely on domestic assumptions. International student support training is essential for any office that works with students, not just international student affairs offices.

Internationalizing Campuses

"Internationalization" is a hot buzzword in promoting the prestige of US colleges and universities. Internationalization is more than the international composition of its students and sometimes faculty. Though a high proportion of international students is the most common marker of internationalization, merely accounting for international enrollment numbers could simply be nothing more than a financial ploy to attract and bring in as many full-fee-paying students as possible. Internationalization should incorporate international perspectives, views, values, and cultures into campus life, both in and outside the classroom. Cultural centers are one obvious area where diversity is central and celebrated. However, these centers tend to focus on the needs of domestic Students of Color, and as such, international students may not feel welcome. For example, previous research has documented ways that African American students might discriminate against African students (Constantine et al., 2005; Lee & Opio, 2011). Thus, it is important to expand the roles of cultural centers to serve students beyond our domestic borders and possibly bridge understandings between US Students of Color and their international student counterparts. In the classroom, faculty and students should be especially attentive to what international students might offer by way of new viewpoints and new interpretations of class materials.

Humanizing International Students

While international students are well aware of their stereotype as "cash cows," the most humanizing approach is getting to know them. Suggestions include asking how they are doing, how they feel, and what their struggles and needs are and showing genuine interest in their experiences. Seeking their opinions such as through meetings, focus groups, or even informal gatherings where students can share their concerns with staff from the university can be highly impactful in regards to obtaining first-hand insights and allowing the students to feel their words matter (Perez-Encinas & Ammigan, 2016; Yu, Isensee, & Kappler, 2016). Naturally, just collecting data is not helpful enough if the institution does not address the students' concerns. However, it is important to design and implement support services that are based on these students' insights as opposed to doing what one imagines is best for the students. Just as important is to understand, as previously discussed, that international students are not a homogeneous group. An 18-year-old first-year student who leaves their parental home and country for the first time to come study in the US will have different needs than a 35-year-old graduate student who moves to the country with a spouse and children.

Most of the recommendations provided here are broadly prescribed but not exhaustive enough to become a recipe for success in student engagement. We invite our readers to involve international students in the process of creating a more hospitable environment where they can truly flourish in the different dimensions of student development that universities intend for their students.

Conclusion

International students are vital as many colleges and universities are seeking to internationalize and establish a global presence. Beyond enrollments, it is critical to understand the unique challenges and needs of this population and to effectively engage them. In this chapter, we discussed ways to better understand international students and offered soft power, neo-racism, and academic hospitality theories to make further sense of their needs and to promote an academic global community on every campus. These recommendations require international consciousness among faculty, student affairs educators, and students, which means stepping beyond comfort zones to educate themselves about international students and employ practices that are attuned to these students' various needs.

International students suffer from particular challenges as outlined in this chapter but are also very resilient and resourceful. For example, Lee (2018) identified ways that international students engage in informal learning practices, referred to as peer-brokering, in order to bridge cultural and knowledge gaps. International student agency was not the focus of this chapter as it potentially excuses institutional responsibilities, but it does provide important insights on less-investigated strategies for success, which might be applicable to domestic populations. International student agency also repositions the college student narrative away from victimhood. However, their challenges are still very real and require institutional interventions to support this still very vulnerable population.

Finally, we would like to bring attention to the importance for higher education institutions to also engage atypical international students. Campuses across the US are filled with students who do not fully fall under the binary of domestic or international students. Some of them are, for many purposes, considered as "domestic students" since they do not need a student visa; however, they share many of the challenges faced by international students. These include refugees, asylees, Jay treaty, and DACA students. In some cases, these students might have been in the US for many years to know how to navigate the higher education system just as any other domestic student. However, in many other cases, these students may also struggle with some of the challenges discussed in this chapter, such as language barriers, discrimination, isolation, and so forth. Due to their atypical status, institutions may not readily offer these students the more personalized follow-up that an international affairs office would provide to international students or the orientation programs intended to help the students set up and create a support community among their peers. We especially encourage all members of the university community to recognize and support this broad range of noncitizen students.

References

Abel, C. F. (2002). Academic success and the international student: Research and recommendations. *New Directions for Higher Education, 117*, 13–20.

Adhikari, S. (2018). Beyond culture: Helping international students avoid plagiarism. *Journal of International Students, 8*(1), 375–388. http://doi.org/http://dx.doi.org/10.5281/zenodo.1134315

Akanwa, E. E. (2015). International students in Western developed countries: History, challenges, and prospects. *Journal of International Students, 5*(3), 271–284. http://doi.org/10.5539/hes.v1n1p2

Amsberry, D. (2009). Deconstructing plagiarism: International students and textual borrowing practices. *The Reference Librarian, 51*(1), 31–44. http://doi.org/10.1080/02763870903362183

Andrade, M. S. (2006). International students in English-speaking universities: Adjustment factors. *Journal of Research in International Education, 5*(2), 131–154. http://doi.org/10.1177/1475240906065589

Australia Department of Education and Training [DET]. (2018). *Research snapshot*. Retrieved from https://internationaleducation.gov.au/research/research-snapshots/pages/default.aspx

Balibar, E. (2005). Racism and nationalism. In P. Spencer & H. Wollman (Eds.), *Nations and nationalism: A reader* (pp. 163–172). Piscataway, NJ: Rutgers University Press.

Balibar, E. (2007). Is there a neo-racism? In T. Das Gupta (Ed.), *Race and racialization: Essential readings* (pp. 83–88). Toronto: Canadian Scholars Press.

BBC. (2011, November 18). *BBC News—alert after foreign students attacked in Lewes*. Retrieved from www.bbc.co.uk/news/uk-england-sussex-15787553

Bennett, J. B. (2000). The academy and hospitality. *Cross Currents, 50*(1–2), 23–35.

Bennett, J. M. (2009). Cultivating intercultural competence: A process perspective. In D. K. Deardorff (Ed.), *The Sage handbook of intercultural competence* (pp. 121–140). Thousand Oaks, CA: SAGE Publications.

Bethany, R. D. (2016). The plagiarism polyconundrum. *Journal of International Students, 6*(4), 1045–1052.

Bianchi, C. (2013). Satisfiers and dissatisfiers for international students of higher education: An exploratory study in Australia. *Journal of Higher Education Policy and Management, 35*(4), 396–409. http://doi.org/10.1080/1360080X.2013.812057

Bound, J., Braga, B., Khanna, G., & Turner, S. (2016). *A passage to America: University funding and international students* (Working Paper Series). Retrieved from www.nber.org/papers/w22981

Byun, K., Chu, H., Kim, M., Park, I., Kim, S., & Jung, J. (2011). English-medium teaching in Korean higher education: Policy debates and reality. *Higher Education, 62*(4), 431–449. http://doi.org/10.1007/s10734-010-9397-4

Campbell, N. (2012). Promoting intercultural contact on campus: A project to connect and engage international and host students. *Journal of Studies in International Education, 16*(3), 205–227. http://doi.org/10.1177/1028315311403936

Cantwell, B., & Lee, J. J. (2010). Unseen workers in the academic among international postdocs in the United States and the United Kingdom. *Harvard Educational Review, 80*(4), 490–517. http://doi.org/10.17763/haer.80.4.w54750105q78p451

Chavajay, P., & Skowronek, J. (2008). Aspects of acculturation stress among international students attending a university in the USA. *Psychological Reports, 103*(3), 827–835. http://doi.org/10.2466/pr0.103.3.827-835

Cheng, R., & Erben, A. (2012). Language anxiety: Experiences of Chinese graduate students at US higher institutions. *Journal of Studies in International Education, 16*(5), 477–497. http://doi.org/10.1177/1028315311421841

Coate, K. (2009). Exploring the unknown: Levinas and international students in English higher education. *Journal of Education Policy, 24*(3), 271–282. http://doi.org/10.1080/02680930802669961

Conlon, G., Ladher, R., & Halterbeck, M. (2017). *The determinants of international demand for UK higher education.* Oxford, UK: Higher Education Policy Institute.

Constantine, M. G., Anderson, G. M., Caldwell, L. D., Berkel, L. A., & Utsey, S. O. (2005). Examining the cultural adjustment experiences of African international college students: A qualitative analysis. *Journal of Counseling Psychology, 52*(1), 3–13. http://doi.org/10.1037/0022-0167.52.1.57

Constantine, M. G., Okazaki, S., & Utsey, S. O. (2004). Self-concealment, social self-efficacy, acculturative stress, and depression in African, Asian, and Latin American international college students. *American Journal of Orthopsychiatry, 74*(3), 230–241. http://doi.org/10.1037/0002-9432.74.3.230

Deardorff, D. K. (2006). Identification and assessment of intercultural competence as a student outcome of internationalization. *Journal of Studies in International Education.* http://doi.org/10.1177/1028315306287002

Deschamps, E., & Lee, J. J. (2015). Internationalization as mergers and acquisitions: Senior international officers' entrepreneurial strategies and activities in public universities. *Journal of Studies in International Education, 19*, 122–139.

Devos, A. (2003). Academic standards, internationalisation, and the discursive construction of "the international student." *Higher Education Research & Development, 22*(2), 155–166. http://doi.org/10.1080/07294360304107

Farrugia, C. A., & Bhandari, R. (2017). *Open doors 2017. Report on international educational exchange.* New York, NY: Institute of International Education.

Gautam, C., Lowery, C. L., Mays, C., & Durant, D. (2016). Challenges for global learners: A qualitative study of the concerns and difficulties of international students. *Journal of International Students, 6*(2), 501–526.

George Mwangi, C. A. (2017). Partner positioning: Examining international higher education partnerships through a mutuality lens. *The Review of Higher Education, 41*(1), 33–60.

George Mwangi, C. A., Changamire, N., & Mosselson, J. (2018). An intersectional understanding of African international graduate students' experiences in US higher education. *Journal of Diversity in Higher Education* (Online First). http://doi.org/10.1037/dhe0000076

Glass, C. R., Buus, S., & Braskamp, L. A. (2013). *Uneven experiences: What's missing and what matters for today's international students.* Global Perspective Institute.

Glass, C. R., & Gesing, P. (2018). The development of social capital through international students' involvement in campus organizations. *Journal of International Mobility, 8*(3), 1274–1292. http://doi.org/10.5281/zenodo.1254580

Glass, C. R., Gómez, E., & Urzua, A. (2014). Recreation, intercultural friendship, and international students' adaptation to college by region of origin. *International Journal of Intercultural Relations, 42*, 104–117. http://doi.org/10.1016/j.ijintrel.2014.05.007

Glass, C. R., & Westmont, C. M. (2014). Comparative effects of belongingness on the academic success and cross-cultural interactions of domestic and international students. *International Journal of Intercultural Relations, 38*, 106–119. http://doi.org/10.1016/j.ijintrel.2013.04.004

Haddal, C. C. (2008). *Foreign students in the United States: Policies and legislation. (CRS Report for Congress). Congressional Research Service, Order Code RL31146.* Retrieved from https://fas.org/sgp/crs/misc/RL31146.pdf

Hanassab, S., & Tidwell, R. (2002). International students in higher education: Identification of needs and implications for policy and practice. *Journal of Studies in International Education,* (6), 305–322. http://doi.org/10.1177/102831502237638

Heggins, W. J., & Jackson, J. F. (2003). Understanding the collegiate experience for Asian international students at a midwestern research university. *College Student Journal, 37*(3), 379–392. http://doi.org/10.1037/a0024821

Hellstén, M. (2007). International student transition: Focusing on researching international pedagogy for educational sustainability. *International Education Journal, 8*(3), 79–90.

Herron, C., Cole, S. P., Corrie, C., & Dubreil, S. (2000). The effectiveness of a video-based curriculum in teaching culture. *Modern Language Journal, 83*(4), 518–533. http://doi.org/10.1111/0026-7902.00038

Hotta, J., & Ting-Toomey, S. (2013). Intercultural adjustment and friendship dialectics in international students: A qualitative study. *International Journal of Intercultural Relations, 37*(5), 550–566. http://doi.org/10.1016/j.ijintrel.2013.06.007

ICEF. (2018). *Turkey to suspend graduate scholarships for study in US.* Retrieved from http://monitor.icef.com/2018/09/turkey-to-suspend-graduate-scholarships-for-study-in-us/

IIE. (2015). *What international students think about US higher education: Attitudes and perceptions of prospective students from around the world.* New York, NY. Retrieved from www.iie.org/Research-and-Insights/Publications/What-International-Students-Think-About-US-Higher-Education

Kiecker Royall, P., & Dodson, A. (2017). *Effect of the current political environment on international student enrollment: Insights for US colleges and universities.* Washington, DC.

Lacina, J. G. (2002). Preparing international students for a successful social experience in higher education. *New Directions for Higher Education,* (117), 21–28. http://doi.org/10.1002/he.43

Lee, J. J. (2010). International students' experiences and attitudes at a US host institution: Self-reports and future recommendations. *Journal of Research in International Education, 9*, 66–84.

Lee, J. J. (2014, December 5). Tides shifting in global soft power influence. *University World News.* Retrieved from www.universityworldnews.com/article.php?story=20141204095256823

Lee, J. J. (2017). Neo-nationalism in higher education: Case of South Africa. *Studies in Higher Education, 42*(5), 869–886. http://doi.org/10.1080/03075079.2017.1293875

Lee, J. J., Jon, J.-E., & Byun, K. (2017). Neo-racism and neo-nationalism within East Asia. *Journal of Studies in International Education, 21*(2), 136–155. http://doi.org/10.1177/1028315316669903

Lee, J. J., & Opio, T. (2011). Coming to America: Challenges and difficulties faced by African student athletes. *Sport, Education and Society, 16*(5), 629–644. http://doi.org/10.1080/13573322.2011.601144

Lee, J. J., & Rice, C. (2007). Welcome to America? International student perceptions of discrimination. *Higher Education, 53*(3), 381–409. http://doi.org/10.1007/s10734-005-4508-3

Lee, S. (2018). Seeking academic help: A case study of peer brokering interactions. *Transitions: Journal of Transient Migration, 2*(1): 149–173.

Leng, P. (2016). Mutuality in Cambodian international university partnerships: Looking beyond the global discourse. *Higher Education, 72*(3), 261–275. http://doi.org/10.1007/s10734-015-9952-0

Leng, P., & Pan, J. (2013). The issue of mutuality in Canada-China educational collaboration. *Canadian and International Education, 42*(2), 1–16.

Li, G., Chen, W., & Duanmu, J.-L. (2010). Determinants of international students' academic performance: A comparison between Chinese and other international students. *Journal of Studies in International Education, 14*(4), 389–405. http://doi.org/10.1177/1028315309331490

Li, X., & Lee, J. J. (2018). Acquisitions or mergers? International students' satisfaction with work availability. *Journal of Student Affairs Research and Practice, 55*(1), 91–104. http://doi.org/10.1080/19496591.2017.1369421

Lin, J. H., Peng, W., Kim, M., Kim, S. Y., & LaRose, R. (2012). Social networking and adjustments among international students. *New Media and Society.* http://doi.org/10.1177/1461444811418627

Maldonado-Maldonado, A., & Cantwell, B. (2007). Rethinking the role of international students in North America: A borderland case study in understanding university collaboration. In *Paper presented at the annual meeting of the Consortium on North American Higher Education Collaboration.* Montreal, Quebec.

Marangell, S., & Arkoudis, S. (2018). Developing a host culture for international students: What does it take? *Journal of International Students, 8*(3), 1440–1458. http://doi.org/10.5281/zenodo.1254607

Marginson, S. (2007). Globalisation, the "idea of a university" and its ethical regimes. *Higher Education Management and Policy, 19*(1), 31–46. http://doi.org/10.1787/hemp-v19-art2-en

Marginson, S., Nyland, C., Sawir, E., Forbes-Mewett, H., Ramia, G., & Smith, S. (2010). *International student security.* Cambridge, UK: Cambridge University Press. http://doi.org/10.1017/CBO9780511751011

McKenzie, P. (2008). *Key international developments affecting Australian education and training.* Melbourne, Australia. Retrieved from https://research.acer.edu.au/ceet/1/

Myles, J., & Cheng, L. (2003). The social and cultural life of non-native English speaking international graduate students at a Canadian university. *Journal of English for Academic Purposes, 2*(3), 247–263. http://doi.org/10.1016/S1475-1585(03)00028-6

NAFSA. (2017). *The United States of America. Benefits from international students.* Washington, DC. Retrieved from www.nafsa.org/_/File/_/econvalue2017_natl.pdf

National Science Foundation (NSF). (2018). *Doctorate recipients from US universities.* Arlington, VA. Retrieved from www.nsf.gov/statistics/2018/nsf18304/static/report/nsf18304-report.pdf

Nye, J. (2002). *The paradox of American power.* Oxford: Oxford University Press.

Nyland, C., Forbes-Mewett, H., & Härtel, C. E. J. (2013). Governing the international student experience: Lessons from the Australian international education model. *Academy of Management Learning & Education, 12*(4), 656–673. http://doi.org/10.5465/amle.2012.0088

OECD. (2018). *Education at a glance 2018: OECD indicators.* Paris, France: OECD. Retrieved from www.oecd-ilibrary.org/education/education-at-a-glance-2018_eag-2018-en

Park, E., Klieve, H., Tsurutani, C., & Harte, W. (2017). International students' accented English— Communication difficulties and developed strategies. *Cogent Education, 4*(1), 1–15. http://doi.org/10.1080/2331186X.2017.1314651

Paton, M. J. (2007). Why international students are at greater risk of failure: An inconvenient truth. *International Journal of Diversity in Organizations, Communities and Nations, 6*(6), 101–111.

Perez-Encinas, A., & Ammigan, R. (2016). Support services at Spanish and US institutions: A driver for international student satisfaction. *Journal of International Students, 6*(4), 984–998. http://jistudents.org/

Pimpa, N. (2003). The influence of family on Thai students' choices of international education. *International Journal of Educational Management, 17*(5), 211–219.

Ploner, J. (2018). International students' transitions to UK Higher Education—revisiting the concept and practice of academic hospitality. *Journal of Research in International Education, 17*(2), 164–178. http://doi.org/10.1177/1475240918786690

Quinton, W. J. (2018). International students unwelcome on campus? Predictors of prejudice against international students. *Journal of Diversity in Higher Education* (Online First). http://doi.org/http://dx.doi.org/10.1037/dhe0000091

Reda, M. (2009). *Between speaking and silence: A study of quiet students.* Albany, NY: State University of New York Press.

Reynolds, A. L., & Constantine, M. G. (2007). Cultural adjustment difficulties and career development of international college students. *Journal of Career Assessment, 15*(3), 338–350. http://doi.org/10.1177/1069072707301218

Ritter, Z. S. (2016). International students' perceptions of race and socio-economic status in an American higher education landscape. *Journal of International Students, 6*(2), 367–393. http://jistudents.org/

Romerhausen, N. J. (2013). Strategies to enhance student success: A discourse analysis of academic advice in international student handbooks. *Journal of International Students, 3*(2), 129–139. http://jistudents.org/

Rose-Redwood, C., & Rose-Redwood, R. (2018). Fostering successful integration and engagement between domestic and international students on college and university campuses. *Journal of International Students, 8*(3), 2162–3104. http://doi.org/10.5281/zenodo.1254578

Rosenthal, D. A., Russell, J., & Thomson, G. (2008). The health and wellbeing of international students at an Australian university. *Higher Education, 55*(1), 51–67. http://doi.org/10.1007/s10734-006-9037-1

Sakurai, Y., Parpala, A., Pyhältö, K., & Lindblom-Ylänne, S. (2016). Engagement in learning: A comparison between Asian and European international university students. *Compare: A Journal of Comparative and International Education, 46*(1), 24–47.

Sawir, E., Marginson, S., Deumert, A., Nyland, C., & Ramia, G. (2008). Loneliness and international students: An Australian study. *Journal of Studies in International Education, 12*(2), 148–180. http://doi.org/10.1177/1028315307299699

Schmitt, M. T., Spears, R., & Branscombe, N. R. (2003). Constructing a minority group identity out of shared rejection: The case of international students. *European Journal of Social Psychology, 33*(1), 1–12. http://doi.org/10.1002/ejsp.131

ShanghaiRanking Consultancy. (2018). *Academic ranking of World Universities 2018.* Retrieved from www.shanghairanking.com/ARWU2018.html

Sherry, M., Thomas, P., & Chui, W. H. (2010). International students: A vulnerable student population. *Higher Education, 60*(1), 33–46. http://doi.org/10.1007/s10734-009-9284-z

Smith, R. A., & Khawaja, N. G. (2011). A review of the acculturation experiences of international students. *International Journal of Intercultural Relations.* http://doi.org/10.1016/j.ijintrel.2011.08.004

Smith, T. B., Bowman, R., & Hsu, S. (2007). Racial attitudes among Asian and European American college students: A cross-cultural examination. *College Student Journal, 41*(2), 436–443.

Southern Poverty Law Center (SPLC). (2016). Update: 1,094 bias-related incidents in the month following the election. Retrieved August 9, 2018, from www.splcenter.org/hatewatch/2016/12/16/update-1094-bias-related-incidents-month-following-election

Stein, S., & Andreotti, V. (2016). Cash, competition, or charity: International students and the global imaginary. *Higher Education, 72*(2), 225–239. http://doi.org/10.1007/s10734-015-9949-8

Su, M. (2018). Work a way out: Breaking monoethnic isolation through on-campus employment. *Journal of International Students, 8*(3), 1363–1385. http://doi.org/10.5281/zenodo.1254596

Times Higher Education. (2018). *World University rankings 2018.* Retrieved from www.timeshighereducation.com/world-university-rankings

United Nations Educational Scientific and Cultural Organisation. (2018). *Outbound internationally mobile students by host region.* Paris, France. Retrieved from http://data.uis.unesco.org

Urias, D., & Yeakey, C. C. (2009). Analysis of the US student visa system: Misperceptions, barriers, and consequences. *Journal of Studies in International Education, 13*(1), 72–109. http://doi.org/10.1177/1028315307308135

Van Horne, S., Lin, S., Anson, M., & Jacobson, W. (2018). Engagement, satisfaction, and belonging of international undergraduates at US research universities. *Journal of International Students, 8*(1), 351–374. http://doi.org/10.5281/zenodo.1134313

Volet, S. E., & Ang, G. (2012). Culturally mixed groups on international campuses: An opportunity for inter-cultural learning. *Higher Education Research & Development, 31*(1), 21–37. http://doi.org/10.1080/07294360.2012.642838

Wang, K. T., Heppner, P. P., Fu, C. C., Zhao, R., Li, F., & Chuang, C. C. (2012). Profiles of acculturative adjustment patterns among Chinese international students. *Journal of Counseling Psychology, 59*(3), 424–436. http://doi.org/10.1037/a0028532

Wilton, L., & Constantine, M. G. (2003). Length of residence, cultural adjustment difficulties, and psychological distress symptoms in Asian and Latin America international College Students. *Journal of College Counseling, 6*(2), 177–187.

Ye, L., & Edwards, V. (2015). Chinese overseas doctoral student narratives of intercultural adaptation. *Journal of Research in International Education, 14*(3), 228–241. http://doi.org/10.1177/1475240915614934

Yeh, C. J., & Inose, M. (2003). International students' reported English fluency, social support satisfaction, and social connectedness as predictors of acculturative stress. *Counselling Psychology Quarterly, 16*(1), 15–28. http://doi.org/10.1080/0951507031000114058

YouAreWelcomeHere.org. (2016). You are welcome here. Retrieved September 9, 2018, from www.youare welcomehereusa.org/read-me/

Yu, X., Isensee, E., & Kappler, B. (2016). Using data wisely to improve international student satisfaction: Insights gained from international student barometer. In K. Bista & C. Foster (Eds.), *Exploring the social and academic experiences of international students in higher education institutions* (pp. 212–232). Hershey, PA: IGI Global.

Zhang, J., & Goodson, P. (2011). Predictors of international students' psychosocial adjustment to life in the United States: A systematic review. *International Journal of Intercultural Relations, 35*(2), 139–162. http://doi.org/10.1016/j.ijintrel.2010.11.011

Zhang, Y., & Mi, Y. (2009). Another look at the language difficulties of international students. *Journal of Studies in International Education, 14*(4), 371–388. http://doi.org/10.1177/1028315309336031

Zhou, J., & Cole, D. (2017). Comparing international and American students: Involvement in college life and overall satisfaction. *Higher Education, 73*(5), 655–672. http://doi.org/10.1007/s10734-016-9982-2

Zhou, Y., Jindal-Snape, D., Topping, K., & Todman, J. (2008). Theoretical models of culture shock and adaptation in international students in higher education. *Studies in Higher Education, 33*(1), 63–75. http://doi.org/10.1080/03075070701794833

Chapter 8
Engaging Undocumented Students

Susana M. Muñoz

I think maybe the opposition that I, that I'm encountering is a lack of support from some of the administrators at the school. I know that I approached someone regarding career services and my colleague and I went up to him on the first day of orientation when he was talking about fellowships, and connecting with alumni. And we said, okay, that's great. How does that apply to us, because we're undocumented. And he sort of looked at us and said, I'm not sure. I'm going to go to a meeting and then we'll see. So I talked to him afterwards and I said, okay, so how did the meeting go? Oh, they basically told me that I'm on my own. And, I think I've asked maybe, maybe once again, and he just doesn't seem, I mean I'm sure he's incredibly busy, but he doesn't seem interested to do that research.

(Angelica, North Carolina, 2013)

The problem is when you go and talk to that same person who's a career development director, you go and ask them "What opportunity do you have for people who are undocumented?" They're like, well, what does that mean? And then you try to explain. They don't really understand . . . And you have this obviously very smart person, very talented, and very prepared person talking about career development for students, so to me its miscommunication. they make everything look so good about you being there, everything's going to work out. But when you actually approach someone and ask them about your situation, either there's structural barriers or they just simply don't know what's going on.

(Ariel, Chicago, 2013)

These excerpts from these undocumented college students depict how both approached student affairs administrators only to be met with apathy and dismissal, which reproduces sentiments of invisibility, loss of personhood, and indignation among undocumented students. Over the course of ten years, I have been working with and for undocumented college students in the areas of identity development, campus climate, and social activism. Time and time again, I hear from them that colleges and universities are swift in taking their tuition dollars but providing adequate and humane support has been slow or nonexistent. In this chapter, I highlight the educational policies that impact undocumented students' access to higher education, college persistence, and employability. I then discuss three theoretical frameworks: legal liminality, legal violence as a form of racist nativist microaggression, and undocufriendly campus climate model. I conclude by providing detailed strategies for college administrators and faculty to better support student engagement for undocumented students.

Education Policies and Undocumented College Students

The fight for educational and human rights for undocumented immigrants in the United States (US) spans many decades. In 1882, the Chinese Exclusionary Act was the first immigration policy passed, banning Chinese immigrants and other people of Asian descent from obtaining employment or establishing businesses, which provided the foundation for xenophobic policies to come by questioning who is deemed worthy of citizenship and who it not. The first time legal status was litigated in the US educational system was the *Plyer v. Doe* (1982) Supreme Court case, which set the precedent for undocumented students' access to education in the US, where they were given the right to a free public K–12 education. However, postsecondary education was not included in the case.

The DREAM Act

The Development, Relief, and Education for Alien Minors (DREAM) Act was the first legislature introduced in 2001 to provide immigrant young adults a pathway to citizenship if they met the following criteria: (1) entered into the United States before the age of 18; (2) lived in the US for at least four years; and (3) are admitted into a college or university, currently attending high school, or working towards a GED, all while passing a criminal background check. Unfortunately, on December 2010, the DREAM Act was filibustered on the Senate floor, and many speculate this failure was due to the lack of unification in the Democratic party (five Democrats voted against the bill) and the conservative side critiquing the DREAM Act as a mass amnesty bill; however, this filibuster ignited an entire community of activists who continue to fight for immigrant rights.

A number of immigration legislative policies have been heard in both the House and Senate chambers without much resolution. At the time of this writing (early 2019), many immigration advocates are pushing a "clean DREAM Act," which would create a pathway to citizenship without using young immigrants as political pawns or harming other immigrant communities in the process. A clean DREAM Act would mean no border wall funding or increased security along the border. On February 15, 2018, the Senate considered several proposals that would have provided a path to citizenship for the more than a million undocumented youth in the United States, but all failed to receive the 60 votes needed to proceed to the Senate.

State DREAM Acts

Individual states cannot grant citizenship status, but many have taken it upon themselves to create in-state tuition policies and state laws that provide in-state tuition (rather than the out-of-state price) for undocumented students who graduated from high school in that particular state. Texas (HB 1403) was the first state to pass an in-state tuition policy for undocumented students who have received the equivalent of a high school diploma, resided in the state within at least three years of the high school graduation date, and provided an affidavit stating that the individual will file an application to become a permanent resident at their earliest opportunity. Since then, 17 additional states (California, Colorado, Connecticut, Florida, Illinois, Kansas, Maryland, Minnesota, Nebraska, New Jersey, New Mexico, New York, Oklahoma, Oregon, Rhode Island, Utah, and Washington) allow undocumented students to pay the same college tuition as other in-state residents if they have attended and graduated from the state's high schools. However, some states, like Georgia, have restrictionist policies that ban undocumented students from admission to five of their selective institutions. In October 2010, the Georgia Board of Regents passed Policy 4.1.6 and Policy 4.3.4, which went into effect in the fall of 2011. Policy 4.1.6 bans undocumented students from applying to the state's top five public universities, and Policy 4.3.4 prohibits them from qualifying for in-state tuition rates at all public universities. These policies indicate that an undocumented person's locality and context matters in how they are able to access higher education.

Deferred Action for Childhood Arrivals (DACA)

On June 15, 2012, under the Obama Administration, the Deferred Action for Childhood Arrivals (DACA) program was created via executive order, allowing a temporary renewable status for undocumented persons who meet certain requirements to apply for a work permit. In theory, it allowed them the opportunity to remain in the country, work lawfully, continue their education or join the armed services, and not face deportation for that period of time. On September 5, 2017, the Trump Administration rescinded the executive order, placing 800,000 recipients at risk of losing their work permits and of deportation, which is indicative of the anti-immigrant sentiment with the Trump Administration. However, three federal judges have blocked the administration from ending DACA, ordering the Department of Homeland Security to continue renewing permits under the program. At the time of this writing (early 2019), people who have or have previously had DACA can apply to renew it. It is important to note that the immigration movement is about more than access to education; it is about fighting for the humane treatment of all immigrants. However, in the next section, I address issues pertaining to undocumented students and their access to higher education as well as their college experiences.

Challenges and Needs of Undocumented and DACA College Students

A recent report (Zong & Batalova, 2019) stated that approximately 98,000 undocumented students graduate from high school every year in the United States, which is a

50% increase from the early 2000s (Passel, 2006); between 200,000 and 225,000 undocumented immigrants are enrolled in US colleges and make up almost 2% of all college students (Suárez-Orozco et al., 2015). The challenges and needs of undocumented college students are well documented in the literature (Abrego, 2006; Buenavista, 2012; Chen & Rhoads, 2016; Garcia & Tierney, 2011; Muñoz & Maldonado, 2011; Muñoz, 2013, 2015; Muñoz & Vigil, 2018; Muñoz, Vigil, Jach, & Rodriguez-Gutierrez, 2018; Pérez, 2009; Pérez, 2011; Suárez-Orozco et al., 2015; Suárez-Orozco et al., 2015; Teranishi, Suarez-Orozco, & Suarez-Orozco, 2015); they include lack of financial aid, disclosure of legal status, and a campus climate hostile toward undocumented students.

Lack of Financial Aid Support

Context matters. Undocumented students who reside in states where they are able to attend higher education through an in-state tuition policy experience higher stop-out rates during their education trajectory than their native-born or permanent-resident counterparts (Terriquez, 2015). One reason may be the difficulty of paying tuition out of pocket due to the lack of a financial aid policy (Pérez Huber, 2010; Terriquez, 2015). Considering that the majority of undocumented families live below the poverty line due to low wages and employment instability (Diaz-Strong et al., 2011; Terriquez, 2015), college access and success are already challenging; on top of that, without a financial aid policy, the dream of completing a college degree becomes more difficult.

Without access to federal financial aid to attend college, many students are drawn to community colleges due to their affordability levels (Diaz-Strong et al., 2011; Kim & Chambers, 2015; Teranishi, Suárez-Orozco, & Suárez-Orozco, 2011; Terriquez, 2015), and although community colleges are an important option, students should have a choice of what type of institution they would like to attend. Community colleges can serve as gateways to four-year universities, yet structural barriers, such as lack of financial aid and student resources within community systems, lead to a tendency for students not to graduate on time and for schools not to have strong transfer and/or graduation rates (Teranishi et al., 2011; Terriquez, 2015). Yet navigating the educational system as an undocumented college student requires to disclosing their legal status, which poses the question "How do undocumented students come to know and understand the meaning behind their legality?"

Disclosure of Legal Status

Some undocumented students choose to be open and public about their immigration status while others find it difficult to share for various reasons (e.g., social context, stigma, personal trauma, or campus climate). My work (Muñoz, 2015) with and for community activists who self-identify as "undocumented and unafraid" reveals that undocumented students often lie about their status to school personnel or avoid speaking about their undocumented identity. These practices are part of the coping skills undocumented students employ to get through college, but they lead to high levels of stress and anxiety. Disclosure of legal status can be an empowering educational tool for students—one that is usually facilitated through peer solidarity groups as well as a sense of liberation, particularly around community organizing for immigrant rights (Muñoz, 2015, 2016; Nicholls, 2013; Seif, 2011). Angelica (from the earlier excerpt), who participated in the identity and social activists project, illuminates this by witnessing how the power of her community to stop deportation made her feel more powerful; she stated,

> To see that power that we have, that for me, it's very encouraging to see that after years of feeling powerless, feeling ashamed, and feeling afraid and to see people who have that courage and that belief and that conviction that they can do something and that they will do something.
>
> (Muñoz, 2015, p. 79)

In some instances, undocumented students are able to identify at least one institutional staff member whom they trust and who can help them throughout their academic journeys (Cervantes, Minero, & Brito, 2015). However, this requires faculty, staff, and administrators to also discourse themselves as allies and advocates.

Hostile Campus Climates

While having an inclusive campus environment helps all students thrive academically and socially (Hurtado, Ruiz Alvarado, & Guillermo-Wann, 2015; Museus & Jayakumar, 2012), it is important to recognize the particular needs of undocumented students and how a hostile campus environment may further marginalize this population. Some colleges and universities may have an overall institutional commitment to serving students around racial, socioeconomic, and gender diversity but often disregard legality as an area of need. Participants in Jauregui and Slate's (2009) study "felt institutions were not doing enough and more support could be provided" to undocumented students (p. 199). Additionally, undocumented students have to consider the political climate and the increase of deportations, which may create more fear and isolation for students and their families. This can put added mental health stress and heightened anxiety on students, which can be detrimental to their college trajectories.

Conceptual Frames for Undocumented Students

The usage of conceptual frames privy to the challenges and social constructs that interrogate legality are imperative to working with and for undocumented college students. The following section highlights four conceptual frames: legal liminality, legal consciousness, legal violence as a form of racist nativism, and the undocufriendly campus climate model.

Legal Liminality

The idea of "illegality" is a socially constructed image, which places immigrants as marginalized people based on the fluid interpretation of immigration laws. Thus, it is imperative to unpack the construct of "illegality" as a social, legal, and political nuanced practice, which reproduces and maintains systems of inequity in contemporary society

(De Genova, 2002; Muñoz, 2015). The concept of liminality is used by Menjívar (2006) to describe the temporariness and fluidity of legal status, which causes ambiguity and uncertainty. This is best described by the recent rescindment of DACA, which paused the application process for those who have reached the age to apply and perhaps resulted in current DACA recipients allowing their DACA status to lapse due to fear of reapplication. Legal liminality is determined by immigration policies and contexts, which shape how immigrants (documented and undocumented) are received by communities (Portes & Zhou, 1993). National and state immigration policies determine who stands inside or outside the law (or in between) and whether immigrants have access to opportunities and resources to fully participate in society (Menjívar, 2000). Liminality can be used as an analytic frame to understand the experiences of DACA and undocumented students in higher education to explore the degree of their tentativeness around their legal status.

Legal Consciouness

Legal consciousness is defined as a process in which an individual's lived experiences and sense of self are constructed, shaped, and influenced by the law or legal norms (Silbey, 2005). A heightened sense of legal consciousness is acquired by experiences within localities and immigration discourses that are often dictated by anti-immigration policies. Anzaldúa's (1987, 1999) notion of *la facultad* describes individuals who live in colonized spaces but choose to navigate rather than resist them. A point of rupture occurs in *la facultad* when one's consciousness opens, and experiences are perceived with a deeper understanding. The notion of "shifting" remains a constant element when Anzaldúa problematizes the conflict between one's cultural values and the values of the dominant culture. This produces the indigenous term "*nepantla*—living between multiple worlds or beliefs" (Calderon et al., 2012, p. 517).

In my previous work (Muñoz, 2018), I use these concepts to analyze how undocumented students come to understand their legal consciousness. In my findings, legal consciousness is negotiated through undocumented students' own understanding of their migration process through their family experiences; how their localities and contexts shape how they navigate disclosure of their status; and how social activism helped them develop critical legal consciousness, which is a heightened understanding of systemic inequities in the US immigration system, which are rooted in White supremacy.

Legal Violence as a Form of Racist Nativist Microaggression

Racist nativism situated within sociopolitical and sociohistorical contexts in the United States may infiltrate different communities of color, depending on who is being perceived as foreign through national political discourse (Pérez Huber, Benavides Lopez, Malagón, Velez, & Solórzano, 2008). Racist nativism connects race and immigration within the current sociohistorical and sociopolitical climate (Pérez Huber et al., 2008). Together, the concept of racist nativist microaggression illustrates the recurring and systemic "forms of racist nativism that are subtle, layered, and cumulative verbal and non-verbal assaults directed toward People of Color that are committed automatically and unconsciously" (Pérez Huber, 2011, p. 388). Racist nativist microaggressions can be used to highlight how everyday occurrences and institutional policies aimed at undocumented and DACA students create legal violence within the campus climate. The term *legal violence* considers the occurrences of harm that negatively impact the livelihood of immigrants and their cumulative effects. Menjívar and Abrego (2012) draw on structural and symbolic violence to contend that legal violence is the implementation of laws and policies that heighten social suffering. They use legal violence to illustrate how contemporary immigration laws "bring to the fore the complex manner in which the law exerts its influence and control . . . [and] the harmful effects of the law that can potentially obstruct and derail immigrants' paths of incorporation" (Menjívar & Abrego, 2012, p. 1383). In my prior work (Muñoz & Vigil, 2018), I use legal violence to illuminate how anti-immigration sentiments ingrained in US society are performed within the context of higher education. Our research highlights institutional ignorance, when administrators and faculty are oblivious to serving undocumented students or lack competencies to serve them; the reproduction of pervasive invisibility, when the undocumented are treated inhumanely or experience erasure of personhood as a result of non-acknowledgment; and how forms of support were hidden or not easily found at their institutions.

Undocufriendly Campus Climate Model

Suárez-Orozco et al.'s (2015) model of undocufriendly campus climates provides an ecological approach to understanding undocumented student experiences. It considers challenges and assets for undocumented students at the student level, the campus level, and the level of state and national policies. Suárez-Orozco et al.'s (2015) model provides concrete examples of the assets and challenges students experience within the microsystems of their daily experiences. Undocumented student challenges at the student level, for instance, include competing responsibilities, possible separation from family, and often first-generation status. Assets at the student level include academic resilience and civic engagement. The campus level considers institutional agent support systems and stressors over financing education, microaggressions, and lack of resources. Taking the microsystems together with the current political climate, this may impact the academic success and performance of undocumented college students.

Engagement Strategies for Working With and for Undocumented Students

It is concerning that administrators, staff, and faculty do not know about the needs and experiences of undocumented students, especially when administrators, staff, and faculty can be influential in making policies and practices to create humane spaces for undocumented students. Next, I offer some strategies for engagement.

- Disseminate knowledge. Campus administrators and faculty need to have accurate information and should provide and attend trainings on undocumented students as an entire unit or department; moreover, these trainings should be part of college-wide onboarding processes. Through these practices, colleges and universities can move beyond having one designated person as the sole holder of this knowledge and minimize the risk of losing that knowledge if that person leaves the institution.

- Fall orientation is an important time for undocumented students to gain understanding and knowledge about key allies and resources for their success. Conduct a welcome event where both students and allies can exchange knowledge and information about campus resources and services. Since many undocumented students never had access to health care or mental health services, they may not know that these services are part of their student fee plan. Colleges and universities should consider creating a first-year experience course for undocumented students, which would create community and provide students with knowledge and awareness of institutional support resources and policies.

- Faculty and administrators can work together intentionally to ensure that undocumented students and their families, despite their immigration status, feel welcomed into all spaces on campus. Creating a university committee to assess and specifically address barriers and challenges that undocumented students encounter can serve as a first step toward fostering a more inclusive campus environment. Representation from offices such as financial aid, admissions, legal services, and the counseling center are most prudent for this university committee.

- Faculty and administrators should keep in mind that the disclosure process is unique for each undocumented student. State, local, and institutional contexts can play a crucial role in whether a student chooses to disclose. For undocumented students, if disclosing their legal status to a campus entity or person is met with ambivalence or the person lacks the knowledge to support undocumented students, then they are unlikely to return to that particular office or person. The lack of institutionalized awareness of undocumented students contributes to their hesitation to disclose their legal status.

- Colleges and universities should consider ways to build solidarity groups among undocumented students—not only as a mechanism to gain and exchange knowledge among peers, but also as a way to establish a supportive presence on college and university campuses. It is important to note that not all undocumented students will be comfortable talking about their legal status, but colleges and universities need to provide space for those dialogues to transpire.

- Community organizations that assist immigrant families and youth can be an asset to colleges and universities. It is important for college administrators to understand their state resources and community entities that provide services to immigrant families, particularly when undocumented students move off campus and may not have a credit history for rent or utilities.

- Understand and address the systemic barriers that exist, depending on the state context. Colleges and universities need to be aware of the hurdles for students wanting to pursue majors that require state licensure. For instance, in April 2019, the State of Arkansas passed a bill that would allow DACA recipients to obtain their nursing licenses and pay in-state tuition. It is important to note that not all undocumented students qualify for DACA and thus may not be eligible for certain opportunities. Also noteworthy are the systemic barriers that exist in graduate school education for undocumented students. Often, financial aid is scarce for graduate students, and even when departments are able to award financial packages to undocumented students, being able to access these funds depends on state context, the funding source, and/or if the student has DACA.

Conclusion

I foresee that, under the Trump Administration, the educational plight of undocumented and DACA students will become more tumultuous. It is imperative that higher education institutions institutionalize practices and policies geared toward supporting the academic endeavors of this population. Colleges and universities must exemplify courage by leading efforts to reshape the dominant anti-immigrant narrative that permeates US society.

References

Abrego, L. J. (2006). "I can't go to college because I don't have papers": Incorporation patterns of Latino undocumented youth. *Latino Studies, 4*(3), 212–231.

Abrego, L. (2011). Legal consciousness of undocumented Latinos: Fear and stigma as barriers to claims making for first and 1.5 generation immigrants. *Law & Society Review, 45*(2), 337–369.

Anzaldúa, G. (1987). *Borderlands/La frontera: The new mestiza*. San Francisco, CA: Aunt Lute Books.

Anzaldúa, G. (1999). *Borderlands/La frontera: The new mestiza* (2nd ed.). San Francisco, CA: Aunt Lute Books.

Buenavista, T. L. (2012). Citizenship at a cost: Undocumented Asian youth perceptions and the militarization of immigration. *Asian American and Pacific Islander Nexus, 10*(1), 101–124.

Calderon, D., Delgado Bernal, D., Velez, V. N., Perez Huber, L., & Malagon, M. C. (2012). A Chicana feminist epistemology revisited: Cultivating ideas a generation later. *Harvard Educational Review, 82*(4), 513–539.

Cervantes, J. M., Minero, L. P., & Brito, E. (2015). Tales of survival 101 for undocumented Latina/o immigrant university students: Commentary and recommendations from qualitative interviews. *Journal of Latina/o Psychology, 3*(4), 1–15.

Chen, A. C., & Rhoads, R. A. (2016). Undocumented student allies and transformative resistance: An ethnographic case study. *The Review of Higher Education, 39*(4), 515–542.

De Genova, N. (2002). Migrant 'illegality' and deportability in everyday life. *Annual Review of Anthropology, 31*, 419–447.

Diaz-Strong, D., Gómez, C., Luna-Duarte, M. E., & Meiners, E. R. (2011). Purged: Undocumented students, financial aid policies, and access to higher education. *Journal of Hispanic Higher Education, 10*(2), 107–119. doi:10.1177/1538192711401917

Garcia, L. D., & Tierney, W. G. (2011). Undocumented immigrants in higher education: A preliminary analysis. *Teachers College Record, 113*(12), 2739–2776.

Hurtado, S., Ruiz Alvarado, A., & Guillermo-Wann, C. (2015). Creating inclusive environments: The mediating effect of faculty and staff validation on the relationship of discrimination/bias to students' sense of belonging. *Journal Committed to Social Change on Race and Ethnicity, 1*(1), 60–80.

Jauregui, J. A., & Slate, J. R. (2009). Texas borderland community colleges and views regarding undocumented students: A qualitative study. *Journal of College Student Retention, 11*(2), 183–210.

Kim. E., & Chambers, J. A. (2015). Undocumented immigrants and institutional admission policy transformation in a community college: Exploring policy-making and its consequences, community. *College Journal of Research and Practice, 39*(1), 55–69. doi: 10.1080/10668926.2013.838914

Muñoz, S. M., & Maldonado, M. M. (2011). Counterstories of college persistence by undocumented Mexicana students: Navigating race, class, gender, and legal status. *International Journal of Qualitative Studies in Education*, 1–23. doi:10.1080/09518398.2010.529850

Menjívar, C. (2000). *Fragmented Ties: Salvadoran Immigrant Networks in America*. Berkeley, CA: University of California Press.

Menjívar, C. (2006). Liminal legality: Salvadoran and Guatemalan immigrants' lives in the United States. *American Journal of Sociology, 111*(4), 999–1037.

Menjívar, C., & Abrego, L. (2012). Legal violence: Immigration law and the lives of Central American immigrants. *American Journal of Sociology, 117*(5), 1380–1421.

Muñoz, S. M. (2013). "I just can't stand being like this anymore": Dilemmas, stressors, and motivators for undocumented Mexican women in higher education. *Journal of Student Affairs Research and Practice, 50*(3), 223–249.

Muñoz, S. M. (2015). *Identity, social activism, and the pursuit of higher education: The journey of undocumented and unafraid community activists*. New York, NY: Peter Lang Publishing.

Muñoz, S. M. (2016). Undocumented and unafraid: Understanding the disclosure management process for undocumented college students and graduates. *Journal of College Student Development, 57*(6), 715–729.

Muñoz, S. M. (2018). Unpacking legality through la facultad and cultural citizenship: Critical and legal consciousness formation for politicized Latinx undocumented youth activists. *Equity & Excellence in Education, 51*(1), 78–91.

Muñoz, S. M., & Maldonado, M. M. (2011). Counterstories of college persistence by undocumented Mexicana students: Navigating race, class, gender, and legal status. *International Journal of Qualitative Studies in Education*, 1–23. doi:10.1080/09518398.2010.529850

Muñoz, S. M., & Vigil, D. (2018). Interrogating racist nativist microaggressions and campus climate: How undocumented and DACA college students experience institutional legal violence in Colorado. *Journal of Diversity in Higher Education, 11*(4), 451–466.

Muñoz, S. M., Vigil, D., Jach, E. M, & Rodriguez-Gutierrez, M. M. (2018). Unpacking resilience and trauma: Examining the "Trump Effect" in higher education for undocumented Latinx college students. *Association of Mexican American Educators Journal, 12*(3), 33–52. doi:10.24974/amae.12.3.405

Museus, S. D., & Jayakumar, U. M. (Eds.). (2012). *Creating campus cultures: Fostering success among racially diverse student populations*. London: Routledge.

Nicholls, W. J. (2013). *The DREAMers: How the undocumented youth movement transformed the immigration rights debate*. Stanford, CA: Stanford University Press.

Passel, J. S. (2006). *The size and characteristics of the unauthorized migrant population in the US* Washington, DC: Pew Hispanic Center. Retrieved from http://pewhispanic.org/files/reports/61.pdf

Pérez, W. (2009). *We are Americans: Undocumented students pursuing the American dream*. Sterling, VA: Stylus.

Pérez Huber, L. (2011). Discourse of racist nativist in California public education: English dominance as a racist nativist microaggressions. *Educational Studies, 47*, 379–401.

Pérez Huber, L., Benavides Lopez, C., Malagón, M., Velez, V., & Solórzano, D. (2008). Getting beyond the "symptom," acknowledging the "disease": Theorizing racist nativism. *Contemporary Justice Review, 11*(1), 39–51.

Pérez Huber, L. (2010). Using Latina/o critical race theory and racist nativism to explore intersectionality in the educational experiences of undocumented Chicana college students. *Educational Foundations, 24*(1), 77–96.

Portes, A., & Zhou, M. (1993). The new second generation: Segmented assimilation and its variants. *The Annals of the American Academy of Political and Social Science, 530*(1), 74–96.

Seif, H. (2011). "Unapologetic and unafraid": Immigration youth come out of the shadows. In C. A. Flanagan & B. D. Christens (Eds.), *Youth civic development: Work at the cutting edge. New Directions for Child and Adolescent Development, 134,* 59–75.

Silbey, S. S. (2005). After legal consciousness. *Annual Review of Law and Social Science, 1*(1), 323–368.

Suárez-Orozco, C., Katsiaficas, D., Birchall, O., Alcantar, C. M., Hernández, E., Garcia, Y., . . . Teranishi, R. T. (2015). Undocumented undergraduate on college campuses: Understanding their challenges and assets and what it takes to make an undocufriendly campus. *Harvard Educational Review, 85,* 427–463.

Teranishi, R. T., Suárez-Orozco, C., & Suárez-Orozco, M. (2011). Immigrants in community colleges. *The Future of Children, 21*(1), 153–169. http://dx.doi.org/10.1353/foc.2011.0009

Teranishi, R. T., Suarez-Orozco, C., & Suarez-Orozco, M. (2015). In the shadows of the ivory tower: Undocumented undergraduates and the liminal state of immigration reform. *The UndocuScholar Project.* Institute for Immigration, Globalization & Education, UCLA.

Terriquez, V. (2015). Dreams delayed: Barriers to degree completion among undocumented community college students. *Journal of Ethnic and Migration Studies, 41*(8), 1302–1323. doi:10.1080/1369183X.2014.968534

Zong, J., & Batalova, J. (2019). *Fact sheet: How many unauthorized immigrants graduate from US high schools annually.* Washington, DC: Migrant Policy Institute.

Chapter 9
Engaging Student Activists

Charles H. F. Davis III, Sy Stokes, and Demetri L. Morgan

Although a well-documented part of higher education's not-so-distant past, student activism has become increasingly visible on college and university campuses in the United States as well as abroad. For example, according to data from the Higher Education Research Institute (HERI) at the University of California, Los Angeles, the self-reported likelihood of protest participation among all entering first-year students reached a 50-year high in 2015 (Eagan, Stolzenberg, Bates, Aragon, & Rios-Aguilar, 2015). Additionally, the authors of the report published findings in which Black students, specifically, were twice as likely to participate in protest than their White counterparts. Still, we caution educators from misunderstanding these data points as a suggestion that activist participation is widely adopted by students on campus today. To the contrary, despite overall increases in participation, student activists still represent a relatively small number of students on campus (Cabrera, Matias, & Montoya, 2017). Students engaged in campus-based and broader sociopolitical change continue to have demonstrable impact on leading institutional and sociopolitical transformation. During the period between 2014 and 2016, students at more than 84 different postsecondary institutions in the United States (and 4 others in Canada) issued detailed demands for institutional change (Chessman & Wayt, 2016; Davis III, Ishimoto, Mustaffa, & Stokes, 2017). As Davis et al. (2017) also found, the demands were largely directed at issues related to campus racial climate, which included calls for requisite training to improve racial literacy among faculty, staff, and students; meaningful integration of racially diverse contributions to the curriculum; and an increase in the recruitment, hiring, and retention of faculty of color across academic fields and disciplines.

In this chapter, we contemplate higher education stakeholders' understanding of contemporary student activism and students as agents of social and institutional change. One notable difference from other student populations discussed in this book is the extent to which student activists are not necessarily defined by a shared *social* identity. Rather, in addition to *who* student activists are, which spans the entire spectrum of overlapping and intersecting identities, we posit student activists are primarily defined by their specific (and sometimes disruptive) political actions (e.g., campus canvassing, building or office occupation, and other forms of protest and demonstration), differentiating them from nonactivist students. Such a distinction is an important one, in part, because engaging student activists contains layers of complication in which accounting for high levels of heterogeneity and interactional diversity are necessary. We revisit this action-oriented framing further in later sections of this chapter.

We begin this chapter by offering a conceptual reframing of student activism within broader discourses regarding students' political and democratic participation. Next, we discuss the various historical and contemporary contexts within which student activists have and continue to engage in the work of transformative institutional and sociopolitical change. Then we discuss useful frameworks for understanding relatively new technological tools employed by contemporary student activists, as well as the measurable impact(s) of activist participation on the emotional and mental health of students. Finally, we offer a series of practical recommendations for college and university faculty, student affairs professionals, and others to engage and support student activists as allies and accomplices in their work.

Student Activism and Political Engagement

Within higher education discourses, student activism and political engagement (i.e., established and accepted forms of political participation in electoral politics) are commonly framed as wholly oppositional (Morgan & Davis 2019). However, in this chapter we offer a reframing of previous dichotomous understandings of the two related phenomena. We first define each concept in relation to the extant higher education literature. Then, building on the aforementioned definitions, we offer a new conceptual frame for understanding contemporary student political engagement within a broader arrangement of political activities, on campus and beyond.

Defining Student Activism

When consulting the fragmented higher education literature on student activism across the decades, determining a singular definition remains challenging. Like other concepts in the study of higher education, student activism suffers from a definitional dilemma in which rival epistemologies often compete on the grounds of what constitutes "authentic" and "legitimate" activism (Altbach, 1989; Biddix, 2014; Kezar, 2010). This has become especially challenging as broadening access to internet communication technologies (ICTs), which are now commonly used by student activists, continues to grow and become more complex. Recently, however, Cabrera et al. (2017) offered a broad set of premises to consider when attempting to understand *what* student activism is rather than *how* it is done. Among the theoretical underpinnings offered, Cabrera et al. (2017) posit the following premises about student activism:

1. Student activism involves an intentional, sustained connection to a larger collective.
2. Student activism involves developing and exercising power.
3. Even though student activism seeks to change the political landscape, it is not the same as political governance (or campaigning) (pp. 404–405, 408).

For the purposes of this chapter, what is most useful from Cabrera et al. (2017) is the precise delineation between activism and other forms of political work. The genesis of this framing was likely to ensure passive political actions, particularly those in online venues and often with little or no associated risk (i.e., advocacy and Slacktivism; see also Gladwell, 2010; Morozov, 2009), are not misunderstood as activist actions. However, with the exception of Cabrera et al.'s third premise, the matter of *how* activism falls in relation to ideas and concepts within broader conceptual frameworks of political engagement and activity remains relatively undiscussed. Before discussing such a relation, it is helpful to first offer some definitional clarity as to what is meant by political engagement.

Conceptualizing Political Engagement

One frequently cited definition refers to political engagement as "activity that has the intent or effect of influencing government action—either directly by affecting the making or implementation of public policy or indirectly by influencing the selection of people who make the policies" (Verba, Scholzman, & Brady, 1995, p. 38). Verba et al.'s use of the operative phrase "government action" has largely limited our understanding of what can and therefore should be considered political engagement to the formal and accepted means of political participation (e.g., voting, campaigning, and other forms of electoral politics) (Morgan & Davis 2019). As a result, myriad practices within and adjacent to these formal political process (e.g., activism) have largely remained without consideration as means of political participation—a lack of consideration despite the documented evidence to the contrary. For example, various processes of sociopolitical change—including processes in postsecondary contexts—often begin with issuing public (or private) demand(s). Through organized and strategic direct action (i.e., protest or demonstration), a key tactical element of any social movement repertoire (Tilly, 2004), demands are offered as both diagnosis and prognosis of asymmetrical power relations between dominant and subordinated groups. Therefore, we invite readers to consider student activism within a more expansive conceptualization of political engagement. In so doing, also consider the broader banner of civic and community-based learning, which are high-impact practices (Kuh, 2008), and how much political work often traverses the boundaries of campus and community. In an effort to reconcile the dialectical tension presented by the aforementioned differences in definition, we further invite readers to consider student activism within our more expansive definition.

Student Activism as Political Engagement

While the aforementioned sections engage activism and political engagement on a relatively discrete basis, our shared perspective is that the two must no longer be considered separate. Instead, activism and traditional political work should be understood in dialectical relation to each other. This bringing together of ostensibly separate dimensions of the broader political universe is not entirely new. In fact, two decades ago, Rhoads (1998) introduced an important and timely reframing of campus-based student activism as a distinct form of democratic participation. Rhoads encouraged higher education stakeholders to reconsider the predominant dichotomous framing of activism and traditional (and accepted) forms of political participation (e.g., voting and other forms of electoral politics). Specifically, Rhoads wrote:

> The efforts of diverse students to forge their own place in campus life through organized demonstrations may also be understood as a form of participatory democracy. Thus, [student activism and unrest] instead may be understood as democracy playing itself out, as diverse students seek to build a truly multicultural society through the colleges and universities they inhabit.
>
> (p. 623)

However, higher education researchers have largely continued advancing a discourse in which activism is considered separate from larger arrangements of political participation by college and university students. A recent exception includes the recent work of Morgan and Davis (2019), in which they explicitly argue for returning to and expanding upon Rhoads's (1998) earlier contribution. In particular, the authors posit student political engagement as a symbiotic process in which the often-disruptive practices undertaken by student activists (i.e., protest, demonstration, and assembly) and other democratic practices mutually constitute one another in a dialectical configuration and exist "within a broad and expansive arrangement of political activities on-campus and beyond" (Morgan & Davis 2019, p. xvii). A key demarcation from Rhoads, which should not be overlooked, is Morgan and Davis' (2019) reference to political engagement *beyond* college and university campuses. We further elucidate the implications of this departure from Rhoads's campus-based framing later. First, however, we broadly discuss the historical antecedents and contemporary contexts of student activism in college.

Historical and Contemporary Issues of Student Activism in the United States

Among the long-standing concerns at the foundation of student-organized resistance—and indeed organized resistance more broadly—are various systems and relationships of power. Broadly speaking, these concerns are related to intersecting issues of systemic and structural bias, prejudice, discrimination, and oppression (e.g., racism, sexism, heterosexism, classism, ableism, religious minoritization). More acutely, however, collectives and coalitions of students engaged in activism also recognize their subaltern structural position as temporary, often transient members of college and university communities (Chesler & Crowfoot, 2010). These compounding experiences and positions of marginality are often key motivating factors for activist participation, especially among students multiply marginalized by systems of oppression (e.g., women of color whom experience both racism and sexism) and/or exploited within higher education (Broadhurst & Martin, 2014; Hurtado, 1992; Linder & Rodriguez, 2012; Renn, 2007).

Given the very nature of how power is structured and consolidated at many postsecondary institutions in the United States, which remain overwhelmingly governed and presided over by affluent, White, and/or male leadership, contentions with institutional power by student activists remain a permanent fixture of postsecondary life. Although greater visibility over the last decade may suggest to some the idea that student activism is relatively new or simply a trend, student activism is as old as higher education itself (Moore, 1997). For example, historians, social scientists, and higher education scholars have long examined student protest, demonstration, campaigns, and movements for social justice issues (Astin, Astin, Bayer, & Bisconti, 1975; Astin et al., 1975; Brax, 1981; Carson, 1995; Moore, 1997; Rhoads, 1998; Rudy, 1996; Vellela, 1988). From the "first student movement" in the 1930s (Brax, 1981), which largely focused on labor exploitation and US involvement (and investment) in war, to the "Golden Era" of protest for civil rights and civil liberties during the 1950s and 1960s, student activism has proven an important indicator of broader sociopolitical discord as well as campus climate issues of the respective eras.

Take, for instance, the work of the Student Nonviolent Coordinating Committee (SNCC), which was founded at Shaw University through the convening power of Ella Baker, a Shaw alumna and executive secretary of the Southern Christian Leadership Conference. The work undertaken by SNCC to register Black voters in Mississippi, which was assisted by volunteer White students from colleges and universities across the US, reflected the need to address the long-standing disenfranchisement of Black citizens from the electoral process and everyday American life (Carson, 1995). During the same period, as many postsecondary institutions were only *beginning* to integrate Black students (and the perspectives of non-White scholars) into their socioacademic environments, such disenfranchisement was also widely reflected on campuses. As such, student activists also were engaged, simultaneously, in campus-based efforts to assuage the impacts and reproduction of injustice in their classrooms, sports teams, residence halls, and governing organizations.

Building on this legacy, contemporary student activists continue to advocate and organize against persistent forces that dismiss, subjugate, and do harm to minoritized and marginalized people. In many ways, student activists at the intersection of campus and community continue to function as frontline political actors in transformative periods of sociopolitical and institutional histories. However, student activists encounter various risks and challenges contending with hierarchical power. As educators, we should not romanticize activist participation (or encourage students to do so). It is important to familiarize ourselves with the documented and possible consequences to which student activists are subjugated in their quest to improve their intersecting lifeworlds as students and people. For example, in reflecting on the aforementioned work of SNCC organizers (and their accomplices), consider the intense racial animus and violent terrorism experienced by student activists attempting to register Black voters in the Deep South. Related, during the SNCC Freedom Rides to resist *de facto* segregation of interstate buses, many student activists (Black and White) were arrested by White police and violently beaten by collectives of White citizens at various stops along the interstate route.

Similar, but different, the use of force by police to intimidate, disrupt, and even violently assault student activists has continued. Let us consider that less than a decade ago, university police in riot gear pepper-sprayed student activists conducting a nonviolent protest at the University of California, Davis (Maira & Sze, 2012). More recently, at Ohio State University in 2016, student activists engaged in a sit-in outside the university president's office were threatened by the administration with expulsion and forcible removal and arrest by campus police for continuing to exercise their right to peaceably assemble (Herner, 2016). At the University of Florida, student protestors expressing their opposition to the presence of hate speech on campus were among those shot at by nonstudent attendees following White supremacist Richard Spencer's address (Levenson, Brannon, Fortney, & Baker, 2007). Lastly, and most notably, the violent clash after White nationalists first confronted student activists on the University of Virginia campus and later marched through Charlottesville, Virginia, in August 2017 left three dead and dozens more injured (Hart & Danner, 2017). Each of the aforementioned examples alludes to various challenges and risks facing contemporary student activists. Additionally, those risks, like student activism, are traversing various contexts within which organized resistance takes place on campus and beyond. Next, we explore those contexts and offer analyses for educators to consider in their attempts to better understand and co-navigate these contexts with the student activists they support. Thereafter, we provide some theoretical and conceptual sense making of other psychosocial needs and opportunities for supporting student activists.

Ecological Contexts of Student Activism

The spaces and places in which students engage in various forms of activism are many and varied. In particular, while sites of student activist participation may be centered on college and university campuses, many students engaged in activism often do so well beyond campus boundaries. Here, these contexts are described to illuminate both the singular and multiple milieus in which contemporary student activism takes shape. Educators should be particularly attentive to the off-campus and digital landscapes in which new and social media play a substantive part in student political engagement. By attentive, we are not merely suggesting a heightened awareness of these contexts, but consideration for educators to similarly traverse the expanded boundaries of where students experience postsecondary life.

Student Activism on Campus

Perhaps the most commonly understood context within which student activism occurs is the college or university campus. This context broadly refers to the relatively predetermined boundaries of a campus within which many students live, work, and learn. This includes, but should not be limited to, administrative buildings, classrooms and other curricular spaces, cultural and other student resource centers, libraries, residence halls, sports stadiums and arenas, student unions and quadrangles, and other socioacademic spaces. Given the contextual limitation of campus spaces, the aforementioned often serve as both incubators for and sites of student activism. For example, racially minoritized students within a residence hall might use common areas or study rooms to host organizing meetings wherein they discuss how to respond to incidents of racism *within* their hall. Similarly, women students may meet in the campus women's center or space provided by the gender and women's studies department to bravely discuss issues of campus sexual violence and predatory behaviors undertaken by physicians at the university's health center. However, these efforts are often also connected to broader movements within contexts off and away from campus. As such, student activists continue to leave campus to engage in political activities in nearby public spaces and surrounding communities.

Activist Participation Beyond the "City Limits"

Davis III (2015, 2019) has encouraged higher education researchers to shift their analytical gaze in the study of student activism in college to include the activist experiences, relationships, and resources derived from settings off and away from campus. As was evident in student activist participation of the past, contemporary student activists continue to traverse the spatial boundaries of postsecondary life to engage with broader movements. For example, both in addition to and separate from campus protest, students continue to be a substantive part of today's overlapping social movements against police brutality and state violence, separation of immigrant families, sexual violence, and other such macro-level political issues. In some cases, these issues are recontextualized by finding connections between the lives of everyday people and students' own lives on campus. As but one example, consider the precarious circumstances facing undocumented youth and their families in the United States, particularly related to access to services and resources reserved for documented citizens. A broad-based movement built around the stories and lived experiences of children born to undocumented immigrant parents in (or brought by them to) the United States, affectionately known as DREAMers, also included college and university students. The identifier of DREAMers referenced those who would have been affected by the Development, Relief, and Education for Alien Minors Act (DREAM Act), which was first introduced in 2001 as a pathway to citizenship but continuously failed to be ratified by the US Senate.

This broader movement provided a foundation for undocumented students organizing in US colleges and universities, especially around issues of college affordability and access to financial aid, campus/public safety (from deportation), and student health services. As issues decidedly situated at the intersection of campus and community, undocumented students were simultaneously raising campus awareness and demanding broader governmental action (e.g., renewal of the Deferred Action on Childhood Arrivals program) to ensure their own safety as well as that of their communities. However, as many educators have attempted to make sense of and respond to the demands of undocumented student activists on campus, too few have broadened their scope of understanding (or experience) to include the everyday lives of undocumented people. This includes the extent to which educators, in supporting student activists, could make space for lifeworlds, worldviews, and the families of the undocumented students they teach, advise, and support.

Social Media and Student Activism Online

Similarly, student affairs educators should shift their observations and understanding of student participation in activism to include their involvement in the emerging digital landscape of alternative and activist new media projects (Lievrouw, 2011) online. Rhoads (1998) signaled student activists' turn toward digital strategies and tactics in reference to the work of the Free Burma Coalition in the late 1990s. That work was continued by Biddix (2008), who examined the roles early social media technologies offered a growing site of possibility for communications efforts in relation to increasing awareness and raising support for students' causes. For example, in 2013 at the University of California, Los Angeles, Sy Stokes and other Black male undergraduates released a video on YouTube entitled "Black Bruins." The video, moderated by Stokes's spoken word art, decried the stark racial inequities in enrollment and student success outcomes experienced by Black male undergraduates, especially their overrepresentation on UCLA's men's basketball and football teams. A scathing public indictment of persistent racism in US higher education, the video went viral, receiving more than one million views online and becoming the subject of higher education news for weeks. Similar online campaigns were waged by others at Harvard (#ITooAmHarvard), wherein Black students recounted their racialized experiences in Cambridge through a collection of digital photos and videos aggregated using social media hashtags and through the campaign's website.

The aforementioned examples of digital activism cannot and should not be reduced by educators to lesser forms of political engagement. In fact, as Lievrouw (2011) articulates, many forms of digital activism and new media projects are decidedly political and impactful in their own right. Nevertheless, digital activism by students is also rooted in on-the-ground efforts (Hope, Keels, & Durkee, 2016), which are merely replicated and amplified using new and social media technologies to organize, mobilize, and document efforts of their resistance. Therefore, it is important for educators to be familiar with and even participatory in these digital spaces. While doing so could ultimately aid and assist student organizers in taking strategic action online, it also serves as a site for receiving up-to-date information regarding students' concerns and desires for greater institutional accountability.

While there are numerous theories and concepts useful for better understanding *what* activism is and *how* activism is done, we turn to those most related to understanding the impact of activism and activist participation on students' psychosocial well-being. In particular, we first engage the role of fatigue as experienced by student activists. Then we offer educators a consideration for understanding student activism as part and parcel of the broader developmental project of critical consciousness in which college and university educators are involved. More specifically, we turn our attention to the production of critical hope as at least one important outcome of student participation in activism.

Activist and Social Justice Advocacy Fatigue

The foundational research concerning experiences with "burnout" was in workplace settings (Freudenberger, 1974; Heinemann & Heinemann, 2017). The concept was later adopted by Gomes and Maslach (1991), who reapplied the concept in the context of laboring for social justice. In their conceptualization, social justice work contains unique characteristics that make activists especially vulnerable to psychological distress. Activists' work, they argue, "involves cultivating and maintaining awareness of large and overwhelming social problems, often carrying a burden of knowledge that society as a whole is unable or unwilling to face" (Gomes & Maslach, 1991, p. 43). Thus, Gomes and Maslach (1991) condense activist burnout into three key parts: (1) exhaustion, the feelings of lethargy and helplessness that lead to discouragement to proceed with the activist work; (2) cynicism, the detachment from the work as a psychological defense mechanism to protect oneself from further mental trauma; and (3) inefficacy, the feeling of a lack of achievement, which leads to doubts about self-worth.

Although there is significant research related to activist burnout in a general sense (Chen & Gorski, 2015; Givens, 2016; Gorski, 2015; Gorski & Chen, 2015; Hope, Velez, Offidani-Bertrand, & Durkee, 2017; Moane, 2006; Rodgers, 2010; Szymanski & Lewis, 2015; Vaccaro & Mena, 2011), there is a considerable dearth of literature that specifically focuses on postsecondary student activists. Stokes and Miller (2019) sought to fill this gap by exploring the concept of activist burnout through a case study analysis of Black undergraduate student activists at the University of California, Los Angeles (UCLA). They found that experiences of Black student activists at UCLA aligned with Gomes and Maslach's (1991) three key parts of activist burnout, but many of their experiences were also student specific. For example, Stokes and Miller (2019) also found that, along with feelings of cynicism, exhaustion, and inefficacy, Black students felt a distrust in university leadership, a declining sense of belonging on their predominantly White campus, and racial battle fatigue (Smith, Allen, & Danley, 2007). By racial battle fatigue, Smith et al. (2007) are broadly referring to the physiological and psychological strain experienced by racially minoritized groups as well as the severe drain of socioemotional energy in an effort to cope with racial microaggressions and other overt experiences of racial trauma. In conjunction with general experiences of activist burnout, student activists of color experience a compounded sense of exhaustion by not merely fighting for racial justice, but also living with the socioemotional and material consequences of racism every day. The consequences are innumerable but include experiences of dissociation, emotional numbness, anxiety, nihilism and despair, and heightened stress, all of which can have a significant effect on student well-being, sense of belonging, and overall student success (Smith et al., 2007). Using Stokes and Miller's (2019) analysis as a point of departure, we next explore what is required from institutional agents to better support student activists further.

Freirian Praxis and Critical Hope

The concept of "critical hope" derives from Paulo Freire's (1970) *Pedagogy of the Oppressed*, in which he describes what is necessary to reject the ideological intent of domineering forms of education. Rather than depending on the mechanisms of an oppressive society to create an equitable social and political order, he argues that a critical consciousness is required on an interpersonal level to achieve such an endeavor. Thus, critical hope is not predicated on a naïve hope that the dominant elites will relinquish their authoritarian positions and abandon their oppressive practices. Rather, critical hope is achieved when education is perceived as a practice of freedom (Freire, 1970). Freire describes the importance of considering liberation as praxis:

> Liberation is a praxis: the action and reflection of men and women upon their world in order to transform it. Those truly committed to the cause of liberation can accept neither the mechanistic concept of consciousness as an empty vessel to be filled, nor the use of banking methods of domination (propaganda, slogans—deposits) in the name of liberation.
>
> (p. 79)

Bozalek, Liebowitz, Carolissen, and Boler (2014) delineate two ways that critical hope can be utilized: 1) "as a unitary and unified concept which cannot be disaggregated into either *hopefulness* or *criticality*" (p. 1), and 2) as an analytical concept that recognizes the political, intellectual, and spiritual aspects of critical hope (i.e., critical empathy, aspirations towards social flourishing and alleviating social injustices that induce human suffering; reevaluation of the present through historical scrutiny, a concern with power relations and their impact on marginality, and; the importance of solidarity). Quaye (2007), Bozalek et al. (2014), and Grain and Lund (2016) emphasize the importance of approaching social justice through a transnational lens. Quaye (2007) posits that through activism, students are able to cultivate their voices, actively listen to and learn about the perspectives of their peers, and realize their connection to a global society. Social justice issues are thus reframed as nonlinear phenomena that are experienced by a multitude of marginalized student populations, resulting in a sense of shared purpose when engaging in student activist work. Thus, utilizing critical hope as a function of activism subsequently enriches students' academic engagement and mitigates feelings of nihilism. Similarly, Grain and Lund (2016) explored how critical hope can be utilized as a tool for social justice service learning by promoting global solidarity against structural forms of oppression. By amalgamating *hopefulness*—a core human value that can serve as a catalyst for social and political action—and *criticality*—a counterhegemonic approach to analyzing and disassembling systemic forms of oppression—students and educators can effectively respond to issues within an oppressive social and political landscape (Grain & Lund, 2016).

In using Freire's concept as a component of our conceptual framework, we turn once more to Quaye's (2007) interpretation of critical hope in the context of student activism. Quaye (2007) describes how "critical hope is not based in a naïve belief that racism, sexism, classism, and other unjust practices can be easily extinguished; instead, it is anchored in the belief that by challenging inequitable behaviors, college students can work to improve their circumstances and those of their current and future peers" (p. 3). A core tenet of critical hope is that it is an ongoing process, one that rejects the evaluative rigidity and welcomes solution-oriented critique for the purpose of achieving a grandiose goal of equity and justice. Rather than allowing oneself to be engulfed by cynicism throughout the tumultuous and seemingly indelible process of pursuing social justice work, critical hope provides a blueprint for resilience by providing a space for peace and affirmation. "Hope . . . does not consist in crossing one's arms and waiting. As long as I fight, I am moved by hope; and if I fight with hope, then I can wait" (Freire, 1970, p. 92).

By using critical hope as a counterbalance to the realities of burnout and fatigue experienced by student activists broadly, and minoritized student activists more specifically, educators have the opportunity to develop and enact socioemotional interventions that interrupt the likely consequences of activist participation. Doing so might also provide a frame for educators to support students in their own experiential sense making, identity development, and overall approaches to social justice praxis. This is particularly important given the implications of student activist burnout and its contribution to the always already-persistent issues of minoritized student recruitment, retention, attrition, and academic success. What is more, as entering first-year students become increasingly exposed to participation in activism prior to enrolling, it is likely student activists will exhibit some symptoms of burnout earlier in their collegiate tenure.

Student Engagement Strategies

In order to support the complex diversity of participants in student activism, on campus and beyond, several strategies are helpful within the context of today's sociopolitical climate. In addition, employing multiple engagement strategies in conjunction rather than in isolation is strongly recommended. As such, we encourage educators to use the strategies offered here as a point of departure for developing their systems and protocols. In so doing, we also encourage educators to use these approaches in close relation to Quaye and Harper's (2015) comprehensive analysis of how to serve students across difference as well as other population-specific (e.g., women of color students) engagement strategies included in this volume. Again, student activists include a broad range of minoritized student populations (as well as their allies and accomplices) and are not reducible to any one social identity or affinity group.

Listening to Student Activists

While it may be considered obvious or even pedestrian to suggest listening to student activists as an engagement strategy, it is perhaps the most overlooked strategy for many campus administrators. In part, administrators are often looking for how to stop disruption or "bad press" quickly through top-down exertions of power. This forecloses opportunities to take more human-centered approaches to building relationships with communities of student activists who, primarily, want to have their grievances heard. Instead of simply prejudging and making assumptions about student activists, which may be based on our own biases and political or ideological differences, actively listening to their concerns while also seeking to understand the underlying issues is critically important. At least one benefit of listening *before* responding is that it signals to student activists that their feelings of concern are valid. An openness to receiving student activists rather than penalizing them as a primary course of action also signals the institution is committed to addressing the issues rather than silencing and suppressing activists.

Intersectional Praxis

Supporting today's student activists, although also important for any generation, requires a more complicated understanding of intersectionality as a solidarity politic (Hancock, 2011). Intersectionality emerges from the work of Kimberlé Crenshaw (1989, 1991), which focuses on how Black women's lives were uniquely forged at the intersection of multiple systems of oppression (i.e., racism and sexism). Building upon that work, Hancock (2011) offers a useful framework for understanding how intersectionality, too, is an important politic for millennials, many of whom are college students. In part, to engage student activists of today, one cannot focus on a single-issue framework for understanding what is most important to disrupters and resisters. Instead, educators should understand that the very concerns about which students are advocating are not single issues because students do not live single-issue lives, and they are increasingly aware of and have language to articulate how political intersectionality can impact which interests are prioritized. As Crenshaw notes, political intersectionality occurs when the political movements working towards justice for different, often separate, groups (e.g., feminism and anti-racism) interact to exclude or marginalize the interests of some subset of the groups, thereby reinforcing another form of injustice. For example, a focus on racial equity and racial justice by college student activists has the opportunity to advance the concerns of Black students in the aggregate. However, a failure to intentionally and deliberately account for the unique concerns of Black women students, Black LGBTQ students, and Black students with disabilities could easily yield demands that seek to only improve the conditions affecting heterosexual, able-bodied, cisgender Black men. Similarly, a focus on issues of sexual violence by student activists, who are primarily women, could just as easily account for and address the raceless concerns of White women students without acknowledging the converging systems of racism and sexism affecting racially minoritized women on campus.

Co-curricular Learning Opportunities

Consider how various programs and courses may offer opportunities for students to engage in understanding and developing strategies and tactics of social change. Although some, but far from most, civic engagement and service learning–style programs are considered spaces in which student activists can develop social justice identities, these sites are often more about advocacy than activism. To be clear, while these programs can and do assist student activists in their development at a broad political level, other co-curricular spaces outside the classroom (e.g., student resource centers and local community meeting spaces) are necessary for deeper and more transformative work. By deep and transformative work, we are referring to opportunities for student activists to explore the root causes of injustice, on campus and elsewhere, as well as to devise strategic and tactical plans for taking action to transform those conditions. Such opportunities can and should be built into existing programs intended to support the political development and engagement of students concerned with social and institutional change. This ensures that student activists are not required, even if encouraged, to seek such development *in addition* to their existing course-related and co-curricular commitments. However, other options could be considered, such as political education–themed wings as living-learning communities in residence halls.

Mental Health Services and Counseling Support

Our analysis of student activist burnout and racial battle fatigue calls for an institutional commitment to mental health services and support that is specifically intended for student activists. Although the support services do not have to be exclusively activist oriented, mental health professionals on campus must, at the very least, have a baseline understanding of the emotional and psychological demands of student activism. Building from Stokes and Miller's (2019) case study, mental health professionals have to be aware of potential feelings of nihilism, exhaustion, distrust in university leaders, declining sense of belonging, and battle fatigue that many student activists face. In turn, mental health professionals should validate student activists when engaging in conversations about this student-specific form of burnout.

The political climate following the election of Donald Trump to the United States presidency has resulted in student activism becoming increasingly racialized. Thus, mental health services must also be able to accommodate a racially diverse population of student activists. According to a study conducted by Nickerson, Helms, and Terrell (1994), Students of Color maintained a level of distrust for White counselors when seeking mental health support from Counseling and Psychological Services (CAPS) on their campus. The authors found that Black students believed the services rendered by White counselors would be less relevant, impactful, and gratifying (Nickerson et al., 1994). There are severe ramifications for these types of insufficiencies that result in academic, emotional, and psychological fractures—a decrease in retention rates (Bonner II & Bailey, 2006), self-harm (Wang, Nyutu, & Tran, 2012), hesitancy to utilize/underutilization of counseling services on campus (Davis & Swartz, 1972; Francis & Horn, 2016), and poor mental health (Duncan & Johnson, 2007). Therefore, a focused commitment to providing support services for student activists must also consider how race impacts their mental health needs.

Faculty and Staff Support and Solidarity

Agua and Pendakur (2019) provide five primary skills for student affairs educators and other higher education staff to develop to effectively serve their students: (1) emotional resilience; (2) authenticity in performativity; (3) values communication; (4) counterpositioning; and (5) rectifying discriminatory practices and policies. Two of these five primary skills—counterpositioning and rectifying discriminatory policies and practices—are especially important for engaging with student activists. Counterpositioning refers to how student affairs educators are subject to a perpetual dilemma of either serving the institutional interests on one end or serving student demands on the other (Agua & Pendakur, 2019). Shifting prioritization to either group can be negatively perceived by the oppositional side. However, rather than trying to balance or compromise between the two, Agua and Pendakur (2019) ask that higher education professionals shift from a "student versus institution" perspective to a "students *and* administrators versus institutional oppression" approach. According to the authors, this proposed shift can mediate mounting tensions between student activists and the institution while also signaling a collective commitment to improving the campus climate.

The second activist-centered skill, rectifying discriminatory policies and practices, is a bit more complex. It asks student affairs educators to challenge the discriminatory policies and practices of the institution that are often enforced by administrators (Agua & Pendakur, 2019). In many ways, it is the greatest signal to student activists that they are supported not only as students, but also as political agents seeking institutional change. Understandably, the efficacy of this particular skill is challenged by power dynamics and organizational hierarchies in one's institution, which can be more difficult to navigate for early-career professionals. For example, a Latinx program coordinator in a campus cultural center might be more reluctant to challenge long-standing discriminatory policies for fear of retribution from a supervisor or senior institutional leader. Whereas a White, tenured sociology professor may not need to be as apprehensive due to their job security and protections under academic freedom. To be sure, most higher education professionals working to support student activists will inevitably be met with seemingly conflicting professional decisions. Although levels of risk will vary, it is still important to act in solidarity with student activists against discriminatory policies and practices whenever possible. As Kezar (2010) has argued, mobilizing for social and institutional change is most effective when higher education professionals collaborate and conspire with student activists.

Conclusion

Contemporary student activists often arrive on campus with either a predisposition to or previous experience with participating in efforts to enable social change, if not both. They represent a complex, heterogeneous group inclusive of all populations of students from margins to center. However, minoritized students remain most likely to participate—and remain at highest risk for retribution for participating—in activism on campus. Student activists are increasingly engaged in political activities off and away from campus, including those online. Thus, the aforementioned engagement strategies are offered with these considerations in mind. These strategies are also intended to shift the perspective of educators from being committed to interventions that may suppress student voices to investing in a collective commitment to addressing the issues underlying student activism. Policies and practices that move away from retributive and punitive responses and toward human-centered approaches of rectification and reconciliation are key to supporting student activists.

References

Agua, J., & Pendakur, S. (2019). From resistance to resilience: Transforming institutional racism from the inside out. In C. H. F. Davis III & D. Morgan. (Eds.), *Student engagement, student services, and supporting student activists*. New York, NY: Routledge.

Astin, A. W., Astin, H. S., Bayer, A. E., & Bisconti, A. S. (1975). *The power of protest*. San Francisco, CA: Jossey-Bass.

Altbach, P. G. (1989). Perspectives on student political activism. *Comparative Education, 25*(1), 97–110.

Biddix, J. P. (2010). Technology uses in campus activism from 2000 to 2008: Implications for civic learning. *Journal of College Student Development, 51*, 679–693. http://dx.doi.org/10.1353/csd.2010 .0019

Biddix, J. P. (2014). Development through dissent: Campus activism as civic learning. *New Directions for Higher Education, 2014*(167), 73–85.

Bonner II, F. A., & Bailey, K. W. (2006). Enhancing the academic climate for African American men. In M. J. Cuyjet (Ed.), *African American men in college*. San Francisco, CA: Jossey-Bass.

Bozalek, V., Leibowitz, B., Carolissen, R., & Boler, M. (Eds.). (2014). *Discerning critical hope in educational practices*. New York, NY: Routledge.

Brax, R. S. (1981). *The first student movement: Student activism during the 1930s*. Port Washington, NY: Kennikat Press.

Broadhurst, C., & Martin, G. L. (2014). Part of the "establishment"? Fostering positive campus climates for student activists. *Journal of College and Character, 15*(2), 75–86.

Cabrera, N. L., Matias, C. E., & Montoya, R. (2017). Activism or slacktivism? The potential and pitfalls of social media in contemporary student activism. *Journal of Diversity in Higher Education, 10*(4), 400–415.

Carson, C. (1995). *In struggle: SNCC and the black awakening of the 1960s*. Cambridge, MA: Harvard University Press.

Chen, C., & Gorski, P. C. (2015). Burnout in social justice and human rights activists: Symptoms, causes and implications. *Journal of Human Rights Practice, 7*(3), 366–390.

Chesler, M., & Crowfoot, J. (2010). An organizational analysis of racism in higher education. In M. Brown, J. Lane, & E. Zamani-Gallaher, *Organization and governance in higher education—ASHE reader series* (6th ed., pp. 932–964). New York, NY: Pearson Learning Solutions.

Chessman, H., & Wayt, L. (2016). *What are students demanding?* Retrieved from www.higheredtoday. org/2016/01/13/what-are-students-demanding/

Crenshaw, K. (1989). Demarginalizing the intersection of race and sex: A Black feminist critique of antidiscrimination doctrine, feminist theory, and antiracist politics. *University of Chicago Legal Forum, 1*(8), 139–167.

Crenshaw, K. (1991). Mapping the margins: Intersectionality, identity politics, and violence against women of color. *Stanford Law Review, 43*(6), 1241–1299.

Davis III, C. H. F. (2015). *Dream defending, on-campus and beyond: A multi-sited ethnography of contemporary student organizing, the social movement repertoire, and social movement organization in college* (Unpublished doctoral dissertation). University of Arizona, Tucson, AZ.

Davis III, C. H. F. (2019). *Expanding the web: The case for shifting the analytical gaze in the study of contemporary student activism.* Manuscript in preparation.

Davis III, C. H. F., Ishimoto, M., Mustaffa, J. B., & Stokes, S. (2017). *Black on-campus: Contemporary Black student activism and demands for institutional change.* Paper presented at the 2017 Association for the Study of Higher Education annual meeting, San Antonio, TX.

Davis, K., & Swartz, J. (1972). Increasing Black students' utilization of mental health services. *American Journal of Orthopsychiatry, 42*(5), 771–776.

Duncan, L. E., & Johnson, D. (2007). Black undergraduate students' attitude toward counseling and counselor preference. *College Student Journal, 41*(3), 696–719.

Eagan, K., Stolzenberg, E. B., Bates, A. K., Aragon, M. C., & Rios-Aguilar, C. (2015). *The American freshman: National norms fall 2015.* Report published by the Higher Education Research Institute at the University of California, Los Angeles.

Francis, P., & Horn, A. (2016). *Campus-based practices for promoting student success: Counseling services.* Midwestern Higher Education Compact. Retrieved from www.mhec.org/sites/mhec.org/files/201602counseling_services.pdf

Freire, P. (1970). *Pedagogy of the oppressed.* New York, NY: The Continuum International Publishing Group Inc.

Freudenberger, H. J. (1974). Staff burn-out. *Journal of Social Issues, 30*(1), 159–165.

Givens, J. R. (2016). The invisible tax: Exploring Black student engagement at historically White institutions. *Berkeley Review of Education, 6*(1), 55–78.

Gladwell, M. (2010, October 4). Small change: Why the revolution will not be tweeted. *The New Yorker.* Retrieved August 6, 2015, from www.newyorker.com/magazine/2010/10/04/small-change-malcolm-gladwell

Gomes, M. E., & C. Maslach (1991). *Commitment and burnout among political activists: An in-depth study.* Paper presented at the International Society of Political Psychology, Helsinki.

Gorski, P. C. (2015). Relieving burnout and the "Martyr Syndrome" among social justice education activists: The implications and effects of mindfulness. *The Urban Review, 47,* 696–716.

Gorski, P. C., & Chen, C. (2015). "Frayed all over:" The causes and consequences of activist burnout among social justice education activists. *Educational Studies, 51*(5), 385–405.

Grain, K. M., & Lund, D. E. (2016). The social justice turn: Cultivating "critical hope" in an age of despair. *Michigan Journal of Community Service Learning, 23*(1), 45–59.

Hancock, A. (2011). *Solidarity politics for millennials: A guide to ending the oppression Olympics.* New York: Palgrave Macmillan.

Hart, B., & Danner, C. (2017). 3 Dead and dozens injured after violent White-nationalist rally in Virginia. *New York Magazine: Intelligencer.* Retrieved from http://nymag.com/intelligencer/2017/08/state-of-emergency-in-va-after-white-nationalist-rally.html

Heinemann, L. V., & Heinemann, T. (2017). Burnout research: Emergence and scientific investigation of a contested diagnosis. *SAGE Open, 7*(1), 1–12.

Herner, H. (2016, April 7). #ReclaimOSU releases statement regarding treatment at sit in. *The Lantern.* Retrieved from www.thelantern.com/2016/04/reclaimosu-releases-statement-regarding-treatment-at-sit-in/

Hope, E. C., Keels, M., & Durkee, M. I. (2016). Participation in Black lives matter and deferred action for childhood arrivals: Modern activism among Black and Latino college students. *Journal of Diversity in Higher Education, 9*(3), 203–215.

Hope, E. C., Velez, G., Offidani-Bertrand, C., & Durkee, M. I. (2017). Political activism and mental health among Black and Latinx college students. *Cultural Diversity and Ethnic Minority Psychology, 24*(1), 26–39.

Hurtado, S. (1992). The campus climate: Context for conflict. *Journal of Higher Education, 63*(5), 539–569.

Kezar, A. J. (2010). Faculty and staff partnering with student activists: Unexplored terrains of interaction and development. *Journal of College Student Development, 51*(5), 451–480.

Kuh, G. D. (2008). *High-impact educational practices: What they are, who has access to them, and why they matter*. Washington, DC: Association of American Colleges and Universities.

Lievrouw, L. A. (2011). *Alternative and activist new media*. Malden, MA: Polity Press.

Linder, C., & Rodriguez, K. L. (2012). Learning from the experiences of self-identified women of color activists. *Journal of College Student Development, 53*(3), 383–398.

Maira, S., & Sze, J. (2012). Dispatches from pepper spray university: Privatization, repression, and revolts. *American Quarterly, 64*(2), 315–330.

Moane, G. (2006). Exploring activism and change: Feminist psychology, liberation psychology, and political psychology. *Feminism & Psychology, 16*(1), 73–78.

Moore, K. M. (1997). Freedom and constraint in eighteenth century Harvard. In L. F. Godchild & H. Wescler (Eds.), *The history of higher education* (2nd ed., pp. 108–114). Need ham Heights, MA: Simon and Schuster.

Morgan, D. L., & Davis III, C. H. F. (Eds.) (2019). *Student activism, political engagement, and campus climates in higher education*. New York, NY: Routledge.

Morozov, E. (2009). *The net delusion: The dark side of internet freedom*. New York, NY: Public Affairs.

Nickerson, K. J., Helms, J. E., & Terrell, F. (1994). Cultural mistrust, opinions about mental illness, and Black students' attitudes toward seeking psychological help from White counselors. *Journal of Counseling Psychology, 41*(3), 378–385.

Quaye, S. J. (2007). Hope and learning: The outcomes of contemporary student activism. *About Campus, 12*(2), 2–9.

Quaye, S. J., & Harper, S. R. (Eds.). (2015). *Student engagement in higher education: Theoretical perspectives and practical approaches for diverse populations* (2nd ed). New York, NY: Routledge.

Renn, K. A. (2007). LGBT student leaders and queer activists: Identities of lesbian, gay, bisexual, transgender, and queer identified college student leaders and activists. *Journal of College Student Development, 48*(3), 311–330.

Rhoads, R. A. (1998). Student protest and multicultural reform: Making sense of campus unrest in the 1990s. *The Journal of Higher Education, 69*(6), 621–646.

Rodgers, K. (2010). "Anger is Why We're All Here": Mobilizing and managing emotions in a professional activist organization. *Social Movement Studies, 9*(3), 273–291.

Rudy, W. (1996). *The campus and a nation in crisis*. Cranberry, NJ: Associated University Presses.

Smith, W. A., Allen, W. R., & Danley, L. L. (2007). "Assume the position . . . you fit the description": Psychosocial experiences and racial battle fatigue among African American male college students. *American Behavioral Scientist, 51*(4), 551–587.

Stokes, S., & Miller, D. (2019). Remembering "The Black Bruins": A case study of supporting activists at UCLA. In C. H. F. Davis III & D. Morgan (Eds.), *Student engagement, student services, and supporting student activists* (pp. 143–163). New York, NY: Routledge.

Szymanski, D. M., & Lewis, J. A. (2015). Race-related stress and racial identity as predictors of African American activism. *Journal of Black Psychology, 41*(2), 170–191.

Tilly, C. (2004). *Social movements: 1768–2004*. London, UK: Paradigm Publishers.

Vaccaro, A., & Mena, J. A. (2011). It's not burnout, it's more: Queer college activists of color and mental health. *Journal of Gay & Lesbian Mental Health, 15*(1), 339–367.

Vellela, T. (1988). *New voices: Student political activism in the '80s and '90s*. Boston, MA: South End Press.

Verba, S., Schlozman, K. L., & Brady, H. E. (1995). *Voice and equality: Civic voluntarism in American politics*. Cambridge, MA: Harvard University Press.

Wang, M. C., Nyutu, P. N., & Tran, K. K. (2012). Coping, reasons for living, and suicide in Black college students. *Journal of Counseling and Development, 90*(1), 459–466.

Chapter 10
Engaging Queer Students

Shaun R. Harper and Kaylan S. Baxter

"Times have changed; things aren't as bad as they used to be," Tom argued to his colleague who was asking for a larger physical space and more money to expand the campus LGBTQ center's programming and services. He went on to suggest that contemporary undergraduates are far more open minded. "I have heard many say that homophobia is stupid, and they don't care if their friends are gay, straight, or whatever," Tom added. Widespread support for same-sex marriage (as indicated in a recent attitudinal survey distributed to undergraduates), as well as the impressive turnout of heterosexual students, faculty, and staff at the college's annual gay pride parade, were examples used to bolster his case. Tom also pointed out that it had been at least a decade since there had been any report of a sexuality-related hate crime or any form of discrimination on campus. "I definitely don't think we should close our LGBTQ center, but we cannot justify increasing its budget," Tom concluded.

PJ, the center's founder and longtime director, grew increasingly frustrated as Tom talked. It disappointed her that this vice president for student affairs, a man who had been her supervisor for so many years, had such a terrible misunderstanding of the condition and experiences of queer students on campus. "Just because no one has spray-painted 'fag' on our LGBTQ center door in the past seven years, not a decade, doesn't mean that our campus is fully inclusive of queer students and that there aren't other manifestations of homophobia and heterosexism."

Tom asked PJ for evidence and again referred back to the recent survey question about support for marriage equality. "More than 90 percent said they support it, therefore there is no homophobia remaining here."

PJ immediately responded by calling attention to the fact that some survey respondents—a full 10% of them—were indeed homophobic. "But besides that, we cannot base our assumptions about the inclusiveness of our campus community on one question in a methodologically flawed attitudinal survey," she maintained. "I work with and on behalf of queer students all day long, every single day, Tom. Of the two of us, I'm the expert on their experiences. I'm telling you that parade attendance and the absence of reported hate incidents are flimsy, incomplete indicators of queer students' satisfaction and sense of belonging here at the college." Tom was ultimately unpersuaded, and therefore denied PJ's proposal for additional space and financial resources.

PJ resigned later that day. Hundreds of queer students, faculty, and staff, along with heterosexual members of the campus community, marched in protest the next day. While the march was occurring, someone vandalized the LGBTQ center and posted homophobic signs all across campus. The student body president, a bisexual woman who delivered a powerful speech on "everyday heterosexism" at the campus rally, received an anonymous death threat. Also, a student released an audio recording of a professor making several homophobic statements during a class discussion several months prior. "I had forgotten that I even had this recording in my cell phone until everything flared up here," he admitted. Many people, including alumni of the college, used social media to call for Tom's resignation and to insist the professor on the recording be somehow reprimanded. Over the course of several days, dozens of television stations and newspapers across the United States highlighted what had quickly erupted into a campus crisis.

In this chapter, we synthesize literature on queer students' experiences in higher education. Our aim is to help readers understand that the absence of hate crimes does not signal the end of homophobia and heterosexism on campuses. Deepening understanding of factors, conditions, and behaviors that undermine the engagement, sense of belonging, psychological and emotional wellness, and academic success of queer students is also a goal of ours. Bronfenbrenner's (1993) Ecological Systems Theory and Vaccaro, Russell, and Koob's (2015) Campus Context Model are used to make sense of these issues. We then introduce our Heterodominance Framework to further show how particular histories, features, and norms of postsecondary institutions negatively shape queer students' experiences. The chapter concludes with eight recommendations for postsecondary faculty members, student affairs professionals, and institutional leaders.

Rather than using LGBTQ+ or some similarly limiting acronym, we use "queer" throughout this chapter to denote an expansive, ever-evolving spectrum beyond heterosexuality. It is important to acknowledge that queer is also a term that transgender, gender-nonconforming, and non-cisgender persons use to identify and form community. Because D. Chase J. Catalano, Z Nicolazzo, and T. J. Jourian write about genderqueer students in the chapter that follows this one, our use of "queer" refers specifically to students' sexualities.

Queer Students' Needs and Experiences

Despite the legalization of same-sex marriage and shifts in homophobic attitudes among adolescents, recent studies show that many queer students still experience overt harassment, microaggressions, mocking, and bullying in college (Bauman & Baldasare, 2015; Moran, Chen, & Tryon, 2018; Woodford, Chonody, Kulick, Brennan, & Renn, 2015;

Woodford, Kulick, Sinco, & Hong, 2014); erasure of their sexual identities in college classrooms and in curricula (Garvey & Rankin, 2015; Garvey, Taylor, & Rankin; 2015); discrimination and hostility in fraternities and on intercollegiate sports teams (Atteberry-Ash & Woodford, 2018; Evans, Nagoshi, Nagoshi, Wheeler, & Henderson, 2017); isolation at religious institutions and in religious spaces on campuses (Craig, Austin, Rashidi, & Adams, 2017; Rockenbach, Lo, & Mayhew, 2017; Woodford, Levy, & Walls, 2013); inadequate services in college and university health centers (Hood, Sherrell, Pfeffer, & Mann, 2019); and comparatively higher rates of intimate partner violence during their undergraduate years (Graham, Jensen, Givens, Bowen, & Rizo, 2019; Reuter, Newcomb, Whitton, & Mustanski, 2017). These are just some of the challenges with which contemporary queer collegians are continually confronted. In this section, we use Bronfenbrenner's (1993) Ecological Systems Theory and Vaccaro et al.'s (2015) Campus Context Model to frame our discussion of queer students' classroom, curricular, and out-of-class experiences.

Bronfenbrenner's Ecological Systems Theory

Bronfenbrenner's (1993) ecological systems theory posits that understanding how people relate to society requires analyses of individual interactions with five systems: microsystem, mesosystem, exosystem, macrosystem, and chronosystem. The theory is most frequently visualized as a set of concentric circles, with the individual at the center, surrounded by microsystem, surrounded by mesosystem, and so on, through chronosystem as the outermost circle. Each system contains norms that influence an individual's psychological development.

A microsystem comprises those groups and institutions that most directly impact the person. In the case of college students, microsystems might include their fellow student organization members or members of the local community in which their institution is situated. A mesosystem consists of interactions between different microsystems, such as connections between students and faculty members. Exosystem incorporates a broader social system with which a person may not directly interact but is nonetheless impacted by its presence. Public policy influenced by the sociopolitical climate for queer individuals, for example, may not be directly influenced by a specific college student; however, the climate might present consequences for the emotional or physical well-being of that student. Finally, the chronosystem accounts for the relationship between the person and time. This might include passage of time during or since an internal event, such as identity development, or an external event like the recent loss of a loved one.

Bronfenbrenner's model is useful to understand the numerous factors that shape the capacity of queer students to engage academically and socially in postsecondary settings (Stewart, Renn, & Brazelton, 2015). As Hurtado, Milem, Clayton-Pederson, and Allen (1999) suggest, factors external to the student, and even the institution, have a substantial influence on how college students experience their environments. Ecological Systems Theory can be used to understand how students are influenced by both internal and external factors, all of which interact across various systems. Development of programs and policies designed to enhance engagement should involve consideration of each system of the model, contextualized by campus environments and by queer students' intersecting identities.

Vaccaro, Russell, and Koob's Campus Context Model

Informed partially by Bronfenbrenner's (1993) ecological model and by research related to campus climate, Vaccaro et al. (2015) present queer students in campus context model as a means of understanding how self interacts with homeplace context, institutional/campus context, sociopolitical contexts, and time contexts to inform the degree to which queer students experience academic and social engagement. While most earlier, related research involved students who specifically identified as gay, lesbian, or bisexual and who mostly attended large public institutions, the Campus Context Model takes into account the presence of queer students at all institution types, including community colleges, and is inclusive of a more expansive array of sexualities.

Incorporating an intersectional sense of self and institutional characteristics unique to postsecondary settings into their model, Vaccaro et al. (2015) present an asset-based framework for understanding queer collegians' experiences. At the center of the model, sense of self includes identity development, personality type, coping skills, and strengths. The influence of family, peers, faith communities, and workplace settings comprise homeplace context, while institutional or campus context consists of institution type and mission, formal policies and programs, and informal events and interactions. Also, the model includes Bronfenbrenner and Morris's (1998) emphasis on time—immediate, recent, and historical—to explain how various societal events shape queer students' experiences. Sociopolitical context—at local, regional, and national levels—also shapes how students experience college. Together, time and sociopolitical context account for life events and broader societal conditions that likely inform how queer students perceive themselves and how they experience classroom, curricular, and out-of-class contexts.

Queer Students' Classroom and Curricular Experiences

Understanding the conditions under which students become academically engaged must involve an intersectional approach, considering the interplay of sexuality, race, socioeconomic status, (dis)ability, and other characteristics with various sociocultural factors within and outside postsecondary institutions (Linley & Nguyen, 2015). Despite greater visibility of queer people in the media, politics, and other aspects of society, most of these narratives center the experiences of White and cisgender individuals. As racially minoritized persons continue to be disproportionately victimized by anti-LGBTQ hate crimes, and discrimination on the basis of gender identity remains yet to be criminalized by federal law, these and other external sociopolitical factors often negatively impact their academic success (Linley & Nguyen, 2015; National Coalition of Anti-Violence Programs, 2017). Because college students are not isolated from our greater society, the sociopolitical climate around issues related to sexuality, gender, and other aspects of identity affect their engagement in classrooms.

The climate of an academic department also influences the degree to which queer students engage with curricula (Linley & Nguyen, 2015). While the "microclimates" of social science and humanities departments are often more affirming to queer collegians, those who major in STEM fields often struggle to establish meaningful relationships with faculty, thereby minimizing their likelihood of benefiting from the positive academic outcomes associated with student-faculty research and mentoring (Brown, Clarke, Gortmaker, & Robinson-Keiling, 2004; Kim & Sax, 2009; Linley, Renn, & Woodford, 2014; Rypisi, Malcom, & Kim, 2009). Research also suggests that collegians in STEM and other fields in which objectivity and positivism are highly valued often perceive their identities as irrelevant to their faculty members; consequently, queer students tend not to disclose their sexualities in class discussions (Linley & Nguyen, 2015). This reluctance to disclose their sexual identities prevents many queer students from engaging as their full selves in their curricular environments. In contrast, students in the social sciences and humanities tend to feel more affirmed in their sexual identities, largely due to the curricular nature of the disciplines, which often include content or intended learning outcomes related to social justice (Linley & Nguyen).

Campus climates, policies, mission statements, and resources also influence classroom experiences (Linley & Nguyen, 2015). The ways in which students experience four institutional dimensions of campus climate—structural diversity, psychological climate, behavioral dynamics, and historical legacy of exclusion and inclusion—influence the degree to which they experience academic and social engagement (Hurtado et al., 1999). The more diverse and equitable that queer students perceive and experience their campus climates, the more likely they are to be academically engaged.

Campus policies influence curricular engagement by signaling to students the values and norms of their institutions (Linley & Nguyen, 2015; Pitcher, Camacho, Renn, & Woodford, 2018; Dirks, 2011). In their studies of historically Black colleges and universities (HBCUs), scholars (e.g., Harper & Gasman, 2008; Patton, 2014; Mobley & Johnson, 2019) found policies that were explicitly homophobic. The presence of institutional policies barring discrimination or harassment on the basis of sexuality is associated with a greater sense of belonging among queer students, regardless of whether such policies actually affect them (Linley & Nguyen, 2015; Pitcher, Camacho, Renn, & Woodford, 2018). Because instances of discrimination or harassment can occur in a curricular context, the presence of protective policies likely contributes to the ability of students to engage academically.

Similarly, an institution's mission statement communicates to internal and external stakeholders its aspirations, values, and priorities (Morphew & Hartley, 2006; Ozdem, 2011). Many missions include a commitment to sustaining a diverse or inclusive environment broadly defined and without explicit mentions of queer members of the campus community. Some faith-affiliated institutions suggest cultural values through their mission statements that implicitly signal unsupportive environments for students, faculty, and staff who are queer (Linley & Nguyen, 2015). Similarly, an institution with a mission that explicitly centers a faith tradition whose membership is largely unaccepting of queer identities likely reinforces the espousal of queerphobic ideals by campus members (Jayakumar, 2009). Both explicit naming of an anti-queer faith tradition as informing the values of an institution and the omission of campus members who are queer as a target population in efforts toward diversity and inclusion are characteristics of a mission statement likely to negatively influence perceptions of campus climate and subsequent curricular engagement.

Professional development opportunities for faculty and staff members to gain the necessary knowledge and skills to support queer populations is associated with more supportive classroom experiences for queer students (Linley & Nguyen, 2015; Woodford, Kolb, Durocher-Radeka, & Javier, 2014). Often called "Safe Zone" programs, the learning outcomes of these initiatives typically include knowledge of basic sexuality-related terminology as well as specific strategies for supporting queer students in classrooms. Upon completion, participants often receive a Safe Zone sticker, or some other tangible symbol, to publicly signal their presence as an ally to queer students (Linley & Nguyen, 2015). Despite the proliferation of such programs, little research has explored their actual impact on queer students' experiences (Worthen, 2011). Scholars have also noted that, despite the potential usefulness of Safe Zone programs in equipping faculty members with the interpersonal skills to engage queer students, most programs lack a critique of the systemic and structural conditions that contribute to the inequitable educational experiences of many marginalized students (Linley & Nguyen; Woodford et al.).

Queer Students' Out-of-Class Experiences

As faculty shift their curricula and pedagogical practices to enhance the experiences of marginalized students, administrators and staff must also assess the nature of co-curricular activities to ensure equitable participation among queer students in such practices as learning communities, community-based learning, study-abroad experiences, and other activities demonstrated as having a high impact on student learning. Kuh (2008) and Harper (2009) note there is often inequitable access to these high-impact activities. Such activities are typically under the leadership of student affairs professionals whose competency around issues of sexuality and adoption of universal design practices are associated with enhanced co-curricular experiences for queer students (Bazarsky, Morrow, & Javier, 2015).

To sustain a campus climate conducive to deep out-of-class engagement among queer collegians, student affairs and academic affairs professionals must understand terms such as *queer*, *sexuality*, *gender identity*, and *sex assigned at birth*, to name a few (Bazarsky et al., 2015). Like faculty in their considerations of curricular design, educators implementing co-curricular programs must take an intersectional approach that considers the multiple identities that students bring to campus and their varying experiences due to systemic power and oppression. Staff members must also stay abreast of evolving sexuality-related terminology to ensure their language, practices, and programming are affirming of students with identities outside the traditional LGBTQ umbrella (Bazarsky et al.).

Beyond the role of individual professionals in enhancing out-of-class experiences, institutions have a responsibility to implement policies and provide resources necessary to sustain equitable campus climates for queer students (Bazarsky et al., 2015). While campus policies cannot guarantee an equitable climate for marginalized students, they can signal institutional values and should provide an accountability protocol for instances during which students experience harm due to their sexualities. Campus leaders should designate adequate resources for ongoing professional development on issues related to sexuality as well as physical modifications to residence halls, recreational facilities, academic buildings, and other student-centered spaces that might enhance experiences of campus climate among queer students.

While many colleges and universities have created LGBTQ student–focused physical spaces (which are typically aimed at support, education, and advocacy), less institutional attention has been given to the ways in which the remaining physical spaces on campus are designed in ways that problematically reinforce dominant norms. Drawing from the work of disability scholars, recent research has proposed universal design as a framework for enhancing campus experiences, including for queer students (Bazarsky et al., 2015). In the context of higher education, universal design should involve approaches to instruction, services, information technology, and physical spaces that maximize effective usage by all members of a diverse population (Burgstahler, 2008). Implementing policies mandating the use of chosen names and pronouns and accessible all-gender restrooms are examples of strategies grounded in universal design and associated with positive campus experiences for queer students. But for these approaches to be effective, campus stakeholders must first undo the dominance of heteronormativity evidenced in just about everything the institution does. In the next section, we present a new framework that could be useful in first understanding and then ultimately disrupting what we are calling "heterodominance."

Conceptual Framework

In the two prior editions of this book, authors of the chapters on queer students (Schueler, Hoffman, & Peterson, 2009; Stewart & Howard-Hamilton, 2014) used theories, models, and frameworks pertaining to human rights, sexual identity development, intersectionality, and multiple dimensions of identities. Stewart and Howard-Hamilton also used Queer Theory to challenge "prescribed internalized beliefs about the social construction of sexual identity" (p. 129). Given our focus on queer students in institutional contexts, we decided against focusing on their sexual identity development during college. To be sure, we deem theoretical examinations of queer students' identities incontestably important and therefore urge readers to consult the previous editions for overviews of useful models and frameworks. But here, we debut a new conceptual framework that shows how the origins and enduring dominance of heterosexism in campus and organizational contexts marginalize queer identities.

Like other frameworks, the one we introduce here is intended to be adapted, critiqued, extended, and revised by scholars (including us) in future publications. Though crafted specially for this chapter on queer students in collegiate contexts, our framework can be used in studies of queer people's experiences in a wide array of social and other organizational contexts, including workplace settings. One of us has conducted qualitative climate assessments on college campuses and in an array of other organizational contexts for 15 years. Our framework is informed by insights from those studies, many of which included queer participants. In addition, our lived experiences as queer people and as professionals who have taught, mentored, and advised queer students over the course of our careers also shaped the insights we offer here.

Heterodominance Framework

Presented in Figure 10.1 is a multiphase conceptual framework that begins at the creation of an institution or organization. It presumes the endurance of queer marginalization within that context, while showing the multitude of ways in which heterosexism and homophobia become functional and entrenched. The framework is also about the function of pervasive heterosexism as well as its impact on queer people. Queer theorists,

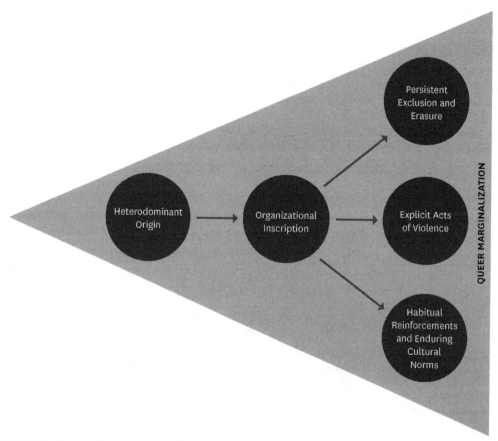

FIGURE 10.1. Heterodominance Framework

feminist scholars, and others (e.g., Butler, 1990; de Freitas Boe & Coykendall, 2016; Herz & Johansson, 2015; Marchia & Sommer, 2019; Rich, 1980; Rubin, 1984; Seidman, 2005; Smith, 2018; Warner, 1991) have written extensively about "heteronormativity." This term is often used to show and critique the widespread mischaracterization of a "normal" sexuality, the one to which most people are socialized and defaulted (Slagle, 2006). In a critique of the term, Jackson (2006) observes that "institutionalized, normative heterosexuality regulates those kept within its boundaries as well as marginalizing and sanctioning those outside them. The term 'heteronormativity' has not always captured this double-sided social regulation" (p. 105). We attempt to respond to this two-sidedness by theorizing the impact of heterosexuality as the dominant foundation of a context on people whose sexualities are outside the boundaries drawn by its heterosexist and homophobic architects.

Heterodominant Origin
Our framework begins with the recognition that colleges and universities in the United States were created without the meaningful participation of significant numbers of persons who publicly identified as anything other than heterosexual. Even though there may have been queer persons involved in the establishment of the colonial colleges and other postsecondary institutions founded throughout the 18th and 19th centuries, very few (if any at all) were permitted to disclose their sexualities and bring their full selves to tables at which decisions were being made about what an institution of higher education would be, how it would be governed and operated, what its curriculum would include, what its architecture would be, and what its long-standing cultural norms would ultimately become. Given this, heterosexual people (exclusively men in the overwhelming majority of cases) created campuses that marginalized queer persons from the start. We theorize that heterodominance is genetic and therefore impossible to fully undo, especially at colleges and universities founded and led by mostly heterosexual men many years ago. It is perhaps possible to eradicate heterodominance in less mature organizational contexts that were not fashioned in the image of heterodominant others.

Organizational Inscription
The next phase in our framework represents the period in an institution's lifespan at which the heteronormativity its earliest stakeholders brought to the original campus design becomes deeply imbedded into its everyday functions and culture. Inscription also occurs at this point through the dominating presence of heterosexual people and the universal presumption of heterosexuality. Because so many students, faculty, and staff on the campus are presumed to be heterosexual, all parts of the institution begin to firmly reflect their interests and privilege their identities. This has marginalizing effects on queer members of the campus community. Historians and other scholars can refer back to archival materials to determine specific moments at which heterodominance became concretized and omnipresent. The next phase of the framework shows three outcomes of the inscription of heterodominance, each of which sustains queer marginality.

Persistent Exclusion and Erasure

Because queer people were not represented in significant numbers when curricula were being developed, the contemporary curriculum at most places excludes queer lives, histories, and epistemologies. In the overwhelming majority of academic fields, queer authors are rarely assigned to students. Moreover, classroom conversations often default to heterosexual viewpoints and examples. Fraternities and sororities on many campuses tend to exclude queer students, both in membership and in the cultures they create. Regarding the latter, even when there are queer members, their sexualities tend to be entirely erased or constantly overshadowed by the dominant representation of heterosexuals. This occurs on many intercollegiate sports teams too. Few queer-centric programs are offered through student activities offices and in residence halls—instead most are offered through LGBTQ centers and organizations specifically for queer students.

Explicit Acts of Violence

Because heterodominance is so long standing and deeply rooted into just about everything an institution does, some members of the campus community react violently to the presence of queer people. They see them as abnormal, not reflective of what is taught and valued on campus. Beyond slogans, pride weeks and parades, upside-down rainbow triangles in various people's offices, and the presence of an LGBTQ center on campus, little else is often done to demonstrate love for queer students. Even less is done to undo the hate and homophobic precollege socialization with which some students enter college. The heterodominant nature of a campus environment gives rise to homophobic cruelty in its myriad forms. These acts of violence range from teasing and name-calling, to bullying in an array of campus spaces and on social media, vandalism of personal property and LGBTQ centers, and physical threats and attacks, to name a few.

Habitual Reinforcements and Enduring Cultural Norms

Through a multitude of everyday acts, members of campus communities sometimes unknowingly uphold an institution's heterodominant origin and the heterodominance that has been inscribed over time. An example is calling one's spouse "first lady" when she is married to a man who serves as president of a college, but not when she is married to a presidential leader who is a woman. Another is the display of portraits throughout campus of wealthy heterosexual couples who donated money to the university, but no images of same-sex couples who played meaningful roles at any point in the institution's history. Even when queer individuals are represented in portraits, busts, or statues, rarely are they acknowledged as being or having been queer. Some other examples are class discussions about families that refer only to mothers and fathers; readings, discussions, and events that consider several dimensions of sex among heterosexuals, but focus only on HIV and "safe sex" practices among queer people; speed dating events that only present heterosexual dating options; romance movie screenings that show only heterosexual lovers; and websites and fliers for spring formals and other dances that only include images of heterosexual couples. Ubiquitous heterodominance compels even the most open-minded and accepting persons on campus to inadvertently adhere to and thereby uphold contradictory cultural norms established in prior periods. These institutional habits have marginalizing effects on queer students, and ultimately undermine their sense of belonging and engagement.

Student Engagement Strategies

We offer in this section eight strategies to address heterodominance and other institutional challenges confronting queer students. Taken together, we hope these recommendations will lead to higher levels of engagement and a host of productive personal and academic outcomes.

Establish a Queer Advisory Council

Presidents, vice presidents, deans, department chairs, and other administrators could benefit from advice on ways to make classrooms, out-of-class environments, and policies more inclusive and responsive to queer people. The formal establishment of an advisory council would be an effective way to solicit feedback and ideas from queer students, faculty, and staff. No one would know better than they what it is like to be queer on campus. Membership on the advisory council would also afford queer students access to potential role models—queer peers, faculty, and staff members whom they may not otherwise encounter elsewhere at the institution. The administrator who commissions the council should regularly meet with its members and take seriously recommendations those experts put forth.

Take Stock of Heterodominance

Queer advisory council members and others (including heterosexual members of the campus community) should be tasked with studying historical and contemporary manifestations of heterodominance. Faculty members in the history department, for example, can work with a team of students to engage archival materials that shed light on the institution's heterodominant origins. Another team comprising students and professors from anthropology, sociology, industrial-organizational psychology, and other fields can identify when and how heterodominance became inscribed into the institution, as well as mapping the ways in which it shows up in curriculum, campus architecture, ceremonies, governance and decision-making, and an expansive array of operations and activities. Teams of students and student affairs professionals could employ a range of methodologies to document the erasure and exclusion of queer identities, myriad forms of violence against queer people, and enduring cultural habits on campus that reinforce heterodominance. Being on one of these teams would be a form of purposeful engagement for queer students who are interested in these topics. Each team's discoveries can and should be used strategically to make the institution less heterodominant and more queer affirming.

Specifically Assess the Climate for Queer Students

Bensimon (2004) asserts that most institutional research practices fail to include assessments of varying outcomes experienced by students across identities. This tends to be true of most campus climate studies. In 2018, the University of Southern California Race and Equity Center launched its National Assessment of Collegiate Campus Climates (NACCC). While the instrument includes demographic questions about sexuality that permit intersectional analyses, its creators are clear that it is a quantitative racial climate study. Broad, all-encompassing qualitative and quantitative climate studies rarely provide sufficiently deep insights into any one group's experiences. Because of this, NACCC questions are specifically about race. Given the relationship between experiences of campus climate and academic and social engagement for queer students (Woodford & Kulick, 2015), it is important to develop instruments and interview protocols that provide deep and specific insights into queer students' appraisals of campus climate.

Rankin and Garvey (2015) propose several methodological approaches to enhance the inclusivity of institutional assessments: (1) regular administration of experiential assessments, rather than overreliance on programmatic outcomes assessments, to provide a better understanding of the campus climate–related behaviors and perceptions of queer students; (2) systematized inclusion of sexuality-related demographic variables on admissions applications, program assessments, and other survey instruments, using best-practice design and terminology; (3) employing tenets of queer theory to resist the rigid and often binary nature of data collection and analysis, creating space for a more fluid and multifaceted understanding of identity; and (4) approaching assessment with an intersectional lens, acknowledging the multiple identities that students hold and the potential salience of a particular aspect(s) of their identities and the fluidity of salience over time. Adoption of these practices by institutional researchers and others leading assessment efforts will allow campus leaders to implement and assess the effectiveness of policies and programs aimed at fostering academic and social support for queer students.

Review and Revise Homophobic Policies

In their study of conservatism at HBCUs, Harper and Gasman (2008) found several homophobic policies. Here is an example from one of the twelve institutions in their study: "Sexual misconduct is defined as including, but not limited to sexual intercourse, adultery, rape, sodomy, and homosexual acts" (p. 343). Similar language was included in written policy documents they analyzed from other HBCUs. While they may have been written in earlier periods, these policies were still active. More recently, Patton (2014) and Mobley and Johnson (2019) conducted analyses of the "Appropriate Attire Policy" at Morehouse College. Much about this policy is homophobic, their studies show. Surely, HBCUs are not the only postsecondary institutions with homophobic policies. In fact, Craig et al. (2017) found several in their study of queer students and alumni who attended religious colleges and universities. The Queer Advisory Council and others on campus should be empowered to point out to institutional leaders policies that are explicitly or implicitly homophobic. These policies ought to be revised or discarded. Student engagement is unlikely to occur in heterodominant environments with policies that prohibit queer students from being their full selves on campus.

Require Evidence of Queer Inclusion

Campus leaders who espouse commitments to fostering and maintaining inclusive campus environments for all students (including queer collegians) must hold themselves and others accountable for consistently furnishing evidence of institutional commitment. In academic schools and departments, this would entail engaging faculty members in reviews of their syllabi to determine how many queer authors are assigned to students; where and how topics pertaining to queer lives, histories, and epistemologies are taught; and where curricular heterodominance is being reinforced. Conversations about how professors are intentionally making their classrooms inclusive and queer affirming could be useful. Topics like these are rarely on faculty meeting agendas—they should be. Chief student affairs officers and other senior leaders should require all directors, not only those who lead LGBTQ centers, to provide specific lists of programs, activities, and resources their respective units offer to engage and support queer students. All the evidence that is amassed from academic units and various offices across the student affairs division should be mapped and made publicly available so that queer students know where they are likeliest to be affirmed. Leaders should also pay attention to units that are not on the list and insist that they produce more evidence to confirm their meaningful participation in institutional efforts to dismantle heterodominance.

Make Culture Centers and LGBTQ Centers More Inclusive

Numerous scholars (e.g., Abes & Jones, 2004; Abes, Jones, & McEwen, 2007; Abes & Kasch, 2007; Harper, Wardell, & McGuire, 2011; Narui, 2014; Patrón, 2019; Patton & Simmons, 2008; Rankin & Garvey, 2015; Thomas-Card & Ropers-Huilman, 2014; Vaccaro, 2012) have written about sexuality as one of many dimensions of queer students' identities. Many have specifically called for more attention to the convergence of racial and sexual identities. One experience that queer Students of Color often report is feeling an insufficient sense of belonging in ethnic culture centers (because of climates of homophobia, heterosexism, and heterodominance) and in LGBTQ centers (because of cultures of whiteness and the dominance of programming catering to white cultural interests). Directors and staff members in culture centers for Asian American and Pacific Islander, Black, Latinx, and Native American collegians, as well as those who work in multicultural centers that serve a multitude of racially minoritized student populations, must intentionally include more activities and services for queer collegians. They also should assess queer students' feelings of belongingness and ask for examples of heterodominance in the center. Similarly, educators working in LGBTQ centers must include more cultural artifacts that reflect a multitude of racialized histories and offer more programs that satisfy racially diverse queer students' needs and expectations. Doing this necessitates collecting data from queer Students of Color. In addition, culture centers and LGBTQ centers should both establish advisory councils composed of queer students and alumni of color.

Establish Queer Inclusion and Engagement Fund

Administrators, as well as student governments and campus activities boards that allocate funds to student organizations, should consider creating a fund focused on increasing queer student engagement and awakening institutional consciousness about the dominance of heteronormativity on campus. This fund could be used to support LGBTQ centers and queer student organizations. But it also should be used to incentivize other offices, centers, and student groups to make their services and activities more queer-inclusive. Institutional dollars could be augmented by money raised through private foundations that place an emphasis on LGBTQ communities, as well as through fundraising campaigns targeted at queer alumni and donors who care deeply about LGBTQ issues.

Launch Campaign to Illuminate Queer People's Lives and Contributions

To bolster feelings of inclusion among queer collegians, a campaign should be created to showcase the lives and contributions of queer students, faculty, and staff—past and present. This campaign could include a special collection in campus libraries and museums; hanging portraits of the first openly queer students and professors in various academic departments and schools, founding LGBTQ center directors, and queer staff members who deeply influenced students; and installations by queer artists who are somehow affiliated with the college or university. The campus might also consider hosting a series that brings queer scholars to campus for colloquia and panels focused on queer people's lives. While LGBTQ center staff should be substantively involved in the planning and execution of this campaign, heterosexual and queer partners across the campus should play serious roles. Moreover, this campaign should not be isolated to LGBTQ+ pride month. Instead, its activities and efforts ought to be distributed across the full academic year. There should be a website, social media strategy, and printed materials (posters, banners, etc.) to publicize the campaign and its activities.

Conclusion

In hindsight, Tom very likely wishes he had approved PJ's request for more money. Several indicators clearly suggest he should have. But honestly, it would have taken much more than a bigger budget and larger physical space to dismantle the omnipresence of heterodominance on their campus. Funds are necessary, but so too are bold strategies, queer-inclusive assessments, revisions and discontinuations of homophobic policies, and most importantly, institutional responsiveness to advice from queer people who navigate the campus each day. Tom and others like him must not only solicit perspectives from an advisory council and data from respondents to a survey about queer students' appraisals of the campus climate, but they must also act with high degrees of intentionality and seriousness to what they hear and learn. Some actions will inevitably require financial resources.

References

Abes, E. S., & Jones, S. R. (2004). Meaning-making capacity and the dynamics of lesbian college students' multiple dimensions of identity. *Journal of College Student Development, 45*(6), 612–632.

Abes, E. S., Jones, S. R., & McEwen, M. K. (2007). Reconceptualizing the model of multiple dimensions of identity: The role of meaning-making capacity in the construction of multiple identities. *Journal of College Student Development, 48*(1), 1–22.

Abes, E. S., & Kasch, D. (2007). Using queer theory to explore lesbian college students' multiple dimensions of identity. *Journal of College Student Development, 48*(6), 619–636.

Atteberry-Ash, B., & Woodford, M. R. (2018). Support for policy protecting LGBT student athletes among heterosexual students participating in club and intercollegiate sports. *Sexuality Research and Social Policy, 15*(2), 151–162.

Bauman, S., & Baldasare, A. (2015). Cyber aggression among college students: Demographic differences, predictors of distress, and the role of the university. *Journal of College Student Development, 56*(4), 317–330.

Bazarsky, D., Morrow, L. K., & Javier, G. C. (2015). Cocurricular and campus contexts. In D. L. Stewart, K. A. Renn, & G. B. Brazelton (Eds.), *Gender and sexual diversity in US higher education: Contexts and opportunities for LGBTQ college students* (New directions for student services, No. 152) (pp. 55–71).

Bensimon, E. M. (2004). The diversity scorecard: A learning approach to institutional change. *Change, 36*(1), 44–52.

Bronfenbrenner, U. (1993). The ecology of cognitive development: Research models and fugitive findings. In R. H. Wozniak & K. W. Fischer (Eds.), *Development in context: Acting and thinking in specific environments* (pp. 3–44). Hillsdale, NJ: Erlbaum.

Bronfenbrenner, U., & Morris, P. A. (1998). The ecology of developmental processes. In W. Damon and R. M. Lerner (Eds.), *Handbook of child psychology, Vol. 1: Theoretical models of human development* (5th ed., pp. 993–1023). New York, NY: Wiley.

Brown, R. D., Clarke, B., Gortmaker, V., & Robinson-Keiling, R. (2004). Assessing the campus climate for gay, lesbian, bisexual, and transgender (GLBT) students using a multiple perspectives approach. *Journal of College Student Development, 45*, 8–26.

Burgstahler, S. E. (2008). Universal design in higher education. In S. E. Burgstahler & R. C. Cory (Eds.), *Universal design in higher education: From principles to practice* (pp. 3–20). Cambridge, MA: Harvard Education Press.

Butler, J. (1990). *Gender trouble*. New York, NY: Routledge.

Craig, S. L., Austin, A., Rashidi, M., & Adams, M. (2017). Fighting for survival: The experiences of lesbian, gay, bisexual, transgender, and questioning students in religious colleges and universities. *Journal of Gay & Lesbian Social Services, 29*(1), 1–24.

de Freitas Boe, A., & Coykendall, A. (Eds.). (2016). *Heteronormativity in eighteenth-century literature and culture*. New York, NY: Routledge.

Dirks, D. A. (2011). *Transgender people on university campuses: A policy discourse analysis*. Unpublished doctoral dissertation.

Evans, R., Nagoshi, J. L., Nagoshi, C., Wheeler, J., & Henderson, J. (2017). Voices from the stories untold: Lesbian, gay, bisexual, trans, and queer college students' experiences with campus climate. *Journal of Gay & Lesbian Social Services, 29*(4), 426–444.

Garvey, J. C., & Rankin, S. R. (2015). Making the grade? Classroom climate for LGBTQ students across gender conformity. *Journal of Student Affairs Research and Practice, 52*(2), 190–203.

Garvey, J. C., Taylor, J. L., & Rankin, S. (2015). An examination of campus climate for LGBTQ community college students. *Community College Journal of Research and Practice, 39*(6), 527–541.

Graham, L. M., Jensen, T. M., Givens, A. D., Bowen, G. L., & Rizo, C. F. (2019). Intimate partner violence among same-sex couples in college: A propensity score analysis. *Journal of Interpersonal Violence, 34*(8), 1583–1610.

Harper, S. R. (2009). Race-conscious student engagement practices and the equitable distribution of enriching educational experiences. *Liberal Education, 95*(4), 38–45.

Harper, S. R., & Gasman, M. (2008). Consequences of conservatism: Black male students and the politics of historically Black colleges and universities. *Journal of Negro Education, 77*(4), 336–351.

Harper, S. R., Wardell, C. C., & McGuire, K. M. (2011). Man of multiple identities: Complex individuality and identity intersectionality among college men. In J. A. Laker & T. Davis (Eds.), *Masculinities in higher education: Theoretical and practical considerations* (pp. 81–96). New York, NY: Routledge.

Herz, M., & Johansson, T. (2015). The normativity of the concept of heteronormativity. *Journal of Homosexuality, 62*(8), 1009–1020.

Hood, L., Sherrell, D., Pfeffer, C. A., & Mann, E. S. (2019). LGBTQ college students' experiences with university health services: An exploratory study. *Journal of Homosexuality, 66*(6), 797–814.

Hurtado, S., Milem, J., Clayton-Pederson, A., & Allen, W. (1999). *Enacting diverse learning environments: Improving the climate for racial/ethnic diversity in higher education.* ASHE-ERIC Higher Education Report 26, Vol. 8. Washington, DC: The George Washington University, Graduate School of Education and Human Development.

Jackson, S. (2006). Gender, sexuality and heterosexuality: The complexity (and limits) of heteronormativity. *Feminist Theory, 7*(1), 105–121.

Jayakumar, U. M. (2009). The invisible rainbow in diversity: Factors influencing sexual prejudice among college students. *Journal of Homosexuality, 56*(6), 675–700.

Kim, Y. K., & Sax, L. J. (2009). Student-faculty interaction in research universities: Differences by student gender, race, social class, and first-generation status. *Research in Higher Education, 50*, 437–459.

Kuh, G. D. (2008). *High-impact educational practices: What they are, who has access to them, and why they matter.* Washington, DC: Association of American Colleges and Universities.

Linley, J., & Nguyen, D. (2015). LGBTQ experiences in curricular contexts. In D. L. Stewart, K. A. Renn, & G. B. Brazelton (Eds.), *Gender and sexual diversity in US higher education: Contexts and opportunities for LGBTQ college students* (New directions for student services, No. 152) (pp. 41–53).

Linley, J. L., Renn, K. A., & Woodford, M. R. (2018). Examining the ecological systems of LGBTQ STEM majors. *Journal of Women and Minorities in Engineering, 24*(1), 1–16.

Marchia, J., & Sommer, J. M. (2019). (Re)defining heteronormativity. *Sexualities, 22*(3), 267–295.

Mobley Jr., S. D., & Johnson, J. M. (2019). "No pumps allowed": The "problem" with gender expression and the Morehouse College "Appropriate Attire Policy." *Journal of Homosexuality, 66*(7), 867–895.

Moran, T. E., Chen, C. Y. C., & Tryon, G. S. (2018). Bully victimization, depression, and the role of protective factors among college LGBTQ students. *Journal of Community Psychology, 46*(7), 871–884.

Morphew, C., & Hartley, M. (2006). Mission statements: A thematic analysis of rhetoric across institutional type. *Journal of Higher Education, 77*(3), 456–471.

Narui, M. (2014). Hidden populations and intersectionality: When race and sexual orientation collide. In D. Mitchell Jr., C. Y. Simmons, & L. A. Greyerbiehl (Eds.), *Intersectionality & higher education: Theory, research, & Praxis* (pp. 185–200). New York, NY: Peter Lang.

National Coalition of Anti-Violence Programs (2017). *Hate violence against lesbian, gay, bisexual, transgender, queer, and HIV-affected communities in the United States in 2016.* New York, NY: Author.

Ozdem, G. (2011). An analysis of the mission and vision statements on the strategic plans of higher education institutions. *Educational Sciences: Theory and Practice, 11*(4), 1887–1894.

Patrón, O. E. (2019). *Reconceptualizing notions of resilience through the experiences of gay Latino male collegians* (Unpublished doctoral dissertation), Pittsburgh, PA: University of Pittsburgh.

Patton, L. D. (2014). Preserving respectability or blatant disrespect? A critical discourse analysis of the Morehouse Appropriate Attire Policy and implications for intersectional approaches to examining campus policies. *International Journal of Qualitative Studies in Education, 27*(6), 724–746.

Patton, L. D., & Simmons, S. L. (2008). Exploring complexities of multiple identities of lesbians in a Black college environment. *Negro Educational Review, 59*(3–4), 197–215.

Pitcher, E. N., Camacho, T. P., Renn, K. A., & Woodford, M. R. (2018). Affirming, policies, programs, and supportive services: Using an organizational perspective to understand LGBTQ+ student success. *Journal of Diversity in Higher Education, 11*(2), 117–132.

Rankin, S., & Garvey, J. C. (2015). Identifying, quantifying, and operationalizing queer-spectrum and transspectrum students: Assessment and research in student affairs. In D. L. Stewart, K. A. Renn, & G. B. Brazelton (Eds.), *Gender and sexual diversity in US higher education: Contexts and opportunities for LGBTQ college students* (New directions for student services, No. 152) (pp. 73–84). San Francisco, CA: Jossey-Bass.

Reuter, T. R., Newcomb, M. E., Whitton, S. W., & Mustanski, B. (2017). Intimate partner violence victimization in LGBT young adults: Demographic differences and associations with health behaviors. *Psychology of Violence, 7*(1), 101–109.

Rich, A. (1980). Compulsory heterosexuality and lesbian existence. *Signs, 5*(4), 631–660.

Rockenbach, A. N., Lo, M. A., & Mayhew, M. J. (2017). How LGBT college students perceive and engage the campus religious and spiritual climate. *Journal of Homosexuality, 64*(4), 488–508.

Rubin, G. (1984). Thinking sex: Notes for a radical theory of the politics of sexuality. In C. S. Vance (Ed.), *Pleasure and danger: Exploring female sexuality* (pp. 267–319). Boston: Routledge & Kegan Paul.

Rypisi, C., Malcom, L. E., & Kim, H. S. (2009). Environmental and developmental approaches to supporting women's success in STEM fields. In S. R. Harper & S. J. Quaye (Eds.), *Student engagement in higher education: Theoretical perspectives and practical approaches for diverse populations* (pp. 117–135). New York, NY: Routledge.

Schueler, L. A., Hoffman, J. A., & Peterson, E. (2009). Fostering safe, engaging campuses for lesbian, gay, bisexual, transgender, and questioning students. In S. R. Harper & S. J. Quaye (Eds.), *Student engagement in higher education: Theoretical perspectives and practical approaches for diverse populations* (pp. 61–79). New York, NY: Routledge.

Seidman, S. (2005). From polluted homosexual to the normal gay: Changing patterns of sexual regulation in America. In C. Ingraham (Ed.), *Thinking straight: New work in critical heterosexuality studies* (pp. 39–62). New York, NY: Routledge.

Slagle, A. R. (2006). Ferment in LGBT studies and queer theory: Personal ruminations on contested terrain. *Journal of Homosexuality, 52*(1–2), 309–328.

Smith, A. (2018). *Gender, heteronormativity, and the American presidency*. New York, NY: Routledge.

Stewart, D. L., & Howard-Hamilton, M. F. (2014). Engaging lesbian, gay, and bisexual students on college campuses. In S. J. Quaye & S. R. Harper (Eds.), *Student engagement in higher education: Theoretical perspectives and practical approaches for diverse populations* (2nd ed., pp. 121–134). New York, NY: Routledge.

Stewart, D. L., Renn, K. A., & Brazelton, G. B. (2015). *Gender and sexual diversity in US higher education: Contexts and opportunities for LGBTQ college students* (New directions for student services, No. 152). San Francisco, CA: Jossey-Bass.

Thomas-Card, T., & Ropers-Huilman, R. (2014). Heteronormativity fractured and fused: Exploring the college experiences of multiple marginalized LGBT students. In D. Mitchell Jr., C. Y. Simmons, & L. A. Greyerbiehl (Eds.), *Intersectionality & higher education: Theory, research, & praxis* (pp. 78–87). New York, NY: Peter Lang.

Vaccaro, A. (2012). Campus microclimates for LGBT faculty, staff, and students: An exploration of the intersections of social identity and campus roles. *Journal of Student Affairs Research and Practice, 49*(4), 359–480.

Vaccaro, A., Russell, E. I. A., & Koob, R. M. (2015). Students with minoritized identities of sexuality and gender in campus contexts: An emergent model. In D. L. Stewart, K. A. Renn, & G. B. Brazelton (Eds.), *Gender and sexual diversity in US higher education: Contexts and opportunities for LGBTQ college students* (New directions for student services, No. 152) (pp. 25–39). San Francisco, CA: Jossey-Bass.

Warner, M. (Ed.). (1991). *Fear of a queer planet: Queer politics and social theory*. Minneapolis, MN: University of Minnesota Press.

Woodford, M. R., Chonody, J. M., Kulick, A., Brennan, D. J., & Renn, K. (2015). The LGBQ microaggressions on campus scale: A scale development and validation study. *Journal of Homosexuality*, *62*(12), 1660–1687.

Woodford, M. R., Kolb, C. L., Durocher-Radeka, G., & Javier, G. (2014). Lesbian, gay, bisexual, and transgender ally training programs on campus: Current variations and future directions. *Journal of College Student Development*, *55*(3), 317–322.

Woodford, M. R., & Kulick, A. (2015). Academic and social integration on campus among sexual minority students: The impacts of psychological and experiential campus climate. *American Journal of Community Psychology*, *55*, 13–24.

Woodford, M. R., Kulick, A., Sinco, B., & Hong, J. (2014). Contemporary heterosexism on campus and psychological distress among LGBQ students: The mediating role of self-acceptance. *American Journal of Orthopsychiatry*, *84*(5), 519–529.

Woodford, M. R., Levy, D., & Walls, N. E. (2013). Sexual prejudice among Christian college students, denominational teachings, and personal religious beliefs. *Review of Religious Research*, *55*(1), 105–130.

Worthen, M. G. F. (2011). College student experiences with an LGBTQ ally training program: A mixed methods study at a university in the southern United States. *Journal of LGBT Youth*, *8*(4), 332–377.

Chapter 11
Engaging Transgender Students

D. Chase J. Catalano, Z Nicolazzo, and T.J. Jourian

We are coming together, here and now, at a moment of increased visibility for trans* people, in pop culture and in the gaze of the state. But at the same time, as we so intimately know, we are witnessing some of the highest rates of violence against our communities ever documented. So, in this moment of violence and visibility, I feel it's urgent to think about what we risk losing when the state, and pop culture, seem to be inviting us in. What do we open ourselves, and our communities, up to when we seek out visibility?

(Grace, 2015, para. 2–3)

Visibility does not always secure certain rights or privileges. I am interested in the demands that visibility makes upon its subjects. We live in a coming out time, a time when mainstream culture asks for complete disclosure from its subjects, but this coming out does have ramifications.

(Green, 2017, p. 320)

Although transgender (trans)[1] students have always taken part in postsecondary education, there has been a recent, increased attention to their presence. Similar to the ways some trans people and communities have become visible through the social sphere, many educators are beginning to think more deeply about gender and the implications of how gender mediates collegiate life. Trans activist Leslie Feinberg (1998) once wrote, "Gender is the poetry each of us makes out of the language we are taught" (p. 10). Arguably, there is no richer time in a person's life than the college years to create that poetry, and no environment more fertile than the contemporary college campus to explore, define, and redefine one's sense of self as a gendered being in the world. As educators, we have the responsibility—and the privilege—to bear witness to and support the poetry making of our students and to be honest and thoughtful about our own process of gender identification. Knowing and understanding the lives of transgender students and constructing environments that affirm all students regardless of gender is what we are called to do. We must know, care, and act to create change to signal that in higher education, all genders are welcome.

However, it would be rash to be overly sanguine about the effects of the increased visibility of transgender students. As noted in the earlier epigraphs, the arrival of transgender people—heralded as the "transgender tipping point" as Laverne Cox graced the cover of *TIME* magazine (Steinmetz, 2014)—is uncomfortably situated with the ongoing realities of threat, violence, and harm. And, as scholars have pointed out, those in higher education cannot abdicate responsibility for this duality; in fact, postsecondary educators may indeed be colluding with the furthering of the systemic violence and transgender oppression (Catalano & Griffin, 2016) trans students must navigate (e.g., Nicolazzo, Marine, & Galarte, 2015). And yet, transgender students continue to forge their own pathways toward engagement on college campuses. That is, despite the social, political, and educational climate built and maintained to *not* support transgender students, trans students continue to practice resilience in ways that allow them to be successful on their own terms as students (Nicolazzo, 2017a).

What, then, are postsecondary college educators (faculty and student affairs educators) to do to engage transgender students further? How can educators recognize their complicity in structural transgender oppression while also deconstructing the false notion of the gender binary? And how can educators know when to intentionally get out of the way and allow transgender students to practice the strategies they developed over time to be successful on their own terms? These are the questions we as authors use to frame this chapter, because while we agree with Feinberg about the poetry of gender, we are also cognizant that one needs practice in understanding, interpreting, and (re)writing that poetry, as well as when to let transgender students themselves take the lead.

Critical Perspectives on Gender

In his 2015 book *Normal Life*, transgender legal scholar Dean Spade laid out a framework that has quickly become a keystone to understanding how discourses of gender restrain life for transgender people. Although not focused on educational contexts, Spade's critical trans politics (CTP) has direct connections to collegiate settings. For example, Spade discussed how transgender oppression influenced one's (in)ability to obtain proper identification documents, access proper sex-segregated facilities, and gain access to health care. These three areas are easily transferable to higher education settings as one can think of the difficulties transgender people—as well as other marginalized populations—often face with changing their names through administrative systems, accessing proper housing and changing rooms on campus, and getting trans-affirmative health care on campus. Toward the end of his book, Spade (2015) articulated that "social justice trickles up, not down," and proposed that readers commit to a course of action in which the "well-being of the most vulnerable will not be compromised for promises of legal and media recognition" (p. 138). In so doing, Spade reminded readers that the promise of social justice—on college campuses and beyond—necessitates centering the needs of those who are most vulnerable, and to do what is needed, not just what may look good in terms of visibility and recognition.

It is with this framework in mind that we approach this chapter. To date, transgender scholars(hip) in the field of higher education has fully embraced CTP, using it to elucidate the machinations of gender binary discourse (Nicolazzo, 2016b, 2017a), or the process by which the gender binary creates (un)written rules that regulate the lives of collegians, with particularly pernicious effects for transgender college students (see Catalano, 2015a, 2015b; Jourian, 2017a, 2017b, 2018; Nicolazzo, 2016b, 2017a). Additionally, CTP serves to remind educators that transgender oppression not only operates on individual and group (interpersonal) levels, but also on institutional and systemic levels as well. Thus, when educators begin to craft and implement more gender-aware practices (Catalano, Wagner, & Davis, 2018), we advise—in concurrence with CTP—that there be multiple strategies that address how to engage transgender students on all three levels. We discuss some of these practices and share resources for educators to do this at the end of this chapter.

Some Important Notes on Language

We do not wish to repeat the various glossaries that exist regarding transgender people and identities (see Catalano & Griffin, 2016; Jourian, 2015a; Nicolazzo, 2017a; Stryker, 2017; Nicolazzo, n.d.). However, we do find it important to spend some time highlighting a few key terms and concepts that will be helpful for understanding this chapter. In fact, we would assert that all researchers, including those who research dominant populations, ought to define terms and concepts as it is a further substantiation of privilege not to do so (Jourian, in press).

Much of the (un)conscious resistance to understanding or generating any agreement on terminology regarding trans identities is rooted in our interchangeable colloquial uses of terms such as "gender" and "sex" (Fausto-Sterling, 2000; Hubbard, 1998; Kessler, 1998; Kessler & McKenna, 1978), including our conflation of these terms throughout postsecondary education (Renn, 2010). Our current understanding of gender roles and expression (masculine and feminine) has become intrinsically linked with biological sex (male and female) (Connell, 2002; Feinberg, 1998). Stryker (2017) pointed out that gender is historical, temporal, geographical, cultural, contingent, and contextual, whereas sex is considered scientifically immutable and fixed, although as Butler (2006) eruditely pointed out, even what we have socially come to understand as "sex" is not nearly as fixed as one may like to believe.

Precisely because the basis of understanding both gender and sex is rooted in faulty binary assumptions, they are unstable constructs. This is often what is meant when people say, "Gender is a social construct"; however, it bears reminding readers that while gender—and sex—are indeed social constructs, and in that sense are fallacies, they also have, to use the words of Patel (2015), "crushingly real consequences" (para. 9). That is, although gender and sex are socially, temporally, and geographically (un)done, they still have the potential to enact serious consequences on those who do not live by their rigid boundaries and rules. These rules and consequences also become heightened when taking various other interlocking systems of oppression and domination into account. For example, anti-Black racism, sexism, and transgender oppression collide to create high vulnerability for trans women as evidenced through empirical literature (James et al., 2016). Similarly, any understanding of how transgender oppression operates for US college students must always take into account the gender binary's roots in settler colonialism. A clear example involves the uncivil "civilizing" project of kidnapping Indigenous youth and regendering them into Western Christian boys and girls in off-reservation boarding schools (Lomawaima, 1993; Lugones, 2007). We expound on these connections not to intentionally confuse or obfuscate, but to disavow readers of the presumptions that there is one monolithic way to come to know who is trans, how trans people understand themselves and each other, and how the current cultural moment shapes trans as a category. In other words, it is important that readers recognize the wide diversity within trans communities, *and* how various systems of oppression overlap with very real—and often asymmetrical, depending on one's identities—effects for these diverse trans people. We must resist the sort of thinking that places transness in the aggregate, into a singular community, which leads to problematic notions of whether someone is "trans enough" (Catalano, 2015b) and belies how transness is one of many multiple social identities trans people hold. Instead, we encourage a pluralistic thinking about trans communities to expand the possibilities of transness and liberatory potentials.

Given these complexities, it is helpful to understand the term *transgender* to encompass a wide range of identities, appearances, and behaviors that blur or cross gender lines. Within this transgender umbrella are transsexuals, who live some or all of the time in a sex different from their assigned sex at birth; cross-dressers (formerly called transvestites), who wear clothes typically associated with the "opposite" gender; drag kings and drag queens, who cross-dress within a specific performance context; and gender radicals (Gagne & Tewksbury, 1999) and genderqueers, who identify outside binary gender or sex systems altogether (Lombardi & Davis, 2006). Additionally, the use of an asterisk with the prefix trans (i.e., trans*) has entered common parlance in research literature. Originally created as a way to denote the capaciousness of the identity category itself (Tompkins, 2014), there have been some who do not use the asterisk, as it has been used in limiting and counterproductive ways (Trans Student Educational Resources, n.d.), while others suggest the use of the asterisk does little to shift antinormative discourse (Titman, 2013). Although we are mindful of the contestation of these terms, we use trans(*) and transgender as umbrella terms because of their current recognition in broader literature. Furthermore, it is important to remember that just as within the breadth and depth of trans communities in our society, college student populations will reflect the multiplicity of trans identities and may create new terms to define their gender.

There are many examples of how all gender identities, but especially trans identities, are "under-construction" (Stryker, 2017, p. 1), especially through a perusal of literature on trans identities. In this chapter, we will use the terms "transgender," "trans," and "trans*" alternately to be inclusive, to resist intergroup or imposed hierarchy (Martin & Yorkin, 2006; Schilt & Waszkiewicz, 2006), and to reflect the broadest possibilities for self-identification. Therefore, "transgender" includes those who subvert the gender binary (Bornstein, 2013) and/or "whose gender identity conflicts with their sex assigned at birth" (Bilodeau, 2005, p. 30). Definitional distinctions are important, but just as important is that we make space for all individuals to "describe and label their own gender identities in whatever ways feel most appropriate to them" (Catalano, McCarthy, & Shlasko, 2007, p. 219).

As previously mentioned, what significantly adds to the confusion around transgender identities, beyond our cultural expectations of gender normativity and sexual orientation binarism (heterosexual and homosexual), is the consistent condensing of lesbian, gay, and bisexual identities with transgender identities (often seen via the moniker LGBT). Thus, mistaking trans identity as a sexual orientation, when in fact it is a gender identity and/or a form of gender expression (Renn, 2010). There is a complex history to the connection between trans identities and marginalized sexual orientations, which is beyond the scope of this chapter; however, for in-depth discussions on the historical linkages and tensions between trans identities and sexual orientations, we refer readers to the work of Minter (2006) and Stryker (2017).

Throughout this chapter, we will also use the term cisgender in reference to those who are not trans identified. "'Cis' is the Latin prefix for 'on the same side,' and indicates an identity for those who experience a match between the gender they were assigned at birth, their bodies, and their personal identity" (Schilt & Westbrook, 2009, p. 461). Additional useful terms to describe the impact of normative gender on trans people include "genderism" (alternately "cissexism") and "transgender oppression." Genderism is the practice of strict adherence to a binary gender system that, by definition, oppresses those who fall outside it—including, but not exclusively, trans* people (Bilodeau, 2005; Hill, 2002; Hill & Willoughby, 2005; Wilchins, 2002). Meanwhile, transgender oppression is the "system of oppression that targets and marginalizes people who are transgender in the broadest sense" (Catalano & Shlasko, 2010, p. 425). While research indicates that genderism and transgender oppression are common experiences of college students who identify as trans (Beemyn, 2005; Bilodeau, 2005; Rankin, Weber, Blumenfeld, & Frazer, 2010), we use the term "transgender oppression" throughout the chapter to keep our attention specifically focused on trans* students.

Who Trans College Students Are

To know how to engage trans* students, it is important to first know who trans students are. While there has been a recent uptick in research centering trans students—much of it done by trans scholars—there are also some persistent gaps in the literature, signaling some not-yet-known potentials for engaging fully the plethora of trans students who are in postsecondary education. In what follows, we review the current literature on trans* collegians, with particular attention paid to how this literature can aid educators' engagement of trans* students. We do so by thinking first about the literature on trans* students as individuals, then on trans* student groups and organizations, as well as on offices that serve trans* students (e.g., LGBTQ centers, residential life, cultural centers). We close by discussing literature focusing on discourses of gender on college campuses as a whole or, put another way, by looking at how institutions are (not) serving trans* students, and on what needs to happen for positive institutional shifts to occur. We then follow this review of the literature with recommendations for postsecondary educators and administrators to consider for furthering gender-aware practice.

Trans Students as Individuals

The past several years have seen a relative explosion of empirical research on trans* students in postsecondary education contexts. While still making up a marginal amount of the total published scholarship on students' gender and sexuality (Garvey, 2014), there is much educators can mine from this recent output. Research regarding trans students spans both curricular (Duran & Nicolazzo, 2017; Pryor, 2015) and co-curricular settings (Case, Kanenberg, Erich, & Tittsworth, 2012; Dugan, Kusel, & Simounet, 2012; Nicolazzo, 2016b). Additionally, researchers have begun to explore interconnections between gender and disability (Miller, 2017), transness and race (Blockett, 2017; Jourian, 2017a; Mobley Jr. & Johnson, 2019; Nicolazzo, 2016a), and transness and sexuality (Jourian, 2018; Nicolazzo, 2017b).

To date, the research focusing on trans students has elucidated the various individual, administrative, institutional, and social barriers trans students confront on college campuses. However, in a turn toward affirmative- and assets-based research, research with trans students has also begun to explore how this student population has continued to find ways of circumventing the oppressive systems and daily microaggressions they face. For example, described as "practices of resilience," Nicolazzo (2016b, 2017a) framed how trans students have always been able to engage a do-it-yourself process of learning how to navigate the campus cultures and systems built without them in mind. Catalano (2015b) noted that participants had a low threshold (low expectations) for what constitutes support on campus; instead, instances of tokenization and exploitation were times when students felt seen or heard. One participant's advice to other trans* men was to "recognize the fact that people are going to ask unfortunate questions." Similarly, Blockett (2017) discussed how Black queer men—a study population that included multiple genderqueer students—engaged in queer world-making practices to reshape their collegiate environments. Jourian (2017b) and Nicolazzo (2016b, 2017a) also wrote about how trans students forge community off-campus, be it virtually or in person. As one participant in Jourian's study emphatically stated, "I don't fuck with campus," and one of Nicolazzo's participants stated, "The internet is basically my hometown." These two short quotations from participants suggest that perhaps engaging trans students in higher education means expanding where and how educators seek to engage them or, rather, that to engage trans students, educators ought to focus on improving their collegiate environments. These quotations also suggest that perhaps there are times when educators need to get out of trans students' ways because they are already engaging themselves in venues that may be more welcoming.

In addition to literature on trans students' (multiple) identities, a development of new theoretical models through which educators can understand trans students now exists. Of particular note, Jourian (2015b) proposed a model "that forwards a dynamic perspective on sex, gender, and sexuality, allowing individuals to embody any of those identities in infinite forms of expression" (p. 464). It does so by not only making room for fluidity in individuals' identities, but by also unsettling the categories themselves, thus acknowledging that the constructs of sex, gender, and sexuality are not static or fixed.

Recognizing the plurality of the trans* student population has become critical to the ongoing project of thinking about how one can engage trans students on campus. In fact, while the literature on trans college students has begun to explore gender alongside other salient social identities as they relate to engagement, there remains much more that ought to be done. For example, little to no empirical work exists regarding various populations of trans Students of Color, including Indigenous, Latinx, Middle Eastern, and Asian Pacific Islander and Desi American (APIDA) trans students; international trans students; transness and spirituality; and trans students with various disabilities. As authors, we would also like to see more research focused on trans women, especially trans women of color, as well as trans students across institutional contexts. For example, at the writing of this chapter, trans students in community college settings are woefully under researched. Additionally, the perspectives and experiences of trans students are often relegated to studies specifically *about* trans students (or to some extent LGBTQ students) rather than integrated across higher education scholarship. This practice others trans students by assuming that the only valuable knowledge that they possess centers on their gender or, at best, that they are afterthoughts or "outliers" to an otherwise binary-constrained student population.

Offices That Serve Trans Students

Marine (2011) traced the emergence of LGBTQ student populations in higher education. In so doing, she was also able to give an account of how LGBTQ affinity spaces developed and became institutionalized on some college campuses. Despite the relatively small number of these offices at four-year institutions (Consortium of Higher Education LGBT Resource Professionals, 2017; Tillapaugh & Catalano, 2018), and their almost complete absence at two-year institutions (Samoff, 2018), it would seem to be all the more crucial that those LGBTQ centers in existence would serve trans students effectively. However, the available literature on this topic shows several pitfalls and oversights in terms of these offices' engaging trans students.

Tillapaugh and Catalano (2018) described the effects of graduate assistants who serve as the singular point of contact for their campuses' LGBTQ centers as: (1) feeling set up to fail; (2) experiencing a paltry amount of onboarding, if any at all; (3) not receiving adequate supervision or professional development; and (4) being (understandably) overwhelmed with the volume of work required of them, all of which they are unable to complete in the 20 hours per week their GA appointment entails, as well as with limited financial resources. In several instances, Tillapaugh and Catalano (2018) talked with GAs who were tracked out of LGBTQ center work as a result of their GA experience. Not only does their study speak to the continued underresourcing of LGBTQ centers on college campuses; it also serves as a reminder of how GAs are disciplined by neoliberal ideologies of "doing more with less," which then translates to their not demanding adequate funding, staffing, support, and/or training they need to fulfill their roles and responsibilities. One might reasonably deduce that in such resource-strapped settings, the ability of GAs to more intentionally engage trans student populations in a disaggregated manner is at best constrained.

Previous literature has also demonstrated that, even when LGBTQ centers exist on college campuses, trans* and gender nonconforming students may be leery of utilizing them (Rankin et al., 2010). While some of this may be based on the overwhelming whiteness of these spaces (Consortium of Higher Education LGBT Resource Professionals, 2016; Nicolazzo, 2016a, 2017a), there is also a demonstrated lack of attention, programming, and services specifically *for* trans students. As Marine and Nicolazzo (2014) found, much of the trans*-related programming done by LGBTQ center staff was *about* and not *for* trans* students. In other words, trans*-related knowledge and programming focused outward to cisgender populations and not internally toward trans* students themselves. While Marine and Nicolazzo (2014) were quick to recognize the importance of outward-facing programming about trans* people and identities, they were justly concerned that the lack of programming for trans* students reproduced the same lack of support and recognition of their realities, albeit more pronounced due to its coming from a space specifically designed with their well-being in mind.

Cultural Theories of Gender in Postsecondary Education

In Nicolazzo's (2017a) book on trans* students' experiences in higher education, she elucidates what she referred to as "twin cultural realities" (p. 80) of gender on campus. Specifically, she discussed *gender binary discourse* and *compulsory heterogenderism* as shaping how educational administrators come to know gender and, as a result, come to un/know trans students. In brief, these cultural realities are (un)written rules that stipulate "appropriate" gender expression (i.e., gender binary discourse) and the use of sexuality-based stereotypes that render one's trans*ness invisible and/or unknowable (e.g., a transfeminine person being misunderstood as an effeminate gay man). Different from being about individual trans* peoples' experiences or groups/organizations/offices, these discourses permeate the entirety of higher education. In other words, gender binary discourse and compulsory heterogenderism are omnipresent in postsecondary education and, as a result, influence how one thinks—or perhaps how one does not think—about trans* students.

Building off Patton's (2016) work elucidating the effects of epistemological racism in higher education, Nicolazzo (2017) developed a way to understand *epistemological trans* oppression*, or the myriad ways the foundations of higher education are structured to disallow one thinking about gender in expansive, trans*-affirmative ways. This inhibiting of thought has far-reaching implications for how one may behave as a result of such (lack of) knowledge. For example, the resistance from cisgender people that trans people are not *really* the gender they identify as means many trans collegians move through collegiate spaces in fear. And when cisgender people's understanding of trans*ness has its roots in fear, then "saving" trans students stems from pity instead of coalitions of empowerment, furthering the othering of trans* people implied via epistemological trans* oppression. And, although they did not use the phrase, Patton (2014) and Mobley Jr. and Johnson (2019) highlighted how epistemological trans* oppression leads to overt forms of policy-based gender policing, as has happened through the Morehouse Appropriate Attire Policy. In her work, Nicolazzo (2017) traces trans* legacies as a way to uncover a trans-centric way of knowing. Similar to the work of Brayboy (2005), Delgado Bernal (2002), and Patton (2016), Nicolazzo's work is a counter-story to how postsecondary education has come to (not) take up gender and illuminates pathways down which educators can both unlearn their own investments in trans* oppression and recognize the full humanity of the trans* people on their campuses.

Far from purely abstract and theoretical, the growing conversations about discourses of gender, as well as epistemological concerns related to how one comes to (not) know gender in expansive ways, is deeply important to how educators can engage trans* students in higher education. As an applied field, student affairs educators face the task of putting empirical research into practice to further student learning and development. What focusing on cultural discourses of gender invites educators to do, however, is think about how one comes to put into practice the knowledge one acquires. For example, Catalano (2015b) wrote about how discourses of gender influence trans men's feeling "not [trans] enough," which then mediates their decisions regarding biomedical transition (e.g., taking testosterone, having top surgery). Here, educators can begin to recognize the ways one (does not) think about gender not only influences trans students' self-conceptions (internal and external recognition), but also how one comes to know transness as a category of difference and, as a result, how to engage trans students. As such, we as authors suggest it is important for postsecondary educators to engage in backward thinking (Tillapaugh & Nicolazzo, 2014), or the practice of recognizing how one came to know what they assert to know, and to think deeply about how their guiding epistemological groundings and the discourses in which they've been socialized influence their thinking and actions.

Coming at our understandings of gender (broadly or of particular identities/expressions) from a trans-centered perspective exposes how "we assume we all know what we are talking about based on dominant and default representations" (Jourian, 2017c, p. 416) of gender. Employing a trans* method or trans* analytic—in other words, a trans way of thinking, knowing, and analysis—forces us to "be more attuned to difference rather than sameness," as well as the "potential to be made anew and undone perpetually that marks ongoing transformation" (Green, 2016, p. 79). Said differently, to think trans* is to unmask and then move away from the default, continuously transforming ourselves in order to transform how we engage trans students. It also promotes a decoupling of gender and sexuality in thought and action, thereby deconstructing compulsory heterogenderism.

Student Engagement Strategies

If critical trans politics is a practice, and if it being a practice means one must continually repeat it—or one must practice "constant reflection and self-evaluation" (Spade, 2015, p. 1)—then to provide a list of best practices becomes a gilded experiment that provides the veneer of progress regarding trans* inclusion but may in its very existence cover up practices, attitudes, and an overall ethos of trans* exclusion.

(Nicolazzo, 2017a, p. 140)

As the epigraph at the start of this section expounds, the idea of providing best practices for trans inclusion is problematic. Given the complexity of campus environments, we must acknowledge how the ecological dynamics of any campus will influence the effectiveness of any given practice-based intervention, as will the diversity and specificities of campus populations. There are limitations about what we know of the experiences of trans students on college campuses and may not map onto various institutional types. However, we offer the following recommendations that allow for reflection and action by student affairs professionals and other educators to potentially improve the experiences, retention, and persistence of trans students and reduce the social and psychological cost of trans oppression.

Engage in Gender-Reflection Work

One of the benefits of doing gender-reflection work is that it allows cisgender and transgender people to communicate about shared experiences of gender socialization and resistance, deepening respect and empathy toward the infinite possibility of genders around us. The utility of everyone doing gender-reflection work is to avoid communication of unintentional microaggressions, verbally or nonverbally, to trans people (Nadal, Rivera, & Corpus, 2010). At a personal level, gender reflection provides an opportunity to give one's self permission to explore all manner of things previously discouraged. Gender reflection also allows us to approach our work from a gender-aware perspective, meaning we consciously consider how gender influences all aspects of our lives and our multiple identities (Catalano, Wagner, & Davis, 2018). Our work as educators means that we must continuously unpack our socialization in an attempt to understand how we came to view the world as we do and how we may change our perceptions towards building more inclusive communities. Educators can begin with a resource, such as *My Gender Workbook: How to Become a Real Man, a Real Woman, the Real*

You, or Something Else Entirely, authored by Kate Bornstein (2013). This book includes numerous exercises and activities for reflection on one's own personal gender journey, including ways to identify significant events in one's life that solidified gender identity and strategies to meaningfully challenge the dominant culture's restrictive definitions of gender. Another resource for facilitation and teaching on trans issues is the chapter on transgender oppression in *Teachings for Diversity and Social Justice* (second edition) (Catalano, McCarthy, & Shlasko, 2007).

Listen to Trans Students

While reading this chapter is an important step on the journey to working meaningfully with trans students, it offers an overview and not a complete picture of the experiences of this diverse student population. The next step in understanding the challenges and supports inherent for any minoritized group is to take the time to seek out and remain open to the perspectives of the affected population, without presuming we already know what they need. To that end, student affairs educators can best understand areas of needed change through a concerted effort to obtain first-person perspectives from trans students in their community. Assurance of confidentiality and safety in these conversations is paramount; students should never have to feel they are "on display" for the learning benefit of others. Putting out the word through related student communities (i.e., women's and gender study programs, LGBT centers, and LGBT student organizations) that you are open and interested in learning more about trans student experiences is a good first step. As noted by Hanson (2010), an institution should only undertake these efforts if the institution is ready to begin acting on the information offered. It is important to avoid tokenizing trans students as there is a balance student affairs educators must find between honoring student voices and agency and expecting their words to speak on behalf of all trans students and communities. In addition to suspending presumptions of our own knowledge as educators of what trans students need, it would behoove us to extend grace and not presume trans students themselves know all that they need, as well as have depth of knowledge about trans*ness or an ability/desire to articulate those needs.

Learn More About Trans Politics, Identities, Interests, and Concerns

Student experiences and narratives are important for context, and we should do our own reading and content learning on broader issues of trans identity. Institutions can support this effort through professional development for staff and faculty. We must seek knowledge beyond the students we work with day to day and educate ourselves about trans politics, histories, and experiences. We can begin this work with seeking information and conversations about how gender functions in our own lives and in our institutions. Trans*ness is complex and dynamic. The impact of transgender oppression, especially as it intersects with other forms of oppression (e.g., racism, femmephobia, misogyny, and classism), means there can be a diverse number of ways for trans individuals' abilities and desires to persist into higher education (James et al., 2016). Educators who invest in complicating their knowledge of trans experiences will help them understand how they may have a limited view of broader trans communities. Hart and Lester (2011) noted that when college communities attempt to engage in conversations on trans issues, there are often superficial responses marked by the power of an institutionally enforced silence, which reveals absences of discourse, policy, and practice changes. Whether our silences are born out of lack of knowledge, assumptions that we have already addressed these issues, or an attempt to wait until we are certain we have trans students at our institution, our silence has the impact of making trans students invisible and ultimately, underserved. If we think about our work with critical trans politics as nuanced and coalition building, then our greater understandings of trans*ness will only increase our potential to create sustainable institutional changes that allow for trans students to be their whole selves (not just trans).

Address Material Realities to Create Trans-Inclusive Campuses

A common refrain when considering how colleges can change their campuses to be more trans inclusive is "Well, how many trans students are there, anyway?" Our response to this question is to ask how often we consider whether the relatively small number of trans students present on our campuses is a function of imposed invisibility and marginality. As noted by Spade (2015), we can focus our attention on three areas of policy to address material needs: health care, identifications, and facilities. Institutions can focus their attention to address trans inclusion as it regards college records and documentation, counseling and health services, bathrooms and locker rooms, campus housing, staff competencies, and support services. Working to include gender identity and expression in your institution's nondiscrimination policy can set an important stage for addressing trans student's visibility. At the same time, policy changes are not a panacea to issues of inclusion and issues of exclusion (intentional or unintentional). If there are not institutional practices to support policy changes along with knowledge about why this policy change occurred, then the policy changes are hollow or nonperformative (Ahmed, 2012). Institutional practices require the application of institutional values in the everyday work of the people who work at the institution.

We encourage an approach that invests in sustainable institutional interventions. Creating a standing task force or committee with institutional power to influence campus policies and other efforts is a starting point for trans-affirming campus culture shifts. The work begins with assessment of current practices and areas for improvement. A thoughtful, diverse group of faculty, staff, and students, committed to the practice of collaborative transformation (Marine, 2011) of the campus, can then work together to identify areas needing improvement, and marshal the human and other resources required to make change (e.g., Case et al., 2012).

Improve Trans-Inclusion Practices of LGBT Resource Centers

Currently, approximately 320 US colleges and universities, representing less than 3% of all institutions, have a professional staff member (working at least half time) or graduate assistant (solely dedicated to LGBT services) to support, advocacy, and education on LGBT student needs (Consortium of Higher Education LGBT Resource Professionals,

2017). Given such limited numbers of staff members, any attempt to be inclusive of all sexualities and genders is an unfair burden for those in these roles to expect they can meet the needs of all LGBT students, let alone specifically trans students. While design of centers was to pull marginalized identities into visibility, we have instead developed centers on the periphery, typically solely responsible for LGBTQ support and advocacy. Broader campus collaborations and investments must occur to avoid the idea of filtering all trans related issues through one office and, in some cases, one staff person. Even when there is a center at a given institution, it does not mean that trans students will go there for advice or support. Trans students may not seek out an LGBT center for a variety of reasons; it is reasonable (and likely) that a trans student with a financial aid problem may go to the financial aid office, and that a trans student struggling with balancing their identity development process and their coursework may seek out an academic advisor instead of the staff of the LGBT center. As legal issues related to trans students begin to play out in the courts and on campus, the staff of the financial aid office needs to be knowledgeable about topics such as the ways that the federal financial aid system might trigger an investigation into a student's record when their assigned and declared gender do not match (Burns, 2011). Additionally, reflective of the broader erasure of trans people and communities (what Spade (2008) refers to as the "LGBfakeT movement"), it is a dangerous assumption that LGBT centers are affirming spaces for trans students, particularly multiply marginalized students.

Note

1 The contestation about language and trans identities, specifically the use of or refusal to use the asterisk, is beyond the scope of this chapter. We use trans, trans*, and transgender interchangeably throughout the chapter to acknowledge these in-community tensions. Some uses directly reflect the language of the works cited, and we honor the choices made by those authors. We also use the asterisk in our writing as a visual reminder to readers to pause and reflect on just who and how they come to know trans* as an identity.

References

Ahmed, S. (2012). *On being included: Racism and diversity in Institutional Life*. Durham, NC: Duke University Press.

Beemyn, B. G. (2005). Trans on campus: Measuring and improving the climate for transgender students. *On Campus with Women, 34*(3). www.aacu.org/ocww/volume34_33/feature.cfm?section=32

Bilodeau, B. (2005). Beyond the gender binary: A case study of two transgender students at a midwestern research university. *Journal of Gay and Lesbian Issues in Education, 3*(1), 29–44.

Blockett, R. A. (2017). "I think it's very much placed on us": Black queer men laboring to forge community at a predominantly White and (hetero)cisnormative research institution. *International Journal of Qualitative Studies in Education, 30*(8), 800–816. doi:10.1080/09518398.2017.1350296

Bornstein, K. (2013). *My new gender workbook*. New York, NY: Routledge.

Brayboy, B. M. J. (2005). Toward a tribal critical race theory in education. *The Urban Review, 37*, 425–446.

Burns, C. (2011). *Unequal aid discriminatory treatment of gay and transgender applicants and families headed by same-sex couples in the higher education financial aid process*. Report for Center for American Progress. Retrieved on October 15, 2011, from www.americanprogress.org/issues/2011/08/pdf/lgbt_higher_ed.pdf

Butler, J. (2006). *Gender trouble: Feminism and the subversion of identity*. New York, NY: Routledge.

Case, K. A., Kanenberg, H., Erich, S. A., & Tittsworth, J. (2012). Transgender inclusion in university non-discrimination statements: Challenging gender-conforming privilege through student activism. *Journal of Social Issues, 68*, 145–161.

Catalano, D. C., McCarthy, L., & Shlasko, D. (2007). Transgender Oppression. In M. Adams, L. A. Bell, & P. Griffin (Eds.), *Teaching for diversity and social justice* (2nd ed., pp. 219–245). New York, NY: Routledge.

Catalano, D. C., & Shlasko, D. (2010). Transgender Oppression. In M. Adams, et al. (Eds.), *Readings for diversity and social justice* (2nd ed., pp. 423–456). New York, NY: Routledge.

Catalano, D. C. J. (2015a). Beyond virtual equality: Liberatory consciousness as a path to achieve trans* inclusion in higher education. *Equity & Excellence in Education, 48*(3), 418–435.

Catalano, D. C. J. (2015b). "Trans enough?": The pressures trans men negotiate in higher education. *TSQ: Transgender Studies Quarterly, 2*(3), 411–430.

Catalano, D. C. J., & Griffin, P. (2016). Sexism, heterosexism, and trans* oppression. In M. Adams, L. A. Bell, D. J. Goodman, & K. Y. Joshi (Eds.), *Teaching for diversity and social justice* (3rd ed., pp. 183–211). New York, NY: Routledge.

Catalano, D. C. J., Wagner, R., & Davis, T. (2018). Approaching masculinities through a gender-aware practice framework. In D. C. J. Catalano, R. Wagner, & T. Davis (Eds.), *Masculinities in student affairs: Intersectional theories in practice* (New Directions in Student Services, No. 164, pp. 11–17). San Francisco, CA: Jossey-Bass.

Connell, R. W. (2002). *Gender*. Cambridge, England: Polity Press.

Consortium of Higher Education LGBT Resource Professionals. (2016, April). *Recommendations for supporting trans and queer students of color* [Report]. Retrieved from https://lgbtcampus.memberclicks.net/assets/tqsoc%20support%202016.pdf

Consortium of Higher Education LGBT Resource Professionals. (2017). *Find an LGBTQ center*. [Website]. Retrieved from www.lgbtcampus.org/find-an-lgbtq-campus-center

Delgado Bernal, D. (2002). Critical race theory, Latino critical theory, and critical raced-gendered epistemologies: Recognizing students of color as holders and creators of knowledge. *Qualitative Inquiry, 8*, 105–126.

Dugan, J. P., Kusel, M. L., & Simounet, D. M. (2012). Transgender college students: An exploratory study of perceptions, engagement, and educational outcomes. *Journal of College Student Development, 53*, 719–736.

Duran, A., & Nicolazzo, Z. (2017). Exploring the ways trans* collegians navigate academic, romantic, and social relationships. *Journal of College Student Development, 58*(4), 526–544. doi:10.1353/csd.2017.0041

Fausto-Sterling, A. (2000). *Sexing the body: Gender politics and the construction of sexuality*. New York, NY: Basic Books.

Feinberg, L. (1998). *Trans Liberation: Beyond Pink or Blue*. Boston, MA: Beacon Press.

Gagne, P., & Tewksbury, R. (1999). Knowledge and power, body, and self: An analysis of knowledge systems and the transgendered self. *Sociological Quarterly, 40*(1), 59–83.

Garvey, J. C. (2014). Demographic information collection in higher education and student affairs survey instruments: Developing a national landscape for intersectionality. In D. Mitchell, Jr., C. Y. Simmons, & L. A. Greyerbiehl (Eds.), *Intersectionality & higher education: Theory, research, and praxis* (pp. 201–216). New York, NY: Peter Lang.

Grace, R. (2015, April 6). *"What are we defending?": Reina's talk at the INCITE! COV4 conference* [Blog post]. Retrieved from www.reinagossett.com/what-are-we-defending-reinas-talk-at-the-incite-cov4-conference/

Green, K. M. (2016). Troubling the waters: Mobilizing a trans* analytic. In E. P. Johnson (Ed.), *No tea, no shade: New writings in Black queer studies* (pp. 65–82). Durham, NC: Duke University Press.

Green, K. M. (2017). Trans* movement/trans* moment: An afterword. *International Journal of Qualitative Studies in Education, 30*(3), 320–321.

Hanson, D. E. (2010, November 10). Institutions can launch assessments of their LGBT climate, but should they? *NetResults: Critical issues for student affairs practitioners*. Retrieved October 4, 2011, from www.naspa.org/membership/mem/pubs/nr/default.cfm?id=1756

Hart, J., & Lester, J. (2011). Starring students: Gender performance at a women's college. *NASPA Journal About Women in Higher Education, 4*(2), 193–217.

Hill, D. B. (2002). Genderism, transphobia, and gender bashing: A framework for interpreting anti-transgender violence. In B. Wallace & R. Carter (Eds.), *Understanding and dealing with violence: A multicultural approach* (pp. 113–136). Thousand Oaks, CA: Sage.

Hill, D. B., & Willoughby, B. L. B. (2005). The development and validation of the genderism and transphobia scale. *Sex Roles, 53*, 531–544.

Hubbard, R. (1998). Gender and genitals: Constructs of sex and gender. In D. Denny (Ed.), *Current concepts in transgender identity* (pp. 45–54). New York, NY: Garland Publishing.

James, S. E., Herman, J. L., Rankin, S., Keisling, M., Mottet, L., & Anafi, M. (2016). *The report of the 2015 US transgender survey.* Washington, DC: National Center for Transgender Equality.

Jourian, T. J. (2015a). *Evolving nature of sexual orientation and gender identity* (New directions for student services, No. 152). pp. 11–23.

Jourian, T. J. (2015b). Queering constructs: Proposing a dynamic gender and sexuality model. *The Educational Forum, 79*(4), 459–474. doi:10.1080/00131725.2015.1068900

Jourian, T. J. (2017a). "Fun and carefree like my polka dot bowtie": Disidentifications of trans*masculine students of color. In J. M. Johnson & G. C. Javier (Eds.), *Queer people of color in higher education* (pp. 123–143). Charlotte, NC: Information Age Publishing.

Jourian, T. J. (2017b). Trans*forming college masculinities: Carving out trans*masculine pathways through the threshold of dominance. *International Journal of Qualitative Studies in Education, 30*(3), 245–265. doi:10.1080/09518398.2016.1257752

Jourian, T. J. (2017c). Trans*ing constructs: Towards a critical trans* methodology. *Dutch Journal of Gender Studies, 20*(4), 415–434.

Jourian, T. J. (2018). Sexua-romanticised pathways of transmasculine college students in the USA. *Sex Education, 18*(4), 360–375.

Jourian, T. J. (in press). Transfeminist methodology: Examining cissexism in higher education and student affairs research. In N. Niemi & M. Weaver-Hightower (Eds.), *The international handbook of gender equity in higher education.*

Kessler, S. J. (1998). *Lessons from the intersexed.* New Brunswick, NJ: Rutgers University Press.

Kessler, S. J., & McKenna, W. (1978). *Gender: An ethnomothodological approach.* Chicago, IL: University of Chicago Press.

Lomawaima, K. T. (1993). Domesticity in the federal Indian schools: The power of authority over mind and body. *American Ethnologist, 20*(2), 227–240.

Lombardi, E., & Davis, S. M. (2006). Transgender health issues. In D. F. Marrow & L. Messinger (Eds.), *Sexual orientation and gender expression in social work practice* (pp. 343–363). New York, NY: Columbia University Press.

Lugones, M. (2007). Heterosexualism and the colonial/modern gender system. *Hypatia, 22*(1), 186–209.

Marine, S. B. (2011). Stonewall's legacy: Bisexual, gay, lesbian, and transgender students in higher education. *ASHE Higher Education Report, 37*(4).

Marine, S. B., & Nicolazzo, Z. (2014). Names that matter: Exploring the complexities of the experiences of trans* individuals in LGBTQ centers. *Journal of Diversity in Higher Education, 7*(4), 265–281. doi:10.1037/a0037990

Martin, J. I., & Yorkin, D. R. (2006). Transgender identity. In D. F. Morrow & L. Messinger (Eds.), *Sexual orientation and gender expression in social work practice: Working with lesbian, gay, bisexual, and transgender people.* New York, NY: Columbia University Press.

Miller, R. A. (2017). "My voice is definitely strongest in online communities": Students using social media for queer and disability identity-making. *Journal of College Student Development, 58*(4), 509–525.

Minter, S. P. (2006). Do transsexuals dream of gay rights? Getting real about transgender inclusion. In P. Currah, R. M. Juang, & S. P. Minter (Eds.), *Transgender rights* (pp. 141–170). Minneapolis, MN: University of Minnesota Press.

Mobley Jr., S. D., & Johnson, J. M. (2019). "No pumps allowed": The "problem" with gender expression and the Morehouse College "Appropriate Attire Policy." *Journal of Homosexuality, 66*(7), 867–895.

Nadal, K. L., Rivera, D. P., & Corpus, M. J. H. (2010). Sexual orientation and transgender microaggressions. In D. W. Sue (Ed.), *Microaggressions and marginality: Manifestations, dynamics, and impact* (pp. 217–240). Hoboken, NJ: Wiley.

Nicolazzo, Z. (2017). Imagining a trans* epistemology: What liberation thinks like in higher education. *Urban Education*. Advanced online publication. doi:10.1177/0042085917697203

Nicolazzo, Z. (2016a). "It's a hard line to walk": Black non-binary trans* collegians' perceptions on passing, realness, and trans*-normativity. *International Journal of Qualitative Studies in Education, 29*(9), 1173–1188. doi:10.1080/09518398.2016.1201612

Nicolazzo, Z. (2016b). "Just go in looking good": The resilience, resistance, and kinship-building of trans* college students. *Journal of College Student Development, 57*(5), 538–556. doi:10.1353/csd.2016.0057

Nicolazzo, Z. (2017a). *Trans* in college: Transgender students' strategies for navigating campus life and the institutional politics of inclusion*. Sterling, VA: Stylus.

Nicolazzo, Z. (2017b). Compulsory heterogenderism: A collective case study. *NASPA Journal About Women in Higher Education, 10*(3), 245–261. doi:10.1080/19407882.2017.1351376

Nicolazzo, Z. (n.d.). *Trans* studies in higher education syllabus*. Retrieved from https://docs.google.com/document/d/1uUFd5pMlLTOigvVtt9uJYmimhH2w4rZL9azrrUiqZJc/edit

Nicolazzo, Z, Marine, S. B., & Galarte, F. J. (2015). Introduction. *TSQ: Transgender Studies Quarterly, 2*(3), 367–375.

Patel, L. (2015, June 17). *Why racial justice is not what we need at this moment* [Blogpost]. Retrieved from https://decolonizing.wordpress.com/2015/06/17/why-racial-justice-is-not-what-we-need-at-this-moment/

Patton, L. D. (2014). Preserving respectability or blatant disrespect?: A critical discourse analysis of the Morehouse Appropriate Attire Policy and implications for intersectional approaches to examining campus policies. *International Journal of Qualitative Studies in Education, 27*(6), 724–746.

Patton, L. D. (2016). Disrupting postsecondary prose: Toward a critical race theory of higher education. *Urban Education, 51*(3), 315–342.

Pryor, J. T. (2015). Out in the classroom: Transgender student experiences at a large public university. *Journal of College Student Development, 56*(5), 440–456.

Rankin, S., Weber, G., Blumenfeld, W., & Frazer, S. (2010). *The state of higher education for lesbian, gay, bisexual, and transgender people*. Campus Pride: Charlotte, NC.

Renn, K. A. (2010). LGBT and queer research in higher education: The state and status of the field. *Educational Researcher, 39*(2), 132–141.

Samoff, S. A. (2018). *Transgender community college students' perceptions of campus climate and inclusiveness* (dissertation), California State University Fullerton.

Schilt, K. R., & Waszkiewicz, E. (2006). *I feel so much more in my body: Challenging the significance of the penis in transsexual men's bodies*. Paper presented at the annual meeting of the American Sociological Association, Montreal Quebec, Canada Online <PDF>. Retrieved October 22, 2008, from www.allacademic.com/meta/p104747_index.html

Schilt, K. R., & Westbrook, L. (2009). Doing gender, doing heteronormativity: "Gender normals," transgender people and the social maintenance of heterosexuality. *Gender & Society, 23*(4), 440–464.

Spade, D. (2008). Fighting to win. In M. Bernstein Sycamore (Ed.), *That's revolting!: Queer strategies for resisting assimilation* (pp. 47–53). Berkeley, CA: Soft Skull Press.

Spade, D. (2015). *Normal life: Administrative violence, critical trans politics, and the limits of law (revised and expanded edition)*. Durham, NC: Duke University Press.

Steinmetz, K. (2014, June 9). The transgender tipping point: America's next civil rights frontier. *Time, 22*(183), 38–46.

Stryker, S. (2017). *Transgender history* (2nd ed.). Berkeley, CA: Seal Press.

Tillapaugh, D., & Catalano, D. C. J. (2018). Structural challenges affecting the experiences of public university LGBT services graduate assistants. *Journal of Diversity in Higher Education*. Advance online publication. http://dx.doi.org/10.1037/dhe0000079

Tillapaugh, D., & Nicolazzo, Z. (2014). Backward thinking: Exploring the relationship among intersectionality, epistemology, and research design. In D. Mitchell Jr., C. Y. Simmons, & L. A. Greyerbiehl (Eds.), *Intersectionality & higher education: Theory, research, & praxis* (pp. 112–122). New York, NY: Peter Lang.

Titman, N. (2013, October 31). *About that often misunderstood asterisk* [Blog post]. Retrieved from http://practicalandrogyny.com/2013/10/31/about-that-often-misunderstood-asterisk/

Tompkins, A. (2014). Asterisk. *Transgender Studies Quarterly, 1*(1/2), 26–27.

Trans Student Educational Resources. (n.d.). *Why we used trans* and why we don't anymore* [Blog post]. Retrieved from www.transstudent.org/asterisk

Wilchins, R. A. (2002). Queerer bodies. In J. Nestle, C. Howell, & R. A. Wilchins (Eds.), *Genderqueer: Voices from beyond the sexual binary* (pp. 33–47). Los Angeles, CA: Alyson books.

Chapter 12
Engaging Cisgender Women and Men Students

Christopher M. Fiorello and Jaime Lester

In a way that has perhaps not been seen since the 1960s and 1970s, gender is at the forefront of contemporary political and social discourse. In the period since the previous edition of this book, the #MeToo movement has spoken with a firm voice, sending waves through Hollywood, media, politics, and business, leading to hundreds of resignations and reshaping these industries as women have assumed nearly half these positions (Carlson et al., 2018). In 2017, the Women's March on Washington showed that collective action and protest about gender is very much alive in US politics. Accompanying the #MeToo movement is the entrance of toxic masculinity into the popular discourse and an increased awareness that men, too, are, as Kimmel and Messner (2007) note, "gendered beings." Simultaneously, there is a backlash. A Gillette commercial aired during the 2019 Superbowl that invoked the #MeToo movement and encouraged men to be their best through words and actions that dismantle toxic masculinity. Their message, "We believe in the best in men," which could have been and should have been a powerful message of support and unity, divided audiences (see Tovia, 2019). Students exist at the nexus of the #MeToo movement, toxic masculinity discourse, and the resistance to both. The events of this time will inform and shape students' gender and identity development. Meaning that, there is an increasing need for student affairs professionals and researchers to engage conversations about gender and identity.

The state of research on gender and student identity development continues to expand. Concepts such as intersectionality, critical race theory, and queer theory are being used to understand the complexity of student identity development (Torres, Jones, & Renn, 2009). In addition, as Torres, Jones, and Renn (2009) argue, long-held psychological and sociological theories are being modified to account for more contemporary ideas that emphasize status versus stage in psychological development theories and the socially constructed nature of identity, for example. Of note in the more recent research is the attention to other populations, such as gay and lesbian students, transgender and gender nonconforming students, students of different socioeconomic statuses, and Students of Color. Each of these identities (race/ethnicity, gender, sexuality, religion, and class) is integral to identity development among college students (Abes, Jones, & McEwen, 2007; Evans, Forney, Guido, Patton, & Renn, 2010; Nicolazzo, 2017).

There are several key areas consistent with the progressive changes in student development that need additional consideration to account for the relationship between gender and student development theory. Consistent with the two theoretical frameworks—feminist poststructuralism and social constructionism—presented in the chapter, three key areas are of note:

1. *Intersection of identity that allows for participants to define and fluidly move between identities.* While there is a burgeoning literature on the multiplicity of identity, these studies often predetermine and strictly define identities. Students are defined by the relationship between and within their race/ethnicity, gender, social class, and so forth.
2. *Integration of power to beyond structural dynamics that limit the ability of students to express their identities.* Critical race theory places oppression as a structure that arises from the sociohistorical marginalization of groups. As we will discuss, poststructuralist ideas of power complicate and expand the sources, presence, and use of power.
3. *Impact of conforming to and performing gender norms on an individual's identity.* Much of the literature notes the impact of gender norms on individuals and shows the limiting nature of norms. However, the literature does little to explain the identity impact. How does the performing of one's gender, the doing of gender, impact their gender identity?

These three areas are of particular importance to the examination of gender and student development theory due to the complex nature of gender social norms in the academy.

Students enter higher education with 18 or more years of gender identity development that is often consistent with sociocultural notions of gender and can have an impact on their collegiate success. Sax (2008) found in her work that women rate themselves lower in mathematical ability, intellectualism, and competitiveness than men. Women are also more likely to conform to gender norms around family, service, and community while men prioritize partying, exercising, and playing video games. Students are also confronting the relationship between and among their various identities in a way that is not predetermined or prescribed. Finally, students encounter the power structures within the academy that are connected to gender norms. These can include cultural definitions of what it means to be masculine and a successful student, the majority/minority of a single gender in the classroom or academic major, and hierarchies that exist in social clubs, Greek life, and other groups on campus. Students are confronting not only their own individual identity development, but also the gender norms present in their new context—a college or university. Gender intersects and interacts with other salient identity dimensions (e.g., race/ethnicity, religion, sexual orientation, etc.) and shapes students' self-concept and the ways in which they experience college contexts (Abes et al., 2007; Evans et al., 2010). Moreover, there is compelling empirical evidence suggesting that students experience a range of challenges and issues (which will be discussed later in this chapter) attributable, in part, to their gender identities. Thus, our focus on gender as a salient construct in student development is warranted. The issues we consider in this chapter have significant implications for the work of college educators, notably faculty and student affairs professionals, in ensuring that students experience the gains and outcomes that are assumed to accompany participation in higher education.

For the purposes of this chapter, we conceptualize identity consistent with social constructivism. We define identity as "the interface between the individual and the world, defining as it does what the individual will stand for and be recognized as" (Josselson, 1987, p. 8). Identity is then constructed based on interactions with others and can change based on contexts; identity is fluid and ever changing. Identity is a central principle to the college student population as traditional-aged students enter college at a time when they are beginning the adult development process. Implicit within these areas is our understanding that gender is neither fixed nor binary. Gender is social practice and performative imitation situated within a given time, place, and culture (Butler, 1990; Connell, 2005). The decision to utilize binary gender within this chapter is our strategic choice as educators. As Linda Alcoff (1988) observes,

> Thus, we can say at one and the same time that gender is not natural, biological, universal, ahistorical, or essential and yet still claim that gender is relevant because we are taking gender as a position from which to act politically.
>
> (p. 433)

This discussion is not about men and women, but rather it is about the dominant social constructs that frame the discussion of gender and student identity development. We adopt this approach in order to address the practical implications of gendered social categories. In utilizing this position, we are careful to state directly that there are many constructions of gender.

We begin this chapter by presenting two theoretical frameworks to address the key areas of need in gender identity development—feminist poststructuralism and social constructionism—and their implications for practice follow. We then outline key issues and challenges in the identity development among men and women in colleges and universities across the United States. Intricate pictures of gender in universities illustrate the complexities of the experiences of men and women students. Finally, we provide an extensive discussion of strategies for applying these perspectives to a college or university setting.

Theoretical Approaches to the Examination of Gender Identity Among Cisgender Women and Men

In this section, we introduce two epistemological approaches to the study of gender among cisgender women and men: feminist poststructuralism and social constructionism. As the name suggests, feminist poststructuralism is an extension of modern feminist thought. Poststructuralism is a response to feminist critiques of essentialism, the ideal that gender is an inherent, single, and immutable essence with which one is born (Weedon, 1997). It offers a framework in which gender is socially constructed through language, and the meanings of identity and power are multiple and fluid. Social constructionism as used in the study of gender similarly responds to essentialist notions. In the social constructionist model, gender is a series of relations constructed within a given time, space, and culture. While both approaches offer anti-essentialist perspectives, they differ in their approaches to notions of power. Social constructionism emphasizes the power of institutions and social structures, whereas poststructuralism emphasizes multiple meanings of power constructed within the discursive with emphasis on the situation, the circumstances, and the speaker. We present feminist poststructuralism as an epistemological approach to the study of women and social constructionism as an epistemological approach to the study of men. We do so because they are more frequently used in this way in the existing literature on gender. However, these approaches are not inherent to the study of either women or men. The question for scholars and practitioners in determining which perspective is best suited to their needs is: How do I interpret the nature of power and identity?

Feminist Poststructuralism

Decades of research on women's student identity development discuss the profound effect that social relationships have in forming and framing identity. Gilligan (1982), Belenky, Clinchy, Goldberger, and Tarule (1986), and Josselson (1987) each challenged the prevailing body of academic research, which assumed men's experiences as universal by focusing on relationships as the site of women's identity development. However, this, too, presupposes a fixed and universal development for all women. The diversity of experience as well as the intersections of class, race, and sexuality and the fluidity of identity development have been largely ignored. In order to provide an alternative perspective of women's identity development, we present a feminist poststructural approach to identity, which claims that identity is fluid, subjective, and contextually bound.

Feminist poststructuralism begins from the assumption that gender is socially constructed in a society that systematically places women in oppressive positions. Feminist poststructuralism argues that language constructs identity and culture, and the social norms that form the basis of identity are expressed in language (Weedon, 1997). This means that identity is fluid, shifting, and unstable, changing as language describes and creates meaning. Language constructs power; signs, symbols, institutions, and social and cultural norms are without power until language assigns power to them (Weedon, 1997). Because language conveys power, multiple constructions of power can exist simultaneously. Language is contextually bound. Specific contexts alter the messages of gender, thus, affecting identity development. Hall and Sandler (1982) and Sadker and Sadker (1994) have documented the ways in which women's voices are silenced and dismissed within the classroom environment. The privileging of men's voices establishes social norms that devalue women's voices.

In feminist poststructuralism, identities are not singular. College students have multiple identities, such as gender, race, sexuality, and class. The multiplicity of identities does not infer that they are separate or can be compartmentalized. Identities tend to intersect, and the feminist poststructural model argues that identities are fluid, contextual, and multiple. Identity is not a fixed category, but one that is constantly constructed. Not only does a feminist poststructural perspective reconceptualize the formation and permanence of identities, but the perspective also assists in connecting individual experience and social structures in new ways. According to Tisdell (2000), one of the basic tenets of feminist poststructuralism includes shifting identities within different social structures. In a sense, each individual has multiple identities that are available based on the particular context. A multiracial undergraduate student, for example, may emphasize her identity as a Black woman in her National Pan-Hellenic Council (NPHC) sorority but her Filipino identity in her hometown, which has a large Filipino community. At the same time, she is never separate from each of these identities. She may emphasize each of these to navigate certain cultural contexts and experiences, but she is simultaneously all these identities and the unique cultural experience of all of them. Poststructuralism emphasizes this type of individual analysis of identity. This model refutes singular and monolithic categories of identity as they relate to gender; identity does not develop in one singular process or at one exacting time. To focus on the complexities of identity development as presented by feminist poststructuralism, studies examine individual experiences and refute the possibility of constructing universal theories. Tisdell (2000) explains that by looking at identity as complex and often times intersecting, research can address identity development in new ways and possibly facilitate social change.

Only a handful of studies use feminist poststructuralism to examine student identity development. Of note is the work of Foor and Walden (2009), who explore the "multiple, dynamic, and competing layers of being and meaning in the construction of gender roles and identities" (p. 45). In their study of female undergraduates in industrial engineering, they found that the discourse of industrial engineering as having a less demanding curriculum and a stronger relationship to business made it more accepting of and for women. Danielson (2011) also employed a feminist poststructural lens to gender and physics and found that female students must contend with masculine gender norms and shifting definitions of how a woman is supposed to be in a physics context. The norms included women being diligent and responsible but unskilled in handling laboratory equipment. These few studies show that feminist poststructuralism has the potential to complicate bounded gender norms by addressing the complexity of meaning and the shifting nature of identity.

The Social Constructionist Model

Early research on men and masculinity focused primarily on examining male "sex roles" and sought to link empirically what were believed to be essential characteristics of masculinity to men's biological and cognitive compositions (Connell, 2005; Kimmel & Messner, 2007). The sex role paradigm fails to acknowledge the "complex social meanings" that are associated with masculinity and the interrelated social processes by which these meanings are produced and reinforced (Kimmel & Messner, 2007, p. xvi). Consequently, this approach was effectively challenged by feminists (e.g., Chodorow, 1978; Gilligan, 1982) and gender performance (e.g., West & Zimmerman, 1987) scholars. This critique led to a body of pro-feminist men's study scholarship, which critiques the power structure of socially prescribed gender roles and serves as the foundation of the social constructionist model. Scholars of men and masculinities frequently utilize the social constructionist model because it emphasizes the power of institutions and social structures that are historically established to benefit men—at least, to benefit men who adhere to the rigid expectations of masculinity. Since so many men experience powerlessness within a structure designed to benefit them, social constructionism reinforces that masculinities should be analyzed with a recognition of institutions and social structures.

Like feminist poststructuralism, the social constructionist model is grounded in the assumption that gender is not a fixed characteristic, but rather one that is produced, negotiated, and reinforced through human interactions and within social structures. Another key assumption of the model is that masculinity is not uniformly expressed and experienced by all groups of men. Race/ethnicity, socioeconomic status, religion, sexual orientation, and a range of other identity dimensions intersect gender and significantly shape men's experiences as men. An important implication follows from this assumption: that is, a single, universal, or normative masculinity does not actually exist. Masculinity is a collection of rules and norms that govern gendered behavior for men in particular contexts.

Connell (2005) describes four masculinities, which exist in relationship to each other and the rules and norms of masculinity. Four masculinities form the basis of the social organization of masculinity: *hegemonic, complicit, subordinated*, and *marginalized masculinities*. Hegemonic masculinity describes the dominant form of gender practice that ensures patriarchal dominance. Hegemonic masculinity is the foundation of rules to which men must ascribe. Connell and Messerschmidt (2005) clarify that hegemonic practices vary within local, regional, and global settings. Thus, hegemonic masculinity and its associated rules are always shifting within particular contexts. Scholars have placed the greatest emphasis on the study of hegemonic performances because of the power these performances wield over men's contextualization of their identities (Connell & Messerschmidt, 2005). Subordinated masculinities are those that are incompatible with traditional definitions of masculinity. In contemporary Western culture, heterosexuality is compulsory for men (Pascoe, 2007). Thus, contemporary Western culture marks gay men as subordinated. Complicit masculinities may not as rigidly maintain the structures of hegemonic masculinity. Connell (2005) notes that complicit masculinity functions as a way to permit men to maintain relationships with women, family, and community. At the same time, complicit masculinity accepts patriarchal dividend and the subordination of women in silence or, at best, without interrogation. Marginalized masculinities experience marginalization through their other identities, such as race, class, ability, and religion. Marginalized masculinities may enact hegemonic masculinity but are subject to the authorization of the hegemonic.

The social organization of masculinity (Connell, 2005) illustrates how the social constructionist model defines gender as a social practice, attends to the social structures and institutions that produce gender, and acknowledges the instability of gender. The social constructionist model focuses on the ways in which masculinities are developed through patterns of gender socialization and reinforced within social structures, such as schools, churches, media, sports, and other institutions. Within these institutions, clear expectations for what constitutes "appropriate" roles and behaviors for men and women are communicated, performed, and maintained. School cultures are inherently gendered through academic competition, testing, team games, dress codes, and patterns of authority (Swain, 2005). Parents, teachers, and students reinforce the gender regime (Gilbert & Gilbert, 1998; Swain, 2005). Alloway (1995) found that teachers interacted more often with boys and girls when they engaged in gender stereotypical activities. Moreover, the tendencies of some educators to track boys toward the sciences and mathematics while encouraging girls to master the humanities and the arts is also a well-documented phenomenon that takes place in schools (Gilbert & Gilbert, 1998). Pollack (2001) described the phenomenon that governs gender performance among adolescent boys as the "boy code" and noted its influence on boys' dispositions toward sexism, homophobia, violence, and misbehavior in schools.

The social constructionist model is a much-needed alternative to the sex role paradigm and other frameworks that rely on biological differences between men and women to make sense of gendered behavior. With regard to college men, this model provides insight into the extent to which the conceptualizations of masculinity that are shared among male undergraduates are both consistent with and divergent from the conceptualizations that are salient within mainstream, noncollegiate male populations.

Articulation of Issues

Cisgender Women's Identity Development in College

College women do not appear to suffer academically while exploring identity development during early adulthood. In fact, since the mid-1970s, the enrollment of women in colleges and universities across the nation has exceeded that of men. In 2016, college women received just over 57% of bachelor's degrees, 59% of master's degrees, and 52% of doctoral degrees (US Department of Education, National Center for Education Statistics, Integrated Postsecondary Education Data System, 2017). The largest gains are in the first-professional and doctoral degrees. Women began entering higher education in greater numbers between 1970 and 1995, making them eligible for graduate programs that require bachelor's degrees.

Disaggregating the statistics by degree completion, however, begins to show a more complex picture of gender disparities across the academy and hints at the complex nature of gender and identity development. While women are larger in number than men in undergraduate and graduate enrollment and have a slightly higher representation in community colleges, their degree completion in specific fields of study illustrates the perpetuation of men- and women-majority disciplines. Women account for only 21% of undergraduate engineers, and the number of women earning a bachelor of science degree in engineering has grown only slightly in the last decade (National Science Foundation, National Center for Science and Engineering Statistics, 2016). Research has noted that increasing the numbers of women in science or engineering is dependent on developing a science identity from adolescence (Brickhouse, Lowery, & Schultz, 2000). However, women in science and engineering classrooms in higher education find an overwhelmingly male-dominated environment and are expected to conform to masculine ways of learning (Tonso, 1996a, 1996b; Margolis & Fisher, 2002). In the field of computer science, Margolis and Fisher (2002) note that the environment is not just male centered and male dominated. The environment is actively hostile toward women by continually questioning their abilities and place in the academic program. Precollege tracking of women by schools and parents away from science and technology means that women enter college with less exposure to science and technology in high school than male counterparts, placing women at a strategic disadvantage in this regard (Margolis & Fisher, 2002). Unfortunately, the underrepresentation of women in these fields has long-term effects. Women who graduate from college are likely to earn incomes that are lower than their male peers with the same credentials. In 2017, the average woman with a bachelor's degree made $46,900 per year, compared to $59,700 for men (NCES, 2018). The discrepancy between average salaries for men and women is attributed to the types of jobs that men and women populate after college graduation. Science and engineering graduates earn significantly higher incomes upon graduation than those with degrees in the social sciences. Aligning academic identity for men and women students alongside the particular disciplines leads to unfair long-term financial disadvantages for women.

Enrollment and degree attainment statistics, however, only provide a small picture of the overall status and experience of women in higher education. Women may enter and complete college at greater rates than men, but the pressure to maintain femininity causes identity conflicts that are not evident in student outcome statistics. These pressures to perform and maintain sociohistorical gender norms impact the experiences of female students and may deter them from specific academic majors. From the first studies that identified a "chilly" classroom climate, the experiences of women in the classroom and their interaction with peers, faculty, and the curriculum does impact their success. Sax (2008) found that women tend to react differently to interactions with faculty. Women who challenge faculty in the classroom experience heightened stress as opposed to men, who have lower levels of stress from the same behaviors. The gender of the instructor also plays a role. Female students in majority female classrooms with male professors find the environment less positive and perceive of less support and encouragement than all female students (Crombie, Pyke, Silverthorn, & Jones, 2003). Experimental studies have shown that even when women express specific interest in faculty mentoring, they are less likely to receive a response than male counterparts (Milkman, Akinola, & Chugh, 2014).

Finally, gender norms are present in the classroom from student perceptions of how they should perform gender to the gender expectations of instructors. Bergvall (1996) found that women in engineering classrooms must confront masculine norms while addressing the expectations of femininity; female students must be masculine engineers and address the shifting expectations of what it means to be a female engineer. Research on student evaluations and gender illustrates the differing expectations for male and female instructors. Sprague and Massoni (2005) found that students perceive their best male teachers as funny and personable and best female teachers as fun and nurturing. Further research indicates that students give higher evaluation scores when they receive higher grades, but the effect is stronger for men than women instructors (Sinclair & Kunda, 2000). Gender plays a strong role in the classroom from the experiences of women students to the gender norm expectations of instructors.

Another area that has an impact on college women's identity relates to participation in activities—sports, sororities, social clubs, or academic organizations—that are designed to increase student academic and social engagement and are found to positively impact student success. Yet women experience identity conflicts related to these activities and exhibit psychological stress and physical symptoms (Rozin, Bauer, & Catanese, 2003). Women are more likely than men to engage in eating disorders (Smolak & Murnen, 2001) due to media images that portray beauty alongside thinness (Levine & Smolak, 1996) and the intense relationship between body image and athletics. For women whose identity is closely related to a sport, particularly a sport that focuses on their bodies, eating disorders have emerged as a significant issue. In a meta-analysis of eating disorders and women athletes, researchers found that women athletes are more at risk for eating problems than non-athletes (Smolak, Murnen, & Ruble, 2000). Sports that emphasize thinness, such as dancing, were found to report larger numbers of students with eating disorders. Another group that has been found to be at risk for eating disorders are women students who belong to sororities (Allison & Park, 2004). In a study of university women, sorority members were more likely to strive for thinness and exhibit eating disorders than non-sorority women (Allison & Park, 2004). The pressure to maintain the ideals of femininity with a thin physique or succumbing to the norms of a group, such as some sororities, has negative effects on women students. Identity conflicts are not unique to women students; as we describe in the next section, men also experience gender-related challenges that impact their development and outcomes.

Cisgender Men's Identity Development in College

An increasing amount of new scholarship on men and masculinities has entered the study of higher education (see Harper and Harris III, 2010; Kellom, 2004; Laker & Davis, 2011), helping to facilitate discussions on college campuses about how to engage and support college men. While it is important to note that college student development theory, which serves as the foundation for student affairs work in higher education, is based on men as research subjects, scholarship has traditionally viewed these subjects as genderless and universal. The new scholarship of men and masculinities is primarily grounded in theories and perspectives from gender studies, psychology, sociology, and education (see Brod & Kaufman, 1994; Connell, 2005; Kimmel & Messner, 2007; Levant, 1996; Pleck, 1981) and has been critical in making sense of the ways in which campus contexts facilitate, constrain, and complicate men's identity development in college. Davis (2002) highlights that men feel constrained and overwhelmed by external pressures to behave in ways that were consistent with stereotypical notions of what it means to be a man in college. Other scholars, notably Edwards and Jones (2009), Harper, Harris III, and Mmeje (2005), and Harris III (2010), have proposed conceptual models that illuminate processes of men's identity development in college and influences with a range of contextual factors. Finally, others have offered empirical and theoretical insights into the identity development and gender-related experiences of men from various subgroups, such as men of color (Brooms, Clark, & Smith, 2017; Estrada & Jimenez, 2018; Guardia & Evans, 2008; Harper, 2004; Harper & Nichols, 2008; Jackson & Hui, 2017; Liu, 2002), male student-athletes (Anderson, 2011; Nelson, 2018; Martin & Harris III, 2006), men in community colleges (Harris III & Harper, 2008), and gay, bisexual, and transgender men (Anderson-Martinez & Vianden, 2014; Dilley, 2005; Holland & Holley, 2011).

At the heart of the issues concerning college men and identity development is the pressure men face to conform to narrowly constructed and stereotypically masculine behavioral norms, which discourage or detract from their engagement in behaviors and activities that lead to desirable outcomes. This phenomenon is perhaps more intensely experienced in college environments, given that most traditional-age college students are in the early phases or in periods of transition in their identity development. While there are cultural and regional considerations when discussing the norms of masculinity, within the context of college men's identity, two main overarching themes emerge: masculinity as performance for other men and the fear of feminization and homophobia.

Men perform masculinity for other men. A significant structure of masculinity is the internal social hierarchy of masculinity (Connell, 2005), in which men compete for position within the hierarchy based on certain performances that conform to narrow expectations of men. Physical ability, sexual relations, power, and dominance are characteristics that offer status within masculinity (Kimmel, 2008; Pascoe, 2007). Being deemed a "nerd," a "sissy," or "unpopular" by one's male peers places boys at the margins of peer culture and puts them at risk of bullying, harassment, or social alienation (Swain, 2005). As Swain (2005) noted, "one of the most urgent dimensions of school life for boys is the need to gain popularity and status. Indeed the search to achieve status is also the search to achieve an acceptable form of masculinity" (p. 218). Sports are one way that men attempt to achieve status. Sports that focus on aggression and physical contact (Crocket, 2012; Young, White, & McTeer, 1994), are extreme versions of traditional sports (Young et al., 1994), or have single-gender "elite" leagues (Crocket, 2012) are prized because they convey the greatest masculine value upon the athlete.

Men's obsession with the accumulation of masculine status may be due to the nature and extent of gender policing among men. Men heavily regulate each other's gender and actions. The clearest rule of masculinity is to "be a man," which largely means that men must resist feminization (Harris III et al., 2011; O'Connor, Ford, & Banos, 2017; O'Neil, 1981). Men are praised for being masculine and punished for being feminine. Homophobia prominently features in male gender policing, which originates from men's fear of being perceived as feminine: "Gay men symbolize parts of the self that do not measure up to cultural standards [of masculinity]; directing hostility at them [gay men] is a way to externalizing the conflict" (Herek, 1987, p. 77). Men weaponize and strategically deploy sexist and homophobic language to regulate the performance of gender (O'Connor et al., 2017; Pascoe, 2007). Homophobia allows boys and men to affirm their heterosexual identities while also differentiating themselves from women and their gay male peers. When sexist or homophobic slurs are insufficient to correct offending behaviors, men utilize physical violence. In school, boys report higher rates of physical bullying and fights than girls (NCES, 2019), and men are more likely to be victims of assault (Tjaden & Theonnes, 2000) and homicide (Sabo, 2010). Physical violence enforces masculine standards and serves as a claim to masculine status for the aggressor. The looming threat of physical violence ensures that men remain silent about or participate in the policing of gender (Kimmel, 2008).

Three trends highlight the concerns about men's identity development: low engagement, alcohol use, and student misconduct. Several published reports (e.g., Cuyjet, 1997; Sax, 2008) indicate that college men are not as engaged in educationally purposeful activities (e.g., leadership in student organizations, study abroad, community service) as the women on their campuses. Men's view of masculinity shapes their participation in activities. For example, the lower participation rate of men in service activities (Salgado, 2003) may be attributable to men's view of service learning as feminized terrain (Foste & Jones, 2018). Male socialization promotes individualistic interests, such as earning money, gaining reputation, and having authority over others, over collective and community interests (Sax & Harper, 2007). Analyses of the Multi-institutional Study of Leadership similarly report that men view of leadership as hierarchical, systematic, and individual (see Dugan, Komives, & Segar, 2008; Haber, 2012; Wielkiewicz, Fischer, Stelzner, Overland, & Sinner, 2012). Given the empirical evidence that connects purposeful campus engagement to a host of positive outcomes for all students (Astin, 1984; Kuh, 1995; Pascarella & Terenzini, 2005), disengagement among college men warrants attention and concern.

While alcohol consumption has been ingrained in the American collegiate experience for decades, alcohol is "male dominated, male identified, and male centered" (Capraro, 2000, p. 307). Men vastly outdrink female peers (Capraro, 2000; Courtenay, 2000a, 2000b), and scholars consistently link this phenomenon to college men's tendencies to embrace stereotypical expectations of masculinity (Capraro, 2000; Courtenay, 2004; Iwamoto, Cheng, Lee, Takamatsu, & Gordon, 2011; Mahalik, Lombardi, Sims, Coley, & Lynch, 2015; McCreary, Newcomb, & Sadave, 1999; O'Neil, 1990; Sabo, 2005). For these reasons alone, it is not surprising that men and women perceive heavy drinking as masculine behavior (Peralta, 2007), which is only further reinforced by the media's focused advertising targeted toward men (Courtenay, 2000b). Men's stories of heavy alcohol consumption offer symbolic status in masculinity (Engstrom, 2012; Peralta, 2007). Through drinking stories, men normalize heavy drinking and view surviving particularly excessive nights as a "badge of honor" (Peralta, 2007). Capraro (2000) argues that the heavy drinking that characterizes college male cultures is a strategy for coping with the "paradox of masculinity." He writes: "My interpretation of a variety of evidence suggests that men may be drinking not only to enact male privilege but also to help them negotiate the emotional hazards of being a man in the contemporary American college" (p. 307).

The last trend we find important to discuss is male misbehavior on college and university campuses. That men are sanctioned more often than women for acts that violate campus conduct policy (nonacademic), including acts of violence, sexual assault, and sexual harassment (Foubert, Newberry, & Tatum, 2007; Hong, 2000), is consistently acknowledged in the published literature on college men and masculinities (e.g., Dannells, 1997; Harper et al., 2005; Ludeman, 2004, 2011; Stimpson & Janosik, 2007). The disparities in these rates are staggering. Stimpson and Janosik (2007) noted that of 226 suspensions at one institution over the course of ten years, 88.5% of those suspended were men. Men's resistance to authority is a factor in their misconduct and disciplinary outcomes (Morris, 2012). Harper et al. (2005) and other scholars correlate male misbehavior with the social construction of masculinity and cultural norms related to gender. They contend that men are more prone to engage in acts that violate campus conduct policy because those acts have been culturally defined as "masculine." Although men who engage in these behaviors are likely to face significant consequences, the perceived pressure to be accepted and granted status within male peer groups and to see one's self as a man are perhaps greater incentives to violate policy than to avoid punishments.

Ludeman (2011) suggested that men's misbehavior may be a consequence of being overwhelmed by the process of identity development. Men are socialized to be unemotional, to avoid seeking help, and to hide feelings of insecurity and vulnerability. Avoidance of help seeking for academic, physical, and emotional concerns is well documented among men (Ang, Lim, Tan, & Yau, 2004; Levant, Wimer, Williams, Smalley, & Noronha, 2009; Wimer & Levant, 2011) as men view help as a sign of weakness, which they deny to even their closest relations (Tang, Oliffe, Galdas, Phinney, & Han, 2014). College men are uneducated and uninformed about the importance of mental health, and the fact that men find help seeking stigmatizing further compounds this concern (Rafal, Gatto, & DeBate, 2018). If men are reluctant or refuse to seek support when they experience challenges or setbacks, the likelihood that they will rely on other, less productive outlets to deal with these issues is perhaps greater.

Our discussion herein has focused primarily on mainstream social constructions of masculinities because society in the United States uses normative White masculinity as the ideal standard and compares men of color's performances to this standard, further perpetuating systems of racism (Wade, 1996). In a study of undergraduate Black men, Mincey, Alfonso, Hackney, and Luque (2014) note that participants conceptualize their identities as men differently than their identities as Black men. While participants' descriptions of being a man mirror traditional notions of masculinity (i.e., White masculinity), their identities as Black men form around pride and strength in Black masculinity and exceeding the boundaries set by racist stereotypes (Mincey et al., 2014).

Scholars have also recognized culturally specific masculine constructions and conceptualizations, which have been most extensively documented among African American and Latino men. Majors and Billson's (1992) concept of "cool pose" describes performance of masculinities among African American men to portray calmness and resolve through unique styles of dressing, speaking, gesturing, shaking hands, and other observable behavioral patterns. While traditional masculinities deprioritize academic achievement (Morris, 2012), Harper (2004) and Harris III, Palmer, and Struve (2011) show that Black masculinity embraces academic achievement among Black male collegians. Morris (2012) made a similar observation but offered the caveat that Black peers encourage academic achievement when the achievement has the appearance of effortlessness and casual exceptionalism, much like Majors and Billson's (1992) cool pose.

Research into the experiences of Latino men also offers insight into culturally specific forms of masculinity. Mirande (2004) deconstructed the concept of macho and discussed its cultural significance in the performance of masculinities among Latino men as both a form of hypermasculinity and a sense of cultural pride and obligation. Piña-Watson, Lorenzo-Blanco, Dornhecker, Martinez, and Nagoshi (2016) separate masculine notions into two distinct concepts: machismo and caballerismo. Another important concept is familismo or familia, a deeply felt familial connection, obligation, and interdependence (Duran & Pérez II, 2017; Suarez-Orozco & Suarez-Orozco, 1995); this concept includes multiple generations and extended family (Suarez-Orozco & Suarez-Orozco, 1995). Familismo may be a factor in the higher utilization of community colleges among Latino men (Zarate & Burciaga, 2010) as community colleges allows them to fulfill obligations to the family while furthering educational pursuits. Duran and Pérez II (2017, 2019) explore the unique ways in which queer, bisexual, and gay men experience familia, especially in the form of chosen familia. Recent research from Pérez II and Sáenz (2017) has begun to challenge deficit models of Latino masculinity, noting that with the right peer and academic support networks, Latino men are thriving in college.

For Asian men, masculinity is intertwined with the myth of the model minority, which idealizes Asian people as the ideal immigrant whose strong values and industry have led to their collective success in the American system (Chua & Fujino, 1999). This myth constructs Asian men as brainy nerds (Huynh & Woo, 2014) or sexually incompetent and lusty (Shek, 2007). Asian men are permitted to embody hegemonic ideals in the narrowest circumstances, primarily through American cinema's interest in martial arts (Nishime, 2017). Nemoto (2008) describes Asian men's strategies for negotiating White masculinities and stereotypes of Asian masculinity in the context of interracial dating relationships. While this research offers insight into how Asian men experience stereotypes of masculinity, the literature on Asian men's identity development in college is lacking but ripe for new voices.

Culturally defined notions of masculinities are employed by marginalized men to help them cope with racial prejudice and alienation and to "mask feelings of inferiority, powerlessness, and failure" (Mirande, 2004, p. 37) stemming from their status as minoritized men (Majors & Billson, 1992; Nemoto, 2008). They facilitate a sense of pride and common identity. One significant challenge for research on marginalized masculinities is the use of totalizing and pan-ethnic identities in which the common and uniting experience is White racism and stereotypes. The field of masculinities research needs more culturally relevant and specific research that acknowledges not only the difference between Black, Latino, and Asian identities, but also the specific regional and ethnic identities that comprise these categories. Moreover, Morris (2012) utilizes intersections of social class and geography as a context for analysis and shows the importance of utilizing a similar approach for White masculinities.

Our comparison and acknowledgement of the gender-related conflicts and issues that challenge college men do not aim to devalue the realities of gender inequities in higher education. We agree that there is a system of patriarchy in higher educational institutions that has historically oppressed women. However, men are also constricted by the same system that privileges patriarchy and stereotypical notions of masculinity. To address the identity development among college men and women, this chapter seeks to apply new ways of considering gender identity development.

Programmatic Strategies

Gender-Specific Recommendations for Student Gender Identity Development

Provide Reflection Opportunities

A basic principle of feminist poststructuralism is the multiplicity of identities. Students have multiple and sometimes conflicting identities that may make identity development difficult or complicated. One suggestion is to provide opportunities for students to have structured and facilitated reflection opportunities about their multiple and complex identities. Reflection gives students a chance to recognize identity intersections and make sense of identity conflicts. Published literature on male gender identity suggests that men are traditionally socialized to believe in hegemonic conceptions of masculinity and to adopt sexist, homophobic, and unhealthy attitudes. Providing opportunities for male students to recognize the effects of traditional male socialization is necessary. It is ever more important because men rarely view themselves as having gender and making gendered choices. Critical self-reflection may encourage some to recognize the role of gender and to seek more productive ways to express their gender identities. Facilitated discussions with peers and professionals with an expertise in gender identity are first steps in this regard.

Offer Group Reflection Opportunities

Similar to the first recommendation, higher education institutions and student affairs programs should consider group reflection opportunities. Encouraging students to talk and collaborate with individuals with different identities and facilitating dialogue across differences encourages reflection and self-understanding (Tierney, 1993). An exploration of the experiences of others also connects individual experiences to social structures (i.e., the college or university).

Develop Student Support Groups

Student support groups that address issues relating to gender identity development, particularly among male students, have proven effective. Intentional collaboration with men's and women's centers, faculty with expertise in gender identity and student development, counseling services, and the student health center will enhance the effectiveness of these groups. In some cases, these groups may need to be homogenous on the basis of gender, given the unique needs and challenges that characterize the identity development process for men and women. Faculty and administrators who advise and facilitate these groups should create strategies for reaching out to Students of Color, student-athletes, and gay and bisexual students as they are typically underrepresented in student support groups. In addition to support groups based broadly on gender, space for intragroup dialogue is necessary. A recent positive trend is student affairs professionals hosting, providing space for, and even participating in culturally specific identity dialogue groups, such as Black men's groups and Latina women's groups. While not discussed in this chapter, intersections of ability, class, first-generation status, and religion provide more opportunities for intragroup discussions about the intersections of students' gendered experiences.

Train Student Affairs Educators

Training is necessary for student affairs educators at all levels. Recent events, such as the #MeToo movement, demonstrate how generations of professionals interpret and make sense of gender activism and discriminatory conduct. Book groups, lunch and learns, and formal training all provide venues to dialogue about gender. Student affairs educators, specifically residential life staff and others serving in peer-supervisory roles, must be adequately trained to support and appropriately refer students who may need or seek assistance with gender-related issues and identity development. While residential communities are frequently gender segregated, conversations about the effects of gender socialization are rarely included in residential life training. Further, while this chapter employs a strategic use of binary gender, student affairs educators have an obligation to further their understanding of issues facing transgender and gender-nonconforming students and colleagues, in order to create spaces that embrace and welcome the diversity of gender.

Policy Change and Interventions

Preferred Names, Name and Sex Designation Changes, and Pronouns

Institutions should examine and facilitate policies that make it easy for students to indicate a preferred name. For example, transgender and gender-nonconforming students may be unable to or uninterested in changing their name for legal, economic, or other reasons. Institutions should also examine how easily they facilitate name changes and gender designations when students utilize legal processes to change one or both. Institutions should permit the use of gender-neutral designations. Institutional policies should use gender-neutral language. Finally, one of the simplest ways to increase dialogue about gender is to institutionalize the use of pronouns within departments, divisions, or universities. Performing introductions at meetings using pronouns raises the visibility of gender issues and creates inclusive spaces.

Restructure Programs to Focus on Identity Development

We suggest that higher educational institutions consider altering the existing programs to create a more explicit focus on identity development. Similarly, these programs can also be enhanced by a stated initiative to support both men and women students. The inclusion of men in these centers creates a more diverse environment where men and women have an opportunity to support each other. Western Illinois University, the University of Massachusetts, and the University of Oregon, to name a few, have opened centers focused on men's health, wellness, and identity development needs. However, it is essential that these centers are connected to women's centers or broader centers for gender inclusivity.

Offer Transition Programs

Programmatic efforts sponsored by offices of orientation, residential life, campus life, and first-year programs focus primarily on assisting students in successful transitions and adjusting to college. However, rarely do these programs focus intentionally on issues directly related to gender identity. Transition programs provide timely opportunities to engage students in discussions involving their gender identities.

Examine Campus Cultural Symbols

In addition to the aforementioned programmatic recommendations, colleges and universities need to consider cultural symbols and discourses that diffuse throughout the institution. Messages that promote idealized notions of gender place students in a dichotomous paradigm. For example, on campuses with high-profile athletics programs, male students may assume that in order to be perceived as masculine, they must perform gender in ways that mirror their male student-athlete peers. However, performing gender in this way may not be a comfortable endeavor for most men on campus. Being mindful and intentional about the messages that are communicated about gender in campus media and other symbolic forms can help infuse well-rounded conceptualizations of gender among students.

Devote Attention to Student Conduct Offices

Scholars have discussed the overrepresentation of male students as respondents in student conduct systems (Harper et al., 2005; Ludeman, 2004, 2011). As we have discussed, men's identity development and socialization encourage heavy drinking, risk taking, resistance to authority, and other behaviors that can prematurely end a student's collegiate career. Therefore, staff who have a role in student conduct are uniquely positioned to encourage men to explore and consider appropriate and healthy ways to express their gender identities. When student conduct staff understand masculinities, they can help men discuss and understand the role of male socialization in their choices. Staff also have the ability to change the gender script. Men expect punishment and may utilize resistance techniques such as silence, armchair lawyering (i.e., arguing the details), and deflecting or blaming others. As well, men do not think that authority figures genuinely care about them or their experiences. These are socialized behaviors. When student conduct staff recognize them, they can reframe conversations and express genuine care. Opportunities exist to infuse critical reflection into the sanctioning process in order to effectively engage students. Many of the articles and books listed in this chapter provide opportunities for reflection-based sanctions about genders. We recommend in-person dialogue after reflection assignments to help male student make sense of the readings. Finally, alternative programs to suspension should incorporate gender socialization discussions into their frameworks.

Recommendations for Curricular or Classroom-Based Support

Integrate Gender Identity Development across Curricula

Conversations about identity development are important in the context of peer groups as described earlier. These conversations need to also occur in the college classroom as an integrated component of curricula. We suggest that higher education institutions infuse the curricula of all courses with opportunities for students to discuss how gender impacts their lives and experiences as college students and to do so with careful attention to intersectionality and multiple formations of gender. Readings, films, guest speakers, case studies, observation assignments, and a range of other teaching and learning strategies should be used accordingly.

Offer Service-Learning Opportunities

Service-learning projects have been very effective in enhancing student learning, primarily by connecting course content outside the classroom (Markus, Howard, & King, 1993). Thus, faculty should develop projects that allow students to examine gender-related issues within and beyond the campus context. Ideally, students will gain some insight into the ways in which gender intersects everyday real-world social issues. Partnerships with local middle and high schools, family shelters, and other contexts in which gender issues are salient correspond logically with this strategy.

We recognize that most of the strategies we offer will require institutions to reinvest or shift resources. While we understand that this may not be possible on some campuses, at the very least, all institutions are capable of providing opportunities for students to confidently and proactively address gender-related issues. One strategy to begin understanding the specific issues within one's college population is to inquire directly of students about their experiences. This will assist in understanding how a particular campus context both hinders and facilitates gender identity development. Campus faculty and administrators who have an interest in gender-related trends and issues can be invited to participate in the inquiry as interviewers, group facilitators, and in other important roles. Campuses have options. With thoughtful and purposeful action on the part of campus leaders, students can receive the support they need to manage the challenging but necessary process of gender identity development.

Conclusion

The challenges and issues that men and women students face during their undergraduate years are noticeably different. Many women are academically successful yet often exhibit eating disorders or other unhealthy habits to "fit in" and maintain the idealized norm of beauty. Women may also succumb to the pressure of traditional occupations and are deterred from math, science, and engineering fields. Men often attempt to maintain and live up to the idealized images of masculinity. As a result, some male students exhibit poor help-seeking behaviors, abuse drugs and alcohol, and perform poorly academically.

In this chapter, we presented two frameworks to consider when addressing gender identity development among college men and women. Each framework extends previous conceptualizations of gender and identity development by focusing on the fluidity of identity and the contextual meaning associated with identities. We suggest that postsecondary leaders consider how their institutional cultures may contribute to gender identity conflicts, as well as designing and implementing innovative strategies to support students in their gender identity development. With a few important programmatic efforts, student affairs educators and faculty can help students successfully manage identity development conflicts.

References

Abes, E. S., Jones, S. R., & McEwen, M. K. (2007). Reconceptualizing the model of multiple dimensions of identity: The role of meaning-making capacity in the construction of multiple identities. *Journal of College Student Development, 48*(1), 1–22. doi:10.1353/csd.2007.0000

Alcoff, L. (1988). Cultural feminism versus post-structuralism: The identity crisis in feminist theory. *Signs, 13*, 405–436. doi:10.1086/494426

Allison, K. C., & Park, C. L. (2004). A prospective study of disordered eating among sorority and nonsorority women. *International Journal of Eating Disorders, 35*(3), 354–358. doi:10.1002/eat.10255

Alloway, N. (1995). *Foundation stones: The construction of gender in early childhood.* Carlton, Australia: Curriculum Corporation.

Anderson, E. (2011). Inclusive masculinities of university soccer players in the American Midwest. *Gender and Education, 23*, 729–744. doi:10.1080/09540253.2010.528377

Anderson-Martinez, R., & Vianden, J. (2014). Restricted and adaptive masculine gender performance in White gay college men. *Journal of Student Affairs Research and Practice, 51*(3), 286–297. doi:10.1515/jsarp-2014-0029

Ang, R. P., Lim, K. M., Tan, A.-G., & Yau, T. Y. (2004). Effects of gender and sex role orientation on help-seeking attitudes. *Current Psychology, 23*(3), 203–214. doi:10.1007/s12144-004-1020-3

Astin, A. W. (1984). Student involvement: A developmental theory for higher education. *Journal of College Student Personnel, 25*, 297–308.

Belenky, M. F., Clinchy, B. M., Goldberger, N. R., & Tarule, J. M. (1986). *Women's ways of knowing: The development of self, voice, and mind.* New York, NY: Basic Books.

Bergvall, V. L. (1996). Constructing and enacting gender through discourse: Negotiating multiple roles as female engineering students. In V. Bergvall, J. M. Bing, and A. Freed (Eds.), *Rethinking language and gender research: Theory and practice* (pp. 172–201). New York, NY: Longman.

Brickhouse, N. W., Lowery, P., & Schultz, K. (2000). What kind of a girl does science? The construction of school science identities. *Journal of Research in Science Teaching, 37*(5), 441–458. doi:10.1002/(sici)1098–2736(200005)37:5<441::aid-tea4>3.0.co;2–3

Brod, H., & Kaufman, M. (Eds.). (1994). *Theorizing masculinities.* Thousand Oaks, CA: Sage.

Brooms, D. R., Clark, J., & Smith, M. (2017). Being and becoming men of character: Exploring Latino and Black males' brotherhood and masculinity through leadership in college. *Journal of Hispanic Higher Education, 17*, 317–331. doi:10.1177/1538192717699048

Butler, J. (1990). *Gender trouble: Feminism and the subversion of identity.* New York, NY: Routledge.

Capraro, R. L. (2000). Why college men drink: Alcohol, adventure, and the paradox of masculinity. *Journal of American College Health, 48*, 307–315. doi:10.1080/07448480009596272

Carlson, A., Salam, M., Miller, C. C., Lu, D., Ngu, A. Patel, J. K., & Wichter, Z. (2018, October 29). #MeToo brought down 201 powerful men. Nearly half of their replacements are women. *The New York Times.* Retrieved from www.nytimes.com/interactive/2018/10/23/us/metoo-replacements.html

Chodorow, N. (1978). *The reproduction of mothering.* Berkeley: University of California.

Chua, P., & Fujino, D. C. (1999). Negotiating new Asian-American masculinities: Attitudes and gender expectations. *The Journal of Men's Studies, 7*, 391–413. doi:10.3149/jms.0703.391

Connell, R. W. (2005). *Masculinities* (2nd ed.). Berkeley, CA: University of California Press.

Connell, R. W., & Messerschmidt, J. W. (2005). Hegemonic masculinity: Rethinking the concept. *Gender & Society, 19*, 829–859. doi:10.1177/0891243205278639

Courtenay, W. H. (2000a). Constructions of masculinity and their influence on men's well-being: A theory of gender and health. *Social Science and Medicine, 50*, 1385–1401. doi:10.1016/s0277–9536(99)00390–1

Courtenay, W. H. (2000b). Engendering health: A social constructionist examination of men's health beliefs and behaviors. *Psychology of Men & Masculinity, 1*(1), 4–15. doi:10.1037//1524–9220.1.1.4

Courtenay, W. H. (2004). Best practices for improving college men's health. *New Directions for Student Services: Developing Effective Programs and Services for College Men, 107*, 59–74. doi:10.1002/ss.133

Crocket, H. (2012). 'This is men's ultimate': (Re)creating multiple masculinities in elite open ultimate frisbee. *International Review for the Sociology of Sport, 48*(3), 318–333. doi:10.1177/1012690211435185

Crombie, G., Pyke, S., Silverthorne, N., & Jones, A. (2003). Students' perceptions of their classroom participation and instructor as a function of gender and context. *The Journal of Higher Education, 74*(1), 51–76. doi:10.1353/jhe.2003.0001

Cuyjet, M. J. (1997). African American men on college campuses: Their needs and their perceptions. *New Directions for Student Services: Helping African American Men Succeed in College, 80*, 79–91. doi:10.1002/ss.8001

Danielson, A. T. (2011). Exploring woman university physics students' 'doing gender' and 'doing physics.' *Gender and Education, 24*(1), 25–39. doi:10.1080/09540253.2011.565040

Dannells, M. (1997). *From discipline to development: Rethinking student conduct in higher education. ASHE-ERIC Higher Education Report* (Vol. 25, No. 2). Washington, DC: The George Washington University Graduate School of Education and Human Development. doi:10.1002/aehe.3640140206

Davis, T. (2002). Voices of gender role conflict: The social construction of college men's identity. *Journal of College Student Development, 43*(4), 508–521.

Dilley, P. (2005). Which way out? A typology of non-heterosexual male collegiate identities. *Journal of Higher Education, 76*, 56–88. doi:10.1353/jhe.2005.0004

Dugan, J. P., Komives, S. R., & Segar, T. C. (2009). College student capacity for socially responsible leadership: Understanding norms and influences of race, gender, and sexual orientation. *Journal of Student Affairs Research and Practice, 45*(4). doi:10.2202/1949–6605.2008.

Duran, A., & Pérez II, D. (2017). Queering la Familia: A phenomenological study reconceptualizing familial capital for queer Latino men. *Journal of College Student Development, 58*(8), 1149–1165. doi:10.1353/csd.2017.0091

Duran, A., & Pérez II, D. (2019). The multiple roles of chosen Familia: Exploring the interconnections of queer Latino men's community cultural wealth. *International Journal of Qualitative Studies in Education, 32*(1), 67–84. doi:10.1080/09518398.2018.1523484

Edwards, K. E., & Jones, S. R. (2009). "Putting my man face on": A grounded theory of college men's gender identity development. *Journal of College Student Development, 50*(2), 210–228. doi:10.1353/csd.0.0063

Engstrom, C. L. (2012). "Yes . . ., but I was drunk": Alcohol references and the (re)production of masculinity on a college campus. *Communication Quarterly, 60*(3), 403–423. doi:10.1080/01463373.2012.688790

Estrada, F., & Jimenez, P. (2018). Machismo and higher education: Examining the relation between caballerismo and ethnic identity, support seeking, and sense of connectedness among college Latinos. *Journal of Latinos and Education, 17*, 215–224. doi:10.1080/15348431.2017.1319367

Evans, N. J., Forney, D. S., Guido, F. M., Patton, L. D., & Renn, K. A. (2010). *Student development in college: Theory, research, and practice* (2nd ed.). San Francisco, CA: Jossey-Bass.

Foor, C. E., & Walden, S. E. (2009). "Imaginary engineering" or "re-imagined engineering": Negotiating gendered identities in the borderland of a college of engineering. *Feminist Formations, 21*(2), 41–64.

Foste, Z., & Jones, S. R. (2018). Isn't that for sorority girls?: Narratives of college men in service-learning. *Journal of Student Affairs Research and Practice, 55*(1), 65–77. doi:10.1080/19496591.2017.1346514

Foubert, J. D., Newberry, J. T., & Tatum, J. (2007). Behavior differences seven months later: Effects of a rape prevention program. *NASPA Journal, 44*(4), 728–749. doi:10.2202/0027–6014.1866

Gilbert, R., & Gilbert, P. (1998). *Masculinity goes to school*. New York, NY: Routledge.

Gilligan, C. (1982). *In a different voice: Psychological theory and women's development*. Cambridge, MA: Harvard University Press.

Guardia, J. R., & Evans, N. J. (2008). The ethnic identity development of Latino fraternity members at a Hispanic serving institution. *Journal of College Student Development, 49*, 163–181.

Haber, P. (2012). Perceptions of leadership: An examination of college students' Understandings of the concept of leadership. *Journal of Leadership Education, 11*(2), 26–51. doi:10.12806/V11/I2/RF2

Hall, R. M., & B. R. Sandler. (1982). *The classroom climate: A chilly one for women?* Washington, DC: Association of American Colleges.

Harper, S. R. (2004). The measure of a man: Conceptualizations of masculinity among high-achieving African American male college students. *Berkeley Journal of Sociology, 48*(1), 89–107.

Harper, S. R., & Harris III, F. (2010). *College men and masculinities: Theory, research, and implications for practice*. San Francisco, CA: Jossey-Bass.

Harper, S. R., Harris III, F., & Mmeje, K. (2005). A theoretical model to explain the overrepresentation of college men among campus judicial offenders: Implications for campus administrators. *NASPA Journal, 42*(4), 565–587. doi:10.2202/0027–6014.1541

Harper, S. R., & Nichols, A. H. (2008). Are they not all the same? Racial heterogeneity among Black male undergraduates. *Journal of College Student Development, 49*(3), 199–214.

Harris III, F. (2010). College men's conceptualizations of masculinities and contextual influences: Toward a conceptual model. *Journal of College Student Development, 51*(3), 297–318.

Harris III, F., & Harper, S. R. (2008). Masculinities go to community college: Understanding male identity socialization and gender role conflict. In J. Lester (Ed.), *Gendered perspectives on community colleges: New directions for community colleges, 142* (pp. 25–35). San Francisco, CA: Jossey-Bass.

Harris III, F., Palmer, R., & Struve, L. E. (2011). "Cool posing" on campus: A qualitative study of masculinities and gender expression among Black men at private research institution. *Journal of Negro Education, 80*(1), 47–62.

Herek, G. M. (1987). On heterosexual masculinity: Some psychical consequences of the social construction of gender and sexuality. In M. Kimmel (Ed.), *Changing men: New directions in research on men and masculinity* (pp. 68–82). Newbury Park, CA: Sage.

Holland, C., & Holley, K. (2011). The experiences of gay male undergraduate students at a traditional women's college. *Journal of Student Affairs Research and Practice, 48*(2), 179–194. doi:10.2202/1949–6605.6156

Hong, L. (2000). Toward a transformed approach to prevention: Breaking the link between masculinity and violence. *Journal of American College Health, 48*, 269–282.

Huynh, K., & Woo, B. (2014). 'Asian fail': Chinese Canadian men talk about race, masculinity, and the nerd stereotype. *Social Identities, 20*(4–5), 363–378. doi:10.1080/13504630.2014.1003205

Iwamoto, D. K., Cheng, A., Lee, C. S., Takamatsu, S., & Gordon, D. (2011). "Man-ing" up and getting drunk: The role of masculine norms, alcohol intoxication and alcohol-related problems among college men. *Addictive Behaviors, 36*, 906–911. doi:10.1016/j.addbeh.2011.04.005

Jackson, B. A., & Hui, M. M. (2017). Looking for brothers: Black male bonding at a predominantly White institution. *The Journal of Negro Education, 86*(4), 463. doi:10.7709/jnegroeducation.86.4.0463

Josselson, R. (1987). *Finding herself: Pathways to identity development in women.* San Francisco, CA: Jossey-Bass.

Kellom, G. E. (Ed.). (2004). *New directions for student services: Developing effective programs and services for college men, 107.* San Francisco, CA: Jossey-Bass.

Kimmel, M. S. (2008). *Guyland: The perilous world where boys become men.* New York, NY: Harper Collins.

Kimmel, M. S., & Messner, M. A. (Eds.). (2007). *Men's lives* (7th ed.). Boston: Allyn & Bacon.

Kuh, G. D. (1995). The other curriculum: Out-of-class experiences associated with student learning and personal development. *Journal of Higher Education, 66*(2), 123–155.

Laker, J., & Davis, T. (Eds.). (2011). *Masculinities in higher education: Theoretical and practical implications.* New York, NY: Routledge.

Levant, R. F. (1996). The new psychology of men. *Professional Psychology: Research and Practice, 27*(3), 259–265. doi:10.1037//0735–7028.27.3.259

Levant, R. F., Wimer, D. J., Williams, C. M., Smalley, K. B., & Noronha, D. (2009). The relationships between masculinity variables, health risk behaviors and attitudes toward seeking psychological help. *International Journal of Men's Health, 8*(1), 3–21. doi:10.3149/jmh.0801.3

Levine, M. P., & Smolak, L. (1996). Media as a context for the development of disordered eating. In L. Smolak, M. P. Levin, & R. Striegel-Moore (Eds.), *The developmental psychopathology of eating disorders* (pp. 235–257). Mahwah, NJ: Erlbaum.

Liu, W. M. (2002). Exploring the lives of Asian American men: Racial identity, male role norms, gender role conflict, and prejudicial attitudes. *Psychology of Men and Masculinity, 3*, 107–118. doi:10.1037//1524–9220.3.2.107

Ludeman, R. B. (2004). Arrested emotional development: Connecting college men, emotions, and misconduct. *New Directions for Student Services: Developing Effective Programs and Services for College Men, 107*, 75–86.

Ludeman, R. B. (2011). Successful judicial interventions with men. In J. Laker & T. L. Davis (Eds.), *Masculinities in higher education: Theoretical and practical implications.* New York, NY: Routledge.

Mahalik, J. R., Lombardi, C. M., Sims, J., Coley, R. L., & Lynch, A. D. (2015). Gender, male-typicality, and social norms predicting adolescent alcohol intoxication and marijuana use. *Social Science & Medicine, 143*, 71–80. doi:10.1016/j.socscimed.2015.08.013

Majors, R. G., & Billson, J. M. (1992). *Cool pose: The dilemmas of Black manhood in America.* New York, NY: Lexington Books.

Margolis, J., & Fisher, A. (2002). *Unlocking the clubhouse: Women in computing.* Cambridge, MA: Massachusetts Institute of Technology Press.

Markus, G., Howard, J., & King, D. (1993). Integrating community service and classroom instruction enhances learning: Results from an experiment. *Educational Evaluation and Policy Analysis, 15*, 410–419. doi:10.2307/1164538

Martin, B. E., & Harris III, F. (2006). Examining productive conceptions of masculinities: Lessons learned from academically driven African American male student-athletes. *Journal of Men's Studies, 14*(3), 359–378. doi:10.3149/jms.1403.359

McCreary, D. R., Newcomb, M. D., & Sadave, S. (1999). The male role, alcohol use, and alcohol problems. *Journal of Counseling Psychology, 46*(1), 109–124.

Milkman, K. L., Akinola, M., & Chugh, D. (2014). What happens before? A field experiment exploring how pay and representation differentially shape bias on the pathway into organizations. *Journal of Applied Psychology.* Advanced online publication. doi:10.2139/ssrn.2063742

Mincey, K., Alfonso, M., Hackney, A., & Luque, J. (2014). Understanding masculinity in undergraduate African American men: A qualitative study. *American Journal of Men's Health, 8*(5), 387–398. doi:10.1177/1557988313515900

Mirande, A. (2004). "Macho": Contemporary conceptions. In M. Kimmel & M. Messner (Eds.), *Men's lives* (6th ed., pp. 28–38). Boston: Allyn & Bacon.

Morris, E. W. (2012). *Learning the hard way: Masculinity, place, and the gender gap in education.* New Brunswick, NJ: Rutgers University Press.

National Center for Education Statistics (2018). *The condition of education 2018* [NCES 2018–144]. Washington, DC: US Department of Education.

National Center for Education Statistics (2019). Annual earnings of young adults. In National Center for Education Statistics, *The condition of education 2018* [NCES 2018–144]. Washington, DC: US Department of Education. Retrieved from https://nces.ed.gov/programs/coe/indicator_cba.asp

National Science Foundation, National Center for Science and Engineering Statistics (2016). *Special tabulations of US Department of Education, National Center for Education Statistics, Integrated Postsecondary Education Data System, Completions Survey, unrevised provisional release data.* [Data Set]. Retrieved from https://ncsesdata.nsf.gov/webcaspar/index.jsp?subHeader=WebCASPARHome

Nelson, J. (2018). "Groupies" and "jersey chasers": Male student-athletes' sexual relationships and perceptions of women. *New Directions for Student Services, 163*, 55–66. doi:10.1002/ss.20270

Nemoto, K. (2008). Climbing the hierarchy of masculinity: Asian American men's cross-racial competition for intimacy with White women. *Gender Issues, 25*(2), 80–100. doi:10.1007/s12147-008-9053-9

Nicolazzo, Z. (2017). *Trans* in college: Transgender students' strategies for navigating campus life and the institutional politics of inclusion.* Sterling, VA: Stylus.

Nishime, L. (2017). Reviving Bruce: Negotiating Asian masculinity through Bruce Lee paratexts in Giant Robot and Angry Asian Man. *Critical Studies in Media Communication, 34*, 120–129. doi:10.1080/15295036.2017.1285420

O'Connor, E. C., Ford, T. E., & Banos, N. C. (2017). Restoring threatened masculinity: The appeal of sexist and anti-gay humor. *Sex Roles, 77*(9–10), 567–580. doi:10.1007/s11199–017–0761-z

O'Neil, J. M. (1981). Patterns of gender role conflict and strain: Sexism and fear of femininity in men's lives. *The Personnel and Guidance Journal, 60*, 203–210. doi:10.1002/j.2164–4918.1981.tb00282.x

O'Neil, J. M. (1990). Assessing men's gender role conflict. In D. Moore & F. Leafgren (Eds.), *Men in conflict: Problem solving strategies and interventions* (pp. 23–38). Alexandria, VA: American Counseling Association.

Pascarella, E. T., & Terenzini, P. (2005). *How college affects students: A third decade of research.* San Francisco, CA: Jossey-Bass.

Pascoe, C. J. (2007). *'Dude, you're a fag': Masculinity and sexuality in high school.* Berkeley, CA: University of California Press

Peralta, R. L. (2007). College alcohol use and the embodiment of hegemonic masculinity among European American men. *Sex Roles, 56*, 741–756. doi:10.1007/s11199-007-9233-1

Pérez, D., & Sáenz, V. B. (2017). Thriving Latino males in selective predominantly White institutions. *Journal of Hispanic Higher Education, 16*(2), 162–186. doi:10.1177/1538192717697754

Piña-Watson, B., Lorenzo-Blanco, E. I., Dornhecker, M., Martinez, A. J., & Nagoshi, J. L. (2016). Moving away from a cultural deficit to a holistic perspective: Traditional gender role values, academic attitudes, and educational goals for Mexican descent adolescents. *Journal of Counseling Psychology, 63*(3), 307–318. doi:10.1037/cou0000133

Pleck, J. H. (1981). *The myth of masculinity.* Cambridge, MA: MIT Press.

Pollack, W., S. (2001). *Real boys' voices.* New York, NY: Random House.

Rafal, G., Gatto, A., & DeBate, R. (2018). Mental health literacy, stigma, and help-seeking behaviors among male college students. *Journal of American College Health, 66*(4), 284–291. doi:10.1080/07448481.2018.1434780

Rozin, P, Bauer, R., & Catanese, D. (2003). Food and life, pleasure and worry, among American college students: Gender differences and regional similarities. *Journal of Personality and Social Psychology, 85*, 132–141.

Sabo, D. (2005). The study of masculinities and men's health: An overview. In M. Kimmel, J. Hearn & R. W. Connell (Eds.), *Handbook of studies on men & masculinities* (pp. 326–352). Thousand Oaks, CA: Sage.

Sabo, D. (2010). Masculinities and men's health: Moving toward post-superman era prevention. In M. S. Kimmel & M. Messner (Eds.), *Men's lives* (8th ed., pp. 243–260). Boston, MA: Pearson.

Sadker, M., & Sadker, D. (1994). *Failing at fairness*. New York, NY: Charles Scribner's Sons.

Salgado, D. M. (2003). *2003 Campus compact annual membership survey.* Retrieved from www.compact. org/wp-content/uploads/pdf/2003_statistics.pdf

Sax, L. J. (2008). *The gender gap in college: Maximizing the developmental potential of women and men.* San Francisco, CA: Jossey-Bass.

Sax, L. J., & Harper, C. E. (2007). Origins of the gender gap: Pre-college and college influences on differences between men and women. *Research in Higher Education, 48*(6), 669–694.

Shek, Y. L. (2007). Asian American masculinity: A review of the literature. *The Journal of Men's Studies, 14*(3), 379–391.

Sinclair, L., & Kunda, Z. (2000). Motivated stereotyping of women: She's fine if she praised me, but incompetent if she criticized me. *Personality and Social Psychology Bulletin, 26*(11), 1329–1342.

Smolak, L., & Murnen, S. K. (2001). Gender and eating problems. In R. H. Striegel-Moore & L. Smolak (Eds.), *Eating disorders: Innovative directions in research and practice* (pp. 91–110). Washington, DC: American Psychological Association.

Smolak, L., Murnen, S. K., & Ruble, A. E. (2000). Female athletes and eating problems: A meta-analysis. *International Journal of Eating Disorders, 27*(4), 371–380.

Sprague, J., & Massoni, K. (2005). Student evaluations and gendered expectations: What we can't count can hurt us. *Sex Roles, 53*(11–12), 779–793.

Stimpson, M. T., & Janosik, S. M. (2007). Characteristics of students who reenroll after serving a disciplinary suspension. *NASPA Journal, 44*, 496–511. doi:10.2202/0027–6014.1833

Suarez-Orozco, C., & Suarez-Orozco, M. (1995). *Transformations: Immigration, family life, and achievement motivation among Latino adolescents.* Stanford, CA: Stanford University Press.

Swain, J. (2005). Masculinities in education. In M. Kimmel, J. Hearn, & R. W. Connell (Eds.), *Handbook of studies on men & masculinities* (pp. 213–229). Thousand Oaks, CA: Sage.

Tang, M. O. T., Oliffe, J. L., Galdas, P. M., Phinney, A., & Han, C. S. (2014). College men's depression-related help-seeking: A gender analysis. *Journal of Mental Health, 23*(5), 219–224. doi:10.3109/09638 237.2014.910639

Tierney, W. G. (1993). An anthropological analysis of student participation in college. *Journal of Higher Education, 63*(6), 603–618.

Tisdell, E. J. (2000). Feminist pedagogies. In E. Hayes & D. D. Flannery (Eds.), *Women as learners: The significance of gender in adult learning* (pp. 155–184). San Francisco, CA: Jossey-Bass.

Tjaden, P., & Theonnes, N. (2000, November). *Full report of the prevalence, incidence, and consequences of violence against women*[NCJ 183781]. Washington, DC: U.S. Department of Justice. Retrieved from https://www.ncjrs.gov/pdffiles1/nij/183781.pdf

Tonso, K. L., (1996a). Student learning and gender. *Journal of Engineering Education, 85*(2), 143–150.

Tonso, K. L. (1996b). The impact of cultural norms on women. *Journal of Engineering Education, 85*(3), 217–225.

Torres, V., Jones, S., & Renn, K. A. (2009). Identity development theories in student affairs: Origins, current status, and new approaches. *Journal of College Student Development, 50*(6), 577–596.

Tovia, S. (2019, January 17). Blacklash erupts after Gillette launches a new #MeToo-inspired ad campaign. *National Public Radio.* Retrieved from www.npr.org/2019/01/17/685976624/backlash-erupts-after-gillette-launches-a-new-metoo-inspired-ad-campaign

US Department of Education, National Center for Education Statistics, Integrated Postsecondary Education Data System (2017). *Completions component, Fall 2016* [Data Set]. Retrieved from https://nces.ed.gov/ipeds/datacenter/

Wade, J. C. (1996). African American men's gender role conflict: The significance of racial identity. *Sex Roles, 34*, 17–33. doi:10.1007/bf01544793

Weedon, C. (1997). *Feminist practice and poststructuralist theory.* Malden. MA: Blackwell Publishers.

West, C., & Zimmerman, D. H. (1987). Doing gender. *Gender & Society, 1*(2), 125–151.

Wielkiewicz, R. M., Fischer, D. V., Stelzner, S. P., Overland, M., & Sinner, A. M. (2012). Leadership attitudes and beliefs of incoming first-year college students: A multi-institutional study of gender differences. *Journal of Leadership Education, 11*(2), 1–25. doi:10.12806/v11/i2/rf1

Wimer, D. J., & Levant, R. F. (2011). The relation of masculinity and help-seeking style with the academic help-seeking behavior of college men. *The Journal of Men's Studies, 19*(3), 256–274. doi:10.3149/jms.1903.256

Young, K., White, P., & McTeer, W. (1994). Body talk: Male athletes reflect on sport, injury, and pain. *Sociology of Sport Journal, 11*(2), 175–194. doi:10.1123/ssj.11.2.175

Zarate, M. E., & Burciaga, R. (2010). Latinos and college access: Trends and future directions. *Journal of College Admission, 209*, 24–29.

Chapter 13
Engaging Religious Minority Students

Shafiqa Ahmadi, Darnell G. Cole, and Bo Lee

The United States of America is the most religiously diverse nation in the world (Eck, 2009). Changes brought about by the 1965 immigration law created opportunities for an emergence of non-European immigrants. With this wave of immigrants came an array of religious traditions from Buddhists to Muslims to Sikhs. While the diversity of these non-Christian religious traditions has grown, their numbers remain relatively small when compared to those who identify religiously with some form of Christianity. According to Bryant (2006), "Colleges and universities provide a microcosm of American society . . . and must endeavour to create campus climates that are welcoming to students from all faith traditions" (p. 2). In an effort to create an inclusive and welcoming campus milieu for religious minority students (i.e., those who identify as non-Christian), we discuss the following in this chapter: (1) the dominant Christian context undergirding the early development of higher education institutions, (2) the continued prevalence of Christian privilege, (3) the role of religion and the experiences of religious minority students (RMS) in college, and (4) conceptual frameworks for understanding the campus climate and aspects of RMS religiousness. These theoretical perspectives are particularly useful for deconstructing students' religiousness and reconstructing individual agency and institutional responsibility toward enhancing the nature and quality of experiences for religious minority students. In the end, we offer recommendations for improving campus climate and the experiences of religious minority students.

College Campuses as Dominant Christian Contexts

Brubacher and Rudy (1997) argue that the most compelling reason for the founding of the colonial colleges was the need for "a literate, college-trained clergy" in early American society (p. 6). In fact, all nine colonial colleges were either founded or were substantially controlled in efforts to train clergy by an organized Christian group like the Anglicans, Lutherans, Presbyterians, Puritans, or Quakers. Consequently, Christian values and traditions lay at the foundation of American higher education. As these early colleges became today's elite institutions, they were often used as models for the development of other higher education institutions (Brubacher & Rudy, 1997; Rudolph, 1990). As the educational leadership of these early colleges slowly changed away from clergy, secularism began taking shape amid colleges and universities (Stamm, 2003; Wuthnow, 2007). While we are almost 400 years removed from the founding of Harvard in 1636, the first American university, most institutions maintain the vestiges of a Christian-centric history. For instance, it is not uncommon to find a chapel on many college campuses, an extensive curriculum about Christianity, and an academic calendar where the institution is closed or classes cancelled to observe Christian holy days. While most of these holidays are also shared within the larger society, religious holidays particular to non-Christian religious groups, like Islam and Judaism, are often not recognized on the academic calendars of colleges and universities (Brubacher & Rudy, 1997; Rudolph, 1990).

The secularization of American higher education has often been attributed to four historical events: (1) denominational diversity, (2) liberal and practical education, (3) access, and (4) the Carnegie pension system. The increase of denominational diversity within the colonies and the continued desire of students for a college education prompted greater flexibility in curricular goals as institutions began catering to students' diverse religious denominations. If nothing else, institutional survival necessitated such flexibility and a general broadening of its religious obligation in students' lives. The first and second Morrill Land Grant Acts were the first federal legislation that provided states with resources to broaden the curriculum and increase access. The first Morrill Land Grant Act of 1862 was the legislation that created, for each eligible state and its citizens, widespread access to a liberal and practical education and, in some instances, military training (Rudolph, 1990). This meant that students were not trained primarily in theology, but in agriculture, mechanics, and/or technology—a secularization of students' education and, substantively, American higher education. Hence, the inclusion of these trades is reflected in the original name of some of the oldest state-specific public institutions, such as Alabama A&M University, Texas A&M University, and Virginia A&M (now known as Virginia Polytechnic Institute and State University or Virginia Tech). The second Morrill Act of 1890, however, extended this state-specific access to Black Americans. Primarily aimed at confederate states, where Black people were denied admissions on the basis of race, monetary resources were used to establish some 70 separate higher education institutions, which contributed to what are federally designated as historically black colleges and universities (HBCUs) today—institutions such as the University of Arkansas at Pine Bluff, Alabama A&M University, and Tuskegee University.

Later in 1905, the Carnegie Foundation established a pension plan for American college professors, which specified that only nondenominational schools could partake in the program, encouraging many institutions to formally drop their religious affiliation

(Kohlbrenner, 1961). The evolution of this retirement investment system is now known as Teachers Insurance and Annuity Association of America (TIAA), which later added the College Retirement Equities Fund (CREF) in the 1950s—hence, TIAA-CREF. Also during the 20th century, scientific inquiry, objectivism, and modernism became more influential within the college curriculum, further secularizing institutions of higher education (Eisenmann, 1999; Marsden, 1994). American colleges and universities came to embody the Western positivistic paradigm, which honored value-free inquiry (Palmer, 1993). By the last half of the 20th century, American colleges and universities began to experience the paradox that while their campuses were becoming more religiously diverse, due to the influx of a diverse student body, religion was simultaneously becoming less essential to the mission of higher education. Furthermore, despite the fact that the number of religious higher education institutions (i.e., colleges and universities with strong faith identities) have been on the rise, religion has become further marginalized on secular college campuses (Riley, 2005).

Christian Privilege

The 2008 American Religious Identification Survey (ARIS) found that of the 228 million people polled, 76% identified as Christian (Table 13.1). The Pew Forum on Religion and Public Life Survey (2008a, 2008b) reported similar results, with about 5% identifying as a religion other than Christian or Catholic (see Table 13.2). Subtle and overt references to Christianity can also be seen throughout American "secular" culture, such as the national celebration of Christmas, "one nation under God" in our pledge of allegiance, and "in God we trust" on our currency (Clark & Brimhall-Vargas, 2003). Due to high numbers in population and historical foundation, Christians typically have more power than all minority religious groups combined on campus, which can create

TABLE 13.1. Self-Described Religious Identification of Adult Population: 1990, 2001, and 2008

Religious Group	1990		2001		2008	
	Estimated Number of People	Percent of People	Estimated Number of People	Percent of People	Estimated Number of People	Percent of People
Catholic	46,004,000	26.2	50,873,000	24.5	57,199,000	25.1
Other Christian	105,221,000	60.0	108,641,000	52.2	116,203,000	50.9
Total Christian (Including Catholic)	151,225,000	86.2	159,514,000	76.7	173,402,000	76.0
Other Religions	5,853,000	3.3	7,740,000	3.7	8,796,000	3.9
Nontheist/ No Religion	14,331,000	8.2	29,481,000	14.1	34,169,000	15.0
Don't know or Decline to State	4,031,000	2.3	11,246,000	5.4	11,815,000	5.2
Total	175,440,000	100	207,983,000	100	228,182,000	100

TABLE 13.2. Statistics on Religion in America

Religious Group	Estimated Percent
Other Religions	4.7
Jewish	1.7
Muslim	0.6
Buddhist	0.7
Hindu	0.4
Other World Religion	< 0.3
Other Faith	1.2
Unaffiliated	16.1
Don't Know or Refuse to State	0.8
Christian	78.4
Protestant	51.3
Evangelical Churches	26.3
Mainline Churches	18.1
Historically Black Churches	6.9
Catholic	23.9
Mormon (LDS)	1.7
Jehovah's Witness	0.7
Orthodox	0.6
Other Christian	0.3

Note: From the Pew Forum on Religion and Public Life (2008b) based on data obtained from the United States Census Bureau (2011).

contexts where religious minorities are vulnerable to oppression and discrimination (Clark & Brimhall-Vargas, 2003; Schlosser, 2003). The commercial proliferation of Christianity into the secular realm is often unrecognized because, like other forms of privilege, it often remains undetected by mainstream society (Clark & Brimhall-Vargas, 2003; McIntosh, 1988).

The conscious and subconscious advantages often afforded to members of the Christian faith identified as Christian privilege can be seen at many colleges and universities (Clark & Brimhall-Vargas, 2003; Schlosser, 2003). The privileged majority is composed solely of Christian denominations, which include mainline Protestant faiths—Episcopalian, Presbyterian, Methodist, Lutheran, and United Church of Christ/Congregational (Bonderud & Fleischer, 2005; Roof & McKinney, 1987). Other relatively privileged Christian groups include Roman Catholic, Baptist, Church of Christ, and other Christians (Bowman & Small, 2010). Religious minorities include those who identify as Buddhist, Hindu, Muslim, Quaker, Jewish, and in some cases LDS (Mormon) and Unitarians (Bowman & Small, 2010) (see Table 13.3).

In institutions of higher education, Christian students enjoy a number of daily advantages including widely accepted positive portrayals of their faith in mainstream media,

TABLE 13.3. Religious Self-Identification of the US Adult Population 1990, 2001, 2008

Religious Group	1990	2001	2008
	Estimated Number of People	Estimated Number of People	Estimated Number of People
Jewish	3,137,000	2,837,000	2,680,000
Muslim	527,000	1,104,000	1,349,000[*]
Buddhist	404,000	1,082,000	1,189,000
Unitarian/Universalist	502,000	629,000	586,000
Hindu	227,000	766,000	582,000
Native American	47,000	103,000	186,000
Sikh	13,000	57,000	78,000
Wiccan	8,000	134,000	342,000
Pagan	N/A	140,000	340,000
Spiritualist	N/A	116,000	426,000
Other Unclassified	991,000	774,000	1,030,000
Total	5,853,000	7,740,000	8,796,000

Note: From the American Religious Identification Survey (ARIS) 200
* The number of Muslims in America has been estimated to be as much as six to seven million
(Cole & Ahmadi, 2010).

privilege in the institution's calendar, and privilege in on-campus dining options (Seifert, 2007). State and federal holidays often coincide with Christian holidays and days of religious observances, while marginalized non-Christian students must negotiate conflicts between their studies and their spiritual practices (Schlosser & Sedlacek, 2003). Christians are also unlikely to know or believe that the American college environment is oppressive because that environment has rarely, if ever, been hostile toward their faith (Schlosser, 2003). Additionally, Christian privilege has the potential to stifle non-Christian students' expression of their spiritual identity while simultaneously forestalling or foreclosing Christian students' critical examination of their privileged position (Seifert, 2007).

Religion in Higher Education

Most administrators and faculty within public institutions of higher education are hesitant to engage students' religious beliefs for fear of alienating students or impinging on students' constitutional rights (Clark, 2003; Jablonski, 2001). Administrators often claim that issues of religion and spirituality are private matters, citing the "separation of church and state" clause as evidence that they cannot promote religion within the public realm on their campuses (Collins et al., 1987; Hamburger, 2002). Public institutions, however, are legally allowed to provide campus space (e.g., meeting room, bulletin boards), non-coercive prayer environments, opportunities to engage in religious and spiritual classroom discussions, and the right to organize—as long as the student organization pursues lawful goals, poses no significant threat of material disruption, and conforms to a reasonable set of school-based policies (Lowery, 2004, 2005). Yet public institutions must remain neutral and "cannot favor or support religion over non-religion" (Kaplin & Lee, 2007, p. 56).

Despite the fear of legal challenges, the consideration of religion in higher education has been shown to promote positive social and cognitive outcomes for students. The Fetzer Institute released a report in 1999, and then a revised version in 2003, which indicates that various dimensions of religiousness and spirituality enhance students' sense of well-being (Ellison, 1991), lower levels of depression and psychological distress (Idler, 1987; Williams et al., 1991), and reduce morbidity and mortality (Levin, 1996). Other scholars have also found a positive link between religiosity and mental/emotional health, which includes life satisfaction, happiness, purpose and meaning, hope, optimism, and lower numbers of instances of depression and anxiety (Bonderud & Fleischer, 2004; Koenig, 2001; Koenig, McCullough, & Larson, 2001).

By cultivating a more conducive space for religious engagement, colleges can contribute to students' development, sense of belonging, and overall satisfaction with college, which is also significantly related to college student persistence (Astin, Astin, & Lindholm, 2011a; Hurtado & Carter, 1997; Mooney, 2005). Astin et al. (2011a) found that increased satisfaction with college is related to equanimity, or the extent to which the student feels at peace and is able to find meaning in times of hardship. While many students report that their religion provides such feelings of peace, identity development, and moments of transcendence, students who engage in spirituality-enhancing activities are also more likely to engage in a broader cross-section of collegiate activities, such as exercising, attending cultural events, and performing community service (Astin, 1993; Bryant, 2006; Kuh & Gonyea, 2005). Furthermore, religious communities can offer young adults supportive mentoring environments that allow questioning and provide challenge and support toward students' overall development in college (Parks, 2000).

Challenges Religious Minority Students Face

Although many colleges and universities have shifted away from their religious foundations, a Christian ethos continues to permeate many campus cultures, which can at times alienate non-Christian students (McEwen, 1996; Schlosser, 2003). Arguably, religious minorities are more likely to experience spiritual struggle during the college years; these struggles are often exacerbated by the lack of support and understanding from those who do not share similar beliefs. By contrast, when students have faculty support for spiritual/religious development, religious engagement, and, to a lesser extent, interactions with others who hold similar religious beliefs, they are more likely to experience positive gains in religious growth and development (Bowman & Small, 2010; Bryant & Astin, 2008). Interestingly, religious minority students are acutely aware of their marginalization and that their ways of viewing the world frequently distinguish them from the majority of Christian students (Small, 2008). Being surrounded by conflicting ideologies can produce cognitive disequilibrium, which, if fostered in a supportive educational environment, can enhance critical thinking skills (Gurin, Dey, Hurtado, & Gurin, 2002; Cole & Ahmadi, 2010) yet students can also experience behavioral barriers and psychological stressors that inhibit their religious and spiritual development (Cole & Ahmadi, 2003, 2010; Mahaffey & Smith, 2009; Schlosser & Sedlacek, 2003).

Religious holidays, dietary restrictions, access to safe spaces for spiritual expression, and other barriers pose significant challenges for religious minority students (Mahaffey & Smith, 2009; Mayhew & Bryant, 2013). The most obvious, as noted earlier, are religious holidays. While many institutions allow excused absences, the burden of proof and obtaining written support from one's religious community is a responsibility completely left up to the non-Christian student (Mahaffey & Smith, 2009; Schlosser & Sedlacek, 2003). For instance, Wesak, celebrated by many Buddhists; Diwali, celebrated by many Hindus; the holy days of Rosh Hashanah and Yom Kippur, celebrated by many Jewish students; and Eid Al-Fitr and Eid Al-Adha, celebrated by many Muslims, require similar accommodations as those taken for granted by many Christians celebrating Christmas during what is typically referred to simply as "winter break." Although some reports indicate an increase in vegan and vegetarian options on college campuses, students whose religious observance requires kosher or *halal* dishes are often unable to find satisfactory dining options on campus (Mahaffey & Smith, 2009; Rifkin, 2004). As a result, dining spaces are not optimally used to facilitate natural conversations regarding the intersections of religious observance and dietary restrictions or opportunities to eat with peers who hold similar restrictions. The access to and a place for spiritual expression extends well beyond lost dining hall conversations. There need to be prayer spaces for communal prayer for Muslim students, for example, and religious study group spaces, akin to Bible study groups.

The psychological stressors religious minority students face are due in large part to the tensions experienced from these campus barriers to religious engagement, in that students become isolated and feel alienated or marginalized through their campus experiences (Mahaffey & Smith, 2009). World events, which inform the sociocultural climate of college campuses, the misinformation (or lack of information) regarding different religious traditions, and religious ideology regarding "truth" provide additional stressors confronting students. Several authors, for instance, have reported on the aftermath of the September 11, 2001, terrorist attacks, when Muslim college students (and those students perceived as Muslim) were threatened, attacked, and beaten (Ahmadi, 2011; Cole & Ahmadi, 2003, 2010). The disclosure of the New York Police Department's (NYPD) undercover surveillance operation of over a dozen college campuses throughout the Northeastern United States further underscores the ongoing Islamophobic zeitgeist that persists not only in our larger social context but also on college campuses (Ahmadi, 2011; Hawley, 2012). The NYPD, "In one report, [had] an undercover officer . . . accompanying 18 Muslim students from the City College of New York on a whitewater rafting trip in upstate New York on April 21, 2008" (Hawley, 2012, para. 8). The perception and misinformation regarding Muslims are that any one of them can be a terrorist. Negative stereotypes like these and others, such as that all Buddhists are Asian, all Muslims are Arab, and all Jews are White, often serve to further alienate students from non-Christian mainline religious traditions. Mayhew and Bryant (2013), for example, assert that "students' perceptions of the psychological climate around religion, spirituality, and ideology on campus create (or undermine) opportunities for curricular and co-curricular engagements and challenging experiences" (p. 65). The psychological climates, where such stressors are pervasive for religious minority students, are likely to exaggerate students' feelings of alienation, which increases the likelihood of becoming isolated.

Theoretical Perspectives

While Fowler (1981) and Parks (2000) provide developmental models often referenced when conceptualizing and discussing faith and spiritual growth, we offer two college impact models useful for examining the effects of college on religious minority students. The first is the campus climate conceptual framework proposed by Hurtado, Milem, Clayton-Pedersen, and Allen (1998) and extended by Milem, Chang, and Antonio (2005). This framework has four original dimensions, which consider both institutional responsibility and individual agency in the complex constructions of college impact on Students of Color. We use these dimensions and extend their application to religious minority students. The second framework is relatively new and offers conceptual measures of spirituality and religiousness. This framework, provided by Astin, Astin, and Lindholm (2011b), allows one to identify and empirically measure students' spirituality and religiousness as growth indices during one of the most important developmental contexts in the lives of young adults—college.

Campus Climate

According to Hurtado and colleagues (1998), students are educated in racial and ethnic campus climates that vary from campus to campus. While campus climate as a conceptual framework has typically been applied to the campus racial climate, we propose a similar utility for understanding the campus climate for religious minority students (Mayhew & Bryant, 2013). The racial and ethnic climate of a campus is shaped by the interaction of external and internal forces (Hurtado et al., 1998). External forces are represented in two domains: (1) governmental policy, programs, and initiatives; and (2) sociohistorical forces (Hurtado et al., 1998). Examples of the former include financial aid policies and programs, court decisions on the desegregation of higher education, and state and federal policies on affirmative action (Hurtado et al., 1998). When applied to the role of religion in postsecondary education, an example of the legal view is the separation of church and state. Sociohistoric forces are events or issues in the larger society that influence how people view racial and ethnic diversity in society (Hurtado et al., 1998). While external forces occur "outside" a college campus, Hurtado et al. (1998) stress that they serve as stimuli for diversity-related discussions and/or activities that occur on campus. In the case of religion, national and world conflicts like the terrorist attacks of September 11 offer such sociohistorical examples.

Internal forces are composed of four interconnected dimensions (Hurtado et al., 1998): (1) historical legacy of inclusion or exclusion, (2) structural diversity, (3) psychological climate, and (4) behavioral climate. The first dimension—an institution's historical legacy of inclusion or exclusion—refers to the institution's initial response to the admission of Students of Color (Hurtado et al., 1998). A college's inclusionary or exclusionary past is relevant because it can determine the prevailing climate and influence current diversity practices (Hurtado et al., 1998). Yet, in the context of religious diversity, we assert that institutional type (public versus private) and religious affiliation (historical versus current) are likely to impact the embedded nature in which cultural values and traditions are recognized or become implicit as the normative backdrop for which institutional policies are derived and maintained with regard to admissions practices, university holidays, and the like. Structural diversity, the second dimension, is an institution's numerical representation of various racial/ethnic groups. An institution's structural diversity is significant because it conveys whether maintaining a multicultural environment is a high institutional priority (Hurtado et al., 1998). Structural diversity in terms of ethnicity can also include the representation of different religious traditions in the campus's student body. In fact, Cole and Ahmadi (2010) found that religiously diverse student groups can extend traditional definitions of diversity beyond race. They found that religious minorities, such as Muslim and Jewish students, were less likely to spend time in prayer when compared to their Christian peers; Muslim students were also more likely to interact with peers different from themselves when compared to both Christian and Jewish students.

The third dimension, psychological climate, focuses on individuals' views of group relations, institutional responses to diversity, perceptions of discrimination, and attitudes toward groups of different racial/ethnic backgrounds (Hurtado et al., 1998). Hurtado et al. (1998) indicate that *who* people are and *where* people are positioned in an institution shape the manner in which they experience and view the institution. Consequently, students' perceptions are a product of the environment and will influence future interactions as well as the outcomes gained by their interactions (Berger & Milem, 1999). These perceptions include the religious values and social dispositions students bring with them to college. The final dimension, the behavioral climate, consists of: (a) the status of social interactions, (b) the nature of interactions between individuals from different racial/ethnic backgrounds, and (c) the quality of intergroup relations (Hurtado et al., 1998). Hence, *when*, with *whom*, and *how* individuals interact serve as indicators of an institution's campus climate, which also consists of the religious activities students create and pursue during college. For instance, Cole and Ahmadi (2003) reported that Muslim women who maintained their veiling practice in the face of harsh campus-related discrimination did so because of their religious commitment and active involvement with members of their religious community on and off campus.

Milem et al. (2005), however, expand Hurtado et al.'s (1998) model and propose a fifth dimension of campus climate. Specifically, this fifth dimension represents the organizational and structural aspects of colleges, which consider among other student services, racial/ethnic community centers and racial/ethnic student organizations. The organizational aspects of college are also represented through religious-oriented student centers and student organizations that are either cultural or dogmatic in their religious affiliation; student centers like Hillel, Chalutzim, Muslim Student Association or Muslim Student Union (MSA or MSU) offer religious minority students the structural and organizational representation to support services specific to their religious engagement on campus.

Spirituality and Religiousness

Astin and colleagues (2011b) have identified ten interrelated measures of spirituality and religiousness—five measures for spirituality and five measures for religiousness— and offer an empirically driven framework for examining and understanding students' spiritual sense of self. The first two measures, constructed as an inward focus of spirituality, include equanimity (i.e., feeling of peace or centering) and spiritual quest (i.e., the search for meaning and/or one's life purpose). Ecumenical worldview, charitable involvement, and ethic of caring comprise the external foci of spirituality and the extent to which students feel connected to people around them. An ecumenical worldview reflects students' interest in other religious traditions and sense of connectedness to a broad construct of humanity. Charitable involvement and ethic of caring is the extent of students' community service and value toward helping others, respectively.

Yet, within the context of this chapter, the constructs guiding students' religiousness may offer a more useful conceptual framework for understanding the role of religion in students' lives. Of the five constructs, religious commitment is considered an inward focus on the essential role of religion and how religious beliefs affect students' daily lives, whereas religious engagement is the external representation of commitment, in that religious engagement considers the type and frequency of religious-related activities such as praying, attending religious services, religious singing, and reading. The other three constructs reflect students' dispositions regarding their religiousness and include social conservatism, skepticism, and struggle. Religious conservatism reflects students' views on social issues, "commitment to proselytize," and "God as a father figure" (Astin et al., 2011b, p. 21). Religious skepticism, however, is perhaps more agnostic in its framing and considers "beliefs such as the 'universe arose by chance' and 'in the future, science will be able to explain everything'" (p. 21). Unlike religious skepticism or conservatism, religious struggle seems to be just that—the extent to which students have questions, are unsettled, or are unsure about their religious beliefs or matters concerning their religious upbringing.

While Astin et al. (2011b) identify the interrelatedness of spirituality and religiousness, there are two critical findings regarding the relationships among these constructs. First, religious commitment, engagement, and social conservatism tend to be highly correlated; students with high commitment are likely to be highly engaged and have conservative social values and dispositions. Accordingly, these students are also likely *not* to be skeptical in their religious beliefs. Students who are struggling, however, are likely "not to show any substantial relationship with other religious or spiritual measures" (p. 22). These constructs provide an organizing conceptual frame for making sense of students' religious experiences while in college but lack a specific focus on the interactions between religious minority students in a nonreligious or dominant religious institutional context.

Student Engagement Strategies

America was founded on the basis of religious freedom. In fact, the establishment clause of the First Amendment states that public institutions must maintain a neutral stance regarding religious beliefs and activities (Kaplin & Lee, 2007). Institutions of higher education may permit noncoercive religious activity. Private institutions, on the other hand, have no obligation of neutrality under the Constitution. If, however, a private institution discriminates based on religion, the federal government can take action (e.g., take the private institution's tax-exempt status away) because it has a compelling interest in eradicating all forms of discrimination. Most institutions of higher education operate from a dominant Christian ideology and Christian privilege, which could be viewed as coercive religious activity. Mayhew and Bryant (2013) assert that higher education administrators and faculty can strive to minimize coercion on campus by formulating noncoercive policies for recognized student religious, spiritual, and ideological organizations on campus; providing opportunities for students to engage one another with respect, compassion, and openness; and modeling the principles of constructive exchange within the classroom and co-curricular programming. (p. 81).

It is within this context of constructive curricular and co-curricular exchange that we identify a number of policy recommendations and best practices. We assert that postsecondary institutions should support underrepresented religious groups where students can have a formal mechanism for organizing themselves under a particular religious denomination or expression like RecKlez, the Harvard Klezmer Band (Ashkenazic Jewish culture), and the Hindu Student Council & Young Jains of America at the University of Pennsylvania. Institutional agents, like faculty and student affairs personnel, can serve as advisors to students interested in participating in a particular religious/spiritual group (Mahaffey & Smith, 2009). Additionally, a list of recognized groups and organizations, widely available, could facilitate students' integration into campus life.

Institutions should sponsor multi-faith programming where students' diverse religious backgrounds offer opportunities to reflect on what it means to engage in multi-faith dialogue, awareness, and questioning in a safe environment. For example, annual inter-faith week, service-learning projects, leadership training, and even a multi-faith student choir like SHANTI at the University of Southern California are the types of activities common among active multi-faith organizations. Offering co-curricular opportunities for nonreligious students to explore their spiritual and existential philosophies (Mayhew & Bryant, 2013) is also essential for creating a safe environment where understanding, respect, and acceptance are of utmost importance. Concurrently, providing resources to support co-curricular experiences linked to religious minorities students' experiences can foster a welcoming environment, which can encourage institutional interconnectedness.

Providing campus spaces for students' religious-related activities such as prayer rooms or programming areas display value for religious minority students and their religious needs. For some, these designated areas may be the only space students have for religious practices as access to nearby outside religious organizations and places for worship may be limited. Institutions can also consider extending hours of availability for students who may have conflicting schedules or limited access during the weekday business hours. In particular, for community college students who only take evening classes or residential students who may not have access off campus, this campus space is critical for their religious needs. Considering the physical structure and scheduling alternatives at fitness facilities (Cole & Ahmadi, 2003; Mahaffey & Smith, 2009) can also make the campus environment inclusive. For example, fitness facilities can schedule gender-specific times for "women-only swim time," which can be helpful to some Muslim and Jewish women who would not use the pool when men are present. Moreover, institutions should provide food options on campus that cater to religious minority students' diet like *halal* or kosher food options. Students may have limited options outside campus or access may conflict with their academic schedule on campus. In addition, other food accommodations for religious practices, like fasting, include providing takeout boxes or expanding late night hours for on-campus dining halls. Committing such institutional resources to meet the needs of religious minority students also has the capacity to communicate more than value, but a fundamental understanding of who these students are in terms of their developing religious identities. This can facilitate meaningful forms of institutional connectedness.

Moreover, traditional institutions with residential housing options should consider sponsoring themed housing where students can have a residential space to live, learn, and eat together creating both intra- and intergroup engagement among students who share either the same category of religious identification or important similarities in diet, modesty, or religious/spiritual interests. Examples include the Jewish Life House at Wheaton College, the Bodhi (Buddhist) House at Earlham, or the Religious Diversity House at Union College. A seamless living-learning campus experience, when both social and academic programs are intentional, can engage the complexities of students' lived experiences and their developing religious identities. Community colleges, on the other hand, are distinct from other institutions of higher education in that they are primarily commuter campuses, often serve as the pathway to four-year universities and colleges, and are disproportionately high in the number of ethnic minorities and first-generation immigrants (Shammas, 2017). Furthermore, community college students spend only one to four hours on campus, during which two-thirds of students spend less than half an hour outside of the classroom (Borglum & Kubala, 2000). Thus, community college students encounter a more varied college experience than a traditional four-year institution student, where community college students' college experience on campus is comparatively limited. Community college specific recommendations include investing and extending multicultural and multi-faith resources, centers, programming, and activities for when community college students can be engaged on campus, specifically in the evening with programs designed for working adults, adults with dependents, and other family and life responsibilities. Moreover, increasing timely access of food options tailored to religious minority students like *halal* or kosher food for those who have a short amount of time between classes or for those who take evening classes would significantly accommodate religious minority students. When accommodations for religious minority students are specific to the community college–going experience, they can help students navigate academic life and their religious identities.

Institutional accommodations for days of religious significance recognize religious minority students and their religious holidays and support students in balancing academic responsibilities and their religious observances and practices. Traditional academic calendars close institutions or cancel classes to observe Christian holy days but non-Christian religious groups are often not recognized on the academic calendars of colleges and universities (Brubacher & Rudy, 1997; Rudolph, 1990). Institutions should include observances of religious minorities in university-wide calendars. Furthermore, faculty can also provide proactive accommodations or resolutions for days of religious significance in their syllabi. Supportive policies, resolutions, or days off can foster a supportive academic environment and improve religious minority students' college experiences.

Initiating dialogue with students (Cole & Ahmadi, 2003; Mahaffey & Smith, 2009; Mayhew & Bryant, 2013) outside the classroom about the nature of their religious interactions and their campus experience(s) can inform existing conversations about religion on campus. Such dialogue can alter feelings or perceptions of being marginalized, particularly if the recommendations derived from those conversations influence institutional policies and practices. These dialogues can have important institutional benefits regarding a university's mission and the quality of students' college experiences.

Providing support to religious minority students can also come in the form of mentoring. Faculty and student affairs educators who identify with these religions can mentor students not just within the context of on-campus religious organizations, but also when students face issues within their academic careers or life's challenges. For instance, the University of Southern California has several positions that allow for support and mentorship, including a Dean of Religious Life, Director of Muslim Student Life, Director of Spirituality and Sexuality, and Director of Hindu Student Life. These directors assist students with religious/spiritual issues. It is important to understand the intersection of identities (Cole & Ahmadi, 2010; Mahaffey & Smith, 2009) and to know that religion is not the only identity that one possesses. For example, the intersection of race, gender, and religion is essential to how some students self-identify. One can be African American, Jewish, and female or Chinese, gay, and Muslim. For some, religious identity is often embedded with ethnic identity, where religion serves as an ethnic identity marker and can assert primacy over individual ethnic identities (Shammas, 2015). Thus, these multiple identities become inseparable, and the intersection of these identities engage the complexities of students' lived experiences and their developing religious identities. In today's global environment, institutions of higher education should strive to celebrate and support the intersection of students' identities.

These recommendations provide possibilities for religious minority students to experience a campus environment that is more attuned to their diverse needs.

References

Ahmadi, S. (2011). The erosion of civil rights: Exploring the effects of the Patriot Act on Muslims in American higher education. *Rutgers Race and the Law Review, 12*(1), 1–56.

Astin, A. W. (1993). *What matters in college? Four critical years revisited.* San Francisco, CA: Jossey-Bass.

Astin, A. W., Astin, H. S., & Lindholm, J. A. (2011a). Assessing students' spiritual and religious qualities. *Journal of College Student Development, 52*(1), 39–61.

Astin, A. W., Astin, H. S., & Lindholm, J. A. (2011b). *Cultivating the spirit: How college can enhance students' inner lives.* San Francisco, CA: Jossey-Bass.

Berger, J. B., & Milem, J. F. (1999). The role of student involvement and perceptions of integration in a causal model of student persistence. *Research in higher Education, 40*(6), 641–664.

Bonderud, K., & Fleischer, M. (2004). *New study of college students finds connection between spirituality, religiousness, and mental health.* Los Angeles, CA: University of California, Los Angeles, Higher Education Research Institute.

Bonderud, K., & Fleischer, M. (2005). *College students report high levels of spirituality and religiousness: Major study has implications for colleges, health, and politics.* Los Angeles, CA: University of California, Los Angeles, Higher Education Research Institute.

Borglum, K., & Kubala, T. (2000). Academic and social integration of community college students: A case study. *Community College Journal of Research and Practice, 24*, 567–576.

Bowman, N. A., & Small, J. L. (2010). Do college students who identify with a privilege religion experience greater spiritual development? Exploring individual and institutional dynamics. *Research in Higher Education, 51*, 595–614.

Brubacher, J. S., & Rudy, W. (1997). *Higher education in transition: A history of American colleges and universities.* Piscataway, NJ: Transaction Publishers.

Bryant, A. N. (2006). Exploring religious pluralism in higher education: Non-majority religious perspectives among entering first-year college students. *Religion & Education, 33*(1), 1–25.

Bryant, A. N., & Astin, H. S. (2008). The correlates of spiritual struggle during the college years. *Journal of Higher Education, 79*(1), 1–28.

Clark, R. T. (2003). The law and spirituality: How the law supports and limits expression of spirituality on the college campus. In M. A. Jablonski (Ed.), *The implications of student spirituality for student affairs practice* (New directions for student services, No. 95, pp. 37–46). San Francisco, CA: Jossey-Bass.

Clark, C., & Brimhall-Vargas, M. (2003). Diversity initiatives in higher education: Secular aspects and international implications of Christian privilege. *Multicultural Education, 11*, 55–57.

Cole, D. G., & Ahmadi, S. (2003). Perspectives and experiences of Muslim women who veil on college campuses. *Journal of College Student Development, 44*(1), 47–66.

Cole, D. G., & Ahmadi, S. (2010). Reconsidering campus diversity: An examination of Muslim students' experience. *The Journal of Higher Education, 81*(2), 121–139.

Collins, J. R., Hurst, J. C., & Jacobsen, J. K. (1987). The blind spot extended: Spirituality. *Journal of College Student Personnel, 28*(3), 274–276.

Eck, D. L. (2009). *A new religious America: How a "Christian country" has become the world's most religiously diverse nation.* New York, NY: HarperCollins.

Eisenmann, L. (1999). Reclaiming religion: New historiographic challenges in the relationship of religion and American higher education. *History of Education Quarterly, 39*(3), 295–306.

Ellison, C. G. (1991). Religious involvement and subjective well-being. *Journal of Health and Social Behavior, 32*, 80–99.

Fetzer Institute/National Institute on Aging Working Group (1999). *Multidimensional measurement of religiousness/spirituality for use in health research: A report of the Fetzer institute/national institute on aging working group* (1st ed.). Kalamazoo, MI: Fetzer Institute.

Fowler, J. W. (1981). *Stages of faith: The psychology of human development and the quest for meaning.* New York, NY: HarperCollins.

Gurin, P., Dey, E. L., Hurtado, S., & Gurin, G. (2002). Diversity and higher education: Theory and impact on educational outcomes. *Harvard Educational Review, 72*(3), 330–366.

Hamburger, P. (2002). *Separation of church and state.* Cambridge, MA: Harvard University Press.

Hawley, C. (2012, February 8). *NYPD monitored Muslim students all over the northeast.* Retrieved on April 1, 2012, from http://ap.org/Content/AP-In-The-News/2012/NYPD-monitored-Muslim-students-all-over-Northeast

Hurtado, S., & Carter, D. F. (1997). Effects of college transition and perceptions of the campus racial climate on Latino college students' sense of belonging. *Sociology of Education, 70*(4), 324–345.

Hurtado, S., Milem, J. F., Clayton-Pedersen, A. R., & Allen, W. R. (1998). Enhancing campus climates for racial/ethnic diversity: Educational policy and practice. *The Review of Higher Education, 21*, 279–302.

Idler, E. L. (1987). Religious involvement and the health of the elderly: Some hypotheses and an initial test. *Social Forces, 66*, 226–238.

Jablonski, M. A. (2001). Editor's notes. In M. A. Jablonski (Ed.), *Implications of student spirituality for student affairs practice* (New directions for student services, No. 95, pp. 1–5). San Francisco, CA: Jossey-Bass.

Kaplin, W. A., & Lee, B. A. (2007). *The law of higher education* (4th ed.). San Francisco, CA: Jossey-Bass.

Koenig, H. G. (2001). Religion and medicine II: Religion, mental health, and related behaviors. *International Journal of Psychiatry in Medicine, 31*(1), 97–109.

Koenig, H. G., McCullough, M., & Larson, D. B. (2001). *Handbook of religion and health.* New York, NY: Oxford University Press.

Kohlbrenner, B. J. (1961). Religion and higher education: An historical perspective. *History of Education Quarterly, 1*(2), 45–56.

Kuh, G. D., & Gonyea, R. M. (2005). *Exploring the relationships between spirituality, liberal learning, and college student engagement.* Bloomington, IN: Indiana University. Retrieved September 16, 2011, from www.nsse.iub.edu/pdf/research_papers/teagle.pdf

Levin, J. S. (1996). How religion influences morbidity and health: Reflections on natural history, salutogenesis and host resistance. *Social Science Medicine, 43*, 849–864.

Lowery, J. W. (2004). Understanding the legal protections and limitations upon religion and spiritual expression on campus. *College Student Affairs Journal, 23*(2), 146–157.

Lowery, J. W. (2005). What higher education law says about spirituality. *New Directions for Teaching and Learning, 104*, 15–22.

Mahaffey, C. J., & Smith, S. A. (2009). Creating welcoming campus environments for students from minority religious groups. In S. R. Harper & S. J. Quaye (Eds.), *Student engagement in higher education: Theoretical perspectives and practical approaches for diverse populations* (pp. 81–97). New York, NY: Routledge.

Marsden, G. M. (1994). *The soul of the American university: From Protestant establishment to established non-belief.* New York, NY: Oxford University Press.

Mayhew, M. J., & Bryant, A. N. (2013). Achievement or arrest? The influence of the collegiate religious and spiritual climate on students' worldview commitment. *Research in Higher Education, 54*(1), 63–84.

McEwen, M. K. (1996). New perspectives on identity development. In S. R. Komives & D. B. Woodard (Eds.), *Student services: A handbook for the profession* (3rd ed., pp. 188–217). San Francisco, CA: Jossey Bass.

McIntosh, P. (1988). *White privilege and male privilege: A personal account of coming to see correspondences through work in women's studies.* Wellesley, MA: Wellesley College Center for Research on Women.

Milem, J. F., Chang, M. J., & Antonio, A. L. (2005). *Making diversity work on campus: A research-based perspective.* Washington, DC: Association of American Colleges and Universities.

Mooney, M. (2005). *Does religion influence college satisfaction of grades earned? Evidence from the National Longitudinal Survey of Freshmen (NLSF).* Manuscript submitted for publication.

Palmer, P. J. (1993). *To know as we are known: Education as spiritual journey*. San Francisco, CA: Harper.

Parks, S. D. (2000). *Big questions, worthy dreams: Mentoring young adults in their search for meaning, purpose, and faith*. San Francisco, CA: Jossey-Bass.

Pew Forum on Religion and Public Life. (2008a). *US religious landscape survey*, Chapter 1: Religious composition of the United States (pp. 10–21). Retrieved November 19, 2011, from http://religions.pew forum.org/pdf/report-religious-landscape-study-chapter-1.pdf

Pew Forum on Religion and Public Life. (2008b). *US religious landscape survey*, Chapter 3: Religious affiliation and demographic group (pp. 40–41). Retrieved September 16, 2011, from http://religions.pewforum.org/pdf/report-religious-landscape-study-chapter-3.pdf

Rifkin, I. (2004). *Spiritual perspectives on globalization: Making sense of economic and cultural upheaval*. Woodstock, VT: SkyLight Paths Publishing.

Riley, N. S. (2005). *God on the quad*. New York, NY: St. Martin's Press.

Roof, W. C., & McKinney, W. (1987). *American mainline religion: Its changing shape and future*. New Brunswick, NJ: Rutgers University Press.

Rudolph, F. (1990). *The American college and university*. Athens, GA: University of Georgia Press.

Schlosser, L. Z. (2003, January). Christian privilege: Breaking a sacred taboo. *Journal of Multicultural Counselling and Development, 31*, 44–51.

Schlosser, L. Z., & Sedlacek, W. (2003). Christian privilege and respect for religious diversity: Religious holidays on campus. *About Campus, 7*(6), 28–29.

Seifert, T. (2007). Understanding Christian privilege: Managing the tensions of spiritual plurality. *About Campus, 12*(2), 10–18.

Shammas, D. (2015). We are not all the same: Arab and Muslim students forging their own campus communities in a post-9/11 America. *Journal of Muslim Minority Affairs, 35*(1), 65–88.

Shammas, D. (2017). Underreporting discrimination among Arab American and Muslim American community college students: Using focus groups to unravel the ambiguities within the survey data. *Journal of Mixed Methods Research, 11*(1), 99–123.

Small, J. L. (2008). *College student religious affiliation and spiritual identity: A qualitative study* (Unpublished doctoral dissertation), University of Michigan, Ann Arbor, MI.

Stamm, L. (2003). Can we bring spirituality back to campus? Higher education's re-engagement with values and spirituality. *Journal of College and Character, 4*(5). www.degruyter.com/view/j/jcc.2003.4.5/jcc.2003.4.5.1354/jcc.2003.4.5.1354.xml?format=INT

United States Census Bureau (2011). *Statistical abstract of the United States: 2012*. Retrieved November 19, 2011, from www.census.gov/compendia/statab/2012/tables/12s0075.pdf

Williams, D. R., Larson, D. B., Buckler, R. E., Heckmann, R. C., & Pyle, C. M., (1991). Religion and psychological distress in a community sample. *Social Science Medicine, 32*, 1257–1262.

Wuthnow, R. (2007). Can faith be more than a slide show in the contemporary academy? In D. Jacobsen & R. H. Jacobsen (Eds.), *The American University in a postsecular age: Religion and higher education* (pp. 31–44). New York, NY: Oxford University Press.

Chapter 14
Engaging Students With Disabilities

Kirsten R. Brown and Ellen M. Broido

Historically underrepresented groups share a common experience: all face unwelcoming environments when initially entering higher education (Hall & Belch, 2000). Ableism (the oppression of people with disabilities) plays a powerful role in shaping the ways students with and without disabilities experience educational environments (Evans, Broido, Brown, & Wilke, 2017). Ableism, like other forms of oppression, operates on multiple levels—individual, institutional, systemic, and social-cultural (Hardiman, Jackson, & Griffin, 2007). An example of ableism at the individual level is when people assume there are few disabled students on campus because they do not see many students using wheelchairs. A college or university not mandating web, print, and video materials be accessible to all users is an example of institutional ableism. Systemic ableism is reflected in reliance on medical diagnosis of disability to obtain disability accommodation. Cultural ableism is evident in privileging typical ways of demonstrating competence (e.g., assuming resident assistants must be able to hear in order to do their jobs when there are other equally effective ways of communicating). Ableism's power lies in the unchallenged assumption that there is one right way to function (e.g., communicate) and specific abilities (e.g., hearing) are necessary (Hutcheon & Wolbring, 2012). Ableism hides the value of interdependence by assigning stigma to certain forms of assistance (e.g., using a tablet to communicate) while portraying other forms of assistance as unremarkable (e.g., using an advisor's help to fill out graduate school applications) (Evans et al., 2017). To create engaging environments for students with disabilities, educators need to identify and address ways in which ableism shapes the experiences of members of campus communities.

Ableism is profoundly shaped by its interaction with other forms of oppression. For example, some behaviors resulting from autism are more likely to be explained by educators as lack of intelligence or self-discipline in Black students but are addressed as indicators of impairment in White students (Mandell et al., 2009). Women with disabilities report far higher rates of sexual violence on college campuses than their nondisabled peers (Brown, Peña, & Rankin, 2017). Queer disabled students often feel invisible (Miller, 2015).

Before moving further, we make a distinction between disability and impairment. We follow the definitions of Evans and Herriott (2009), who use *impairment* to refer to "any condition that results in a way of functioning or results in behavior that differs from the expected level of performance in any given area" (p. 29); essentially, impairments are ways people's bodies or minds differ from what society defines as normal. *Disability* is defined in multiple ways, depending on the theoretical perspective one uses. In this chapter, we use the term to refer to the consequences of the interaction between society's response to people with impairments, particularly ways that exclude, discriminate against, or stigmatize people with disabilities (Sherry, 2004); the impairment itself; and the choices the disabled person makes regarding self-care and their own views of disability and impairment (Evans & Broido, 2011). Disabilities are consequences of three things: ableist attitudes, physical or social environments that support only putatively normal ways of functioning (Griffin, Peters, & Smith, 2007), and the impacts of impairment on people's minds and bodies (Evans et al., 2017; Shakespeare, 2014).

The language used to describe disability adds a further layer of complication. Specifically, different groups prefer identity-first language (e.g., autistic person) or person-first (e.g., person with autism) (Dunn & Andrews, 2015). Identity-first labels are a way of reclaiming formerly derogatory disability-related terms (e.g., cripple) (Dunn & Andrews, 2015), showing pride in an aspect of one's identity, and eschewing language that implies disability is something that "should be hidden" behind statements of personhood (Collier, 2012, p. E939). Conversely, person-first language foregrounds the individual rather than the disability, thereby linguistically recognizing disability as only one facet of the individual (Hall & Belch, 2000). We, and others, advocate for person-preferred language when possible (Peña et al., 2018) and use disability- and identity-first language interchangeably to reflect the preferences of the authors we cite.

Enrollment and Demographic Trends

National longitudinal studies conducted by researchers at the US Department of Education demonstrate a substantive increase in postsecondary students with disabilities since the passage of the Americans with Disabilities Act (ADA) in 1990, although their enrollment rates still lag behind those of nondisabled peers. In 1995 only 26% of high school students with disabilities reported continuing on to college (Newman, Wagner, Cameto, Knokey, & Shaver, 2010); that number rose to 46% in 2005 (Newman et al., 2010) and 60% in 2009 (Newman et al., 2011). Currently, about 11% of college students identify themselves to their postsecondary institution as having a disability (National Center for Education Statistics, 2016). However, this often-cited 11% statistic masks the much larger population of individuals who choose not to disclose their disability to their institutions. Specifically, only 35% of students who received special education services in high school self-identify to their postsecondary institution (Newman & Madaus, 2015a).

Enrollment patterns of disabled students vary by institution type; while students with disabilities attend all types of postsecondary institutions, national studies (e.g., NTLS-2, NCES) indicate between half and three-quarters of undergraduate students with disabilities who attended postsecondary institutions enrolled at a public two-year college (Raue & Lewis, 2011; Snyder, deBrey, & Dillow, 2016). Studies following students with disabilities for up to eight years after they left high school indicated that, of those who enrolled in postsecondary education, about 44% attended a two-year college, 31% attended a vocational/technical college, and 18% attended a four-year university (Newman et al., 2011; Snyder et al., 2016). Because disability status changes over the lifespan, reports from the National Center for Education Statistics do not reflect all students with disabilities.

Disabled students differ from each other in numerous ways—including life experiences and demographic characteristics. Data from the 2014 National Center for Education Statistics Digest (the most recent with disability statistics) indicated that veterans are more likely to self-identify as disabled (21%) than undergraduates who are not veterans (11%) (Snyder et al., 2016). Although there were not significant differences in self-identification by gender,[1] the same is not true for race: Asian (8%) students report lower rates of disability than their Hispanic (10%), White (11%), Black (12%), multiracial (14%), American Indian/Alaska Native (14%), and Pacific Islander (15%) peers (Snyder et al., 2016). Family income is critical for disabled students' access to postsecondary education and their access to accommodations once enrolled. Only 50% of disabled high school students with household incomes of $25,000 or less enrolled in postsecondary education while 70% of their peers with household incomes of $50,000 or more enrolled in postsecondary education (Newman et al., 2011). Disabled students from households with less than $25,000 in annual income were less likely to use accommodations than disabled students with household incomes larger than $50,000 (Newman & Madaus, 2015b).

Students with disabilities also differ from each other by their type of impairment and the extent, duration, and continuity of their impairment (Evans et al., 2017). Mention the term *disabled student* and many people picture a student using a wheelchair or perhaps a guide dog. However, most college students with disabilities have nonapparent impairments, such as learning disabilities, psychological disabilities, attention deficit disorder, chronic health conditions, and neurologic impairments (Snyder et al., 2016). Other peoples' perceptions have substantive implications for disabled students; although it is illegal to discriminate by disability type, students with impairments that are more apparent to others (e.g., hearing, visual, orthopedic) were more likely to receive accommodations (Newman & Madaus, 2015b). Some people are born with impairments, but many develop them over the course of their lifespan, including just before or while they are college students. Some impairments require medical management, but many do not.

Some people's impairments are stable over their lives, and others experience periods in which the impairment is more or less intrusive. Some people strongly identify as having a disability, and many others eschew this term. For all these reasons, it is important not to generalize about students (or other members of the campus community) with disabilities and to understand the goals of the particular people with whom one works.

Theoretical Perspectives on Disability

The medical, minority group, and social models are three conventional theoretical paradigms to understanding disability (Evans et al., 2017). The medical model aligns with a positivistic, scientific approach that defines disability as biological deficiencies that interventions or medical services are designed to rectify. This model frames disability as an individual experience, defined and verified by medical professionals (Smart & Smart, 2006). The medical model ignores social and environmental components; the problem is located within the student.

A second paradigm, the minority group paradigm, focuses on issues of relative social privilege, power, and oppression (Evans et al., 2017). Proponents of the minority group paradigm perceive prejudice and discrimination found in broader society as greater obstacles than medical impairments (Smart & Smart, 2006). The minority model is useful for shifting the focus toward political action. Critics point out that this paradigm depends on individuals with disabilities consciously identifying themselves with a minority group (Smart & Smart, 2006).

The social construction paradigm considers impairment as a part of normal human variation (Denhart, 2008) and shifts the focus to societal factors such as inaccessible environments and discrimination (Jones, 1996). The social construction paradigm encourages student affairs practitioners to consider the environment and to align programming with both individual and social factors (Hall & Belch, 2000).

The fields of disability studies, deaf studies, autistic studies, and rhetoric offer several critical paradigms that challenge and upend traditional student affairs theoretical perspectives on disability. Here, we briefly describe one perspective, critical disability theory (CDT), and direct interested readers to Brown, Peña, Broido, Stapleton, and Evans (2019), and Peña et al. (2018) for further discussions of critical theories. CDT argues that disability fluctuates over time and setting (Shildrick, 2009); individuals can acquire a disability while in college (e.g., a student-athlete may experience post concussive syndrome), individuals can be diagnosed with a disability while in college (e.g., a first-generation student may gain access to testing for learning disabilities that was previously unavailable in their low-income secondary school), or individuals can experience a change of impact from an existing disability due to the college environment (e.g., a student with a mobility impairment may find the hilly campus terrain, poor snow removal, and limited parking options impede their ability to engage with the campus community). CDT allows practitioners to understand disability as including both the impairment and the environment (Evans et al., 2017).

Critical and Intersectional Perspectives

Engagement, like other concepts (e.g., assessment, student development theory), has its origins in White power structures (Patton, Harper, & Harris, 2015). Patton et al. (2015) explained the power associated with who decides "which experiences and activities add value to a student's college experience" (p. 210). We agree that traditional perspectives on engagement do not reflect the lived experience of disabled students and, thus, may reproduce ableism. Specifically, traditional conceptions of engagement assume that all students have the same levels of energy, use the same modes of communication, have access to the same transportation options, and take the same amount of time on daily living tasks. In reality, students with disabilities may make intentional choices based on their level of energy (e.g., spoon theory) (Miserandino, 2003), may use multiple modes of communication (e.g., American Sign Language), may have limited forms of transportation (e.g., wheelchair accessible bus), and may need to spend more time on daily living tasks (e.g., use of a personal assistant to get dressed, checking blood sugar values, calculating carbohydrates, and administering insulin before eating) and negotiating institutional barriers (e.g., requesting an interpreter to go on a hiking trip sponsored by a student organization). Some disabled students may define engagement very differently (e.g., independent living) than nondisabled practitioners (e.g., serving on hall council), and both definitions are valued and valuable (Wilke, Varland, Brown, Evans, & Broido, 2018).

Disability often "erases" others' awareness of disabled students' multiple social identities; people often attend to nothing other than the students' impairment (Abes & Wallace, 2018). There is a small but growing body of research on how disabled college students experience their own multiple social identities (see Abes & Wallace, 2018; Miller, 2015; Stapleton, 2015) and the ways in which others (rarely) do and (often) do not see their racial, gender, religious/spiritual, sexual orientation, economic class, and additional social identities. Abes and Wallace, Miller, and Stapleton all make compelling arguments that practitioners must recognize that disability is a form of social identity and that the experience of disability always shapes and is shaped by students' additional social identities. Abes and Wallace (2018) conclude that "We must name these systems that render students invisible, create space for them to bring their whole bodies, and value disability as an intersectional social identity" (p. 560).

Engagement

Like all students, disabled students benefit from academic and co-curricular engagement. Although we present research findings in subsections for clarity, it is important to understand that students' lives are integrated across their campus experiences. Further, accommodations and accessibility should not be interpreted as inclusion (Abes & Wallace, 2018); just because one can (literally or metaphorically) get in the door does not mean one is welcomed, affirmed, or included in decision-making processes.

Academic Engagement

Data on six-year graduation rates of students with disabilities provides mixed results; institution-level studies that use students who self-identify as disabled find comparable graduation rates, whereas national-level studies that use students who are identified in high school find lower graduation rates. For instance, Knight, Wessel, and Markle (2018) explored graduation rates at a midwestern research university and found no overall difference in the retention and graduation rates of students with a disability compared to those without a disability. However, Knight et al. (2018) reported that disabled students took significantly longer (4.4 years) to graduate than students without disabilities (4.2 years, a statistically significant difference). There were also non–statistically significant differences in time to graduation by disability type: students with apparent disabilities graduated in 4.3 years, and students with non-apparent disabilities graduated in 4.5 years.

In contrast, nationally representative longitudinal surveys conducted by the US Department of Education (NLTS-2) found that completion rates for disabled students (41%) were lower than nondisabled peers (52%) (Newman et al., 2011); note these data were collected eight years after completion of high school. However, completion rates differed by institution type: at four-year colleges students with disabilities (34%) were less likely to graduate than their abled peers (51%), but at two-year institutions, disabled students were more likely to graduate (41%) than nondisabled students (22%) (Newman et al., 2011). When interpreting these data, it is important to remember that students studying at two-year institutions and technical colleges may have academic goals that are not associated with graduation (e.g., learning a second language, completing general education requirements, transferring to another institution).

Unsurprisingly, academic engagement predicts retention for students with disabilities; between the first and second year, disabled students who had at least minimal academic involvement were significantly more likely to be retained than students with disabilities who reported no academic involvement (78% versus 69%) (Mamiseishvili & Koch, 2011). Students with disabilities reported a higher level of student-faculty interaction than did students without disabilities and levels of academic challenges and active and collaborative learning comparable to their nondisabled peers (Hedrick, Dizén, Collins, Evans, & Grayson, 2010). However, as we describe later, students did not always perceive faculty interaction as facilitating their success.

Co-Curricular Engagement

Despite strong evidence of the importance of out-of-class engagement for the general student population (Mayhew, Rockenbach, Bowman, Seifert, & Wolniak, 2016), co-curricular aspects of campus life for disabled students have received considerably less attention (Evans et al., 2017). The limited existing research indicates that social engagement is a significant predictor of persistence; disabled students with at least some level of social engagement were almost 10% more likely to persist from their first to their second year of college than their uninvolved classmates (81.1% versus 72.6%)

(Mamiseishvili & Koch, 2011). In their grounded theory study with eight first-year students with mostly nonapparent disabilities, Vaccaro, Daly-Cano, and Newman (2015) found that sense of belonging was interrelated with and connected to social relationships, self-advocacy, and mastery of the student role. Students with physical disabilities who were involved in collegiate athletic clubs had higher levels of social interactions, reported greater levels of independence and self-confidence, and created or strengthened friendships (Wessel, Wentz, & Markle, 2011). Living in a campus residence hall and participating in intermural sports were statistically significant predictors of retention for students with disabilities between their first and second years of college (Mamiseishvili & Koch, 2011).

Some evidence supports the notion that engagement is influenced by the kinds of impairments students have. For example, students with learning disabilities may have fewer opportunities to participate in co-curricular activities because they allocate more time to academic engagement (e.g., studying) than their nondisabled peers do (Markoulakis & Kirsh, 2013). Additionally, Evans and Broido (2011) found that students with psychiatric disabilities often faced attitudinal barriers to co-curricular involvement, felt pressure from their families to focus solely on academics, or feared the stigma that others might ascribe to their disability.

Barriers to Engagement

In this section, we call attention to barriers to engagement for disabled students. We focus on topics salient to social justice—ablest attitudes and discriminatory actions, lack of knowledge, legal barriers, physical barriers, and unwelcoming campus environments.

Ableist Attitudes and Discriminatory Behavior

Attitudinal barriers for students with disabilities generally are based on four assumptions. First, ableism leads to the presumption that accommodations for disabilities hold people to lower standards. For example, Beilke and Yssel (1999) found multiple instances in the media in which faculty and administrators indicated they believed many students were claiming to be disabled so they would not have to work as hard or perform to the same level as other students. Ableist beliefs translate into discriminatory actions; Cawthon and Cole (2010) found 21% of students with a learning disability indicated they experienced obstacles, most often from faculty unwilling to make accommodations. Faculty report holding more negative attitudes about providing accommodations for students with mental health disabilities or attention disorders than students with apparent physical or learning disabilities (Baker, Boland, & Nowik, 2012), and faculty thought including students with specific disabilities (e.g., autism) would disturb class routines and take more time (Gibbons, Cihak, Mynatt, & Wilhoit, 2015).

Second, ablest attitudes, stemming from a medical model of disability, inaccurately presume that "typical" ways of functioning are the only appropriate ways, that most accommodations are expensive to the institution and/or burdensome to those providing the accommodation, believe disability "trumps" other social identities, and fail to perceive that everyone benefits from environments designed for universal access (Griffin et al., 2007). These attitudes make it more likely that administrators will relegate responsibility for disability access to one office (Huger, 2011) and make it less likely institutions will proactively seek ways to expand access or view disability as a form of diversity. Further, considering disability only through the lens of accommodation erases disabled students' intersectional identities (Abes & Wallace, 2018) by ignoring the complex ways that ableism is connected to racism, sexism, heteronormativity, transphobia, and other systemic forms of oppression (Lewis, 2019). If educators solely focus on accommodations, they will not recognize that "the same disability is held and expressed differently by different people and communities" (Lewis, 2019, para. 5) and that people's bodies and minds are policed unequally. Stopping the discussion at accommodations dismisses the disproportional harm that racially minoritized students experience across multiple social systems (e.g., education system, medical system, and legal system).

Third, the social construction of stigma creates the assumption that students with disabilities are not capable and, therefore, need to be saved from their limitations. It is important that student affairs personnel possess "the ability to empower rather than rescue students" (Brown, 1994, p. 104). Fourth, disability stigma means that disabled students may need to be the first to initiate friendship or make nondisabled peers, faculty, and staff comfortable with their disability during social interactions (Myers & Bastian, 2010). Miller (2015) found that disabled LGBTQ students experienced microaggressions in the classroom, felt invisible, negotiated faculty and peer perceptions, and made strategic choices about when to disclose their identities. Green's (2018) qualitative exploration indicated that disabled students experience bullying from peers and faculty and disabled students recognized negative social consequences (e.g., ostracization) for using college policies to report the bullying. Thus, practitioners must work to change ablest attitudes held by individuals across campus and challenge discriminatory behavior to remove barriers for disabled students while still respecting their autonomy.

Lack of Knowledge

Lack of knowledge about disability and the absence of systematic disability-specific training or educational programs are barriers to student engagement (Evans et al., 2017). Burgstahler and Moore (2009) examined challenges that students with disabilities face when using student services and found that students perceived support personnel outside disability resource offices (DROs) as insufficiently knowledgeable about disability or accommodations. Additionally, faculty report feeling like they are underprepared to teach students with specific disabilities (e.g., autistic students) (McKeon, Alpern, & Zager, 2013). Given the marginalization of disability research within higher education scholarship (Peña, 2014), it is very possible that disability was not part of the curriculum in many graduate preparation programs.

Legal Barriers

The law is often perceived as a protection for students with disabilities. It is important to honor the hard-fought battles for civil rights that occurred with the passage of federal legislation (e.g., Section 504 of the Rehabilitation Act of 1973 [Section 504]) and also acknowledge that the law functions as a regulatory social mechanism (Spade, 2011) that enforces normality from a predominantly medical perspective (Evans et al., 2017). The law requires a baseline criterion of equal access, but minimum standards are not sufficient to foster engagement. Further, as political climates shift, attention must be paid to the mechanisms used to enforce legislation (e.g., Office for Civil Rights [OCR] case-processing policies) and subregulatory processes (e.g., Department of Justice [DOJ] *Dear Colleague Letters*). An in-depth legal analysis is beyond the scope of this chapter; thus, we briefly describe federal legislation and emphasize that legal rights are not synonymous with equality or inclusion.

Federal Legislation

Three major pieces of federal legislation provide guidance related to engagement for students with disabilities. Section 504 mandates equal access for people with disabilities to public and private postsecondary institutions, stipulating that programs or activities that receive federal funding cannot deny participation in, benefits of, or discriminate against any otherwise qualified person due to their disability (Hall & Belch, 2000). The ADA (1990) extended the protections offered in Section 504 to private employers, places of public accommodation, and programs provided by state or local governments. The ADA defines discrimination to include:

> (1) the use of criteria that unnecessarily screen out or tend to screen out individuals with disabilities from the use and enjoyment of goods and services, (2) the failure to make non-fundamental, reasonable modifications of policies, practices or procedures when such modification is necessary to accommodate disabled persons, and (3) the failure to take necessary steps to ensure that no individual with a disability is excluded, denied services, segregated or otherwise treated differently than other individuals.
>
> (42 USC sec. 12182)

The Americans with Disabilities Act Amendments Act (ADAAA, 2008) clarified the definition of disability and reduced the amount of documentation individuals must offer when establishing they have a disability (Heyward, 2011). Federal legislation mandates that disabled students have the same opportunities for engagement as students without disabilities. Yet, OCR complaints (e.g., snow blocking accessible parking and campus routes) (OCR, 2015), consent decrees (e.g., screen reader–inaccessible websites and curricular materials) (DOJ, 2016), and civil suits (e.g., lack of captions for basketball and football games) (National Association of the Deaf, 2010) demonstrate that, despite this legislation, postsecondary institutions do not automatically provide equal access.

One implication of the ADAAA is that in order to access accommodations, students must identify themselves as disabled to their institutions, which many eligible students do not do (Newman & Madaus, 2015a), even when accommodations would make engagement more likely. There are a variety of reasons students may not self-identify. Students may be anxious for a "new beginning," not want to feel labeled, decide to wait until they have academic problems (Getzel & Thoma, 2008), or may not view their impairment as a disability and, thus, are unaware that accommodations are available (e.g., Type 1 diabetes) (Broido, 2006). Disabled students experience a legal transition from their K–12 environment, where teachers and parents identified and advocated for them, and the postsecondary environment, where they must self-identify and self-advocate to access accommodations. Self-identification is a skill set legally required of no other student population; thus, practitioners should be aware that the law sets up inequitable expectations for this minoritized group.

Physical Barriers

Physical aspects of campus environments often function as barriers to engagement for students with a variety of disabilities. Most obvious are lack of curb cuts, insufficiently wide doors, lack of elevators and automatically opening doors, insufficient and inconveniently located accessible parking spaces, and inaccessible bathrooms that restrict the access of students with mobility impairments. Less obvious barriers are inadequate snow removal, elevator buttons and reception desks at heights that cannot be reached by people using wheelchairs, software incompatible with screen readers, computer and standard desks that cannot be raised and lowered for students who have orthopedic impairments, absence of Braille signage, and lack of software and advertising for campus events readable by those with visual impairments (Evans et al., 2017). All these make it difficult, frustrating, and sometimes impossible for students to fully engage with curricular and co-curricular aspects of the campus and, even when possible, often preclude the spontaneity so characteristic of traditionally aged college students.

Unwelcoming Campus Climates

The campus climate also presents barriers to the engagement of disabled students. In a national study, students with disabilities reported similar levels of engagement in enriching educational experiences to nondisabled classmates, but they perceived their campus environments as significantly less supportive than did students without disabilities (Hedrick et al., 2010). Campus climate studies, a metric of campus environment that measures how comfortable students feel, demonstrate that disabled students feel less welcome on campus (Nachman & Brown, 2019; Zehner, 2018). Using data from 15 public research institutions, Zehner (2018) found that disabled students feel less valued (46% versus 32%), less respected (70% versus 42%), and less satisfied with their social experiences than nondisabled peers (56% versus 42%). Extending campus climate into digital spaces, Nachman and Brown described how college websites are spaces of exclusion and othering. The lack of inclusion is pervasive and noticed by nondisabled students; about half the undergraduate students (49%) in Bruder and Mogro-Wilson's (2010) survey at a single institution believed that the university did a poor to fair job of including disabled students in social organizations and co-curricular activities. Student affairs practitioners play an important role in making sure that the campus climate and specific functional areas under their purview are welcoming to all students.

Recommendations for Practice

In this section, we focus on six specific methods to enhance the engagement of students with disabilities. In making these recommendations, we also recognize that ableism takes many different forms, and each institutional culture is unique. Part of the power of ableism is found within the concept of normalcy, which is inherently embedded in recommendations for practice. Thus, in offering these recommendations, we challenge student affairs practitioners to go beyond a prescriptive list, to confront the unique subtleties of ableism woven into institutional fabrics, and to find ways to foster engagement within their own campus cultures and communities.

Universal Design

One method of engaging students, with and without disabilities, is to institute policies that support universal design (UD). UD is "the design of products and environments to be usable by all people, to the greatest extent possible, without the need for adaptation or specialized design" (Center for Universal Design, 2011, para. 1). Three fundamental principles of UD are multiple means of representation of information, multiple means of expression of knowledge, and multiple means of engagement in the learning process (Schelly, Davies, & Spooner, 2011). UD brings a specific focus to inclusion as a primary and unifying goal (Higbee, 2004). A full review (including critique) of UD is beyond the scope of this chapter; here we describe applications of UD to engagement and direct interested readers to Evans et al. (2017).

One of the benefits for disabled students stems from UD's proactive approach, which may allow students to circumvent the effort associated with requesting and scheduling accommodations because access has already been built into the environment. Further, because UD prioritizes providing access to all students, UD offers the potential to support the engagement of disabled students who choose not to self-identify to their institutions or may be unaware of their disability, as well as disabled students who choose to self-identify and the diversity of nondisabled students who benefit from multiple ways to become engaged in their campus environments (Burgstahler & Moore, 2009).

Training faculty to implement UD supports the academic engagement of students with disabilities (Schelly et al., 2011). Effective strategies include allowing students to demonstrate learning in multiple ways, rather than just by tests, or essays, or any singular approach. All videos should be captioned and have oral description; all readings should work with screen-reading software. All course and training materials and university documents and forms should be run through accessibility-checking software to ensure they can be accessed by all students (Palmer & Caputo, n.d.). Expanding the use of live streaming, videoconferencing, and recording presentations will enable disabled students (and others) to access events at times and for durations that work with their needs. This expands access, given many students with disabilities have less free time and less flexible time than nondisabled students (Samuels, 2017).

Students reported their instructors who received UD training made multiple changes, such as those listed here, to their teaching that supported students' academic success (Raue & Lewis, 2011). Further, faculty from multiple institutions in the United States who received UD training and implemented UD principles reported higher student course evaluations and student pass rates, for both students with and without disabilities (Higbee, 2009). However, due to inadequate staff resources, it is rare that faculty receive training; approximately half of two-year and four-year public institutions and only one-third of private four-year institutions provide UD training (Raue & Lewis, 2011). By advocating for training and implementation of UD concepts, practitioners support an empirically demonstrated way of improving engagement for all students on their campus, including those with disabilities.

UD also applies to student development programs and services (Burgstahler & Moore, 2009; Higbee, 2004), including institutional and departmental websites (Harper & DeWaters, 2008). Higbee (2004) outlined nine UD principles for student development programs and services: (a) create welcoming spaces; (b) develop, implement, and evaluate pathways for communication; (c) promote interaction among students and between staff and students; (d) ensure equal opportunities for learning and growth; (e) communicate clear expectations; (f) use methods that consider diverse learning styles; (g) provide natural supports for learning; (h) ensure confidentiality; and (i) define service quality, establish benchmarks, and evaluate services. For example, practitioners can consider how admissions tours on their campus may or may not be accessible or welcoming and consider diverse learning styles by assessing multiple means of movement across campus, not just walking; multiple means of communicating information, not just speaking; and whether or not the DRO is highlighted as part of the tour.

Collaboration With Disability Resource Offices

Student affairs practitioners can create engaging opportunities for students with disabilities by collaborating with DRO staff on their campus. Practitioners should attend educational events sponsored by the DRO to gain a better understanding of students with disabilities and existing resources to support them. Further, practitioners can seek out educational opportunities beyond their campus via conferences and webinars hosted by professional organizations such as the Association on Higher Education and Disability (AHEAD). Practitioners must work collaboratively with DRO staff to ensure that events and programs that their department sponsors are accessible and welcoming to students with disabilities. Pragmatically, this means that advertisements for events are sent out to the campus community via multiple manners, the physical space in which programs are hosted is accessible, and content provided during the program is presented in formats that are varied and accessible. Moreover, when purchasing new technology (hardware and software programs and products), it is imperative that practitioners collaborate with both DRO staff and information technology offices to ensure the technology is usable by students with and without disabilities.

Bridge, Career, and Mentorship Programs

Bridge, career, and mentorship programs can be effective engagement techniques. It is important that programs align with students' definitions of success and do not employ patronizing or deficit-based models (Evans et al., 2017); therefore, student affairs practitioners are encouraged to plan programs in conjunction with the disabled community.

Bridge programs play an important role in helping students and their families navigate the legal, social, and philosophical changes that occur when moving from K–12 schools to postsecondary education. In secondary education, students with disabilities are covered by legislation that guarantees evaluation, remediation, and accommodation of impairments and designates parents and education providers as the individuals responsible for securing these services (Wolf, Brown, & Bork, 2009). "As students move forward to higher education, however, the legal focus shifts from entitlement and remediation to *protection from discrimination and equal access*" (Wolf et al., 2009, p. 72, italics in original). Thus, disabled students must transition to a new learning environment and negotiate self-advocacy. Since the majority of disabled students attend two-year institutions (Snyder et al., 2016), practitioners developing bridge programs need to consider ways to engage traditional-age learners, adult learners, parenting students, and transfer students (Evans et al., 2017).

Although transition programs generally are thought of as supporting students as they enter the college or university setting, engagement opportunities that target the transition to career or graduate school are equally important because disabled individuals face discrimination in hiring and admissions processes. Hence, internships and programs that promote networking skills via mentoring connections with alumni are vital. Ideally, career preparation programs match individual strengths with viable career paths through engagement in career assessment, internships, co-ops, and on-campus employment opportunities. Excellent examples can be found in California's WorkAbility III (for community colleges) and WorkAbility IV (for four-year institutions) programs. Practitioners working in career services must also acquire the knowledge to coach students with disabilities as they negotiate the decision to disclose their disability status and potentially request or use accommodations during the interview process.

Mentor programs are a way to support engagement for disabled students. Practitioners designing mentoring programs must take a non-deficit-based approach to programming and supporting interpersonal connections. Mentoring programs can take a variety of forms; one-to-one models typically pair disabled students with an older peer, a faculty member in an area of academic interest, or a community member with career connections. If peer mentors are used, disabled students should have the opportunity to be both a mentee and a mentor. Group mentoring models generally pair a faculty member or career-related community member with a small group of students. Practitioners interested in creating a mentor program are encouraged to explore Disability Rights, Education Activism, and Mentoring (DREAM), which is sponsored by the National Center for College Students with Disabilities.

Campus Climate Assessment

Climate assessments may take a variety of different formats (focus groups, surveys), target different levels (institutional, departmental), and seek information from various populations (faculty, students). As described earlier, results from multi-institutional studies (e.g., Zehner, 2018) indicated that students with disabilities face unwelcoming campus climates. Therefore, student affairs practitioners should be attuned to and assess the climate within their own departments and review their own institutions' climate assessment data. While the design, collection, and analysis of data regarding the climate for students with disabilities can itself provide important awareness and knowledge about the climate, it is imperative to act on the findings (Upcraft & Schuh, 1996) or risk losing the trust and future involvement of those participating in the assessment. Climate assessment data must be used to inform policy decisions and direct funding to create a more welcoming environment for disabled students.

Disability Culture

Institutional support for disability identity and disability culture are critical components of a diverse campus. Practitioners and postsecondary institutions must honor and support disability identity as part of the complex and intersectional ways that students with disabilities learn and develop (Abes & Wallace, 2018). Forber-Pratt (2018) posited that disability community and culture were critical to the development of a disability identity. Forber-Pratt found that disability culture made students "feel less isolated," "feel more in control over their own lives," and promoted "a healthy self-image" (p. 9). Disability studies programs and disability cultural centers (DCCs) are specific avenues to engage with disability identity within curricular and co-curricular spaces. In particular, the creation of and commitment to ongoing fiscal support for a DCC is one step that campus leaders can take toward recognizing disability as an identity and fostering the engagement of disabled students. Practitioners who are interested in models for DCCs should consult the University of Arizona, the University of North Carolina at Asheville, the University of Illinois at Chicago, or Syracuse University.

Recognize Variability in Disability

Disability is experienced differently in different student populations (see in particular Chapter 5 in Evans et al., 2017). Programming that recognizes the intersection of disability with other forms of social identity in affirming, non-deficit ways has the potential to enhance the experiences of students in all aspects of their social identities. Unfortunately, as of yet there are few models within higher education for doing so. On campuses that do not have designated disability cultural spaces, educators can engage students by intentionally including disability in multicultural conversations, programs, and campus-wide events and encourage programming that addresses two or more marginalized identities simultaneously. For example, the Sins Invalid art group provides performances and lectures highlighting the intersection of disabled, queer, racially minoritized experiences.

There are many online sites and groups that address disability in conjunction with other minoritized social identities, but few are specific to higher education. An exception is a consortium of HBCU DROs, in conjunction with the Association on Higher Education And Disability (AHEAD), which hosts the website Black, Disabled, and Proud (www.blackdisabledandproud.org), an online community to support Black disabled high school and college students, their families, and faculty.

Conclusion

Research indicates two of the most important pieces in academic success are the empowerment of students with a disability and the education of others about disability (Evans et al., 2017). In working with students with disabilities, the goal is to begin by providing equal access in all areas of the campus and to continue by creating environments that encourage, affirm, and support the development of students. To accomplish this goal, practitioners must actively educate themselves on current issues and work to infuse the campus community with this knowledge. Access is not limited to classroom learning, but rather, the entire campus environment should be shaped according to principals of universal design. Disability service offices are responsible for keeping accurate records, assisting students in receiving reasonable accommodations, and educating other campus members including faculty and staff about support for students with disabilities. However, all campus personnel working with students have a responsibility to create inclusive environments. From the institutional level, leadership must view disability as an important aspect of campus diversity and allocate funding to support educational initiatives. Finally, the values of human dignity and self-advocacy must be honored in working with students with disabilities.

Note

1   Several studies demonstrate that many students with disabilities do not ascribe to a gender binary (see Nicolazzo, 2016). Here, we are limited to binary concepts by the methods that national survey research centers employ to collect and disseminate data on gender.

References

Abes, E. S., & Wallace, M. M. (2018). "People see me, but they don't see me": An intersectional study of college students with physical disabilities. *Journal of College Student Development*, *59*(5), 545–562.

Americans with Disabilities Act Amendments Act of 2008. (2008). *Public Law*, 110–325, 122 Stat. 3553.

Americans with Disabilities Act of 1990, 42 USC sec. 12102 (2010).

Baker, K. Q., Boland, K., & Nowik, C. M. (2012). Survey of faculty and student perceptions of persons with disabilities. *Journal of Postsecondary Education and Disability*, *25*(4), 309–329.

Beilke, J. R., & Yssel, N. (1999). The chilly climate for students with disabilities in higher education. *College Student Journal, 33*(3), 364–371.

Broido, E. M. (2006). *Diabetes as case study: Experiences of students with disabilities*. Presentation made at the American College Personnel Association conference, Indianapolis, IN.

Brown, J. T. (1994). Effective disability support service programs. In D. Ryan & M. McCarthy (Eds.), *A student affairs guide to the ADA & disability issues* (pp. 98–110). Washington, DC: National Association of Student Personnel Administrators.

Brown, K. R., Peña, E. V., Broido, E. M., Stapleton, L. D., & Evans., N. J. (2019). Understanding disability frameworks in higher education research. In J. Huisman & M. Tight (Eds.), *Research in higher education. International perspectives on theory, policy, and practice* (Vol. 5, pp. 19–36). London, UK: Routledge.

Brown, K. R., Peña, E. V., & Rankin, S. (2017). Unwanted sexual contact: Students with autism and other disabilities at greater risk. *Journal of College Student Development, 58*(5), 771–776.

Bruder, M. B., & Mogro-Wilson, C. (2010). Student and faculty awareness and attitudes about students with disabilities. *Review of Disability Studies, 6*(2), 3–13.

Burgstahler, S., & Moore, E. (2009). Making student services welcoming and accessible through accommodations and universal design. *Journal of Postsecondary Education and Disability, 21*(3), 151–174.

Cawthon, S. W., & Cole, E. V. (2010). Postsecondary students who have a learning disability: Student perspectives on accommodations access and obstacles. *Journal of Postsecondary Education and Disability, 23*(2), 112–128.

Center for Universal Design. (2011). *The principles of universal design*. Retrieved from www.ncsu.edu/project/design-projects/udi/center-for-universal-design/the-principles-of-universal-design/

Collier, R. (2012). Person-first language: Laudable cause, horrible prose. *CMAJ: Canadian Medical Association Journal, 184*(18), E939–E940. doi:10.1503/cmaj.109–4338

Cory, R. C. (2011). Disability services offices for students with disabilities: A campus resource. In W. S. Harbour & J. W. Madaus (Eds.), *Disability and campus dynamics* (New Directions for Higher Education, No. 154, pp. 27–36). San Francisco, CA: Jossey-Bass.

Denhart, H. (2008). Deconstructing barriers: Perceptions of students labeled with learning disabilities in higher education. *Journal of Learning Disabilities, 41*(6), 483–497.

Department of Justice. (2016). *Consent decree, The United States of America and Dudley v. Miami University*, No. 1:14-cv-38 (D.D.C. October 17, 2016). Retrieved from https://www.ada.gov/miami_university_cd.html

DO-IT: Disabilities, Opportunities, Internetworking, and Technology. (n. d.). *University of Washington*. Retrieved from www.washington.edu/doit/

Dunn, D. S., & Andrews, E. E. (2015). Person-first and identity-first language: Developing psychologists' cultural competence using disability language. *American Psychologist, 70*(3), 255–264.

Evans, N. J., & Broido, E. M. (2011). *Social involvement and identity development of students with disabilities*. Poster presented at the conference of the Association for the Study of Higher Education, Charlotte, NC.

Evans, N. J., Broido, E. M., Brown, K. R., & Wilke, A. (2017). *Disability in higher education: A social justice approach*. San Francisco, CA: Jossey-Bass.

Evans, N. J., & Herriott, T. K. (2009). Philosophical and theoretical approaches to disability. In J. L. Higbee & A. A. Mitchell (Eds.), *Making good on the promise: Student affairs professionals with disabilities* (pp. 27–40). Lanham, MD: University Press of America.

Forber-Pratt, A. J. (2018). (Re) defining disability culture: Perspectives from the Americans with disabilities act generation. *Culture & Psychology*, Advance online publication. doi:1354067X18799714

Getzel, E. E., & Thoma, C. A. (2008). Experiences of college students with disabilities and the importance of self-determination in higher education settings. *Career Development for Exceptional Individuals, 31*(2), 77–84.

Gibbons, M. M., Cihak, D. F., Mynatt, B., & Wilhoit, B. E. (2015). Faculty and student attitudes toward postsecondary education for students with intellectual disabilities and autism. *Journal of Postsecondary Education and Disability, 28*, 149–162.

Green, B. (2018). A qualitative investigation of bullying of individuals with disabilities on a college campus. *Journal of Postsecondary Education and Disability, 31*(2), 135–147.

Griffin, P., Peters, M. L., & Smith, R. M. (2007). Ableism curriculum design. In M. Adams, L. A. Bell, & P. Griffin (Eds.), *Teaching for diversity and social justice* (2nd ed., pp. 335–358). New York, NY: Routledge.

Hall, L. M., & Belch, H. A. (2000). Setting the context: Reconsidering the principles of full participation and meaningful access for students with disabilities. In H. A. Belch (Ed.), *Serving students with disabilities* (New Directions for Student Services, No. 91, pp. 4–17). San Francisco, CA: Jossey-Bass.

Hardiman, R., Jackson, B., & Griffin, P. (2007). Conceptual foundations for social justice education. In M. Adams, L. Bell, & P. Griffin (Eds.), *Teaching for diversity and social justice* (2nd ed., pp. 35–66). New York, NY: Routledge.

Harper, K. A., & DeWaters, J. (2008). A quest for website accessibility in higher education institutions. *Internet & Higher Education, 11*(3/4), 160–164. doi:10.1016/j.iheduc.2008.06.007

Hedrick, B., Dizén, M., Collins, K., Evans, J., & Grayson, T. (2010). Perceptions of college students with and without disabilities and effects of STEM and non-STEM enrollment on student engagement and institutional involvement. *Journal of Postsecondary Education and Disability, 23*(2), 129–136.

Heyward, S. (2011). Legal challenges and opportunities. In W. S. Harbour & J. W. Madaus (Eds.), *Disability and campus dynamics* (New Directions for Higher Education, No. 154, pp. 55–64). San Francisco, CA: Jossey-Bass.

Higbee, J. L. (2004). Universal design principles of student development programs and services. In J. L. Higbee & E. Goff (Eds.), *Pedagogy and student services of institutional transformation: Implementing universal design in higher education* (pp. 195–204). Minneapolis, MN: National College Learning Center Association. Retrieved from https://files.eric.ed.gov/fulltext/ED503835.pdf

Higbee, J. L. (2009). Implementing universal instructional design in postsecondary courses and curricula. *Journal of College Teaching & Learning, 6*(8), 65–77.

Huger, M. S. (2011). Fostering a disability-friendly institutional climate. In M. S. Huger (Ed.), *Fostering the increased integration of students with disabilities* (New Directions for Student Services, No. 134, pp. 3–11). San Francisco, CA: Jossey-Bass.

Hutcheon, E. J., & Wolbring, G. (2012). Voices of "disabled" post secondary students: Examining higher education "disability" policy using an ableism lens. *Journal of Diversity in Higher Education, 5*(1), 39–49.

Jones, S. R. (1996). Toward inclusive theory: Disability as a social construction. *NASPA Journal, 33*, 347–354.

Knight, W., Wessel, R. D., & Markle, L. (2018). Persistence to graduation for students with disabilities: Implications for performance-based outcomes. *Journal of College Student Retention: Research, Theory & Practice, 19*(4), 362–380.

Lewis, T. A. (2019, March 5). *Longmore lecture: Context, clarity & grounding* [Blog post]. Retrieved from www.talilalewis.com/blog/longmore-lecture-context-clarity-grounding

Mamiseishvili, K., & Koch, L. C. (2011). First-to-second-year persistence of students with disabilities in postsecondary institutions in the United States. *Rehabilitation Counseling Bulletin, 53*(2), 93–105.

Mandell, D. S., Wiggins, L. D., Carpenter, L. A., Daniels, J., DiGuiseppi, C., Durkin, M. S., . . . & Shattuck, P. T. (2009). Racial/ethnic disparities in the identification of children with autism spectrum disorders. *American Journal of Public Health, 99*(3), 493–498.

Markoulakis, R., & Kirsh, B. (2013). Difficulties for university students with mental health problems: A critical interpretive synthesis. *Review of Higher Education, 37*(1), 77–100.

Mayhew, M. J., Rockenbach, A. B., Bowman, N. A., Seifert, T. A., & Wolniak, G. C. (2016). *How college affects students: 21st century evidence that higher education works (Vol. 3)*. San Francisco, CA: Jossey-Bass.

McKeon, B., Alpern, C. S., & Zager, D. (2013). Promoting academic engagement for college students with Autism Spectrum Disorder. *Journal of Postsecondary Education and Disability, 26*(4), 353–366.

Miller, R. A. (2015). "Sometimes you feel invisible": Performing queer/disabled in the university classroom. *The Educational Forum, 79*(4), 377–393. doi:10.1080/00131725.2015.1068417

Miserandino, C. (2003). *The spoon theory*. Retrieved from https://butyoudontlooksick.com/articles/written-by-christine/the-spoon-theory/

Myers, K. A., & Bastian, J. J. (2010). Understanding communication preferences of college students with visual disabilities. *Journal of College Student Development, 51*(3), 265–278.

Nachman, B., & Brown, K. R. (2019). Omission and othering: Constructing Autism on college websites. *Community College Journal of Research and Practice.* Advanced online publication. https://doi.org/10.1080/10668926.2019.1565845

National Association of the Deaf. (2010). *Score for accessibility: OSU to provide in-stadium captions.* Retrieved from http://nad.org/news/2010/11/score-accessibility-osu-provide-stadiumcaptions

National Center for Education Statistics. (2016). *Digest of education statistics, 2015 (2016–014).* Retrieved from https://nces.ed.gov/fastfacts/display.asp?id=60

Newman, L. A., & Madaus, J. W. (2015a). Reported accommodations and supports provided to secondary and postsecondary students with disabilities: National perspective. *Career Development and Transition for Exceptional Individuals, 38*(3), 173–181.

Newman, L. A., & Madaus, J. W. (2015b). An analysis of factors related to receipt of accommodations and services by postsecondary students with disabilities. *Remedial and Special Education, 36*(4), 208–219.

Newman, L. A., Wagner, M., Cameto, R., Knokey, A. M., & Shaver, D. (2010). *Comparisons across time of the outcomes of youth with disabilities up to 4 years after high school. A report of findings from the National Longitudinal Transition Study (NLTS) and the National Longitudinal Transition Study-2 (NLTS-2).* Prepared for the US Department of Education (NCSER2010–3008). Menlo Park, CA: SRI International. Retrieved from www.nlts2.org/reports/2010_09/nlts2_report_2010_09_complete.pdf

Newman, L. A., Wagner, M., Knokey, A.-M., Marder, C., Nagle, K., Shaver, D., & Schwarting, M. (2011). *The post-high school outcomes of youth with disabilities up to 8 years after high school. A report from the National Longitudinal Transition Study-2 (NLTS-2)* (NCSER 2011–3005). Menlo Park, CA: SRI International. Retrieved from http://files.eric.ed.gov/fulltext/ED524044.pdf

Nicolazzo, Z. (2016). "Just go in looking good": The resilience, resistance, and kinship-building of trans* college students. *Journal of College Student Development, 57*(5), 538–556. doi:10.1353/csd.2016.0057.

Office for Civil Rights. (2015). *Letter to Indiana University of Pennsylvania* (No. 03152020). Retrieved from http://ahead.wiley.com:8080/ahead/files/338

Palmer, J., & Caputo, A. (n.d.). *The universal instructional design implementation guide.* Guelph, ON: University of Guelph. Retrieved from https://opened.uoguelph.ca/instructor-resources/resources/uid-implimentation-guide-v13.pdf

Patton, L. D., Harper, S. R., & Harris, J. (2015). Using critical race theory to (re) interpret widely studied topics related to students in US higher education. In A. M. Martínez-Alemán, B. Pusser, & E. M. Bensimon (Eds.), *Critical approaches to the study of higher education* (pp. 193–219). Baltimore: MA, Johns Hopkins University.

Peña, E., Stapleton, L., Brown, K., Stygles, K., Broido, E., & Rankin, S. (2018). A Universal Research Design for student affairs scholars and practitioners. *College Student Affairs Journal, 36*(2), 1–14. doi:10.1353/csj.2018.0012.

Peña, E. V. (2014). Marginalization of published scholarship on students with disabilities in higher education journals. *Journal of College Student Development, 55,* 30–40.

Raue, K., & Lewis, L. (2011). *Students with disabilities at degree-granting postsecondary institutions* (NCES 2011–018). US Department of Education, National Center for Education Statistics. Washington, DC: US Government Printing Office.

Samuels, E. (2017). Six ways of looking at crip time. *Disability Studies Quarterly, 37*(3). http://dsq-sds.org/article/view/5824/4684

Schelly, C. L., Davies, P. L., & Spooner, C. L. (2011). Student perceptions of faculty implementation of universal design for learning. *Journal of Postsecondary Education and Disability, 24*(1), 17–28.

Section 504 of the Rehabilitation Act of 1973, 29 U.S.C. sec. 794. Retrieved from www.dol.gov/oasam/regs/statutes/sec504.htm

Shakespeare, T. (2014). *Disability rights and wrongs revisited* (2nd ed.). New York, NY: Routledge.

Sherry, M. (2004). Overlaps and contradictions between queer theory and disability studies. *Disability & Society, 19,* 769–785.

Shildrick, M. (2009). *Dangerous discourses of disability, subjectivity and sexuality.* Basingstoke, NY: Palgrave Macmillan.

Smart, J. F., & Smart, D. W. (2006). Models of disability: Implications for the counseling profession. *Journal of Counseling & Development, 84*, 29–40.

Snyder, T. D., deBrey, C., & Dillow, S. A. (2016). *Digest of education statistics 2014, NCES 2016–006.* Washington, DC: National Center for Education Statistics.

Spade, D. (2011). *Normal life: Administrative violence, critical trans politics and the limits of the law.* Brooklyn, NY: South End Press.

Stapleton, L. (2015). When Being deaf is centered: d/Deaf women of color's experiences with racial/ethnic and d/Deaf identities in college. *Journal of College Student Development, 56*(6), 570–586.

Upcraft, M. L., & Schuh, J. H. (1996). *Assessment in student affairs: A guide for practitioners.* San Francisco, CA: Jossey-Bass.

Vaccaro, A., Daly-Cano, M., & Newman, B. (2015). A sense of belonging among college students with disabilities: An emergent theoretical model. *Journal of College Student Development, 56*(7), 670–686. doi:10.1353/csd.20150072

Wessel, R. D., Wentz, J., & Markle, L. L. (2011). Power soccer: Experiences of students using power wheelchairs in a collegiate athletic club. *Journal of Postsecondary Education and Disability, 24*(2), 147–159.

Wilke, A., Varland, C., Brown, K., Evans, N., & Broido, E. M., (2018). *Integration and success: Disabled students living on campus.* Tampa, FL: Association for the Study of Higher Education.

Wolf, L. E., Brown, J. T., & Bork, G. R. (2009). *Students with Asperger Syndrome: A guide for college personnel.* Shawnee Mission, KS: Autism Asperger.

Zehner, A. L. (2018). Perceptions of campus climate at the intersections of disability and LGBTQ identities. In K. Soria (Ed.), *Evaluating campus climate at US research universities: Opportunities for diversity and inclusion* (pp. 125–149). New York, NY: Palgrave Macmillan.

Chapter 15
Engaging Student-Athletes

Joy Gaston Gayles and Rebecca E. Crandall

Headlines tell of widespread student-athlete academic fraud (e.g., Stripling, 2014) and public debate highlights questions surrounding the exploitation of student-athletes (e.g., Chavez, 2014). Further, the fair treatment and welfare of student-athletes has been an issue of concern since the earliest days of intercollegiate athletic competition. One aspect of this debate concerns the extent to which participation in college sports influences and shapes desired outcomes of undergraduate education for student-athletes (Gayles & Hu, 2009; Harper, Williams, & Blackman, 2013; Shulman & Bowen, 2001). Of particular interest in research, amongst athletic administrators, and for institutions of higher education is the extent to which student-athletes are involved and engaged within the college environment and experience positive gains in educational outcomes during their college years. Namely, are student-athletes involved in the college experience, and do colleges and universities engage them in ways that have a positive impact on learning and personal growth?

Student engagement happens when the college environment produces conditions that lead individuals to make psychological and behavioral investments to enhance their learning and personal growth. Student engagement includes involvement in academic and social activities both inside and outside the classroom, as well as the level and intensity of such involvement (Astin, 1993; Kuh, Schuh, Whitt, & Associates, 2005; Mayhew et al., 2016). Interacting with faculty; participating in student groups and organizations; reading, writing, and studying for class; attending class; and other curricular and co-curricular activities are all considered to be high-impact practices and forms of engagement (Mayhew et al., 2016; Pascarella & Terenzini, 1991; 2005). The extent to which students participate in such activities is a function of both the person and the college environment (Evans, Forney, Guido, Patton, & Renn, 2010; Kuh et al., 2005). In other words, engagement requires student effort as well as institutional support through policies and practices that facilitate active participation in educational activities.

Relevant to students' level of engagement is the reality that balancing the academic and social demands of the college experience can be challenging for all students. Attending class, completing homework, studying, and academically achieving are all aspects of the college experience that every student must balance to be successful. Student-athletes, however, have the added responsibility of managing athletic demands (e.g., daily practice, competitions, injuries) along with academic and social demands that take up a considerable amount of time (e.g., Broughton & Neyer, 2001; Gayles & Baker, 2015; Jolly, 2008; NCAA Research, 2016; Parham, 1993; Watt & Moore, 2001). Given the demands on their time and energy, scholars have raised serious questions about the impact that participation in college sports has on important outcomes such as persistence, degree completion, and academic performance (Bowen & Levin, 2003; Clotfelter, 2011; Shulman & Bowen, 2001). Moreover, despite recent reform efforts (see NCAA, 2017), concerns remain regarding the time required to participate in intercollegiate athletics and how such demands potentially limit the degree to which student-athletes can become involved within and connected to the college environment (e.g., Gayles & Hu, 2009; Solomon, 2017).

In recent years, scholars have raised questions about the extent to which the organizational structure (e.g., rules, policies, regulations) that governs college sports infringes on the rights and well-being of student-athletes in ways that ultimately have implications for involvement and engagement on campus (Gayles, Comeaux, Ofoegbu, & Grummert, 2018). Using critical frameworks to better understand structural barriers and inequities that exist and intersect within the culture of intercollegiate athletics is important for the overall well-being and fair treatment of student-athletes. When the experiences of student-athletes, particularly those who hold marginalized identities, are centered within the context of intersecting structural inequities, a counternarrative emerges that brings to light stories that are not often told and how systems of privilege and power operate in ways that infringe on the rights and fair treatment of underserved populations.

In this chapter, we take more of a critical approach to understanding student-athletes' engagement in college. In addition to discussing current issues for student-athletes' engagement and success, we also include an overview of barriers to engagement across institutional contexts to underscore the diversity of experience within intercollegiate athletic programs. To address some of these challenges in ways that disrupt the status quo, we discuss critical perspectives that have implications for rethinking and holding institutions responsible for engaging student-athletes on college campuses. We conclude the chapter with a set of recommendations on inclusive ways to engage student-athletes within the campus environment that maximize fair treatment and overall well-being during their postsecondary years.

Issues for Student-Athletes in the 21st Century

Regardless of the institutional setting, student-athletes who participate in college sports face many obstacles that can impact the extent to which they become engaged in the college environment. All the challenges associated with sports on college campuses are too numerous to cover in this chapter. Therefore, we will focus on two major issues that have persisted over time as challenges for student-athletes.

Balancing Academics and Athletics

Balancing academic and athletic responsibilities in order to make progress toward degree completion and maintain eligibility is one of the major issues facing college athletes (Broughton & Neyer, 2001; Parham, 1993). National studies of student-athlete experiences (NCAA Research, 2016; Potuto & O'Hanlon, 2006) consistently show that intercollegiate athletes at four-year institutions would prefer to spend more time on academics. Similarly, though not the perspective of the majority, large numbers of student-athletes report that athletics participation precludes them from taking full advantage of educational opportunities, including enrolling in their desired major, taking classes that they wanted to take, and study-abroad programs (NCAA Research, 2016). Further, many student-athletes struggle to balance their dual roles of "student" and "athlete," leading some, particularly football players and men's basketball players, to see themselves as more "athlete" than "student" (e.g., Adler & Adler, 1987; Linnemeyer & Brown, 2010; Potuto & O'Hanlon, 2006).

Student-athletes are often considered to be a special population of college students, given the unique rules and requirements that they must adhere to during their college years. Selecting a major within two years, scheduling the appropriate number of hours per semester, passing a required number of degree hours per semester, and earning a minimum grade-point average are distinct requirements for student-athletes at both community colleges and four-year institutions. Further, keeping track of the many conference rules and regulations requires support from the university to assist student-athletes with balancing academic, personal, and athletic demands (Broughton & Neyer, 2001; Jolly, 2008).

To date, much of the extant research on student-athlete engagement centers on four-year institutions. Community college student-athletes experience many of the same challenges to balancing athletics and academics as their peers at four-year institutions; however, the community college athletics experience is, in some ways, distinct. For example, although some student-athletes choose to start their college career at a community college for non-academic-related reasons (see, for example, Horton, 2009), a number of community college student-athletes are academically ineligible for four-year institutions' athletics programs. Concurrently, many community college student-athletes aspire to transfer to a four-year institution and compete in that context. Research reveals that campus support mechanisms exist to support community college athletes (e.g., Horton, 2009; Keim & Strickland, 2004); however, because courses must be "transferable credit hours" (NCAA, n.d.-a, p. 15) (i.e., remedial credits do not count), the biggest barriers to achieving an academics-athletics balance may be those faced by academically vulnerable student-athletes for whom remedial education is necessary but perhaps seen as a barrier to their athletics-related goals (see Hagedorn & Horton, 2009a).

Academic Performance and Navigating the "Dumb Jock" Stigma

Academic performance of college athletes has been an issue of concern throughout the history of intercollegiate athletics. Eligibility standards for the NCAA and the National Junior College Athletic Association (NJCAA) were adapted in the 1980s in an attempt to better align the goals of intercollegiate athletics with the goals of higher education. Since then, athletics-governing agencies have instituted other academic standards to ensure that student-athletes make timely progress toward degree completion.

As a result of low academic performance and increased standards for play, scholars began to examine the academic performance of college athletes to understand how student-athletes were performing in the classroom relative to their peers. Many of the early studies found that student-athletes were less prepared academically for college than their non-athlete peers (Hood, Craig, Ferguson, 1992; Purdy, Eitzen, & Hufnagel, 1985; Stuart, 1985), findings that have been echoed in more recent studies (Aries, McCarthy, Salovey, & Banaji, 2004; Bowen & Levin, 2003; Shulman & Bowen, 2001). Notably, level of sport commitment appears to play a role in the precollege preparation of student-athletes, with those who were highly committed to their sport arriving on campus less academically equipped than other student-athletes (Aries et al., 2004; Bowen & Levin, 2003; Shulman & Bowen, 2001).

Complementing the body of scholarship on the precollege academic preparation of student-athletes are studies exploring the ways in which athletes differ from their non-athlete peers in measures of academic performance. Whereas research proposes that student-athletes at highly selective colleges may not perform lower academically than nonathletes of similar backgrounds (Aries et al., 2004), quasi-experimental research using nationally representative data suggests that athletics participation does have a negative effect, albeit small, on the GPA of student-athletes relative to their non-athlete counterparts (Routon & Walker, 2014). Umbach, Palmer, Kuh, and Hannah's (2006) research on the educational experiences of student-athletes also highlights potential GPA disparities for student-athletes, specifically males.

Likely influencing academic outcomes for intercollegiate athletes are the perceptions that faculty members have of student-athletes, attitudes tied, in part, to stereotypes about student-athletes' academic ability and motivation (Engstrom, Sedlacek, & McEwen, 1995; Harrison et al., 2009). Stereotyping them as "dumb jocks," faculty members often perceive student-athletes as caring only about academics insomuch as they meet eligibility requirements to play their sport. Studies underscore the prevalence of stigmatization for Black male student-athletes, particularly those who compete in revenue sports (e.g., Adler & Adler, 1985; Engstrom et al., 1995; Harper et al., 2013; Simons, Bosworth, Fujita, & Jensen, 2007). However, the "dumb jock" stereotype is one that Simons et al. (2007) found haunts all intercollegiate athletes on some level, regardless of sex, race, or sport profile.

When it comes to the ultimate measure of academic performance, graduation, student-athletes at four-year institutions graduate at higher rates than students in the general population (NCAA, n.d.-b). However, success in graduation rates is not consistent across gender, race/ethnicity, and sport, patterns that remain even when using the NCAA's designed method for calculating graduation rates that does not penalize institutions for student-athletes who transfer to another institution in good standing. NCAA academic reforms have helped facilitate marked improvements in academic performance gaps; yet some subpopulations of student-athletes, namely African American males in revenue-producing sports, still graduate at rates lower than their student-athlete peers (e.g., Harper, 2018a, 2018b; NCAA Research Staff, 2017). Related disparities also manifest at the community college level, with research highlighting marked differences between Black male athletes and other student-athletes in the percentage of attempted credit hours earned, GPA, and degree completion (Horton, 2015). Ultimately, as Harper (2006) states, "Perhaps nowhere in higher education is the disenfranchisement of Black male students more insidious than in college athletics" (p. 6).

Structural Challenges in Intercollegiate Athletics and Higher Education

In many ways, the extent to which students are engaged in the college experience depends on the campus environment. We know from decades of research on the college student experience that behavior is a function of people and the environment; therefore, it is important to consider problematic aspects of campus environments that may hinder, rather than facilitate, student-athlete engagement. In relation to intercollegiate athletics, scholars have used critical theory to examine how various aspects of the organized environment are problematic for the overall well-being and holistic development of student-athletes. A recent volume of *New Directions for Student Services* examined critical issues for student-athletes through discussing topics such as legal issues, stereotypes and hyper-surveillance, transgender student-athletes, mental health, and social media policies. All of these topics are considered taboo and rarely discussed; yet they play a critical role in the lives of many student-athletes on college campuses and can shape the extent to which student-athletes engage within the campus and athletic environments. By structural challenges, we mean systemic barriers at the institutional level that potentially impede student engagement. From an institutional perspective, rules, regulations, and guidelines are put in place to protect the well-being of student-athletes and ensure fair play and progress towards degree attainment. However, these same rules can have unintended or intended consequences that infringe on the rights and fair treatment of student-athletes. Where applicable in our discussion, we integrate information specific to distinct institutional types.

History of Structural Challenges

Since their inception in the 1800s, college sports have evolved from a student-organized activity into a highly commercialized enterprise (Duderstadt, 2003). As such, many have questioned the amateur status of college sports and the premise that intercollegiate athletes "should be motivated primarily by education and by the physical, mental, and social benefits" (NCAA, 2018, p. 4) of their participation (see Epstein & Anderson, 2016). Similarly, greater attention has been placed on the extent to which student-athletes are isolated from the overall campus culture and whether they are benefitting from the college experience in ways comparable to their non-athlete peers (e.g., Gayles & Hu, 2009; Routon & Walker, 2014; Umbach et al., 2006). Intercollegiate athletics is deeply embedded into the culture of US higher education; yet for many institutions—primarily four-year colleges and universities—clear conflicts exist between the goals and functions of intercollegiate athletics programs and the educational mission of higher education (Bok, 2004; Bowen & Levin, 2003; Clotfelter, 2011; Duderstadt, 2003; (Harper & Donnor, 2017). There is even concern that the rules and regulations, policies, and overall structure of intercollegiate athletics in higher education are in conflict with the fair treatment and well-being of student athletes. In October 2018, the North Carolina Legislature created the Legislative Commission on the Fair Treatment of College Student-Athletes. Discussions have centered on injuries and negligence, mental health, and sexual assault, to name a few.

Student-Athlete Engagement Across Institutional Types

Given the athletic, academic and social demands placed on student athletes' time and energy, there is concern about whether or not student-athletes are engaging in the types of activities that lead to desired learning and personal development outcomes. Illuminating nuances not fully captured in Bowen and Levin's (2003) premise on the growing divide between intercollegiate athletics and the mission of higher education, a few studies have examined the extent to which student-athletes at four-year institutions are engaged in the college experience. For instance, Umbach et al. (2006), using data from the National Survey of Student Engagement (NSSE), found that, on average, student-athletes were just as likely to engage in educational purposeful activities as their nonathlete peers. In doing so, Umbach and colleagues paint a contrasting picture of the college experience for intercollegiate athletes.

Despite evidence suggesting that student-athletes are generally no less engaged in "effective educational practices" (Umbach et al., 2006, p. 709) than other students, research reveals that student-athlete engagement is not uniform, thus highlighting potential barriers to engagement for those who compete on the Division I and Division II levels. Specifically, the results of Umbach et al.'s (2006) study suggest that Division III student-athletes are more engaged academically than their peers at Division I and II institutions, a pattern perhaps reflective of the resolute academics-first focus of the NCAA's Division III (NCAA, n.d.-c). Other studies support this finding, showing that athletes at Division III institutions tend to be engaged in both their sport and campus life despite the fact that it may be more difficult to participate due to athletic time constraints (Richards & Aries, 1999; Schroeder, 2000).

Extending extant research by distinctly focusing on Division I athletes, Gayles and Hu (2009) examined the impact of engagement on cognitive and affective outcomes and the extent to which the impact varied in magnitude across levels of sport (Gayles &

Hu, 2009). Their findings suggest that interaction with peers other than teammates is the most common means of engagement for Division I athletes. Notably, the influence of this type of engagement mattered most for students in sports other than football and men's basketball. More research is needed to understand what types of involvement are most meaningful for students in high-profile sports. In addition, more research is needed to better understand the nature and types of educational experiences that matter most for various subgroups of student-athletes.

For the greater part of a century, intercollegiate athletics have existed in community college contexts (NJCAA, n.d.). What started in a single state (Lawrence, Mullin, & Horton, 2009) now exists at community colleges across the country. As of 2016, there are 569 nonprofit community colleges hosting at least one varsity sports team (US Department of Education, n.d.). Despite this long history, relatively little is known about the experiences of student-athletes in these settings. In recent years, scholars (see Hagedorn & Horton, 2009b) have begun to focus more on this athlete subpopulation, but much remains to be learned about the nearly 80,000 community college athletes who participate in varsity sports each year (US Department of Education, n.d.).

Despite a clear lack of research related to student-athlete engagement in community college settings, current scholarship illuminates potential gaps between athletics at community colleges and the mission and priorities of those institutions (e.g., Hagedorn & Horton, 2009a; Williams & Pennington, 2006). As suggested in Williams and Pennington's (2006) study of community college presidents' perceptions of intercollegiate athletics, varsity sports can foster a sense of school pride for students and the community alike, and they may play a positive role in the institution's reputation. However, the question of whether athletics within community colleges is truly mission supportive remains contested. Notably, community college presidents themselves disagree on whether athletics contributes to their institutional mission (Williams & Pennington, 2006). Even more striking, though community colleges provide opportunities for individuals who are academically ineligible to participate in four-year-college sports, and community college athletics may contribute in meaningful ways to some student-athletes' academic journeys (e.g., Horton, 2009), the aspirations that many community college athletes have of successfully transferring to four-year institutions and their sports programs often go unmet (e.g., Acevedo-Gil, 2018; Hagedorn & Horton, 2009a; Harper, 2009). Simply put, while the sports that these students play likely enhance institutional outcomes, the student-athletes themselves may not receive adequate support to achieve their educational and athletics-related goals.

Opportunities for participation in sports at historically black colleges and universities have existed since HBCUs were established during the mid-twentieth century (Cooper, Cavil, & Cheeks, 2014). HBCUs were founded to provide educational opportunities and advancement for African Americans who experienced discrimination and exclusion from educational opportunities at predominantly White institutions (Allen & Jewel, 2002; Fleming, 1984). Opportunities for African Americans to participate in college sports were virtually nonexistent at PWIs. During this period in history, HBCUs provided a space for the cultivation and holistic development of students through sports, as well as entertainment and economic advancement for the surrounding community (Wiggins & Miller, 2003). College sports at HBCUs suffered from some of the same structural and governance issues experienced at PWIs. The lack of oversight of college sports led to a number of abuses and misconduct, injuries, and uneven competition experiences (Miller, 1995). Desegregation and the civil rights movement during the mid- to late 1900s changed the landscape for athletic competition at HBCUs (Cooper et al., 2014). Instead of an integrated approach to ending segregation, talented Black athletes were recruited away from HBCUs to play at predominately White institutions.

Theoretical Perspectives

For decades there has been concern about the quality of the educational experiences of student-athletes and the extent to which this goal can be achieved within the context of highly commercialized market-driven athletics programs on some college campuses. In many ways, the market-driven values that control intercollegiate athletics run contrary to initiatives, such as student engagement, designed to increase gains in desired outcomes of undergraduate education. While power brokers such as coaches, athletics directors, corporate sponsors, television networks, and other privileged stakeholders benefit greatly from the capital generated from big-time college sports programs, student-athletes, without whom there would be no revenue generation, can exit this enterprise without a college degree or a positive educational experience. Unfortunately, this kind of culture situated within academic institutions places an emphasis on profit generation, which takes precedence over important academic values such as attitudes and behaviors aligned with the pursuit of knowledge, equity, and intellectual freedom (Giroux, 2002).

Neoliberal Capitalism

The term *neoliberal capitalism* has been used to describe and critique intercollegiate athletics programs (Gayles et al., 2018). Neoliberal capitalism in the United States represents a particular form of capitalism that places a premium on individual entrepreneurial freedom, property rights, free markets, and free trade (Harvey, 2007). When values and behaviors such as these exist within academic institutions, conditions currently present in intercollegiate athletic programs emerge, characterized by commercial entertainment industries with large sums of revenue generated and large payouts. Further, student-athletes function more as employees of athletics programs rather than as students, which contributes to the concerns about the quality of educational experiences for this population (Comeaux, 2015; McCormick & McCormick, 2006).

Neoliberal capitalism shows up in college sports in many ways and has negative consequences for student-athletes. Critics argue that the organizational culture of intercollegiate athletics is like a market-driven enterprise that devalues education by placing significant time demands on student-athletes who are the primary sources of revenue generation (Jayakumar & Comeaux, 2016; Wolverton, 2008). Student-athletes devote over 40 hours per week, which leaves little to no time and energy for academic and social engagement (Comeaux, Speer, Taustine, & Harrison, 2011; Wolverton, 2008). These forms of engagement (e.g., spending time with peers in student groups and organizations and participating in study groups) are important kinds of involvement that are related to student success and personal development (Gayles & Hu, 2009).

Another consequence of intercollegiate athletics operating within the context of a market-driven culture is that such values can translate into major clustering, defined as large percentages of student-athletes majoring in select disciplines, and academic misconduct (Wolverton, 2007). Disciplines that are overly populated with student-athletes tend to be characterized as less labor intensive in order to "help" student-athletes maintain their academic eligibility to compete. A recent example of this phenomenon occurred at the University of North Carolina at Chapel Hill. Large numbers of high-profile student-athletes were found to be enrolled in fake classes in the African, African American, and Diaspora studies department for several years (Zimmer & Harper, 2017). Such gross misconduct at the institutional level led to UNC Chapel Hill being placed on accreditation probation for a year. Unfortunately, academic scandals and misconduct send the message that student-athletes' interests are not valued nearly as much as the market interest. Further, when scandals and other forms of misconduct occur, student-athletes are blamed at the individual level instead of taking a critical look at the power structures in place that drive policies, practices, and behavior (Giroux & Giroux, 2009).

The market-driven nature of intercollegiate athletics within higher education institutions also has consequences for who should (and can) provide oversight to ensure that student-athletes are engaging and benefitting in positive ways. As commercialism and revenue generation has increased exponentially over time, the traditional faculty governance structure used to oversee co-curricular activities on campus no longer holds. Questions about who should govern and have oversight of athletic enterprises on college campuses are long standing, given the increase in abuses, scandals and other forms of unsportsmanlike conduct that have threatened the reputation and integrity of academic institutions (Harper & Donnor, 2017). The faculty governance structure is further complicated by higher education institutions shifting from hiring full-time tenure-track professors to hiring more part-time, contingent faculty (Kezar & Gehrke, 2014). This kind of shift has the potential to weaken faculty leadership to the detriment of higher education institutions (Hanlon, 2019). With fewer full-time faculty, as a consequence of market-driven values, institutions can expect declines in faculty oversight. Without faculty leadership and oversight to help hold universities and athletics departments accountable and regulate problematic policies and practices, the unfair treatment and lack of well-being for student-athletes will likely continue in ways that are harmful to students and institutions alike (Harper & Donnor, 2017).

Based on the systemic challenges in intercollegiate athletics informed by neoliberal capitalism discussed earlier, we conclude this chapter with a set of recommendations for effectively engaging student-athletes in the overall college experience. This is not an exhaustive list of recommendations as there is much work to be done to change policies and practices to facilitate student-athlete engagement and overall well-being. Some of these recommendations hold true from the first iteration of this chapter, whereas others are more informed by structural challenges at the institutional level.

Utilize Existing Data to Explore Potential Engagement Opportunities

Each year, campuses administer a host of assessments in hopes of understanding more about the ways in which students are engaged academically and socially. These existing data provide a logical first step in efforts to foster student-athletes engagement. Disaggregating data based on participation in athletics will provide an initial snapshot of the ways in which certain subpopulations of students experience and engage in the campus and yield insight into patterns that deviate from their nonathlete peers in comparison. Considering these data within the context of institutional-level data (e.g., campus climate; selectivity) can provide a more complete picture of the ways in which aspects of the college environment shape the engagement and for whom.

Rethink Practices That Can Harm Student-Athletes

In an effort to ensure student-athletes maintain their eligibility to compete, academic support services use intrusive advising practices that can potentially be harmful for some student-athletes. Comeaux (2018) discusses the problematic nature of a common practice used in athletics to make sure student-athletes attend class. When race is centered, one can more clearly understand how the surveillance of student-athletes, particularly Black student-athletes, can impact the overall educational experience. We live in a culture where Black people are profiled and targeted unfairly because of their race. Many innocent Black people have lost their lives because of stereotypes, bias, and unacceptable mistakes informed by ill-informed judgments. Experiencing subtle (or not so subtle) forms of surveillance and control motivated neoliberal values to generate revenue is not in the best interest of student-athletes and detracts from their overall well-being and development. Athletics administrators can be more intentional about working alongside and learning from scholars who conduct research using critical perspectives in order to check their subconscious bias that can and has informed many of the policies and practices that create structural inequities.

Collaboration Between Student Affairs and Athletic Support Services

Athletic department administrators who are responsible for student-athlete support services should regularly collaborate with student affairs offices on campus to develop programs that facilitate greater involvement with the campus community for student-athletes. Such collaborative efforts will help eliminate duplication of services and programs, as well as create opportunities for increased peer interaction between athletes and nonathletes. Further, sharing of resources and information can be useful across functional areas in ways that help student affairs understand the experiences of student-athletes, and athletics administrators can be better informed about the ways in which the campus community is working to create inclusive environments for all students.

Foster Nonathlete Peer Interaction

Campus administrators should actively seek ways to engage student-athletes with their nonathlete peers. Research suggests that this type of engagement is important, particularly for student-athletes who are limited by time demands associated with their sport (Gayles & Hu, 2009). Peer interaction is one of the major ways of successfully integrating into the academic and social systems of the campus culture (Comeaux & Harrison, 2011). Thus, college administrators should partner to identify ways to get student-athletes involved in service activities, academic clubs and organizations, and other student-based activities on campus.

Increase Faculty Interaction

Faculty interaction both inside and outside the classroom is an important form of engagement for student-athletes and should be highly encouraged. One suggestion is to provide opportunities for faculty to learn about the athletics program at the institution by inviting them to sit in on a practice or a home game. Faculty perceptions of student-athletes' experiences are not always favorable (Engstrom et al., 1995; Howard-Hamilton & Sina, 2001; Jolly, 2008; Simons et al., 2007). Therefore, providing opportunities for faculty to experience a day in the life of a student-athlete might help shape their perspective, facilitate a connection, and encourage increased interaction between student-athletes and faculty. In addition to inviting faculty to visit the athletic department, initiatives such as mentoring programs may help bridge divides between student-athletes and faculty as establishing those relationships may also lead to heightened engagement with other, nonmentoring faculty.

Conclusion

Student-athletes face many challenges that can potentially impact the quality and frequency of their engagement with the campus community. This chapter provides an overview of some of the structural challenges that can negatively shape student-athletes' engagement on college campuses. Although not exhaustive, the culture of intercollegiate athletics within the context of higher education; the demands of academics and athletics; and academic performance barriers, including the "dumb jock" stigma, are all key aspects of the environment that can shape student-athletes' experience that if unchecked can be detrimental to their success as students and athletes. The critical theoretical perspectives discussed in this chapter have the potential to help higher education and athletics administrators reshape policies and practices in ways that better serve student-athletes and foster student engagement.

References

Acevedo-Gil, N. (2018). Postsecondary pathways of Latinas/os: A review of student experiences in the community college. *Journal for the Study of Sports and Athletes in Education, 12*(1), 4–13. doi:10.1080/19357397.2018.1444699

Adler, P., & Adler, P. A. (1985). From idealism to pragmatic detachment: The academic performance of college athletes. *Sociology of Education, 58*(4), 241–250.

Adler, P., & Adler, P. A. (1987). Role conflict and identity salience: College athletics and the academic role. *The Social Science Journal, 24*(4), 443–455.

Allen, W. R., & Jewel, J. O. (2002). A backward glance forward: Past, present, and future perspectives on historically Black colleges and universities. *Review of Higher Education, 25*(3), 241–261.

Aries, E., McCarthy, D., Salovey, P., & Banaji, M. R. (2004). A comparison of athletes and non-athletes at highly selective colleges: Academic performance and personal development. *Research in Higher Education, 45*(6), 577–602.

Astin, A. W. (1993). *What matters in college: Four critical years revisited.* San Francisco, CA: Jossey-Bass.

Bok, D. (2004). The benefits and costs of commercialization of the academy. In D. G. Stein (Ed.), *Buying in or selling out? The commercialization of the American research university* (pp. 32–47). New Brunswick, NJ: Rutgers University Press.

Bowen, W. G., & Levin, S. A. (2003). *Reclaiming the game: College sports educational values.* Princeton, NJ: Princeton University Press.

Broughton, E., & Neyer, M. (2001). Advising and counseling student athletes. *New Directions for Student Services, 93*, 47–53.

Chavez, L. (2014, March 28). How colleges exploit athletes. *New York Post.* Retrieved from http://nypost.com/2014/03/28/how-colleges-exploit-athletes/

Clotfelter, C. (2011). *Big-time sports in American universities.* New York, NY: Cambridge University Press.

Comeaux, E. (2015). Innovative research into practice in support centers for college athletes: Implications for the academic progress rate initiative. *Journal of College Student Development, 56*(3), 274–279.

Comeaux, E. (2018). Stereotypes, control, hyper-surveillance, and disposability of NCAA Division I Black male athletes. *New Directions for Student Services, 2018*(163), 33–42.

Comeaux, E., & Harrison, C. K. (2011). A conceptual model of academic success for student—athletes. *Educational Researcher, 40*(5), 235–245.

Comeaux, E., Speer, L., Taustine, M., & Harrison, C. K. (2011). Purposeful engagement of first-year Division I student-athletes. *Journal of the First-Year Experience & Students in Transition, 23*(1), 35–52.

Cooper, J. N., Cavil, J. K., & Cheeks, G. (2014). The state of intercollegiate athletics at Historically Black Colleges and Universities (HBCUs): Past, present, & persistence. *Journal of Issues in Intercollegiate Athletics, 7*(1), 307–332.

Duderstadt, J. J. (2003). *Intercollegiate athletics and the American university.* Ann Arbor: University of Michigan Press.

Engstrom, C. H., Sedlacek, W. E., & McEwen, M. L. (1995). Faculty attitudes toward male revenue and nonrevenue student-athletes. *The Journal of College Student Development, 36*(3), 215–225.

Epstein, A., & Anderson, P. M. (2016). The relationship between a collegiate student-athlete and the university: An historical and legal perspective. *Marquette Sports Law Review, 26*, 287–300.

Evans, N. J., Forney, D. S., Guido, F. M., Patton, L. D., & Renn, K. A. (2010). *Student development in college: Theory, research, and practice.* San Francisco, CA: Jossey-Bass.

Fleming, J. (1984). *Blacks in college: A comparative study of student success in Black and White institutions.* San Francisco, CA: Jossey-Bass.

Gayles, J. G., & Baker, A. R. (2015). Opportunities and challenges for first-year student-athletes transitioning from high school to college. *New Directions for Student Leadership, 2015*(147), 43–51.

Gayles, J. G., Comeaux, E., Ofoegbu, E., & Grummert, S. (2018). Neoliberal capitalism and racism in college athletics: Critical approaches for supporting Student-Athletes. *New Directions for Student Services, 2018*(163), 11–21.

Gayles, J. G., & Hu, S. (2009). The influence of student engagement and sport participation on college outcomes among Division I student athletes. *The Journal of Higher Education, 80*(3), 315–333.

Giroux, H. (2002). Neoliberalism, corporate culture, and the promise of higher education: The university as a democratic public sphere. *Harvard Educational Review, 72*(4), 425–464.

Giroux, H. A., & Giroux, S. S. (2009). Beyond bailouts: On the politics of education after neoliberalism. *Policy Futures in Education, 7*(1), 1–4. doi:10.2304/pfie.2009.7.1.1

Hagedorn, L. S., & Horton, Jr., D. (2009a). Conclusions and parting words from the editors. *New Directions for Community Colleges, 147*, 85–92.

Hagedorn, L. S., & Horton, Jr., D. (Eds.). (2009b). Student athletes and athletics. *New Directions for Community Colleges, 147*.

Hanlon, A. (2019, April 16). The university is a ticking time bomb. *The Chronicle of Higher Education.* Retrieved from www.chronicle.com/article/The-University-Is-a-Ticking/246119

Harper, S. R. (2006). Black male students at public universities in the US: Status, trends and implications for policy and practice. Washington, DC: Joint Center for Political and Economic Studies.

Harper, S. R. (2009). Race, interest convergence, and transfer outcomes for Black male student athletes. *New Directions for Community Colleges, 147*(Fall 2009), 29–37.

Harper, S. R. (2018a). *Black male student-athletes and racial inequities in NCAA Division I college sports: 2018 edition.* Los Angeles: University of Southern California, Race and Equity Center.

Harper, S. R. (2018b). *2018 Graduation Success Rates supplement: Black male student-athletes and racial inequities in NCAA Division I college sports.* Los Angeles: University of Southern California, Race and Equity Center.

Harper, S. R., & Donnor, J. K. (2017). *Scandals in college sports.* New York, NY: Routledge.

Harper, S. R., Williams, C. D., & Blackman, H. W. (2013). Black male student-athletes and racial inequities in NCAA Division I college sports. Philadelphia: University of Pennsylvania, Center for the Study of Race & Equity in Education.

Harrison, C. K., Stone, J., Shapiro, J., Yee, S., Boyd, J. A., Rullan, V. (2009). The role of gender identities and stereotype salience with the academic performance of male and female college athletes. *Journal of Sport and Social Issues, 33*(1), 78–96.

Harvey, D. (2007). *A brief history of neoliberalism.* New York, NY: Oxford University Press.

Hood, A. B., Craig, A. F., & Ferguson, B. W. (1992). The impact of athletics, part-time employment, and other activities on academic achievement. *Journal of College Student Development, 33*, 447–453.

Horton, Jr., D. (2009). Class and cleats: Community college student athletes and academic success. *New Directions for Community Colleges, 147*, 15–26.

Horton, Jr. D. (2015). Between a ball and a harsh place: A study of Black male community college student-athletes and academic progress. *Community College Review, 43*(3), 287–305.

Howard-Hamilton, M. F., & Sina, J. A. (2001). How college affects student athletes. In M. F. Howard-Hamilton and S. K. Watt (Eds.), *Student services for student athletes* (New directions for student services, No. 93, pp. 35–45). San Francisco, CA: Jossey-Bass.

Jayakumar, U. M., & Comeaux, E. (2016). The cultural cover-up of college athletics: How organizational culture perpetuates an unrealistic and idealized balancing act. *The Journal of Higher Education, 87*(4), 488–515.

Jolly, J. C. (2008). Raising the Question #9: Is the student-athlete population unique? And why should we care? *Communication Education, 57*(1), 145–151.

Keim, M. C., & Strickland, J. M. (2004). Support services for two-year college student-athletes. *College Student Journal, 38*(1), 36–43.

Kezar, A., & Gehrke, S. (2014). Why are we hiring so many non-tenure-track faculty? *Liberal Education, 100*(1), n1.

Kuh, G. D., Schuh, J. H., Whitt, E. J., & Associates (2005). *Student success in college: Creating conditions that matter.* San Francisco, CA: Jossey-Bass.

Lawrence, H. J., Mullin, C. M., & Horton, Jr., D. (2009). Considerations for expanding, eliminating, and maintaining community college athletic teams and programs. *New Directions for Community Colleges, 147*, 39–51.

Linnemeyer, R. M., & Brown, C. (2010). Career maturity and foreclosure in student athletes, fine arts students, and general college students. *Journal of Career Development, 37*(3), 616–634. doi:10.1177/0894845309357049

Mayhew, M. J., Pascarella, E. T., Bowman, N. A., Rockenbach, A. N., Seifert, T. A., Terenzini, P. T., & Wolniak, G. C. (2016). *How college affects students: 21st century evidence that higher education works* (Vol. 3). San Francisco, CA: Jossey-Bass.

McCormick, R. A., & McCormick, A. C. (2006). Myth of the student-athlete: The college athlete as employee. *Washington Law Review*, *81*, 71.

Miller, P. B. (1995). To bring the race along rapidly: Sport, student culture, and educational mission at historically Black colleges during the interwar years. *History of Education Quarterly*, *35*, 111–133.

NCAA. (n.d.-a). *2017–18 guide for two-year transfers* [PDF document]. Retrieved from www.ncaa.org/sites/default/files/201718_Transfer_Guide_2_Year_20170721.pdf

NCAA. (n.d.-b). *DI African-American student-athletes graduate at record rates*. Retrieved from www.ncaa.org/about/resources/media-center/news/di-african-american-student-athletes-graduate-record-rates

NCAA. (n.d.-c). *NCAA Division III*. Retrieved from www.ncaa.org/about?division=d3

NCAA. (2017, January 18). *DI council approves time commitment legislation*. Retrieved from www.ncaa.org/about/resources/media-center/news/di-council-approves-time-commitment-legislation

NCAA. (2018). *2018–19 Division I manual*. Retrieved from www.ncaapublications.com/productdownloads/D119.pdf

NCAA Research. (2016, January). *Results from the 2015 GOALS study of the student-athlete experience*. Retrieved from www.ncaa.org/sites/default/files/GOALS_convention_slidebank_jan2016_public.pdf

NCAA Research Staff. (2017, November). *Trends in graduation success rates and federal graduation rates at NCAA Division I institutions*. Retrieved from www.ncaa.org/sites/default/files/2017D1RES_Grad_Rate_Trends_FINAL_20171108.pdf

NJCAA. (n.d.). *NJCAA history*. Retrieved from https://d2o2figo6ddd0g.cloudfront.net/a/o/l4s1wdrl6n1xvy/NJCAA_History_8_2_18.pdf

Parham, W. D. (1993). The intercollegiate athletes: A 1990s profile. *The Counseling Psychologist*, *21*(3), 411–429.

Pascarella, E. T., & Terenzini, P. T. (1991). *How college affects students*. San Francisco, CA: Jossey-Bass.

Pascarella, E. T., & Terenzini, P. T. (2005). *How college affects students: A third decade of research*. San Francisco, CA: Jossey-Bass.

Potuto, J. R., & O'Hanlon, J. (2006). *National study of student athletes regarding their experiences as college students*. Retrieved from www.ncaapublications.com/p-4086-national-study-of-student-athletes-regarding-their-experiences-as-college-students.aspx

Purdy, D. A., Eitzen, D. S., & Hufnagel, R. (1985). Are athletes also students? The educational attainment of college athletes. In D. Chu, J. O. Segrave, G. J. Becker (Eds.), *Sport in higher education* (pp. 221–234). Champaign, IL: Human Kinetics.

Richards, S., & Aries, E. (1999). The Division III student-athlete: Academic performance, campus involvement and growth. *Journal of College Student Development*, *40*(3), 211–218.

Routon, P. W., & Walker, J. K. (2014). Student-athletes? The impact of intercollegiate sports participation on academic outcomes. *Eastern Economic Journal*, *2014*, 1–20. doi:10.1057/eej.2014.32

Schroeder, P. J. (2000). An assessment of student involvement among selected NCAA Division III basketball players. *Journal of College Student Development*, *41*(6), 616–626.

Shulman, J. L., & Bowen, W. G. (2001). *The game of life: College sports and educational values*. Princeton, NJ: Princeton University.

Simons, H. D., Bosworth, C., Fujita, S., Jensen, M. (2007). The athlete stigma in higher education. *College Student Journal*, *41*(2), 251–273.

Solomon, J. (2017, January 20). *NCAA time demands rules ignore the biggest problem in the situation: The games*. Retrieved from www.cbssports.com/college-football/news/ncaa-time-demands-rules-ignore-the-biggest-problem-in-the-situation-the-games

Stripling, J. (2014, October 23). *Widespread nature of Chapel Hill's academic fraud is laid bare*. Retrieved from www.chronicle.com/article/Widespread-Nature-of-Chapel/149603

Stuart, D. (1985). Academic preparation and subsequent performance of intercollegiate football players. *Journal of College Student Personnel*, *26*(2), 124–129.

Umbach, P. D., Palmer, M. M., Kuh, G. D., Hannah, S. J. (2006). Intercollegiate athletics and effective educational practices: Winning combination or losing effort? *Research in Higher Education, 47*(6), 709–733.

US Department of Education. (n.d.). *Equity in athletics data analysis*. Retrieved from https://ope.ed.gov/athletics/#

Watt, S. K., & Moore, J. L. (2001). Who are student athletes? In M. F. Howard-Hamilton and S. K. Watt (Eds.), *Student services for student athletes* (New directions for student services, No. 93, pp. 7–18). San Francisco, CA: Jossey-Bass.

Wiggins, D. K., & Miller, P. B. (2003). *The unlevel playing field: A documentary history of the African American experience in sport* (Vol. 114). Urbana, IL: University of Illinois Press.

Williams, M. R., & Pennington, K. (2006). Community college presidents' perceptions of intercollegiate athletics. *The Community College Enterprise, 12*(2), 91–104.

Wolverton, B. (2007). Athletics participation prevents many players from choosing majors they want. *Chronicle of Higher Education, 53*(20).

Wolverton, B. (2008). Athletes' hours renew debate over college sports. *Chronicle of Higher Education, 54*(20).

Zimmer, T., & Harper, S. R. (2017). Fake "paper classes" at UNC Chapel Hill. In S. R. Harper & J. K. Donnor (Eds.), *Scandals in college sports* (pp. 96–101). New York, NY: Routledge.

Chapter 16
Engaging Justice-Involved Students

Royel M. Johnson and Joshua Abreu

In the United States there are an estimated 6.6 million people under the supervision of the adult correctional system, of which 2.2 million people are in jail or prison—a 500% increase over the past forty years. National estimates also suggest that there are about 70 million Americans with criminal records (US Department of Education, 2016). That racial disparities exist in the US criminal justice system is not new information either (Alexander, 2012). Consider that Black and Latinx men are about 6 and 2.7 times more likely to be incarcerated than White men, respectively (Sentencing Project, 2015). Mass incarceration in the US has been described by some as yet another form of racialized social control that operates and functions in ways strikingly similar to Jim Crow (Alexander, 2012). Consider the complex web of laws and regulations, which are powerfully influenced by social stigma, that relegate formerly incarcerated people and those with criminal histories, hereafter referred to as *justice-involved*,[1] to the margins of society, denying or limiting their access to public benefits like higher education.

One clear example of how justice-involved people are restricted access to the well-documented benefits of higher education (see Ma, Pender, & Welch, 2016) is through the use of criminal justice information in college admissions. In a study of 273 colleges and universities, roughly 55% reported collecting and using criminal justice information in the admissions process (Weissman, Rosenthal, Warth, Wolf, & Messina-Yauchzy, 2010). This practice often has in a chilling effect, deterring applicants with criminal records from applying. For instance, one study found that two-thirds of people with a felony record discontinued their college application to the State University of New York (SUNY) after being asked about their criminal history (Rosenthal, NaPier, Warth, & Weissman, 2015). In light of these challenges, the US Department of Education (2016) announced a high-profile campaign aimed at improving postsecondary education outcomes for justice-involved students. "Beyond the Box"—a corollary to another national campaign, "Ban the Box," in the employment sector—discourages institutions from inquiring about an applicant's criminal history during the college admissions process.

The Beyond the Box campaign is a necessary strategy, but it's insufficient alone to reduce barriers to college access and success for justice-involved students. Research, albeit limited, offers troubling insight about the condition and experiences of justice-involved students who gain access to higher education, such as stigma (e.g., Strayhorn, Johnson, & Barrett, 2013). This stigma may limit their academic and social engagement, thwart belongingness, and place students at risk for early departure. Even worse is that faculty and academic and student affairs administrators in higher education are often either unaware of and/or ill-prepared to meet the needs of this growing subset of the college student population. Thus, the purpose of this chapter is to raise the specter on the challenges facing justice-involved students in college and offer strategies for increasing their success. In the following section, we present a brief review of literature, followed by a set of theories and concepts that inform the recommendations in the final section.

Challenges of Justice-Involved College Students

Before presenting major findings and themes From existing research, several important points deserve mention. First, research on the experiences of justice-involved students in college is sorely underdeveloped. We encourage scholars and emerging researchers to take up this important work in critical, emancipatory, and socially responsible ways. Second, while we use the term "justice-involved" to refer to a broad range of contact and involvement with the criminal justice system, we also recognize and appreciate the diversity that exists among students' criminal experiences and its impact on their educational experiences. When necessary, we make distinctions between formerly incarcerated students' education experiences and students with a criminal record as a result of an arrest. Nevertheless, we present four major findings related to challenges justice-involved students experience in college: (a) academic barriers, (b) access to campus housing, (c) financial aid, and (d) stigma.

Academic Barriers

Justice-involved students experience a number of academic challenges that can serve as barriers to their postsecondary education access and success. While their education levels and academic preparation vary, those who are returning from jail or prison are in large part undereducated in comparison to the general population (Crayton & Neusteter, 2008). The 1994 Violent Crime Control and Law Enforcement Act (Pub. L. No. 103–322) effectively blocked students from accessing federal Pell grants while incarcerated, and access to postsecondary education programming and training subsequently decreased (Brazzell et al., 2009; Castro & Zamani-Gallaher, 2018). As a result, incarcerated people preparing for community reentry frequently report little confidence in their academic skills and preparation (Fields & Abrams, 2010). In Dreger's (2017) study of justice-involved students at community colleges, participants discussed concerns regarding their academic underpreparation for college, which they attributed to long gaps in school attendance as a result of time spent in jail or prison.

Other academic challenges justice-involved students experience are related to instructional and pedagogical difficulties in the classroom. For students returning from long stints in jail or prison, access and usage of technology can serve as a barrier. Participants in Dreger's (2017) study reported challenges using required instructional technologies, such as the internet, email, Blackboard, Microsoft Office, smartphones, flash drives, and other modern technologies like tablets and wireless printers. These challenges are exacerbated by the stigma associated with their identities as justice-involved students, which may reduce their help-seeking behavior. Group discussion, activities, and assignments can also serve as an academic barrier for justice-involved students, given documented difficulties interacting with peers and navigating disclosure of their identities (Strayhorn et al., 2013). Thus, it is not surprising that Custer (2013) found that students with felony records on average earned below-average grade-point averages and 50% drop out after a quarter.

Access to Campus Housing

Access to campus housing is another barrier that some justice-involved students experience in college. In Custer's (2018) review of state statutes and policies, he found that in Texas, South Carolina, South Dakota, and Tennessee, sex offenders are prohibited from living on campus. The same is true for drug offenders in South Dakota. Generally, however, a growing number of institutions around the country conduct background checks during the housing application process, prohibiting those with criminal histories from living in campus residence halls. Prior research has consistently linked living in a residence hall to a number of positive academic outcomes such as increased involvement, engagement on campus, and academic performance (Astin, 1984; López Turley & Wodtke, 2010; Pascarella & Terenzini, 2005). Denying justice-involved students access to campus housing conspires in their disengagement and academic success by facilitating a basic-need insecurity. Certainly, institutions of higher education must balance often legitimate concerns regarding safety and security in the residence halls; however, they must also make sure that *all students* have equitable opportunities for *full participation* in the academic and social spheres of campus life.

Financial Aid

Depending on the nature of one's offense, significant barriers abound as it relates to access to financial aid. For instance, students who are convicted of a sexual offense (forcible or non-forcible), and who are subject to an involuntary civil commitment after completing a sentence of incarceration for that offense, are ineligible to receive a federal Pell Grant to support their education ("Federal Pell Grants," 2019). Additionally, students who are charged with and convicted of drug-related crimes (e.g., possession or sale of illegal drugs) at the time of receiving federal student aid (e.g., grants, loans, work-study) may have their eligibility suspended. The Free Application for Federal

Student Aid (FASFA) provides a special worksheet for applicants to complete that helps determine whether their conviction affects their eligibility for federal student aid ("Student with Criminal Conviction," 2019). In addition to federal student aid restrictions, Custer (2018) reports that a number of state financial aid policies also pose barriers for justice-involved students. For instance, popular merit-based programs such as Florida's Bright Futures Scholarship denies students with any felony conviction from participation. So, too, does Georgia's Hope Award, which restricts applicants with drug felony convictions for one term following the conviction (Custer, 2018).

Stigma

Another significant challenge justice-involved college students experience is related to the stigma associated with their criminal history. Stigma has been defined as "an attribute that is significantly discrediting, which in the eyes of society, serves to reduce the person who possesses it" (Goffman, 1963, p. 13). Some scholars have described the stigma that justice-involved people experience as an *invisible stripe* (LeBel, 2012; Maruna, 2011), "referring to the lifelong label of 'criminal' that gets inscribed on the bodies of ex-offenders" (Halkovic & Greene, 2015, p. 765). For justice-involved students who overcome the negative stigmatizing effects of being probed about their criminal history in the college admissions process and enroll, a new set of challenges awaits them. Indeed, justice-involved students often face the dilemma of whether to disclose or conceal their stigmatized identity (i.e., having a criminal record) (Strayhorn et al., 2013). Negotiating this dilemma can serve as a social barrier for justice-involved college students at a time when establishing supportive relationships with faculty, peers, and administrators is critical to their success. Concealing one's stigmatized identity is also associated with a number of negative effects, such as diminished self-esteem (Crocker & Major, 1989) and thwarted belongingness (Strayhorn, 2012).

Some justice-involved students in college also report feeling like outsiders, especially in the classroom (Copenhaver, Edwards-Willey, & Byers, 2007). Halkovic and Greene (2015) argue that "the cultures of college classrooms . . . rarely invite students with criminal records to share their experiences, leaving them too often to keep their pasts . . . secret" (p. 769). One participant in Halkovic and Greene's study described the experience of stigma on campus as similar to wearing an invisible coat "that may or may not be seen by the other students" (p. 769). This invisible weight may induce anxiety; negatively affect their interactions with faculty, staff, and peers; and reduce engagement in curricular and co-curricular activities on campus. Copenhaver et al. (2007) found that justice-involved students feared the consequences of identity disclosure, which also heightened their fears about developing relationships with peers on campus. Interestingly, however, Strayhorn et al. (2013) reported that some justice-involved students in college derive motivation to persist academically in light of negative stereotypes and low expectations of them. Finally, stigma associated with one's criminal history may be exacerbated by other marginalizing and stigmatizing identities, such as race, gender, first-generation status, adult learner status, and sexual orientation, among others.

Taken together, the sections here only begin to capture the numerous and complex challenges facing justice-involved students in higher education. Additional barriers may include limited access to student employment due to background checks and restrictions in studying abroad, service-learning projects, and other activities that may involve working with children, traveling, or visiting places like schools or hospitals (Custer, 2018). Such restrictions and challenges deny justice-involved students the opportunity of full participation (and engagement) in campus life and may lead to early departure from college before earning their degree.

Theories and Concepts

Presented in this section is a set of theories and concepts that can offer a framework for understanding the experiences of justice-involved students while also guiding higher education policy and practice. They help form the basis for the engagement strategies presented in the following section.

Sense of Belonging

One theoretical perspective that can be used to understand the experiences and outcomes of justice-involved students in college, as well as shape policy and practice efforts to fully engage them, is a sense of belonging. As a concept, belongingness can be traced back to Maslow's (1943, 1954) theory of human motivation. In his widely cited (and often debated) five-stage pyramid model, Maslow argued that all people have basic human needs that must be satisfied for maximum psychological health: physiological needs, safety needs, belongingness and love needs, esteem needs, and self-actualization. Scholars have drawn on Maslow's early work to understand how one's sense of identification with or membership in a community, such as a school, can impact other outcomes and behaviors like academic performance, motivation and retention (Baumeister & Leary, 1995; Hagerty et al., 2002, Hurtado & Carter, 1997; Strayhorn, 2008).

In higher education research, Strayhorn (2012, 2019) has theorized about the importance of sense of belonging for college students. He defines it as a "students' perceived social support on campus, a feeling or sensation of connectedness, the experience of mattering or feeling cared about, accepted, respected, valued by, and important to the group (e.g., campus community) or others on campus (e.g., faculty, peers)" (Strayhorn, 2012, p. 3). Seven core elements constitute Strayhorn's model. Drawing on Maslow's motivational research, he *first* argues that sense of belonging is a basic human need that must be met before higher-order needs like self-actualization and self-esteem are met (which he argues represent some of the desired outcomes of college education). This is important for justice-involved students, particularly those returning from long stints in jail or prison who often experience financial and housing insecurities. These basic needs must be met before higher-order-level needs like belongingness emerges. *Second*, a student's desire to belong, Strayhorn argues, may drive or influence their decision-making and engagement on campus. Indeed, a desire to belong may compel justice-involved students, for instance, to join clubs and organizations, especially those with others who share their background experiences and identities. Conversely, one's desire to belong can also result in antisocial behaviors. And college students who feel alienated or unsupported by peers, faculty, or administrators may dis-identify with school or disinvest from their academic goals (Strayhorn, 2012; Tinto, 1975).

The *third* core element of Strayhorn's model posits that sense of belonging is context specific (e.g., in a classroom) and has the greatest impact on one's outcomes in that particular area (e.g., academic achievement). Sense of belonging also takes on heightened importance at particular times (e.g., during a life transition) and among certain populations (e.g., Students of Color). As an example, formerly incarcerated Black males may experience a sense of belonging at the Black cultural center on campus, which leads to the development of supportive relationships with peers and staff. They may simultaneously experience alienation in a predominantly White classroom, where they are often invited to share about their experiences being incarcerated. *Next*, Strayhorn argues that sense of belonging is an antecedent of mattering. In order for justice-involved students, for instance, to have their belongingness needs met, they must feel that they matter; that is, feel valued, respected, and appreciated by others. The *fifth* element suggests that the confluence of one's social identities intersect and affect one's sense of belonging. Strayhorn notes that in order "To understand students' belonging experiences, one must pay close attention to issues of identity, identity salience or 'core self,' ascendancy of certain motives, and even social contexts that exert influence on these considerations" (p. 38).

The *sixth* element of Strayhorn's model posits that sense of belonging can engender positive outcomes like motivation, academic achievement, and retention. *Finally*, sense of belonging must be satisfied on a continual basis, particularly as one's circumstances, conditions, and contexts change (Strayhorn, 2012). Taken together, the seven core elements that constitute Strayhorn's model offer a useful framework for understanding and explaining how college contexts; relationships with peers, faculty, and administrators; and identity coalesce in shaping the experiences of justice-involved students and their sense of belonging.

Intersectionality

Another useful framework for understanding the experiences of justice-involved college students and guiding policies and practices to engage them is intersectionality. As Strayhorn's (2012) model suggests, to understand sense of belonging among students, one must pay attention to the ways in which social identities converge and impact their experiences in college. This is, in part, the essence of intersectionality, which traces its origins to Black feminists such as Audre Lorde (1984), Kimberle Crenshaw (1991), and Patricia Hill Collins (1998). Intersectionality can be defined as the "relationships among multiple social dimensions and modalities of social relations and subject formations" (McCall, 2005, p. 1771). Similarly, Bowleg (2008) argues that one's social identities are both interdependent and mutually constitutive (i.e., intersectional). Crenshaw (1991) emphasizes the importance of understanding the impact of multiple subordination across race, gender, social class, and other socially constructed categories sustained by social structures and systems. In other words, intersectionality can highlight people's experiences with oppression and/or privilege by examining how the spaces they occupy grant advantages based on a person's various social identities (Crenshaw, 1991).

Higher education scholars are increasingly drawing on intersectionality as a framework for understanding the experiences of—and offering recommendations for—supporting marginalized college students (Bhopal & Preston, 2012; Johnson, 2013; Museus & Griffin, 2011; Strayhorn, 2013; Tillapaugh & Nicolazzo, 2014). It is particularly useful in guiding the formulation of policies and practices that engage justice-involved college students in more holistic ways. As an example, formerly incarcerated Black women in college may simultaneously experience racism and patriarchy, in addition to the stigma and discrimination that might accompany having a criminal record.

It is also important to acknowledge that not all criminal records (and convictions) are equal. Some crimes are deemed more respectable than others, with fewer systemic barriers to successful reentry. Take, for instance, "white-collar" crimes, which refer to nonviolent, financially motivated offenses, often committed by (White) business and government professionals. White-collar crimes usually carry with them lighter sentences and less stigma (Holtfreter et al., 2008) than nonviolent, drug-related crimes, in which Blacks experience overrepresentation (despite having rates of drug use similar to Whites). An intersectional framework brings to one's attention the ways in which the experiences of justice-involved students are simultaneously raced and gendered and also shaped by the nature of their history with the criminal justice system. Policies and practices that are designed to engage justice-involved students in college that do not take into consideration such nuances are likely to be ineffective.

Critical Reflexivity

Critical reflexivity is another concept that can be useful for engaging justice-involved students. We refer to critical reflexivity as the process by which one interrogates their own positionality, as well as their assumptions, actions, decisions, and interactions. Critical reflexivity is particularly relevant for college educators as it provides an opportunity for them to interrogate their own roles in perpetuating hegemonic policies and practices (MacBeth, 2001). This process of deconstruction and reconstruction is important for both college educators and justice-involved students as it can lead to changes in one's values, beliefs, and behaviors such as engagement in "regressive practices" (e.g., homophobia, misogyny, and racism) and it can also help facilitate critical consciousness (Paris & Alim, 2014, p. 92).

Critical reflexivity is an important practice for college educators as it provides an opportunity for them to interrogate what assumptions and perspectives they have about justice-involved students (which may be steeped in White hegemony, capitalism, and racism) that may inhibit their capacity to fully support and engage them in college. It is also a useful practice for justice-involved students, particularly those who have been incarcerated, given the coercive and authoritarian nature of carceral contexts (Castro &

Brawn, 2017). Some justice-involved students may also be working through the impact of the crimes they may (or may not) have committed (LeBel, Richie, & Maduna, 2015; harm they may have caused to their victims, themselves, and their families (McTier Jr., Santa-Ramirez, & McGuire, 2017); and the impact of their socialization in a carceral context on their values, beliefs, and behaviors. Thus, critical reflexivity not only provides an opportunity for college educators to strengthen their capacity to support and engage justice-involved students, but can also serve as a restorative practice for the students themselves.

Student Engagement Strategies

Given some of the challenges facing justice-involved students and the theoretical perspectives and concepts discussed here, we propose seven strategies for effectively engaging them in college.

Humanizing Language

As we described in a previous section, the stigma associated with having criminal record can pose significant challenges for students' sense of belonging and their subsequent engagement on campus. When working with or referring to justice-involved students and any aspect of their criminal history, we recommend the usage of humanizing, person-first language. Here we rely on a list of recommendations offered by a group of formerly incarcerated and system-impacted scholars at the University of California, Berkeley, who identify as the Underground Scholars Initiative (USI). In lieu of terms and labels like *prisoner* (which they argue attaches a permanent identity to an often-temporary status) or *convict*, they recommend the usage of *incarcerated person* as it makes no claim about guilt or innocence. Another example includes *formerly incarcerated person* rather than terms like *ex-convict* or *ex-felon*. A full list of the scholar's terminology guide can be accessed at https://undergroundscholars.berkeley.edu. Faculty, as well as higher education and student affairs administrators, should familiarize themselves with the recommendations offered by USI and take heed in their subsequent interactions. As described in an earlier section, stigma and stigmatizing language can hijack a student's confidence, reduce their belonging, and lead to disengagement.

Provide Opportunities for Choice

Justice-involved students—especially those who have been incarcerated—have experienced a lack of choices. They are often told what time to wake up, what rehab and/or educational programs to attend, the frequency of their attendance, and other obligations that accompany probation and/or jail terms. Any divergence from these obligations can result in additional probation and/or jail time. Thus, in an educational setting, choice can be emancipatory for justice-involved students (Sandoval, Baumgartner, & Clark, 2016). By the time they are attending college classes, they have made multiple choices regarding courses and possible career tracks. Educators can expand on the emancipatory power of choice within the classroom by providing multiple options on assignments and various ways to engage during class time. Sandoval, Baumgartner, and Clark (2016) show how an educational program for incarcerated women established a core curriculum but integrated choice by allowing women to choose from a variety of elective courses. Additionally, the program educators provided the space for various forms of expression (e.g., dance, art, talk). This autonomy can be liberating for justice-involved students as they transition into a life without constant monitoring (Baumgartner & Sandoval, 2018).

Provision of Financial Aid Resources

As described in an earlier section, justice-involved students, especially those with certain drug and sex-related convictions, may experience difficulty paying for college, given federal and state student aid restrictions. College educators and administrators should consider this and advocate for the provision of resources for institutional scholarships, grants, emergency funds, and even access to student employment on *campus*, for justice-involved students. As Strayhorn (2012, 2019) theorizes, it is difficult to find community and experience belonging in college when you are worried about your basic needs being met. Thus, to ensure their full participation and engagement on campus, justice-involved students, particularly those from low-income backgrounds, will need access to substantial financial resources to pursue their education without interruption.

Critical Self-Reflection in the Classroom

Through critical self-reflections, justice-involved students are able to examine their beliefs and behaviors and better understand how they may be beneficial or detrimental to their development (LeBel, Richie, & Maruna, 2015; Sandoval, Baumgartner, & Clark, 2016). In other words, the classroom can serve as a safe environment for students to reflect and imagine a better future (Baumgartner & Sandoval, 2018). This process is essential for instructors to engage students in critical reflexivity (Brookfield, 2009; Mezirow, 2006). However, given the probable trauma of many justice-involved students, critical self-reflections may elicit a range of narratives and emotions filled with violence and victimization (Sandoval, Baumgartner, & Clark, 2016). Therefore, educators must be equipped with the skills and tools to facilitate difficult conversations in a productive manner. One way to maximize student learning is by connecting the knowledge from students' reflections into the course content (Castillo-Montoya, 2018). This way, the classroom instructor deconstructs the traditional teacher-student power dynamics as the course content is also generated by students' insights, which can be empowering and validating for students.

Academic and Social Support Services and Programs

Access to higher education without requisite supports and services to ensure the success of justice-involved students is negligent and irresponsible on the part of the institution. College educators and administrators should make sure that justice-involved students on campus are aware of and know how to access academic and social support services and programs available to them. As such, faculty and administrators must also be knowledgeable and prepared to support the complex and multifaceted lives and demands of justice-involved students (e.g., mandatory court appearances, meetings with parole officers), and/or appoint/hire someone who can. Campus-based initiatives such as the Berkeley Underground Scholars (BUS) program serves as an excellent model for other colleges and universities to consider replicating, especially as a strategy for facilitating students' sense of belonging. In short, BUS has not only created a pathway for justice-involved students into higher education, but also supports them through a comprehensive set of academic and co-curricular support services with dedicated staff and resources.

Professional Development and Support

Justice-involved people often consider their ability to secure employment and become financially self-reliant as a significant part of their reintegration (Heidemann, Ceder-baum, & Martinez, 2016; LeBel et al., 2015). However, employment opportunities can vary drastically, depending on the student's identity and criminal record. White offenders are more likely to be employed than Black offenders; those who have been incarcerated are less likely to find employment than offenders who have not been incarcerated; and white-collar offenders are more likely to regain and maintain employment than street-level offenders (Apel & Sweeten, 2010; Kerley & Copes, 2004; Lyons & Pettit, 2011).

Given these employment challenges, college educators and practitioners can play a critical role in helping students explore their professional opportunities and reduce recidivism rates (LeBel et al., 2015; Ray, Grommon, & Rydberg, 2016). First, justice-involved students can be encouraged to take part in reintegration programs that help with resumes, interviewing, and job searching. Also, faculty and instructors can position students to reflect on their vocational and transferable skills as a way to acknowledge their strengths, enhance their confidence, and develop their professional identity.

Mentorship

Another strategy to further engage justice-involved students is through mentorship programs, specifically those that pair successful justice-involved students with newly enrolled justice-involved students (Heidemann, Cederbaum, Martinez, & LeBel, 2016; LeBel et al., 2015). This peer-to-peer strategy entails mentoring justice-involved students on navigating personal, educational, and social contexts without the structure and demands of the criminal justice system. As cited by Schnappauf and DiDonato (2017), this approach can be effective as justice-involved people "often feel the most comfortable addressing the real issues preventing them from a successful reentry into society when they do not feel the negative presence of stigma and discrimination" (Schnittker, 2014, p. 4). Furthermore, justice-involved students can possibly provide each other with information and resources unavailable or unknown to criminal justice and college practitioners (LeBel et al., 2015). This strategy may also prove beneficial for the mentors as well. Indeed, some scholars have noted that such programs help facilitate a sense of purpose among mentors, who often maintain a desire to help and give back to their communities (LeBel et al., 2015). As such, justice-involved students—via mentorship—can begin to establish a social network of peers, which is essential to cultivating a sense of belonging, identify resources, and actualize successful reintegration (Pickering, Sputek, & Rutherford, 2016; Schnappauf & DiDonato, 2017).

Conclusion

As more justice-involved students pursue higher education as a viable pathway to upward economic and social mobility, it is important that those who work in higher education are prepared to meet their multifaceted and complex needs. In this chapter, we provide a very brief overview of just some of the challenges facing justice-involved students that may impact the nature and frequency of their engagement on campus. In addition, we discuss three theoretical perspectives and concepts that we hope college educators will draw on as they interrogate existing, and formulate new, policies and practices on campus. We also offer a set of recommendations that are grounded in published research and scholarship, which faculty and campus administrators might draw on as they work to enhance their capacity to support justice-involved students in college.

Note

1 In this chapter we use the term "justice-involved" to refer to a wide range of a person's involvement with the criminal justice system, including, but not limited to, incarceration in jail or prison, parole, probation, and mandatory supervision, to name a few

References

Alexander, M. (2012). *The new Jim Crow: Mass incarceration in the age of colorblindness*. New York, NY: The New Press.

Apel, R., & Sweeten, G. (2010). The impact of incarceration on employment during the transition to adulthood. *Social Problems, 57*(3), 448–479.

Astin, A. W. (1984). Student involvement: A developmental theory for higher education. *Journal of college student personnel, 25*(4), 297–308.

Baumeister, R. F., & Leary, M. R. (1995). The need to belong: Desire for interpersonal attachments as a fundamental human motivation. *Psychological Bulletin, 117*(3), 497–529.

Baumgartner, L. M., & Sandoval, C. L. (2018). "Being a presence to each other": Adult educators who foster empowerment with incarcerated women. *Adult Education Quarterly, 68*(4), 263–279. doi:10.1177/0741713618774412

Bhopal, K., & Preston, J. (2012). *Intersectionality and race in education*. London: Routledge.

Bowleg, L. (2008). When Black+ lesbian+ woman≠ Black lesbian woman: The methodological challenges of qualitative and quantitative intersectionality research. *Sex Roles, 59*(5–6), 312–325.

Brazzell, D., Crayton, A., Mukamal, D. A., Solomon, A. L., & Lindahl, N. (2009). *From the classroom to the community: Exploring the role of education during incarceration and reentry*. Washington, DC: The Urban Institute.

Brookfield, S. D. (2009). Engaging critical reflection in corporate America. In J. Mezirow & E. W. Taylor (Eds.), *Transformative learning in practice: Insights from community, workplace, and higher education* (pp. 125–135). San Francisco, CA: Jossey-Bass.

Castillo-Montoya, M. (2018). Rigor revisited: Scaffolding college student learning by incorporating their lived experiences. *New Directions for Higher Education, 2018*(181), 37–46.

Castro, E. L., & Brawn, M. (2017). Critiquing critical pedagogies inside the prison classroom: A dialogue between student and teacher. *Harvard Educational Review, 87*(1), 99–121.

Castro, E. L., & Zamani-Gallaher, E. M. (2018). *Expanding quality higher education for currently and formerly incarcerated people: Committing to equity and protecting against exploitation (ASHE-NITE Report Series)*. Las Vegas, NV: Association for the Student of Higher Education.

Collins, P. H. (1998). It's all in the family: Intersections of gender, race, and nation. *Hypatia, 13*(3), 62–82.

Copenhaver, A., Edwards-Willey, T. L., & Byers, B. D. (2007). Journeys in social stigma: The lives of formerly incarcerated felons in higher education. *Journal of Correctional Education, 58*, 268–283.

Crayton, A., & Neusteter, S. R. (2008). *The current state of correctional education*. Paper presented at the Reentry Roundtable on Education, John Jay College of Criminal Justice, New York, NY.

Crenshaw, K. (1991). Mapping the margins: Intersectionality, identity politics, and violence against women of color. *Stanford Law Review, 43*(6), 1241–1299.

Crocker, J., & Major, B. (1989). Social stigma and self-esteem: The self-protective properties of stigma. *Psychological Review, 96*(4), 608.

Custer, B. D. (2013). Why college admissions policies for students with felony convictions are not working at one institution. *College and University, 88*(4), 28.

Custer, B. D. (2018). Reconsidering policy barriers for justice-involved college students. *Journal of College Access, 4*(1), 51–63.

Dreger, M. L. (2017). *Barriers to postsecondary education participation experienced by formerly incarcerated community college students* (Unpublished doctoral dissertation). Hartford, CT: University of Hartford.

Federal Pell Grants. (2019, April 14). Retrieved from https://studentaid.ed.gov/sa/types/grants-scholarships/pell

Fields, D., & Abrams, L. S. (2010). Gender differences in the perceived needs and barriers of youth offenders preparing for community reentry. *Child & Youth Care Forum, 39*(4), 253–269.

Goffman, E. (1963). *Stigma. Notes on a spoiled identity*. Englewood Cliffs, NJ: Prentice-Hall.

Hagerty, B. M., Williams, R. A., & Oe, H. (2002). Childhood antecedents of adult sense of belonging. *Journal of Clinical Psychology, 58*(7), 793–801.

Halkovic, A., & Greene, A. C. (2015). Bearing stigma, carrying gifts: What colleges can learn from students with incarceration experience. *The Urban Review, 47*(4), 759–782.

Heidemann, G., Cederbaum, J. A., & Martinez, S. (2016). Beyond recidivism: How formerly incarcerated women define success. *Affilia, 31*(1), 24–40.

Heidemann, G., Cederbaum, J. A., Martinez, S., & LeBel, T. P. (2016). Wounded healers: How formerly incarcerated women help themselves by helping others. *Punishment & Society, 18*(1), 3–26.

Holtfreter, K., Van Slyke, S., Bratton, J., & Gertz, M. (2008). Public perceptions of White-collar crime and punishment. *Journal of Criminal Justice, 36*(1), 50–60.

Hurtado, S., & Carter, D. F. (1997). Effects of college transition and perceptions of the campus racial climate on Latino college students' sense of belonging. *Sociology of Education, 70*(4), 324–345.

Johnson, R. M. (2013). Black and male on campus: An autoethnographic account. *Journal of African American Males in Education, 4*(2), 25–45.

Kerley, K. R., & Copes, H. (2004). The effects of criminal justice contact on employment stability for white-collar and street-level offenders. *International Journal of Offender Therapy and Comparative Criminology, 48*(1), 65–84. doi:10.1177/0306624X03256660

LeBel, T. P. (2012). Invisible stripes? Formerly incarcerated persons' perceptions of stigma. *Deviant Behavior, 33*(2), 89–107.

LeBel, T. P., Richie, M., & Maruna, S. (2015). Helping others as a response to reconcile a criminal past: The role of the wounded healer in prisoner reentry programs. *Criminal Justice and Behavior, 42*(1), 108–120.

Levenson, J. S., Brannon, Y. N., Fortney, T., & Baker, J. (2007). Public perceptions about sex offenders and community protection policies. *Analyses of Social Issues and Public Policy, 7*, 137–161.

López Turley, R. N., & Wodtke, G. (2010). College residence and academic performance: Who benefits from living on campus? *Urban Education, 45*(4), 506–532.

Lorde, A. (1984). *Sister outsider: Essays and speeches*. Trumansburg, NY: Crossing Press.

Lyons, C. J., & Pettit, B. (2011). Compounded disadvantage: Race, incarceration, and wage growth. *Social Problems, 58*(2), 257–280.

Ma, J., Pender, M., & Welch, M. (2016). *Education pays 2016: The benefits of higher education for individuals and society. Trends in higher education series*. New York, NY: The College Board.

Macbeth, D. (2001). On "reflexivity" in qualitative research: Two readings, and a third. *Qualitative Inquiry, 7*(1), 35–68.

Maruna, S. (2011). Reentry as a rite of passage. *Punishment & Society, 13*(1), 3–28.

Maslow, A. H. (1943). A theory of human motivation. *Psychological Review, 50*(4), 370–396.

Maslow, A. H. (1954). *Motivation and personality*. New York, NY: Harper.

McCall, L. (2005). The complexity of intersectionality. *Signs, 30*(3), 1771–1800. doi:10.1086/426800

McTier, T. S., Santa-Ramirez, S., & McGuire, K. M. (2017). A prison to school pipeline. *Journal of Underrepresented & Minority Progress, 1*(1), 8–22.

Mezirow, J. (2006). Chapter 6: An overview of transformative learning. In P. Sutherland & J. Crowther (Eds.), *Lifelong learning: Concepts and contexts* (pp. 24–38). New York, NY: Routledge.

Museus, S. D., & Griffin, K. A. (2011). Mapping the margins in higher education: On the promise of intersectionality frameworks in research and discourse. *New Directions for Institutional Research, 2011*(151), 5–13.

Paris, D., & Alim, H. S. (2014). What are we seeking to sustain through culturally sustaining pedagogy? A loving critique forward. *Harvard Educational Review, 84*(1), 85–100.

Pascarella, E. T., & Terenzini, P. T. (2005). *How college affects students: A third decade of research* (Vol. 2). San Francisco, CA: Jossey-Bass.

Pickering, B. J., Sputek, J., & Rutherford, G. (2016). Peers engaging in empowering research (PEER): Finding Women's voices after prison. *International Journal of Nursing and Clinical Practices, 3*(193). Article 2.

Ray, B., Grommon, E., & Rydberg, J. (2016). Anticipated stigma and defensive individualism during post-incarceration job searching. *Sociological Inquiry, 86*(3), 348–371.

Rosenthal, A., NaPier, E., Warth, P., & Weissman, M. (2015). *Boxed out: Criminal history screening and college application attrition*. Retrieved from Center for Community Alternatives, Inc., website: www.communityalternatives.org/fb/boxed-out.html

Sandoval, C. L., Baumgartner, L. M., & Clark, M. C. (2016). Paving paths toward transformation with incarcerated women. *Journal of Transformative Education, 14*(1), 34–52. doi:10.1177/1541344615602758

Schnappauf, E. M., & DiDonato, T. E. (2017). From solitary to solidarity: Belonging, social support, and the problem of women's recidivism. *Modern Psychological Studies, 23*(1), Article 7.

Schnittker, J. (2014). The psychological dimensions and the social consequences of incarceration. *The ANNALS of the American Academy of Political and Social Science, 651*(1), 122–138.

Sentencing Project. (2015). *Trends in US corrections*. Washington, DC: Author. Retrieved from http://sentencingproject.org/wp-content/uploads/2016/01/Trends-in-US-Corrections.pdf

Strayhorn, T. L. (2008). Fittin' in: Do diverse interactions with peers affect sense of belonging for Black men at predominantly White institutions? *NASPA Journal, 45*(4), 501–527.

Strayhorn, T. L. (2012). *College students' sense of belonging: A key to educational success*. New York, NY: Routledge.

Strayhorn, T. L. (2019). *College students' sense of belonging: A key to educational success* (2nd ed.). New York, NY: Routledge.

Strayhorn, T. L., Johnson, R. M., & Barrett, B. A. (2013). Investigating the college adjustment and transition experiences of formerly incarcerated Black male collegians at predominantly White institutions. *Spectrum: A Journal on Black Men, 2*(1), 73–98.

Students with criminal conviction. (2019, April 14). Retrieved from https://studentaid.ed.gov/sa/eligibility/criminal-convictions

Tillapaugh, D., & Nicolazzo, Z. (2014). Backward thinking: Exploring the relationship among intersectionality, epistemology, and research design In D. Mitchell Jr., C. Y. Simmons, & L. A. Greyerbiehl (Eds.), *Intersectionality and higher education: Theory, research, and praxis*. New York, NY: Peter Lang.

Tinto, V. (1975). Dropout from higher education: A theoretical synthesis of recent research. *Review of educational research, 45*(1), 89–125.

US Department of Education. (2016). *Beyond the box: Increasing access to higher education for justice-involved individuals.* Washington, DC: US Department of Education.

Weissman, M., Rosenthal, A., Warth, P., Wolf, E., & Messina-Yauchzy, M. (2010). *The use of criminal history records in college admissions reconsidered.* New York, NY: Center for Community Alternatives.

Chapter 17
Engaging First-Generation Students

Georgia Kouzoukas

Higher education leaders and administrators are constantly evolving their campuses as the college-age population in the United States is becoming increasingly more diverse (Baum, Ma, & Payea, 2013; Zumeta, Breneman, Callan, & Finney, 2012). Considerable attention has more recently been given to first-generation students, who can be simply defined as people who are the first in their families to attend college (Gofen, 2009; Pascarella, Pierson, Wolniak, & Terenzini, 2004). While the first-generation-student label may not have been ubiquitously utilized on college campuses over a decade ago, it is now common nomenclature. Conversations regarding the first-generation student population either formally in higher education research or informally across campuses, are a trending topic. The common themes surrounding first-generation college-goers, I argue, revolve around their experiences in terms of college access, persistence, and retention, given that the student population is less likely to enroll in higher education, and those who do enter, are less likely to graduate (Choy, 2001; Saenz, Hurtado, Barrera, Wolf, & Yeung, 2007). With higher education policymakers focusing on increasing America's degree completion rates, including those of first-generation students (Zumeta et al., 2012), administrators have been tasked with creating and employing strategies to proactively ameliorate such issues. Since engagement in both curricular and co-curricular experiences in college is positively related to student outcomes, including persistence (Astin, 1975, 1993; Pascarella & Terenzini, 2005; Tinto, 1993, 2000, 2005), educational practices have been customized in ways to engage first-generation learners.

In this chapter, I focus on examining the first-generation student population as commonly depicted through longitudinal and national statistical research and the institutional resources that have been created in response. However, I argue that, although first-generation student scholarship and recommendations for practice are of critical importance, they also assume that first-generation college-goers are a homogenous student population with generalized experiences. Yet not all first-generation students are nontraditional collegians from disadvantaged and underrepresented populations with academic and social deficits in the college context (Choy, 2001; Saenz et al., 2007). Moreover, strategies for first-generation students should not follow a one-size-fits-all mindset.

To fully engage first-generation students in the college experience, there needs to be a better understanding of each student within and outside their first-generation group membership. Given the complexity and multidimensionality of the student population, higher education administrators should thoughtfully engage first-generation students in identity exploration in addition to standard engagement practices. Since identity is shaped by how a person organizes their experiences within the environments that they are part of (Erikson, 1959/1994) and is a balance between oneself and others (Kroger, 2004), the college experience and context are crucial to moving students through identity development (Chickering & Reisser, 1993; Deaux, 1993; Moran, 2003). By providing students with opportunities for self-definition and a critical examination of their abilities, values, objectives, and relationships, students can better ascertain how their intersecting identities (e.g., race/ethnicity, income, gender, sexual orientation) influence and are influenced by their college experience. In addition, stakeholders can identify how first-generation students are navigating their unique institutional context and how resources are being utilized and understand the meanings students associate with their experiences, the positive or negative impact this reflection has on their self-concept, and ultimately its influence on student's holistic well-being (Torres, 2011).

As such, the chapter continues with a focus on the guiding theoretical frameworks of identity development and identity intersectionality to help administrators focus on the uniqueness of each first-generation college-goer and the importance of developing the whole student. Finally, I conclude by utilizing identity intersectionality as a framework to propose strategies to engage students in identity exploration and development. By affording first-generation students the ability to uncover their multidimensional needs, higher education administrators can better facilitate the acquisition of tools needed in order to be holistically engaged in the environment, persist until degree completion, enter adulthood with a life of meaning, and be contributing members of society.

The "Typical" First-Generation Student

The term *first-generation student* was initially formulated by the federal government as an eligibility designation for federally funded programs for underserved students and is defined as collegians whose parents have not obtained a degree from a postsecondary institution (Ward, Siegel, & Davenport, 2012). Other researchers (e.g., Gofen, 2009; Pascarella et al., 2004) have since adopted a more stringent approach, categorizing first-generation learners as students enrolling in and/or completing an undergraduate degree despite neither parent having attended a college or university. Depending on the definition used by a higher education institution, either those presented here or the many others adopted, the number of first-generation collegians in the United States varies. To provide some context in an ambiguous territory, according to data from the National Center for Education Statistics (NCES), approximately one-third of undergraduates during the 2011–2012 academic year have parents who did not attend a college or university (Cataldi, Bennett, & Chen, 2018; Skomsvold, 2015).

If a college or university does not have a clear definition of first-generation students, campus leaders and administrators are not familiar with or able to properly assist the first-generation college-goers who are enrolled in their institution and, instead, resort to viewing the population based on information found in research, which I present here. Although inconsistencies in the statistical proportion of students deemed first-generation are evident, first-generation college-goers experience intersecting sites of oppression since the generalized population is overrepresented within marginalized racial, gender, and socioeconomic groups (Lohfink & Paulsen, 2005). Data from the NCES (Radwin, Wine, Siegel, & Bryan, 2013) found that 28% of White students were first-generation, compared to 42% of Black or African American collegians, 47.8% of Hispanic students, and 32.8% of Asians. Similar to findings in other studies (e.g., Bui, 2002; Pascarella et al., 2004; Ward et al., 2012), first-generation students are more likely to be Students of Color.

Another common demographic characteristic of the student population is in regards to socioeconomic status and a more frequent tendency to come from low-income backgrounds than peers with parents who have had some college experience or completed postsecondary degrees (Choy, 2001; Radwin et al., 2013; Ward et al., 2012). Gender differences are also evident, with statistics from the 2011–2012 National Postsecondary Student Aid Study reporting that 35.2% of college women had parents who either did not complete high school or whose highest level of education was a high school diploma, compared to 31.1% of college men (Radwin et al., 2013). While a seemingly minimal difference, first-generation college-goers have been more likely to be women since the 1980s (Saenz et al., 2007), which is consistent with the general trend of an increased college participation rate for women (Freeman, 2004; Snyder & Dillow, 2015). Scholars (e.g., Choy, 2001) have found first-generation students to be older than the traditional college-age population, with an age of 24 years or older. Students who are the first in their families to attend college are also more likely to have parents whose native language is not English (Bui, 2002; Pascarella et al., 2004; Ward et al., 2012).

College Access and Transition

Compared to traditional collegians, first-generation students are less likely to enroll in a college or university (Choy, 2001; Gofen, 2009). Issues of access into higher education for underserved populations have been well researched (e.g., Perna, 2000; Perna & Kurban, 2013), with first-generation students echoing college affordability concerns (Horn, Chen, & Chapman, 2003), inadequate targeted college counseling in secondary schooling (Bruce & Bridgeland, 2012), and an unfamiliarity with or inadequate knowledge of the college-going process (Perna & Kurban, 2013), due to their lack of social and cultural capital (Pascarella et al., 2004). However, first-generation learners choose to pursue higher education for familial reasons, as well as to achieve financial stability through the achievement of their career aspirations (Bui, 2002).

In terms of institution type, first-generation learners are more likely to select two-year colleges than continuing-generation students (Choy, 2001; Ward et al., 2012). Low-income first-generation students in particular are overrepresented in not only public two-year colleges, but also for-profit institutions (Engle & Tinto, 2008). Even those deemed academically qualified are less likely to choose a rigorous selective postsecondary institution (Pascarella et al., 2004; Ward et al., 2012). Due to the characteristics of first-generation students, two-year colleges provide a less expensive and more accommodating means for the student population to pursue higher education while attending to personal and familial needs (Ward et al., 2012). For similar reasons, not only are first-generation college-goers more likely to enroll in a college or university on a part-time basis (Choy, 2001; Pascarella et al., 2004; Saenz et al., 2007), but a higher percentage of the student population also works full time in comparison to continuing-generation students (Warburton, Bugarin, & Nuñez, 2001) and are more likely to live off campus (Pascarella et al., 2004). It is important to note, though, that first-generation learners are more likely to receive a bachelor's degree if directly enrolled in a four-year institution when beginning their collegiate career (Choy, 2001; Pascarella et al., 2004; Ward et al., 2012).

First-Generation Curricular and Co-Curricular Engagement

Due to a number of factors, first-generation students typically experience difficulty within the postsecondary institutional context, do not perform as well academically as continuing-generation peers, and have lower degree completion rates (Pascarella et al., 2004). Academically, first-generation college-goers are more likely to require remedial assistance, are less equipped to handle the academic rigor of college (Chen & Carroll, 2005), and find it difficult to interpret faculty expectations and understand course syllabi (Collier & Morgan, 2008). Regarding undergraduate major, students who are the first in their families to attend college have a more difficult time choosing an academic field of interest. Chen and Carroll (2005) reported that 33% of first-generation students did not have a declared major after entering college. When deciding on a major, first-generation college students may be limited to certain fields because of inadequate academic preparation but aim to pursue a career that will provide a lucrative salary upon entering the workforce. The most popular majors for first-generation collegians, including low-income first-generation learners, are business, health science, and the social sciences (Chen & Carroll, 2005; Engle & Tinto, 2008).

Despite scholastic difficulties, specific academic disciplines are developmentally beneficial in terms of "internal locus of attribution for academic success" (Pascarella et al., 2004, p. 274). For example, coursework in the arts and humanities, mathematics, social sciences, natural sciences, and engineering has positive effects on first-generation students' writing skills and educational plans. The number of courses taken in these disciplines also has significant positive effects on first-generation collegians' writing skills and educational plans, compared to peers whose parents had postsecondary experience. Further, engagement in academic activities, including the amount of time spent studying and the number of papers written, have positively affected first-generation students in terms of critical thinking, writing skills, and learning for personal understanding (Pascarella et al., 2004).

With limited time on campus, the first-generation student population is less likely to take part in extracurricular activities, volunteer efforts, and athletic groups during the second year of college (Pascarella et al., 2004). Further, during the third year, first-generation students tend to have less peer interaction outside classroom activities. While time constraints and place of residence do not allow participation in certain aspects of campus life, the first-generation student population reaps the most benefits from co-curricular and peer engagement when compared to other collegians (Lohfink & Paulsen, 2005; Pascarella et al., 2004). Specifically, such engagement positively affects first-generation students' critical thinking abilities and degree plans (Pascarella et al., 2004). Further, interacting with fellow students outside the classroom positively impacts first-generation students' writing abilities and science reasoning.

Other reasons contributing to first-generation college-goers' lower levels of engagement may be due to their discomfort on campus with peers (Arzy, Davies, & Harbour, 2006). First-generation students are less likely to have a social support system at their postsecondary institution (Barry, Hudley, Kelly, & Cho, 2009). Without emotional support from others, first-generation college-goers are unable to successfully cope, leading to feeling overwhelmed (Phinney & Haas, 2003). Feeling socially isolated and unable to approach parents since they cannot relate to their situation, first-generation learners become less confident in how to succeed within the college environment.

Institutional Resources for First-Generation Students

Utilizing the research on first-generation students, strategies for improving their experiences have primarily focused on the following areas: pre-entry attributes and transition into the postsecondary context (Collier & Morgan, 2008; Pascarella et al., 2004); adjustment and engagement in college; and academic preparation, self-efficacy, and motivation (Pascarella et al., 2004; Ramos-Sanchez & Nichols, 2007). Summer bridge programs or transition programs have been utilized in colleges and universities to provide access to and assist in retaining and graduating low-income students, Students of Color, and first-generation students (Ackerman, 1991; Walpole et al., 2008). During the summer prior to a learners' first year as a collegian, first-generation students in the program are provided with academic and personal support, as well as social development through a residential experience on campus at the institution (Ackerman, 1991; Pascarella & Terenzini, 2005), to enhance their understanding of and comfort level in the college environment (Wathington et al., 2011). While the effects of participation in summer bridge programs have been inconsistent, students note an increased familiarity with campus resources and time management development and form a sense of community (Suzuki, Amrein-Beardsley, & Perry, 2012).

Living-learning communities have also been utilized to assist first-generation college-goers in their transition into higher education; however, faculty participation, academic advising, mentoring, and programming are more robust since students reside together during the academic year (Pascarella & Terenzini, 2005). First-generation students participating in a living-learning community indicate a positive academic transition to the college context due to available faculty interaction and resources in the residence hall (Inkelas, Daver, Vogt, & Leonard, 2007). Living-learning communities also allow first-generation students to have a more successful social transition.

Additional strategies for higher education institutions have also been considered. Recommendations include increasing classroom engagement for first-generation students, as well as developing study groups that allow for a system of social support (Engle & Tinto, 2008). Providing opportunities for mentorship and coaching from peers, faculty, and administrators has also been positively impactful (Bettinger & Baker, 2011; Whitley, Benson, & Wesaw, 2018). Instead of emphasizing the needs of first-generation learners from a deficit perspective, an asset-based lens that celebrates their strengths is suggested (Whitley et al., 2018). Similarly, institutions are advised to become student ready as opposed to college ready, which focuses not on a student's level of preparedness when entering the institutional context, but on how prepared a campus is to successfully engage collegians.

First-Generation Student Identity

Although there is great utility in the institutional resources created from the aforementioned research, there is minimal information focused on identity development and incorporating identity intersectionality into such strategies. Researchers (e.g., Orbe, 2004; Wildhagen, 2015) have examined first-generation students and how a multifaceted identity is both constructed and understood within the college context. Utilizing a qualitative approach with first-generation college-goers of all races/ethnicities and genders, Orbe (2004) examined the saliency of first-generation status based on experiences, situational context, and interactions with others. Notably, students were incognizant of a first-generation identity if attending an institution predominantly composed of other first-generation learners. A first-generation status was instead more salient outside the college context, when intersecting identities were more pronounced and noticeable. For example, Black and Latino students reported disparate experiences in regards to their first-generation status when at home—either celebrated because of their representation of the larger community or met with contention and jealously, similar to family achievement guilt (Covarrubias & Fryberg, 2015). Within the home environment, first-generation status was typically seen as unavoidable; however, the higher education context allowed the identity to be invisible unless explicitly made known (Orbe, 2004). For example, some students willingly disclosed being a first-generation student, while others chose not to enact this identity due to the perceived stigma attached. Further, saliency depends on the level of privilege associated with students' other social identities, with first-generation status being on the periphery of some students' self-concept if they also identified with being White, a man, and of a middle to upper socioeconomic status. Although Orbe (2004) adds to the nascent topic of first-generation student identity formation, parental education status was the most critically examined, warranting more extensive research on the complexity of multidimensionality and how first-generation students understand the intersection of their identities.

Theoretical Approaches

I review identity development frameworks in this section to illustrate the evolution of a siloed focus on identities to a multidimensional and intersectional approach, which serves as a foundation or lens for the engagement strategies I present in the forthcoming section.

Identity Development in Higher Education

Psychosocial identity development theories have focused on the psychological and experiential issues people face at different junctures throughout their lifespan (Evans, 2011). Initially derived from Erikson (1980), development from adolescence to adulthood is seen to occur through eight stages, each of which has a crisis an individual resolves that enables them to move forward and handle subsequent issues later in life. Ultimately, crisis resolution, in conjunction with contextual forces, allows for the development of self-concept, an understanding of how the self relates to others, and a consistently changing and more established identity.

Expanding on Erikson's (1980) conception of identity, Chickering's (1969) theory of identity development, introduced in the 1960s, became a foundational framework in understanding psychosocial development as it pertains to college students specifically (Evans, Forney, Guido, Patton, & Renn, 2010). Seven vectors were introduced to comprehensively understand the establishment of identity while in the postsecondary context: developing competence, managing emotions, moving through autonomy toward interdependence, developing mature interpersonal relationships, establishing identity, developing purpose, and developing integrity (Chickering, 1969; Chickering & Reisser, 1993; Evans et al., 2010, pp. 67–69). Establishing a positive identity even more specifically includes the following:

> Comfort with body and appearance; comfort with gender and sexual orientation; sense of self in a social, historical, and cultural context; clarification of self-concept through roles and responsibilities; sense of self in response to feedback from valued others; self-acceptance and self-esteem; and personal stability and integration.
>
> (Chickering & Reisser, 1993, p. 38)

As opposed to sequential stages, the theory emphasizes that collegians move through vectors or developmental tasks at different rates and have the ability to reexamine issues that were previously addressed (Chickering & Reisser, 1993). However, the vectors can build off one another as a means toward intellectual, emotional, and interpersonal development and ultimately individuation. Recently, the theory has been revised to include the development of diverse populations; however, at the time of its inception, identity development based on gender, race, and other social identities was not considered.

Consequently, psychosocial theories evolved into social identity theories as a means to further understand the critical years of adolescence, especially within the college context, as well as to address the various dimensions of identity (e.g., race, gender, socioeconomic status) (Torres, 2011). Given the diversity on college campuses and the larger sociohistorical context of the United States, the development of both privileged/ dominant groups and oppressed/minoritized groups has been researched within social identity theoretical frameworks. Racial identity development models (e.g., Cross, 1991) focus on the process of developing a Black identity, from low race salience to a more complex meaning of race based upon encounters with racism in societal and institutional contexts (Torres, 2011). In addition, White identity theories (e.g., Helms, 1990) primarily emphasize the privilege associated with being in the racial majority and acknowledge how such privilege influences the relationship, or rather distance, between diverse races (Evans et al., 2010; Torres, 2011). Although well-established racial identity development models have been created for Black, White, Latinx (e.g., Ferdman & Gallegos, 2001), and Asian people (e.g., Kim, 2001), the frameworks examine identity formation strictly from a catchall racial/ethnic perspective, not taking into account other social identities, such as gender and socioeconomic status. Similarly, gender identity theories (e.g., Josselson, 1987, 1996) primarily focus on understanding gender from a social constructivist perspective, without considering dimensions of race and income (Torres, 2011).

Ultimately, social identity theories have contributed to the knowledge base on student development and how collegians understand themselves in relation to others; however, the frameworks view people as separate entities based on gender or race. Understanding students' experiences based on one social identity is problematic since it reinforces essentialized perceptions (Harper, Wardell, & McGuire, 2011) and disregards other dimensions that may be specifically salient to collegians and their development. The Multidimensional Identity Model initiated the importance of understanding how people from various group memberships experience and negotiate multiple oppressions (Reynolds & Pope, 1991). Jones and McEwen (2000) expanded the framework, developing a fluid and dynamic three-dimensional model that emphasizes consistent identity construction influenced by context. Specifically, the contextual influences of family background, sociocultural conditions, and current experiences impact the level of importance different dimensions of identity (e.g., race, gender, income status) have on a person's core sense of self. Abes, Jones, and McEwen (2007) then reconceptualized the model to emphasize how a person's developmental stage impacts meaning-making capacity and, ultimately, the perception of their multiple identities. A more complex understanding of self lessens the influence of contextual elements on identity development while a weaker meaning-making capacity can lead people to formulate an identity based on the context as opposed to their inner selves. The model allows people to not only recognize their multiple identities, but also understand the manner in which identities are perceived and influenced by cognitive, interpersonal, and intrapersonal domains (Abes & Jones, 2004; Abes et al., 2007).

Identity Intersectionality

The theoretical approach of intersectionality, credited to Crenshaw (1991), provides a more comprehensive understanding of multiple identities in terms of privilege, power, and oppression (Jones, 2009). Rooted in Black feminist thought (Collins, 2000), Crenshaw emphasized structural, political, and representational intersectionality when specifically addressing Black women's experiences of subordination, the practice of ignoring their experiences within racial or gender inequality discussions, and the depiction of women of color based upon common racial and gender stereotypes (Brunn-Bevel, Joy Davis, & Olive, 2015; Crenshaw, 1991). Although Crenshaw's (1991) research was initially situated in the exploration of how race and gender intersect, she acknowledged that other frameworks, such as income and sexuality, are critical in understanding the integration of all aspects of identity.

Research on intersectionality is, therefore, characterized through the following: examining the lived experiences of people, including those from marginalized groups; understanding identity in terms of the individual and their group associations; exploring the saliency of identity based on the conception of privilege; and ultimately aiming to promote social justice (Brunn-Bevel et al., 2015; Dill & Zambrana, 2009). Moreover, intersectionality recognizes the experiences of an individual as part of homogenous and essentialized social identity groups (e.g., Black, Latino, woman) yet pushes against an additive approach (e.g., Latino/a + woman = Latina woman) that compels people to choose one identity over another (Crenshaw, 1991; Winkle-Wagner & McCoy, 2013). For example, although studies (e.g., Stewart, 2008, 2009) indicate that Black collegians perceive themselves as multifaceted, opting to choose multiple salient identities to reflect their self-concept as opposed to one, some students express the need to negotiate and choose aspects of their identities, depending on whether the environmental climate is deemed supportive (Stewart, 2008). Conversely, through multiple case studies, Winkle-Wagner and McCoy (2013) found that Black first-generation students typically discuss their identities as intersecting, unable to disentangle their race, income, gender, and first-generation status when reflecting on their college experience and graduate school aspirations.

Ultimately, scholarship on intersectionality has predominantly focused on People of Color, in particular women, since they overlap multiple sites of oppression, yet the framework can be more critically examined by studying people with other minoritized identities. Since the purpose of intersectionality, as argued by Strayhorn (2013), is to examine the experiences of people who are situated within multiple social dimensions (i.e., race, gender, income status) as a means to understand the influence of oppression and privilege on social inequalities, such as access to higher education, aspirations while in the college context, and post-college outcomes, the theoretical perspective can be used as a guide to understanding first-generation collegians. With first-generation students being categorized as a student population with generalized experiences yet cutting across various racial/ethnic and socioeconomic backgrounds, an intersectional approach allows for an understanding of how people may have common identities yet also have distinctive and unique differences, avoiding the insinuation that the experiences of a collective group are the same (Crenshaw, 1991; Winkle-Wagner & McCoy, 2013) and instead highlight the unique lived experiences of students.

Incorporating an intersectional approach in relation to first-generation students can assist in providing avenues for them to participate in self-reflection, understand their first-generation status in relation to and independent of their group association, give them the opportunity to validate their other multiple identities (privileged and oppressed), and create their own self-definition based on the impact of their relationships and experiences in the college context. In doing so, higher education administrators can more accurately understand how students navigate their postsecondary environment, assist in their holistic development throughout the college years, and reap the benefits associated with identity formation, such as intercultural maturity (King & Baxter Magolda, 2005) and student learning (King & Baxter Magolda, 1996), as well as those related to curricular and co-curricular engagement (Astin, 1975, 1993; Pascarella & Terenzini, 2005; Tinto, 1993, 2000, 2005).

Student Engagement Strategies

The aforementioned research on first-generation students has informed administrators to create prevalent and impactful strategies to engage the student population based on their common identities. In this section, I suggest approaches for institutional stakeholders to develop the whole first-generation student and embrace their heterogeneity by utilizing an intersectional approach to engage them in thoughtful identity development.

Define First-Generation Student

As previously addressed, the definition of a first-generation student varies across and within institutions (Whitley et al., 2018). Some institutions may choose to adopt the required definition needed to align with funded programs (e.g., students whose parents have not obtained a degree from a postsecondary institution) (Ward et al., 2012), while offices on campus may elect varying definitions based on their specific missions. It is important that institutional leaders focus on a first-generation definition that is specific to the students on their campus and not simply because it aligns with that found in research. An initial step is to determine how first-generation students are defined across each office on campus and the reason behind the definition. By doing so, campus stakeholders can better understand any inconsistencies and the messaging being sent to prospective and current students.

University leaders can also take the pulse of their collegians by surveying them to indicate what they view the definition of a first-generation student to be and their corresponding thoughts, if they identify with the term, and whether they identify as being a first-generation student based on a different variation of the definition. Any negative connotations can then be determined. Specifically, practitioners should be mindful of whether there is a stigma associated with being a first-generation college-goer on a particular campus that would lead students to not associate with the term to the extent that they felt uncomfortable accessing resources geared toward them. Conversely, it is important to consider whether a prescribed definition excludes first-generation students. For example, higher education institutions that utilize a first-generation, low-income stance may inadvertently exclude students who are the first in their families to attend college but identify with another income bracket and believe the resources are only available for those students who are both first-generation and low-income.

The intent behind the first-generation, low-income example is positive since it attempts to recognize the multidimensionality of first-generation students. Other institutions have taken a different approach by utilizing the term "first-gen plus" (Whitley et al., 2018) to appreciate students' multiple identities in addition to being first-generation. However, the approach is an additive one and not necessarily intersectional. To clarify, a "first-gen plus" model indicates that, for example, a student is a first-generation student + a woman + middle-income + Black. An intersectional approach views the same student as a Black first-generation woman who is middle-income. The difference between the approaches is that the former examines the student in compartmentalized ways, whereas the latter views both the intersection and intrasection of identities. Higher education institutions can utilize a more intersectional approach to the first-generation label or definition by recognizing students' multiple layers of identity, including both social identities or membership categories with which people associate and personal identities, including behaviors and characteristics that are connected with identity categories (Deaux, 1993). Having a more clearly defined first-generation student definition and utilizing an intersectional approach can assist university leaders in determining the number of first-generation students on campus, who they are, their strengths and needs, and how funding can be allocated to create resources that assist in their engagement at the institution.

Assess Institutional Resources

While it may be a daunting undertaking, especially depending on the institution type and size, higher education leaders can review how each campus office is working with first-generation students (Keeling, 2006; Ward et al., 2012; Whitley et al., 2018). Whether or not a college or university has a center specifically for the first-generation student population, engaging first-generation college-goers may be done in silos across campus. Create a committee of dedicated people who are passionate and energetic about first-generation students and are perhaps voluntarily willing to incorporate this task in their everyday work, especially if the campus does not have the resources to designate specific people for this endeavor. The committee can be tasked with surveying not just campus resource centers, which are typically geared toward first-generation learners, but all academic and non-academic offices students utilize. Through an in-depth list of how offices collaborate with first-generation learners, either through one-on-one advising, group workshops, or events, the committee can determine where there may be overlap and how offices can collaborate to maximize time, effort, and impact. By joining forces with multiple offices, resources can be better advertised and made more visible. Providing this list to all campus partners and not simply creating an internal document for the committee to utilize can be beneficial, especially because practitioners are typically liaisons between students and the campus at large. Specifically, first-generation students may prefer to speak directly with certain administrators and/or faculty members, and if these people are cognizant of all campus resources, they can discuss and direct students to them.

An audit of resources can also ascertain if identity development and exploration are direct learning outcomes in the engagement practices for first-generation college-goers on campus or simply a happenstance result of educational activities. Knowing whether you and your institutional colleagues are strategically incorporating experiences for students to continuously develop their self-definition may seem like an ambiguous endeavor and cause them to question what exactly constitutes identity intersectionality programming. To provide some clarity, two suggestions should be considered. Foremost, institutional stakeholders can determine what it means to promote identity development on their specific campus, especially as it relates to the institution's mission, vision, and values. For example, if developing students to be contributing citizens is weaved within the fabric of the institution, find ways for students to reflect on what community means to them and who they are as members of their hometown communities, as well as their new institutional community.

With the many resources available on campuses, another initial step in this process is to assess already-established institutional programs for first-generation learners specifically, and all students in general, utilizing a combination of both Chickering and Reisser's (1993) vectors of development and the main tenets of identity intersectionality. Identity intersectionality programming can be ascertained as an activity or experience that allows a student to critically think about themselves in relation to others; the saliency of their identities; the forces that impact how they define themselves; and how their self-concept impacts their learning, objectives, and goals, both presently and in the future. More specific examples are incorporated throughout the forthcoming recommendations.

Incorporate Identity Intersectionality in Established Resources

Since program assessment and/or creation is time intensive, especially considering the competing demands, resources, and finances within higher education institutional contexts, incorporate the following identity intersectionality ideas within preexisting resources on campus. Summer bridge programs and living-learning communities are examples of those geared primarily toward first-generation learners and are direct avenues to facilitating engagement. With first-generation college-goers commonly addressing concerns related to social adjustment on campus (see Arzy et al., 2006; Barry et al., 2009; Phinney & Haas, 2003), the programs are effective in creating a sense of community (Suzuki et al., 2012). To maximize impact and foster a sense of belonging that situates first-generation students as part of the institution and not a student population on the margins, especially given the effects of marginality on student learning and retention within higher education (Schlossberg, 1989), summer bridge programs and living-learning communities can incorporate reflective practices, invite speakers such as first-generation graduates to discuss their experiences, and have workshops addressing inclusivity. Since participants are with other first-generation learners, these resources allow for a secure space to reflect on the first-generation identity sans stigma, which can parlay into deeper conversations about identity intersectionality. By creating a community at the start of their educational career and providing information about identities and intersectionality, first-generation students can seek out other, similar opportunities and begin to proactively participate in their own development.

Other co-curricular engagement practices that are geared toward all students can also be considered as avenues for identity development. Faculty- or staff-led conversations about identity during orientation programs introduce first-generation students to the topic and signals that identity development is a valued competency and part of the learning experience at the institution. To further solidify an institutional culture of developing the whole student, administrators can consider creating reorientations for each class year. By forming an online orientation site, for example, at the start of a student's second, third, and fourth years, important information and activities can be addressed (e.g., academic deadlines, internship processes, research opportunities), and suggestions for resources, courses, and events that promote self-reflection and learning about social identities can be incorporated. Given that the transition and adjustment to college for first-generation students tend to be difficult (Pascarella et al., 2004), finding more opportunities to engage students with the university throughout their entire college career may be impactful.

In addition, faculty and administrators can utilize an intersectional lens when considering the accessibility and learning objectives of high-impact education practices (Kuh, 2008). Addressing financial and logistical concerns for first-generation learners who are less likely to participate in co-curricular activities (Pascarella et al., 2004) will allow them to reap the benefits associated with such engagement generally. In addition, participating in and writing blogs about volunteer activities and study-abroad experiences in particular can contribute to diversity and global learning, as well as an understanding of oneself in relation to the worldviews of others.

Higher education institutions can also ensure that identity intersectionality is addressed in spaces that are typically compartmentalized and dedicated to one social dimension. Cultural centers should discuss not only issues related to race/ethnicity and the generalized and nuanced experiences of those who identify with a group, but also the unique identities of each student. Since collegians can seek counsel from each compartmentalized center at their college or university that addresses an aspect of their identity, it is more streamlined when a student can confide in the administrators at the one center at which they feel most comfortable and supported.

Establish Identity Intersectionality Development as a Shared Responsibility

Engaging first-generation students in identity exploration and development is a shared responsibility, and the onus should not solely be on a single department or the offices that are viewed as more student affairs focused. If a first-generation student is on a decentralized campus or is only at the institution for short periods of time due to other commitments, practitioners can find strategic ways to engage them in identity reflection. As a means to do so, institutional leaders can first promote that student-facing practitioners, regardless of their position, be knowledgeable of intersectionality and how to assist students in all aspects of either identity reflection or conflict. Areas of higher education to consider, and for which I provide suggestions, include academic advising, career counseling, and work-study employment environments.

Depending on the academic advising approach at a particular institution, academic advisors can be integral to adjusting first-generation learners to the college context. An active and intrusive advising philosophy has been found to be particularly impactful in regards to retention of underserved student populations since advisors meet with students at multiple points throughout the year, track their progress, and focus on the whole student (Muraskin, 1997; Engle & Tinto, 2008). In addition to providing information on campus resources, academic advisors, whether assigned at the division, department, or faculty level, can supplement their student meetings by suggesting academic courses that allow for an exploration of social identities generally (e.g., a gender studies course) or are geared toward their own culture or heritage (e.g., supporting a student interested in learning a language from their family's country of origin). If the general requirements at one's institution include a broad liberal arts education, a variety of course options may be available to recommend. If the ratio of students to academic advisors is a concern in having such conversations, advisors can still propose these targeted course options to all their students through electronic communication and/or a newsletter.

In addition, offices specific to career services can be paramount in assisting first-generation students, who are more likely to have a difficult time choosing an academic field of interest and believe their career options are limited due to their level of academic preparation (Chen & Carroll, 2005) or are influenced by familial ties and perceptions (Tate et al., 2015). Career counselors can include identity reflection in their conversations regarding career exploration, as well as bolstering their lacking professional network to understand the career development process (Tate et al., 2015). By understanding how a student views their identities, career counselors can better coach first-generation college-goers in their professional identity; process any stereotypes that they may have as they pertain to career choices; and provide teachings on gender role attitudes, work-life balance, and salary negotiation, to name a few.

Furthermore, work-study environments may be an underutilized experience, especially considering that first-generation students are more likely to be employed while in college, as well as persist if they acquire a work-study position (Lohfink & Paulsen, 2005). Work-study supervisors can dedicate time within students' work schedules to discussing their experiences at the institution; the ways in which the work-study position relates to their short- and long-term goals; and how the supervisor can be a supportive resource, especially in terms of goal achievement and transferable skills. The work-study experience can be utilized as a learning model for the professional world, allowing supervisors to engage in dialogues with students regarding any preconceived notions they may have about experiences in their future career, as well as managing relationships, emotions, and potential conflicts in the workplace.

Encourage Faculty to Incorporate Identity Intersectionality Into the Curriculum

Given that the focus of attending a higher education institution is to complete the academic requirements needed to graduate, and one would assume that first-generation students attend courses to reach this goal, collaborating with faculty members is the most straightforward way to engage first-generation students in identity reflection, regardless of the institution type. With first-generation learners typically being apprehensive to communicate with faculty (Collier & Morgan, 2008), it is important to encourage faculty partnerships, not just with those who identify as being a first-generation student themselves (Whitley et al., 2018). To create a classroom community and engaging learning environment, academic departments can collaborate with student affairs administrators (Kuh, 2011) who can provide information on the experiences of first-generation students and identity theories, as well as a knowledge base for identity intersectionality. In addition, faculty members can utilize teaching and/or learning resource centers on campus to assist in aspects of pedagogy and suggestions for intertwining identity intersectionality with their curriculum, even if for a brief portion of the course. Providing readings on identity theories and diversity issues, as well as understanding privilege and oppression, within- and between-group differences, and identity intersectionality educates students on the topics. Assigning group projects, papers, in-class exercises that allow students to get to know each other's stories and perspectives on who they are, or informal journal-writing activities in these areas allows students meaningful personal and group reflection, as well as the opportunity to critically examine their beliefs and understand themselves in relation to and independent of others. Collegians should not only be engaged in such reflection with their peers, but faculty members should also take these opportunities to discuss their own personal identities as a means to relate to students, showcase the importance of these conversations, and substantiate identity development as not simply a required exercise but a learning objective in the curriculum. While all faculty should be involved in incorporating identity intersectionality in their courses, academic department heads can choose one required course in a major with which to establish this strategy, the intention being that it will be used as a model for other faculty members.

Create Programs With First-Generation Students

First-generation students need more spaces for their identities to be directly discussed and processed throughout their college experience since identity development is an evolving process (Torres, 2011). Instead of creating programs for first-generation students, create programs with them. If a first-generation student group or center exists on campus, engage them in discussions. If not, ask educators at the institution to refer first-generation students who would be interested in getting involved. Higher education faculty and administrators can also normalize the concept of directly asking first-generation college-goers what types of support would be most beneficial to them as they progress in college not only as students, but also as holistic people. Academic advisors and faculty can ask this question during their first correspondence with first-generation students as a means to initiate conversations and find ways to promote academic, co-curricular, and identity engagement.

Conclusion

Although higher education institutions purport an appreciation for diversity within their campuses, especially as the student population is becoming more diverse, first-generation students are typically seen as a homogenous population. The concerns and issues surrounding first-generation students commonly cited in research and across campuses are real, and considerable attention should be given to the many engagement strategies that can be employed to positively impact their experiences and completion rates. First-generation college-goers are also complex people, and educators can improve their experiences by not only recognizing students' multiple identities, but also acknowledging how their identities intrasect and intersect. By engaging first-generation students in identity exploration and development, students can unpack who they are and understand how their identities influence and are influenced by their collegiate experiences. The strategies suggested in this chapter are meant to remind higher education administrators that first-generation students are unique people, and incorporating an intersectional approach in engagement strategies can be impactful in holistically developing students as they traverse the college context and prepare for lives of meaning.

References

Abes, E. S., & Jones, S. R. (2004). Meaning-making capacity and the dynamics of lesbian college students' multiple dimensions of identity. *Journal of College Student Development*, 45(6), 612–632.

Abes, E. S., Jones, S. R. & McEwen, M. K. (2007). Reconceptualizing the model of multiple dimensions of identity: The roles of meaning-making capacity in the construction of multiple identities. *Journal of College Student Development*, 48(1), 1–22.

Ackerman, S. P. (1991). The benefits of summer bridge programs for underrepresented and low-income students. *College & University*, 66(4), 201–208.

Arzy, M. R., Davies, T. G., & Harbour, C. P. (2006). Low income students: Their lived university campus experiences pursuing baccalaureate degrees with private foundation scholarship assistance. *College Student Journal*, 40(4), 750–766.

Astin, A. W. (1975). *Preventing students from dropping out*. San Francisco, CA: Jossey-Bass.

Astin, A. W. (1993). *What matters in college? Four critical years revisited*. San Francisco, CA: Jossey-Bass.

Barry, L. M., Hudley, C., Kelly, M., & Cho, S. J. (2009). Differences in self-reported disclosure of college experiences by first-generation college student status. *Adolescence, 44*(173), 55–68.

Baum, S., Ma, J., & Payea, K. (2013). *Education pays 2013: The benefits of higher education for individuals and society*. New York, NY: College Board Advocacy & Policy Center.

Bettinger, E., & Baker, R. (2011). *The effects of student coaching in college: An evaluation of a randomized experiment in student mentoring*. National Bureau of Economic Research (No. w16881). www.nber.org/papers/w16881.pdf

Bruce, M., & Bridgeland, J. (2012). *2012 national survey of school counselors. True North: Charting the course to college and career readiness*. New York, NY: College Board Advocacy & Policy Center. Retrieved from https://secure-media.collegeboard.org/digitalServices/pdf/nosca/true-north.pdf

Brunn-Bevel, R. J., Joy Davis, D., & Olive, J. L. (2015). *Intersectionality in educational research*. Sterling, VA: Stylus Publishing.

Bui, K. V. T. (2002). First-generation college students at a four-year university: Background characteristics, reasons for pursuing higher education, and first-year experiences. *College Student Journal, 36*(1), 3–11.

Cataldi, E. F., Bennett, C. T., & Chen, X. (2018). First-generation students: College access, persistence, and post bachelor's outcomes. *Stats in Brief* (NCES 2018–421). Washington, DC: National Center for Education Statistics. Retrieved from https://nces.ed.gov/pubs2018/2018421.pdf

Chen, X., & Carroll, C. D. (2005). *First-generation students in postsecondary education: A look at their college transcripts*. Washington, DC: US Department of Education, National Center for Education Statistics. Retrieved from http://nces.ed.gov/pubs2005/2005171.pdf

Chickering, A. W. (1969). *Education and identity*. San Francisco, CA: Jossey-Bass.

Chickering, A. W., & Reisser, L. (1993). *Education and identity* (2nd ed.). San Francisco, CA: Jossey-Bass.

Choy, S. P. (2001). *Students whose parents did not go to college: Postsecondary access, persistence, and attainment* (NCES 2001–126). Washington, DC: US Department of Education, National Center for Education Statistics. Retrieved from http://nces.ed.gov/pubs2001/2001126.pdf

Collier, P. J., & Morgan, D. L. (2008). "Is that paper really due today?": Differences in first-generation and traditional college students' understandings of faculty expectations. *Higher Education, 55*, 425–446.

Collins, P. H. (2000). *Black feminist thought: Knowledge, consciousness, and the politics of empowerment* (2nd ed.). New York, NY: Routledge.

Covarrubias, R., & Fryberg, S. A. (2015). Movin' on up (to college): First-generation college students' experiences with family achievement guilt. *Cultural Diversity and Ethnic Minority Psychology, 21*(3), 420–429.

Crenshaw, K. (1991). Mapping the margins: Intersectionality, identity politics, and violence against women of color. *Stanford Law Review, 43*(6), 1241–1299.

Cross, W. E., Jr. (1991). *Shades of Black: Diversity in African American identity*. Philadelphia: Temple University Press.

Deaux, K. (1993). Reconstructing social identity. *Personality and Social Psychological Bulletin, 19*, 4–12.

Dill, B. T., & Zambrana, R. E. (Eds.). (2009). *Emerging intersections: Race, class, and gender in theory, policy, and practice*. New Brunswick, NJ: Rutgers University Press.

Engle, J., & Tinto, V. (2008). *Moving beyond access: College success for low-income, first-generation students*. Washington, DC: The Pell Institute.

Erikson, E. H. (1980). *Identity and the life cycle*. New York, NY: W. W. Norton.

Erikson, E. H. (1994). *Identity and the life cycle*. New York, NY: W. W. Norton. (Original work published 1959).

Evans, N. J. (2011). Psychosocial and cognitive-structural perspectives on student development. In J. H. Schuh, S. R. Jones, S. R. Harper, & Associates (Eds.), *Student services: A handbook for the profession* (pp. 168–186). San Francisco, CA: Jossey-Bass.

Evans, N. J., Forney, D. S., Guido, F. M., Patton, L. D., & Renn, K. A. (2010). *Student development in college: Theory, research, and practice* (2nd ed.). San Francisco, CA: Jossey-Bass.

Ferdman, B. M., & Gallegos, P. I. (2001). Racial identity development and Latinos in the United States. In C. L. Wijeyesinghe & B. W. Jackson III (Eds.), *New perspectives on racial identity development: A theoretical and practical anthology* (pp. 32–66). New York, NY: New York University Press.

Freeman, C. E. (2004). *Trends in educational equity of girls & women: 2004*. Washington, DC: US Department of Education, National Center for Education Statistics.

Gofen, A. (2009). Family capital: How first-generation higher education students break the intergenerational cycle. *Family Relations, 58*, 104–120.

Harper, S. R., Wardell, C. C., & McGuire, K. M. (2011). Man of multiple identities: Complex individuality and identity intersectionality among college men. In J. A. Laker & T. Davis (Eds.), *Masculinities in higher education: Theoretical and practical considerations* (pp. 81–96). New York, NY: Routledge.

Helms, J. E. (1990). *Black and White racial identity theory, research, and practice*. Westport, CT: Praeger.

Horn, L. J., Chen, X., & Chapman, C. (2003). *Getting ready to pay for college. What students and their parents know about the cost of college tuition and what they are doing to find out*. Washington, DC: US Department of Education, National Center for Education Statistics.

Inkelas, K. K., Daver, Z. E., Vogt, K. E., & Leonard, J. B. (2007). Living-learning programs and first-generation college students' academic and social transition to college. *Research in Higher Education, 48*(4), 403–434.

Jones, S. R. (2009). Constructing identities at the intersections: An autoethnographic exploration of multiple dimensions of identity. *Journal of College Student Development, 50*, 267–304.

Jones, S. R., & McEwen, S. R. (2000). A conceptual model of multiple dimensions of identity. *Journal of College Student Development, 41*(4), 405–414.

Josselson, R. (1987). *Finding herself: Pathways to identity development in women*. San Francisco, CA: Jossey-Bass.

Josselson, R. (1996). *Revising herself: The story of women's identity from college to midlife*. New York, NY: Oxford University Press.

Keeling, R. (2006). *Learning reconsidered 2: A practical guide to implementing a campus-wide focus on the student experience*. Washington, DC: American College Personnel Association & National Association of Student Personnel Administrators.

Kim, J. (2001). Asian American identity development theory. In C. L. Wijeyesinghe & B. W. Jackson III (Eds.), *New perspectives on racial identity development: A theoretical and practical anthology* (pp. 67–90). New York, NY: New York University Press.

King, N, P., & Baxter Magolda, M. B. (2005). A developmental model of intercultural maturity. *Journal of College Student Development, 46*(6), 571–592.

King, P. M., & Baxter Magolda, M. B. (1996). A developmental perspective on learning. *Journal of College Student Development, 37*(2), 163–173.

Kroger, J. (2004). *Identity and adolescence: The balance between self and other* (3rd ed.). London: Routledge.

Kuh, G. D. (2008). *High-impact educational practices. What they are, who has access to them, and why they matter*. Washington, DC: Association of American Colleges and Universities.

Kuh, G. D. (2011). Student success. In J. H. Schuh, S. R. Jones, S. R. Harper, & Associates (Eds.), *Student services: A handbook for the profession* (pp. 168–186). San Francisco, CA: Jossey-Bass.

Lohfink, M. M., & Paulsen, M. B. (2005). Comparing the determinants of persistence for first-generation and continuing generation students. *Journal of College Student Development, 46*(4), 409–428.

Moran, C. (2003). Nourishing and thwarting effects of contextual influences upon multiple dimensions of identity: Does gender matter? *NASPA Journal, 40*, 113–131.

Muraskin, L. (1997). *"Best practices" in Student Support Services: A study of five exemplary sites*. Washington, DC: US Department of Education.

Orbe, M. P. (2004). Negotiating multiple identities within multiple frames: An analysis of first-generation college students. *Communication Education, 53*(2), 131–149.

Pascarella, E. T., Pierson, C. T., Wolniak, G. C., & Terenzini, P. T. (2004). First-generation college students: Additional evidence on college experiences and outcomes. *The Journal of Higher Education, 75*(3), 249–284.

Pascarella, E. T., & Terenzini, P. T. (2005). *How college affects students: Volume II, A third decade of research.* San Francisco, CA: Jossey-Bass.

Perna, L. W. (2000). Differences in the decision to attend college among African Americans, Hispanics, and Whites. *The Journal of Higher Education, 71*(2), 117–141.

Perna, L. W., & Kurban, E. R. (2013). Improving college access and choice. In L. W. Perna & A. P. Jones (Eds.), *The state of college access and completion* (pp. 10–33). New York, NY: Routledge.

Phinney, J. S., & Haas, K. (2003). The process of coping among ethnic minority first-generation college freshmen: A narrative approach. *The Journal of Social Psychology, 143*(6), 707–726.

Radwin, D., Wine, J., Siegel, P., & Bryan, M. (2013). *2011–2012 National postsecondary student aid study (NPSAS:12): Student financial aid estimates for 2011–12.* Washington, DC: US Department of Education, National Center for Education Statistics.

Ramos-Sanchez, L., & Nichols, L. (2007). Self-efficacy of first-generation and non-first generation college students: The relationship with academic performance and college adjustment. *Journal of College Counseling, 10,* 6–18.

Reynolds, A. L., & Pope, R. L. (1991). The complexities of diversity: Exploring multiple oppressions. *Journal of Counseling & Development, 70*(1), 174–180.

Saenz, V. B., Hurtado, S., Barrera, D., Wolf, D., & Yeung, F. (2007). *First in my family: A profile of first-generation college students at four-year institutions since 1971.* Los Angeles: Higher Education Research Institute. Retrieved from www.heri.ucla.edu/PDFs/pubs/TFS/Special/Monographs/FirstIn-MyFamily.pdf

Schlossberg, N. K. (1989). Mattering and marginality: Key issues in building community. In D. C. Roberts (Ed.), *Designing campus activities to foster a sense of community* (New directions for student services, No. 48, pp. 5–15). San Francisco, CA: Jossey-Bass.

Skomsvold, P. (2015). *Web tables-profiles of undergraduate students. 2011–12.* US Department of Education. Washington, DC: National Center for Education Statistics. Retrieved from https://nces.ed.gov/pubs2015/2015167.pdf

Snyder, T. D., & Dillow, S. A. (2015). *Digest of education statistics 2013.* Washington, DC: US Department of Education. Washington, DC: National Center for Education Statistics.

Stewart, D. L. (2008). Being all of me: Black students negotiating multiple identities. *The Journal of Higher Education, 79*(2), 183–207.

Stewart, D. L. (2009). Perceptions of multiple identities among Black college students. *Journal of College Student Development, 50*(3), 253–270.

Strayhorn, T. L. (2013). Introduction. In T. L. Strayhorn (Ed.), *Living at the intersections: Social identities and Black collegians* (pp. 1–20). Charlotte, NC: Information Age Publishing Inc.

Suzuki, A., Amrein-Beardsley, A., & Perry, N. J. (2012). A summer bridge program for underprepared first-year students: Confidence, community, and re-enrollment. *Journal of the First-Year Experience & Students in Transition, 24*(2), 85–106.

Tate, K. A., Caperton, W., Kaiser, D., Pruitt, N. T., White, H. & Hall, E. (2015). An exploration of first-generation college students' career development beliefs and experiences. *Journal of Career Development, 42*(2), 294–310.

Tinto, V. (1993). *Leaving college: Rethinking the causes and cures of student attrition* (2nd ed.). Chicago, IL: University of Chicago Press.

Tinto, V. (2000). Taking retention seriously: Rethinking the first year of college. *NACADA Journal, 19*(2), 5–10.

Tinto, V. (2005). Moving from theory to action. In A. Seidman (Ed.), *College Student retention: Formula for student success* (pp. 371–333). Washington, DC: American Council on Education and Praeger.

Torres, V. (2011). Perspectives on identity development. In J. H. Schuh, S. R. Jones, S. R. Harper, & Associates (Eds.), *Student services: A handbook for the profession* (pp. 187–206). San Francisco, CA: Jossey-Bass.

Walpole, M., Simmerman, H., Mack, C., Mills, J. T., Scales, M., & Albano, D. (2008). Bridge to success: Insight into summer bridge program students' college transition. *Journal of the First-Year Experience & Students in Transition, 20*(1), 11–30.

Warburton, E. C., Bugarin, R., & Nuñez, A. (2001). *Bridging the gap: Academic preparation and postsecondary success of first-generation students.* Washington, DC: US Department of Education, National Center for Education Statistics.

Ward, L., Siegel, M. J., & Davenport, Z. (2012). *First-generation college students: Understanding and improving the experience from recruitment to commencement.* San Francisco, CA: Jossey-Bass.

Wathington, H. D., Barnett, E. A., Weissman, E., Teres, J., Pretlow, J., & Nakanishi, A. (2011). Getting ready for college: An implementation and early impacts study of eight Texas developmental summer bridge programs. *National Center for Postsecondary Research.* Retrieved from http://www.postsecondaryresearch.org/pdf/DSBReport.pdf

Whitley, S. E., Benson, G. & Wesaw, A. (2018). *First-generation student success: A landscape analysis of programs and services at four-year institutions.* Center for First-Generation Student Success: NASPA-Student Affairs Administrators in Higher Education. Retrieved from http://cmmedia.hs.llnwd.net/v1/naspa_firstgen/dmfile/NASPA-First-generation-Student-Success-FULL-REPORT.pdf

Wildhagen, T. (2015). "Not your typical student": The social construction of the "first-generation" college student. *Qualitative Sociology, 38*(3), 285–303.

Winkle-Wagner, R., & McCoy, D. L. (2013). Many into one: Using intersectional perspectives to understand Black first-generation college student identities. In T. L. Strayhorn (Ed.), *Living at the intersections: Social identities and Black collegians* (pp. 41–60). Charlotte, NC: Information Age Publishing Inc.

Zumeta, W., Breneman, D. W., Callan, P. M., & Finney, J. E. (2012). *Financing American higher education in the era of globalization.* Cambridge, MA: Harvard University Press.

Chapter 18
Engaging Poor and Working-Class Students

Sonja Ardoin

Broadly understood, student engagement describes if, and how, students holistically interact with their educational environment—academically, through the co-curricular, and socially. These interactions suggest a relationship between parties (e.g., students and institutions) and hint that individual-, group-, and system-level dynamics are associated with student engagement. Focusing on these multiple dynamics, student engagement is often framed through the National Survey of Student Engagement (NSSE) definition of "educational practices that are strongly associated with high levels of learning and personal development" (Kuh, 2001, p. 12), including academic challenge, learning with peers, experiences with faculty, and campus environment (NSSE, 2014). Involvement theory also highlights how students who are engaged on campus typically perform better academically, persist at the institution, and have greater success (Astin, 1984), particularly when engaging in specific types of involvement deemed to be high quality (e.g., academic involvement, involvement with peers, involvement with student peers, involvement in work, Astin, 1993) and over longer durations of time (Museus & Yi, 2015; Soria, Gipson, & Mitchell Jr., 2015). In short, most educators would agree that student engagement generally fosters positive educational outcomes.

However, students' singular and combined identity dimensions can influence their ability to be engaged at colleges and universities because of differential time and physical and psychological energy; inequitable opportunities; and systemic barriers based on race, ethnicity, gender, ability, sexuality, religion, age, and—of particular interest to this chapter—social class. Education, including higher education, is a "harsh version of basic training . . . about class, class conflict, and differing class values," which can foster "class shame and embarrassment" for students from the poor and working classes (Collins, Ladd, Seider, & Yeskel, 2014, p. 56). Further, Barratt (2011) emphasizes how "social class is a powerful and often unrecognized influence on student participation in the extracurriculum" (p. 1).

Social class is left out of many conversations in higher education, being seen as a complex and convoluted "taboo topic" to be avoided (Ardoin, 2019; Ardoin & Martinez, 2019; Liu, 2011; Martin & Elkins, 2018). hooks (2014) emphasized that "nowhere is there more intense silence about the reality of class differences than in educational settings" (p. 144). When a semblance of this identity does appear in higher education literature and conversation, it is routinely relegated to only income or socioeconomic status and not the comprehensive conceptualization of social class identity (Ardoin, 2019; Ardoin & Martinez, 2019; Barratt, 2011; hooks, 2000; Martin & Elkins, 2018). As such, educators and students often have limited awareness, language, and understanding regarding social class as an identity (Martin, Williams, & Young, 2018) and how it influences student engagement.

Liu, Soleck, Hopps, Dunston, and Pickett (2004) invite educators to consider social class as the values, beliefs, customs, norms, language, and expectations tied to one's socioeconomic culture (rather than only income) within a contextual environment, such as higher education, and the complex system of classism (Liu, 2011). Social class provides individuals with access to forms of capital (e.g., economic, cultural, social) that either provide power and privilege, in the case of the middle and upper classes, or do not, in the case of the poor and working classes (Bourdieu, 1984). For example, *cultural capital*, or knowledge, skills, and tastes, can include one's experience with things such as books, travel, museums, and foods, while *social capital* describes the networks of individuals to whom one has access, such as business leaders, health care professionals, educators, farmers, military members, or tradespeople. Social class is often cyclical and intergenerational (Chetty, Hendren, Lin, Majerovitz, & Scuderi, 2016; Strunk, Locke, & Martin, 2017). While social class is one of the less visible and more fluid forms of identity (Liu, 2011), children as young as six are able to discern different social classes based on cues such as materials and goods (Ramsey, 1991). So, while people may refrain from or be uncomfortable with talking about social class, it is recognizable and ever present in both daily life and higher education, sometimes in the form of classism. Classism is defined by Liu (2011) as "a behavior acted on others, an experience of discrimination to the self, and an internalized dissonance that occurs when individual[s] perceive [themselves] to be out of accord with others" based on social class identity; he contends that classism occurs across social class elements, "not just income," and across the lifespan, happening "because a child does not have the right kinds of shoes, an adolescent has to go to a public swimming pool instead of a private pool, or an adult may not live in the right neighborhood" (p. 179).

Higher Education's Historical and Present-Day Elitism

Higher education in the US was and is set up not only with financial barriers but also with social, cultural, and linguistic barriers (among others) that perpetuate systemic classism and favor middle and affluent classes from access and admission to engagement and completion. While some might subscribe to the mantra that education is an equalizer, and it can be at times, it is clear that higher education often amplifies the power and privilege of the elite.

Higher Education's Historical Elitism

Educational processes in the US have always been class based (Ardoin, 2019; Hurst, 2012), and higher education is no exception. From its beginnings at Harvard in 1636, US higher education has been rooted in class inequity (Ardoin, 2018b, 2019). Colleges and universities were created as an acculturation process "shaped by aristocratic traditions" to ensure white, straight, Christian elite men became both scholars and gentlemen (Rudolph, 1990, p. 7). Thus, poor and working-class populations were deterred, and sometimes barred, from pursuing higher education because of financial and labor costs, geography, and the inattention to practical learning (Ardoin, 2019). Essentially, the US higher education system generated more opportunities (e.g., knowledge, connections, and cultural experiences) for those who already had racial, gender, religious, and class-based privileges.

It was not until the Morrill Acts of 1862 and 1890 and the opening of Joliet Junior College in 1901 that this focus would start to shift, simultaneously allowing higher education to be more widely accessible, while also expecting all who attended to assimilate to "aristocratic values" (Rudolph, 1990 p. 465), and cementing class stratification among institutional types (Serna & Woulfe, 2017; Stich, 2012; Thelin, 2011). Yet, the "massification of higher education" would not truly begin until the Servicemen's Readjustment Act of 1964, the Civil Rights Act of 1965, and the Higher Education Act of 1965 all became law (Stich, 2012, pp. 5–7).

Higher Education's Present-Day Social Class Barriers and Buoys

The historical elitism rooted in class bias and classist customs is still present today, although it is often less overt (Locke & Trolian, 2018). Students from poor and working-class backgrounds remain underrepresented in every aspect of higher education, from access to engagement to completion, particularly at four-year institutions and elite institutions (Soria, 2015a). Some completely forgo higher education due to both perceived and realistic economic factors (Serna & Woulfe, 2017; Soria, Stebleton, & Huseman, 2013), while those who do enroll typically attend community colleges, less selective four-year universities, or for-profit institutions and focus their studies on practical and professional majors that directly link to jobs or career pathways (Ardoin, 2019; Poutré, Rorison, & Voight, 2017; Martin, 2015b). Despite making enrollment decisions that defray costs, many students from poor and working classes face daunting challenges to afford the "indirect costs" of higher education, which account for approximately 60% of the total cost of attendance (Lumina, 2018, p. 2). These costs include, but are not limited to, basic needs (e.g., food and housing security); books, course materials, and technology required for academic study; and child or elder care. Subsequently, more than "58 percent of today's students work while enrolled in school to manage costs, with about 40 percent of community college students and 20 percent of bachelor's degree students working more than 20 hours per week" (Lumina, 2018, p. 1).

Stich and Freie (2016) also note how "the working-classes arguably remain devalued and pathologized within our contemporary [higher education] context" (p. 9). Students with poor and working-class backgrounds encounter stereotypes, stigmatization, micro-aggressions, shame, and pressure to behave—or perform social class—in certain ways (Buckley & Park, 2019; Garrison & Liu, 2018; hooks, 2000; Housel & Harvey, 2009; Locke & Trolian, 2018; Soria, 2015b; Yee, 2016). These barriers are created by faculty members, administrators, and peers who have both assumptions about and lower expectations for this student population (Soria & Bultmann, 2014; Soria, 2015b). Accordingly, some students from poor and working-class backgrounds attempt to hide their social class by carefully selecting how they speak and dress so that it is less detected (Ardoin, 2019; Martin, 2015a; Soria & Bultmann, 2014; Soria, 2015b). Additionally, students from poor and working-class backgrounds frequently face financial and time resource constraints and sense of belonging challenges that hamper their ability to fully engage in their educational experience, including, but not limited to, study groups and tutoring, course materials and technology, co-curricular activities, and social opportunities (Buckley & Park, 2019; Locke & Trolian, 2018; Walpole, 2003). Students may also be unaware that campus resources (e.g., health centers, counseling centers) are included in their tuition and fees or believe that seeking assistance from such services is a sign of being ill equipped (Ardoin, 2019). Collectively, these challenges result in a completion gap; only 11% of students living below the poverty line graduate within six years of enrollment (Lumina, n.d.). Moreover, 77% of students from high-income backgrounds have a bachelor's degree by age 24, compared to only 9% of students from poor and working-class backgrounds (Lumina, 2016).

Despite these barriers, there are proven practices that educators can use to buoy engagement for students from poor and working-class backgrounds. Studying working-class students' engagement with high-impact practices (Kuh, 2008) at four-year research universities, Soria (2015a) found that "participation in common book-reading programs, enrollment in writing intensive courses and courses related to diversity or global learning; and participation in internships, study abroad, and undergraduate research" were all positively related to academic achievement (p. 51). It is also known that co-curricular involvement strengthens students' sense of belonging and retention at an institution, yet Martin (2015b) discovered how students from poor and working-class backgrounds were less engaged in student organizations and campus activities due to work and family obligations. The challenge is that some of these engagement practices come at high economic and time costs that may impede interest and involvement for students from poor or working-class backgrounds. Therefore, even though educators may know how to bolster student engagement for those from poor and working-class backgrounds, the structures and policies may not be in place to support engagement in those practices. Knowing that social class shows up in persistent and pervasive ways in higher education and that students from poor and working-class backgrounds account for at least 33% of the student population (Lumina, 2018), the "unwillingness to name social class as an identity, with both privileged and minoritized members, does a disserve to students and further entrenches the inequitable campus environments that many [educators] strive to disrupt" (Martin et al., 2018, p. 16).

It is also essential to recognize that social class identity is not experienced uniformly or in isolation. Social class is layered with one's race, ethnicity, gender, sexuality, ability, religion, and age and will be experienced differently based on the unique combination of identities one holds. Buckley and Park (2019) highlight how "a focus on class must also be mindful of the diversity of individuals within different social classes and wary of approaches to mitigate classism that avoid attention to race, sex, and other aspects of identity" (p. 274). For example, scholars have found that White students across social class were often unaware of social class differences or eluded social class conversations in an effort to not call attention to any disadvantage they or others might experience (Buckley & Park, 2019; Martin, 2015a), while Students of Color, particularly women, experienced shame or guilt in relation to their social class (Buckley & Park, 2019; hooks, 1989). This speaks to how students who hold multiple marginalized identities may more readily recognize social class inequities but may also feel pressure to overlook those inequities to pretend their campuses are social class homogenous (Buckley & Park, 2019).

Additionally, there can be conflation between race and class, where individuals of certain races—primarily People of Color—are assumed to belong to a particular social class. Buckley and Park (2019) point out how "Students of Color, therefore, had added burdens of psychologically negotiating microaggressions of class, no matter their class status" and experience the "compounding nature of microaggressions that may further burden minoritized students across class lines" (p. 285). As such, educators should not pretend social class is a race-neutral concept or pay attention solely to class—often in lieu of race—because that can isolate identities in ways that negate students' lived experiences on campuses.

Theoretical Frameworks

To better comprehend both social class as a form of identity and how it influences students' ability to engage in higher education, educators can utilize three frameworks that offer insights into why social class shapes one's worldview, how colleges and universities replicate social stratification and classism, and what institutions can do to create more culturally engaged environments.

Liu et al. (2004) and Liu (2011) Social Class Worldview Model

From counseling psychology, the Social Class Worldview Model, in both its original and revised versions (Liu et al., 2004; Liu, 2011), provides a lens through which individuals can "make sense of their social class perspectives, feelings, economic environments, and cultures" through both internal and external dimensions (Liu et al., 2004, p. 103), explore classism, and reflect on the amount of privilege or oppression derived from their social class identity. Liu's (2011) Social Class Worldview Model-Revised (SCWM-R) frames one's social class worldview—or lens—as an interactive process between an individual, their environment, and their relationships with others in that environment. This interactive process of SCWM-R begins with the economic culture of the environment, such as a college or university. This economic culture impresses expectations and demands upon those within it to abide by particular social class capitals, which Liu (2011) consolidates into human, social, and cultural capitals. In higher education, the expectations reflect the middle- and upper-class forms of capital. These capitals are filtered into two forces that help shape individuals' worldview: 1) socialization messages, which are the "implicit and explicit communications" and cross-class interactions that create our social class "script" (Liu, 2011, p. 83) and 2) social class and classism consciousness, which is the "level of awareness people [have] around their own social class experiences" (Liu, 2011, p. 87).

These messages and consciousness influence one's level of materialism, behaviors, and lifestyle considerations (e.g., how one spends their time and resources), which feed into three forms of classism: 1) downward, or against those from perceived lower classes; 2) upward, or against those from perceived higher classes; and 3) lateral, or comparison to those perceived to be in a similar social class. Engaging in any of these three forms of classism can result in a fourth form of classism called internalized classism, which is when someone accepts stereotypes about their social class that influence feelings about oneself (Liu, 2011).

The SCWM-R highlights the importance of context, complexity of individuals' social class identification and understanding, and challenge in cross-class interactions such as colleges and universities. This can be aptly applied to the higher education environment, exploring the explicit and implicit social class expectations; how each student possesses different capitals, messages, levels of consciousness, and ways of being; and the various kinds of classism that influence student engagement.

Bourdieu's (1977, 1986) Social Reproduction Theory

The theory of social reproduction explains how social class materializes over time and context. Bourdieu (1977, 1986) and Bourdieu and Passeron (1990) describes how individuals possess attitudes and dispositions (*habitus*), as well as financial resources (*economic capital*), knowledge, skills, and tastes (*cultural capital*), and networks of individuals (*social capital*), which determine one's status and strategies in a given context (*field*). While there are people who hold education—particularly higher education—as the great equalizer and opportunity to interrupt intergenerational social class dynamics, others believe that colleges and universities are actually "reproducing social advantage instead of serving as engines of mobility" (Leonhardt, 2004, p. A1) and regard "schooling as a primary means for the perpetuation of the dominant class's ideologies, values, and power" (Serna & Woulfe, 2017, p. 1).

While one set of attitudes, dispositions, knowledge, skills, and tastes are not inherently more valuable than another (Yee, 2016), colleges and universities often subscribe to middle- and upper-class ways of being and doing as "ordinary or desirable" (Hurst, 2010, Ostrove, 2003, p. 177; Stuber, 2011), including manifestations of the "right" kinds of cultural and social capital, including, but not limited to participating in particular activities (e.g., visiting museums, attending theater), engaging in leisurely and educational travel, reading specific books, and knowing certain kinds of people (Locke & Trolian, 2018). Having these experiences (i.e., cultural capital) and connections (i.e., social capital) allows middle- and upper-class students to comprehend the rules of engagement, and possessing economic capital provides time and finances to engage (Barratt, 2012; Yee, 2016). As such, higher education furthers "reproduction of the power relationship between classes by systematically excluding working class students who do not fit into the elite middle [and upper] class habitus of higher education" (Soria, 2015a, p. 46). Yee (2016) proposes that educators use Bourdieu's (1977, 1986) theories and concepts "to not only understand why students engage in the ways that they do, but also to understand why their engagement strategies are more or less effective in the university setting" (p. 834); essentially, examining not only individuals' actions but also their interactions with their college or university (i.e., field) as influential on both desire and practices of engagement.

Museus's (2014) Culturally Engaged Campus Environments (CECE) Model

Responding to critiques that existing involvement and engagement theories omit how identity and culture influence students' educational opportunities at colleges and universities, Museus (2014) developed the CECE model to offer an explanation of how external influences and precollege characteristics can shape individual influences and college success outcomes. The model lists nine indicators of culturally engaging campus environments within two frames: cultural relevance and cultural responsiveness. Cultural relevance includes: 1) cultural familiarity, 2) culturally relevant knowledge, 3) cultural community service, 4) meaningful cross-cultural engagement, and 5) culturally validating environments. Cultural responsiveness includes: 6) collectivist cultural orientations, 7) humanized educational environments, 8) proactive philosophies, 9) holistic support (Museus, 2014). While the CECE model is primarily used with and for racially and ethnically underserved populations to lead to "positive experiences for diverse students" (Museus & Yi, 2015, p. 17), it also presents insights that can be utilized for recognizing how to better engage students from poor and working-class backgrounds and advance equity around social class in higher education.

Individually, each of these frameworks provides educators with a lens for exploring individual- and systems-level social class elements that influence student engagement. Even selecting one of these to analyze a campus environment and culture would be beneficial in reducing barriers. When layered together, though, Liu's (2004, 2011) Social Class Worldview Model, Bourdieu's (1977, 1986) Social Reproduction Theory, and Museus's (2014) Culturally Engaged Campus Environments (CECE) Model allow educators to fully examine why students from poor and working-class backgrounds may engage differently or not at all, in what ways campuses may be complicit in hindering engagement and replicating classist systems, and how to reimagine higher education engagement practices and environments to be more social class conscious and inclusive.

Recommendations for Educators and Institutions

There is a need to examine policies, practices, and supports systems across higher education—including both two-year and four-year institutions—to determine how educational systems might be creating social class–based barriers and what can be done to reduce classism and increase support structures and engagement opportunities for students from poor and working-class backgrounds. Using the frameworks offered in this chapter, the following recommendations are offered as examples of how educators might shift approaches to advance student engagement and social class equity on their campuses.

Increase Awareness of and Training on Social Class Identity

Knowing that social class is a less visible and more fluid identity and sometimes one that people avoid discussing, it is key that educators engage in consciousness building and training around this identity dimension. First and foremost, educators should engage in self-exploration around their own social class identity and how it influenced their ability to engage as a student (Ardoin & Martinez, 2019; Liu, 2011). Reflecting on one's consciousness, saliency, and attitude—or awareness, importance, and feelings—about social class; one's behaviors, lifestyle, and relationship to property; and one's referent, or comparison, groups will allow an individual to better grasp how their social class is shaping the lens through which they see the world (Liu et al., 2004; Liu, 2011).

Once self-work has begun, educators can examine social class from the interactional and institutional frames (Bourdieu, 1977, 1986, 1990; Liu, 2011). This includes exploring:

- existing institutional data on students' social classes (e.g., Pell Grant data; guardian, income, and education level) and how social class interacts with other identity factors (e.g., race, gender, ability) (Lumina, 2018);
- how one's social class worldview may be impacting interactions with students (Martin & Elkins, 2018); and
- one's ability to recognize where microaggressive behaviors and classism may show up in their roles, departments, and institutions and deter student engagement (Liu, 2011; Locke & Trolian, 2018).

Educators need to be aware of the everyday classism and cultural mismatch that poor and working-class students may experience at their institutions in order to create more opportunities for student engagement through cultural relevance and cultural responsiveness (Museus, 2014). Cultural mismatch is when the cultural norms (e.g., middle- and upper-class ways of being) in mainstream institutions, such as colleges and universities, are mismatched with the norms prevalent among poor and working classes (Stephens, Fryberg, Markus, Johnson, & Covarrubias, 2012; Stephens, Townsend, Markus, &

Phillips, 2012). Cultural mismatch can compromise sense of belonging and create social class inequity (Stephens et al., 2012a; Stephens et al., 2012b).

Provide Connection Points to Peers, Administrators, and Faculty From Poor or Working-Class Backgrounds

Conceding that the presence of poor and working-class folks in academia is consistently "more of the exception than the rule" (Hurst, 2012, p. 24), finding ways to connect students from the poor and working classes with peers, administrators, and faculty members from similar backgrounds can reduce imposter syndrome and increase sense of belonging and engagement. These connections would be beneficial prior to admission to introduce students to potential role models and resources at the college or university who "get it" and encourage them to pursue enrollment. Employing admissions counselors and financial aid officers from a multitude of class backgrounds can assist in this effort, along with creating websites to highlight educators on campus who come from different backgrounds. Then, maintaining these types of connection points through orientation, first-year or transfer programming, living-learning programs, student organizations, and/or campus identity centers would provide continuity and community to encourage student engagement throughout their duration at the institution.

Martin et al. (2018) emphasize the importance of "providing financial and spatial support for peer networks" (Martin et al., 2018, p. 15). This will obviously look different depending on the institution, but cultivating resources to foster formal and informal student engagement around social class, such as the Working Class Student Union at the University of Wisconsin-Madison, the First Generation/Working Class Club at Whitman College, the Low-Income Student Center at Brown University, or the crowdsourced "guides to not being rich" at the University of Texas and Michigan State University, can create a sense of connection and camaraderie for students from poor and working-class backgrounds, which aligns with Museus's (2014) CECE factors of cultural familiarity, culturally validating environments, and humanized educational experiences.

Examine Policies and Practices for Classism

If educators have increased their class consciousness, they will hopefully be able to analyze existing policies and practices for "unintended negative consequences (academic, financial, or otherwise)" (Lumina, 2018, p. 4) and elements of classism. It is also valuable to invite students and families from poor and working-class backgrounds into the review process because they are the ones living with the student engagement barriers educators have erected or reproduced (Bourdieu, 1977, 1986, 1990; Locke & Trolian, 2018) and can shed light on whether policies and practices are culturally relevant and responsive or not (Museus, 2014). Focusing on student engagement, examples of policies to scrutinize might include:

- Registration policies: Might it be possible to allow those who have to work specific hours or provide caregiving responsibilities to schedule first to allow them to secure course times that allow them to engage more fully?

- Fining practices: In what ways do fines (e.g., parking, residence hall, conduct, student organizations) inhibit students' ability to engage academically and co-curricularly? Might there be other accountability measures to offer to students from poor and working classes since fines disproportionately impact this population?
- Fee increase policies and practices: When considering student and other fee increases, do educators discuss options with students from poor and working-class backgrounds or consider allowing students to opt out of fees for services they do not, or will not, utilize?
- Student organization funding/reimbursement policies and practices: If the institution expects student organization officers to front money for expenses and then get reimbursement afterwards from the college or university, how might this be deterring students from poor and working-class backgrounds from joining or leading these groups?
- Qualifications for scholarships or awards: When creating these qualifications or reviewing applications, do educators knowingly or subconsciously preference certain types of engagement over others? For example, is serving on the student government seen as "better" than working 30-hour weeks as an on-campus employee or off-campus server or caretaker when, in fact, students may gain similar skills from a variety of experiences?
- Resource and networking practices: Do educators always expect students to initiate engagement with educators or campus offices? How might this be limiting for students from poor and working-class backgrounds who subscribe to an independent stance or believe that help-seeking behaviors show weakness due to internalized classism (Liu, 2011)?
- Internship policies and practices: Considering variations in students' economic and social capitals (Bourdieu, 1977, 1986, 1990; Liu, 2011), if a student's academic area requires or encourages them to engage in an internship, how are institutions ensuring that students from different social classes have equitable opportunities to engage in applied learning?

This sampling highlights how educators and collaborators can review any policy or practice within their sphere of influence for classist tendencies and inequities and contemplate how to rethink, shift, or discard institutional structures that impede student engagement. Then, educators can (re)create policies and practices to be culturally relevant and responsive for the poor and working classes and foster student engagement (Museus, 2014).

Shift Hours of Operation or Format of Engagement

One particular practice to be interrogated is college and university hours of operation. A simple, but not easy, way to increase engagement of students from the poor and working classes is to shift hours of operation for offices and programs on campus. It is simple because it is in educators' purview to change, but it's certainly not easy as it involves human resources, facilities, and other campus partners and interrupts the traditional way of "doing business" (e.g., 8AM–5PM) in higher education. However, since students from poor and working-class backgrounds often work many hours, typically corresponding with institutional hours of operation, instituting different shifts for college and university offices and services would allow more students access to engage with educators and resources. While contemplating this time shift, another idea is to offer different means of engaging with educators and resources; in-person attendance might not be possible for some students, so might educators and offices invite students to engage with them via phone or video streaming? While there might be some confidentiality measures to work out, providing a multitude of formats extends opportunities for students to engage in the ways they are able.

Consider Basic Needs

For some students from poor and working-class backgrounds, basic needs are a major impediment to engaging on campus. The work of Goldrick-Rab (2016) and Cady (2017) provides insight into the harrowing realities of food and housing insecurities (e.g., property relationships; Liu, 2011) that students valiantly confront in order to pursue higher education. It should not come as a surprise to anyone that students who manage basic needs worries also face challenges in student engagement. If a student is unsure where they will be sleeping that night or when their next meal might happen, studying for an exam or attending a campus program are likely much farther down their to-do list. In order to assist students in securing basic needs, institutions should scrutinize funding and financial aid structures, campus employment offerings, food, housing, and clothing programs.

Many scholarships—both institutional and statewide—tend to be focused more on merit-based aid instead of need-based aid (Ardoin, 2018a); Sacks (2007) points out the scarcity of this type of aid, offered by only 34% of public institutions and 27% of private institutions, and that state merit aid is essentially a subsidy "from the states to relatively affluent taxpayers, offered under the legitimizing guise of academic merit" (p. 184). A shift to more need-based aid on both levels would open up more funding streams for students from poor and working-class backgrounds and has the potential to support students' basic needs and, correspondingly, their ability to be more engaged. Further, emergency funding programs are also emerging in higher education; these are one-time funds that students can apply for when there are unexpected or dire circumstances that threaten their ability to stay enrolled at the institution. The hope is that the emergency funds will be a stop-gap that will assist the student until they locate more secure funding options; however, these funds are sometimes not well advertised, and thus, students may not be aware of this resource.

Because students from poor and working-class backgrounds often have to work one or more jobs and campus employment typically extends more flexibility for students while fostering campus engagement, institutions might consider how to offer more of these positions—outside of work-study roles—to this population. This could aid in basic needs acquirement, fulfill students' need to work, and keep them on campus where they can interact with peers, administrators, and faculty members.

Institutions might also consider joining the growing trend of colleges and universities that are supporting food, housing, and clothing programs to assist students with obtaining basic needs. Thanks to Clare Cady and the work of the College and University Food Bank Alliance, numerous two-year and four-year institutions now host food pantries or other food programs on their campuses and/or in conjunction with local food organizations to provide meals or snacks for students in need. This practice alone increases student engagement because fueling one's body allows one's brain to better work, learn, and interact with others. Some institutions are also providing temporary on-campus housing or opening campus buildings early (e.g., student union, library, recreation center) for students who are housing insecure to be able to get some sleep or utilize restrooms, while others are partnering with local nonprofit and community organizations that offer low-cost or free temporary housing options. Additionally, career centers are contributing to basic needs by offering "clothing closets" with "professional" attire (e.g., suits, briefcases) on loan to students who need these items to engage in internship or job interviews.

Finally, colleges and universities might mirror their two-year institutional peers who are collaborating with state and federal agencies to streamline application processes that qualify students for governmental food, housing, health, and childcare benefits. Some community colleges—such as Central Piedmont Community College in North Carolina, Bunker Hill Community College in Boston, City University of New York, Delgado Community College in New Orleans, and Miami Dade College in Florida—are identifying students who may qualify through their enrollment practices and then creating space for representatives to come to campus to help students navigate the application process without having to spend time, money, and energy traveling around to different agencies. This streamlining constructs a "one-stop shop" for students and allows institutions that might have limited capacity to still assist in the securement of basic needs. It is also one way that institutions can interrupt social reproduction (Bourdieu, 1977, 1986, 1990) and be more culturally relevant and responsive to student needs by providing proactive philosophies and holistic support (Museus, 2014).

Incorporate Social Class Into the Curriculum

First and foremost, those who teach courses should consider social class during their course material selection process, both in whose voices they are inviting into their classrooms (or not) through readings and the corresponding costs of books and other materials required to engage and be successful in the course. Working with campus librarians to diversify reading selections and ensure materials can be put on reserve or accessed electronically for free are great tactics to becoming more class conscious in material selection. Faculty can also build high-impact practices/costs (e.g., study abroad, research, service learning) into academic courses in order for students to qualify for grants or loans to cover costs. On the other hand, instructors should ruminate on how their assignments may pose social class issues: for example, if a project requires students to utilize technology or art supplies, is there somewhere on campus students can obtain these for little to no cost? Or if an assignment necessitates that students travel somewhere to gather information or have an experience, might the educator be able to secure a vehicle from the campus for students to use and offer varying time options to allow flexibility with students' work schedules? Considering how to set up courses so that students across the social class spectrum can be successful is essential in creating a more equitable student engagement experience.

Next, when facilitating class discussion or grading assignments, educators can foster engagement by inviting "examination of [social class] identity from a place of value and encourage students to draw from their personal experiences . . . [which] can validate students' knowledge and capitals, nurture their confidence, and advance their ability to both share and grow" (Ardoin, 2019, p. 210). Additionally, being conscious of linguistic preferences based in social class (e.g., dialect, word choice) can be helpful in determining if a student's writing or discussion comments are truly off base or merely more aligned with a social class different from that of the instructor.

Lastly, while few campuses offer working-class or poverty studies (Gilbert, 2008; Grassi, Armon, & Barker, 2008), colleges and universities can look to the example set by the University of Michigan, championed by a student and supported by faculty in women's studies, which is the first institution to offer a minor in social class and inequality studies. However, if this is not a realistic option or if the process will take years to come to fruition, educators can consider how to build social class elements into existing courses through the content (e.g., readings, videos, assignments) they select, the examples they use to clarify concepts or frame case studies, and the way they address classist happenings in the classroom.

Reduce Costs and/or Offer Differential Pricing for Student Involvement

Higher education comes at a high base cost, literally and figuratively (Goldrick-Rab, 2016), and students often have to incur additional costs to become involved in student organizations and activities, such as dues, registration fees, uniforms, and equipment. How might educators work with their colleagues and with students to inventory the co-curricular costs that might impede student engagement, as a first step, and then brainstorm ways to reduce or eliminate those costs to provide more equitable opportunities? This is another way of examining policies and practices for classism that is centered on the co-curricular environment.

And, if that is not possible based on present institutional dynamics, what is the possibility of offering a sliding scale for student organization membership fees and/or campus event rates? While this is not generally a popular recommendation because of its logistical complications and seeming appearance of unfairness, this practice could assist students in their student involvement and co-curricular engagement. For students who receive Pell Grants or have other indicators highlighting their poor or working-class identity, might offices take into account the systemic barriers—like cost—that inhibit student engagement and act on that recognition to completely eliminate costs or offer sliding-scale pricing based on social class? Although this may seem unfair at first glance, it is actually a culturally responsive way (Museus, 2014) to create more equitable opportunities for student engagement and disrupts social reproduction by introducing more pathways for students from poor and working-class backgrounds to acquire additional cultural and social capital (Bourdieu, 1977, 1986, 1990; Liu, 2011). Would this be challenging to explain to other students, caregivers, and legislators? Absolutely. However, if educators desire to break cycles and reinvent systems, daring measures are sometimes necessary.

Help Students Recognize Their Assets

As Liu's (2011) model shows, referent groups—or social class comparison groups—and internalized classism can shape one's social class worldview. Additionally, social reproduction highlights how higher education favors middle- and upper-class forms of capital (Bourdieu, 1977, 1986, 1990), thus alienating students from the poor and working classes. Holding both of these frameworks, educators need to understand the "importance of reframing deficit thinking regarding social class within higher education in favor of an asset-based approach that honors the values and experiences students bring with them to college" (Martin, Smith, & Williams, 2018, p. 87). Helping students see the utility of their social class strengths, such as work ethic, responsibility, strategy, creativity, and resiliency, and the value and transferability of their work and caregiving experiences can lessen the impact of internalized classism, better scaffold students' referent groups, and honor their social class worldviews (Garrison & Liu, 2018; Liu, 2011; Walpole, 2011). Facilitating students' understanding of their social class assets constructs a culturally validating and humanized educational environment that allows students to recognize their culturally relevant knowledge (Museus, 2014).

Conclusion

If students from poor and working-class backgrounds are expected to engage with their educational environment—academically, through the co-curricular, and socially—educators have to acknowledge the systemic barriers created historically and currently that hinder that student engagement and work to disrupt social reproduction (Bourdieu, 1977, 1986, 1990), recognize multiple social class worldviews (Liu et al., 2004; Liu, 2011), and design more culturally relevant and responsive educational environments (Museus, 2014). It is the role of all educators at every institutional type to incorporate social class into the engagement and equity conversation and not only offer "educational practices that are strongly associated with high levels of learning and personal development" (Kuh, 2001, p. 12), but also ensure that student engagement opportunities advance equity for students from poor and working-class backgrounds. This will drive colleges and universities toward the potential to become "instruments of social justice" (Serna & Woulfe, 2017, p. 4).

References

Ardoin, S. (2018a). *College aspirations and access in working-class rural communities: The mixed signals, challenges, and new language first-generation students encounter.* Lanham, MD: Lexington Books.

Ardoin, S. (2018b). Helping poor and working class students create their own sense of belonging. *New Directions for Student Services, 162,* 75–86.

Ardoin, S. (2019). Social class influences on student learning. In P. Magolda, M. B. Baxter Magolda, & R. Carducci (Eds.), *Contested issues in troubled times: Student affairs dialogues about equity, civility, and safety* (pp. 203–214). Sterling, VA: Stylus Publishing.

Ardoin, S., & Martinez, B. (2019). *Straddling class in the academy: 26 stories of students, administrators, and faculty from poor and working class backgrounds and their compelling lessons for higher education policy and practice.* Sterling, VA: Stylus Publishing.

Astin, A. W. (1984). Student involvement: A developmental theory in higher education. *Journal of College Student Personnel, 25,* 297–307.

Barratt, W. (2011). *Social class on campus: Theories and manifestations.* Sterling, VA: Stylus.

Barratt, W. (2012). Social class and the extracurriculum. *Journal of College and Character, 33*(3), 1–7.

Bourdieu, P. (1977). *Outline of a theory of practice.* Cambridge: Cambridge University Press.

Bourdieu, P. (1984). *Distinction: A social critique of the judgement of taste.* Cambridge, MA: Harvard University Press.

Bourdieu, P. (1986). The forms of capital. In J. Richardson (Ed.), *Handbook of theory and research for the sociology of education* (pp. 241–258). Westport, CT: Greenwood.

Bourdieu, P., & Passeron, J. (1990). *Reproduction in education, society, and culture.* London: Sage Publications.

Buckley, J. B., & Park, J. J. (2019). "When you don't really focus on it": Campus climate for social class diversity and identity awareness. *Journal of College Student Development, 60*(3), pp. 271–289.

Cady, C. (2017, August 14). Your student leaders are back. *Medium.* Retrieved from https://medium.com/@saragoldrickrab/your-student-leaders-are-back-c01ba552b619

Chetty, R., Hendren, N., Lin, F., Majerovitz, J., & Scuderi, B. (2016). Childhood environment and gender taps in adulthood. *American Economic Review, 106,* 282–288.

Collins, C., Ladd, J., Seider, M., & Yeskel, F. (2014). *Class lives: Stories from across our economic divide.* Ithaca, NY: Cornell University Press.

Garrison, Y. L., & Liu, W. M. (2018). Using the social class worldview model in student affairs. *New Directions for Student Services, 162,* 19–33.

Gilbert, R. (2008). Raising awareness of class privilege among students. *Diversity Digest, 11*(3). Washington, DC: Association of American Colleges and Universities.

Goldrick-Rab, S. (2016). *Paying the price: College costs, financial aid, and the betrayal of the American dream.* Chicago, IL: The University of Chicago Press.

Grassi, E., Armon, J., & Barker, B. (2008). Don't lose your working-class students. *Diversity Digest, 11*(3). Washington, DC: Association of American Colleges and Universities.

hooks, b. (1989). *Talking back: Thinking feminist, thinking Black.* Boston, MA: South End Press.

hooks, b. (2000). *Where we stand: Class matters.* New York, NY: Routledge.

hooks, b. (2014). *Teaching to transgress.* New York, NY: Routledge.

Housel, T. H., & Harvey, V. L. (2009). *The invisibility factor: Administrators and faculty reach out to first-generation college students.* Boca Raton, FL: BrownWalker Press.

Hurst, A. L. (2010). *The burdens of academic success: Loyalists, renegades, and double agents.* New York, NY: Rowman & Littlefield.

Hurst, A. L. (2012). *College and the working class: What it takes to make it.* Boston, MA: Sense.

Kuh, G. D. (2001). Assessing what really matters to student learning: Inside the National Survey of Student Engagement. *Change, 33*(3), 10–17, 66.

Kuh, G. D. (2008). *High impact educational practices: What are they, who has access to them, and why they matter.* Washington, DC: American Association of Colleges & Universities.

Leonhardt, D. (2004, April 22). As wealthy fill top colleges, concerns grow over fairness. *New York Times,* p. A1.

Liu, W. M. (2011). *Social class and classism in the helping professions: Research, theory, and practice.* Thousand Oaks, CA: Sage.

Liu, W. M., Soleck, G., Hopps, J., Dunston, K., & Pickett, T. (2004). A new framework to understand social class in counseling: The social class worldview model and modern classism theory. *Journal of Multicultural Counseling and Development, 32,* 95–122.

Locke, L. A., & Trolian, T. L. (2018). Microaggressions and social class identity in higher education and student affairs. *New Directions for Student Services, 162,* 63–74.

Lumina Foundation. (2016). *A stronger nation: An annual report of Lumina Foundation.* Indianapolis, IN: Author. Retrieved from www.luminafoundation.org/files/publications/stronger_nation/2016/A_Stronger_Nation-2016-Full.pdf

Lumina Foundation. (n.d.). *Today's reality: Statistics compiled by Lumina Foundation.* Retrieved from www.luminafoundation.org/todays-student-statistics

Lumina Foundation. (2018). *Beyond financial aid: How colleges can strengthen the financial stability of low-income students and improve student outcomes.* Indianapolis, IN: Author. Retrieved from www.luminafoundation.org/beyond-financial-aid

Martin, G. L. (2015a). "Always in my face": An exploration of social class consciousness, salience, and values. *Journal of College Student Development, 56*(5), 471–487.

Martin, G. L. (2015b). "Tightly wound rubber bands": Exploring the college experiences of low-income, first-generation White students. *Journal of Student Affairs Research and Practice, 52*(3), 275–286,

Martin, G. L., & Elkins, B. (2018). Editor's notes. *New Directions for Student Services, 162,* 5–8.

Martin, G. L., Smith, M., & Williams, B. (2018). Reframing deficit thinking on social class. *New Directions for Student Services, 162,* 87–93.

Martin, G. L., Williams, B., & Young, C. R. (2018). Understanding social class as identity. *New Directions for Student Services, 162,* 9–18.

Museus, S. D. (2014). The culturally engaging campus environments (CECE) model: A new theory of college success among racially diverse student populations. In M. B. Paulsen (Ed.), *Higher education: A handbook of theory and research* (pp. 189–227). New York, NY: Springer.

Museus, S. D., & Yi, V. (2015). Rethinking student involvement and engagement: Cultivating culturally relevant and responsive contexts for campus participation. In D. Mitchell Jr., K. M. Soria, E. A. Daniele, & J. A. Gipson (Eds.), *Student involvement and academic outcomes: Implications for diverse college student populations* (pp. 12–24). New York, NY: Peter Lang.

National Survey of Student Engagement (NSSE). (2014). *From benchmarks to indicators and high impact practices.* Retrieved from http://nsse.indiana.edu/pdf/Benchmarks%20to%20Indicators.pdf

Ostrove, J. M. (2003). Belonging and wanting: Meanings of social class background for women's constructions of their college experience. *Journal of Social Issues, 59,* 771–784.

Poutré, A., Rorison, J., & Voight, M. (2017). *Limited means, limited options: College remains unaffordable for many Americans.* Washington, DC: Institute for Higher Education Policy.

Ramsey, P. G. (1991). Young children's awareness and understanding of social class differences. *The Journal of Genetic Psychology, 152,* 71–82.

Rudolph, F. (1990). *The American college and university: A history.* Athens, GA: The University of Georgia Press.

Sacks, P. (2007). *Tearing down the gates: Confronting the class divide in American education.* Berkeley, CA: University of California Press.

Serna, G. R., & Woulfe, R. (2017). Social reproduction and college access: Current evidence, context, and potential alternatives. *Critical Questions in Education, 8*(1), 1–16.

Soria, K. M. (2015a). Elevating the academic success of working-class college students through high-impact educational practices. In D. Mitchell Jr., K. M. Soria, E. A. Daniele, & J. A. Gipson (Eds.), *Student involvement and academic outcomes: Implications for diverse college student populations* (pp. 41–56). New York, NY: Peter Lang.

Soria, K. M. (2015b). *Welcoming blue collar scholars to the ivory tower: Developing class-conscious strategies for student success.* Columbia, SC: University of South Carolina, National Resource Center for The First-Year Experience and Students in Transition.

Soria, K. M., & Bultmann, M. (2014). Supporting working-class students in higher education. *NACADA Journal, 34*(2), 51–62.

Soria, K. M., Gipson, J. A., & Mitchell Jr., D. (2015). Introduction. In D. Mitchell Jr., K. M. Soria, E. A. Daniele, & J. A. Gipson (Eds.), *Student involvement and academic outcomes: Implications for diverse college student populations* (pp. 1–8). New York, NY: Peter Lang.

Soria, K. M., Stebleton, M. J., & Huseman, Jr. R. L. (2013). Class counts: Exploring differences in academic and social integration between working-class and middle/upper class students at large, public research universities. *Journal of College Student Retention, 15*(2), 215–242.

Stephens, N. M., Fryberg, S. A., Markus, H. R., Johnson, C. S., & Covarrubias, R. (2012). Unseen disadvantage: How American universities' focus on independence undermines the academic performance of first-generation college students. *Journal of Personality and Social Psychology, 102*(6), 1178–1197.

Stephens, N. M., Townsend, S. S. M., Markus, H. R., & Phillips, T. (2012). A cultural mismatch: Independent cultural norms produce greater increases in cortisol and more negative emotions among first-generation college students. *Journal of Experimental Social Psychology, 48*, 1389–1393.

Stich, A. E. (2012). *Access to inequality: Reconsidering class, knowledge, and capital in higher education.* Lanham, MD: Lexington Books.

Stich, A. E., & Freie, C. (2016). The working classes and higher education: An introduction to a complicated relationship. In A. E. Stich & C. Freie (Eds.), *The working classes and higher education* (pp. 1–10). New York, NY: Routledge.

Strunk, K. K., Locke, L. A., & Martin, G. L. (2017). *Oppression and resistance in southern higher and adult education: Mississippi and the dynamics of equity and social justice.* New York, NY: Palgrave Macmillan.

Stuber, J. M. (2011). *Inside the college gates: How class and culture matter in higher education.* Lanham, MD: Lexington.

Thelin, J. R. (2011). *A history of American higher education* (2nd ed.). Baltimore, MD: The John Hopkins University Press.

Walpole, M. (2003). Socioeconomic status and college: How SES affects college experiences and outcomes. *Review of Higher Education, 27*, 45–73.

Walpole, M. (2011). Academics, campus administration, and social interaction: Examining campus structures using post-structural theory. In A. J. Kezar (Ed.), *Recognizing and serving low-income students in higher education* (pp. 99–120). New York, NY: Routledge.

Yee, A. (2016). The unwritten rules of engagement: Social class differences in undergraduates' academic strategies. *Journal of Higher Education, 87*(6), 831–858.

Chapter 19
Engaging Commuter, Part-Time, and Returning Adult Students

Barbara Jacoby

Although only 15% of today's college students are of traditional age, attend full time, and live on campus, too little is known about the 85% majority and their college experiences (US Department of Education, 2015). Even less is known about differences that exist within this diverse student population, which includes all commuter, part-time, and returning adult students. Much of the scant existing research treats commuter students as homogenous and ignores the need to examine within-group differences (Jacoby & Garland, 2004; Biddix, 2015). One result of this dearth of knowledge is the application of what Pascarella (2006) refers to as "rational myths," or the adoption of programs and policies that lack empirical evidence of effectiveness but that seem to make logical or intuitive sense (p. 513). Rational myths include the continued utilization of programs and interventions designed for resident students to serve commuter students, assuming that the effect on learning will be equivalent. Another result is that the programs and interventions that are most likely to promote student engagement may not be offered at all to commuter, part-time, or returning adult students.

The unique needs of commuter students have been neither adequately understood nor appropriately incorporated into policies, programs, and practices (Jacoby, 1989). Despite their numbers, the residential traditions dominant in American higher education have impeded institutional response to their presence. This chapter describes how to use what we know about commuter, part-time, and returning adult students to design and implement strategies that enhance their success. It begins with a snapshot of the extraordinary diversity of this population and their common needs and concerns. It then offers several theoretical frameworks that are useful in understanding these students and the nature of their interactions with institutional environments. In this chapter, the term "commuter students" is used interchangeably with "commuter, part-time, and returning adult students" for simplicity and to avoid repetition.

Although some institutions' definitions differ, the most common and broadest definition of commuter students is those who do not live in institution-owned housing on campus (Jacoby, 1989, 2000). Over the last several years, the traditional distinction between resident students (those who live in institution-owned housing on campus) and commuter students (those who do not) has become considerably blurred. Some institutions consider students who live in privately owned housing within a university "zone" or students who live in institution-owned housing a distance away from the campus as commuters; others do not. Like the definition of "commuter student," the definition of "part-time student" is also complicated because it varies by institution. According to the US Department of Education, part-time students are enrolled for fewer than 12 credits per semester. Adult returning students are those 25 years of age and older who enter college after a gap in their education, either between high school and college or following a period of college enrollment (US Department of Education, 2015).

Of the 19,977,000 college students in the most recent National Center for Educational Statistics dataset, 8,141,000 are 25 years of age or older (US Department of Education, 2015). As for part-time students in four-year institutions, the most recent federal data reveals that there are 108,000 part-time, first-time students and 378,000 part-time, non-first-time students. In two-year institutions, there are 396,000 part-time, first-time students and 311,944 part-time, non-first-time students. Twenty-three percent of undergraduates at four-year institutions attended part time, while 61% of undergraduates at two-year colleges attended part time. The number of part-time students rose 16% between 2004 and 2014. (US Department of Education, 2015).

Only about one-quarter of exclusively part-time students earn a degree within eight years of starting college. Just more than half of students who attend part time during some of their college career eventually earn a degree, in comparison to about 80% of exclusively full-time students who attain a degree. Four in ten students who attend college exclusively part time in their first-year are not enrolled in classes the next year. It is not surprising that part-time students are far less engaged in their college education than full-time students (Bombardieri, 2017).

More than 40% of full-time students work and 80% of part-time students work while enrolled in college. Part-time and returning adult students tend to think of themselves as employees first and students second. Twenty-seven percent of full-time students work more than 20 hours per week and will, as a result, suffer negative consequences related to grade-point average, level of engagement, persistence, and degree completion (Carnevale, Smith, Melton, & Price, 2015).

Transfer students comprise another group of students who are almost all commuters. A report of the National Student Clearinghouse Research Center of students who started college in fall 2008 documents the prevalence of transfer and captures the complexity of student mobility across institutions and state lines. Over 32% of these students transferred at least once within six years. Among those who transfer, almost half (45%) transferred more than once (2015). Many commuter students "stop out" of college to focus their time and energy on family or work issues. And, to further complicate matters, a majority of college students attend more than one institution of higher education. This phenomenon, known as "swirling," is becoming more prevalent, particularly among part-time students. Nearly 60% of undergraduates attend at least two institutions, and more than 20% have attended three or more. "Swirling" significantly reduces the likelihood of attaining a degree. Seventy-two percent of students who attended only one college obtained a bachelor's degree within six years, compared to 46% who attended more than one. Only 34% who attended more than three colleges obtained a bachelor's degree within six years (National Student Clearinghouse Research Center, 2015).

A group of commuter students has been growing behind the scenes and is now being highlighted by professional associations, foundations, and higher education institutions: post-traditional students. Post-traditional students are defined as individuals already in the workforce without a postsecondary credential yet determined to pursue further knowledge and skills while balancing work, life, and education responsibilities. Post-traditional students are needed wage earners for themselves and their families; pursue knowledge, skills, or credentials that employers will recognize and compensate; and are more likely to require developmental education in order to be successful. What is important to note is that post-traditional students are just as likely to be under the age of 25 as over the age of 25 (Soares, 2013).

Another rapidly trending phenomenon is student-parents. There are almost five million students who are also parents, representing more than one-quarter of the undergraduate population. The number of college students with children grew by more than one million, or 30%, between 2004 and 2012. Nearly 40% of African American women attending college are single mothers (Berman, 2017).

Sadly, another trend is growing: very low-income students who deal with food and housing insecurity. A large-scale survey reveals that nearly half of college students experience food insecurity or struggle to access enough affordable nutritious food. That includes 22% of students who experienced such low levels of food insecurity in the 30 days prior to the survey period that they qualified as hungry. In addition, 36% of students were housing insecure, meaning they had missed rent payments or couch-surfed from place to place (Goldrick-Rab, Richardson, Schneider, Hernandez, & Cady, 2018). A similarly large-scale study of community college students found that more than 13% were homeless, and about half were housing insecure. The survey also found that two-thirds of community college students were food insecure (Goldrick-Rab, Richardson, & Hernandez, 2017).

It is clear that there is nothing simple about the commuter student population. Commuter students include students of traditional age who live with their parents, those who live in rental housing near the campus, adults with full-time careers, and parents whose lives intersect with one or more of the previous characteristics. Although they have always been present on college campuses, commuter students have always been and continue to be viewed as "nontraditional." Their needs are diverse, and they have perennially been underserved. The diversity of the commuter student population is increasing in several other dimensions as more Students of Color and first-generation college students enter the general college population. In addition, many of the military-connected students, transfer students, undocumented students, delayed-entry students, and older students—whose numbers are also growing—are commuter students.

There is a powerful reality that emerges above and beyond any differences among commuter students: *No matter where commuter students live or what type of institution they attend, the fact that they commute to the college campus and/or attend part time profoundly influences the nature of their educational experience.* This is particularly true of students who, for a variety of reasons, never live on campus or in nearby student housing. Actually, the educational goals of many commuter students may be quite similar to those of full-time residential students. They may be just as likely to seek to be engaged in their learning and in the campus community; however, their lives consist of balancing many competing commitments, including work, family, and other responsibilities. As a result, they may *appear* to be less committed to, and engaged in, their education. There are certainly both part- and full-time, commuter and residential, students who seek minimal engagement while earning a degree. The critical point is not to assume that this is more likely true of commuter students. Despite their commitment, many commuter students simply cannot always make their college education their primary focus.

Further, most campus policies, programs, and practices fail to address the most current information about the multiple complexities of their commuter students' lives. In fact, unintentional barriers and burdens exist at most institutions. Part-time, returning adult, and commuter students continue to feel "othered," that they are "other" or different from the mainstream of the institution's students.

Common Needs and Concerns of Commuter Students

Although commuter students are extraordinarily diverse, a common core of needs and concerns can be identified (Jacoby, 1989). The following set of core needs have been used by the NCCP and many institutions as a basis for the design of services, programs, and needs assessment instruments for commuter students. Since virtually all part-time students commute, these needs and concerns are applicable to that population.

Transportation

The most obvious concerns shared by commuter students are those related to transportation: parking, traffic, fixed transportation schedules, inclement weather, vehicle maintenance, transportation costs, and locating alternative means of transportation when their primary means fails. No matter the mode, commuting to and from campus places demands on students' time and energy. As a result, they frequently concentrate their classes into blocks, take some classes online, and have little free time to spend on campus. The convenience of classes, services, and programs is of paramount importance. (Wilmes & Quade, 1986).

Multiple Life Roles

For most commuter students, being a student is only one of several important and time-consuming roles. As mentioned earlier, most commuter students work to defray the costs associated with higher education. Many work the equivalent of full time and at more than one job. In addition, many have responsibilities for managing households including children, siblings, and relatives. Commuter students' time is a critical and finite resource that directly impacts their ability to engage in academic and out-of-class activities. By necessity, they select their campus involvements carefully. The relative value of a campus activity when compared with other priorities is a major factor in their decision to participate. (Wilmes & Quade, 1986).

Integrating Support Networks

Commuter students often lack the supportive campus environment that has been identified as one of the benchmarks of effective educational practice of the National Survey of Student Engagement (Kuh, Gonyea, & Palmer, 2001). As a result, the support networks for commuter students generally exist off, rather than on, campus, including partners, parents, children, siblings, employers, coworkers, and friends. Although these individuals can be supportive, students must negotiate with family, employers, and others to establish priorities, responsibilities, and time commitments. These negotiations are more difficult if significant others do not understand both the challenges and the opportunities of higher education, as do campus-based advisors, counselors, and others who generally provide support to students.

Sense of Belonging

Students who commute often lack a sense of belonging to, or of feeling wanted by, the institution. Some institutions fail to provide even the most basic facilities, such as lockers and lounges, which allow students to feel physically connected to campus. In many cases, there are inadequate opportunities for commuter students to develop relationships with faculty, staff, and peers. Individuals rarely feel connected to a place where they have no significant relationships. Students who do not have a sense of belonging may complain that their college experience is like "stopping at the mall" to get what they need on the way to somewhere else (Wilmes & Quade, 1986; Jacoby, 2000).

In recognition of the realities of commuter and part-time students' busy lives, Astin (1985) summarizes the challenges that higher education institutions face in increasing their engagement in learning: "Educators are in reality competing with other forces in the student's life for a share of that finite time and energy. The student's investment in matters relating to family, friends, job and other outside activities represents a reduction in the time and energy the student has to devote to his or her education development" (p. 143). Astin further asserts that, as a result, colleges and universities must recognize that almost every institutional policy and practice can affect how students spend their time and how much effort they devote to their education.

Theoretical Perspectives

Although theories and models cannot capture the complexity of human beings or environments, they can serve as lenses that bring situations and relationships into sharper focus (Jacoby, 2015). Several theoretical frameworks have direct application to commuter student success. Maslow's (1982) hierarchy of needs is not one of the frameworks covered in this chapter, but it is helpful in thinking about the experience of commuter and part-time students both on and off the campus. Because of their various life situations, they are often preoccupied with satisfying their most fundamental needs. As a result, it is essential for institutions to provide services to help meet students' basic needs for housing, transportation, food, security, health care, and childcare. On the next level, students need to feel a sense of membership in and acceptance by the campus community. Before students can take full advantage of the institution to achieve self-actualization, their need for esteem must be met.

Mattering and Marginality

The concept of mattering (Rosenberg & McCullough, 1981) is related to the needs for belonging and esteem described by Maslow (1982). Mattering is "the feeling that others depend on us, are interested in us, [and] are concerned with our fate" (Rosenberg & McCullough, 1981, p. 165). Schlossberg, Lynch, and Chickering (1989) applied this concept to colleges by developing a mattering scale for use in determining to what extent policies, practices, and classroom activities are geared toward making adult students feel that they matter. In 1991, the Commission on Commuter Students and Adult Learners of the American College Personnel Association broadened this application to include all types of commuter students by adopting "All Students Matter" as its slogan.

Schlossberg (1985) identified the construct of marginality as the polar opposite of mattering. Commuter and part-time students have been, and have felt, marginal in colleges and universities since first participating in and engaging higher education. Although feeling marginal during a period of transition into a new environment is to be expected, institutions should employ policies and practices that make all students feel that they matter—that they are central rather than marginal.

Transition Theory

Schlossberg et al. (1989) define a transition as any event or non-event that changes relationships, routines, assumptions, and roles. For some students, their transitions are obvious, traditional, and well-marked, such as when a first-time college student leaves home and moves into a residence hall to begin a new life on campus. For commuter, part-time, and returning adult students and those close to them, their transitions are often perceived as "non-events," such as when a fully employed adult begins taking courses at the local community college on a part-time basis while keeping most other aspects of her life intact. Many students returning to school after a break in their education do so because of some sort of life transition. Such transitioners include employed or unemployed individuals trying to keep up with an increasingly competitive job market, homemakers whose children have grown up, or spouses and partners who suddenly find themselves single parents. Students transferring from community colleges to four-year institutions and those who alternate between semesters of full- and part-time enrollment also may perceive these transitions as "non-events." First-time, full-time commuter students may feel that going to college while continuing to work at the job they had in high school, eating dinner and participating in social activities with their family, living in the same house, and hanging out with their high school friends is not much of a transition. Regardless of whether students realize that they are in transition, transitions that are both "events" and "non-events" are challenging, and colleges need to recognize these transitions and provide appropriate supports.

Student Engagement

Research indicates that the more time and effort students invest in their learning and the more intensely they engage in their own education, the greater will be their achievement, growth, and satisfaction with the college experience. Investment in learning also increases the likelihood of persistence toward attainment of educational goals (Study Group on the Conditions of Excellence in American Higher Education, 1984). The concept of student engagement includes activities that are traditionally associated with learning, such as reading and writing, preparing for class, and other key activities that more recently have emerged as being important, such as collaborating with peers on projects and community service.

Kuh et al. (2001), in an analysis of data from the National Survey of Student Engagement, compare three categories of students: on-campus residents, walking commuters, and driving commuters. They found that both first-year students and seniors who lived on campus had higher scores on all the benchmarks of effective educational practice, although many of the differences were relatively small. Some of the largest differences were found in the benchmarks of interactions with faculty members and enriching educational experiences. The latter benchmark includes complementary learning experiences inside and outside the classroom, experiencing diversity, using technology, and opportunities to synthesize and apply knowledge. Results also indicated that, although many commuter students' time is constrained by work and family matters, they put forth just as much effort as resident students in areas that relate directly to the classroom.

Astin (1984) explicitly states that the effectiveness of all educational policies and practices is directly related to their capacity to increase student engagement. However, many commuter, part-time, and returning adult students cannot become involved in the same ways that traditional-age, full-time, residential students can. Nevertheless, by using what we know about commuter students, we can create opportunities to enhance their engagement in learning in ways that meet their needs. Rather than expecting commuter students to adjust their lifestyles and schedules, it is the responsibility of colleges and universities to develop strategies specifically and intentionally to involve them deeply and intentionally in learning.

Schlossberg, Lynch, and Chickering describe the transitions of adult students within higher education in terms of moving in, moving through, and moving on (1989). In fact, all commuter, part-time, and returning adult students experience multiple challenging transitions that require a range of support strategies. This section highlights promising practices that support students at all points in their college experience.

Guided Pathways

One of the greatest challenges of engagement from the commuter, part-time, or returning adult student's viewpoint is finding one's way into (or back into) college; understanding its plentiful opportunities, figuring out how things work, and then making the college experience part of one's life require a new set of complex learnings. Whether they enter college after a period of full-time work or homemaking, a community college or high school, commuter students must make the transition from a world in which they felt comfortable and in control to a new world in which they feel like strangers. They are faced with opportunities, along with uncertainties and risks. They may lack confidence in their ability to handle the academic work at the new institution and may have doubts about whether they can meet their professors' expectations. If their pathway to achieving their educational goals—or, even worse, if their goals themselves—are not clear, their likelihood of completion is substantially reduced.

In this light, both community colleges and four-year institutions are building clear and comprehensive pathways to success for their students. Both the American Association of Community Colleges (AACC, 2018) and the Association of American Colleges and Universities (AACU, 2018) have initiated and provide support to institutions to develop such pathways (Schmidt, 2016; AACU, 2018). All 30 of the colleges in AACC's program have implemented or are moving toward implementation of, a meta-major structure, which combines like programs together under broad umbrellas so that students have fewer but clearer choices upon entering the institution. The colleges are examining and restructuring theirs advising models to help students make informed choices earlier in their academic career but also implementing new structures in a way that fits their local environment and culture (AACC, 2018).

For example, the Alamo Colleges in Texas, which are five individual colleges, each with a distinct culture and no on-campus housing, have implemented the MyMAP (Monitoring Academic Progress) pathway project. MyMAP is notable in that it provides a common, interactive web interface that begins by outlining the steps to enrollment and leads students through a web-based process to introduce academic and career opportunities and the potential pathways they involve. This web-based process is accompanied by advising, registration, and orientation at the individual campuses in a high-touch manner. An outstanding feature of Alamo's roadmaps is that they include the Career Coach web-assisted career exploration and development program. This program includes workforce data, regional economic analysis, potential earnings, and the like, together with a "personal GPS" for career preparation and placement (Mendiola-Perez & Dalrymple, 2015).

Other innovations related to pathways include built-in systems to alert advisors and students of need for early intervention when things are not going well, together with notifications to celebrate achievement of milestones along the way; electronic portfolios that enable students to view their goal achievements over time, shape their learning, and demonstrate their accomplishments and competencies to employers; a bold graphic design using a ribbon theme that illustrates pathways that are displayed on large posters all around the campus and on a mobile app; and a virtual game model providing video and audio content along with degree audits, access to online tutoring, library support, and career services.

In another easily replicable example, the Adult, Commuter, and Transfer Services website at East Tennessee State University contains a link to the Buc Path for College Success. (They are the ETSU Buccaneers.) Buc Path is a series of online visual time-lines that highlight the essential elements to identifying and realizing academic and career goals. It is a guide to knowing when key academic requirements are due; when and where students should seek support; applications, deadlines, and tasks related to financial aid and scholarship opportunities; and what out-of-class experiences students should consider at what point to enrich their journey to degree (East Tennessee State University, 2018).

Financial Aid

Commuter, part-time, and returning adult students are disproportionately at risk of stopping out, or dropping out, of college as a result of financial struggles. Although colleges expect families to financially support their children while they attend college, the reverse is also happening—low-income children are supporting their parents, grandparents, and even siblings. Financial issues negatively affect the success of most commuter students, causing derailment of educational goals and a great deal of stress and worry (Goldrick-Rab, 2016). Needless to say, students who are financially challenged are unlikely to seek or take advantage of engagement opportunities.

Limited financial aid frequently forces commuter students to seek or return to work full time (Steele & Erisman, 2016). Some students without jobs are searching for work they can't find. Others are holding down two or even three minimum-wage jobs to try to make enough, and too many students are working the graveyard shift because it pays more, going from work straight to class without a night's sleep.

Loans are intended to permit students to afford college, focus on their studies, and repay their debt later. However, that is often not how they work in reality. Loans affect students long before they come due. When student borrowers feel that loans are their only option and that their prospects of graduating from college, let alone getting a good job afterward, are uncertain, feeling forced into borrowing surely contributes to stress during college (Goldrick-Rab, 2016).

Financial aid officers should ensure that expense budgets used to determine the amount of financial need realistically reflect costs, including transportation, rent, childcare, and food. The way the federal government, and consequently institutions, measure financial need for part-time and even full-time commuter students' is misleading and even flat-out wrong (Goldrick-Rab, 2016). It overstates a family's ability to pay for college by ignoring debt and the hardships that go with it and grossly understates the actual costs of attending college, including living off campus, childcare, and transportation. While some federal financial aid is available to part-time students, it is woefully inadequate. Institution-based scholarships for specific subgroups of the commuter population (e.g., adult, part-time, transfer, first-generation, and veteran students) should be established, and eligible students should be contacted in a timely manner and strongly encouraged to apply. Financial aid officers should be aware that students who find attending a brick-and-mortar campus challenging may consider online degrees offered by for-profit colleges. The programs at these institutions are very costly, their dropout rate is very high, and their students have the highest debt burdens. Sharing this information with students, together with helping them find ways to persist at our institutions and earn their degrees, is critical.

Textbooks are a formidable expense for many students, and too often they simply do not purchase them. Over the past decade, textbook costs have risen more than four times the rate of inflation. Tidewater Community College is a pioneer in the use of openly licensed, high-quality electronic textbooks and other educational materials for the completion of an entire two-year associate degree. These materials are open educational resources, which are freely accessible for teaching, learning, assessment, and research. TCC's Z-Degree—the "Z" stands for "zero"—means students can save as much as $2,500 on the cost of their degree (Tidewater Community College, 2018). All types of higher education institutions are exploring and training faculty members to use open educational resources (OER), which include textbooks, classroom modules, lesson plans, video content, and other media that are openly licensed and freely accessible. OER are especially useful for faculty members to enable access to a range of underserved students, including those with low socioeconomic status and those with disabilities (Yale University, 2018).

Many colleges have created emergency loan programs. Emergency loans can make a huge difference in helping students over a sudden, one-time hurdle, such as a sudden health emergency, unexpected loss of income, death or other family emergency, rent in arrears and risk of eviction, or natural disaster (Kruger, Parnell, & Wesaw, 2016). Some institutions include support for emergency loans among their fundraising priorities for capital campaigns. But most raise funds for these loans through small contributions through donation boxes at campus shops and eateries or various crowdfunding mechanisms. However, emergency loans and other services for students in crisis or with critical needs such as food banks are only helpful if students know about them. In addition to prolific signage and social media, institutions should encourage (or require) faculty members to include information about emergency assistance on their syllabi and to mention this information as they go over other syllabus details.

It is also incumbent upon higher education institutions to support student-parents, who now number almost five million (Berman, 2017). BestColleges.com has published a list of the 50 best colleges for students with children. These are colleges that provide a specific set of amenities for student-parents, while still managing to be relatively inexpensive in terms of tuition and other costs. For example, the University of Washington has a comprehensive Student Parent Resource Center. In addition to providing a sense of community and a wide range of resources, it offers the Childcare Assistance Program that assists students in covering the costs of licensed childcare for their children from birth to 12 years old (University of Washington, 2018). Commuter student advocates could work with the student-parents on their campuses to lobby their student governments to adopt a similar fee. The University of Michigan offers Kids Kare at Home for parents whose child is mildly ill or if their regular childcare is unavailable on short notice, and they must be at work or on campus. It is available at the full rate of $22.00 per hour, but depending on annual household income, the university may subsidize the cost with rates starting at $6.00 per hour (2018).

Work in College as a High-Impact Practice

As described earlier, work during college is a reality for the vast majority of commuter, part-time, and returning adult students. A range of innovative approaches are enabling students to integrate work into their college experience in meaningful ways. First, commuter students who must work should be strongly encouraged to work on, rather than off, campus. They should be informed about the advantages of on-campus employment: avoiding the "three-point" commute between home, campus, and work; flexible scheduling around and between classes; supervisors' willingness to modify work hours at times of heavy academic work; and the work setting as a place to learn about the campus, meet people, and find a "home away from home" on campus. Through campus jobs, students make friends and build support systems. In addition, some campus jobs pay the same or more for work that students do off campus. More and more colleges are taking important steps to making on-campus jobs more meaningful, even the most mundane ones. One of the most ambitious efforts is Ryerson University's Career Boost program. Ryerson has reviewed hundreds of student jobs to ensure that they're teaching the skills that Canadian employers (Ryerson is in Toronto) say they value most. If a position is found to be lacking in opportunities for skill development, staff members will add duties to the job description. A student working at the front desk in the gym, for example, might be asked to write a report categorizing the types of questions they receive. In Ryerson's system, each job—from varsity equipment and uniform manager to peer support—comes with a list of learning outcomes. Supervisors meet regularly with student employees to discuss their progress toward these outcomes, and both student and supervisor evaluate the student's development at the end of the year (O'Connor, 2016).

Iowa GROW (Guided Reflection on Work) uses brief, structured conversations between student employees and their supervisors to help students connect the skills and knowledge they are gaining in the classroom with the work they are doing and vice versa. Iowa GROW was created to make student employment a "high-impact activity"—one that requires students to reflect on their learning and connect their learning within and beyond the classroom (University of Iowa, 2018).

At other institutions, large employers like dining services, facilities management, student unions, and libraries are building into job descriptions tasks like creating and maintaining social media campaigns, organizing and conducting focus groups, peer education, and supervision of other student employees. Others are having their student employees complete strengths inventories and reflect on their weaknesses and what knowledge and skills they would like to develop. Opportunities are then offered to the students to utilize their strengths, develop skills, and address their weaknesses. For example, students with writing and graphic design skills (and majors) can do very useful work other than serving food or shelving books. Students with language skills can serve as speaking partners with employees who are immigrants who would like to practice their English.

We can also help students find value in the most mundane work, whether on or off campus. Inviting career services staff to work with student employees to help them develop resumes and prepare for job interviews by describing not only what they did in a job but also what they learned, what transferable skills they have acquired, and how they learn.

Learning Communities

Learning communities are without doubt one of the most effective of the high-impact educational practices for student engagement. However, at mixed resident-commuter institutions, many of these are living-learning communities. Most operate under the assumption that "commuters are welcome." However, commuter students generally do not feel welcome when the other members of the community live together in a residence hall and hold community events during the evenings and on weekends. Curricular learning communities can be developed that work particularly well for commuter students. One of the simplest learning community models is linked, or paired, courses. A paired-course learning community usually involves 20 to 30 students who enroll as a cohort in two courses that generally meet back to back. This sometimes includes a first-year seminar with a challenging introductory course, such as composition or chemistry. An innovative spin on this model is to schedule the two courses immediately before and after the lunch hour. It is ideal if the courses are taught in the same classroom, which is blocked during the hour in between so the students can use that time and space to eat, study, and just connect.

Another promising model is creating a learning community within the classroom of a single course, which works well to engage students of any age who work full time during typical weekday work hours. The faculty member teaching a three-credit, semester-long course could organize it so that it meets every other Saturday for eight hours each and two Friday evenings, one at the beginning of the course and one at the end. This totals the requisite 45 hours for a three-credit course but is formatted to enable students who work full time to participate (Chickering, 2000).

The benefits of this model for part-time, commuter, or fully employed students include allowing students a week between classes for reading and preparation, reducing commute time by meeting less frequently and at non–rush hour times, and enabling students to develop a sense of community among themselves and with the faculty member. This course design also enables the faculty member to develop and implement engaging experiential activities that are more complex and take longer than the traditional 50-minute class session, both inside and outside the classroom. With three-hour blocks on Friday nights and eight-hour blocks on Saturdays, the class can go as a group on field trips to museums, performances, and community service sites. Among the pedagogical benefits are allowing students to work together in teams for extended periods of time inside the classroom without having to find time in their busy schedules for group meetings outside class. The teams can also consult with each other. Also, the instructor can observe group interactions for direct assessment of problem-solving and teamwork skills.

In a more complex and comprehensive model, Chattanooga State Community College offers an intense college learning community program for students who are over the age of 25. The cohorts are for those who plan to complete undergraduate degrees and transfer to a Tennessee university or college using Tennessee Transfer Pathways. Notably, the program receives support from academic affairs, learning support, academic advisors, student support personnel, and faculty. Students participate in two to four cohort courses over six academic terms, agree to enroll in college-level courses the following fall term, and agree to enroll in at least 12 hours for fall and spring and 6 credit hours for the summer terms (Chattanooga State Community College, 2018).

Faculty Practices to Increase Classroom Engagement

Unless their courses are exclusively online, the one experience all commuter students share is the classroom, and the one group of campus personnel they see are faculty members. The Education Advisory Board reports that faculty members are critical agents in student success but are surprisingly underemployed in that effort. Their study found that, without engagement among faculty, most top-down student success initiatives are doomed to failure, either through outright opposition or because of disuse. If administrators do not communicate their expectations about supporting students to faculty members, practices that could be helpful are not used or used only in pockets around campus. For example, early-warning systems to identify at-risk students have been purchased or developed by three-quarters of colleges and universities, but they're often not being used. Faculty members often do not know about them or do not use them because they simply do not know how. Provosts, deans, and department heads need to reinforce the importance of early alerts and other support systems to faculty, demonstrate how they can get help to students in a timely manner, and make sure they know how to use them (Education Advisory Board, 2016).

In addition, faculty members need to know the realities of commuter, part-time, and returning adult students' lives. Likewise, student affairs administrators need to learn from them what they have found effective in working with commuter students so they can help get that information into the hands of other faculty and staff members. Partnering with the campus center for teaching and learning is key. For example, many centers for teaching and learning regularly offer workshops for faculty presented by student affairs professionals on topics such as diversity and inclusion, students with disabilities, academic integrity, and student mental health issues. Such centers should also offer workshops on what faculty need to know about commuter, part-time, and returning adult students in general and specifically about subgroups of students including student-parents, veterans, and first-generation students.

Faculty members can use this information in many ways to enhance the classroom experience of commuter—and all—students. A lot of teaching that works well for commuter, part-time, and returning adult students is good teaching for all students. For example, they can develop high-impact practices such as collaborative assignments and projects, through which students learn important workplace skills such as communication, problem solving, collaboration, working across difference, and responsibility. To make group projects accessible to commuter students with complex lives, this means using class time to allow students to work on their group projects instead of the traditional mode of assigning group projects to be completed outside class time. In such a "flipped classroom," faculty members deliver course material via online platforms so that students can view lectures any time, even watching parts of them more than once.

In addition, it helps students focus in class if faculty members tell them what to expect. This is really helpful for students for whom college is not their only focus or who are returning to college after a break in their education. Faculty members can email or text students before each class session to tell them what topics or questions they will cover, how they should prepare, and what they'll be expected to do. When students have time to prepare and can prepare purposefully, they are often more likely to do so and to be invested in the discussion and willing to participate.

Another simple thing faculty members can do is to give students a moment to write down their answers when they pose a question in class. Cold calling can intimidate students who are not used to being in a classroom, introverts, and those for whom English is not their first language. It can cause fear and feel to them like a "gotcha" exercise. An alternative is to pose a thought-provoking, relevant question and give students a few minutes to write down their thoughts/answers. Students are much more likely to participate without feeling like they are put on the spot.

"Nudges," interventions that encourage but do not mandate a certain behavior, have caught on as a way to help students through the many complex processes of higher education. For example, a faculty member at the University of Arizona uses them as a low-touch way to intervene with students who fail the first exam in her course. She sends an email explaining that the student did not do as well as expected on the exam, but it is still early in the semester, and changing habits now could turn their grade around. She sends the message from her own email address and personalizes it using each student's name. The message does not directly offer any additional support to its recipients. Rather, it asks if the student knows why they did not perform well on the exam and whether they were taking advantage of existing resources, like office hours and study groups. Many students are grateful for the "nudge" and take greater responsibility for their learning, while some also take advantage of the resources suggested in the message (Cohen, 2018).

Faculty members also can make a determined effort to arrive a few minutes before class and speak with an individual student or two each day, rotating around the room so that eventually they chat with all of them. The conversation can be very brief, such as "How are you doing?" or "What's your major?" These simple interactions prompt students to be more talkative in discussions and encourage students who normally stay in the back row to ask questions.

Finally, faculty members often require students to turn off their cell phones during class. However, student-parents whose children are in daycare are highly stressed without their phones in case their child becomes ill or some emergency arises that requires them to pick up their child immediately. Another thing faculty members need to know is that keeping students even a few minutes after class may be costly to students who must clock in on time for their shift or they cannot work it. And student-parents who often have to pick up their child from daycare at a specific time or pay an exorbitant fee, sometimes up to $5.00 per minute late.

Conclusion

As commuter, part-time, and returning adult students become more numerous and diverse and attend an increasingly wider variety of institutions, educators must develop a thorough understanding of their needs, useful theoretical frameworks, and strategies that increase their success and retention. The frameworks and strategies described in this chapter are readily adaptable to institutions and their various populations of commuter students. In the current climate in which institutions of higher education are held accountable for translating policies, practices, and programs into degree completion and success for all students, these frameworks and strategies will enable institutions to comprehensively and effectively enhance the educational experience of all students.

References

American Association of Community Colleges. (2018). *AACC pathways project*. Retrieved from www.aacc.nche.edu/programs/aacc-pathways-project

Association of American Colleges and Universities. (2018). *Guided learning pathways*. Retrieved from www.aacu.org/toolkit/guided-learning-pathways

Astin, A. W. (1984). Student involvement: A developmental theory for higher education. *Journal of College Student Development, 25*, 297–308.

Astin, A. W. (1985). *Achieving educational excellence*. San Francisco, CA: Jossey-Bass.

Berman, J. (2017). The number of single moms in college has soared, yet they struggle to graduate. *MarketWatch*. Retrieved from www.marketwatch.com/story/more-than-1-in-10-college-students-is-a-single-mom-2017-09-20

Bombardieri, M. (2017). *Hidden in plain sight: Understanding part-time college students in America.* Center for American Progress. Retrieved from www.americanprogress.org/issues/education-postsecondary/reports/2017/09/06/438341/hidden-plain-sight

Carnevale, A. P., Smith, N., Melton, M., & Price, E. W. (2015). *Learning while earning: The new normal.* Washington, DC: Georgetown University Center for Education and the Workforce.

Chattanooga State Community College. (2018). *Non-traditional learning community.* Retrieved from http://live-chattstate14.pantheonsite.io/sites/default/files/imported/academics/degree-express/pdf/non-traditional.pdf

Chickering, A. W. (2000). Creating community within individual courses. In B. Jacoby (Ed.), *Involving commuter students in learning* (New Directions for Higher Education No. 109, pp. 23–32). San Francisco, CA: Jossey-Bass, 2000.

Cohen, Z. (2018). *Small changes, large rewards: How individualized emails increase classroom performance.* Retrieved from https://evolllution.com/attracting-students/retention/small-changes-large-rewards-how-individualized-emails-increase-classroom-performance/?elqTrackId=2245bda9a1ce490e8e79dccb4694a108&elq=1ce2a85a239c4ddda7b4f7820b733fc7&elqaid=20066&elqat=1&elqCampaignId=9348

East Tennessee State University. *Buc path.* Retrieved from www.etsu.edu/students/bucpath

Education Advisory Board. (2016). *The evolving role of faculty in student success.* Retrieved from http://ns.eab.com/DefiningtheFacultyRoleinStudentSuccess

Goldrick-Rab, S. (2016). *Paying the price*: College costs, financial aid, and the betrayal of the American dream. Chicago, IL: University of Chicago Press.

Goldrick-Rab, S., Richardson, J., & Hernandez, A. (2017). *Hungry and homeless in college: Results from a national study of basic needs insecurity in higher education.* Retrieved from www.wihopelab.com/publications/Hungry-and-Homeless-in-College-Report.pdf

Goldrick-Rab, S., Richardson, J., Schneider, J., Hernandez, A., & Cady, C. (2018). *Still hungry and homeless in college.* Retrieved from http://wihopelab.com/publications/Wisconsin-HOPE-Lab-Still-Hungry-and-Homeless.pdf

Jacoby, B. (1989). *The student as commuter: Developing a comprehensive institutional response.* ASHE-ERIC Higher Education Report, no. 7. Washington, DC: School of Education and Human Development, George Washington University.

Jacoby, B. (2000). *Involving commuter students in learning* (New Directions for Higher Education No. 109). San Francisco, CA: Jossey-Bass.

Jacoby, B. (2015). Enhancing commuter student success: What's theory got to do with it? In P. Biddix (Ed.), *Understanding and addressing commuter student needs* (New directions for student services, No. 150). San Francisco, CA: Jossey-Bass.

Jacoby, B., & Garland, J. (2004). Strategies for enhancing commuter student success. *Journal of College Student Retention, 6*(1).

Kruger, K., Parnell, A., & Wesaw, A. (2016). *Landscape analysis of emergency aid programs.* Retrieved from www.naspa.org/rpi/reports/landscape-analysis-of-emergency-aid-programs

Kuh, G. D., Gonyea, R. M., & Palmer, M. (2001). The disengaged commuter student: Fact or fiction. *Commuter Perspectives, 27*(1), 2–5.

Maslow, A. H. (1982). *Toward a psychology of being* (2nd ed.). New York, NY: Van Nostrand Reinhold.

Mendiola-Perez, C., & Dalrymple, R. (2015). *Collaborative approach to advising and pathways integration using MyMAP.* Retrieved from www.alamo.edu/uploadedFiles/District/About_Us/Chancellor/AACC-Presentation-2015.pdf

National Student Clearinghouse Research Center (2015). *Transfer & mobility, 2015.* Retrieved from https://nscresearchcenter.org/signaturereport9

O'Connor, M. (2016). *How to transform student employment into meaningful career development.* Education Advisory Board. Retrieved from www.eab.com/research-and-insights/student-affairs-forum/expert-insights/2016/career-boost-student-employee-program

Pascarella, E. T. (2006). How college affects students: Ten directions for future research. *Journal of College Student Development, 47*(5), 508–520.

Rosenberg, M., & McCullough, B. C. (1981). Mattering: Inferred significance and mental health among adolescents. In R. Simmons (Ed.), *Research in community and mental health* (Vol. 2). Greenwich, CT: JAI Press.

Schlossberg, N. K. (1985). *Marginality and mattering: A life span approach.* Paper presented at the annual meeting of the American Psychological Association. Los Angeles, CA.

Schlossberg, N. K., Lynch, A. Q., & Chickering, A. W. (1989). *Improving higher education environments for adults.* San Francisco, CA: Jossey-Bass.

Schmidt, G. (2016). *Guided pathways project becomes a movement.* American Association of Community Colleges. Retrieved from www.aacc21stcenturycenter.org/article/pathways-project-becomes-a-movement

Soares, L. (2013). *Post-traditional learners and the transformation of postsecondary education: A manifesto for college leaders.* Retrieved from www.acenet.edu/news-room/Documents/Post-Traditional-Learners.pdf

Steele, P., & Erisman, W. (2016). Addressing the college attainment gap for working adults with prior college credit. *Change: The Magazine of Higher Learning, 48*(2), 46–53.

Study Group on the Conditions of Excellence in American Higher Education. (1984). *Involvement in learning: Realizing the potential of American higher education.* Washington, DC: US Department of Education.

Tidewater Community College. (2018). *Textbook-free degree.* Retrieved from www.tcc.edu/academics/degrees/textbook-free

University of Iowa. (2018). *Iowa GROW.* Retrieved from https://vp.studentlife.uiowa.edu/priorities/grow

University of Michigan. (2018). *Sick or backup ChildCare Service.* Retrieved from https://hr.umich.edu/benefits-wellness/work-life/child-care-resources/sick-or-backup-child-care-service

University of Washington. (2018). *The Student Parent Resource Center.* Retrieved from https://osfa.washington.edu/wp/sprc

US Department of Education (2015). *Demographic and enrollment characteristics of nontraditional undergraduates: 2011–2012.* Retrieved from https://nces.ed.gov/pubs2015/2015025.pdf

Wilmes, M. B., & Quade, S. L. (1986). Perspectives on programming for commuters: Examples of good practice. *NASPA Journal, 24*(1), 25–35.

Yale University. (2018). Center for Teaching and Learning. *Open educational resources.* Retrieved from https://ctl.yale.edu/faculty-resources/instructional-tools/open-educational-resources

Chapter 20
Engaging Military-Connected Students

Stephanie Bondi, Denise N. Williams-Klotz,
Ann M. Gansemer-Topf, and Corey B. Rumann

Military-connected students, defined by Molina and Morse (2015) as active duty personnel, reservists, veterans or members of the National Guard, are a growing student population in higher education. The number of enrolled military-connected students at institutions of higher education is expected to continue to increase as more and more of them use their military educational benefits to attend college and pursue college degrees (Cate, 2014; Cook & Kim, 2009; Sander, 2012). Although the focus on military-connected students in higher education is gaining increased attention, there is still some question as to how to best serve this population and increase opportunity for engagement (Collins, Biniecki, & Polson, 2016; Gregg, Kitzman, & Shordike, 2016; Jenner, 2017; Jenson, Petri, & Day, 2017; NSSE, 2010). This chapter addresses military-connected student engagement in higher education by first providing a snapshot of this population. In addition, Abes, Jones, and McEwen's (2007) reconceptualized model of multiple identities will help readers understand the complex nature of military-connected students' identities and how multiple social identities must be considered in our work with this population. The chapter includes a brief discussion of current research on military-connected students, much of which focuses on their transition experiences. Using Rendón's (1994) Validation Theory as a guiding framework, the chapter concludes with recommendations for promoting military-connected student engagement.

Who are Military-Connected Students?

Student veterans and military servicemembers (on active duty and reserve) comprise about 4% of undergraduates at institutions of higher education (Henke & Paslov, 2016). According to a 2013 national survey of 1,650 higher education institutions, 96% of institutions have at least one military-connected service member or dependent enrolled at their institution (Queen & Lewis, 2014). Data collected from the National Center for Education Statistics (NCES) illustrate similarities and differences between military-connected students and their nonmilitary-connected peers. Both populations have similar percentages of students who identify as Black (17% versus 16%), Hispanic (15% versus 16%), American Indian or Pacific Islander (1% versus 1%), and two or more races (3% versus 3%). Slightly higher percentages of military-connected students identify as White (60% versus 58%), and a lower percentage identify as Asian (3% versus 6%) (Henke & Paslov, 2016). More significant differences also exist. A higher percentage of military-connected students identify as male (78% versus 41%), are less likely to have parents who have earned a bachelor's degree (30% versus 39%), are more likely to be married (50% versus 16%), have children (52% versus 16%), work full time (46% versus 25%), and attend a for-profit institution (26% versus 11%) (Henke & Paslov, 2016). Many of these same characteristics are also negatively associated with degree attainment rates and the data mirror this phenomenon as well. Nationally, the low percentage of all students who achieve a degree is concerning. This concern is amplified for military-connected students: of those who begin an associate's degree program, 14% achieve an associate's degree within six years, and 11% of those who begin a Bachelor's degree program graduate within six years (NCES, 2011).

Institutional Efforts

Recognizing the challenges faced by military-connected students, institutions have developed programs and policies to support their success. An NCES report (Queen & Lewis, 2014) provided some key findings in this area. For this report, institutions were asked to include information for active-duty service members, reservists, members of the National Guard, veterans, and dependents of military service members (Queen & Lewis, 2014). It is not surprising that many institutions identify military-connected students as those who receive financial education benefits—which can be active duty, veterans, or their dependents—and fewer than 70% of institutions distinguish between dependents, veterans, and other military-connected students (Queen & Lewis, 2014). It is important to consider this detail when collecting and interpreting data on military-connected students.

Data on institutional efforts coupled with data on demographics and graduate rates highlight a common challenge regarding this population of students: military-connected students have a continued interest in pursuing higher education, institutions are working to meet the needs of this population, but military-connected students still face challenges within higher education, and not all institutions provide the same level of support (Queen & Lewis, 2014). Fortunately, research and institutional efforts are evolving to provide more information about this population of students and the ways that people, programs, and policies can best support their success.

Recent Research on Military-Connected Students

There is a growing body of literature about the experiences of military-connected students. Barry, Whiteman, and MacDermid (2014) conducted a review of literature and found research related to military-connected students on the following topics: mental health, coping strategies, PTSD and relationship to combat experience, time away from school, importance of support from military peers, military pride, and stereotypes. The most significant body of research on contemporary military-connected students has focused on their transition experiences to the higher education environment (see, for example, Bauman, 2009, 2013; DiRamio, Ackerman, & Mitchell, 2008; Livingston, Havice, Cawthon, & Fleming, 2011; Mendez, Witowsky, Morris, Brosseau, & Nicholson, 2018; Rumann & Hamrick, 2010; Williams-Klotz & Gansemer-Topf, 2017a, 2017b, 2018). Some common themes of these studies help explain military-connected students' experiences. For example, military-connected students tend to feel more mature and report a more focused approach to their academic and career goals than their nonmilitary peers (DiRamio et al., 2008; Rumann & Hamrick, 2010; Wheeler, 2012). This increased level of maturity can help military-connected students be more successful in college, but it can also lead them to feel more alienated from their nonmilitary college student peers (DiRamio & Jarvis, 2011; Livingston, 2009; Rumann, 2010; Schiavone & Gentry, 2014; Wheeler, 2012).

Regarding the transition process itself, military-connected students are navigating an environment (i.e., the college environment) that is very different from the military environment. The military environment tends to be much more structured than college, and military-connected students have reported challenges adjusting or readjusting to the academic experience (Bauman, 2013; Blaauw-Hara, 2016; Jones, 2013, 2017; Livingston et al., 2011; Williams-Klotz & Gansemer-Topf, 2017a; Wheeler, 2012), though De Sawal (2013) found student veterans have better study habits and spend more time studying than non-military-connected peers. Additionally, Wheeler (2012) found that veterans at one community college reported their military service had positively contributed to their academic success, instilling in them skills to plan their studies, execute the plan, and learn from the experience.

Further complicating this process is the disconnect military-connected students may feel from their nonmilitary student peers as well as faculty and staff at the institution (DiRamio et al., 2008; Williams-Klotz & Gansemer-Topf, 2017a). As they navigate the collegiate environment, military-connected students tend to seek each other out for support and understanding in hopes of finding someone who understands their experiences (Hammond, 2015; Rumann, 2010; Rumann & Hamrick, 2010; Williams-Klotz & Gansemer-Topf, 2017a, 2017b, 2018). Simultaneously, many military-connected students who have completed their service are learning what being a veteran means to them in relation to their other social identities (DiRamio, Jarvis, Iverson, Seher, & Anderson, 2015; Schiavone & Gentry, 2014). This negotiation and meaning-making process will be discussed in a future section.

The research to date on military-connected students helps faculty and staff understand how policies, practices, and initiatives can help ease the transition of military-connected students at institutions of higher education and make recommendations about how to engage military-connected students in college, which is distilled and expanded in this chapter.

Military-Connected Student Engagement Data

Campuses are investing in programs and resources to engage military-connected students, although the level of investment differs from institution to institution. With these efforts in mind, the American Council of Education utilized data from the National Survey of Student Engagement to understand student veterans/services members' views on their level of engagement (Cole & Kim, 2013). In comparison with their non-military-connected peers, military-connected students spend more time preparing for class, working off campus, and caring for children. They are more likely to report that their relationships with faculty members and administrative staff are friendly and supportive (61% versus 54%; 46% versus 36%, but a lower percentage report having friendly supportive relationships with other students (58% versus 62%). Military-connected students are less likely to connect with other students outside the classroom, but a slightly higher percentage mention they often or very often have serious conversations with students of a different race or ethnicity (58% versus 54%) or students with different religious beliefs, political opinions, or personal values (58% versus 55%) (Cole & Kim, 2013). Overall, the report highlights that military-connected students are engaged with their institutions but are more likely to be engaged academically than socially. Additionally, Durdella and Kim (2012) found that for military-connected students, the academic engagement may not lead to the outcomes experienced by civilian peers. Their research similarly showed that military-connected students are engaged more academically than civilian peers but that the military-connected students had lower GPAs as a group than non-military-connected peers. They suggest that military-connected students' hours working and transfer student status may mediate the effects of academic engagement for this population. These findings highlight the importance of faculty engagement and academic support for this population of students.

Theories and Concepts

Multiple theoretical models have emerged in the last decade to examine the student development, success, and engagement of military-connected students, including DiRamio and Jarvis's (2011) adaptation of Tinto's longitudinal model, Livingston et al.'s (2011) Student Veteran Academic and Social Transition Model, and Vacchi and Berger's (2014) Model for Student Veteran Support.

DiRamio and Jarvis (2011) offer an adaptation of Tinto's (1993) longitudinal model of student departure to apply to student veterans. In this theoretical model, the goal for integration with the larger campus community is often facilitated by military-connected student peer groups. Integration into civilian culture, including civilian professional environments, is facilitated through interactions with campus career services units. Vacchi, Hammond, and Diamond (2017) are critical of this approach, which can become deficit oriented for military-connected students. Instead of focusing on how military-connected students are not like civilian students, educators could focus on their strengths and finding or creating places to leverage them for success.

Livingston et al.'s (2011) Student Veteran Academic and Social Transition model describes the way multiple factors influence student veteran navigation of the reenrollment process and how that process, in turn, influences student engagement opportunities. They found that military socialization influences the use of peers and support systems (auxiliary aids) and the transition of veterans which, in turn, influence the navigation of reenrollment following deployment. Livingston et al. (2011) included in this transition (a) making sense of a lack of structure and routine, (b) financial considerations, (c) reacclimating to civilian life, and (d) use of support structures. Livingston et al. illustrate the interconnectedness of experiences that frame military-connected and student veteran transition.

Vacchi and Berger (2014) summarize Vacchi's Model for Student Veteran Support including peer support, delivery of services, academic interactions, and transition support. This model draws from an ecological perspective to illustrate the complex way in which military-connected students engage with their environment and are influenced by a myriad of interactions with institutional agents (Vacchi et al., 2017). Like Livingston et al. (2011), this model takes into consideration the multiple levels of support and interaction for military-connected students transitioning to campus.

Multiple Identities and Intersectionality

Theories on intersecting identities among college students and the outcomes that accrue when undergraduates are appropriately validated in campus environments are useful for determining how to effectively engage military-connected students in higher education. Hammond's (2015) Combat Veteran Conceptual Identity Model explores student veteran identity existing simultaneously with other identities such as combat veteran, citizen and peer. Hammond's model reveals a nonlinear approach to identity development and formation for military-connected students dependent on environmental interactions (Vacchi et al., 2017). Hammond (2015) includes five components including perception of self, perception of others, connection to other veterans, and inferred perception of self.

At times, military-connected students may be viewed as a homogenous group, which is not accurate (Iverson & Anderson, 2013; Williams-Klotz & Gansemer-Topf, 2018). Each military-connected student is unique and brings with them a different set of experiences and social identities. People often assume military-connected students are White, heterosexual, 25-year-old men. In reality, military-connected students traverse almost all demographic groups. While a paucity of research on military-connected students exists on the experiences of People of Color and military-connected students in the LGBTQIA+ community (Iverson & Anderson, 2013), a growing body of literature is emerging on the experiences of women military-connected students (see Demers, 2013; DiRamio et al., 2015; Elliott, 2014; Schiavone & Gentry, 2014).

Abes et al. (2007) describe how students negotiate and make sense of multiple intersecting identities through a meaning-making filter acknowledging the "changing contexts and relative salience" of their lives (p. 3). Their model illustrates multiple identities as intersecting circles surrounding a core or inner self. Military-connected students possess multiple identities, and so their experiences may differ greatly. For example, military-connected Students of Color and students who are religious minorities in the US may feel marginalized in a predominantly White institution. People who are bisexual, lesbian, transgender, gay, or queer may develop a vigilance for self-protection (Gonzales, Ramirez, & Galupo, 2018). They may become preoccupied with concerns about their own or friends' safety or may be anxious about the rollback of legal protections (Gonzales et al., 2018).

Transgender and gender diverse (TGD) students specifically may be seeking or developing kinship networks (Nicolazzo, 2017). TGD individuals could also be negotiating how, when, and with whom to share their gender identity in an environment where TGD people are banned from joining the military unless they are willing to serve in what the government describes as their biological sex or if they had already been serving openly prior to the ban. Female military-connected students may struggle transitioning from a male-dominated military culture and lack same-gender role models to assist them in their transition (Baechtold & De Sawal, 2009).

It is also important to know that many military-connected students returning from wartime deployment are trying to make meaning of their experiences and how that influences their other social identities (Rumann, 2010; Rumann & Hamrick, 2010). The salience of these identities follows Abes et al.'s (2007) model indicating students work to make meaning of salient identities through a meaning-making filter influenced by the context (e.g., college, military). In the next section, we discuss Validation Theory, which says that the key to success for some students includes validating their identities and demonstrating to them they have the skills to be academically successful. Educators who want to connect with and support military-connected students must understand these intersecting identities in order to successfully provide that validation.

Validation Theory

To offer recommendations for engaging military-connected students, we turn to a theory of supporting nontraditional college students: Validation Theory (Rendón, 1994; Rendón & Muñoz, 2011). Rendón advocates this theory for any nontraditional students who are unsure about their ability to be successful in college or are unfamiliar with college values (L. Rendón, personal communication, March 19, 2012). Since military-connected students are often older than nonmilitary students and have taken time away from college to serve in the military, many military-connected students fit within the nontraditional student classification. Additionally as discussed earlier, military-connected students have multiple identities and may identify with other social identity groups associated with nontraditional students (Vaccaro, 2015).

Validation Theory was developed from the results of a larger study of the factors contributing to student learning and retention in higher education (Rendón, 1994). During the study, nontraditional students reported validation allayed doubts about their ability to learn and was important to their academic success. Rendón (1994) found the opposite of the prevailing belief that college students would take advantage of opportunities provided for them. She found many nontraditional students would not engage in opportunities without validation. Nontraditional students require validation to overcome existing anxieties, fears, and prior invalidations. Validation serves as an important foundation for involvement, academic success, and development in college (Rendón, 2002; Rendón & Muñoz, 2011).

Validation Theory suggests nontraditional students experience incongruence between their experiences and those of peers. For military-connected students, as mentioned earlier, the incongruence may arise from being more serious about their academics, having more life experiences outside college than peers, and/or raising a family. It could also be related to the differences between the structured, team-oriented military culture and the less structured, individualized academic culture. The incongruence may also be related to one of the military-connected student's other social identities, such as socioeconomic status, age, or race. Additionally, many nontraditional students have experienced prior academic invalidation and need support in order to believe they can be successful learners (Rendón, 1994). Military-connected students may perceive the lack of recognition for their military training and roles as academic invalidation. Or they may have received academic invalidation because of other social identities (e.g., class, race, gender).

Rendón suggests validation is the support nontraditional students need. It takes the form of someone actively encouraging the students. Validation counters the notion that college students must navigate the college system relying primarily on themselves, where faculty and staff serve primarily to hold students accountable. Validation should be reframed from unnecessary coddling to necessary support for nontraditional students.

Validation is grouped into two categories: interpersonal and academic (Rendón, 1994; Rendón & Muñoz, 2011). In the classroom, faculty can provide interpersonal validation through personal connections with students and through genuine concern for them (Rendón & Muñoz, 2011). This means developing opportunities for military-connected students to connect with faculty, staff, and each other is vital to their engagement on campus. Faculty and staff must take initiative to nurture connections with military-connected students and must be knowledgeable about and available to military-connected students (Heineman, 2016). Instructors and staff who practice academic validation create therapeutic learning environments (Ezeonu, 2011) and opportunities for students to experience success (Rendón, 1994). They also provide valuable feedback (Rendón, 2002). Another tactic used to validate students is to provide opportunities for students to connect their life experiences with the academic experiences (Rendón, 1994). These connections can be made through recognition of military skills, education, and accomplishments (Naphan & Elliott, 2015); discussion; in- or out-of-class activities; or assignments.

The timing of validation should be early within the academic experience and continue as a part of ongoing student development (Rendón & Muñoz, 2011). A lack of validation for military-connected students could be a potential barrier to engagement, and this is significant because engagement has been shown to be a predictor of success in college. Therefore, validation is an important prerequisite for many military-connected students' engagement and success in college. There are many possibilities for validating nontraditional students interpersonally and academically. In this chapter we have named just a few. We use these elements of validation to offer strategies to increase military-connected student engagement.

Student Engagement Strategies

Elements of validation (Rendón, 1994) are used in this section to offer a set of recommendations for more effectively engaging military-connected students on college and university campuses, inside and outside classrooms. First, validation is a supportive, enabling process fostered by in- and out-of-class validation agents. Second, validated students feel capable of academic success and that their life experiences are valued. Finally, validation is part of an ongoing process that is most critical early in students' academic careers. The following strategies address these elements of validation.

Ensure Opportunities Reflect Military-Connected Students' Experiences

Validating military-connected students' experiences requires acknowledging their experiences. Student veteran demographics indicate they are more likely to have dependents and work more hours than traditional students. Educators should consider these characteristics when planning academic and co-curricular opportunities. Faculty may assign a project to be due the next day, assuming that students will be able to complete it within a day, but military-connected students, who are more likely to have dependents and work more hours than non-military-connected students, may not be able to complete assignments within this time frame. When activities and assignments are planned for students who are not parenting or working fewer hours, it invalidates the experiences of parenting and working students like many military-connected students. Creating more opportunities for military-connected and other working and parenting students (e.g., family picnics, brown-bag lunch speakers, flexible support hours, assignments with flexibility, etc.) can show support for their experiences and provide evidence that military-connected students are expected and belong in college.

Since military-connected students, like other nontraditional students, may be more likely to question their academic capabilities based on their prior invalidating experiences and perceived differences from traditional students (Rendón, 1994), their life experiences must be recognized by staff and faculty as valuable and contributing to their preparedness for college and academic success. Williams-Klotz and Gansemer-Topf (2018) found that feeling academically prepared prior to enrollment was associated with academic success for military-connected students. Validating students' academic ability prior to entry can potentially bolster academic engagement. Students should also have the opportunity to connect their experiences within and outside the military with classroom discussion, projects, and/or co-curricular activities. Incorporating student experiences in the classroom may require some faculty to reform their pedagogies since many rely on lecturing and have a stock set of examples. Instructors need to create opportunities to connect the course concepts to situations that resonate with military-connected students. Instructors can accomplish this by providing examples that reflect military-connected students' experiences, making time for discussion in the classroom, or asking students to relate classroom concepts or problems to their own lives. For instance, in a math course, students may be asked to find examples of how they could use the math concepts to help them address problems they face in their daily lives or future professions.

While discussion in class can be a useful tool, educators are cautioned that calling on military-connected students in group settings may put them on the spot or make them feel like they are expected to be experts on the military experience. Faculty and staff may invite students to share their personal experiences to the extent they feel comfortable while remembering students cannot speak to the experiences of all military-connected students. Educators should ask students in private how comfortable they are sharing their experiences in class or make general solicitations for sharing (e.g., "Does anyone have personal experiences being in the military they would like to share with the group?"). Soliciting contributions from military-connected students about their experiences outside the military is as important as focusing on their experiences within the military because military-connected students are more than their military experience.

Acknowledge Military-Connected Students' Complex Multiple Identities

When getting to know military-connected students, it is important that staff and faculty not only understand their experiences directly related to being students and connected to the military, but their other life experiences as well (e.g., as a family member, community member, member of a minoritized group). Focusing only on military-connected students' experiences as military servicemembers essentializes their experiences and is likely to ignore salient aspects of their lives. Faculty and staff should provide opportunities for the students to explore how their identities intersect. For example, educators can provide opportunities for them to pursue questions such as (a) What does it mean to be a Latina member of the Army National Guard and be in a STEM field? (b) How does being gay shape your networking and job-searching strategies? or (c) What strategies do military-connected student-parents use to be successful in college? Military-connected students who are able to explore their multiple intersecting identities are more likely to understand how their identities influence their experiences in the differing military and academic cultures, which may contribute to their sense of validation and engagement. Student development theory suggests that students with a strong understanding of their identities may be more likely to pursue connections with similar peers and mentors and also better accept and interact with people who are different. All of these things have been shown to be important developmentally.

Create Opportunities to Validate Through Academic Success

Another way to validate military-connected students so that they feel capable of success is by affording opportunities to experience success in the classroom (Rendón, 2002). One method for helping students experience success is to have students complete tasks while in the presence of supportive faculty and staff. Faculty and staff should demonstrate to students their abilities to complete college tasks and provide useful feedback (Rendón, 2002). Additionally providing clear and accessible instructions for all students provides military-connected students the opportunity to access the information and manage their learning independently, a trait trained and valued in military training (Griffin & Gilbert, 2015; Williams-Klotz & Gansemer-Topf, 2017a). When the in-class and out-of-class agents at the college or university have validated military-connected students, these students are more likely to have increased confidence in their academic abilities. In a course, validation could be accomplished by providing a writing task in the classroom and pointing out to students that they can write, citing that exercise as an example, prior to expecting a larger writing project to be completed. In a lab course, teaching assistants or a lab technician could review students' lab notes and give positive feedback in areas where students are on the right track. They could provide encouragement that students have the tools, including support people to answer questions, to be successful in the course. Additionally, understanding academic expectations has been found to be central to military-connected student academic success, so these interactions could serve to clarify expectations and confirm with the student they have been met (Williams-Klotz & Gansemer-Topf, 2017b). Military-connected students are more likely to imagine themselves succeeding in college and persisting to graduation once they have been able to see their own academic success.

Recognize and Reward Faculty and Staff for Validating Students

Faculty and staff are often rewarded for creation of well-attended programs, for generating a high number of publications, and for serving on multiple campus initiatives, but they are rarely recognized and compensated to the same extent for validating students. Institutions committed to supporting the engagement of military-connected students and other nontraditional students should devote resources to recognizing and rewarding faculty and staff in ways that will promote more opportunities to experience success, connections with validating agents, and experiences that reflect military-connected student experiences. If faculty and staff are not recognized for validation efforts, institutions are severely limiting the validation military-connected students will be able to receive through campus agents.

Train Educators to Validate Military-Connected Students

To have validation agents across campus, faculty and staff need to be trained to validate students (Rendón, 1994). Training should provide demographics and unique concerns of military-connected students. Educators also need information about issues specific to military-connected students, such as access to military educational benefits, the structured military culture, military credit transfer, deployment and active duty interruptions, and service-related injuries and disabilities such as PTSD, mobility constraints, and traumatic brain injuries. A key piece of this training should include helping faculty and staff understand military culture (see www.ptsd.va.gov/professional/ptsd101/course-modules/military_culture.asp). Educators should be cautioned during training that military servicemembers have experiences, abilities, and concerns going beyond their military-connected identity related to their other identities and responsibilities. Essentializing military-connected students to servicemembers could be as harmful as ignoring their military experiences.

In addition to learning about military-connected student demographics and common concerns, faculty and staff need training on validation. Faculty and staff need to learn how to initiate and build genuine interpersonal connections with military-connected students. They may need tips on how to build and maintain relationships when other obligations for instruction, research, and service monopolize their time. Instructors may need examples of how to incorporate student experiences in the classroom. They may also need ideas on how to create a caring, supportive environment where students are more likely to feel capable of and experience academic success.

Another strategy is to discuss the importance of validation and the role of Validation Theory in education and the success of nontraditional students such as military-connected students during staff development and in higher education and student affairs preparation programs. Validation Theory should be included as part of the curriculum for new professionals and those enhancing their professional education. Retention theories like Tinto's based on traditional students' experiences are often included in the canon. Educators should add Validation Theory concepts related to military-connected student transition and success to address the experiences of these students in the academy.

Develop Mentoring Programs in Spaces Where Military-Connected Students Are

Validation must begin in places where military-connected students already are present. Assess your institution to identify where military-connected students can be found. This may be a cafeteria, required courses, advising in the military-connected students' office, or a space on campus like a veteran's lounge. Go to these spaces and offer mentoring in the form of ongoing regular contact with faculty, staff, and/or more advanced military-connected students. The mentors should be trained about military-connected students' concerns, campus climate issues related to military-connected students, academic and other resources available for support on campus and in the community, and validation practices. Goals of the mentoring program should be to support students personally and academically. Mentors can help by showing military-connected students how to harness life experiences for academic success and acknowledging and celebrating those successes throughout their academic journey. Mentors can help military-connected students build and maintain a strong sense of academic self-confidence and interpersonal connection.

Connecting Off-Campus Validation Agents With the Institution

In addition to all the on-campus agents like faculty and staff, parents, siblings, children, and community members are prime candidates to validate military-connected students. Family and community members may already be validating military-connected students, regardless of institutional efforts to validate. Family and community members may promote feelings of connectedness, competence, and self-worth through their personal, genuine relationships with military-connected students. The institution should consider how to promote connections with these out-of-class agents to strengthen the impact of validation on academic pursuits. For example, the institution could provide a newsletter, website, social media space, or listserv of opportunities on campus to military-connected students' family members because these validating agents may be able to encourage military-connected students to engage in these activities. These groups may be especially important agents for validation since research suggests family members (Romero, Riggs, & Ruggero, 2015) and other veterans are significant sources of support during their transitions to college (Rumann, 2010).

Conclusion

Military-connected students are an increasing population in higher education who share many characteristics with other nontraditional students. They come to college with rich personal histories and salient life experiences that institutions should utilize to engage them. Validation in the form of creating supportive environments, building genuine interpersonal connections, and offering opportunities to incorporate personal experiences within classroom and co-curricular activities will help military-connected students engage in college. Validating agents across campus and in the community should be trained and practice validation early in the military-connected students' college experience and at various time throughout, encouraging them to get involved and reinforcing their capability for success in college.

References

Abes, E. S., Jones, S. R., & McEwen, M. K. (2007). Reconceptualizing the model of multiple dimensions of identity: The role of meaning-making capacity in the construction of multiple identities. *Journal of College Student Development, 27*(1), 1–22. doi:10.1353/csd.2007.0000

Baechtold, M., & De Sawal, D. M. (2009). Meeting the needs of women veterans. *New Directions for Student Services, 2009*(126), 35–43.

Barry, A. E., Whiteman, S. D., & MacDermid Wadsworth, S. (2014). Student service members/veterans in higher education: A systematic review. *Journal of Student Affairs Research and Practice, 51*(1), 30–42. https://doi.org/10.1515/jsarp-2014-0003

Bauman, M. (2009). *Called to serve: The military mobilization of undergraduates* (Doctoral dissertation). The Pennsylvania State University, State College. Retrieved from ProQuest Digital Dissertations (AAT 3380873).

Bauman, M. (2013). From the box to the pasture: Student-veterans returning to campus. *College Student Affairs Journal, 31*(1), 41–53.

Blaauw-Hara, M. (2016). "The military taught me how to study, how to work hard": Helping student-veterans transition by building on their strengths. *Community College Journal of Research and Practice, 40*(10), 809–823.

Cate, C. A. (2014). *Million records project: Research from Student Veterans of America.* Washington, DC: Student Veterans of America.

Cole, J. S., & Kim, Y. M. (2013). *Student veterans/service members' engagement in college and university life and education.* Washington, DC: American Council on Education.

Collins, R. A., Biniecki, S. Y., & Polson, C. (2016). Social justice education and US military and adult learners. In *Adult education research conference.* Charlotte, NC: New Prairie Press.

Cook, B. J., & Kim, Y. (2009). *From soldier to student: Easing the transition of service members on campus.* Retrieved from The American Council on Education website: www.acenet.edu/AM/Template. cfm?Section=HENA&Template=/CM/ContentDisplay.cfm&6;ContentID=33233

De Sawal, D. D. (2013). Contemporary student veterans and service members. In F. A. Hamrick & C. B. Rumann (Eds.), *Called to serve: A handbook on student veterans and higher education* (pp. 71–88). San Francisco, CA: Jossey-Bass.

Demers, A. L. (2013). From death to life: Female veterans, identity negotiation, and reintegration into society. *Journal of Humanistic Psychology, 53*(4), 489–515. doi:10.1177/0022167812472395

DiRamio, D., Ackerman, R., & Mitchell, R. L. (2008). From combat to campus: Voices of student-veterans. *NASPA Journal, 45*(1), 73–102.

DiRamio, D., & Jarvis, K. (2011). Veterans in higher education: When Johnny and Jane come marching to campus. *ASHE Higher Education Report, 37*(3).

DiRamio, D., Jarvis, K., Iverson, S., Seher, C., & Anderson, R. (2015). Out from the shadows: Female student veterans and help-seeking. *College Student Journal, 49*(1), 49–68.

Durdella, N., & Kim, Y. K. (2012). Understanding patterns of college outcomes among student veterans. *Journal of Studies in Education, 2*(2), 109–129. https://doi.org/10.5296/jse.v2i2.1469

Elliott, J. D. (2014). Women veterans in higher education. In American Association of Collegiate Registrars and Admissions Officers (AACRO) (Ed.), *Helping veterans succeed: A handbook for higher education administrators* (pp. 35–49). Washington, DC: AACRO.

Ezeonu, R. F. (2011). Fostering a therapeutic learning environment: Highline Community College. *Enrollment Management Journal, 5*(2), 148–156.

Gonzales, K. A., Ramirez, J. L., & Galupo, M. P. (2018). Increase in GLBTQ minority stress following the 2016 US presidential election. *Journal of GLBT Family Studies, 14*(1–2), 130–151. https://doi.org/10.1 080/1550428X.2017.1420849

Gregg, B. T., Kitzman, P. H., & Shordike, A. (2016). Well-being and coping of student veterans readjusting into academia: A pilot survey. *Occupational Therapy in Mental Health, 32*(1), 86–107. https://doi.org/ 10.1080/0164212X.2015.1082081

Griffin, K. A., & Gilbert, C. K. (2015). Better transitions for troops: An application for Schlossberg's transition framework to analyses of barriers and institutional support structures for student veterans. *The Journal of Higher Education, 86*(1), 71–97. doi:10.1353/jhe

Hammond, S. P. (2015). Complex perceptions of identity: The experience of student combat veterans in community colleges. *Community College Journal of Research and Practice, 40*(2), 146–159. doi:10.10 80/10668926.2015.1017891

Heineman, J. A. (2016). Supporting veterans: Creating a "military friendly" community college campus. *Community College Journal of Research and Practice, 40*(3), 219–227. doi:10.1080/10668926.2015.1 112318

Henke, R. R., & Paslov, J. (2016). *Web tables: A profile of military undergraduates: 2011–12. (NCES Report: 2016–415).* Retrieved from https://nces.ed.gov/pubs2016/2016415.pdf

Iverson, S. V., & Anderson, R. (2013). The complexity of veteran identity: Understanding the role of gender, race and sexuality. In F. A. Hamrick & C. B. Rumann (Eds.), *Called to serve: A handbook on student veterans military-connected students and higher education* (pp. 89–115). San Francisco, CA: Jossey-Bass.

Jenner, B. M. (2017). Student veterans and the transition to higher education: Integrating existing literatures. *Journal of Veterans Studies, 2*(2).

Jenson, R., Petri, A., & Day, A. (2017). Veterans in STEM: Supporting the transition from military culture to the culture of college. *Advances in Intelligent Systems and Computing*, 43–53. doi:10.1007/978-3-319-60747-4_5

Jones, K. C. (2013). Understanding student veterans in transition. *The Qualitative Report*, *18*(37), Article 2. Retrieved from http://nsuworks.nova.edu/tqr/vol18/iss37/2

Jones, K. C. (2017). Understanding transition experiences of combat veterans attending community college. *Community College Journal of Research and Practice*, *41*(2), 107–123.

Livingston, W., Havice, P., Cawthon, T., & Fleming, D. (2011). Coming home: Student veterans' articulation of college re-enrollment. *Journal of Student Affairs Research and Practice*, *48*(3), 315–331. doi:10.2202/1949–6605.6292

Livingston, W. G. (2009). *Discovering the academic and social transitions of re-enrolling student veterans at one institution: A grounded theory* (Doctoral dissertation). Clemson University, Clemson, SC. Retrieved from ProQuest Digital Dissertations (AAT 3355150).

Mendez, S. L., Witowsky, P., Morris, P., Brosseau, J., & Nicholson, H. (2018). Student veteran experiences in a transition seminar course: Exploring the thriving transition cycle. *Journal of Veteran Studies*, *3*(2), 1–18.

Molina, D., & Morse, A. (2015). *Military-connected undergraduates: Exploring differences between National Guard, reserve, active duty and veterans in higher education*. Washington, DC: American Council on Education and NASPA-Student Affairs Administrators in Higher Education.

Naphan, D., & Elliot, M. (2015). Role exit from the military: Student veterans' perceptions of transitioning from the US military to higher education. *The Qualitative Report*, *20*(2), 36–48.

National Center for Education Statistics (NCES). (2011). *Data table: Degree completion by veteran status*. Retrieved from https://nces.ed.gov/surveys/npsas/tablesaddl.asp

National Survey of Student Engagement. (2010). *Major differences: Examining student engagement by field of study—Annual results 2010*. Bloomington, IN: Indiana University Center for Postsecondary Research.

Nicolazzo, Z. (2017). *Trans* in college: Transgender students' strategies for navigating campus life and the institutional politics of inclusion*. Sterling, VA: Stylus.

Queen, B., & Lewis, L. (2014). *Services and support programs for military service members and veterans at postsecondary institutions, 2012–13. First Look. NCES 2014–017*. National Center for Education Statistics. Retrieved from http://nces.ed.gov/pubs2014/2014017.pdf

Rendón, L. I. (1994). Validating culturally diverse students: Towards a new model of learning and student development. *Innovative Higher Education*, *19*(1), 33–51. http://doi.org/10.1007/BF01191156

Rendón, L. I. (2002). Community College Puente: A validating model of education. *Educational Policy*, *16*(4), 642–667. doi:10.1177/0895904802016004010

Rendón, L., & Muñoz, S. (2011). Revisiting validation theory: Theoretical foundations, applications, and extensions. *Enrollment Management Journal*, *5*(2), 12–33.

Romero, D. H., Riggs, S. A., & Ruggero, C. (2015). Coping, family social support, and psychological symptoms among student veterans. *Journal of Counseling Psychology*, *62*(2), 242–252. https://doi.org/10.1037/cou0000061

Rumann, C. B. (2010). *Student veterans returning to a community college: Understanding their transitions* (Doctoral dissertation). Iowa State University, Ames. Retrieved from ProQuest Digital Dissertations (AAT 3403830).

Rumann, C. B., & Hamrick, F. A. (2010). Student veterans in transition: Re-enrolling after war zone deployments. *Journal of Higher Education*, *81*(4), 431–458. http://doi.org/10.1353/jhe.0.0103

Sander, L. (2012, March 1). The post-9/11 GI Bill, explained. *The Chronicle of Higher Education*. Retrieved from https://www.chronicle.com

Schiavone, V., & Gentry, D. (2014). Veteran-students in transition at a Midwestern university. *Journal of Continuing Higher Education*, *62*(1), 29–38.

Tinto, V. (1993). *Leaving college: Rethinking the causes and cures of student attrition*. Chicago, IL: University of Chicago Press.

Vaccaro, A. (2015). "It's not one size fits all": Diversity among student veterans. *Journal of Student Affairs Research and Practice*, *52*, 347–358.

Vacchi, D., & Berger, J. (2014). Student veterans in higher education. In M. Paulsen (Ed.), *Higher education: Handbook of theory and research* (Vol. 29). New York, NY: Springer.

Vacchi, D., Hammond, D., & Diamond, A. (2017). Conceptual models of student veteran college experiences. *New Directions for Institutional Research, 171*, 23–41. doi:10.1002/ir.20192

Wheeler, H. A. (2012). Veterans' transitions to community college: A case study. *Community College Journal of Research and Practice, 36*(10), 775–792. https://doi.org/10.1080/10668926.2012.679457

Williams-Klotz, D. N., & Gansemer-Topf, A. M. (2017a). Identifying the camouflage: Uncovering and supporting the transition experiences of military and veteran students. *Journal of First-Year Experience and Students in Transition, 29*(1), 83–98.

Williams-Klotz, D. N., & Gansemer-Topf, A. M. (2017b). Military-connected student academic success at four-year institutions: A multi-institution study. *Journal of College Student Development, 58*(7), 96–982.

Williams-Klotz, D. N., & Gansemer-Topf, A. M. (2018). Examining factors related to academic success of military-connected students at community colleges. *Community College Journal of Research and Practice, 42*(6), 422–438. doi:10.1080/10668926.2017.1339647

Chapter 21
Engaging Graduate and Professional Students

Susan K. Gardner and Marco J. Barker

Despite representing over 14% of the total student enrollment in higher education in the United States (US Department of Education, 2017a), relatively little is known about graduate and professional students when compared to undergraduate students and their engagement. We can define graduate students as those students seeking post-baccalaureate degrees, including academic master's degrees and research doctoral degrees, and professional students as those pursuing post-baccalaureate degrees in professional areas such as medicine and law (Council of Graduate Schools, 2004). These individuals represent a significant proportion of the student population on many university campuses and present higher education professionals with many opportunities for engagement. In this chapter, we discuss this diverse population of students, the issues they face in higher education institutions, theoretical perspectives for working with them, and practical strategies for engaging them on our campuses.

Defining Graduate and Professional Education

The goals, scope, and aims of graduate and professional education are quite different from undergraduate education and merit some explanation. Unlike undergraduate education, which serves to provide students with a wide range of subjects of study and the opportunity to gain skills such as effective reading, writing, and argument skills, graduate education is "focused on a specific area of interest and acquiring specialized skills to practice a profession or do advanced research" (Kidwell & Flagg, 2004, p. 2). More specifically, two kinds of graduate degrees exist: (1) professional degrees and (2) research degrees at the two levels of degrees (master's and doctoral). In addition, post-baccalaureate certificate programs exist that are short term and specialized, often to meet career needs, and require two or three semesters to complete (Kidwell & Flagg, 2004).

At the master's level, students pursuing a professional degree find a program focused on "a specific set of skills needed to practice a particular profession" (Kidwell & Flagg, 2004, p. 2). These are typically final or terminal degrees. Many professional master's degrees are found in areas such as education, business, engineering, fine arts, social work, or other professional areas. The research master's degree, on the other hand, provides experience in research and scholarship and may be either a final degree or a step toward a doctorate (p. 2). In either type of master's degree, study usually lasts one or two years of full-time enrollment.

The doctoral level also features research and professional degrees. Most commonly, we think of professional doctorates as those including the MD for medicine and JD for legal practice. Research doctoral degrees, such as the PhD, generally include both coursework and a major research project, which encompass five to seven years of full-time study (Kidwell & Flagg, 2004). Additionally, the research doctorate involves a close academic relationship between the student and a faculty research advisor (Lovitts, 2001).

As such, the focus of the graduate and professional student in higher education will be much more centered on professional and career goals than the undergraduate student may be. What this means is that the home of the graduate and professional student is generally found in the program or department, rather than the larger university like the undergraduate may be. The implications for this differing focus will be discussed later in this chapter.

Who Are Graduate and Professional Students?

Graduate and professional students represent a significant portion of the higher education student population. A recent report from the US Department of Education (McFarland et al., 2018) documents that enrollment of graduate and professional students rose by 36% from 2000 and 2010 and continued to grow through 2017; even more, this enrollment growth is not predicted to dwindle. When compared to the 45% growth in undergraduate enrollment in the same time period, it is important for those working in higher education to become more aware of the graduate and professional student population on their campuses. Importantly, the most significant gains in graduate enrollment in the past 18 years have been among Students of Color (McFarland et al., 2018).

One thing is certain: graduate and professional students encompass as many different subpopulations of students as those discussed in the remainder of this book. Whether speaking of age, gender, race, nationality, ability, religious affiliation, socioeconomic status, or enrollment status, graduate and professional students represent a wide array of diversity in US higher education.

For example, while the average age of graduate and professional students is obviously older than the typical undergraduate, a great diversity of age range exists among these students. As presented in Table 21.1, a larger percentage of students 25 years of age and older tend to enroll part-time in their programs; however, there still exist significant variation in ages among degree programs and concentrations.

TABLE 21.1. Graduate student enrollment by age and status, 2016

Age	Full-time	Part-time
20–24	34.9%	10.7%
25–34	48.7%	44.9%
35+	16.4%	44.3%
Total enrollment	2,261,000	1,394,000

Source: US Census Bureau (2016)

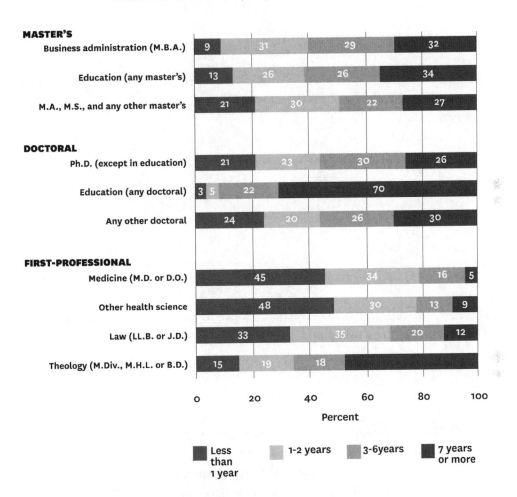

FIGURE 21.1. Enrollment delay after bachelor's degree for graduate and first professional students, by degree program: 2007–08 (Choy & Cataldi, 2011)

Another such example is in business master's degree programs (e.g., MBA), wherein the majority of students will delay their enrollment for seven or more years after receiving their bachelor's degrees and will continue to work full time while pursuing the degree (Choy & Cataldi, 2011). In contrast, the majority of students pursuing professional degree programs in medicine or dentistry enroll in these programs less

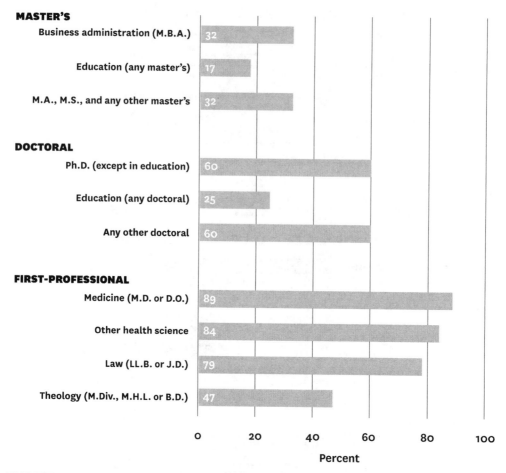

MASTER'S

Business administration (M.B.A.) — 32

Education (any master's) — 17

M.A., M.S., and any other master's — 32

DOCTORAL

Ph.D. (except in education) — 60

Education (any doctoral) — 25

Any other doctoral — 60

FIRST-PROFESSIONAL

Medicine (M.D. or D.O.) — 89

Other health science — 84

Law (LL.B. or J.D.) — 79

Theology (M.Div., M.H.L. or B.D.) — 47

Percent: 0   20   40   60   80   100

FIGURE 21.2. Percentage of graduate and first-professional students who enrolled full time, full year, by degree program: 2007–08 (Choy & Cataldi, 2011)

than two years after receiving the bachelor's degree and will enroll full time (Choy & Cataldi, 2011).

Due to the frequent part-time status of many graduate and professional students, it is often difficult to determine exact numbers in terms of enrollment but a recent snapshot of earned degrees by sex, race, and nationality demonstrates some of the other diverse elements of this population in comparison to the undergraduate population.

As seen here in Table 21.2, much like undergraduate enrollment, more women than men are currently pursuing and receiving graduate degrees in almost equal numbers among graduate degrees. For some racial and ethnic groups, there are significant differences in representation among type of degree received. For example, international students and Asian Americans receive a larger proportion of degrees at the graduate level than at the undergraduate level. Hispanic or Latinx students and American Indian graduate students earn less than 10% of degrees conferred at the master's and doctorate levels, whereas Asian American master's level students and Black doctoral students

TABLE 21.2. Degrees conferred by sex, race, and ethnic group, 2014–2015

	Total	% American Indian	% Asian	% Black	% Hispanic	% White	% Nonresident Alien
Associate							
Males	396,613	0.9	5.8	12.2	17.8	60.8	2.5
Females	617,358	1.1	4.8	14.9	18.3	58.3	1.6
Total	1,013,971	1.0	5.2	13.8	18.1	59.3	1.8
Bachelor's							
Males	812,669	0.5	7.9	9.0	11.2	68.6	4.7
Females	1,082,265	0.6	7.0	11.8	12.5	65.0	3.4
Total	1,894,934	0.6	7.4	10.6	12.0	66.5	3.9
Master's							
Males	306,590	0.5	8.1	10.9	8.8	69.5	21.0
Females	452,118	0.5	6.2	15.3	9.3	66.3	11.6
Total	758,708	0.5	6.9	13.6	9.1	67.5	15.4
Doctorate							
Men	84,921	0.6	11.6	6.2	7.0	72.3	15.3
Women	93,626	0.6	12.7	10.3	7.3	66.7	14.9
Total	178,547	0.6	12.2	8.4	7.2	69.3	11.9

Source: US Department of Education (2017b)

earn less than 10% of degrees conferred at the master's and doctorate level, respectively. These data indicate the importance of examining the recruitment and retention of graduate and professional Students of Color.

Issues Among Graduate and Professional Studies

Across all graduate and professional student populations, however, one concern is prevalent: retention. Many higher education professionals may believe retention issues are less prevalent among graduate and professional students. Surprisingly, doctoral students national completion rates hover only around 50% (Council of Graduate Schools, 2008). While the reasons for student departure at the graduate level are multifaceted, research has found a number of general issues. The Council of Graduate Schools summarizes these influences on graduate student retention in Figure 21.3.

Viewing the attrition-completion kaleidoscope, there are certain issues over which educators and administrators will have control while others will be in the control or experience of the student. Funding, for example, is a common issue for graduate and professional students. Since the majority of financial support to graduate students is often earmarked for full-time students (Nora & Snyder, 2007; Syverson, 1999), part-time students must often find their own resources to subsidize their graduate work. Further, the debt burden for graduate students is often much higher than for undergraduates,

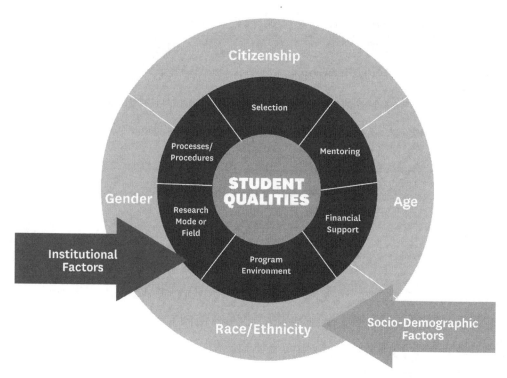

FIGURE 21.3. The Ph.D. Completion-Attrition Kaleidoscope (Council of Graduate Schools, 2004)

given the lack of federal grants and subsidies to assist these students (Choy & Cataldi, 2011). Indeed, federal loans make up 67% of all graduate student aid, compared to 38% for undergraduate students (Belasco, Trivette, & Webber, 2014). Full-time graduate students may also rely on assistantships, which presents the additional challenge of maintaining a healthy working relationship where the student is not exploited (Bargar & Mayo-Chamberlain, 1983; Liddell, Wilson, Pasquesi, Hirschy, & Boyle, 2014). Much of this financial context is dependent, however, on disciplinary cultures, wherein graduate students in STEM fields may be less likely to hold debt while those in the social sciences and humanities are much more likely to do so (Kim & Otts, 2010).

Because of their older age and often part-time enrollment, many graduate and professional students will face issues related to balancing their studies with family responsibilities as well as professional obligations (Choy & Cataldi, 2006; Curran, 1987; Davis & McCuen, 1995; Smith, 2000; Watts, 2008). Gardner and Gopaul (2011) found that part-time doctoral students in particular had a difficult time balancing the many responsibilities in their lives. Further, part-time graduate students tend to express concern at the lack of services available to them on campus that take into consideration their varied hours and these other responsibilities in their lives (Cohen & Greenberg, 2011).

Another issue among graduate and professional students is the resulting stress that accompanies these distinct concerns in their lives. For example, graduate students have been found to have more negative life events, greater depression, and higher anxiety levels than their undergraduate peers (Mallinckrodt & Leong, 1992; Stubb, Pyhältö, & Lonka, 2011; Wyatt & Oswalt, 2013) but also do not tend to take care of themselves as well, given their many stressors (Caple, 1995; Kidwell & Flagg, 2004). At the same time, graduate students will wait longer before seeking help than undergraduates (Caple, 1995), even though they are more likely to seek out mental health support than undergraduates (Wyatt & Oswalt, 2013). Nevertheless, one study found that 67% of the graduate students at the University of California-Berkeley reported feeling hopeless at least once in the past year, and 54% reported feeling so depressed that they had a hard time functioning. In fact, nearly 10% said that they had considered suicide. At the same time, nearly 25% of those same students said they were unaware of mental health services on their campus (Fogg, 2009). According to Baird (1990), when compared to undergraduate study, "graduate study is much less structured, much more individualized, and consequently often much more unclear and ambiguous in its demands on students. These demands call for unusual coping strategies and are met at an emotional cost" (p. 371). Furthermore, the graduate experience may be made more stressful for students from underrepresented populations (Barker, 2011).

Graduate and professional students from diverse backgrounds are also more likely to experience issues with isolation, exclusion, and microaggressions, which often negatively influence their sense of belonging in graduate programs (Winkle-Wagner, Johnson, Morelon-Quainoo, & Santiague, 2010). Graduate Students of Color not only experience forms of racism and discrimination but may also experience challenges in navigating graduate programs in ways that allow them to find their academic voice reflective of their identity and that appreciates them for their racial and cultural interests. In Christman, Pepion, Bowman, and Dixon's (2015) study on Native American doctoral students and González's (2006; 2009) studies on Latina doctoral and professional school students, the students addressed concerns about the lack of inclusion of their culture and the Eurocentric curriculum in their programs. Students described an evident dominant ideology (i.e., Western, White, and hegemonic) present in their programs and the effort they had to put forth to resist such ideologies and avoid cultural assimilation—abandoning their racial and ethnic heritage. These experiences become increasingly challenging for women of color who must navigate these patriarchal spaces at the intersection of race and gender (González, 2006, 2009; Sulé, 2009). Barker's (2014, 2016) and Felder and Barker's (2013) collective work calls for an examination of graduate education through a critical race lens in order to critique and redesign doctoral experiences to reflect the cultural and racial needs and concerns of students and the racial exclusionary history of predominantly white institutions.

For some doctoral students, there is a type of twoness that emerges—navigating graduate programs as a Person of Color and as a graduate student. Black doctoral students in Barker's (2012) study reported consciously and continuously having to decide if and when they would discuss issues related to race and how open or vulnerable they could be with their White faculty advisors. Asian American doctoral students often experience a duality of invisibility in their programs—only seen as foreign on one hand and not thought of as experiencing racism from Whites on the other hand (Poon & Hune, 2009). In addition to Students of Color, international students also experience microaggressions or microassults in both covert and overt ways. For example, Gomez, Khurshid, Freitag, and Lachuk (2011) found that international students and US Students of Color teaching assistants often encountered resistance from primarily White students through their nonparticipation in class or low ratings on teaching evaluations. Taken together, these experiences indicate that Students of Color continue to face stress and racial battle fatigue in matriculating through graduate and professional programs (Truong & Museus, 2012) and are still in search of a sense of belonging (Winkle-Wagner et al., 2010). Gay (2004) advocated for graduate programs to assist graduate Students of Color in managing "the power and politics of professional service" while "living in academe without losing [their] cultural and ethnic self" (p. 285).

Doctoral students from low socioeconomic status or who are first-generation also face challenges in graduate programs. Ostrove, Stewart, and Curtin (2011) found a correlation between social class and sense of belonging. According to the researchers, the lower the social class, the greater the financial struggle and the greater the financial struggle, the lower the sense of belonging. This finding suggests that eliminating financial barriers not only has implications for access, but also has implications for increasing a graduate students' sense of belonging. First-generation students, whose identity may intersect with others, encounter challenges that are similar to and distinct from the aforementioned groups. Gardner (2013) noted four areas that prove difficult for first-generation doctoral students. These included "understanding the system of graduate education" or understanding how to navigate and meet faculty, departmental, and disciplinary expectations; managing "financial constraints" or managing the financial costs or debt associated with pursuing a graduate degree and finding financial resources that may support (e.g., fellowships and assistantships) or hinder (e.g., full-time jobs) their matriculation; feeling as an "other" or feeling as if they do not share the same history or advantages as peers; and encountering the "imposter phenomenon" or feeling as if they are not fully prepared or qualified to be a doctoral student and fearing being discovered for this (p. 51).

To summarize, graduate and professional students are a distinct and yet diverse population in higher education. Their reasons for pursuing an advanced degree are often quite different from undergraduate students and thus require a different focus and understanding by higher education professionals and educators. In the next section, we provide a few theoretical lenses that assist professionals in better serving and engaging this student population.

Theoretical Perspectives

Given the distinct needs of graduate and professional students, their advanced age while in graduate and professional school, and their educational goals, different theoretical perspectives are also warranted. Here we present three such theoretical lenses: (a) adult learning theory, or andragogy; (2) socialization theory; and (3) graduate student development.

Adult Learning Theory

One appropriate theory for working with this student population is adult learning theory. Also known as andragogy, adult learning theory focuses on the different needs of adult learners. Adult learning is built upon five assumptions, according to Merriam (2001, p. 5). First, an adult learner is someone who has an independent self-concept and who can direct his or her own learning. Second, the adult learner has accumulated a reservoir of learning experiences that is a rich resource for learning. Third, the adult learner has learning needs closely related to changing social roles. Fourth, the adult learner is problem centered and interested in immediate application of knowledge. And, fifth, the adult learner is motivated to learn by internal rather than external forces.

This theory is particularly helpful when considering designing programming for graduate and professional students, such as orientation programs. For example, the first assumption of adult learning would be encompassed in such a program by providing a cafeteria-style approach to an orientation, allowing the student to pick and choose from multiple programs and topics that suit their needs (Barker, Felstehausen, Couch, & Henry, 1997). The second assumption would be included in an orientation program that allows students themselves to share their knowledge in a panel. The third assumption might be incorporated through a peer-mentoring program that allows for more advanced students to share their expertise with others. Similarly, assumption four might be included in an orientation program that allows for immediate application of concepts and knowledge that students may need in their first few days and weeks of graduate school. Finally, it is important to realize that adult learners may attend an orientation program for their own benefit and may not be as motivated by the contests, giveaways, and external motivators that may compel younger undergraduates, for example. At the same time, such orientations have been found to significantly reduce anxiety levels among graduate students (Hullinger & Hogan, 2014).

Socialization

Given the frequent career and professional focus of graduate students, a second fitting theoretical lens to understand this population is socialization theory. Socialization in the graduate education context is described by Golde (1998) as a process "in which a newcomer is made a member of a community—in the case of graduate students, the community of an academic department in a particular discipline" (p. 56). She continues, "The socialization of graduate students is an unusual double socialization. New students are simultaneously directly socialized into the role of graduate student and are given preparatory socialization into graduate student life and the future career common to most doctoral students" (p. 56). This socialization tends to occur in stages or developmental phases throughout the education of the graduate student (Baird, 1993).

Therefore, much like other models of undergraduate student development, socialization for graduate students is also developmental as students change their roles and relationships to their discipline and to their future profession (Bragg, 1976; Weidman, Twale, & Stein, 2001).

One such model of socialization in graduate school is that of Weidman et al. (2001). Weidman, Twale, and Stein described graduate student socialization as "the processes through which individuals gain the knowledge, skills, and values necessary for successful entry into a professional career requiring an advanced level of specialized knowledge and skills" (p. iii). According to these theorists, socialization for graduate students occurs in four developmental stages: Anticipatory, Formal, Informal, and Personal.

The Anticipatory Stage occurs primarily as students enter the program and need to learn new roles, procedures, and agendas to be followed. These students will tend to seek information and listen carefully to directions. This stage can be described as the student becoming "aware of the behavioral, attitudinal, and cognitive expectations held for a role incumbent" (Weidman et al., 2001, p. 12).

The Formal Stage is characterized by the graduate student observing roles of incumbents and older students while learning about role expectations and how they are carried out. Students in this stage are primarily concerned about task issues, and communication at this stage is informative through course material, regulative through embracing normative expectations, and integrative through faculty and student interactions (Weidman et al., 2001).

The Informal Stage is described as the stage in which "the novice learns of the informal role expectations transmitted by interactions with others who are current role incumbents" (Weidman et al., 2001, p. 14). At this stage, the graduate student receives behavioral cues, observes acceptable behavior, and subsequently responds and reacts accordingly. Many of these cues will be received from the student's cohort, those with whom most interaction occurs at this stage. Through the lessons learned in the Informal Stage, the student will then begin feeling less "student-like" and more professional.

Finally, the Personal Stage is the time in which the student's "individual and social roles, personalities and social structures become fused and the role is internalized" (Weidman et al., 2001, p. 14). During this final stage, the graduate student accepts a value orientation and relinquishes their former ways. The conflict impeding the total role transformation is resolved, and the graduate student will be able to separate from the department in search of their own identity.

Such a theory is useful in understanding how graduate and professional students will have changing needs and concerns as they progress through their degree programs. Again, the focus on the professional skills and knowledge will be emphasized for these students rather than a broad experience that might interest undergraduate populations. In this way, providing social opportunities that emphasize career and professional development may be more opportune for this population, including existing co-curricular involvement experiences (Gardner & Barnes, 2007) and professional associations (Andrew, Richards, Eberline, & Templin, 2016).

Graduate Student Development

A large focus of the literature on undergraduate students reflects their development (Evans, Forney, & Guido-DiBrito, 1998) and does not extend beyond graduation. Naturally, graduate and professional students will continue to have developmental experiences through their educational experiences (Gardner, 2009). Gardner's theory of graduate student development encompasses many of the theoretical perspectives discussed earlier, including adult learning and socialization, as well as the distinct concerns and issues facing graduate students at different turning points in their educational experience.

As illustrated in Figure 21.4, graduate student development occurs in three phases. The three phases of the model incorporate what is described as Phase I, or Entry; Phase II, or Integration; and Phase III, or Candidacy, with overarching identity development or possible program departure occurring throughout these phases (Gardner, 2009). Phase I is described as the time leading up to admission into the graduate program until the period when coursework begins. This phase generally only lasts a few months but,

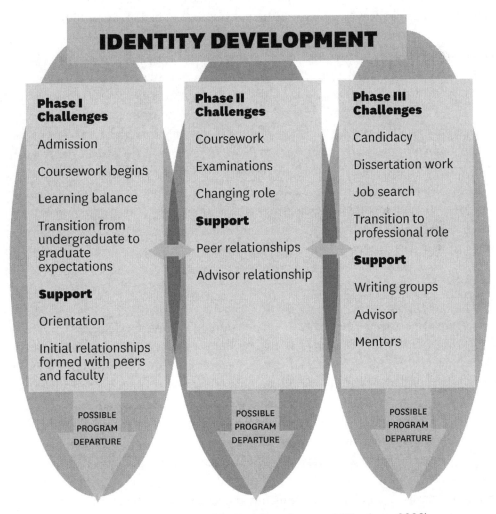

FIGURE 21.4.   Model of Graduate Student Development (Gardner, 2009)

according to many students (Gardner, 2007, 2008a, 2008b), impresses greatly upon the rest of their program, solidifies their decision to attend one institution over another, and even influences their decision to persist to doctoral education altogether.

Phase I presents multiple sources of challenge to the new student, including applying to prospective programs and institutions; submitting requisite materials to programs; visiting campuses; meeting and talking with faculty members, staff, and graduate students in these prospective programs; making a final decision in regard to the program of choice; moving to the new location; beginning course work; learning to balance the demands of life and graduate school; and understanding the changing expectations of the graduate student role. To mitigate these challenges, however, are several sources of support for new graduate students, including students they will meet during orientation, the faculty with whom they will connect and have in their initial courses, and the staff who provide support and direction through the beginning months (Gardner, 2009).

Phase II generally encompasses time in coursework but also represents much of the social and academic integration that the students will experience as they progress toward candidacy. The challenges facing students in Phase II include demonstrating competency and skills; this challenge occurs first in their coursework and then through the examination process. During this phase, students are transitioning from being knowledge consumers to knowledge producers through demonstrating skills in the research process. Students face the additional challenges of forming deeper relationships with both peers and faculty. Supportive relationships with these individuals are therefore imperative to student success and development in this phase (Gardner, 2009).

After moving through the challenges of Phase II, students move into the final phase of their graduate experience. Phase III marks the period after which students have passed their examinations or candidacy status. At this phase, students encounter the daunting challenge of completing independent research in the thesis or dissertation experience and may also begin seeking professional positions. During this phase in the process, students may have less accessible support, whether through close peer relationships in coursework or daily interaction with faculty, intensifying any challenges associated with the research process (Gardner, 2009).

As students progress through the three phases, they also experience personal identity development in response to potential challenges and support mechanisms. As seen in Figure 21.4, the identity development that occurs is as fluid as the phases, wherein the student may confront developmental challenges or issues directly related to the experiences within the three phases or may be simply experiencing overarching developmental issues external to the graduate student experience. For example, a student might enroll in a course that emphasizes issues related to social justice, thereby facilitating racial identity development or intercultural sensitivity. At the same time, a student may experience issues external to the graduate program, such as a changing recognition of their own sexuality, which might facilitate sexual identity development. Whether enrolled in graduate education or not, of course, identity development continues throughout adulthood (Merriam & Clark, 2006).

Such an understanding of graduate student development may be helpful to higher education professionals designing programming for this population. For example, professionals will benefit from understanding that students in early phases may be more interested in connecting with peers in similar circumstances through professional associations or in campus student organizations; in contrast, more advanced graduate students in Phase III may require more career-development assistance or job-seeking assistance through a career center.

Student Engagement Strategies

In this section, we utilize the theoretical frameworks provided earlier to address the unique needs of graduate and professional student populations. It is important to reiterate that there is varying diversity among graduate and professional students, and each student represents a unique experience. We do not recommend here a "one-size-fits-all" approach; rather, we highlight overarching strategies to engage these students on campus and beyond.

Services

Professionals should keep in mind that graduate and professional students are often very degree focused and, in some cases, may rarely leave their departments or programs. Moreover, the many part-time and online-only students among this population may visit the campus infrequently. The types of services utilized by these students must be easily accessible, available beyond typical working hours, and cognizant of these students' often hectic schedules and conflicting responsibilities (e.g., balancing family and school). For example, graduate and professional students who utilize financial aid may require assistance after typical working hours. User-friendly websites and mobile- or chat-enabled technologies may prove beneficial to these students. Beyond these types of services, these students will also be focused on using the library and related technologies. Universities should consider the accessibility of these services by off-campus students and what services exist to orient students to these services if they cannot make it to campus.

Engagement

There is often a misconception that graduate and professional students do not want to become engaged on their campuses. While not all students will be able to engage in co-curricular organizations and activities, some students will actively seek involvement opportunities. In particular, students from underrepresented populations may seek out connections with others on campus, such as students with children, Students of Color, or students with disabilities. Moreover, graduate and professional students tend to be driven more by professional development activities than by leadership development activities. Hence, providing career development and professional networking opportunities may be the one method for engaging these students (Gardner & Barnes, 2007).

Finally, graduate student affairs professionals should consider the spectrum of students, including students with families, and design family-oriented programs and events that occur outside a typical nine-to-five work schedule.

Counseling and Support

The graduate and professional student population has distinct stressors that result in mental health needs. Being purposeful in advertising free or low-cost counseling and therapy services available on campus provides another support system for students and may positively impact this population. In addition, initiating support groups for these students at different developmental phases may be helpful. For example, providing dissertation support groups for students in Phase III or comprehensive or qualifying exam support groups for students in Phase II. Much like other services, universities must consider how to provide remote (e.g., online) counseling support outside typical business hours to reach this unique population. Counseling may also extend to career counseling. According to the Council on Graduate Schools (2010; 2012), there is a growing demand and opportunity for graduate students to receive career guidance and professional development that prepares them for a variety of careers as opposed to traditional career pathways—especially for doctoral students. Given the job-search process that occurs in Phase III and the shift to a more "knowledge-based economy" (CGS, 2010, p. 17), it is important for graduate programs to ensure that graduate students receive career counseling or advisement and transferable skills (e.g., project management) during their program so they might better understand and prepare for a range of career options.

Orientation

While many graduate and professional students will receive specific orientations in their respective degree programs, campus-wide orientation sessions and opportunities are also warranted. Often, these types of sessions focus on bureaucratic policies and procedures rather than student services and development. Developing orientation sessions using a cafeteria-style approach (Barker et al., 1997) maximizes students' time and allows for intentional interactions, including opportunities for existing students to share their expertise with incoming and less advanced students. This approach incorporates adult learning strategies and creates meaningful experiences for graduate and professional students and adult learners.

Peer Mentoring Programs

Similarly, institutions can offer these diverse students a myriad of peer mentoring programs suited to specific needs. Some examples include peer mentoring programs for graduate Students of Color on a predominately White campus, a program for graduate student-parents, or a program for working professionals. Particularly as many graduate students will rely on their peers for advice in the early stages of their programs (Gardner, 2009), these structured programs may go a long way in providing support to these students.

Financial Aid

The high rate of student debt among graduate students is worrisome (Belasco et al., 2014; Ekstrom, Goertz, Pollack, & Rock, 1991; Heller, 2001), particularly given the very sparse need-based aid for these students. For part-time students, in particular, the cost of pursuing an advanced degree can be astronomical, particularly if their place of employment does not subsidize these costs. Institutions should consider more need-based aid for graduate and professional students, including the expansion of grants and scholarships for part-time and full-time students. However, such opportunities must be well advertised, accessible after traditional working hours, and visible (e.g., in orientation programs or websites) in order to reach graduate and professional students and prove reliable.

Faculty Development

Institutions, and particularly faculty, tend to assume that graduate and professional students begin programs with a full knowledge of how to navigate the degree program (Golde, 2005). However, these students sometimes struggle with navigating the institution and the department and attempt to understand their new roles as graduate and professional students. Additionally, these students undergo both personal and professional developmental challenges, ultimately facing identity development issues. It is essential that faculty and specifically advisors participate in professional development opportunities that focus on graduate student development and responding to the diverse demographic of graduate and professional students. These professional development seminars should provide faculty and departmental staff with recommendations for creating positive developmental environments for this population. Aforementioned strategies may serve as a starting point, but strategies and programs should account for the unique culture and context of the student, department, institution, and geography.

Holistic Assessment

In this chapter, we highlighted the diversity of graduate and professional students. While universities may capture graduate student enrollment and completion, including demographic data, institutional research should also capture the day-to-day experiences of these students. Institutional assessments should provide opportunities for students to report their overall experiences on campus to gain greater insight into issues that may be specific to the institution. For example, students may report that they prefer weekend courses to weekly courses, due to work or family obligations. Additionally, climate assessments specifically may allow for a more focused and in-depth analysis of how the institution, department, or both create inclusive learning environments and a sense of belonging among their students. Investing time and resources into campus climates has implications for improving student learning and outcomes (Reason, 2013).

Institutional Culture

Overall, there is a need to incorporate graduate and professional students in institutional student affairs practices. Considering the recommendations in this chapter, institutions should assess how institutionalized practices or campus-wide programs either neglect or discount the participation of graduate and professional students. Additional consideration should be given to subpopulations (e.g., women, ethnic minorities, persons with disabilities, etc.) who experience the campus through multiple lenses reflective of their identity. Graduate schools also have a tremendous responsibility to advocate for these students and make the needs of this population salient to other campus constituencies. Lastly, institutional type is connected to institutional culture and shapes graduate school environments directly or indirectly. Directly, the type of institution may lend itself to providing greater cultural affirmation and role models who reflect the identity of graduate students, as might be the case for historically Black colleges and universities (Fry Brown, Flowers, Hilton, & Dejohnette, 2018; Joseph, 2013; Ross-Sheriff, Edwards, & Orme, 2017) that offer graduate programs. Indirectly, it is important to note that minority-serving institutions may also be conduits for graduate school programs at predominantly White institutions, or PWIs. For example, between 2005 and 2010, 26% of Black PhD STEM degree recipients who were US citizens earned their bachelor's degree from an HBCU and their PhD at a PWI (Joseph, 2013). This means that PWIs, in particular, must be aware and critical of their history of exclusion and develop intentional strategies for equity and inclusion if they are to create environments that are welcoming and supportive, foster access, and are committed to the success of graduate students from diverse backgrounds, lived experiences, and other institutional types.

Conclusion

In conversations about student development and campus life on our campuses, the lives of graduate and professional students tend to go ignored or are rarely considered in decision-making processes. When, in fact, this population comprises a significant percentage of the student body whose enrollment is steadily increasing. While undergraduate enrollment constitutes the larger demographic on college campuses, it is important to note that 40% of undergraduate completers enroll in graduate or professional degree programs (Choy & Cataldi, 2011). In this chapter, we sought to first define and distinguish graduate and professional students and then to bring greater attention to the diversity and dynamics of graduate and professional students while providing theoretical and practical considerations for practitioners and scholars. Additionally, we included Gardner's (2009) theory of graduate student development to further explore the relationship between student identity and the mechanics of graduate education.

Graduate and professional education includes a series of milestones or benchmarks in conjunction with a socialization process in which students must not only successfully complete steps prior to moving forward in their education, but also orient themselves to better understand and become immersed in their chosen profession. This hybrid developmental relationship is further complicated when we consider the unique background of those enrolled in graduate and professional programs.

Issues facing graduate and professional students represent institutional and sociodemographic factors related to the institution, the department, and the individual. Depending on the department and the background of the student, some issues for this population may include budgeting the financial costs of their education; balancing work, family, and school; managing stress; and dealing with day-to-day experiences. We presented three theoretical frameworks that provide lenses for understanding this population: adult learning theory, socialization, and graduate student development. Adult learning theory is a useful theory in understanding the ways in which adults make sense of the world and form knowledge. This takes the form of forming a sense of self, drawing from lived experiences, changing one's social role, developing and applying knowledge to real-world and immediate situations, and being intrinsically motivated to learn. Socialization is the belief that and the process by which students learn the norms, culture, and traditions within their chosen profession or discipline. This process may occur through stages or phases but remains organic in the sense that the individual is learning their new role as a member of the academic or professional community.

Similarly, Gardner's (2009) theory of graduate student development explains the dual journey that students take during their graduate and professional programs. Once a student commits to beginning their program, they begin a process of completing the major phases of the program (i.e., coursework, general examinations, and defense) and, simultaneously, begins the process of acclimating to the profession. During these processes, students encounter both internal and external factors and continuously reconcile their identity as individuals, students, and professionals in their field. Although the process of navigating graduate and professional studies and negotiating one's identity may be challenging for some students, there are clear, intentional strategies that may assist students' transition and successful completion. Providing support services, peer mentoring, counseling, and student involvement opportunities for this population may assist students in forming connections to the campus and in establishing a support network. However, these services and opportunities must consider the unique demographics of most students, offering after-hours contact or remote access, and address the special needs of subgroups within the population. Additionally, student- and activity-centered orientations provide opportunities for students to learn more about the psychosocial support mechanisms on campus and stimulate the learning process of adult learners.

This chapter ended with institutional initiatives and campus environment strategies that can have a positive effect on graduate and professional students. We proposed that institutions establish financial aid policies that increase need-based aid funding sources, promote professional development for faculty who work with this population, conduct more holistic-student outcome assessments beyond retention and completion data, and incorporate graduate and professional students in institutional conversations on student development, persistence, and success (i.e., completion).

Graduate and professional education dates back to the late 1800s with the adoption of the German research university. This model of education and professional training is responsible for shaping the modern-day research university. However, in its formation, the research university has failed to adequately address the personal identities and experiences of students in these programs. Consequently, this population is at risk, and it hinges on universities and colleges to develop effective strategies to support and develop the social and academic lives of graduate and professional students.

References

Andrew, K., Richards, R., Eberline, A. D., & Templin, T. J. (2016). Secondary professional socialization through professional organizations: An exploratory study. *Journal of Teaching in Physical Education, 35*(1), 70–75.

Baird, L. L. (1990). The melancholy of anatomy: The personal and professional development of graduate and professional school students. In J. C. Smart (Ed.), *Higher education: Handbook of theory and research* (Vol. 6, pp. 361–392). New York, NY: Agathon Press.

Baird, L. L. (1993). Using research and theoretical models of graduate student progress. In L. L. Baird (Ed.), *Increasing graduate student retention and degree attainment* (pp. 3–12). San Francisco, CA: Jossey-Bass.

Bargar, R. R., & Mayo-Chamberlain, J. (1983). Advisor and advisee issues in doctoral education. *The Journal of Higher Education, 54*, 407–432.

Barker, M. (2011). Racial context, currency, and connections: Black doctoral student and White faculty advisor perspectives on cross-race advising. *Innovative Education & Teaching International, 48*(4), 387–400.

Barker, M. (2012). An exploration of racial identity among Black doctoral students involved in cross-race advising relationships. In J. Sullivan & A. Esmail (Eds.), *African American identity: Racial and cultural dimensions of the Black experience.* Lanham, MC: Lexington Books.

Barker, M. J. (2014). Critiquing doctoral education: Moving toward a cross-race doctoral advising model. In P. P. Felder & E. P. St. John (Eds.), *Supporting graduate students in the 21st century: Implications for policy and practice* (Vol. 27, pp. 109–134). New York, NY: AMS Press.

Barker, M. J. (2016). The doctorate in Black and White: Exploring the engagemetn of Black doctoral students in cross race advising relationships with White faculty. *The Western Juornal of Black Studies, 40*(2), 126–140.

Barker, S., Felstehausen, G., Couch, S., & Henry, J. (1997). Orientation programs for older and delayed-entry graduate students. *NASPA Journal, 35*, 57–68.

Belasco, A. S., Trivette, M. J., & Webber, K. L. (2014). Advanced degrees of debt: Analyzing the patterns and determinants of graduate student borrowing. *The Review of Higher Education, 37*(4), 469–497.

Bragg, A. K. (1976). *The socialization process in higher education.* Washington, DC: The George Washington University.

Caple, R. B. (1995). Counseling graduate students. In A. S. Pruitt-Logan & P. D. Isaac (Eds.), *Student services for the changing graduate student population* (pp. 43–50). San Francisco, CA: Jossey-Bass.

Choy, S. P., & Cataldi, E. F. (2006). *Student financing of graduate and first-professional education, 2003–04 (No. NCES 2006–185).* Washington, DC. Retrieved from https://nces.ed.gov/pubsearch/pubsinfo.asp?pubid=2006185

Choy, S. P., & Cataldi, E. F. (2011). *Graduate and first-professional students: 2007–08.* Washington, DC. Retrieved from https://nces.ed.gov/pubs2011/2011174.pdf

Christman, D. E., Pepion, D., Bowman, C., & Dixon, B. (2015). Native American doctoral students: Establishing legitimacy in higher education. In D. Aguilera-Black Bear & J. W. Tippeconnic III (Eds.), *Voices of resistance and renewal: Indigenous leadrship in education* (pp. 116–141). Norman, OK: University of Oklahoma Press.

Cohen, M. A., & Greenberg, S. (2011). The struggle to succeed: Factors associated with the persistence of part-time adult students seeking a master's degree. *Continuing Higher Education Review, 75*, 101–112.

Council of Graduate Schools. (2004). *Organization and administration of graduate education.* Washington, DC.

Council of Graduate Schools. (2008). *Ph.D. completion and attrition: Analysis of baseline program data from the Ph.D. completion project.* Washington, DC.

Council of Graduate Schools. (2010). *Ph.D. Completion and attrition: Policies and practices to promote student success*. Retrieved from www.phdcompletion.org/information/executive_summary_student_success_book_iv.pdf

Council of Graduate Schools and Educational Testing Service. (2012). *Pathways through graduate school and into careers*. Report from the Commission on Pathways Through Graduate School and Into Careers. Princeton, NJ: Educational Testing Service. Retreieved from: http://pathwaysreport.org/rsc/pdf/19089_PathwaysRept_Links.pdf

Curran, C. C. (1987). Dealing with the distant learner as part-time learner. *Journal of Education for Library and Information Science, 27*, 240–246.

Davis, A. P., & McCuen, R. H. (1995). Part-time graduate education: Obstacles, conflicts, and suggestions. *Journal of Professional Issues in Engineering Education and Practice, 121*(2), 108–113.

Ekstrom, R., Goertz, M., Pollack, J., & Rock, D. (1991). *Undergraduate debt and participation in graduate education: The relationship between educational debt and graduate school aspirations, applications, and attendance among students wiht a pattern of full-time, continuous postsecondary education.* Retrieved from Princeton, NJ.

Evans, N. J., Forney, D. S., & Guido-DiBrito, F. (1998). *Student development in college: Theory, research, and practice.* San Francisco, CA: Jossey-Bass.

Felder, P. P., & Barker, M. J. (2013). Extending bell's concept of interest convergence: A framework for understanding the African American doctoral student experience. *International Journal of Doctoral Studies, 8*, 1–20.

Fogg, P. (2009, February 20). Grad-school blues. *The Chronicle Review*, pp. B13–B14.

Fry Brown, R. L., Flowers, A. M., Hilton, A. A., & Dejohnette, M. (2018). Beyond respectable: Why earn an advanced degree from an historically Black college and university. In T. F. Boykin, A. A. Hilton, & R. T. Palmer (Eds.), *Professional education at historically Black colleges and universities* (pp. 123–140). New York, NY: Routledge Publishing.

Gardner, S. K. (2007). "I heard it through the grapevine": Doctoral student socialization in chemistry and history. *Higher Education, 54*, 723–740.

Gardner, S. K. (2008a). *Contrasting the socialization experiences of doctoral students in high- and low-completing departments: A qualitative analysis of disciplinary and institutional contexts.* Paper presented at the annual meeting of the Association for the Study of Higher Education, Jacksonville, FL.

Gardner, S. K. (2008b). "What's too much and what's too little?": The process of becoming an independent researcher in doctoral education. *The Journal of Higher Education, 79*, 326–350.

Gardner, S. K. (2009). *Doctoral student development: Phases of challenge and support.* San Francisco, CA: Jossey-Bass.

Gardner, S. K. (2013). The challenges of first-generation doctoral students. In K. A. Holley & J. Joseph (Eds.), *New Directions for Higher Eduation. Increasing diversity in dotoral education: Implicantions for theory and practice* (pp. 43–54). San Francisco, CA: Jossey-Bass.

Gardner, S. K., & Barnes, B. J. (2007). Graduate student involvement: Socialization for the professional role. *The Journal of College Student Development, 48*, 369–387.

Gardner, S. K., & Gopaul, B. (2011). *The part-time doctoral student experience.* Orono: University of Maine.

Gay, G. (2004). Navigating marginality en route to the professoriate: Graduate students of color learning and living in academia. *International Journal of Qualitative Studies in Education, 17*(2), 265–288.

Golde, C. M. (1998). Beginning graduate school: Explaining first-year doctoral attrition. In M. S. Anderson (Ed.), *The experience of being in graduate school: An exploration* (pp. 55–64). San Francisco, CA: Jossey-Bass.

Golde, C. M. (2005). The role of the department and discipline in doctoral student attrition: Lessons from four departments. *The Journal of Higher Education, 76*(6), 669.

Gomez, M. L., Khurshid, A., Freitag, M. B., & Lachuk, A. J. (2011). Microaggressions in graduate students' lives: How they are encountered and their consequences. *Teaching and Teacher Education, 27*, 1189–1199.

González, J. C. (2006). Academic socialization experiences of Latina doctoral students: A qualitative understnading of support systems that aid and challenges that hinder the process. *Journal of Hispanic Higher Education, 5*(4), 347–365.

González, J. C. (2009). Latinas in doctoral and professional programs: Similarities and differences in support systems and challenges. In M. F. Howard-Hamilton, C. L. Morelon-Quainoo, S. D. Johnson, R. Winkle-Wagner, & L. Santiague (Eds.), *Standing on the outside looking in* (pp. 103–123). Sterling, VA: Stylus.

Heller, D. (2001). *Debt and decisions: Student loans and their relationship to graduate school and career choice*. Indianapolis, IN: Lumina Foundation.

Hullinger, M., & Hogan, R. L. (2014). Student anxiety: Effects of a new graduate student orientation program. *Administrative Issues Journal, 4*(2), 5.

Joseph, J. (2013). The impact of historicaly Black colleges and universities on doctoral students. In K. A. Holley & J. Joseph (Eds.), *New Directions for Higher Eduation. Increasing diversity in dotoral education: Implicantions for theory and practice* (pp. 67–76). San Francisco, CA: Jossey-Bass.

Kidwell, C. S., Flagg, C. A., & Stites-Doe. (2004). *Graduate school and you: A guide for prospective graduate students*. Washington, DC. Retrieved from https://www.shu.edu/graduate-affairs/upload/CGS_Graduate-School-and-You-2014.PDF

Kim, D., & Otts, C. (2010). The effect of loans on time to doctorate degree: Differences by race/ethnicity, field of study, and institutional characteristics. *The Journal of Higher Education, 81*(1), 1–32.

Liddell, D. L., Wilson, M. E., Pasquesi, K., Hirschy, A. S., & Boyle, K. M. (2014). Development of professional identity through socialization in graduate school. *Journal of Student Affairs Research and Practice, 51*(1), 69–84.

Lovitts, B. E. (2001). *Leaving the ivory tower: The causes and consequences of departure from doctoral study*. Lanham, MD: Rowman & Littlefield Publishers.

Mallinckrodt, B., & Leong, F. T. L. (1992). International graduate students, stress, and social support. *Journal of College Student Development, 33*, 71–78.

McFarland, J., Hussar, B., Wang, X., Zhang, J., Wang, K., Rathbun, A., . . . Bullock Mann, F. (2018). *The condition of education 2018*. Retrieved from Washington, DC: https://nces.ed.gov/pubsearch/pubsinfo.asp?pubid=2018144

Merriam, S. B. (2001). Andragogy and self-directed learning: Pillars of adult learning theory. *New Directions for Adult and Continuing Education, 89*, 3–13.

Merriam, S. B., & Clark, M. C. (2006). Learning and development: The connection in adulthood. In C. Hoare (Ed.), *Handbook of adult development and learning* (pp. 27–51). Oxford: Oxford University Press.

Nora, A., & Snyder, B. P. (2007). *Structural differences in scholarly engagement among full- and part-time doctoral students*. Paper presented at the annual meeting of the American Educational Research Association, Chicago, IL.

Ostrove, J. M., Stewart, A. J., & Curtin, N. L. (2011). Social class and belonging: Implications for graduate students' career aspirations. *Journal of Higher Education, 82*(6), 748–774.

Poon, O. A., & Hune, S. (2009). Countering master narratives of the "perpetual foreigner" and "model minority": The hidden injuries of race and Asian American doctoral students. In M. F. Howard-Hamilton, C. L. Morelon-Quainoo, S. D. Johnson, R. Winkle-Wagner, & L. Santiague (Eds.), *Standing on the outside looking in* (pp. 103–123). Sterling, VA: Stylus.

Reason, R. D. (2013). Creating and assessing campus climate that support personal and social responsibility. *Liberal Education, 99*(1). Retrieved from Association of American Colleges & Universities: www.aacu.org/publications-research/periodicals/creating-and-assessing-campus-climates-support-personal-and-social

Ross-Sheriff, F., Edwards, J. B., & Orme, J. (2017). Relational mentoring of doctoral social work students at historically Black colleges and universities. *Journal of Teaching in Social Work, 37*(1), 55–70.

Smith, P. R. (2000). A meeting of cultures: Part-time students in an Ed.D. program. *International Journal of Leadership in Education, 3*, 359–380.

Stubb, J., Pyhältö, K., & Lonka, K. (2011). Balancing between inspiration and exhaustion: PhD students' experienced socio-psychological well-being. *Studies in Continuing Education, 33*(1), 33–50.

Sulé, V. T. (2009). Oppositional stances of Black female graduate students. In M. F. Howard-Hamilton, C. L. Morelon-Quainoo, S. D. Johnson, R. Winkle-Wagner, & L. Santiague (Eds.), *Standing on the outside looking in* (pp. 147–168). Sterling, VA: Stylus.

Syverson, P. D. (1999). Part-time study plus full-time employment: The new way to go to graduate school. *Education Statistics Quarterly, 1*(3), 13–15.

Truong, K. A., & Museus, S. D. (2012). Responding to racism and racial trauma in doctoral study: An inventory for copnig and mediating relationships. *Harvard Educational Review, 82*(2), 226–254.

US Census Bureau. (2016). *School enrollment in the United States: October 2016.* Retrieved from Washington, DC: www.census.gov/data/tables/2016/demo/school-enrollment/2016-cps.html

US Department of Education. (2017a). *Enrollment and employees in postsecondary institutions, Fall 2016.* Retrieved from Washington, DC: http://nces.ed.gov/pubsearch

US Department of Education. (2017b). *Status and trends in the education of racial and ethnic groups 2017.* Retrieved from Washington, DC: https://nces.ed.gov/fastfacts/display.asp?id=72

Upton, R., & Tanenbaum, C. (2014). The role of historically Black colleges and universities as pathway providers: Institutional pathways to the STEM PhD among Black students. *American Institutes for Research Broadening Participation in STEM Graduate Education Issue Brief.* Retrieved from American Institutes for Research: www.air.org/sites/default/files/downloads/report/Role

Watts, J. H. (2008). Challenges of supervising part-time PhD students: Towards student-centered practice. *Teaching in Higher Education, 13,* 369–373.

Weidman, J. C., Twale, D. J., & Stein, E. L. (2001). *Socialization of graduate and professional students in higher education: A perilous passage?* San Francisco, CA: Jossey-Bass.

Winkle-Wagner, R., Johnson, S. D., Morelon-Quainoo, C., & Santiague, L. (2010). A sense of belonging: Socialization factors that influence the transitions of students of color into advanced-degree programs. In S. K. Gardner & P. Mendoza (Eds.), *On becoming a scholar: Socialization and development in doctoral education* (pp. 179–199). Sterling, VA: Stylus Publishing.

Wyatt, T., & Oswalt, S. B. (2013). Comparing mental health issues among undergraduate and graduate students. *American Journal of Health Education, 44*(2), 96–107.

Chapter 22
Engaging Student-Parents

Margaret W. Sallee

Although the media and popular imagination still suggest that the average undergraduate is between the ages of 18 and 24 with no dependents of their own, statistics suggest otherwise. Of relevance to this chapter, one in four undergraduates in the United States is a student-parent (Gault, Reichlin, & Roman, 2014). Yet higher education is not designed to cater to their needs. Those who differ from the norm struggle to navigate institutions that, at best, offer add-on services targeted toward them or, at worst, ignore them completely. Student-parents contend with colleges and universities' "carefree" environments (Moreau & Kerner, 2015), which operate under the assumption that students have no familial obligations that might interfere with their schooling. Such assumptions and lack of integrated attention to the needs of student-parents only create more barriers for a population that already struggles.

This lack of attention may stem from the fact that student-parents tend to be single women of color, a historically marginalized group. Women represent 71% of the student-parent population (Gault, Reichlin, Reynolds, & Froehner, 2014). Additionally, student-parents tend to be single parents; 43% of all student-parents are single mothers (Gault, Reichlin, Reynolds et al., 2014), which brings its own set of challenges. In addition to being a woman, the average student-parent is more likely to be a woman of color. Nearly 50% of African American women, 49% of Native American women, and just over 31% of Latina college students are parents (Gault, Reichlin, & Roman, 2014). Student-parents are also more likely to be first-generation; 49% of student-parents versus 29% of nonparents identify as first-generation (Nelson, Froehner, & Gault, 2013). Colleges and universities, and indeed society in general, is not designed to support the needs of this group.

The academic road is a difficult one for student-parents, as they are more likely to have SAT verbal scores below 400 and are more likely to take developmental courses once in college (Miller, 2010). Many student-parents also struggle to complete their degrees. Only one out of three student-parents completes a degree or certificate within six years of enrolling (Gault, Reichlin, Reynolds et al., 2014).

Perhaps because of their academic difficulties and, as I discuss later, their financial constraints, student-parents are concentrated at community colleges and for-profit institutions. Nearly half of all student-parents attend community colleges, accounting for 30% of the entire community college student body. One-quarter of student-parents attend for-profit institutions, comprising half of all students at these institutions. The remaining 25% attend four-year institutions, though they account for a significantly smaller percentage (15%) of the overall student body (Gault, Reichlin, Reynolds et al., 2014). Despite their significant representation at all institutional types, student-parents still tend to be overlooked in policy and practice.

In this chapter, I examine how student-parents are frequently marginalized at colleges and universities. I begin by providing an overview of national policy and societal assumptions about the role of care and those who provide it, as they shape how student-parents' experiences unfold. I then discuss organizational and individual barriers they face, as well as actors who support them. I offer two theories that might be useful in making sense of how student-parents respond to the challenges that they face. I conclude by providing suggestions for ways that institutions might better support this marginalized population. Although campuses can offer a series of targeted supports to student-parents, long-lasting change will only come through transforming societal assumptions and practices.

The Normative Student on the Carefree Campus

As highlighted in the introduction, colleges and universities operate under the assumption that the average student is a traditional-age student with no familial responsibilities. (As other chapters in this volume highlight, the average student is often assumed to be White, cisgender, heterosexual, and able-bodied as well.) These assumptions work against student-parents, who are often asked to leave their parenting responsibilities off campus, both literally and figuratively. These assumptions stem from the fact that colleges and universities operate as if all students are the normative student (Estes, 2011; Moreau, 2016; Moreau & Kerner, 2015). As Moreau and Kerner (2015) suggested, these assumptions are deeply gendered, given that women continue to perform the majority of care work.

Certainly not all institutions respond to students in the same way. Some institutions support student-parents more than others. Moreau (2016) suggested that institutions might take one of three approaches to student-parents. *Careblind* institutions offer little to no provisions for student-parents and might not even acknowledge student-parents' needs. Some institutions might mention student-parents insofar as to prohibit them from bringing their children to campus (Moreau, 2016; Wilson & Cox, 2011). Such actions ignore the realities of combining parenthood with studenthood. More campuses, however, might take a *targeted* approach, in which they offer targeted, though limited, support to students with children. Such campuses might reference the needs of student-parents in particular capacities. This often takes the form of childcare centers (Moreau, 2016), though as I discuss shortly, most campus childcare centers do not meet student needs. However, campuses that adopt a targeted approach might fail to recognize the way that parenting can affect all aspects of students' lives and not integrate attention to their needs in other areas, such as the classroom or other campus support services. Finally, *mainstreaming* campuses are those that have attempted to incorporate the needs of student-parents into all types of policies (Moreau, 2016). Such institutions make care visible across the campus. As Moreau (2016) argued, campuses that offer careblind and targeted approaches, with ostensibly neutral policies, perpetuate normative assumptions about the appropriate student identity while simultaneously othering student-parents. Such campuses may also contribute to stigmatizing the student-parent identity.

Given that the normative student has been constructed as childless, many student-parents report feeling stigmatized for their identities (Estes, 2011; Haleman, 2004; Kensinger & Minnick, 2018). Participants in Haleman's (2004) study of single mothers noted negative societal connotations associated with single motherhood; African American mothers in the sample reported how these connotations were further compounded by their racial identities. Such experiences extend to higher education. In one study, staff labeled students with children as unprepared for university life, suggesting that it was an individual and not an organizational imperative to adapt (Brooks, 2012). Encountering such attitudes is likely discouraging for student-parents. As I discuss later in the chapter, faculty and staff can play a critical role in either promoting or enacting barriers to student-parents' success.

Policy Barriers

This careblind approach and constructions of the normative student identity stem from larger societal discussions on the role that the state should play in supporting families, particularly those on the margins. Many student-parents fall within this group. Among single parents, 59% earn less than $10,000 per year while 38% earn less than $5,000 per year (Goldrick-Rab & Sorensen, 2010). The challenges are compounded for all student-parents of color; 71% of Black student-parents and 68% of Latinx student-parents live at or below 200% of the poverty line compared with 49% of White student-parents (Gault, Reichlin, & Roman, 2014). Whereas the United States once provided generous aid to assist with living and educational expenses, aid has diminished over the past two decades. In particular, welfare was radically overhauled in 1996 with the introduction of Temporary Assistance to Needy Families (TANF). As Wilson (2011) summarized, as a result of this reform, "the cost of the welfare entitlement grant was cut in half, the number of recipients using the program was cut in half, and the monetary support for women seeking post-secondary education was largely eliminated" (p. 52). In particular, TANF only provides support for the pursuit of a degree for 12 months, effectively channeling recipients into certificate programs and away from four-year degrees. Additionally, TANF recipients are required to engage in work-related activities for 30 hours per week to obtain aid. TANF gives discretion to states to determine how they want to interpret "work-related activities"; in some states, recipients are able to count time engaged in higher education as work related while others cannot. However, this work requirement causes significant stress to those trying to juggle school, work, and parenting (Katz, 2013).

As one might suspect, welfare reform significantly impacted the ability of parents to pursue higher education. In 1995, 136,000 welfare recipients were enrolled in higher education. After welfare reform, only 54,000 recipients were (Jacobs & Winslow, 2003). Additionally, those pursuing higher education were more likely to be funneled into certificate programs instead of two- or four-year degrees, given the time limits placed on the use of welfare funds for higher education. Under TANF, welfare recipients are 3.6 times more likely to be enrolled in certificate programs than nonrecipients (Jacobs & Winslow, 2003). This creates problems for those who want to pursue two- or four-year degrees but have limited resources.

Student-parents draw on a number of sources of aid, including food stamps, WIC benefits, and Section 8 housing vouchers, as well as educational grants and loans. All provide important day-to-day assistance for students who are able to access them (Goldrick-Rab & Sorensen, 2010; Haleman, 2004; Katz, 2013; Sallee & Cox, 2019; Wilson, 2011; Wilson & Cox, 2011). Because of their low incomes, student-parents are more likely than those without children to have an Expected Family Contribution (EFC) of $0 toward their federal financial aid; 61% of students with children compared with 30% of students without children have an EFC of 0 (Gault, Reichlin, & Roman, 2014). With no expected family contribution, student-parents are therefore eligible for maximum financial aid.

However, most sources of aid are difficult to access, often leaving students to rely on loans and supplement their incomes by working. In fact, loans have replaced grants as the most common type of aid for paying for college (Goldrick-Rab & Sorensen, 2010). For low-income students, this stems from the welfare system's unwillingness to pay for two- and four-year degrees, thus driving students into significant debt (Katz, 2013). Student-mothers leave college with $3,800 more debt than women without children (Gault, Reichlin, Reynolds et al., 2014). Yet access to grant aid can affect students' access and persistence. In one study of single mothers in community college, nine of the ten participants relied on Pell Grants to facilitate their college attendance; all reported that they were unsure how they would finance the rest of their education once they transferred to a four-year institution, as the Pell Grant does not provide enough money to pay for four-year institutions' tuition and living expenses (Wilson, 2011).

However, many student-parents are likely to seek out additional employment (Goldrick-Rab & Sorensen, 2010). Nearly three-quarters of all full-time single student-parents work at least 15 hours a week; 30% work 40 hours or more per week. Spending more time engaged in paid work reduces the time student-parents are able to spend on their schoolwork and with their children. Of pertinence to this discussion, it also increases their EFC, which therefore reduces the amount of aid for which they are eligible. Student-parents are penalized for engaging in paid work. Earning income from work also can impact their eligibility for social assistance programs.

The mounting costs of college shape students' access to higher education. For example, 30% of participants in one study noted that low finances or an inability to pay for books had interfered with their education (Cerven, Park, Nations, & Nielsen, 2013). Although the costs of college are particularly challenging for student-parents from low SES backgrounds (Moreau & Kerner, 2015), many student-parents struggle with the costs of attendance, including international students (Myers-Walls, Frias, Kwon, Ko, & Lu, 2011), undergraduates (Robertson & Weiner, 2013), and graduate students (Lynch, 2008). For example, over half of the participants in Lynch's (2008) study of graduate student mothers who had received an assistantship still needed to work either part-time or full-time outside the university to pay for their living expenses, including the formidable costs of childcare.

Given that many student-parents—and potential student-parents—live on the margins, they rely on social assistance programs and student aid to meet their needs. Students who wish to pursue postsecondary education can only rely on TANF support for 12 months; others can try to cobble together living expenses from the Pell Grant and other forms of aid. However, sometimes these financial barriers are too big to overcome. In essence, national conversations suggest that low-income people should be trained for jobs, thus likely funneling them into a lifetime of low-wage work, rather than professional careers that a four-year college degree is more likely to open up.

Organizational Barriers and Supports

As the preceding discussion suggests, national policies enact barriers that impede many student-parents' access to higher education. Once they arrive on campus, however, student-parents face organizational factors that can either impede or facilitate their persistence. Student-parents are primarily challenged by a lack of affordable childcare, though they also find that general campus student services vary in their ability to meet their needs. In part, student-parents have mixed experience with interactions with faculty and staff but frequently find that campus-based support networks play an important role in their persistence.

Campus Services

Student-parents across institutional types note a lack of available and affordable childcare (Brown & Nichols, 2013; Kensinger & Minnick, 2018; Lynch, 2008; Sallee & Cox, 2019). One study estimated that campus childcare centers only meet one-tenth of demand (Goldrick-Rab & Sorensen, 2010). Access to affordable childcare has declined across the country (Gault, Milli, & Cruse, 2018). For example, only 47% of community colleges had campus childcare centers in 2012, a 10% decrease from 2002 (Nelson et al., 2013). Although some campuses might offer childcare centers, student-parents typically report that they are prohibitively expensive or the waitlists are too long.

Instead, student-parents often resort to private daycare centers or rely on family and friends to provide care (Lynch, 2008).

However, the lack of available and affordable care might deter potential students from matriculating in the first place (Brooks, 2012) and impede the persistence of those who do (Cerven et al., 2013). The inverse is also true: many student-parents credit affordable childcare for facilitating their persistence (Cerven, 2013; Christopher, 2004; Sallee & Cox, 2019). Single mothers at one university had their childcare costs covered by a community-based organization; all noted that this program allowed them to persist in college (Christopher, 2004). Similarly, American participants in Sallee and Cox's (2019) study of student-parents at two community colleges in the US and Canada noted that the campus childcare center, which charged just $15 per week in tuition due to a federal subsidy, provided a safe place to send their children while they were in class. And evidence suggests that use of campus childcare centers facilitates student progress; according to one study, student-parents who used a campus childcare center "had more than triple the on-time graduation rate of student-parents who did not use the center" (Gault et al., 2018, p. 6). In part, these increased graduation rates might be attributed to staff members who often provide extra support and parenting advice to students (Cox & Sallee, 2016; Fadale & Winter, 1991), thus facilitating their success both in the classroom and at home.

Yet even when they are affordable and have space available, campus childcare centers do not always meet the needs of student-parents. Many colleges and universities now offer classes in the evenings, yet childcare centers' hours do not always extend beyond a standard workday, thus leaving student-parents to seek alternative arrangements. Student-parents in one study reported that a lack of evening and drop-in care made participation in evening academic activities difficult (Robertson & Weiner, 2013). Such limitations may lead them to either scramble to find backup childcare or alternative course options or, in the worst case, drop out. Although campus childcare is indeed a useful resource, the evidence suggests that it fails to meet the needs of most student-parents.

Although childcare is critical for facilitating access, student-parents would most benefit from a mainstreamed campus in which their needs are integrated throughout all campus programs or, in other words, if campuses took a holistic approach to their development and experiences. Student-parents who have access to these sorts of programs gain valuable assistance navigating the campus environment (Cerven, 2013; Cerven et al., 2013; Sallee & Cox, 2019). For example, student-mothers at one community college in California who were enrolled in a support program that provided counselors to address all educational concerns noted that they received more targeted attention that exceeded the types of advice gained from campus support services (Cerven, 2013; Cerven et al., 2013). In addition to meeting with counselors, students in the program had access to affordable childcare, work-study opportunities, tutoring, priority registration, and book vouchers, among other benefits (Cerven et al., 2013). This program clearly attended to all parts of students' identities and not just those associated with their status as parents. Similarly, Sallee and Cox (2019) noted that the Aboriginal advising office at a Canadian community college provided a variety of benefits to students, including counseling, tutoring, and referral to campus and community resources. These programs and others illustrate how student-parents' needs cannot be addressed in isolation, as each identity affects the other.

Campus Actors

Faculty and staff can play an important role in supporting student-parents' persistence and engagement; however, evidence is mixed as to whether they always do so. Some have found faculty and staff to be quite helpful to student-parents (Austin & McDermott, 2003–2004; Estes, 2011; Katz, 2013; Kensinger & Minnick, 2018). For example, nearly all of the 27 participants in a study of student-mothers reported that faculty were mostly or always understanding of parents' needs (Kensinger & Minnick, 2018). Student-parents in other studies also discussed the important role that faculty advisors and staff members played in helping them navigate academic issues as well as career choices (Austin & McDermott, 2003–2004). However, positive faculty experiences were not universal as some wished that faculty exhibited greater understanding and more knowledge of the demands facing student-parents (Brown & Nichols, 2013; Lynch, 2008; Robertson & Weiner, 2013; Springer, Parker, & Leviten-Reid, 2009). For example, participants in Robertson and Weiner's (2013) study felt that faculty did not understand when family emergencies, such as a child's illness, interfered with their ability to attend class or submit an assignment on time. These mixed experiences point to the important role that faculty and staff play in supporting student-parents on campus.

Although faculty and staff play an important role, so, too, can peers, both parents and nonparents alike (Austin & McDermott, 2003–2004; Bloom, 2009; Cerven, 2013; Fadale & Winter, 1991). In particular, campuses and other organizations have recognized the power of peer networks and have intentionally designed support networks for these students. For example, one community-based organization that supports single mothers' pursuit of higher education established weekly meetings for all participants, designed to share information but also to foster a sense of community. Doing so, organizers hoped, would reduce social isolation—a barrier for student-parents as well as for those living in poverty (Bloom, 2009). Others noted the importance that informal networks played in facilitating students' success in college (Cerven, 2013). Such networks extend beyond campus to include students' families and friends. I discuss the important role that these groups play in the section that follows.

Individual Barriers and Supports

Although societal and organizational factors shape student-parents' experience in higher education, so, too, do individual factors. In particular, many note a significant lack of time due to their multiple responsibilities, often leading to role conflict. However, family members can play a significant role in helping alleviate this conflict. Many student-parents simply do not have enough hours in the day to fulfill their competing responsibilities (Christopher, 2004) or to attend to their own needs (Moreau & Kerner, 2015). From attending classes to studying to working to taking care of their children, their days are full—and far busier than those of nonparents. Studies estimate that at least one in three student-parents works and pursues higher education full time (Goldrick-Rab & Sorensen, 2010; Nelson et al., 2013). In addition to working full time, over half of student-parents spend at least 30 hours per week on caregiving (Nelson et al., 2013). The demands are even more intense for those with young children; students with children under the age of six spend 86 more hours per week on tasks, including paid work, housework, and childcare, than students without young children (Wladis, Hachey, & Conway, 2018). The majority of these hours are those spent on child-related tasks, though parents also spend more time working and on housework. As a result, student-parents rate the quality of time they have available for study as significantly poorer than their nonparent peers (Wladis et al., 2018).

Due to these competing obligations, student-parents are likely to experience role conflict or role strain (Bonnycastle & Prentice, 2011; Christopher, 2004; Moreau, 2016; Moreau & Kerner, 2015; Sallee, 2015). And, as others have pointed out, the role of mother and student are often in direct conflict (Lynch, 2008; Moreau, 2016; Moreau & Kerner, 2015). Drawing on Coser's (1974) work, Moreau (2016; Moreau & Kerner, 2015) argued that both academia and parenting are greedy institutions—requiring work that never ends. As a result, a student-parent always has responsibilities related to their children and nearly always has work related to their schooling. Thus, these roles are rarely not in conflict. Similarly, Lynch (2008) argued that the role of mother and student conflict, thus leading people to devise ways to downplay each identity in various situations. For example, student-parents might downplay their identity as mothers in school and downplay their student identity in their personal life. Such strategies suggest that the two identities are incompatible—and given the carefree nature of higher education and society at general, such an assumption has a firm hold in dominant US culture.

Yet, student-parents who can rely on family members for assistance may find ways to mitigate role conflict. Student-parents tend to rely on family members for assistance in different capacities (Austin & McDermott, 2003–2004; Cerven, 2013; Christopher, 2004; Estes, 2011; Katz, 2013; Kensinger & Minnick, 2018; Plageman & Sabina, 2010). Given the prohibitive costs of childcare centers, many student-parents turn to their parents and sometimes their partners for help with childcare (Christopher, 2004; Estes, 2011; Wilsey, 2013). Although students' mothers provide a consistent source of support, the evidence is mixed as to whether partners are always helpful. For example, one-third of single mothers in Christopher's (2004) study noted that their children's father helped with childcare, though they were not always consistent in doing so. Some boyfriends and other family members were noted for not just being unhelpful, but for actively working against student-parents' pursuit of a college degree. In one study of student-mothers, participants mentioned that their boyfriends forbade them to attend college (Cerven, 2013). These examples underscore that, while family can be helpful, they can also work against student-parents' best interests.

Although childcare help is pivotal, many student-parents also turn to family for emotional as well as logistical support with navigating college (Austin & McDermott, 2003–2004; Cerven, 2013; Kensinger & Minnick, 2018; Plageman & Sabina, 2010). Some student-parents note that the emotional support that their family members provide is more significant than financial support (Kensinger & Minnick, 2018). Others might rely on family members for help with demystifying the college-going process, seeking them out for advice on financial aid and other college-related questions (Cerven, 2013). Through the types of help they provide, family members can play a critical role in facilitating student-parents' academic integration into campus (Austin & McDermott, 2003–2004) as well as attendance and persistence (Plageman & Sabina, 2010).

Student-parents face a variety of barriers in their pursuit of higher education. They encounter a society that suggests that childcare is a private issue and that students are to be "carefree." They navigate an increasingly austere policy environment where federal aid—for both social programs and educational support—has been severely curtailed and primarily filters students to vocational programs. Once on campus, student-parents struggle to access affordable childcare and find time to study. However, a variety of actors, including family, faculty, staff, and other student-parents, can play a critical role in helping students overcome these challenges.

Theoretical Perspectives

Given that student-parents face a variety of societal, organizational, and individual obstacles, understanding their experiences requires adopting multiple lenses. As such, I offer two different approaches: the ideal worker (Acker, 1990; Williams, 1989), a concept derived from organizational studies, and role strain (Goode, 1960), a theory that focuses on the way that an individual copes with multiple burdens. The first theory acknowledges the role that organizational structures and norms play in shaping student-parents' experiences while the second focuses on how student-parents might individually respond to their multiple roles.

Ideal Worker

First coined by Joan Williams (1989) and elaborated on by Joan Acker (1990), the ideal worker suggests that the ideal employee is always working and has no familial responsibilities in the home or, at the least, has a wife at home to take care of these responsibilities. As this description suggests, the ideal worker is a gendered construct, as only men were expected to be ideal workers. Women, in particular, are not able to live up to ideal worker norms as society expects them to be engaged mothers while simultaneously penalizing them if they are too engaged. Although the ideal worker initially was used to describe employees in generic organizations, it has since been applied to faculty (Sallee, 2014), staff (Wilk, 2016), and students (Beeler, 2016; Sallee, 2016). For students, the consequences of the ideal worker are the same: students are expected to be able to devote themselves to their academic pursuits with no other demands on their time, including childcare, paid work, or any other tasks that will distract from their focus. Yet, as I have suggested in this chapter, student-parents do not have that luxury. In addition to bearing responsibility for their children, many also are employed in part- and full-time positions, thus ensuring that they are unable to live up to ideal worker norms.

Described as an "abstract, bodiless worker," the ideal worker also "has no sexuality, no emotions, and does not procreate" (Acker, 1990, p. 151). This description clearly marks student-parents as the not-ideal worker, as their status as parents illustrates. Further, pregnant students defy ideal worker expectations through their physical embodiment. Ideal worker norms suggest that organizations can treat all employees the same—and that one employee is interchangeable with the next. Extending this metaphor to students would suggest that all students have similar needs. However, as the chapters in this volume underscore, students come to college with a variety of backgrounds and needs. Yet colleges and universities seem to target their services to respond to the perceived needs of the traditional, or ideal, student. As this discussion suggests, the ideal student is one who thrives on the carefree campus (Moreau, 2016). However, student-parents—and all students who do not embody the ideal student—may experience significant challenges in their pursuit of higher education.

Role Strain

While the ideal worker points to organizational consequences for student-parents' ability to navigate school and family, Goode's (1960) theory of role strain focuses on how individuals navigate multiple roles. Role strain is built on four premises. First, role demands are required at different times and places. With rare exception, a student-parent cannot be in the classroom and parenting at the same time. Second, all individuals enter into multiple role relationships; a person might be a parent, a student, an employee, and a child all at the same time. However, these various relationships may sometimes come into conflict as the previous example suggests. Third, each role relationship may call for multiple, and sometimes conflicting, responses. For example, a parent may limit her child's screen time, which may upset the child, thus creating tension in the household. Finally, many roles are part of "role sets," in which an individual might engage in several role relationships with different individuals. For example, a mother with two children likely has a different relationship with each of them, depending on their needs, personalities, and ages.

Individuals can adopt a variety of strategies in response to role strain, including compartmentalization, delegation, elimination of relationships, and extension. With compartmentalization, an individual focuses on one role demand to the exclusion of all others. A student who has a paper due the next day may only focus on that assignment and not finish reading for another class; in the process, the student may also neglect all other roles, including that of parent, child, and partner. With delegation, an individual identifies another person to take on one or more of their roles. That same student working on the paper might ask her mother to take care of her children, so that she can more readily devote herself to her student responsibilities without distraction. With role elimination, an individual might eliminate one or more burdensome relationships. The student who becomes overwhelmed with coursework might drop a class—or out of college entirely. Alternatively, students with unsupportive partners may break up with them. Finally, with role extension, an individual might take on even more roles, sometimes as an excuse for failing to live up to the demands required of their other roles. However, an individual might also take on additional roles as a way to facilitate completion of existing roles. For example, an individual might join a support program for student-parents that provides academic support and counseling. Although participation in the program might add to the student-parent's total role set, the new role should complement existing roles. Role strain points out how student-parents hold multiple identities that might come into conflict and may occasionally adopt both effective and ineffective strategies for reducing that conflict.

Student Engagement Strategies

Based on the preceding literature review, I offer a number of ways that institutions and the actors who populate them might support student-parents.

Replace the Careblind Campus With the Caring Campus

As I suggested in this chapter, most colleges and universities operate as if students are carefree, when, in reality, one in four undergraduates has dependent children (Gault, Reichlin, & Roman, 2014). Thus, campuses that want to support student-parents should transform themselves from careblind campuses to caring campuses or, using Moreau's (2016) language, mainstream care. In essence, Such an approach amounts to adopting universal design in programs and services that considers student-parents' needs. This would include actively welcoming children in all spaces, except where it might be dangerous, such as science labs. Additionally, campuses might provide changing tables in all men's and women's bathrooms for student-parents and others to use. Campuses can also build in supports for student-parents, such as providing those women who give birth mid-semester with accommodations, such as automatic incompletes. Additional interventions might include training all faculty and staff to be more responsive to student-parents' needs, as well as encouraging faculty and staff to make their own care responsibilities visible. Interventions on the caring campus attend to all parts of student-parents' identities as the role demands of each identity can affect the demands on the others.

Provide Affordable and Accessible Childcare

Childcare is the most significant barrier to student-parents' access and persistence. Not all campuses offer on-site childcare, yet those that do bring significant benefits to student-parents, including gaining access to safe and frequently affordable care for their children, receiving parenting and academic advice from childcare staff, and having a greater likelihood of on-time graduation rates than students who do not use on-campus childcare (Cox & Sallee, 2016; Fadale & Winter, 1991; Gault et al., 2018). Campuses with existing childcare centers should take steps to ensure access for student-parents. This entails both reserving spots for the children of student-parents and offering scholarships to subsidize the often-costly fees. At a minimum, all institutions should make a list of childcare centers in the nearby community readily available to all who ask. Ideally, institutions might help subsidize the cost of off-campus childcare through a series of scholarships.

Given that colleges and universities are increasingly offering classes at night, campuses might offer evening hours for their on-site childcare as well as a drop-in service for students who want to study or have meetings for group projects. Finally, institutions might also offer backup childcare that student-parents can use if their children are sick. Such a program sends a bonded (i.e., having insurance) professional into the home who will watch children on an hourly basis. Some institutions even subsidize the cost so that students and others with low incomes pay a lower fee. Only when student-parents know that their children are taken care of can they be mentally and physically freed up to focus on their academic responsibilities.

Establish a Liaison Between Campus Financial Aid and Welfare

As I have suggested in this chapter, many student-parents are living in poverty and rely on both social assistance and educational aid to finance their educations. Yet the two systems are confusing and often difficult to reconcile. Campuses might establish an official liaison between the welfare office and the financial aid office to help student-parents navigate the two systems. Larger campuses might even house a welfare worker on site so that student-parents could meet with them while on campus. Smaller institutions could ensure that financial aid officers receive training in how the two systems work together so that staff might be better able to advise students.

Capitalize on the Power of Peer Support

Persisting in education is not an individual undertaking; rather, student-parents succeed with the help of a support network. Institutions can help student-parents develop a support system by offering a student-parent support group. Such a group might bring student-parents together on a weekly or bi-weekly basis to allow them to discuss both academic and personal concerns and support one another. Student-parents should be supported in bringing their children to the meetings, particularly if they would be unable to attend otherwise. This peer support program could also be a part of the larger intervention discussed next.

Offer a Comprehensive Support Program

Many of the recommendations reviewed so far have focused on singular aspects of student-parents' identities. Yet, as this chapter has made clear, student-parents need to be supported in both their personal and academic lives. As a result, campuses might create programs that help students navigate the variety of concerns that they face. Such a program might offer academic advising and counseling to address educational issues.

The program might also offer workshops on a variety of topics, including time management, reconciling financial aid and social assistance programs, parenting strategies for various age groups, and tips for academic success. Additionally, given that the preponderance of student-parents are women of color, the program might offer regular sessions to encourage participants to discuss the challenges of navigating their multiple identities (as women, mothers, People of Color, to name but a few) in a society that was designed to attend to the needs of White, childless men. Such a program might also pair students with a more senior student-parent mentor to offer formalized support around navigating issues related to their intersecting identities. Finally, the program might also help student-parents who need to work find jobs on campus, as the literature suggests that those who are involved in more on-campus activities are better integrated and, thus, more likely to persist (Kuh, Kinzie, Schuh, & Whitt, 2010). Attending to all aspects of students' identities will help facilitate success in each realm.

Conclusion

Although student-parents comprise a sizable portion of the undergraduate population, they are frequently neglected by campus programming efforts. However, given that many work at least part time while taking classes and caring for their children, student-parents frequently do not have the time to participate in activities outside of coursework. Additionally, since nearly half of student-parents are first-generation students (Nelson et al., 2013) and the majority are women of color (Gault, Reichlin, & Roman, 2014), this group may also not know how to or feel uncomfortable seeking out help, particularly on predominantly White campuses. However, as the aforementioned interventions suggest, there are a number of ways that campuses might rethink their practices to provide assistance to student-parents to facilitate their persistence.

The normative student needs to be redefined. No longer is the typical undergraduate 18 to 24 with no family responsibilities. Perhaps we need to do away with the language of the normative or typical student altogether to better serve students. Rather, campuses need to learn to respond to the varying demands, interests, and skills that all students bring by creating a campus that cares for all.

References

Acker, J. (1990). Hierarchies, jobs, bodies: A theory of gendered organizations. *Gender & Society, 4*(2), 139–158.

Austin, S. A., & McDermott, K. A. (2003–2004). College persistence among single mothers after welfare reform: An exploratory study. *Journal of College Student Retention, 5*(2), 93–113.

Beeler, S. (2016). Undergraduate single mothers' experience in postsecondary education. *New Directions for Higher Education, 2016*(176), 37–51.

Bloom, L. R. (2009). 'When one person makes it, we all make it': A study of Beyond Welfare, a women-centered community-based organization that helps low-income mothers achieve personal and academic success. *International Journal of Qualitative Studies in Education, 22*(4), 485–503.

Bonnycastle, C., & Prentice, S. (2011). Childcare and caregiving: Overlooked barriers for northern postsecondary women learners. *The Canadian Journal of Native Studies, 31*(1), 1–16.

Brooks, R. (2012). Student-parents and higher education: A cross-national comparison. *Journal of Education Policy, 27*(3), 423–439.

Brown, V., & Nichols, T. R. (2013). Pregnant and parenting students on campus: Policy and program implications for a growing population. *Educational Policy, 27*(3), 499–530.

Cerven, C. (2013). Public and private lives: Institutional structures and personal supports in low-income single mothers' educational pursuits. *Education Policy Analysis Archives, 21*(17), 1–26.

Cerven, C., Park, V., Nations, J., & Nielsen, K. (2013). *College can be complicated: Low-income single mothers' experiences in postsecondary education*. Pathways to Postsecondary Success. Los Angeles, CA: All Campus Consortium on Research for Diversity (UC/ACCORD). Retrieved from http://pathways.gseis.ucla.edu/publications/MLSES_PolicyBrief.pdf.

Christopher, K. (2004). Welfare recipients attending college: The interplay of oppression and resistance. *Journal of Sociology and Social Welfare, 32*(3), 165–186.

Coser, L. A. (1974). *Greedy institutions: Patterns of undivided commitment*. New York, NY: Free Press.

Cox, R. D., & Sallee, M. W. (2016, November). *Navigating competing responsibilities: Community college student-parents, support networks, and institutional agents*. Paper presented at the Annual Meeting of the Association for the Study of Higher Education, Columbus, OH.

Estes, D. K. (2011). Managing the student-parent dilemma: Mothers and fathers in higher education. *Symbolic Interaction, 34*(2), 198–219.

Fadale, L. M., & Winter, G. M. (1991). Campus-based child care and the academic success of student parents. *Community/Junior College Quarterly of Research and Practice, 15*(2), 115–123.

Gault, B., Milli, J., & Cruse, L. R. (2018). *Investing in single mothers' higher education: Costs and benefits to individuals, families, and society*. Washington, DC: Institute for Women's Policy Research.

Gault, B., Reichlin, L., Reynolds, E., & Froehner, M. (2014). *4.8 million college students are raising children*. IWPR No. C424. Washington, DC: Institute for Women's Policy Research.

Gault, B., Reichlin, L., & Roman, S. (2014). *College affordability for low-income adults: Improving returns on investment for families and society*. Washington, DC: Institute for Women's Policy Research. Retrieved from www.iwpr.org/publications/pubs/college-affordability-forlow-income-adults-improving-returns-on-investment-for-families-and-society/

Goldrick-Rab, S., & Sorensen, K. (2010). Unmarried parents in college. *The Future of Children, 20*(2), 179–203.

Goode, W. J. (1960). A theory of role strain. *American Sociological Review, 25*(4), 483–496.

Haleman, D. L. (2004). Great expectations: Single mothers in higher education. *International Journal of Qualitative Studies in Education, 17*(6), 769–784.

Jacobs, J. A., & Winslow, S. (2003). Welfare reform and enrollment in postsecondary education. *The Annals of the American Academy of Political and Social Science, 586*, 194–217.

Katz, S. (2013). "Give us a chance to get an education": Single mothers' survival narratives and strategies for pursuing higher education on welfare. *Journal of Poverty, 17*, 273–304.

Kensinger, C., & Minnick, D. J. (2018). The invisible village: An exploration of undergraduate student mothers' experiences. *Journal of Family and Economic Issues, 39*(1), 132–144.

Kuh, G. D., Kinzie, J., Schuh, J. H., & Whitt, E. J. (2010). *Student success in college: Creating conditions that matter*. Hoboken, NJ: John Wiley & Sons.

Lynch, K. D. (2008). Gender roles and the American academe: A case study of graduate student mothers. *Gender and Education, 20*(6), 585–605.

Miller, K. (2010). *Student parents face significant challenges to postsecondary success*. Washington, DC: Institute for Women's Policy Research.

Moreau, M. P. (2016). Regulating the student body/ies: University policies and student parents. *British Educational Research Journal, 42*(5), 906–925.

Moreau, M. P., & Kerner, C. (2015). Care in academia: An exploration of student parents' experiences. *British Journal of Sociology of Education, 36*(2), 215–233.

Myers-Walls, J. A., Frias, L. V., Kwon, K. A., Ko, M. J. M., & Lu, T. (2011). Living life in two worlds: Acculturative stress among Asian international graduate student parents and spouses. *Journal of Comparative Family Studies, 42*(4), 455–478.

Nelson, B., Froehner, M., & Gault, B. (2013). *College students with children are common and face many challenges in completing higher education*. Washington, DC: Institute for Women's Policy Research.

Plageman, P. M., & Sabina, C. (2010). Perceived family influence on undergraduate adult female students. *The Journal of Continuing Higher Education, 58*, 156–166.

Robertson, A. S., & Weiner, A. (2013). Building community for student-parents and their families: A social justice challenge for higher education. *Journal of Academic Perspectives, 2013*(2), 1–21.

Sallee, M. W. (2014). *Faculty fathers: Toward a new ideal in the research university*. Albany, NY: The State University of New York Press.

Sallee, M. W. (2015). Adding academics to the work/family puzzle: Graduate student parents in higher education and student affairs. *Journal of Student Affairs Research and Practice, 52*(4), 401–413.

Sallee, M. (2016). Ideal for whom?: A cultural analysis of ideal worker norms in higher education and student affairs graduate programs. *New Directions for Higher Education, 176*, 53–67.

Sallee, M. W., & Cox, R. D. (2019). Thinking beyond childcare: Supporting student-parents. *American Journal of Education, 125*, 621–645.

Springer, K. W., Parker, B. K., & Leviten-Reid, C. (2009). Making space for graduate student parents: Practice and politics. *Journal of Family Issues, 30*(4), 435–457.

Wilk, K. E. (2016). Work-life balance and ideal worker expectations for administrators. *New Directions for Higher Education, 2016*(176), 37–51.

Williams, J. C. (1989). Deconstructing gender. *Michigan Law Review, 87*(4), 797–845.

Wilsey, S. A. (2013). Comparisons of adult and traditional college-age student mothers: Reasons for college enrollment and views of how enrollment affects children. *Journal of College Student Development, 54*(2), 209–214.

Wilson, K. (2011). If not welfare, then what?: How single mothers finance college post-welfare reform. *Journal of Sociology & Social Welfare, 38*(4), 51–76.

Wilson, K. B., & Cox, E. M. (2011). No kids allowed: Transforming community colleges to support mothering. *NASPA Journal About Women in Higher Education, 4*(2), 218–241.

Wladis, C., Hachey, A. C., & Conway, K. (2018). No time for college? An investigation of time poverty and parenthood. *The Journal of Higher Education, 89*(6), 807–831.

Afterword

Higher education was not designed to serve the tremendous diversity of students who now find themselves pursuing degrees at postsecondary institutions. In truth, colleges and universities were historically designed to serve a very narrow segment of learners, from able-bodied students to White students to students without children of their own to cisgender students to students from middle- and upper-income families. Today, many institutions find themselves serving a student body that is far from this historical norm, with myriad markers of difference. This schism between higher education's historic *normal* student and today's robust heterogeneity manifests not just as compositional diversity that deserves applause, but also as an equity chasm. For while faculty, student affairs educators, and administrators at colleges and universities have done an increasingly admirable job of admitting a broad diversity of students, they have not invested in a proportional commitment to educational equity. This shift in access, without an attendant equity mission, leaves many students at colleges and universities deeply underserved and vulnerable. This marginalization appears in a number of measurable phenomena, from lower retention and graduation rates to increased prevalence of mental health and wellness crises to a decreased sense of belonging for the communities that live in the equity chasm.

Faculty, student affairs educators, and administrators have begun the critical journey of changing their *who*, but they are still in the infancy of changing their *how*. This third edition of *Student Engagement in Higher Education* is a vital blueprint for faculty, administrators, and student affairs educators to more successfully center marginalized, vulnerable, and underserved communities in their work and approach engaging these communities with an equity frame. The opportunities for postsecondary education to be completely transformational in students' lives are endless, but only if institutional leaders first transform their praxis. The theoretical models, engagement strategies, programmatic initiatives, and assessment plans have to be employed with marginalized and vulnerable student communities at the center of leaders' thinking, rather than simply adapted at a late hour when institutions finally decide to serve these groups. This text offers a chapter-by-chapter tactical playbook on how to do just this.

This updated edition couldn't come at a more urgent time. Here in the United States, and in many places around the world, we are seeing a resurgence of many ideologies that appeared to have been tested and rejected in the great contests of the 20th century. The recent rise of nativism, religious fundamentalism, protofascism, and White supremacy as mainstream, politically viable constructs should electrify all of us who believe in a transformative, liberatory higher education to recommit to the task of dismantling policies, systems, and environments that norm otherness and marginality. As we watch our nations and communities wrestle with some very basic and fundamental questions of human rights and human dignity, we would be naïve to think that these high-stakes contests will not find their way onto campuses. Quaye, Harper, and Pendakur have assembled a panoply of chapters, from a diverse and talented group of contributing authors, which position us to contribute to this critical moment in human history. Our ability to not simply help marginalized students survive higher education, but to empower them to thrive in our midst is intimately connected to the struggle playing out on the world's stage. If we can successfully engage, transform, and graduate an increasing diversity of students in higher education, we can effectively seed our democracies with critical thinkers who champion human rights, equity, and social justice.

This book also gives me hope on a personal level. It's been nearly 20 years since I graduated from college, but I still distinctly remember the dissonance I felt when interacting with staff at my alma mater. As an Asian American man of color, I had many questions about the campus climate, a visceral sense of otherness and alienation based on interactions with my peers and faculty, and anger about how the institution seemed to want to brush significant acts of bigotry and intolerance under the rug, rather than acknowledge these moments as emblematic of a larger cultural problem. When I interacted with staff in leadership programs, the residence halls, or the student union, they often became uncomfortable when I raised these points and tried to shift the conversations towards how college is the "best four years of your life" and how there were so many opportunities to have fun at my institution. To be clear, I do not think that they were operating from a place of intentional malice or active invalidation. I think they were honestly using the tools they'd been offered in their higher education graduate programs to engage with me . . . and these tools had underequipped them to meet me where I stood and forge authentic, transformative relationships. It wasn't until I wandered into the campus Multicultural Student Center as a senior that I met staff that seemed to, oddly enough, have a different approach to working with me. I didn't understand what was happening at the time, but I understand now that these agents of change were employing a praxis that centered my experience, often because of their own lived experience of difference.

I know that much has changed in the nearly two decades since I finished my undergraduate degree, and I am thrilled with most of the change. The third edition of *Student*

Engagement in Higher Education represents an important part of the epistemological shift in higher education administration training programs. Today, graduate students encounter numerous courses and texts that focus on serving historically underserved populations. There is a rapidly growing body of scholarship that looks to incorporate the gains of decades of critical theory into the canonical frameworks of psychosocial development that are the bedrock of our field. This gives me tremendous joy and hope. I look forward to a time when a student doesn't have to find a specialty center, staffed by educators employing counternarrative praxis, to be seen and engaged with dignity. I look forward to a time when this is the co-curricular experience for all students, in all campus spaces and places. And with works like what Quaye, Harper, and Pendakur have assembled here, that time is closer now than ever before.

Vijay Pendakur

Cornell University

April 15, 2019

Contributor Bios

Joshua Abreu is a doctoral candidate in the Department of Educational Leadership at the University of Connecticut (UCONN), USA. His research centers on equity-based teaching and learning and professional development in higher education.

Shafiqa Ahmadi is an associate professor of clinical education and co-director for the Center for Education, Identity, and Social Justice at the University of Southern California (USC) Rossier School of Education (Rossier), USA. Her research focuses on diversity and legal protection of underrepresented students, specifically Muslim students, bias and hate crimes, and sexual assault survivors. She has also taught at USC Gould School of Law and was a visiting researcher at the Center for Urban Education at Rossier.

Sonja Ardoin is a higher education scholar-practitioner and an assistant professor of student affairs administration at Appalachian State University, USA. She studies social class identity, first-generation college students, and rurality, among other research interests.

Aeriel A. Ashlee is assistant professor of college counseling and student development at St. Cloud State University, USA. She has written and presented on transracial Asian American adoptee collegians and Asian American college student engagement at various national conferences including the American Educational Research Association (AERA), American Educational Studies Association (AESA), Association for Asian American Studies (AAAS), Association for the Study of Higher Education (ASHE), Critical Mixed Race Studies (CMRS), and National Conference on Race/Ethnicity in Higher Education (NCORE).

Marco Barker is the inaugural vice chancellor for diversity and inclusion and associate professor of practice for educational administration at the University of Nebraska-Lincoln, USA.

Kaylan S. Baxter is a research associate at the USC Race and Equity Center and doctoral student in the Rossier School of Education at the University of Southern California, USA.

Stephanie Bondi is assistant professor of practice at the University of Nebraska-Lincoln, USA, in the Department of Educational Administration.

Ellen M. Broido is professor of higher education and student affairs at Bowling Green State University, USA.

Kirsten R. Brown is a research faculty member in the Educational Leadership Doctoral Program at Edgewood College, USA.

Nolan L. Cabrera is an associate professor at the University of Arizona, USA, where he studies Whiteness on college campuses. He is the author of over 60 scholarly publications, including the award winning book *White Guys on Campus*. Nolan was one of three expert witnesses in the Tucson Mexican American Studies federal trial, and he was the only academic featured in the MTV documentary *White People*.

Santiago Castiello-Gutiérrez is a doctoral candidate at the Center for the Study of Higher Education at the University of Arizona, USA. He is also the Mobility Programs Coordinator for the CONAHEC Consortium and a coordinator for short-term international programs at the University of Arizona. He currently serves as the graduate student representative for the Council of International Higher Education of the Association for the Study of Higher Education (ASHE) and is a 2019 recipient of the Harold Josephson Award for Professional Promise in International Education of the Association of International Education Administrators (AIEA).

D. Chase J. Catalano is an assistant professor in higher education in the School of Education at Virginia Polytechnic Institute and University (Virginia Tech), USA.

Darnell G. Cole is an associate professor of education with an emphasis in higher education and education psychology at the University of Southern California (USC) Rossier School of Education (Rossier), USA. He also serves as co-director for the Center for Education, Identity and Social Justice at the USC Rossier School of Education. His areas of research include race/ethnicity, diversity, college student experiences, and learning. He serves on several review boards, including the *Journal of College Student Development*.

Chris Corces-Zimmerman is a doctoral candidate in the Center for the Study of Higher Education at the University of Arizona, USA. His research is rooted in critical Whiteness studies and explores various aspects of Whiteness and the ways that it impacts the form and function of institutions of higher education at both systemic and individual levels.

Rebecca E. Crandall is clinical assistant professor of higher education and student affairs at The Ohio State University, USA. She also serves as coordinator of the Student Personnel Assistantship program at The Ohio State University.

Charles H. F. Davis III is an assistant professor of clinical education at the University of Southern California, USA, and chief strategy officer of the USC Race and Equity Center. Charles is co-editor of *Student Activism, Politics, and Campus Climate in Higher Education*.

Christopher M. Fiorello is a doctoral candidate in the higher education program at George Mason University, USA. His research focuses on performance of masculinities among college men. He is also a student affairs professional working in student conduct and academic integrity.

Ann M. Gansemer-Topf is an associate professor of student affairs and higher education at Iowa State University, USA, and a faculty fellow for the Center for Excellence in Learning and Teaching at Iowa State University

Susan K. Gardner is director of the Rising Tide Center and women's, gender, and sexuality studies and professor of higher education at the University of Maine, USA.

Joy Gaston Gayles is professor of higher education and university faculty scholar at North Carolina State University, USA. Her research focuses on student success in post-secondary education.

Kimberly A. Griffin is associate professor of higher education, student affairs, and international education policy at the University of Maryland, USA. She is the editor of the *Journal of Diversity in Higher Education*.

Shaun R. Harper is the Clifford and Betty Allen Professor and executive director of the Race and Equity Center at the University of Southern California, USA.

Barbara Jacoby is a higher education consultant with Barbara Jacoby Consulting. She has served the University of Maryland, USA, for more than 40 years in several roles focusing on service learning, civic engagement, and commuter students. She has authored seven books and serves as consulting editor for *College Teaching* and as contributing editor for the *Journal of College and Character*. She is an active speaker and consultant throughout the US and around the world.

Royel M. Johnson is assistant professor and research associate in the Center for the Study of Higher Education at Pennsylvania State University, USA. He also holds a courtesy appointment in the Department of African American Studies. His research interests broadly focus on students' pathways into and through college, with a particular focus on vulnerable and unserved populations.

Marc P. Johnston-Guerrero is associate professor of higher education and student affairs and affiliated faculty with the Asian American Studies program at The Ohio State University, USA. He also serves as an associate editor of *The Journal of Higher Education* and part of the governing board for ACPA: College Student Educators International.

T.J. Jourian is an independent scholar, consultant, and trainer.

Georgia Kouzoukas is an associate director of undergraduate academic affairs at the University of Pennsylvania, USA. She received her doctorate in higher education at the University of Pennsylvania, focusing her dissertation on first-generation women and identity intersectionality.

Bo Lee is a graduate student at Columbia University's quantitative methods in the social sciences master's program, USA. Most recently, she was a project specialist at USC Rosser's Center for Education, Identity and Social Justice. Previously, she was a program and talent development assistant at United Talent Agency, working on diversity and inclusion initiatives in the entertainment and media industry.

Jenny J. Lee is a professor at the Center for the Study of Higher Education at the University of Arizona, USA. She is currently a NAFSA senior fellow, associate editor of *The Review of Higher Education*, and co-editor of the book series *Studies in Global Higher Education*. She formerly served as the chair for the Council of International Higher Education and on the board of directors for the Association for the Study of Higher Education (ASHE).

Jaime Lester is a professor in the higher education program in the College of Humanities and Social Sciences at George Mason University, USA. She is the editor of *Community College Review* and a fellow in the Office of Faculty Development and Affairs at Mason. Her research focuses on organizational change and leadership in higher education.

Demetri L. Morgan is an assistant professor of higher education at Loyola University Chicago, USA, and co-editor of *Student Activism, Politics, and Campus Climate in Higher Education*.

Susana M. Muñoz is associate professor of higher education and coordinator of the Higher Education Leadership doctoral program at Colorado State University (CSU), USA. She also serves as the co-coordinator for CSU initiatives for the Race and Intersectional Studies in Educational Equity (RISE) Center.

Samuel D. Museus is professor of education studies at the University of California, San Diego, USA. (UCSD). He is also founding director of the National Institute for Transformation and Equity (NITE).

Z Nicolazzo is an assistant professor of trans* studies in education in the Center for the Study of Higher Education and co-chair of the Transgender Studies Research Cluster at the University of Arizona, USA.

C. Casey Ozaki is an associate professor of education, health, and behavior studies at the University of North Dakota, USA, while also serving as a faculty fellow for inclusive excellence, where her role is to provide education and consultation for faculty and departments on the development and integration of inclusive and equitable practices in their teaching and learning.

Sumun L. Pendakur is the chief learning officer and director of the USC Equity Institutes at the USC Race and Equity Center. She also serves on the board of directors for NADOHE, the national chief diversity officers' association.

Stephen John Quaye is associate professor of higher education and student affairs at The Ohio State University, USA, and associate editor of the *Journal of Diversity in Higher Education*. He is also past president of ACPA: College Student Educators International.

Kristen A. Renn is professor of higher, adult, and lifelong education at Michigan State University, USA, where she also serves as associate dean of undergraduate studies for student success research. Her research focuses on college student learning, development, and success, with a focus on minoritized students.

Corey B. Rumann is an assistant professor of practice in the Department of Educational Administration at the University of Nebraska-Lincoln, USA.

Margaret W. Sallee is associate professor of higher education at the University at Buffalo, USA, and co-editor of *Journal of Women and Gender in Higher Education*.

Heather J. Shotton is a citizen of the Wichita & Affiliated Tribes and is an associate professor of Native American Studies at the University of Oklahoma, USA. She is also past president of the National Indian Education Association.

Sy Stokes is a doctoral student at the University of Southern California's Rossier School of Education, USA, and a research associate at the USC Race and Equity Center. Sy was formerly a nationally recognized student activist at the University of California, Los Angeles, as the lead organizer for the "Black Bruins" digital media campaign.

Jamie R. Utt is a doctoral candidate in teaching, learning, and sociocultural studies at the University of Arizona, USA, where he studies intersections of race and schooling. His past research has focused on White teacher racial identity development, and his dissertation research investigates the racialized effects of school resource officers, police officer stationed in schools.

Denise N. Williams-Klotz is the assistant director of multicultural student affairs at Iowa State University, USA.

Erin Kahunawaika'ala Wright is a fifth-generation resident of Kalihi, O'ahu, Hawai'i, now caring for the fourth-generation and raising the sixth-generation on the lands of her maternal great-great grandmother. She brings her professional background in Native Hawaiian student affairs to her current work, serving as an assistant professor of educational administration at the University of Hawai'i at Mānoa, USA.

Index